KU-566-691

Energy and Engineering Science Series

FLOWFIELD MODELING AND DIAGNOSTICS

ENERGY AND ENGINEERING
SCIENCE SERIES

Editors:
A. K. Gupta. Department of Mechanical Engineering, University of Maryland, MD, USA

D. G. Lilley, School of Mechanical and Aerospace Engineering,
Oklahoma State University, USA

Titles Already Published or in Preparation

Flame Combustion Processes in Industry
A. Stambuleanu

Modeling of Furnaces and Combustors
E. E. Khalil

Swirl Flows
A. K. Gupta, D. G. Lilley, and N. Syred

Flowfield Modeling and Diagnostics
A. K. Gupta and D. G. Lilley

Fluidic Flows Control
J. R. Tippetts

Fuels and Combustion in Gas Turbines
J. Odgers and D. Kretschmer

Spatially Precise Laser Diagnostics for Combustion Temperature and Species
A. C. Eckbreth

Heat Conduction
D. G. Lilley

H 12550323

FLOWFIELD MODELING AND DIAGNOSTICS

A. K. Gupta
Department of Mechanical Engineering
University of Maryland

D. G. Lilley
School of Mechanical and Aerospace Engineering
Oklahoma State University

ABACUS PRESS

First Published in 1985 by Abacus Press.
Abacus House, Speldhurst Road. Tunbridge Wells, Kent TN4 OHU

© Abacus Press 1985
All rights reserved. No part of this publication may be reproduced, stored in a retrieval system, or transmitted in any form or by any means, electronic, mechanical, or otherwise, without prior permission of Abacus Press.

BL British Library Cataloguing in Publication Data

Gupta, A. K.
Flowfield modeling and diagnostics.
1. Combustion engineering – Mathematical models
I. Title II. Lilley, D. G.
621.402'3 TJ254.5

ISBN 0-85626-328-1

Printed in the Philippines
APO PRODUCTION UNIT, INC.

D
621·4023
FLO

CONTENTS

PREFACE

This book is intended to serve as a basis for undergraduate and graduate students and research workers in all branches of Fluid Mechanics and Combustion, including Aeronautical, Chemical, Mechanical and Civil Engineers in academic and industrial environments. The aim is to provide a comprehensive and critical account of present technological knowledge for experimental and theoretical flowfield diagnostics. This is achieved in two ways: firstly, by providing a firm foundation for those who intend to carry out research and development work, and, secondly, by providing a comprehensive compendium of knowledge to those who need to understand and apply the diagnostic techniques to their particular problems.

The basic objective of the text is to communicate knowledge relevant to the theoretical and experimental treatment of fluid dynamics and, more specifically, to provide readers with an understanding of the principles and practice of the subject. The designer of practical equipment has a formidable problem, and the modeling and diagnostic task is to provide a route which leads to the accomplishment of design objectives more quickly and less expensively than current practice permits. The theoretical modeling of fluid flows with particular application to practical design is discussed in Chapter 2.

The emphasis is on flowfields in cylindrical polar coordinates, since most practical flows conform to this configuration, and the case of swirl about the axis is included fully, both in its non-axisymmetric and its axisymmetric form. Where possible a detailed analysis leads to a simpler physical model. Since predictions are realistic only if the physical processes are correctly expressed in mathematical form, suitable simulation models to effect closure of the governing equations are included for turbulence, radiative transfer, chemical reaction, multiphase phenomena, etc. An appreciation is also given for complexities associated with alternate fuels, complex chemistry and pollutant formation.

Attention is then given to solving the differential equations which the mathematical models have supplied. Chapter 3 is concerned with predictive techniques available for flowfield investigation. Simplified approaches, and scaling and modeling criteria are followed by discussion of direct numerical prediction for an ascending complexity of flows: axisymmetric with boundary layer assumptions, axisymmetric with recirculation, and fully 3-D flows. Generally, the partial differential equations are expressed in finite difference form (using finite difference of finite element techniques for discretization) and solved via a suitable algorithm and computer program.

In Chapter 4 experimental diagnostic techniques are extensively studied and assessed. Recommendations are given for suitable methods for the measurement of velocity and turbulence, temperature, pressure, density, species concentration, and particle and droplet size distribution. An emphasis is placed upon the understanding of physical principles and the manner in which the methods can be employed. The conventional intrusive and more recent developments in non-intrusive optical diagnostic techniques are described. Various conventional types of measuring techniques, together with the modern optical diagnostic techniques in simple or complex single and two-phase flows, both with and without combustion, are reviewed. Various experimental techniques are described with the main objective of establishing fluid flow patterns, particle/droplet size, velocities and trajectories, flow visualization and flow density in isothermal flows, and rates of transfer of heat, mass and momentum and rates of generation and consumption of chemical species in reacting flows.

The final chapter (Chapter 5) is concerned with problems and progress associated with flowfield investigation. Many current problems involve pollutant emission and techniques for their reduction. Alternate fuels and fuel blends possess their own specific needs. Application areas for the theoretical and experimental techniques of Chapters 2, 3, and 4 are appraised, and the chapter closes with a view of problem areas for application of the techniques presented earlier in the text.

The present book serves as a foundation text in the Energy and Engineering Science series. It deals in a comprehensive manner with modeling and diagnostics: recent and current advances, projected developments and trends, and areas of practical application. Our chief contribution has been to select, abstract and reframe material suitable for exemplifying the principles and techniques, and to produce a text which appeals to the man wishing to understand and apply these ideas to his particular practical problems. A special attribute offered by the present book is its strong practical emphasis of its portrayal of these concepts. Recent advanced ideas on experimental diagnostic techniques and theoretical simulation and solution techniques are fully integrated in the discussion. We have tried to strike the best balance between the mathematical, physical and practical aspects.

We would like to thank all those who have assisted us in the preparation of the book. Our gratitude goes to our colleagues throughout the world who have provided us with information and figures for inclusion. Specific acknowledgment to authors and sources is made in the text and in the lists of references. Our secretaries – Alice Biladeau, Becky Farrell and Janet Torrance – deserve special mention for their unfailing patience and diligence in the preparation of the manuscript. Finally, our thanks go to Abacus Press for their help and cooperation, for encouraging us to complete the text, and for their subsequent transformation of the manuscript into its present form.

A.K. GUPTA and *D.G. LILLEY*

NOMENCLATURE

Symbol	Meaning
a	constant, fringe spacing
a, b, c, d	coefficients in finite difference equations
A, B, C, D	coefficients in finite difference equations
A	area
b	constant
c	speed of sound, specific heat, constant
C	capacitance
C, U, V	control cell volumes for ρ, u, v
C_{R}	eddy break-up constant
d	diameter
D	differential operator, diameter
D/Dt	substantial time derivative
E	activation cncrgy
f	frequency
F	frequency response improvement factor, fuel mass fraction
H	hydrogen, heat of combustion
h	stagnation enthalpy
I, J	mesh point
J	turbulent flux vector
k	eddy wave number, kinetic energy of turbulence $= \frac{1}{2}(\overline{u'^2} + \overline{v'^2} + \overline{w'^2})$
K	constant, reaction rate constant, impact pressure constant of pitot probe, mixing length
ℓ	length
L	length
m	mass fraction
$\dot{m}'$	mass transfer rate across a boundary
$\dot{m}_{\mathrm{net}}$	net outflow of mass from cell
M	total mass, molecular weight
$\dot{M}, \dot{m}$	mass flow rate
n	constant, order of reaction, eddy frequency, normal direction

Symbol	Meaning
O	oxygen
p	pressure, point in flowfield
P	total pressure
Pe	Pecklet number
ΔP	pressure drop
PVC	precessing vortex core
q	dynamic head, heat produced per unit mass of combustible mixture
Q	heat flux, volumetric flow rate
r	radius, radial distance, cylindrical coordinate
R	resistance, gas constant, radius, residual source, mass rate of creation per unit volume
R_c	resistance
Re	Reynolds number
Ri	modified Richardson number
s	stoichiometric ox/fu ratio, fringe spacing
S	swirl number $= G_\theta/(G_x R)$
S_p, S_u	components of linearized source term
S_L	laminar burning velocity
S_T	turbulent burning velocity
t	time
T	temperature
u	time mean axial velocity
v	time mean radial velocity, volume
ΔV	small element of volume
w	time mean tangential velocity
x	amount of conversion, amplitude of temperature fluctuation
x, r, θ	axial, radial, polar coordinates
X	axial distance
y	amplitude of pressure fluctuation, cross stream coordinate, distance normal to a wall, typical function $y = y(x)$
z	coordinate
Z	a plane z

Greek Symbols

ϕ	general dependent variable, equivalence ratio (= 1/mixture ratio)
υ	kinematic viscosity
ρ	time mean density
μ	dynamic viscosity, turbulent viscosity
ϵ	emissivity, turbulence energy dissipation rate, small quantity
o	polar coordinate
δ	displacement
δx	axial distance between two neighboring mesh points

Symbol	Meaning
δx, δz	small distance in r- and z- coordinates
ζ	pressure loss coefficient
η	efficiency
σ	Stefan Boltzmann constant = 5.67 x 10^{-5} erg/cm^{2}K^4 sec, Prandtl-Schmidt number
ξ	non-dimensional radial coordinate (= r/(z + a))
θ	angle between the velocity vector and probe axis
γ	azimuth angle, expresion involving ratio of forward step length to cross-stream length squared
ψ	stream function, angle between the two beams, concentration
∇^2	Laplacian operator $= \frac{\partial^2}{\partial x_1{}^2} + \frac{\partial^2}{\partial x_2{}^2} + \frac{\partial^2}{\partial x_3{}^2}$
β	implicit weighting factor in finite difference system
α	jet half angle
α'	volume of air/volume of fuel
λ	mixing length parameter, wavelength
τ	shear stress, time constant, time, turbulent stress (momentum flux) tensor
Γ	turbulent exchange coefficient, circulation
ω	vorticity, angular frequency, non-dimensional stream function, angular velocity

Subscripts

a	axial, air, atmospheric
av	average
b	backward (or reverse)
c	critical, compensator
D	doppler frequency
e	effective, throat conditions, exit, entrained
E	external boundary of layer
f	forward, fuel, furnace conditions
fu, ox, pr	fuel, oxidant, products (including inerts)
fo	relating to composite quantity $m_{ox} - sm_{fu}$
g	gas
h	enthalpy
i	incident ith component of fluid velocity, nodal point xi = x + ih
I	internal boundary of layer
j	jth species equation, chemical species j
ℓ	laminar
m	maximum, maximum value at a particular axial station
m_o	maximum values (initial or at orifice)
n, s, e, w	north, south, east, west faces of cell
N	relating to Nth grid point across layer
o	reference value, inlet value, ambient conditions

Symbol	Meaning
p	constant pressure, dust particle
P, N, S, E, W	point, north, south, east, west neighbors
r	radial, recirculated
rx etc.	rx component of second-order tensor, etc.
rms	root mean square
s	static, stirred reactor, stoichiometric oxidant/fuel ratio
sh	frequency shift
st	stagnant
t	total
T	turbulent, temperature
W	thermocouple wire
z, x, θ	direction z, x, θ
μ	relating to turbulent viscosity
ϕ	dependent variable

Superscript

′	refers to fluctuating quantities, correction value to u*, v*, p* to get u, v, p
—	refers to averaged quantities
old	last iterate value
*	preliminary u, v, and p field based on estimate pressure field p*

CHAPTER 1

INTRODUCTION

1.1 THE CHALLENGE OF FLOWFIELD MODELING AND DIAGNOSTICS

Flowfield Manifestation

Flowfields typically encountered in turbulent reacting or nonreacting flows are usually quite complex, and an understanding of their fluid dynamics calls for a knowledge of the temporal and spatial values of flow parameters. The insight into a physical process can always be improved if the physical structure produced by, or related to that process can be analyzed with the aid of experimental diagnostics, or theoretical modeling, or both. There are several reasons for studying flowfields and turbulence experimentally; for example, one experimentalist may wish to have a general physical picture of mean flow and turbulence in order to generate an empirical or semi-empirical relationship that may be used as a direct practical application to the problem under investigation. Another experimentalist, however, may require detailed results relating to fine structures in order to develop and test a theoretical model. These varying needs can be satisfied by using a variety of diagnostic techniques; for example, invasive physical probes and non-invasive optical probes. An overall view of flow structure produced in a physical process can be observed by using aids to visualization. In order to trace the fluid motion, one must employ a technique by means of which the flowfield can be manifested; for example, optics. Flow visualization methods play an important role in understanding fluid dynamics by revealing the mean streamline flow patterns that show the main flow directions and relative components of velocity. Such techniques yield information about the complete flowfield under study without physically interfering with the flow. In contrast, a single measuring instrument such as a velocity, temperature, pressure or concentration probe, provides information about only one point in the flowfield. Furthermore its physical presence disturbs the flow and can significantly affect experimental results. Intrusive pressure, thermocouple, and hot-wire probes, besides introducing disturbances into the flow, have two other disadvantages: low frequency response, and the signal response are affected by both velocity and density. At any point in a reacting flowfield, time-mean values of velocity and density parameters are constant during quasi-steady operation of a combustion system, but they may fluctuate independently and in uncertain correlation.

Intrusive probes have the advantage of being less fragile and can be used in flames of large size. To reduce the basic difficulties, continuous efforts have been made to miniaturize the measuring probes and to improve the quantitative interpretation of flow visualization techniques, which have played an important role in the comprehension of complex fluid mechanical problems in several areas; for example, jet flows both with and without swirl, mixing layers, boundary layers, and turbulent shear layers[1-5].

A method of flow visualization entails the addition of foreign particles into the optically-transparent flowfield, which may be gaseous or liquid. By selecting particles of suitable size, the motion of these particles, both in magnitude and direction, can be assumed to be the same as that of the flowfield under investigation. An important feature of many flow visualization techniques is that one can derive semi-quantitative or quantitative information from the resulting flow picture. The visualization method is, therefore, an indirect method since observation is made of the foreign particles instead of the fluid flow. The difference between the velocity of fluid and foreign particles can be minimized, but not made zero, by selecting particles of the same density as that of the fluid. These methods yield satisfactory results in steady flows but for unsteady flows, in reciprocating engines and pulsejet engines; for example, the error can be large because of the inertia of the particles. The method can also give erroneous results if the fluid flow is compressible and the thermodynamic state of the fluid in the flowfield varies. For other flow visualization principles, readers are referred to the excellent text by Merzkirch[3]. Many turbulent flow systems possess large eddy structures, whereas, the fine, microstructures are common to all turbulent systems. In order to categorize a flow system, examination of large and fine microstructures for their formation, growth and convection requires diagnostic tools that physically interfere only minimally or not at all with the fluid flow. Large eddy structures, of sizes comparable to the width of mixing zones, have been identified in many flow systems.

Several different optical phenomena have been utilized as the basis for specific instruments, scattered light methods being the most popular. The light-scattering detection techniques can be separated into two categories: those that make size measurements of single particles, and systems that measure the light scattered by a collection of particles in the collimated laser beam. Multiple-scatter detection systems can typically make size measurements in particle fields that have a higher number density than corresponding single particle counters can handle. Unfortunately, the method does not provide a good spatial resolution and it does not measure the velocity of the droplets, thus limiting its application in spray nozzle measurements. In addition, the method assumes *a priori* particle size distribution which it fits mathematically. Optical methods have their own limitations, a major one being the need for high quality optical access to the test region. The limited dynamic range of these instruments is also of concern. The electrical aerosol analyzer measures the *in-situ* size, distribution in the range below that of the light-scattering method, that is, below that of 0.3 μm. The operating principle of this analyzer is that the mean electrical mobility of a diffusionally-charged particle is a function of particle size. No method, of course, is completely free of ambiguity and none yields ample information to characterize the local properties of the spray completely. As yet, no single instrument has proved to be completely satisfactory for use over a wide size range, although recent developments indicate that this feature will eventually be available.

Turbulent Flow Problems

In turbulent flow the eddies extract energy from the mean flow and retain it for a while before dissipating it in small eddies. The turbulent kinetic energy found in eddies is directly proportional to the sum of the normal Reynolds stresses ($\overline{u'^2}$, $\overline{v'^2}$. and $\overline{w'^2}$). The smaller eddies are much weaker than those that produce most of the Reynolds stress, since most of the energy is immediately transferred to the smallest eddies which are quickly dissipated by viscosity. The apparent mean stresses in turbulent flow are determined by the velocity fluctuations which depend upon the flow history.

In turbulent combustion processes, knowledge of the time-mean properties (for example velocity, temperature, pressure, concentration, etc.) are useful but insufficient to determine the reaction rate. The temporal characteristics of a turbulent flow are important since they govern not only the mixing process, but also the way in which the combustible mixture reacts and heat is transferred to the surroundings. They also yield a great deal of insight into pollutant emissions from, and combustion efficiency of, the system. A small increase in overall combustion efficiency can save many millions of dollars on a national scale. For the modeling and prediction of the spatial distribution of reaction rates, it is desirable to know the turbulence properties of the fuel and oxygen concentrations.

Instantaneous and local measurements within turbulent reacting flows are now possible with pulsed or chopped laser light sources, which can be tuned to selected wavelengths for minimizing spectral interferences. Many of these techniques and their potential for yielding the information required by more detailed models are examined by Lapp and Hartley[6], p. 135. Their application to studies of combustive flows should allow the measurement of single and joint probability density functions of fluctuating properties. Recent developments in laser probes clearly reveal that it is not unrealistic to measure directly one-point time-averaged correlation such as components of the Reynolds stress tensor $\tau_{ij} = -\overline{(\rho u_i)'u_j'}$, the turbulent heat flux vector $J_{hi} = +\overline{(\rho u_i)'h'}$ and the turbulent mass flux vector for the j-th chemical species $J_{m_j i} = +\overline{(\rho u_i)'m_j'}$. These stress and flux expressions occur in the time-averaged equations of conservation of momentum, energy and chemical species, respectively, where ρ is the density, u_i is the ith velocity component, h is the stagnation enthalpy, and m_j is the mass fraction of the jth chemical species.

The determination of these and other correlations of fluctuating quantities can then be incorporated into models of reacting flows. To date, most methods for the prediction of local changes in the distribution of reaction rate, temperature, concentration, etc are based on empirical or semi-empirical relationships. Significant developments have been made in laser-based experimental diagnostics, which are now widely used to measure time-mean and RMS velocity, temperature and concentration[6-8]. Techniques for measuring fluctuating local temperature and concentration would be highly desirable. The development of a detailed microscopically-based understanding of the chemistry of combustion presents a considerable challenge. This is because in a combustion system several chemical and physical processes interact together and proceed simultaneously. What we know is that a flame involves a large chemical reaction network through which heat is produced. The process results in steep gradients of both molecular concentrations and temperature; the reaction rates and mechanistic paths of the whole network are sensitively dependent upon the above parameters. It is clear therefore that the chemistry is woven inextricably with heat transfer and diffusion of reactive species throughout the flowfield. All these aspects must be considered with care, and attention given to the proper selection of the molecular input parameters; for example, transport coefficients and rate constants, as well as detailed un-ambiguous verification of the results. This is not a small task and, at present, we have the capability of picturing only very simple flames. The desire for accomplishing a microscopically-based description for turbulent diffusion flames of larger size of industrial importance is just now becoming feasible.

Combustion Problems

In flows with chemical reaction the flow characteristics are further complicated by non-linear interactions between chemical and fluid dynamical processes. The usual concept of a turbulent flame front is that of a laminar flame front with irregularities caused by fluctuating velocity components, leading to the formation of a wrinkled flame front which has a larger surface area than the corresponding laminar flame front. Schlieren and shadow photographs of the flame fronts reveal that the irregularities in the flame front are a product of turbulent scale and intensity in the flow. The question of flame-generated turbulence has been a topic of interest at several symposia and meetings. Ignition of the combustible mixture in confined flows results in expansion and acceleration of the flow. Acceleration increases the shear and strain and it is not clear whether there are any additional mechanisms that influence the increase in turbulence intensity. In unconfined flows, however, the lack of dynamic confinement results in very little, if any, increase in pressure. Experimental results of mean and RMS velocity in confined flows clearly show expansion and acceleration. Relatively small increases in turbulence intensity appear to be primarily associated with increases in strain and the associated velocity gradients. It is possible that combustion occurs in microexplosions which, in turn, cause turbulence and local pressure increases.

In two-phase flows, accurate size and velocity measurements of liquid sprays or solid particles are important for a broad spectrum of applications. General areas of application include characterization of fuel sprays, agricultural sprays, soot formation and growth, diesel engines, aerosols, pigments, evaluation of scrubbers, etc. Fuel spray applications are of current interest in combustion research because of the need to improve the combustion efficiency and to reduce the particulate and emission levels of other pollutants.

Fuel sprays are complex dynamic phenomena, entailing atomization, coagulation, dispersion, heat and mass transfer, and chemistry, which are subject to intimate interactions within a gaseous flowfield. Research into fuel atomization and fuel-air preparation requires the measurement of fuel droplet size, velocity-size correlations, and mean and RMS velocities of air and fuel. Complete characterization of local properties in a spray includes such attributes as particle size distribution and number density, a velocity distribution function related to droplets of different sizes, mean velocity of the gas phase, local gas and liquid temperatures, composition of both the gas and liquid phases, turbulence properties, and so on. The reliable measurement of any one of the above properties is not trivial.

Sampling techniques can, of course, be used to withdraw a representative sample from a particle-laden flow. The sampling process always disturbs the flowfield to some extent even if the sample is withdrawn isokinetically. In reacting flowfields at high turbulence levels it is particularly difficult to extract a representative sample with any degree of confidence. Particle agglomeration and deposition in a sampling system can alter the size distribution prior to measurement. In addition, real-time measurements are not possible with sampling methods and in some cases sample preparation and analysis can be time-consuming. Despite the above limitations, sampling methods are still useful in many instances. The increased need for non-perturbing real-time *in-situ* measurements of particle size has motivated the development of a wide variety of optical methods. Only in recent years have serious attempts been made to obtain *in-situ* particle-size measurements.

Where the particles are large enough, the direct image photographic method is least ambiguous and most reliable but, unfortunately, it is rather slow and can be employed only for sprays of a continuous nature. Video systems can be used for particle analysis, but even then the systems are intrinsically slow because of limitations imposed by the standard video framing rate. The related problem of solid particulate size measurements is of interest in smoke, particulate and pollutants reduction, fluidized bed combustion, pigments manufacture and other similar areas.

In flame combustion processes the efficient utilization of energy requires maximization of the overall energy efficiency. In a boiler plant, the biggest heat loss is associated with the flue gases. In general, improvements in overall energy efficiency of processes require careful examination of combustion, mechanical and thermodynamic efficiency. The thermal efficiency is the ratio of heat gained by the load to the energy supplied via fuel and is influenced by the rates of heat transfer from flames to the combustion chamber walls and, hence, on temperature distributions within the combustion chamber. Control of the distributions of temperatures within the combustion chamber therefore has a potential that can lead to improvements in overall thermal efficiency. In an electrically heated system, approximately two thirds of the original fuel energy is lost in the power generation and transmission stages, so that an efficiency in excess of 33 per cent is difficult to achieve.

The primary concern of a combustion engineer is to achieve maximum combustion efficiency with minimum or no pollutant emissions. High combustion efficiency requires complete combustion of fuel supplied to the combustor. Any unburned fuel leaving the system contributes not only to combustion inefficiency but also to the pollutant emission levels, since it is also considered to be a pollutant. The incentive for complete combustion of fuel is therefore twofold—increased combustion efficiency and reduced emission of pollutants. In a combustion system, combustion efficiency close to 100 per cent can be achieved provided the fuel is maintained at elevated temperatures in the presence of an oxidizer for a long enough residence time. Combustion efficiencies lower than 100 per cent are primarily due to other design considerations—a typical example being refineries and oil wells where Coanda flares are used for the incineration of explosive gases.

1.2 PURPOSE OF THE TEXT

The present text in the Energy and Engineering Science series covers the interaction between fluid dynamics and combustion, pointing out where theoretical and experimental techniques are applicable in the design, development and operation of practical combustion processes. A number of textbooks that cover various aspects of flowfield diagnostics, modeling, and fluid dynamics of combustion[1-41] are available. The present text complements these and attempts to combine the arts of experimental and theoretical diagnostics for application to systems both with and without chemical reaction. The text is intended to be a comprehensive and illustrated introduction to problems and progress in flowfields investigation: techniques, their practical application, recent research, and projected developments and trends. Application ideas are complemented by full details about modeling and experimental techniques, and available possibilities are extensively surveyed.

The importance of the current subject matter can be easily recognized by considering the following applications in the general areas of science and engineering:

1. Power production—using solid, liquid or gaseous fuels for central power stations and vehicle propulsion.
2. Process industry—for iron, steel and many non-ferrous metals, glass and ceramics, cement, and refined fuels, carbon black, and other hydrocarbon derivatives.
3. Domestic and industrial heating—for homes, factories, offices, etc.
4. Turbulent flows in engineering—channel flows, developing flows, shear flows, and coherent structures.

Although nuclear, hydro and geothermal energy sources are being utilized extensively, it falls upon gas, oil and coal to serve as principal fuels. When their energy extraction is via burning, it is invariably provoked by a supply of oxidant (and a means of initiating and/or sustaining chemical reaction) and the coupling between fluid flow and heat release becomes of paramount importance. The combustion engineer focuses his attention on efficiency of combustion, reduction of costs (capital and running costs of equipment) and emission level and temperature control of the exhausted gases. Theory and experiment combine to aid the diagnostician in this endeavor, for his subject is unusually complex and embraces a multiplicity of disciplines from the fundamental sciences which have to be integrated via models, algorithms and computers, and applied to specific practical engineering processes. Many years have been spent on maximizing the understanding of complex flowfields in turbulent flows both with and without chemical reaction. Fortunately, the requirement for low pollution is compatible with high combustion efficiency (excepting, perhaps, noise pollution), although advanced technology is needed to attain both goals simultaneously. Theoretical and experimental evidence must combine in the effective design, development and operation of most complex practical equipment with 3-D multicomponent flowfields, in which the inter-dependent phenomena of turbulence, chemical kinetics, fuel droplet evaporation and heat transfer (conduction, convection and radiation) are all occurring simultaneously. Clearly the combustion designer has a formidable problem in aerothermochemistry, and the task is to provide a route which leads to the accomplishment of design objectives more quickly and less expensively than current practice permits.

1.3 FLUID DYNAMICS OF COMBUSTION

Complexity of Combustion Processes

The subject of combustion aerodynamics may conveniently be categorized into three areas[37], each at a different level of applicability:

1. *Engineering Practice,* – for example, gasoline engines, diesel engines, gas turbine engines, rockets, industrial boilers and furnaces, open hearth steel furnaces, blast furnaces, fluidized bed combustors, and hot-flame cutting equipment.
2. *Mathematical Models,* – for example, flame propagation, compression ignition, flame stabilization, detonation, spark ignition, gaseous, liquid, solid or liquid-solid fuel combustion, laminar and turbulent jets and flames, particle evaporation and combustion, recirculating reactor and catalytic combustion.
3. *Fundamental Sciences,* – for example, thermodynamics, fluid mechanics, heat and mass transfer, and chemical kinetics.

These areas are connected via a variety of paths, the fundamental sciences providing a basis for mathematical modeling with a view to providing application in engineering practice. Recent trends are influencing engineering practice (alternate fuels, pollution control, efficiency and heat transfer), mathematical models (computer methods, validation and utilization) and fundamental sciences (including chemical kinetics and numerical mathematics).

In *steady-flow* systems, coal may be burned as lumps on a grate as in domestic heating units, small industrial boilers, and blast furnaces, or as powder, suspended in an air stream, as in large industrial boilers, fluidized bed combustors and cement kilns. Light fuel oils, for example: kerosine, gas, oil, light coal liquids (SRC-II, EDS), may be used, as vapor from a heated tube or pot, for example: as in primus stoves, small aircraft gas turbines, and small domestic boilers, as a spray of droplets from a rotating cup as in aircraft gas turbines. Kerosine, gas oil or light coal liquids may also be sprayed from a swirl atomizer as in industrial gas turbines and large domestic and industrial boilers, or impelled by steam as a jet of droplets as in open-hearth furnaces. Rocket propellants in liquid form are atomized by the impingement of liquid jets in large rocket engines and in solid form are burned in perforated blocks at free surfaces in small rocket engines. In *unsteady flow* equipment, gasoline is vaporized by contact with air and hot surfaces in spark-ignition internal combustion engines. Gas oil is sprayed by injection through small orifices in compression-ignition diesel engines.

In introductory articles to recent conferences, Swithenbank[26] pointed out the current unknown fluid mechanics of combustion, and Chigier[41] emphasized the strong interaction between fluid mechanics and combustion by considering recent progress and problems in practical applications, and assessing the extent to which research on combustion aerodynamics has succeeded in influencing the design and performance of practical combustion systems.

Combustion

Combustion is typically viewed as the exothermic chemical reaction of a fuel and oxidant, and three regimes can be easily distinguished:

1. Slow oxidation *preflame combustion* occurs throughout extended volume at low temperatures.
2. *Detonative combustion*—combustion shock wave propagates supersonically through the mixture.
3. *Flame combustion* occurs as a fast process with a thin reaction zone which propagates as a combustion wave at flame speed through the reaction volume, called a

steady state *deflagration flame,* or occurs in a closed vessel with exponential reaction rate increase and pressure explosion, called a thermal or *branching chain explosion.*

Most practical combustion applications involve deflagrative flames, in which the exothermic reaction results in an increase of volume (and temperature), a decrease of density and a small decrease in pressure across the flame front. Two distinct applications can be distinguished:

1. *Heating Applications.* Here it is required to transfer heat from the burning gases to boiler tubes, metal ingots, etc. The achievement of high flame radiation from the burning gases is highly desirable.
2. *Propulsion Applications.* The aim is to increase the volume, velocity and kinetic energy of the fluid stream, in order to provide direct jet propulsion, or to drive a turbine. Since *gas* heating is required, flame radiation is unnecessary, and usually undesirable.

Although a flame can propagate through a static combustible gas mixture, it is usual to stabilize the flame at a fixed point by supplying a continuous flow of combustible mixture. Under these conditions, flames can be divided into two main classes:

1. *Premixed flames* in which the reactants are completely mixed on a molecular level prior to ignition and combustion. These are kinetically controlled and the rate of flame propagation, called the burning velocity, is dependent upon chemical composition and rates of chemical reaction. Completely premixed flames are seldom found in practice for reasons of safety, (for example flashback and blow-off) and stability.
2. *Diffusion flames* in which the reactants mix by diffusion into a thin flame zone, and reaction rates are diffusion controlled. They are preferred in industrial practice, gas turbines, internal combustion engines, etc. being safer since the fuel and oxidant are kept separate, as well as providing greater flexibility in controlling flame size and shape and combustion intensity. Fuel and air may be preheated and partially premixed, with additional or secondary air supplied through a separate section of the combustor.

In both the premixed and diffusion flames, transfer of heat, mass and momentum play important roles. The transfer will be by molecular diffusion in *laminar flames* and the flow of gases follows streamlines in the flow without turbulent transport. The transfer will be by turbulent diffusion in *turbulent flames* and the scale and intensity of turbulence affect the burning rates. In practice the need for high combustion efficiency and intensity or high heat release rates associated with turbulent combustion requires information on physical structure of turbulent flow, flame fronts, flame generated turbulence, probability density functions, flame propagation, pollution and noise generation. The discussion leads naturally to the aerodynamic effect on combustion processes and the strong interaction between them.

Burning Techniques

Fuel and oxidant are admitted into combustion chambers via *burners.* Gaseous fuels can be pumped directly, but liquid, solid fuels, coal-oil, coal-water mixtures and slurries require preparation. Liquid fuels are admitted as an atomized spray or cloud of finely dispersed droplets, and preheating to reduce viscosity is a common practice. Solid fuels are often pulverized, or they can be burned on grates or in fixed or fluid beds. Solid, liquid and solid-liquid slurries undergo *heterogeneous combustion.* This process, involving release of combustible gases from the solid or liquid phases, may be superimposed on the general flame zone concepts. Phenomena of interest include: atomization processes, spray characteristics, vaporization rates, and combustion. Fuel and oxidant are rarely completely premixed in the burner; they are injected separately or, more often, the fuel is mixed with a small proportion of the combustion air (primary air) on its path through the burner. The splitting of the combustion air into primary and secondary streams is made for reasons of flame stability and safety, such as prevention of flash back and explosion in the fuel supply lines. It also enables elevated preheat temperatures to be utilized in the secondary air which, in turn, may favorably affect the thermodynamic efficiency of the system.

Staged combustion and associated *stratified charge engines* separate the combustion into stages, that is two or more distinct regions, usually a first stage where the mixture is fuel-rich followed by a second stage where it is fuel-lean. Typically, there is a prechamber followed by a main chamber. In each, mixture rates, mean temperature and concentrations or reactants and products are maintained at particular levels. Lower temperatures result, since stoichiometric conditions are avoided, and hence lower rates of production of oxides of nitrogen, from thermal fixation of atmospheric N_2, are found. Fuel rich conditions in the first stage are also favorable for reducing NO_X levels from high nitrogen bearing fuels.

Fluid Dynamics

Turbulent jets of fuel and air issuing from burners in a multi-burner system play a dominant role in mixing processes. These jets interact with transverse jets and recirculation zones and provide flow and mixing patterns for directing flame zones and heating, which, in turn, determine local air/fuel ratios, flame zones and combustion rates. *Round jets* are most common and come about by fluid issuing from circular cross-section pipes and nozzles. Even at low flow rates and small burner diameters, the jet flow soon becomes turbulent. In practice, most burners have sizes and velocities that give rise to turbulent conditions at the exit. *Annular jets* frequently surround primary fuel jets or oil guns for secondary air delivery. Sometimes, bluff bodies are placed centrally in the path of air nozzles, so forming an annular flow with central recirculation zone which assists flame stabilization. The combination of a round jet and surrounding annular jet is called a *double concentric jet.* Farther downstream the combined mass flow rates and jet momenta characterize the coalesced flow, but near the burner the size and geometry of the separation interface strongly influences mixing, with pronounced effects on flame stability.

Flame stabilizing recirculation zones may also be provoked by strong adverse pressure gradients caused by spiraling motion imparted to the jet flow, thus forming a *swirling jet.* The swirl velocity component (also known as tangential or azimuthal velocity component) may be imparted via the use of swirl vanes, an axial-plus-tangential entry swirl generator or direct tangential entry into the combustor. The swirl strength has a large-scale effect on a flowfield: jet growth, entrainment and decay (for inert jets) and flame size, shape, stability and combustion intensity (for reacting flows)[4]. In particular, higher mixing rates, higher turbulence intensities and higher combustion intensities result. The degree of swirl also offers an effective control of the proportion of nozzle fluid mass recirculated and hence chamber residence time distribution. Good approximations of combustion performance can be made, and it is extremely satisfying to be able to optimize combustion performance via adjustment of swirl strength and resulting residence time distribution. A companion text[4] (entitled *Swirl Flows*, in the Energy and Engineering Science Series) provides extensive details of the many aspects of these complex swirl flow phenomena.

Throttling entrainment to a turbulent jet by confinment in a chamber results in a *confined jet* with associated recirculation zone(s), outside the jet stream. Jets penetrating into a main stream flow at some angle are called *transverse jets.* They have frequent application as secondary and dilution air injection into, for example, gas turbine combustor flames. Usually, the prediction of their behavior for design purposes (the jet path, its penetration into and mixing with the main stream) proceeds via detailed experimentation or a semi-empirical approach. Recent improvements in theoretical predictive capability reveal that direct prediction of this and other fluid dynamic phenomena in flows both with and without chemical reaction is possible.

1.4 PRACTICAL COMBUSTION AERODYNAMIC APPLICATIONS

In practical design situations, the combustion engineer has to seek an optimum path between design and performance parameters. The general aim of most investigations is to provide information that is useful to designers by 'characterizing' or 'modeling' certain features of the phenomenon in question. Investigations may be theoretical or experimental; the two approaches are complementary. Up to now, designers have relied heavily on the experimental approach, although the mathematical modeling approach is now finding favor and is being used to supplement existing design procedures, and clearly computer modeling of combustion processes is now an established fact. The processes of interest occur in furnaces and combustors, gasoline engines, diesel engines, gas turbine engines, pulsejet, ramjet and scramjet engines, solid- and liquid- propellant rockets.

Gasoline and diesel engines are of the reciprocating kind, with transient features and intermittent ignition and combustion. Similar transient features occur in pulsejet combustion deliberately, and during problem instabilities in the other processes which generally involve quasi-steady continuous combustion.

The Gasoline Engine

Here the combustion system must guarantee ignition by spark, and burn fuel completely under all conditions with minimum heat loss[42-47]. Demands for efficiency led to high compression ratios and the process of 'knock'—an uncontrolled ignition of the gaseous mixture in the cylinder causing excessive heating, noise, and mechanical strain to the engine. Design changes and lead-based fuel additives were introduced to eliminate this unwanted process, but today unleaded fuel is preferred for pollutant reduction reasons. A schematic of the piston-cylinder assembly and its working cycle appears in Fig. 1.1.

Consider the operation of the gasoline engine on its four-stroke Otto cycle:

1. The induction (or charging) stroke. The downward motion of the piston with the inlet valve open, draws the fuel-air mixture into the cylinder from the carburetor.

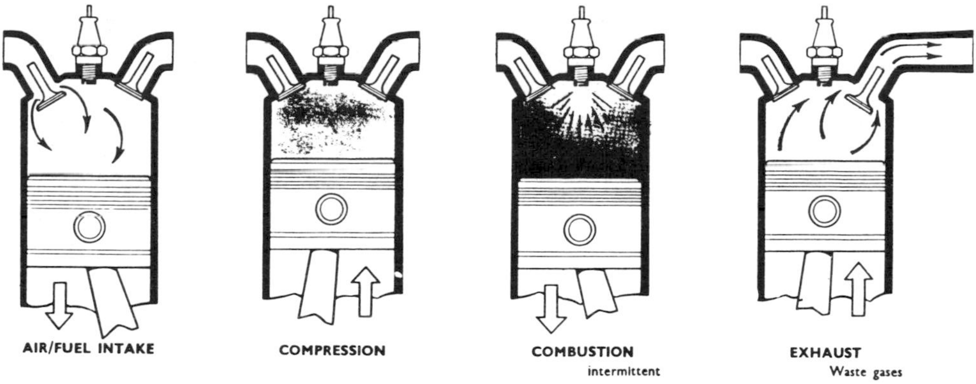

Figure 1.1 The gasoline engine piston-cylinder assembly and four stroke Otto cycle.[68]

2. The compression stroke. The mixture is compressed and heated adiabatically, the inlet valve being closed. Just before top dead center, TDC, the ignition from spark plug initiates a flame and combustion proceeds essentially to completion before the piston has moved appreciably downward. This is essentially a *constant volume* combustion.
3. The power stroke. The hot high-pressure gas drives the piston downward, thus extracting some mechanical energy from the chemical energy of the fuel.
4. The exhaust stroke. The upward motion of the cylinder with the exhaust valve open expels the burnt gases.

Experiment and theory are required to help the designer to determine the influence of boundary shape, gap between and around piston rings, location of spark plug and spark energy, fuel properties and wall temperature on ignition behavior, charge lodged and gas flows in engine crevices[46], pressure-volume-time (indicator diagram) variations, tendency to 'knock', thin layer of the unburned mixture on the cool cylinder walls, and the final gas composition. Past, present and future of the gasoline engine and pollutant emission problems and solutions are discussed in Wheeler[47] and Heywood[48].

Stratified charge engines, SCEs, include both *swirl* and *squish* motions and address two problems simultaneously—pollutant reduction and efficiency. Internal combustion, IC, engines of this type are illustrated schematically in Fig. 1.2 where a cylinder and piston (equipped with a 'cup' in order to produce squish) are drawn. Some piston heads are 'cupped' as shown, so forcing the flow inward during the final stages of the compression stroke, a phenomenon known as 'squish'. The arrangement is such that the fuel/air ratio, FAR, in the vicinity of the spark plug is much richer than elsewhere in the combustion chamber. Combustion is 'gentle' with mixture remote from the spark plug acting like a cushion. Operation with this arrangement is possible with overall FAR well below the operating limit (set by ignitability considerations) for conventional engines, and this leanness feature makes for economy. Further, power is controlled entirely by the rate of fuel flow, and not the wasteful throttling technique of conventional engines where the engine works against itself. The SCE runs always at 'full throttle' with fuel flow limitation controlling the action. High pressure is favorable for the ignition of the fuel, which

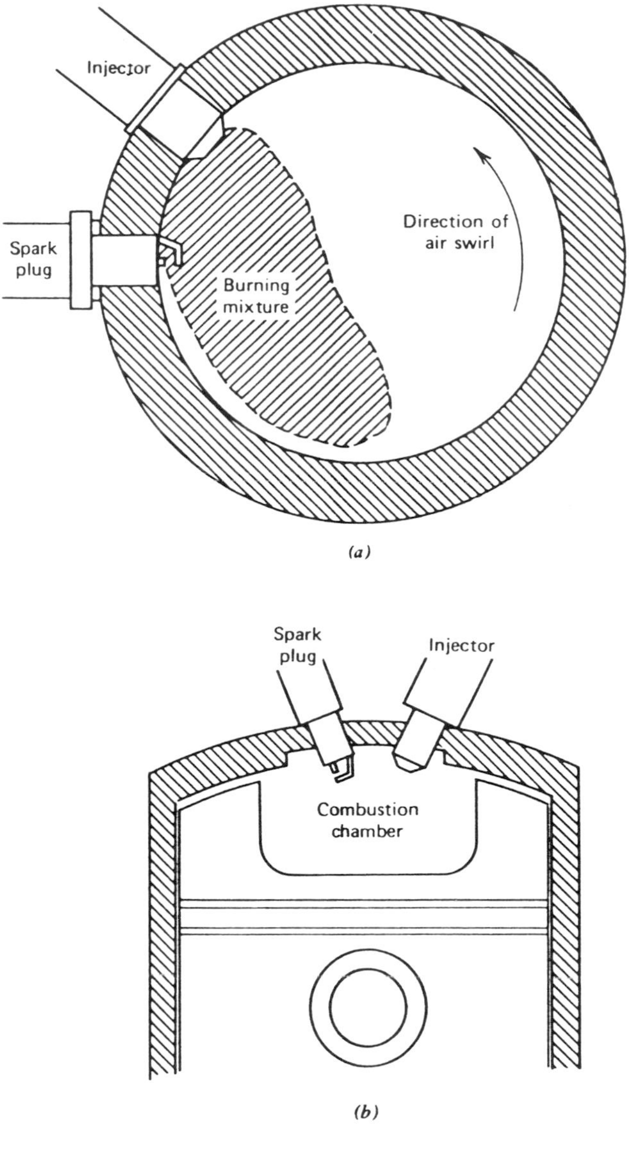

Figure 1.2 Stratified charge engine geometry. (a) Arrangement of injector and spark plug in a stratified charge engine. (b) Cupped piston in stratified charge engine, which produces "squish".[45]

is directly injected through the cylinder head. Swirling air mixes with fuel and carries the mixture past the spark plug. The burning region is highly localized, and comprises a rich mixture with good ignitability in an overall lean mixture. Further discussion of swirl and squish air motions in gasoline engines and their effect in combustion chamber design are given in Wheeler[47]. Discussion includes the Ricardo 'bathtub' chamber, the Heron 'bowl-in-piston' chamber and the high-compression high-turbulence chamber designs. The SCE design possibilities are interpreted in terms of swirl, squish and vortices for the Ricardo spark-ignited comet, the Honda CVCC, the MAN-FM and the Ford PROCO systems. Applications of SCEs to pollutant formation and control in spark-ignition engines are thoroughly covered by Heywood[48], including open chamber (Ford PROCO and Texaco TCCS for example) and divided chamber (Honda small pre-chamber and other two-chamber concepts) systems. Further work is discussed in Chapter 5 on problems and progress.

The Diesel Engine

As compared with the gasoline engine, the compression ratio of the diesel engine is high in order to auto-ignite the fuel since there is no spark in the engine and combustion level is controlled by the rate of liquid fuel spray injection. Maximization of the engine power by using up all the available air tends to yield excessive smoke, an unwanted pollutant. Recent advances in rotary (Wankel) and stratified charge engines, SCEs, have been stimulated through desire for efficient clean combustion.

In the four-stroke diesel engine, the chemical energy of the fuel is partially transformed into mechanical work in four phases, in a manner similar to the spark-ignition engine, but now there is no spark plug—combustion is initiated automatically via high compression. The four phases are:

1. The charging stroke. Air enters through the inlet valve and fills the engine cylinder.
2. The compression stroke and beginning of combustion. The enclosed air is compressed to high pressure, and as the piston approaches top dead center TDC fuel is sprayed into the combustion chamber via rapid pressure injection.
3. The combustion and working (or expansion) stroke. Combustion initiated automatically by compression just before TDC continues for some time after TDC, and high pressure is maintained. This is *constant pressure* combustion. The piston is driven further downward, and pressure and temperature then reduce.
4. The exhaust stroke. The combustion products (plus any excess air or fuel) are expelled via the exhaust (outlet) valve.

Now high compression must provide smooth ignition, use all available oxygen, reduce heat transfer, reduce pumping power (work needed for exhausting and drawing in gases), and emit no or little smoke. It is desirable for the inlet flow to possess a *swirl motion* about the central axis of the cylinder and the bowl-in-piston (or cup-in-piston) arrangement gives the *squish* phenomenon as the piston nears the top of the cylinder. The radial extent of the volume of swirling flow is suddenly restricted, and conservation of swirl momentum causes a dramatic increase in the swirl velocity, increasing turbulence and mixing levels. Researchers need to know the influences of chamber boundary shape, inlet air movement, fuel spray injector characteristics and fuel properties on ignition delay, pressure-volume-time variation, heat transfer to the piston and smoke production. The application of *swirl* and *squish* to gas motion in diesel engines is included in the review and prospects given recently by Shahed *et al.*[49]. These concepts are also used in stratified charge engines of the gasoline variety.

Consider now what theory may contribute in the optimization of design and development. Increasing demands for both thermal efficiency and lower pollutant output provide incentive for better methods of analyzing the aerothermodynamics in internal combustion, IC, engines. The most general approach is to compute as a function of three-space coordinates and time the complete flowfield between the top of the cylinder and the face of the piston throughout the complete four-stroke cycle—intake, compression, power and exhaust stroke—with the intake and exhaust valves opening and closing appropriately. In the gasoline engine, spark ignition initiates the combustion of the compressed gaseous mixture at the beginning of the power stroke; in the diesel engine, on the other hand, ignition of the fuel droplet spray is brought about via the high compression achieved on the compression stroke, and modeling is then a more difficult task. In both cases, it is a major effort to diagnose experimentally and apply computational fluid dynamics in order to analyze and understand the complex flowfield patterns in reciprocating engines for subsequent aid in their design and development.

Recent discussions of the problems of directly computing multidimensional chemically-reacting flows in IC engines are available elsewhere[50-61]. Until recently, most models of IC engines were basically thermodynamic models—the combustion chamber was considered as a control volume, fluid dynamic motion was neglected and energy release rate specified[50-53]. Many such successful applications have been made. Nevertheless, interest in more realistic approaches is essential in understanding and solving current problems in, for example, stratified charge engines, and development of spatial models are necessary[54-61]. More advanced work appears in Chapter 5.

Furnaces

Flame control is especially important in providing specified distributions of radiant and convective heat transfer, complete combustion, freedom from noise and oscillation, and insensitivity to fuel changes. Fig. 1.3 illustrates four ways in which coal may be burned in industrial furnaces. In furnace design, a multitude of practical configurations are involved, and typical problems and requirements are distinctly opposite to those of engine designers; for example, carbon particulates are needed to generate large radiant heat fluxes, but it is desirable to consume them all before the gases leave the furnace. Heat transfer rates must be high and fluxes must be distributed in an optimum manner.

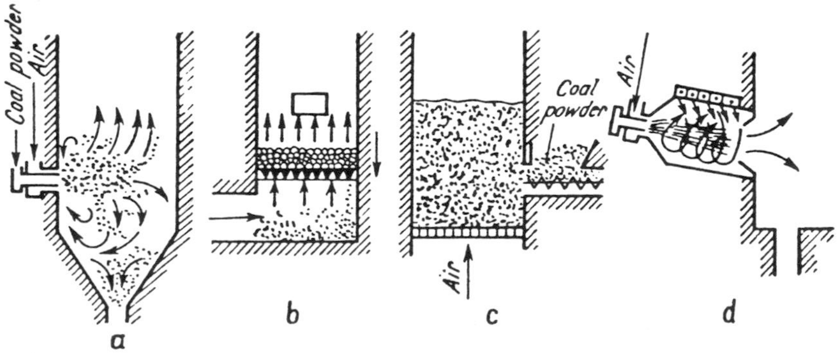

Figure 1.3 Coal combustion in industrial furnaces
a. as pulverized coal
b. in a fixed bed
c. in a fluidized bed
d. in a cyclone furnance[32]

Many different types of furnaces exist—the power station boiler furnace is somewhat different from the furnaces of the metallurgical and process industries, for example. The furnace takes on a role of central importance in modern society and its efficiency and pollution characteristics have far-reaching consequences. In all cases, though, flame control is especially important in providing specified distributions of radiant and convective heat transfer, complete combustion, freedom from noise and oscillation, and insensitivity to fuel changes, in particular future fuels, that is, low-grade fuels, coal liquids, coal-oil or water mixtures.

Most furnace flames are given a degree of *swirl* for improved stability, while others; for example, the tangentially-fired boiler, have inlet streams which are directed so as to aim tangentially at the fireball in the center of the chamber, producing a weak *cyclone* effect in the furnace about the geometric axis of the equipment. The process causes a particular temperature, heat-flux distribution to the walls and combustion efficiency. These are intimately connected with production of pollutants such as soot, particulates, polycyclic aromatic hydrocarbons[62], noise and oxides of nitrogen and sulfur (soot is formed by thermal decomposition of hydrocarbon molecules and consumed by oxidation and PAH are preferentially attached onto soot; both of these are complex chemical-kinetic processes). The designer and operator would like to know how these depend on fuel type, fuel-jet momentum and angle, temperature of preheated air and the shape of the chamber. Needless to say, the simulation problem becomes quite complex, involving the interaction of turbulent combustion of many chemical species, multi-phase processes and radiative heat transfer. As detailed elsewhere, modeling to some extent affects particle-size distributions, flux or zone models of radiation heat transfer, soot and polycyclic aromatic hydrocarbon distribution. Reviews of progress in this areas are available, and the work of the International Flame Research Foundation, Ijmuiden, Holland and the Associated American Flame Research Committee is to be noted[62-67].

Fluidized Bed Combustion

Fluidized combustion shows excellent potential for burning coal and low-grade fuels in industry and utility boilers. Its development is already in the initial stages of commercialization. In operation the fluidizing air is passed through a perforated distributor plate and up through the bed material which consists mainly of inert ash or limestone or dolomite capable of capturing the sulfur introduced with the fuel. In single-stage operation the burning particles account for less than 2 per cent by weight of the total bed solids. Part of the air passes through the interstices between the particles, and the remainder forms bubbles which grow by coalescence as they flow up through the bed. The coal or fuel is fed through a series of points and is rapidly dispersed through the bed as it burns. Bed temperature (typically in the range 975-1275 K) is controlled by the heat transfer tubes immersed in the bed. Some of the solids splash into the freeboard (combustion space above the bed) as the bubbles burst and are elutriated with the combustion products but the majority of the solid removal from the bed is via overflow weirs. In order to increase the carbon combustion efficiency some of the combustible particulates elutriated from the bed are collected by cyclones and re-injected into the bed. The combustion products leaving the bed surface contain some combustible gases and char particles, which rise in the freeboard for the completion of combustion. Some of the major advantages of fluidized combustion over suspension firing include *in-situ* desulfurization of combustion products, high volumetric heat release rates and heat transfer rates to heat exchange surfaces immersed in the bed, insensitivity to fuel quality variation, good temperature control of bed particles, reduction in the vaporization of potentially toxic compounds and the elimination of ash clinkering and slag fouling.

A complete quantitative description of fluidized combustion requires that the processes of combustion, pollutants formation, and elutriation be considered together with the fluid dynamic (including bubble growth and bursting) and chemical properties of the bed several of which are still unknown. The conditions in the bed primarily determine the conditions at entrance to the freeboard. The major combustion losses from fluidized coal combustors are CO and unburned carbon in the effluent from the freeboard and carbon lost with solids removed from the bed. In order to estimate carbon combustion efficiency it is, therefore, necessary to determine carbon loading and particle size distribution within the bed, the rate of elutriation of different size fractions from the bed, and the extent of burn-out in the freeboard of the elutriated carbon. Experimental data are needed to determine the effect of geometric and input parameters upon bubble size and growth, gas-emulsion exchange coefficients, size distribution of ascending and descending particles in the bed, transient temperature variations in the bed and fuel feed location, combustion efficiency and pollutants emission including NO_x and polycyclic aromatic hydrocarbons. Theoretical elutriation models are needed for calculating the net loss of carbon from the freeboard and for modeling freeboard reactions which are strongly dependent upon solids loading in the freeboard. Present models are generally for steady-state operation and models are therefore needed to include transients and stability limits.

The Gas Turbine

The cycle for gas turbine combustion (the Brayton cycle) is similar to that of the reciprocating four-stroke internal combustion engine, *see* Fig. 1.1, except that continuous rather than intermittent burning is involved and the combustion takes place at *constant pressure* rather than at constant volume. Fig. 1.4 illustrates the gas turbine turbojet engine. The cycles of both are made up of four strokes: the charging, compressing, combusting and exhausting strokes. In the reciprocating engine the four strokes take place successively in the same cylinder, *see* Fig. 1.1; in the gas turbine they take place simultaneously in different parts of the engine, via the compressor (with charging system), the combustion

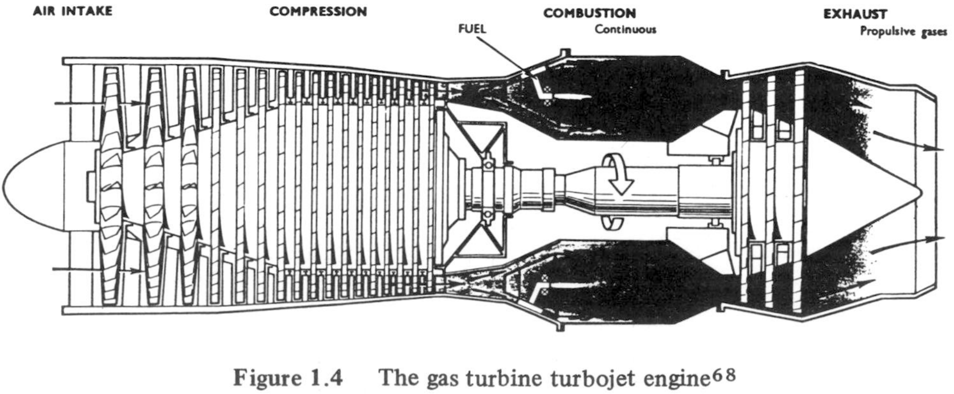

Figure 1.4 The gas turbine turbojet engine[68]

chamber, the turbine (with expansion), and the exhaust system. The continuous smooth steady state rotary motion of the gas turbine led to its wide use in stationary and mobile power plants, most noticeably in aircraft applications, in the form of the turbojet (pure jet), turboprop (most work going to the propeller) and turbofan (some work going to a large fan with 'by-pass' facility). The gas turbine produces, among other things, smoke. Industrial automotive application makes all these pollutants even less tolerable than aircraft applications.

The combustion chamber of a gas turbine engine performs an essential task of high intensity combustion, and designers strive to reduce its length without making the flame too easily extinguishable, and to reduce its pressure drop without adversely affecting the degree of mixing in the gases that exhaust through the turbine. In industry experimentation, 'trial and error' (or so-called 'cut and try' or 'cut and weld') methods are often used for optimization of the basic design.

Basic features of a can-type combustion chamber are shown in Fig. 1.5[68]. Although its construction is quite simple, its design and development are haphazard. Details of its operation are quite complex and present knowledge of the internal aerodynamics is incomplete. Notice that although the figure refers to a combustor can flame tube, it may also be thought of as cross-sectional views of annular combustors. It may also represent directly the flame tube of a cannular system. These systems find their place in high intensity combustion engines, in which the combustor must burn fuel completely, cause little pressure drop, produce gases of nearly uniform temperature, occupy small volume, and maintain stable combustion over a wide range of operating conditions. The combustor has the difficult task of burning large quantities of various types of fuel, introduced in a highly atomized spray from a specially designed nozzle, with extensive volumes of air, which flows in through an upstream annular *swirler.* This task must be accomplished subject to certain performance requirements.

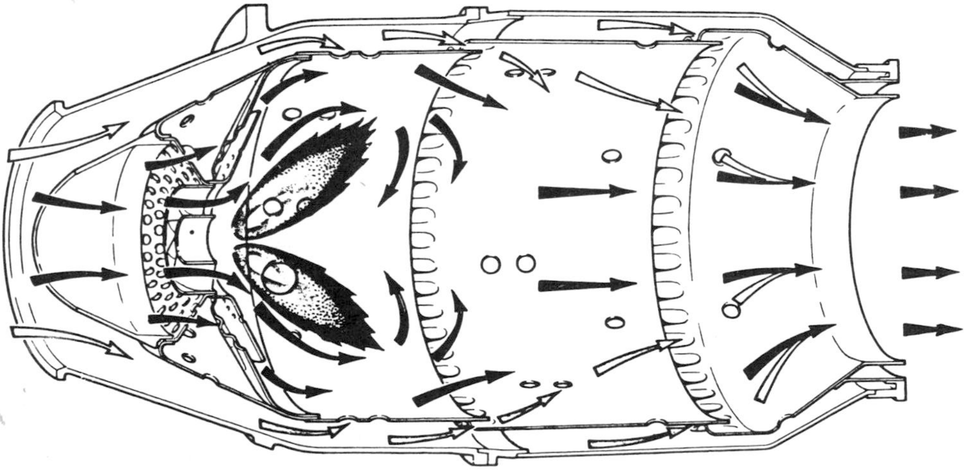

Figure 1.5 Schematic flame stabilization and general flow pattern in a typical axisymmetric can-type combustion chamber of a gas turbine engine.[68]

In a combustor can, typically, 18 per cent or so of the air stream enters through swirl vanes at an angle of about 70 degrees to the main flow direction. This results in strong 'centrifugal' effects on entry to the combustor and very low pressure in the primary zone, resulting in the formation of a *central toroidal recirculation zone,* CTRZ. The central hub of the swirler includes a fuel spray nozzle, and a conical spray of liquid kerosine droplets is projected to the CTRZ, resulting in high-intensity burning. Stability is enhanced by the recirculation of hot combustion products, and additional primary zone air entering via lateral injection holes. The designer needs to know how the host of requirements are influenced by the pressure and temperature of the inlet air, the location and size of other holes and film-cooling slots, swirl strength, boundary geometry, fuel spray angle and properties, and many other parameters. Reviews and recent advances are documented elsewhere[69-77] and further discussion appears in Chapter 5.

Pulsejet Engines

Intermittent combustion is the principle used in the pulsejet engine, of which a schematic is seen in Fig. 1.6. The duct inlet has a series of inlet valves which are spring-loaded into the open position. Air flows in through the open valves and passes into the combustion chamber where it is heated by the burning of fuel injected into the chamber. The resulting pressure rise causes the valves to close and the hot expanded gases are ejected rearward through the propelling nozzle at high speed, thus providing propulsive force. But the frontal air entry is now closed off, and as the exhausting gases escape a rarefaction occurs, thus allowing the valves to open and the cycle to re-start. Some designs dispense with inlet valves by careful ducting aimed at controlling the changing pressures of the resonating cycle. The pulsejet has not been found suitable for aircraft propulsion because of its low thermal efficiency, high fuel consumption and lack of performance in comparison to gas turbine propulsion. It was, however, the power plant of the V-1 flying bomb during the Second World War because of its simple and inexpensive construction[32,44,68,78,79].

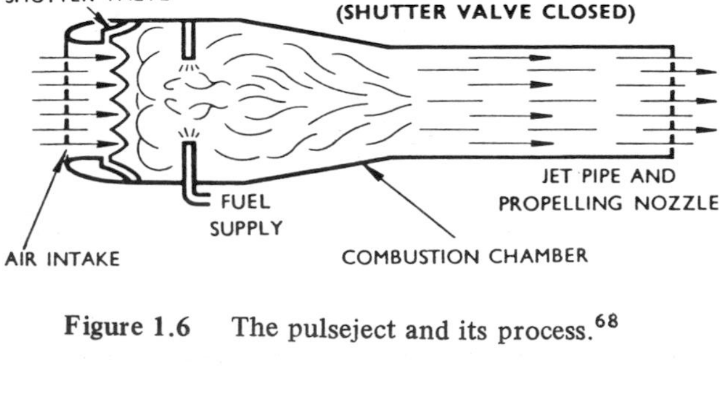

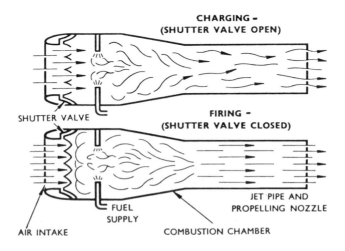

Figure 1.6 The pulseject and its process.[68]

Ramjet and Scramjet Engines

Ramjet combustion offers a high specific impulse (range and speed capability), making it a favored choice for today's light and compact missiles[78-84]. A schematic of a typical ramjet engine is shown in Fig. 1.7. Its propulsion system is conceptually simple, containing no moving parts but requiring a high operating speed so as to compress the intake air by ram effect in the intake section (labeled ∞-1 in the Figure). The air is delivered to a combustion chamber where fuel is injected and burned in the presence of flame stabilizers to provide efficient combustion in the region marked 1-2 in Fig. 1.7. The hot expanded gases leave the engine at high velocities by way of a propelling nozzle thus producing the forward thrust in the region marked 2-3 in Fig. 1.7. The high initial velocity is usually provided by booster rockets or a launch aircraft. A recent technology has evolved concerning the integral rocket ramjet, IRR, concept, where sequential use is made of the ramjet chamber as a solid rocket combustion chamber (during the initial stages of flight) followed by its later use as a ramjet combustion chamber (after a high velocity has been attained and the solid propellant has been burnt). It operates as a completely integrated propulsion system. Initially during the rocket boost, the ramjet fuel is sealed off and the ramjet air inlets are covered with blow-off plugs. When the rocket burns out, the blow-off fairings, inlet plugs and rocket nozzle are ejected, leaving a ramjet propulsion system which is then ignited.

One of the possibilities for powering hypersonic vehicles with an air-breathing engine is the scramjet (or supersonic combustion ramjet)[85-86]. Its basic components are shown in Fig. 1.8 and consist of air intake, a combustion chamber and a propelling nozzle. Many variants of this geometry are available.

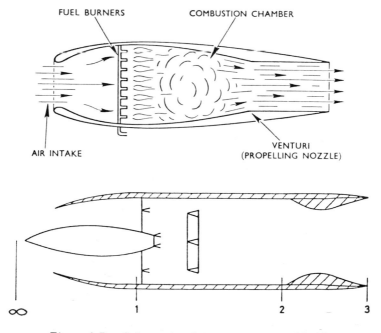

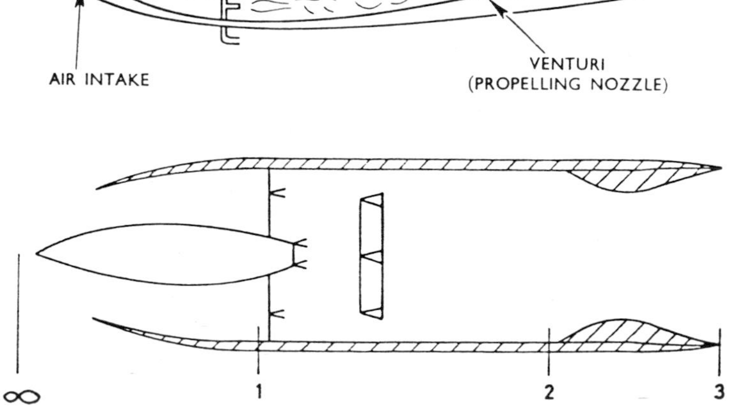

Figure 1.7 Schematic of the ramjet engine.[44, 68]

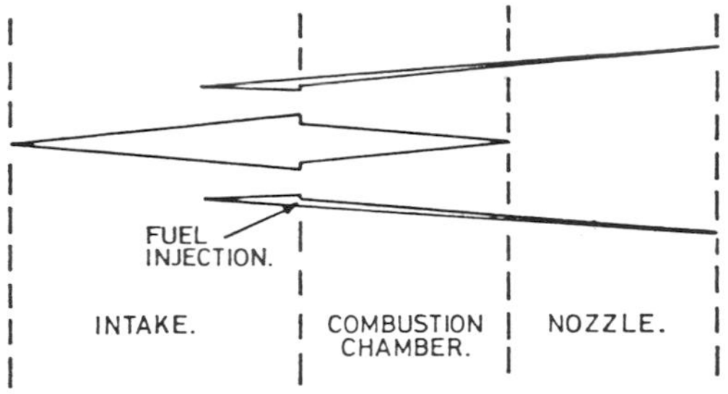

Figure 1.8 Schematic of the scramjet engine.[85]

Rocket Engines

Rocket engines do not use atmospheric air as their working fluid and thus they are able to function outside the earth's atmosphere, if desired[32,44,68,78-80,87-90]. They also provide propulsive force at a vehicle velocity of zero, direct from the launch pad, in contrast to the ramjet which requires a high forward velocity to function. Both liquid and solid-propellant rocket engines are used.

Figure 1.9 shows the basics of a liquid rocket engine. Both fuel and oxidant are carried on board. Typical fuels are hydrogen, hydrazine, ethyl alcohol and kerosine; typical oxidants are oxygen, hydrogen peroxide and flourine. They are carried in liquid form in tanks and are fed to the combustion chamber via injectors (*see* Region 1-2 in Fig. 1.9). Sometimes a pump is used to inject the liquids, as shown, but, alternatively, highly pressurized tanks can provide direct injection. Often the fuel being pumped passes through a double wall construction of nozzle and combustion chamber to provide some degree of cooling for these very high temperature components. In the combustion chamber (region 2-3), the reaction produces high temperature, high pressure and low density products of the chemical reaction. The gases expand in the convergent-divergent nozzle (region 3-4) and are exhausted at high velocity to the surroundings, so producing the propulsive force.

In the solid-propellant rocket engine, the charge of solid-propellant grain, in the form of a cartridge, occupies most of the combustion chamber volume. Propellants fall into two main classes known as 'double-based' and 'composite' types. The former is a homo-

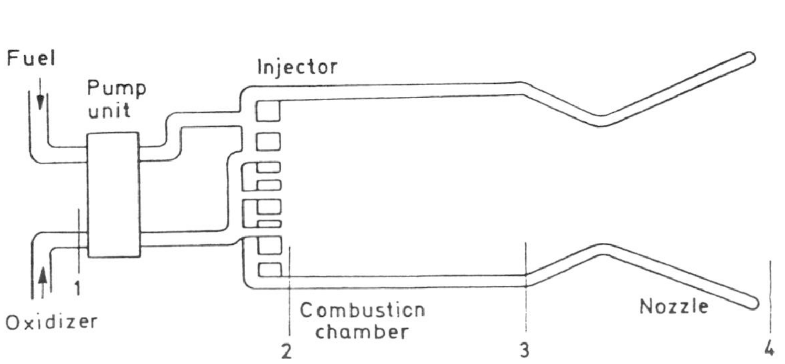

Figure 1.9 Schematic of the liquid rocket engine.[78]

geneous colloidal mixture of nitrocellulose and an explosive plasticizer, usually nitroglycerine. The latter consists of a heterogeneous structure of particles of an oxidizer (such as ammonium nitrate or lithium perchlorate) dispersed through a plastic reducing agent which acts as the fuel. Shown in Fig. 1.10 is a schematic of the solid-propellant rocket engine with its main features. Fig. 1.11 shows typical surface shapes of solid-propellant grain, chosen so that certain burning surface areas and void volume temporal changes may be achieved to be consistent with engine thrust requirements.

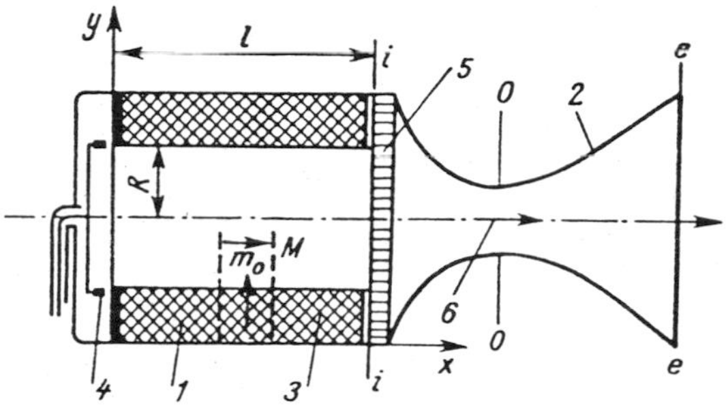

Figure 1.10 Schematic of the solid-propellant rocket.[32]
1. the engine frame
2. the exhaust nozzle
3. the solid-propellant grain charge
4. the electric ignition device
5. the flow uniformisation grate of the burned gases towards the exhaust nozzle
6. the nozzle throat

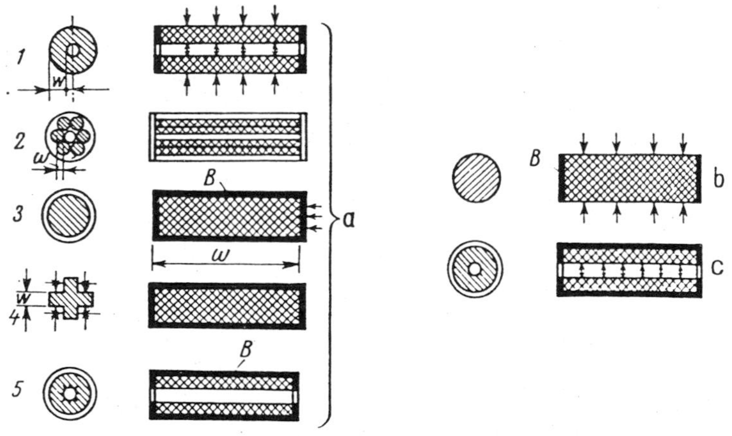

Figure 1.11 Typical surface shapes of solid-propellant grain in a rocket engine.[32]
a. for neutral burning
b. for regressive burning
c. for progressive burning; B – surface inhibited.

1.5 THEORETICAL TECHNIQUES

In order to complement experimental studies, the development, improvement and use of theoretical approaches for evaluation of the combustion process is extremely attractive. The mathematical modeler must interact with his practical counterpart. An appropriate level of complexity of the simulation must be chosen, with judicious matching of physical detail and mathematical tractability. The combustion designer is tempted to fall back on past experience and obtain improvements in efficiency and intensity by redesign of existing systems and scale-up of laboratory experiments. Nevertheless, for the purposes of pollution control, involving both reducing species (hydrocarbons, carbon monoxide) and oxidizing species (oxides of nitrogen and sulfur), better understanding of the combustion process is required. A common feature of many models is the prediction of trends; that is, the prediction of the relative change of some performance parameter caused by a relative change in some geometric or operating parameter. Basic chemical mechanisms are focused upon, since models recommended for pressure and temperature conditions in one device may be completely inadequate when applied to a different device. A basic practice in the formation of a model is the identification of the critical rate-limiting steps, which must be modeled very carefully: effects of processes that are very fast compared to this rate-limiting step can be estimated from equilibrium considerations (mechanical, thermal or chemical); effects of processes that are too slow to have a significant effect can be ignored.

It is in this spirit that simplifications to chemical-kinetics, and idealized flow models for application, have evolved. Excellent reviews are available[6,90] with emphasis on pollution modeling (Bowman[88], Caretto[91]), mixing theories (Pratt[94]), spark-ignition internal combustion IC engines (Wheeler[47], Heywood[48]), diesel engines (Henein[38]), furnaces (Godridge and Read[65]), gas turbines (Jones[69], Mellor[72]), numerical simulation of combustion (Boni[97]). It may be noted that the most common simplified models of mixing processes in common are[91]:

1. piston—and combustion—induced compression and expansion in piston engines,
2. perfectly stirred reactor, PSR, analysis for recirculation regions of combustors,
3. plug flow analysis for furnaces and dilution zones of gas turbine combustors.

Computer modeling of combustion processes is now an established fact[91-97]. It is, however, becoming increasingly clear from recent workshops and conferences on fluid dynamics and combustion that there is still a very large gap between the *needs* in practice and the applicability to the proposed research *tasks* of the researcher, in his desire to make a contribution on the modeling front. Nevertheless, improvements and new developments can and should be made. Accurate mathematical descriptions are required for gas phase and heterogeneous chemical kinetics, for the combustion of fuel droplets in sprays, and for the nucleation, agglomeration, and oxidation of particulates such as soot. Currently available finite-difference computer codes in conjunction with two- and three- equation turbulence models, quasi-global chemical models can be fruitfully employed to elucidate many aspects of turbulent flowfields and combustion[96], but full-scale simulation is still some years away. The accuracy and general applicability of such an undertaking is currently limited by the assumptions and validity of the sub-scale models, which in many circumstances are unknown. Modeling efforts should therefore be concurrent with well-coordinated experimental programs. Numerical simulation will eventually result in detailed space and time resolved predictions of temperature, pressure, species concentrations, turbulent intensity and turbulent length scale throughout the flame. The diagnostic techniques, therefore, must also be capable of yielding unambiguous space and time resolved information.

There is today a certain emphasis on the more sophisticated and more mathematical approaches[23,96-99]. One is then concerned with the status and prospects for computer simulation of combustion processes via rigorous description by partial differential equations, PDEs, of heat, mass, momentum and other phenomena taking place. Economical design, development, and operation can be greatly facilitated by the availability of prior predictions of the flowfield, obtained via the use of a mathematical model incorporating a numerical prediction procedure. Some phenomena, for example, pollutant formation are more sensitive to detailed design changes than is the overall heat transfer or power output of the system. Then, detailed predictions of velocity, concentrations, temperature distributions, etc. are particularly valuable. Notice that this work combines the rapidly developing fields of theoretical combustion aerodynamics and computational fluid dynamics; and its improvement and use will significantly reduce the time and cost of development programs.

A mathematical solution of these flows should provide results, if possible, more cheaply, quickly and proficiently than is possible by other means (for example, experimenting on real-life systems or models). For liquid fuel combustion systems one is interested in; for example, influences and trends, combustor performance, etc., optimum fuel spray angle, swirl strength, combustor can shape, etc. In order to achieve this the model should simulate the flow in all its important respects (geometry, boundary conditions, physical properties of gases, turbulence, combustion, etc.) and quantitatively solve the governing equations. Principal elements of the technique are shown in Fig. 1.12. Mathematical models of steadily increasing realism and refinement are being developed, both in the dimensionality of the model (together with the computational procedures) and in problems associated with the simulation of the physical processes occurring[113,114]. Clearly, there are two areas of difficulty: the simulation and the solution.

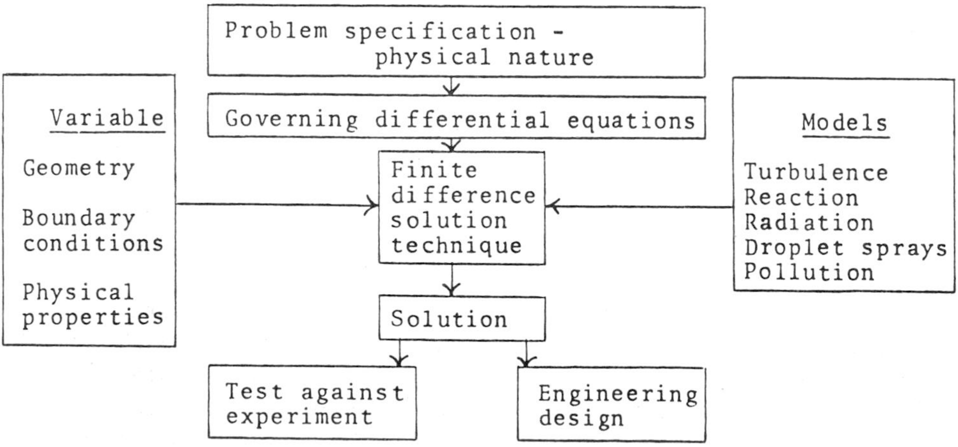

Figure 1.12 Principal elements of numerical prediction[100]

The Flowfield Simulation Problem

In the modeling and prediction of combustor flowfields, the problem is simulated by simultaneous nonlinear partial differential equations. These may be parabolic (boundary layer type) but are more often elliptic (recirculating type) and the solution scheme differs according to the category. Weakly swirling jets and flames without axial recirculation fall into the former category. More often, combustion geometry encourages strongly curved streamlines and recirculation zones (for example, corner recirculation zones, CRZs) even in the absence of swirl, and then problems present themselves in the latter category. Needless to say, flows with strong swirl, sufficient to cause a central toroidal recirculation zone, CTRZ, also belong to this latter elliptic category. In either case (parabolic or elliptic) many approaches proceed with the following basic ideas, for which a comprehensive discussion appears in Chapter 2.

Several previous publications discuss these problems at length, in terms of practical application[4,36-41], turbulence modeling[102-104] and numerical solution of 2-D axisymmetric problems via the stream function ~ vorticity or primitive pressure ~ velocity approach[9,10,100,101,105,106]. Whereas the former approach, used in the 1968 computer program from Imperial College, for example[107], reduces by one the number of equations to be solved and eliminated the troublesome pressure (at the expense of trouble with the vorticity equation), the preferred approach now is SIMPLE (mnemonic for Semi-Implicit Method for Pressure Linked Equations) which focuses attention directly on the latter approach. Because it possesses many advantages, many studies have been developed immediately on this new technique, the basic ideas of which have been embodied into the 1974 Imperial College TEACH (Teaching Elliptic Axisymmetric Characteristics Heuristically) computer program[108]. Advances to this code have been portrayed elsewhere and applied to other 2-D[109-120] and 3-D[121-125] problems of interest to the combustor designer.

The turbulent (Reynolds) equations of conservation of mass, momentum, stagnation enthalpy, and chemical species, which govern the flow of turbulent chemically-reacting multi-component mixtures, may be solved for time-mean pressure, velocity, temperature, and species mass fractions, provided the further thermodynamic and turbulent flux unknowns are specified prior to solution. Often, consideration is given to a simplified main exothermic reaction between just two species, fuel and oxidant; this and other assumptions lead to many simplifications. The reaction is then characterized by equations for:

1. m_{fu} (mass fraction of fuel), h (stagnation enthalpy), and f (mixture fraction which is a normalized value of $m_{ox} - sm_{fu}$, where s is the stoichiometric ratio) for a premixed flame;
2. h and f for a diffusion flame;
3. f for a diffusion flame in an adiabatic, nonreacting, and impervious chamber with only two inlet streams of fuel and oxidant.

Solution for a variable g (mean square fluctuating component of fuel concentration or of mixture fraction) allows a turbulent diffusion flame to have a thick reaction zone or a premixed flame to burn fuel at a rate dependent on eddy-break-up concepts.

Further equations are required to simulate turbulence, two-phase effects, radiation, pollutant formation, etc. but a central point of the theory is that all these equations are similar to laminar flow ones, but the variables are time-mean quantities and the fluxes for momentum, stagnation enthalpy and the chemical species are composed of two parts, the laminar and turbulent parts, the latter of which are related to correlations of turbulent fluctuations. These must be specified via a turbulence model, often, by analogy with the laws of Newton, Fourier, and Fick for laminar flows, using turbulent exchange coefficients relating fluxes to local gradients and then Prandtl, Schmidt, viscosity numbers relating other exchange coefficients to the primary component of turbulent viscosity, μ_{rx}. In turbulence theory, isotropy is the term that connotes the existence of a scalar turbulent viscosity at points in the flowfield. If the turbulent viscosity is not equal with regard to different stress-rate of strain directions, the term nonisotropy is used, and the ratios of the other component with the primary component of turbulent viscosity are called $r\theta$-(and other-) viscosity numbers, by analogy with Prandtl-Schmidt numbers.

All these linkages and complexities in the equations provide a high degree of nonlinearity in the total problem, and give the numerical analysis of fluid flow its peculiar difficulty and flavor. The similarity between the differential equations and their diffusional relations allows them all to be put in the common form

$$\frac{\partial}{\partial t}(\rho\,\phi) + \mathrm{div}\,(\rho\,v\,\phi) = \mathrm{div}\,(\Gamma_\phi\ \mathrm{grad}\,\phi) + S_\phi$$

where the exchange coefficient assumptions have been invoked. Here ϕ is a general dependent variable and equations may be solved for ϕ equal to time-mean axial, radial, and swirl velocities u, v, w, stagnation enthalpy h, fuel mass fraction m_{fu}, mixture fraction f, turbulent kinetic energy k and dissipation rate ϵ, and mean square fluctuating component of fuel concentration $g = \overline{m'_{fu}{}^2}$ or of a mixture fraction $\overline{f'^2}$ (and other variables as well). The equations differ primarily in their final source terms S_ϕ and also in their exchange coefficients.

Closure and completeness of the governing equation set are effected by means of models of the physical processes taking place within the combustion system. Either our knowledge of the processes or computer size limitations can restrict the degree of sophistication to be used in any simulation. The problems of simulation and an introduction to the extensive literature are given in Chapter 2 for the main processes to be modeled.

1.6 EXPERIMENTAL TECHNIQUES

Problems

The development of analytical and numerical methods for predicting flows, both with and without chemical reaction, depends a great deal on the physical and chemical properties of the flow. The accuracy of analytical and numerical predictions is usually tested by comparison with experiment. In a number of cases the predicted results are adjusted or made to conform to the experimental results on the assumption that experimental data is correct.

Real combustion systems possess a complex interaction between turbulent fluid mechanics, heat transfer, thermodynamics and chemical kinetics and it is well-known that modeling of the basic processes must be carried out if a quantitative description of the system is to be achieved. The experimental verification of models describing the combustion of the full spectrum of fuels used in practical combustion systems is urgently required. This urgency has been emphasized by the need to supplement current sources of fuel with low-grade fuels and derived liquid fuels.

Most flows occurring in engineering and nature are turbulent; for example, boundary layer in earth atmosphere, cumulus clouds, water current below the surface of the oceans (Gulf Stream), intersteller gas clouds, wakes of aircrafts, ships, boats and cars, flows of water in rivers and canals. Chemical engineers use turbulence to mix and homogenize fluid mixtures, and to accelerate chemical reaction rates in liquids and gases. The study of turbulence clearly is an interdisciplinary activity, that has a very wide range of applications. Turbulence is rotational, three-dimensional, and always dissipative and is characterized by high levels of fluctuating vorticity. For this reason, vorticity dynamics play an essential role in the description of turbulent flows. The random vorticity fluctuations that characterize turbulence could not maintain themselves if the velocity fluctuations were two-dimensional, since an important vorticity-maintenance mechanism, often called vortex stretching is absent in two-dimensional flows.

Turbulent Flow Measurements

In turbulent flows, measurements are required of instantaneous values that can be separated into time-mean and fluctuating values, which, in conjunction with the time-average correlations, can then be used for the determination of local values of heat, mass, and momentum flux. The temporal characteristics of the flow in the combustion system greatly influence the way in which the combustibles react and the products are produced, and the heat so evolved from the exothermic reactions is transferred to the surroundings. Up to now, the gross properties of the diffusion flames [for example, distribution of mean temperatures, local distribution of reaction rates, flame size, etc.] have been based mostly upon empirical or semi-empirical relationships. More detailed information on the process of turbulent mixing is, therefore, necessary and desirable. In the past, most of the work, particularly in gas turbine combustors, has been based on the time-mean values. This has given some interesting results for turbulent macromixing and general flame characteristics. Nevertheless, intimate molecular mixing takes place in the final stages of chemical interaction. Unfortunately, the simulation of this in turbulent flows is not clear, since it is known that the time-mean reaction rate is not simply related to time-mean flow properties.

In principle, the time-resolved properties of a flow can be determined by solving the relevant conservation equations with appropriate initial and boundary conditions for the case of simple flows. The effect of combustion upon turbulent flows is complex and their prediction requires correct selection of the physical model with the relevant basic equations for the flow system under analysis. In general, the physical properties of turbulent flames, particularly diffusion flames, can be predicted today only approximately by using empirical or semi-empirical relationships.

Intrusive Methods

Experimental diagnostics applied to turbulent flows both with and without combustion assists in understanding the complex fluid dynamics and physical phenomena[3,5-8,126-134]. The diagnostics of swirl combustion has to contend, in addition, with the constraints and limitations imposed or inherent in any other field, with the additional very serious constraint of its hostile environment. Probe techniques for the measurements of temperature, composition, pressure and velocity are inherently simple and easy to use and certainly less expensive than optical methods. For this reason they will and should continue to be used. The presence of a physical probe can alter the flowfield and combustion patterns so that measurements are not being made of the combustion system it was intended to investigate. An important consideration in measurement techniques is whether the acquired signal is dependent on properties other than the particular one of interest. Typically, a pitot tube measurement will yield velocity in homotropic flows only if the density of fluid is known. Also optical absorption and scattering are strongly influenced by pressure- and temperature-controlled broadening mechanisms. An independent measurement of temperature is, therefore, often necessary.

Fluid mechanic disturbances are likely to be most serious when probing recirculation zones and swirl flows with an intrusive probe[4]. It is a well-known observation in fluid mechanics that the introduction of a probe radially into a vortex flow, in a chamber, can have a drastic effect on the flow. The large radial static pressure gradient assists mixing of the reactants. Any probe presents a blockage to the flow and the flow streamlines must alter its course to go around the probe. In fact, they deviate more easily into regions with low dynamic pressure. This often gives an ambiguity in the measurement position. The physical probe can also act as a flameholder and this observation has been made by many combustion engineers. In spray combustors, probes can act as collectors, agglomerators, atomizers, vaporizers and, generally, as fuel redistributors. A large cooled probe can also act as a heat sink so as to alter significantly the rate of chemical reactions.

In streamlined flows without flow reversals (governed by parabolic equations), probe disturbances can be kept to a minimum. A good rule of thumb is to keep the probe diameter to less than one tenth of the integral length scale of the turbulence. The flow disturbance is confined to the region up to about seven effective diameters upstream of the probe or its support. The usual arrangement is in the form of a right-angled pitot probe. In this case the probe should project ahead of the support tube by approximately seven support tube diameters. For static pressure measurements the distance should be even more. The business end of the probe should be as slender as possible. Position error effects due to stream-tube displacement in a dynamic pressure gradient will be of the order of half the diameter of the equivalent square-nosed cylinder. In swirl flows (governed by elliptic equations), disturbances from the probe will always propagate upstream into the flow.

The basic methods for sample collection in common use are the aerodynamic type and the convective type. The phenomenology of sample collection with sonic orifice probes is not completely understood. According to the theory developed for isokinetic sampling the bias toward the light fractions should be extremely large. This will, nevertheless, be offset by the effects of the blunt nose shape which in some cases may dominate the situation so as to bias towards the heavy fractions. The sampling flow velocity at the probe orifice throat varies with the local speed of sound. For quartz microprobes this effect may be significant when the outside diameter of the probe tip is of the order of the Kolmogoroff microscale or smaller. The isokinetic sample probably obtains a Favre averaged composition, $\overline{\rho m_j}/\overline{\rho}$, where m_j is the mass fraction of the jth species. Most theoretical modes will in fact predict Favre mean, and the difference between the true mean and Favre mean can easily be as much as 40 per cent in some parts of the flow.

In gas turbine combustors, a characteristic aspect is its relatively small size enclosed geometry where complex and potentially material-destructive phenomena take place. Hence, a small flow disturbance might lead to a significant change in the energy transfer pattern, possibly destructive to the liner. The diagnostician is therefore faced with the challenge of devising a probe that does not melt and that disturbs neither the flow nor the walls of the combustion chamber.

Non-Intrusive Methods

The search for new and improved methods has been the ongoing task in many research organizations and universities for flowfield diagnostics applicable to flows both with and without chemical reaction. The ultimate aim is always a method or methods that could provide all or most of the necessary information remotely in a nonperturbing and non-intrusive manner, and, if possible, instantaneously. These requirements always steer the experimentalist towards optical techniques[5-8,126-134]. Intrusive methods; for example, pressure probes, bare-wire thermocouples, etc., suffer from the disadvantage of causing disturbances to the flowfield and vice versa, in addition to their relatively low frequency response (excluding hot-wire probes which have fairly good frequency response).

Laser velocimetry, LV, is the only system that can measure a velocity field in a combustion environment accurately with excellent spatial resolution. Its interference with the flow is negligible and better than that of probes. The accuracy and spatial resolution are of the order of 1 per cent and 1 mm^3 respectively. Time resolution is limited by the number of scattering particles that cross the control volume in any given interval of time. In real time turbulence measurements, for instance, one requires near continuous signals. The proper injection and distribution of seeding particles presents interpretation problems (drag/mass problems, sampling bias) and the possibility that the flow chemistry will be affected. Also one can establish enough correlations over a period of time, by double pulsing, for instance, in order to reconstruct the turbulence spectrum.

The specificity of LV is also much better in intrusive probes in the sense that it can pick all the components of the velocity vector, positive or negative—an essential feature in the recirculation zone or in the highly turbulent primary zone. This, of course, is impossible with either pitot probe or hot-wire anemometer. It also measures velocity directly (by counting particle crossing rate) and requires no calibration or additional flow properties.

A difficulty with LV is the refractive index fluctuations on the path of the laser beam. It can be a serious problem when measuring two velocity components simultaneously. Forward scattering, which offers a signal gain of two or three orders of magnitude over the back scattering mode, requires an optical path through the flame. Many combustors do not provide this flexibility. The presence of natural particulates (soot, droplets) creates both a measurement and a background problem. A number of these shortcomings can be overcome by the use of high powered lasers, but these are limited by the electrical breakdown threshold (ionization), which is problematic in dusty flows.

It is often useful to measure and display the properties of the whole flowfield instantaneously, especially if an understanding of its overall features and their time evolution is required. The common form of imaging method is based on the path measurement of the refraction properties of the flow. Such are the well-known techniques of interferometry, schlieren photography and shadowgraphy. These methods yield a signal proportional to the density, the density gradient across the path, and its second derivative, respectively. In more trivial photographic form, shadow methods yield pictures of liquid or solid objects, such as droplets, sprays or particulate clouds, at a desired focal plane. This plane can be moved with time to cover the whole depth of field, or this information can be gathered instantaneously by a hologram. The accuracy is good but the automation needs to eliminate the tediousness of manual data. Reduction is quite expensive.

Qualitative information on the flow structure can also be obtained non-intrusively, using high intensity light sources [for example, water model studies, schlieren and shadowgraph methods, tracer techniques, holography, high-speed photography, velocity measurement with small tracer particles, etc.] In water model studies, the flowfield is investigated by the motion of polystyrene tracer particles, which have the same density as water. A high-intensity slit light beam is used to visualize the desired cross-section of the flow. Further discussions on various experimental techniques appear in Chapter 4. Optical methods that can be used to study flow structure by schlieren, interferometric and holographic methods are given by Merzkirch[3] and Vest[5]. Laser probes for isothermal flow and combustion applications are given in Goulard[6], Crosley[7], Durst *et al*[123] and Lapp and Penney[129].

Finally, References[135-152] provide a selection of the many useful journals containing research articles on various aspects of modeling, diagnostics and the fluid dynamics of combustion.

References to Chapter One

1. Prandtl, L., Tietjens, O.: *Hydro- und Aeromechanik* (based on Prandtl's lectures), **I** and **II**, Berlin, 1929 and 1931. English Trans. by L. Rosenhead **I** and J. P. den Hartog **II**, New York, 1934.
2. Schlichting, H.: *Boundary-Layer Theory,* McGraw-Hill, New York, 1968.
3. Merzkirch, Wolfgang: *Flow Visualization,* Academic Press Inc., 1974.
4. Gupta, A. K., Lilley, D. G., and Syred, N.: *Swirl Flows,* Abacus Press, Tunbridge Wells, England, 1984.
5. Vest, C. M.: *Holographic Interferometry,* Wiley, New York, 1979.
6. Goulard, R. (Ed.): *Combustion Measurements,* A Project SQUID Workshop, Hemisphere Publishing Corp., 1976.
7. Crosley, D. R. (Ed.): *Laser Probes in Combustion Chemistry,* ACS Symposium Series 134, American Chemical Society, Washington, D.C., 1980.
8. Zinn, B. T. (Ed.): *Experimental Diagnostics in Gas Phase Combustion Systems,* AIAA, **53**, Prog. in Astro. and Aero., 1977. *See also AIAA* **63,** 1978.
9. Chow, C-Y: *An Introduction to Computational Fluid Mechanics,* Wiley, 1979.
10. Roache, P. J.: *Computational Fluid Dynamics,* Hermosa Publishers, Albuquerque, NM, 1972.
11. Probstein, R. F., and Hicks, R.E.: *Synthetic Fuels,* McGraw-Hill, 1981.
12. Smith, M.L. and Stinson, K. W.: *Fuels and Combustion,* McGraw-Hill, New York, 1952.
13. Spalding, D. B.: *Some Fundamentals of Combustion,* Butterworths, London, 1955.
14. Gaydon, A. G. and Wolfhard, H. G.: *Flames—Their Structure, Radiation and Temperature,* 4th edn., Chapman & Hall, London, 1979. [1st edn. 1953].
15. Lewis, B. R. and von Elbe, G.: *Combustion, Flames and Explosions of Gases,* Academic Press, New York, 1961.
16. Williams, F. A., *Combustion Theory:* Addison-Wesley, Reading, Mass. 1965.
17. Fristrom, R. M. and Westenberg, A. A.: *Flame Structure,* McGraw-Hill, New York, 1965.
18. Strehlow, R. A.: *Fundamentals of Combustion,* Krieger Publishing Co., NY, 1979 [Original edition, 1968].
19. Smith, I. E. (Ed.): *Combustion in Advanced Gas Turbine Systems,* Pergamon, London, 1968.
20. Bradley, J. N.: *Flame and Combustion Phenomena,* Methuen, London, 1969.
21. Norster, E. R. (Ed.): *Combustion and Heat Transfer in Gas Turbine Systems,* Pergamon, London, 1971.

22. Cornelius, W. and Agnew, W. G. (Ed.): *Emissions from Continuous Combustion Systems,* Plenum Press, New York, 1972.
23. *Proc. of 4th Symp. of Flames and Industry,* British Flame Res. Comm. and Inst. of Fuel, Predictive Methods for Industrial Flames, held at I. C., London, Sept. 19-20, 1972.
24. Beér, J. M. and Chigier, N.A.: *Combustion Aerodynamics,* Applied Science, London and Halsted-Wiley, New York, 1972.
25. Edwards, J. B.: *Combustion,* Ann Arbor Science Press, Michigan, 1974.
26. Dussourd, J. L., Lohmann, R. P., and Uram, E. M. (Ed.): *Fluid Mechanics of Combustion* (Papers presented at Conference held in Montreal, Canada, May 13-15, 1974) ASME Book No. I00034, 1974.
27. Gunther, R.: Verbrennung and Feuerungen [in German], Springer-Verlag, Berlin.
28. Palmer, H. B. and Beér, J. M. (Ed.): *Combustion Technology: Some Modern Developments,* Academic Press, New York, 1974.
29. Afgan, N. H. and Beér, J. M. (Ed.): *Heat Transfer in Flames,* Scripta Book Co., (Hemisphere-Wiley), Washington, D.C., 1974.
30. Kanury, A. M.: *Introduction to Combustion Phenomena,* Gordon and Breach, New York, 1975.
31. Murthy, S. N. B. (Ed.): *Turbulent Mixing in Nonreactive and Reactive Flow,* A Project SQUID Workshop, Plenum Press, New York, 1975.
32. Stambuleanu, A.: *Flame Combustion Processes in Industry,* Abacus Press, Tunbridge Wells, England, 1976.
33. Glassman, I.: *Combustion,* Academic Press, New York, 1977.
34. Goodger, E. M.: *Combustion Calculations,* MacMillan, London, 1977. See also *Hydrocarbon Fuels,* MacMillan, London, 1979.
35. Kennedy, L.A. (Ed.): *Turbulent Combustion, Prog. in Astro. and Aero.,* **58**, AIAA, New York, 1978.
36. Oates, G. C.: *The Aerothermodynamics of Aircraft Gas Turbine Engines,* AFAPL-TR-78-52, 1978.
37. Spalding, D. B.: *Combustion and Mass Transfer,* Pergamon, London, 1979.
38. Chigier, N. A. (Ed.): *Prog. Energy Comb. Sci.,* **1**, 1976 onward.
39. Lefebvre, A. H. (Ed.): *Gas Turbine Combustor Design Problems,* Hemisphere-McGraw-Hill, New York, 1980.
40. Chigier, N. A.: *Energy, Combustion, and Environment,* McGraw-Hill, New York, 1981.
41. Morel, T., Lohmann, R. P. and Rackley, J. M. (Ed.): *Fluid Mechanics of Combustion Systems.* (Papers presented at Conference held at Boulder, Colorado, June 22-24, 1981), ASME, 1981.
42. Spalding, D. B.: *J. Inst. Fuel,* **44**, April 1971, p. 196.
43. Spalding, D. B.: *Combustion Theory Applied to Engineering,* Dept. of Mech. Eng., Report No. HTS/77/1, Imperial College, London, 1977.
44. Lichty, L. C.: *Combustion Engine Processes,* McGraw-Hill, New York, 1967.
45. Campbell, A. S.: *Thermodynamic Analysis of Combustion Engines,* Wiley, New York, 1979.
46. Namazian, M.: Ph.D. Thesis, MIT, 1981.
47. Wheeler, R. W.: Gasoline Combustion Past, Present and Future. Paper D. P. 78/212 presented at CI/CSS Spring Technical Meeting held at Purdue University, W. Lafayette, Indiana, April 3-4, 1978.
48. Heywood, J. B.: *Prog. in Energy and Comb. Sci.,* **1**, 1976, p. 135.
49. Shahed, S. M., Flynn, P. F. and Lyn, W. T.: Diesel Combustion: Review and Prospects. Paper presented at DI/CSS Spring Technical Meeting, held at Purdue University, W. Lafayette, Indiana, April 3-4, 1978.
50. Lavoie, G. A., Heywood, J. B. and Keck, J. C.: *Comb. Sci. and Tech.*, **I**, 1970, p. 313.
51. Bracco, F. V. (issue editor): Special Issue on Stratified Charge Engines. *Comb. Sci. and Tech.* **8**, 1 & 2, 1973, p. 1.
52. Blumberg, P. N.: *Comb. Sci. and Tech.,* 1973, p. 5-24.
53. Tabaczynski, R. J.: A Review of Pollution Control in Internal Combustion Engines. Paper presented at the Workshop on the Numerical Simulation of Combustion for Application to Spark and Compression Ignition Engines, NSF/RANN Report, 3-79-3-104, Oct. 1975.
54. Diwakar, R.: Ph.D. Thesis, Department of Aerospace Engineering, University of Maryland, 1977.
55. Griffin, M. D.: Ph.D. Thesis, Dept. of Aerospace Engineering, University of Maryland, 1977.
56. Sirignano, W. A.: One-Dimensional Analysis of Combustion in a Spark-Ignition Engine. *SAE Paper 719010* presented at the 1971 Intersociety Energy Conversion Conference, Boston, Mass., 1971.
57. Rosentweig-Bellan, J. and Sirignano, W. A.: *Comb. Sci. and Tech.*, **8**, 1973, p. 51.
58. Bracco, F. V.: *Comb. Sci. and Tech.,* **8**, 1973, p. 69.

59. Bracco, F. V.: Introducing a New Generation of More Informative Combustion Models. *SAE Paper No. 741174* presented at the International Stratified Charge Engine Conference, Troy, Michigan, 1974.
60. Boni, A. A., Chapman, M. and Schneyer, G. P.: A One-Dimensional Variable Area Computer Simulation of Combustion in a Divided-Chamber Stratified Charge Engine. *ASME Paper No. 75-WA/DGP-1,* 1975.
61. Bracco, F. V., Gupta, H. C., Krishnamurthy, L., Santavicca, D. A., Steinberger, R. L. and Warshaw, V.: Two-Phase, Two-Dimensional, Unsteady Combustion in Internal Combustion Engines; Preliminary Theoretical-Experimental Results. Paper presented at the Automotive Exposition, Detroit, Michigan, *SAE Paper No. 760114,* Feb., 1976.
62. Particulate Polycyclic Organic Matter, Biologic effects of atmospheric pollutants, *National Academy of Sciences,* Washington, D.C., 1972.
63. Michelfelder, S.: Annual Report of the Activity of the Research Station, Ijmuiden during 1976. *Doc. No. F01/a/93, IFRF, Ijmuiden, Holland,* June, 1977. Repeated and updated annually.
64. Beér, J. M.: *J. Inst. Fuel,* **45**, July, 1972, p. 370.
65. Godridge, A. M., and Read, A. W.: *Prog. in Energy and Comb. Sci.,* **2**, 1976, p. 83.
66. Patankar, S. V., and Spalding, D. B.: Mathematical Models of Fluid Flow and Heat Transfer in Furnaces: A Review. Paper in Ref. 53, p. 13.
67. Perry, R. H. and Chilton, C. H.: *Chemical Engineers' Handbook.* 5th edn. McGraw-Hill, New York, 1973.
68. Anon: *The Jet Engine,* Rolls Royce, Derby, England, 1972.
69. Jones, R. E.: *Prog. in Energy and Comb. Sci.,* **4**, 1978, p. 73.
70. Osgerby, I. T.: *AIAA Journal,* **12**, **6**, June, 1974, p. 743.
71. Odgers, J.: Combustor Modelling within Gas Turbine Engines. *AIAA Paper No. 77-52,* Los Angeles, Calif., Jan. 24-26, 1977.
72. Mellor, A. M.: *17th Symp. (Intl.) on Comb.,* The Comb. Inst., 1979, p. 377.
73. Odgers, J.: *15th Symp. (Intl.) on Comb.,* The Comb. Inst., 1975, p. 1321.
74. Lefebvre, A. H.: *15th Symp. (Intl.) on Comb.,* The Comb. Inst., 1975, p. 1169.
75. Mellor, A. M.: *Prog. in Energy and Comb. Sci.,* **1**, 1976, p. 111.
76. Gradon, K., and Miller, S. C.: *Combustion Development on the Rolls-Royce Spey Engine,* Paper in Combustion in Advanced Gas Turbines (I.E. Smith, Ed.), Pergamon Press, New York, 1967, p. 45.
77. Lefebvre, A. H.; *Design Considerations in Advanced Gas Turbine Combustion Chambers,* Paper in Combustion in Advanced Gas Turbines (I.E. Smith, Ed.), Pergamon Press, New York, 1967, p. 45.
78. McMahon, P. J.: *Aircraft Propulsion,* Barnes and Noble Books, London [A Division of Harper and Row, New York], 1971.
79. Zucrow, M. J.: *Aircraft and Missile Propulsion,* **I** and **II**, Wiley, New York, 1958.
80. Zucrow, M. J.: Thermal-Jet and Rocket-Jet Propulsion, Section 23 of *Handbook of Fluid Dynamics* (V.L. Streeter, Ed.), McGraw-Hill, New York, 1961.
81. Dugger, G. L., (Ed.): Ramjets, *AIAA Selected Reprints,* **VI**, 1969.
82. Drewry, J. E.: *AIAA Journal,* **16**, 4, April 1978, p. 313.
83. Choudhury, P. R.: *AIAA Journal,* **18**, **4**, April, 1980, p. 450.
84. Edelman, R. B., and Harsha, P. T.: Analytical Modeling of Sudden Expansion Burners. *CPIA Publication 287, Chemical Propulsion Information Agency,* the Johns Hopkins Univ., Laurel, MD, June, 1977.
85. Swithenbank, J.: *Prog. in Aero. Sci.,* **8**, (D. Kuchemann, Ed.), 1966, p. 229.
86. Stewart, W. L. (Conf. Chairman): Aeropropulsion 1979. Conference held at NASA Lewis Research Center, Cleveland, OH, May 15-16, 1979.
87. Penner, S. S.: *Chemical Rocket Propulsion and Combustion Research.* Gordon and Breach, New York, 1962.
88. Bowman, C. T., and Seery, D. G.: *Emissions from Continuous Combustion Systems* [Cornelius, W., and Agnew, W. G., (Ed.)], Plenum Press, New York, 1972, p. 123.
89. Streeter, V. L.: *Handbook of Fluid Dynamics,* McGraw-Hill, New York, 1961.
90. Chigier, N. A. (Ed.): *Progress in Energy and Combustion Science,* 1976+.
91. Caretto, L. A.: Modeling Pollutant Formation in Combustion Processes, *14th Symp. (Intl.) on Comb.,* The Comb. Inst., 1973.
92. Lilley, D. G.: *J. of Energy,* **3**, July-Aug., 1979, p. 193.
93. Lilley, D. G.: Prospects for Computer Modeling in Ramjet Combustors, *AIAA Paper No. 80-1189,* Hartford, Ct. June 30-July 2, 1980.
94. Pratt, D. *T.: 15th Symp. (Intl.) on Comb.,* The Comb. Inst., 1974, p. 1339.

95. Lilley, D. G.: Swirl Flows in Combustion: A Review, *AIAA Journal,* **15**, 8, August, 1977, p. 1063.
96. Prediction of Turbulent Reacting Flows in Practical Systems, *ASME Fluids Engineering Conference,* Boulder, CO, June 22-24, 1981.
97. Boni, A. A. (Chairman): SAI/NSF (RANN) Workshop on the Numerical Simulation of Combustion for Application to Spark and Compression Ignition Engines, held in La Jolla, Calif., April 23-25, 1975.
98. Gerstein, M. (Ed.): Fundamentals of Gas Turbine Combustion, NASA-CP-2087, 1979. Workshop held at NASA Lewis Research Center, Cleveland, OH, Feb. 6-7, 1979.
99. Murthy, S. N. B.: Summary Report DOD Colloquium on Gas Turbine Combustor Modeling, *Project SQUID Technical Report PU-Rl-79,* School of Mech. Eng.. Purdue University [for ONR], Nov., 1979.
100. Lilley, D. G.: *Acta Astro.,* **I**, 9, Sept., 1974, p. 1129.
101. Gupta, A. K., Beér, J. M., Louis, J. F., Busnaina, A. A., and Lilley, D. G.: Flow Aerodynamics Modeling of a MHD Swirl Combustor: Calculations and Experimental Verification, *ASME Symposium on Fluid Mechanics of Combustion Systems,* Boulder, CO, June 1981.
102. Launder, B. E. and Spalding, D. B.: *Mathematical Models of Turbulence,* Academic Press, London, 1972.
103. Launder, B. E. and Spalding, D. B.: *Comp. Methods in Appl. Mech. and Engre.,* **3**, March, 1974, p. 269.
104. Tennekes, H., and Lumley, J. L.: *A First Course in Turbulence,* MIT Press, Cambridge, MA 1978.
105. Combustor Modeling, *AGARD Conference Proceedings No. 275,* Feb., 1980.
106. Patankar, S. V.: *Numerical Heat Transfer and Fluid Flow,* Hemisphere-McGraw-Hill, New York, 1980.
107. Gosman, A. D., Pun, W. M., Runchal, A. K., Spalding, D. B., and Wolfshtein, M. W.: *Heat and Mass Transfer in Recirculating Flows,* Academic Press, London, 1969.
108. Gosman, A. D., and Pun, W. M.: Calculation of Recirculating Flows, *Rept. No. HTS/74/12,* Dept. of Mech. Eng., I. C., London, 1974.
109. Gosman, A. D. and Ideriah, F. J. K.: TEACH-2E: A General Computer Program for Two-Dimensional, Turbulent, Recirculating Flows, Report, Dept. of Mech. Eng., I.C., London, June, 1976.
110. Lilley, D. G.: *AIAA Journal,* **14**, June, 1976, p. 749.
111. Khalil, E. E., Spalding, D. B. and Whitelaw, J. H.: *Int. J. Heat Mass. Trans.,* **18**, 1975, p. 775.
112. Novick, A. S., Miles, G. A., and Lilley, D. G.: *J. of Energy,* **3**, 2, March-April, 1979, p. 95.
113. Wuerer, J. E. and Samuelsen, G. S.: Predictive Modeling of Backmixed Combustor Flows: Mass and Momentum Transport, *AIAA Paper 79-0215,* New Orleans, LA, Jan. 15-17, 1979.
114. Habib, M. A. and Whitelaw, J. H.: Velocity Characteristics of Confined Coaxial Jets With and Without Swirl, *ASME Paper No. 79-WA/FE/21,* New York, Dec. 2-7, 1979.
115. El Banhawy, Y. and Whitelaw, J. H.: *AIAA J.,* **18**, 2, Dec. 1980, p. 1503.
116. Srinivasan, R. and Mongia, H. C.: Numerical Computations of Swirling Recirculating Flows, Final Report, *NASA-CR-165196,* Sept., 1980.
117. Rhode, D. L., Lilley, D. G. and McLaughlin, D. K.: On the Prediction of Swirling Flowfields Found in Axisymmetric Combustor Geometries, *ASME Symposium on Fluid Mechanics of Combustion Systems,* held in Boulder, CO, June 22-24, 1981.
118. Sturgess, G. J., Syed, S. A. and Sepulveda, D.: Application of Numerical Modeling to Gas Turbine Combustor Development Problems, Ibid., 1981.
119. Lilley, D. G., Busnaina, A. A., and Gupta, A. K.: Modeling Parameter Influences on MHD Swirl Combustor Nozzle Design *AIAA/ASME Fluids and Heat Transfer Conference,* St. Louis, MO, June 7-11, 1982.
120. Lilley, D. G., Rhode, D. L. and Samples, J. W.: Prediction of Swirling Reacting Flow in Ramjet Combustors, *AIAA Paper No. 81-1485,* Colorado Springs, CO, July 27-29, 1981.
121. Patankar, S. V. and Spalding, D. B.: *14th Symp. (Intl.) on Comb.,* The Comb. Inst., 1973, p. 605.
122. Serag-Eldin, M. A. and Spalding, D. B.: *Trans. ASME J. of Eng. for Power,* **101**, July 1979, p. 326.
123. Mongia, H. C. and Reynolds, R. S.: Combustor Design Criteria Validation **III** – User's Manual, *Report USARTL-TR-78-55C,* U.S. Army Res. and Tech. Lab., Ft. Eustis, VA, Feb. 1979. [See also **I** and **II**].
124. Swithenbank, J., Turan, A. and Felton, P. G.: Three-Dimensional Two-Phase Mathematical Modeling of Gas Turbine Combustors, In *Gas Turbine Combustor Design Problems* [Lefebvre, A. H., (Ed.)], Hemisphere-McGraw-Hill, New York, 1980, p. 249.

125. Khalil, E. E.: *Modelling of Furnaces and Combustors,* Abacus Press, Tunbridge Wells, England, 1982.
126. Gupta, A. K., Swithenbank, J., and Beér, J. M.: *J. Inst. Fuel,* Dec., 1977, p. 163.
127. Durst, F., Melling, A., and Whitelaw, J. H.; *Principles and Practice of Laser-Doppler Anemometry,* Academic Press, London, 1976.
128. Weinberg, F. J.: *Optics of Flames,* Butterworths, London, 1963.
129. Lapp, M. and Penney, C. M. (Ed.): *Laser Raman Gas Diagnostics:* A Project SQUID Workshop, Plenum Press, 1974.
130. Thompson, H. D. and Stevenson, W. H. (Ed.): *Third International Workshop on Laser Velocimetry and Particle Sizing,* Hemisphere Publishing Corporation, 1978.
131. Gupta, A. K., and Rossi, I.: *J. Inst. Energy,* England, Dec., 1981, p. 197.
132. Gaydon, A. G.: *The Spectroscopy of Flames,* Chapman and Hall, London, 1974.
133. Eckbreth, A. C.: CARS Thermometry in Practical Combustors, Paper to be published in Combustion and Flame, 1980. See also 18th Symp. (Intl.) on Comb., The Comb. Inst., 1981.
134. Hecht, E., and Zajac, A.: *Optics,* Addison-Wesley, Reading, MA, 1976.
135. *AIAA Journal*
136. *AIAA Journal of Energy*
137. *Journal of the Institute of Energy* [UK] [formerly: Institute of Fuel]
138. *ASME Journal of Heat Transfer*
139. *ASME Journal of Fluids Engineering*
140. *Int. Journal of Numerical Methods in Engineering*
141. *Journal of Fluid Mechanics*
142. *Annual Reviews of Fluid Mechanics*
143. *Fluid Dynamics*
144. *Computers and Fluids*
145. *Journal of Computational Physics*
146. *Fuel*
147. *Fuel and Energy Abstracts*
148. *Applied Mechanics Reviews*
149. *Progress in Energy and Combustion Science*
150. *Chemical Engineering Science*
151. *Combustion Science and Technology*
152. *International Symposia on Combustion*

CHAPTER 2

THEORETICAL COMBUSTION AERODYNAMICS

Theoretical predictive techniques serve to assist the designer of nonreacting and reacting flow equipment by providing understanding of the key features and input parameter effects that influence this process. The combustion designer has a formidable problem in aerothermochemistry, and the task is to provide a route that leads to the accomplishment of design objectives more quickly and less expensively than current practice permits. One desirable possibility is the computer simulation of combustion problems in practical combustion chamber design and development, and an objective view of the status and prospects is the main theme throughout Chapters 2 and 3. Major features of the mathematical modeling and prediction of turbulent reacting flows include simulation of the physical processes (in the present chapter) and solution schemes for the appropriate level of sophistication of the resulting equations (as discussed in Chapter 3). Emphasis is on application to practical combustion equipment, including reciprocating engines, industrial furnaces, and gas turbine combustors. The difficulties, developments and demonstrations of useful prediction are to be exemplified further, by providing, in Chapter 5, discussion of particular sample predictions in order to demonstrate current capabilities.

Recent demands for the conservation of fossil fuels and the association of atmospheric pollution with undesirable byproducts of combustion and the products of inefficient combustion has forced a re-assessment of the state-of-the-art in this field. Observation of the sequence of events occurring in a combustion process leads to the inevitable conclusion that fluid dynamics play a critical role. It is interesting to point out the recent evolution of combustion-related fluid dynamic technology.

Most profound changes have been in the use of numerical computations to simulate the details of combustion flowfields. Earlier numerical solutions of the relevant turbulent flow equations had been restricted to nonrecirculating nonreacting flows, but, recently, authors have expounded on their successes in more complex situations. A prerequisite to this has been improved knowledge of the turbulent structure and its interactions with chemical reactions. This knowledge has been obtained by the availability of significant improvements in intrusive and nonintrusive instrumentation for measurement of these parameters (as discussed in Chapter 4). Nevertheless, in spite of these refinements in analytic capability and expanded knowledge, some problems must be resolved by empirical developments, especially those in connection with very practical equipment.

Most practical flowfields are in cylindrical polar coordinates, and this is emphasized in the text. Both nonaxisymmetric (fully three-dimensional 3-D) and axisymmetric (two-dimensional 2-D) cases are of special interest in other texts in the Energy and Engineering Series. In either case, flows with swirl (rotation in the θ-direction about the main x-axis) are also of special importance and are thus again given special emphasis in the present foundation text.

2.1 TURBULENT CHEMICALLY REACTING MULTICOMPONENT MIXTURES

Conservation Laws

Theoretical contribution to the simulation and solution of problems in aerothermochemistry starts from hypotheses about the fundamental processes. Basic partial differential equations (PDEs) describe the flowfield of turbulent chemically-reacting multicomponent mixtures, in which heat, mass and momentum transfer are taking place simultaneously. The PDEs express mathematically the appropriate scientific conservation laws for mass, momentum, stagnation enthalpy h, chemical species mass fractions m_j, etc.[1-27] As the two-equation k-ϵ turbulence model[28] is to be featured later, it is convenient here to carry through the discussion on the additional conservation equations for kinetic energy of turbulence per unit mass k and turbulence dissipation rate per unit volume ϵ. Furthermore, in turbulent flow it may be assumed that *time-mean* values obey the governing PDEs provided that the diffusion flux terms are composed of laminar and turbulent parts (resulting in *effective* flux terms) and the source terms may give rise to additional terms[28-49]. The equations are all very similar, for example:[5]

1. *Conservation of Total Mass*: Rate of increase of density ρ equals net rate of inflow of mass into unit volume:

$$\partial\rho/\partial t + \text{div}\,(\rho v) = 0$$

Here, further definitions include time t and time-mean velocity vector v.

2. *Conservation of x-direction Momentum*: Rate of increase of u (= x-direction momentum per unit volume) equals net rate of inflow of ρu plus net force per unit volume. [u is the x-direction velocity component.]

Similar expressions hold in the other two directions, leading to a combined equation for the time-mean velocity vector v:

$$\partial\,(\rho v)/\partial t + \text{div}\,(\rho v v) = \text{div}\,(\underline{\underline{\tau}}) - \text{grad}\,p$$

where τ is the effective stress tensor, and p is the time-mean static pressure. Body forces have been omitted.

3. *Conservation of Energy*: Rate of increase of the sum of internal and kinetic energy equals net rate of convective inflow of stagnation enthalpy plus net rate of energy inflow by thermal and mass transfer diffusion, all per unit volume. [In combustion simulation, other terms accounting for shear work, radiation and other sources are usually neg-

lected.] Additional rearrangement, amalgamation of the diffusive flux terms into the effective stagnation enthalpy flux vector J_h and neglect of a kinetic energy term on the right leads to:

$$\partial (\rho h)/\partial t + \text{div}(\rho v h) = -\text{div}(J_h)$$

4. *Conservation of Chemical Species*: Rate of increase of mass of chemical species *j* equals net rate of convective and diffusive inflow plus net rate of chemical species production R_j, all per unit volume:

$$\partial (\rho m_j)/\partial t + \text{div}(\rho v m_j) = -\text{div}(J_j) + R_j$$

where J_j is effective flux vector for chemical species *j*.

5. *Conservation of k and* ϵ: Similar statements hold.

$$\partial (\rho k)/\partial t + \text{div}(\rho v k) = -\text{div}(J_k) + G_k - \rho\epsilon$$

$$\partial (\rho\epsilon)/\partial t + \text{div}(\rho v \epsilon) = -\text{div}(J_\epsilon) + C_1 \epsilon G_k/k - C_2 \rho\epsilon^2/k$$

where J_k and J_ϵ are effective diffusive flux vectors for k and ϵ, g_k is the volumetric rate of generation of k [$= \mu_{eff}\ 2\underline{\underline{\Delta}}:\underline{\underline{\Delta}}$ later, where μ_{eff} is the effective viscosity] and C_1 and C_2 are turbulence constants:

$$C_1 = 1.44$$

$$C_2 = 1.92$$

These transport equations are all similar and contain terms for the convection and diffusion (via effective flux terms) and source S_ϕ of a general variable ϕ (which contains terms describing the generation (creation) and consumption (dissipation) of ϕ). In fact, they all conform to

$$\partial (\rho\phi)/\partial t + \text{div}(\rho v \phi) = -\text{div}(J_\phi) + S_\phi \tag{2.1}$$

and the equations differ not only in their effective diffusive flux vectors J_ϕ but also, and primarily, in their final source terms S_ϕ as inspection of the summary Table 2.1 reveals. If they are to be solved for time-mean pressure p, velocity v, temperature T and chemical species mass fractions m_j, then the further thermodynamic unknowns (density ρ, stagnation enthalpy h and the mass rates of creation of species j per unit volume R_j) and effective flux unknowns (effective stress tensor τ and effective flux vectors J_ϕ for transported fluid scalar properties $\phi = h, m_j, k$, and ϵ) must be specified prior to solution. It is convenient now to consider the problem of closure of the equations.

TABLE 2.1

Governing differential equations – tensoral version

ϕ	J_ϕ	S_ϕ
1	0	0
ν	$-\tau$	$-$ grad p
h	J_h	0
m_j	J_j	R_j
k	J_k	$G_k - \rho\epsilon$
ϵ	J_ϵ	$C_1 \epsilon G_k/k - C_2 \rho \epsilon^2/k$

where

$G_k = \mu\ [2\Delta{:}\Delta]$

μ = effective viscosity

C_1 = 1.44 and C_2 = 1.92 are turbulence model constants

The next two subsections discuss the problem of closure, via flux laws (including effective viscosity μ and turbulence models) and the combustion simulation, and how the concepts fit into the governing equation scheme. Sections 2.4 and 2.5, on the other hand, are concerned with the general modeling developments in turbulence and combustion.

Flux Laws

The PDEs of conservation already given may be taken to hold for *time-mean* values, provided that the stress tensor τ (for momentum) and diffusive flux vectors J_ϕ (for general transported fluid scalar properties ϕ = h, m_j, etc.) are considered to be *effective* values, composed of laminar and turbulent contributions[28]. The latter are related to correlations of turbulent fluctuations and, neglecting the density fluctuation terms, the appropriate expressions are

$$\underline{\underline{\tau}} = \underline{\underline{\tau}}_{\text{lam}} - \rho\overline{\nu'\nu'}$$

$$J_\phi = J_{\phi\,\text{lam}} + \rho\overline{\nu'\phi'} \qquad (2.2)$$

The term $-\overline{\rho\nu'\nu'}$ is known as the turbulent (Reynolds) stress tensor. It is these terms that are not known and their specification that assists in closing the system and allowing predictions to be made. Specification can be in terms of other time-mean variables already in the equation set. Alternatively, and in a more complex manner, specification can be in terms of other variables not in the current equation set, which must then be made the subject of further PDEs to be solved simultaneously with the others. Thus, the

Reynolds equations are often given the turbulent (or eddy) viscosity concept, suitably generalized to the multicomponent system equations. Turbulent diffusion is approximated by gradient laws (of time-mean values of the variable in question) with enlarged and variable transport coefficients.

The flux-gradient transport laws of Newton, Fourier and Fick for momentum, heat and mass transfer provided most useful unifying assumptions:

1. *Newton's Constitutive Stress-Strain Relation*: Dependence of momentum transport by viscosity on velocity gradients. [The value of the momentum flux tensor is the negative of the value of the stress tensor.]
2. *Fourier's Law of Heat Conduction*: Dependence of heat (energy) transport by conduction on temperature gradients.
3. *Fick's Law of Diffusion*: Dependence of chemical species transport by diffusion on concentration gradients.

In the multicomponent flow case the analogy leads to effective exchange coefficients μ and Γ_ϕ being defined, approximately, by

$$\underline{\underline{\tau}} = 2\mu\underline{\underline{\Delta}} - \frac{2}{3}\mu(\text{div } v)\underline{\underline{I}} - \frac{2}{3}\rho k\underline{\underline{I}}$$

$$J\phi = -\Gamma_\phi \text{ grad } \phi$$

for $\phi = h, m_j$, etc. Here $\underline{\underline{\Delta}}$ is the time-mean rate of strain tensor and $\underline{\underline{I}}$ is the identity tensor[27]. These effective exchange coefficients are composed of laminar and turbulent parts:

$$\mu = \mu_{\text{lam}} + \mu_{\text{turb}}$$

$$\Gamma_\phi = \Gamma_{\phi\text{lam}} + \Gamma_{\phi\text{turb}}$$

and are connected to other fluid properties such as density, temperature, composition, and turbulence characteristics by a variety of algebraic relations. If isotropy is assumed, often, constant Prandtl, Schmidt and rθ (and other) viscosity numbers relate other exchange coefficients to the primary component of effective viscosity $\mu \equiv \mu_{rx}$; these are defined by

$$\sigma_\phi = \mu / \Gamma_\phi$$

$$\sigma_{r\theta} = \mu / \mu_{r\theta} \quad \text{(and similarly for other components)}$$

where often the former are taken near 0.7 and the latter as unity (isotropic)[39]. To describe the turbulent transport, the two-equation k-ϵ turbulence model[28] may be used, whereby the turbulent viscosity is calculated from

$$\mu_{turb} = C_\mu \rho k^2 / \epsilon \tag{2.3}$$

and two differential equations are solved for the two turbulence quantities k and ϵ. Schmidt numbers for these two turbulence equations are generally taken as

$$\sigma_k = 1.0$$

$$\sigma_\epsilon = 1.21$$

and the final turbulence constant is taken as

$$C_\mu = 0.09$$

Of course, a simpler turbulence hypothesis may be made: perhaps a variant of the Prandtl mixing length PML model may be sufficient for the case in question. Then, the two PDEs for k and ϵ are not needed, and specification of μ_{turb} is via a simple algebraic formula. Other techniques are available[28-46].

In the interest of uniformity of the governing equation set it is convenient to keep diffusion in a certain direction related to gradients in that direction *only*, in the *main diffusion terms*. In the case of transported fluid scalar properties ϕ, this is immediate, but if there is a diffusional component normal to this direction, it must be expressed as part of S_ϕ. The transport of momentum is via the stress tensor τ, which cannot be expressed in so simple a manner as the transport of ϕ by diffusion; or rather, it can be, but first the whole expression must be considered, and only then those unwanted components, which do not vanish in view of the continuity equation, transferred into the source terms. The details will become clear very soon.[11, 22-26]

The Simple Exothermic Combustion Simulation

Various standard thermodynamic considerations provide some of the necessary extra equations to close the system; these may be taken as[5, 22-24]

$$\begin{aligned}
p &= \rho\, RT/M \text{ where } 1/M = \sum_j (m_j/M_j) \\
h &= c_p\, T + \sum_j (H_j\, m_j) + v^2/2 \\
R_j &= \text{provided by reaction model} \\
\sum_j m_j &= 1
\end{aligned} \tag{2.4}$$

where R is the universal gas constant, M is the mean mixture molecular weight which may be calculated from m_j and the molecular weight of species j, M_j, c_p is the mean mixture specific heat at constant pressure, and H_j is the heat of combustion of species j (also called heat of reaction and calorific value). To reduce the number of chemical species PDEs, consideration is often given to a simplified main exothermic reaction between just two species, fuel *fu* and oxidant *ox*, combining with a stoichiometric oxidant/fuel ratio of *s* to form product pr plus release of energy. Only the fuel is now supposed to possess a heat of combustion, each kilogram of fuel releasing H_{fu} Joules of energy on burning. Most hydrocarbon fuels have heats of combustion of about 40 x 10^6 J/kg of fuel. This and other assumptions lead to the simplifying equations[5]:

$$1\ \text{kg}\ fu + s\ \text{kg}\ ox \rightarrow (1 + s)\ \text{kg}\ pr + H_{fu}$$

$$h = c_p T + H_{fu}\, m_{fu} + v^2 / 2 \tag{2.5}$$

$$m_{fu} + m_{ox} + m_{pr} = 1$$

In view of the last of these algebraic equations, only two chemical species PDEs need be solved, for *fu* and *ox* (say). But a further simplification follows, since the rates of reaction of *fu* and *ox* are intimately related. That is, for every kilogram of *fu* that burns, so also does *s* kilograms of *ox*. Thus,

$$R_{fu} = R_{ox}/s$$

and a PDE for the combined concentration quantity.

$$f = m_{fu} - m_{ox}/s \qquad \text{(conserved property)}$$

may readily be deduced by eliminating the source term from the *fu* and *ox* PDEs. The assumption of equal exchange coefficients is also needed. Finally, it is to be noted that the equation for *f* so deduced is rather simple: it is a conserved quantity (otherwise, called a passive scalar, a Shvab Zeldovich function or simply a variable that obeys the general PDE and possesses no source term). Hence, it is convenient to solve PDEs for m_{fu} and f (rather than m_{fu} and m_{ox}), from which everything else can be deduced. Thus, solution for m_{fu}, f and h enables a simple premixed chemical reaction to be simulated with the influence of chemical-kinetics included—fuel and oxidant may coexist at a point in the flow and the consumption rate of fuel ($-R_{fu}$) is calculated, depending on local species concentrations, temperature and turbulence levels[50,51]. For this one can use either the time-averaged Arrhenius model or eddy-breakup reaction model[5]:

$$R_{fu} = -P\, p^2\, m_{fu}\, m_{ox} \exp(-E/(R\,T))$$

$$R_{fu} = -C_{EBU}\ \rho\, g^{1/2}\, \epsilon / k \tag{2.6}$$

P, E/R and C_{EBU} are constants for turbulent premixed flames of high temperature and high Reynolds numbers. The value of the latter model is that it tries to assert the effect of turbulence on the reaction, the time to heat up the premixed mixture by eddies of hot combustion product being related to the rate of dissipation of the concentration. In many cases this is the limiting factor in controlling the reaction and not the final stages of molecular processes governed by an instantaneous Arrhenius expression. The variable g (mean square fluctuating component of concentration $g = \overline{f'^2}$) may be obtained from its governing equation or, with the assumption that generation equals dissipation, its reduced algebraic equation

$$g = \frac{C_{g1}\,\mu\,k}{C_{g2}\,\rho\,\epsilon}\;[\,(\text{grad f})\cdot(\text{grad f})\,]$$

where $C_{g1} = 2.8$ and $C_{g2} = 2.0$ are constants. Generally, the lower of the two reaction rate values are used. Some workers take eddy-breakup concepts with m_{fu} replacing f in these expressions with appropriate changes to the constants. Table 2-2 extends the previous Table 2-1 to include the new details.

TABLE 2.2

Governing differential equations – tensoral version – additional equations for combustion

ϕ	J_ϕ	S_ϕ
m_{fu}	J_{fu}	R_{fu}
f	J_f	0
g	J_g	$G_g - C_{g2}\rho\epsilon_g/k$

where

$G_g = C_{g1}\mu_{eff}[\,(\text{grad f})\cdot(\text{grad f})\,]$

$C_{g1} = 2.8$

$C_{g2} = 2.0$

In view of the above discussion, it is clear that similarity between basic PDEs for time-mean properties and their diffusional relations allows them all to be put in the common form

$$\partial(\rho\phi)/\partial t + \text{div}\,(\rho\,v\,\phi) = \text{div}\,(\Gamma_\phi\,\text{grad}\,\phi) + S_\phi \tag{2.7}$$

for $\phi = 1, v$, h, m_{fu}, f, k, and ϵ, and the equations differ in their specification of their effective exchange coefficients Γ_ϕ and their final source terms S_ϕ, as inspection of

Table 2-3 reveals. If ϕ is put equal to unity and Γ_ϕ and S_ϕ to zero, this equation stands for the continuity (overall mass conservation) equation. In the case of the momentum equation for the vector velocity v there is some complexity in that part of div τ has been retained as the main diffusion term, and the remaining part has been transferred to the source term. The remaining equations are unchanged.

TABLE 2.3

Governing differential equations – tensoral version – with exchange coefficient assumptions

ϕ	Γ_ϕ	S_ϕ
1	0	0
v	μ	div τ – div (μ grad v) – grad p
h	μ/σ_h	0
m_{fu}	μ/σ_{fu}	R_{fu}
f	μ/σ_f	0
g	μ/σ_g	$G_g - C_{g2}\rho\epsilon_g/k$
k	μ/σ_k	$G_k - \rho\epsilon$
ϵ	μ/σ_ϵ	$C_1\epsilon G_k/k - C_2\rho\epsilon^2/k$

The basic equations may be written in any coordinate system using appropriate vector and tensor operator theories, although complexities abound where operators on tensors are concerned, and many extra terms arise – like the Corriolis and centripetal accelerations in the convection terms, and additional terms in the diffusion expressions. Although most combustor flows of practical interest are generally fully three-dimensional 3-D, often the boundary geometry conforms to the cylindrical polar coordinate system (sometimes with axisymmetry) and it is the input boundary conditions that have given rise to nonaxisymmetric events. Typical swirl flows are thus handled more accurately and conveniently in this system, although notable exceptions (like a swirl flow entering a rectangular furnace) occur. Often nonaxisymmetries are not too dramatic, and then the axisymmetric assertion leads to a reduction in the number of terms in each PDE, as in the subsequent section. In either case, boundary layer assumptions may be invoked, thus restricting the flow to possess no recirculation in the main stream direction. Then other simplifications arise in the equations, as illustrated in the later discussion.

2.2 CYLINDRICAL POLAR COORDINATE VERSION OF THE GOVERNING EQUATIONS

3-D Cylindrical Polar Coordinate Form of Equations

Let u, v, w be time-mean velocity components in x, r, θ cylindrical polar coordinates. [The Cartesian x, y, z coordinate equations can readily be derived from the following by letting r tend to infinity and replacing $r\partial\theta$ by ∂z. The equations simplify, and indeed the analogy may be exploited by idealizing a segment of an annular combustion chamber, for example, to be taken as a 3-D rectangular region.] Taking

$$\operatorname{div}(\rho \nu \phi) = \frac{1}{r}\left[\frac{\partial}{\partial x}(r\rho u \phi) + \frac{\partial}{\partial r}(r\rho v\phi) + \frac{\partial}{\partial \theta}(\rho w \phi)\right]$$

$$\operatorname{div}(J_\phi) = \frac{\partial}{\partial x}(J_{\phi x}) + \frac{1}{r}\frac{\partial}{\partial r}(r J_{\phi r}) + \frac{1}{r}\frac{\partial}{\partial \theta}(J_{\phi\theta})$$

$$\operatorname{div}(\Gamma_\phi \operatorname{grad}\phi) = \frac{1}{r}\left[\frac{\partial}{\partial x}\left(r\Gamma_\phi \frac{\partial \phi}{\partial x}\right) + \frac{\partial}{\partial r}\left(r\Gamma_\phi \frac{\partial \phi}{\partial r}\right) + \frac{\partial}{\partial \theta}\left(\Gamma_\phi \frac{1}{r}\frac{\partial \phi}{\partial \theta}\right)\right]$$

the general equation in 3-D cylindrical polar coordinates takes the form[22-24]

$$\frac{\partial}{\partial t}(\rho\phi) + \frac{1}{r}\left[\frac{\partial}{\partial x}(r\rho u\phi) + \frac{\partial}{\partial r}(r\rho v\phi) + \frac{\partial}{\partial \theta}(\rho w\phi)\right]$$
$$= \frac{1}{r}\left[\frac{\partial}{\partial x}\left(r\Gamma_\phi \frac{\partial \phi}{\partial x}\right) + \frac{\partial}{\partial r}\left(r\Gamma_\phi \frac{\partial \phi}{\partial r}\right) + \frac{\partial}{\partial \theta}\left(\Gamma_\phi \frac{1}{r}\frac{\partial \phi}{\partial \theta}\right)\right] + S_\phi \qquad (2.8)$$

where ϕ stands for any of the dependent variables, and the corresponding values of Γ_ϕ and S_ϕ are indicated in Table 2-4. The associated model constants appear in Table 2-5.

TABLE 2.4

Governing differential equations – 3-D cylindrical polar coordinate form

ϕ	Γ_ϕ	S_ϕ
1	0	0
u	μ	$-\frac{\partial p}{\partial x} + \frac{\partial}{\partial x}\left(\mu\frac{\partial u}{\partial x}\right) + \frac{1}{r}\frac{\partial}{\partial r}\left(r\mu\frac{\partial v}{\partial x}\right) + \frac{1}{r}\frac{\partial}{\partial \theta}\left(\mu\frac{\partial w}{\partial x}\right) - \frac{2}{3}\frac{\partial}{\partial x}\left[\mu(\operatorname{div}\nu) + \rho k\right]$
v	μ	$-\frac{\partial p}{\partial r} + \frac{\partial}{\partial x}\left(\mu\frac{\partial u}{\partial r}\right) + \frac{1}{r}\frac{\partial}{\partial r}\left(r\mu\frac{\partial v}{\partial r}\right) + \frac{1}{r}\frac{\partial}{\partial \theta}\left(\mu r\frac{\partial}{\partial r}\left(\frac{w}{r}\right)\right) - 2\frac{\mu}{r}\left(\frac{1}{r}\frac{\partial w}{\partial \theta} + \frac{v}{r}\right)$

TABLE 2.4 (Continued)

ϕ	Γ_ϕ	S_ϕ
		$-\frac{2}{3}\frac{\partial}{\partial r}\left[\mu(\mathrm{div}\,\nu)+\rho k\right]+\rho\frac{w^2}{r}$
w	μ	$-\frac{1}{r}\frac{\partial p}{\partial \theta}+\frac{\partial}{\partial x}\left(\mu\frac{1}{r}\frac{\partial u}{\partial \theta}\right)-\frac{w}{r^2}\frac{\partial}{\partial r}(r\mu)$ $+\frac{1}{r^2}\frac{\partial}{\partial r}\left(r^2\mu\frac{1}{r}\frac{\partial v}{\partial \theta}\right)+\frac{1}{r}\frac{\partial}{\partial \theta}\left(\mu\frac{1}{r}\frac{\partial w}{\partial \theta}+2\mu\frac{v}{r}\right)$ $-\frac{2}{3}\frac{1}{r}\frac{\partial}{\partial \theta}\left[\mu(\mathrm{div}\,\nu)+\rho k\right]-\rho\frac{vw}{r}$
h	μ/σ_h	0
m_{fu}	μ/σ_{fu}	R_{fu}
f	μ/σ_f	0
g	μ/σ_g	$G_g - C_{g2}\rho\epsilon g/k$
k	μ/σ_k	$G_k - \rho\epsilon$
ϵ	μ/σ_ϵ	$C_1\epsilon G_k/k - C_2\rho\epsilon^2/k$

where

$$\mu = \mu_{lam} + \mu_{turb}$$

$$\mu_{turb} = C_\mu \rho k^2/\epsilon$$

$$G_g = C_{g1}\mu\left[\left(\frac{\partial f}{\partial x}\right)^2+\left(\frac{\partial f}{\partial r}\right)^2+\left(\frac{1}{r}\frac{\partial f}{\partial \theta}\right)^2\right]$$

$$G_k = \mu\left[2\left\{\left(\frac{\partial u}{\partial x}\right)^2+\left(\frac{\partial v}{\partial r}\right)^2+\left(\frac{1}{r}\frac{\partial w}{\partial \theta}+\frac{v}{r}\right)^2\right\}\right.$$
$$+\left(\frac{\partial u}{\partial r}+\frac{\partial v}{\partial x}\right)^2+\left(\frac{1}{r}\frac{\partial v}{\partial \theta}+r\frac{\partial}{\partial r}\left(\frac{w}{r}\right)\right)^2$$
$$\left.+\left(\frac{1}{r}\frac{\partial u}{\partial \theta}+\frac{\partial w}{\partial x}\right)^2\right]$$

$$\mathrm{div}\,\nu = \frac{\partial u}{\partial x}+\frac{1}{r}\frac{\partial}{\partial r}(rv)+\frac{1}{r}\frac{\partial w}{\partial \theta}$$

TABLE 2.5
Model constants

Prandtl – Schmidt numbers	σ_h	0.7	
	σ_{fu}	0.7	
	σ_f	0.7	
	σ_g	0.7	
	σ_k	1.0	
	σ_ϵ	1.3 *	(*see* footnote)
Reaction model constants	C_{g1}	2.8	
	C_{g2}	2.0	
Turbulence model constants	C_1	1.44	
	C_2	1.92	
	C_μ	0.09	

* Note that σ_ϵ is assigned a value consistent with

$$\sigma_\epsilon = \frac{x^2}{(C_2 - C_1)\, C_\mu^{1/2}}$$

where x is von Karman's constant taken as 0.4

Written out in full, the more usual forms of the equations are:

$$\frac{\partial \rho}{\partial t} + \frac{\partial}{\partial x}(\rho u) + \frac{1}{r}\frac{\partial}{\partial r}(r \rho v) + \frac{1}{r}\frac{\partial}{\partial \theta}(\rho w) = 0$$

$$\frac{\partial}{\partial t}(\rho u) + \frac{\partial}{\partial x}(\rho u^2) + \frac{1}{r}\frac{\partial}{\partial r}(r\rho v u) + \frac{1}{r}\frac{\partial}{\partial \theta}(\rho w u)$$

$$= -\frac{\partial p}{\partial x} + \frac{\partial}{\partial x}(\tau_{xx}) + \frac{1}{r}\frac{\partial}{\partial r}(r\,\tau_{rx}) + \frac{1}{r}\frac{\partial}{\partial \theta}(\tau_{\theta x})$$

$$\frac{\partial}{\partial t}(\rho v) + \frac{\partial}{\partial x}(\rho u v) + \frac{1}{r}\frac{\partial}{\partial r}(r\rho v^2) + \frac{1}{r}\frac{\partial}{\partial \theta}(\rho w v) - \frac{\rho w^2}{r} \qquad (2.9)$$

$$= -\frac{\partial p}{\partial r} + \frac{\partial}{\partial x}(\tau_{xr}) + \frac{1}{r}\frac{\partial}{\partial r}(r\,\tau_{rr}) + \frac{1}{r}\frac{\partial}{\partial \theta}(\tau_{\theta r}) - \frac{\tau_{\theta\theta}}{r}$$

$$\frac{\partial}{\partial t}(\rho w) + \frac{\partial}{\partial x}(\rho u w) + \frac{1}{r}\frac{\partial}{\partial r}(r\rho v w) + \frac{1}{r}\frac{\partial}{\partial \theta}(\rho w^2) + \frac{\rho v w}{r}$$

$$= -\frac{1}{r}\frac{\partial p}{\partial \theta} + \frac{\partial}{\partial x}(\tau_{x\theta}) + \frac{1}{r^2}\frac{\partial}{\partial r}(r^2\,\tau_{r\theta}) + \frac{1}{r}\frac{\partial}{\partial \theta}(\tau_{\theta\theta})$$

$$\frac{\partial}{\partial t}(\rho\theta) + \frac{\partial}{\partial x}(\rho u \phi) + \frac{1}{r}\frac{\partial}{\partial r}(r\rho v \phi) + \frac{1}{r}\frac{\partial}{\partial \theta}(\rho w \phi)$$

$$= -\left[\frac{\partial}{\partial x}(J_{\phi x}) + \frac{1}{r}\frac{\partial}{\partial r}(r\,J_{\phi r}) + \frac{1}{r}\frac{\partial}{\partial \theta}(J_{\phi\theta})\right] + S_\phi$$

for the continuity equation, the three momenta equations and the equation for typical transported fluid scalar properties $\phi = h$, m_{fu}, etc. Notice here that the convection terms of the left-hand sides have been kept in conservative form: most textbooks present the alternative form, which may be derived from the present version by differentiating the products and cancelling half the terms in view of the continuity equation[3]. Then the convection terms of the three momenta equations appear as:

$$\rho\left(\frac{\partial u}{\partial t} + u\frac{\partial u}{\partial x} + v\frac{\partial u}{\partial r} + \frac{w}{r}\frac{\partial u}{\partial \theta}\right)$$

$$\rho\left(\frac{\partial v}{\partial t} + u\frac{\partial v}{\partial x} + v\frac{\partial v}{\partial r} + \frac{w}{r}\frac{\partial v}{\partial \theta} - \frac{w^2}{r}\right)$$

$$\rho\left(\frac{\partial w}{\partial t} + u\frac{\partial w}{\partial x} + v\frac{\partial w}{\partial r} + \frac{w}{r}\frac{\partial w}{\partial \theta} + \frac{vw}{r}\right)$$

The effective stress tensor $\underline{\underline{\tau}}$ and effective flux vector J_ϕ have components in this system given by[3]

$$\begin{aligned}
\tau_{xx} &= \tau_{xx\,\mathrm{lam}} - \rho\overline{u'^2} \\
\tau_{rr} &= \tau_{rr\,\mathrm{lam}} - \rho\overline{v'^2} \\
\tau_{\theta\theta} &= \tau_{\theta\theta\,\mathrm{lam}} - \rho\overline{w'^2} \\
\tau_{rx} &= \tau_{xr} = \tau_{rx\,\mathrm{lam}} - \rho\overline{v'u'} \\
\tau_{r\theta} &= \tau_{\theta r} = \tau_{r\theta\,\mathrm{lam}} - \rho\overline{v'w'} \\
\tau_{x\theta} &= \tau_{\theta x} = \tau_{x\theta\,\mathrm{lam}} - \rho\overline{u'w'}
\end{aligned} \tag{2.10}$$

$$J_{\phi x} = J_{\phi x\ lam} + \overline{\rho u'\phi'}$$

$$J_{\phi r} = J_{\phi r\ lam} + \overline{\rho v'\phi'}$$

$$J_{\phi \theta} = J_{\phi \theta\ lam} + \overline{\rho w'\phi'}$$

The $-\rho\overline{u'^2}$ etc. terms are the turbulent (Reynolds) normal stresses; the $-\rho\overline{v'u'}$ etc. terms are the turbulent (Reynolds) shear stresses.

Closure is often obtained by way of introduction of effective viscosity μ and effective exchange coefficients Γ_ϕ. Constitutive assumptions for the isotropic case arc:

$$\begin{aligned}
\tau_{xx} &= 2\mu \frac{\partial u}{\partial x} - \frac{2}{3}\mu\,(\mathrm{div}\,\nu) - \frac{2}{3}\rho k \\
\tau_{rr} &= 2\mu \frac{\partial v}{\partial r} - \frac{2}{3}\mu\,(\mathrm{div}\,\nu) - \frac{2}{3}\rho k \\
\tau_{\theta\theta} &= 2\mu \left(\frac{1}{r}\frac{\partial w}{\partial \theta} + \frac{v}{r}\right) - \frac{2}{3}\mu\,(\mathrm{div}\,\nu) - \frac{2}{3}\rho k \\
\tau_{rx} &= \tau_{xr} = \mu \left(\frac{\partial u}{\partial r} + \frac{\partial v}{\partial x}\right) \\
\tau_{r\theta} &= \tau_{\theta r} = \mu \left(\frac{1}{r}\frac{\partial v}{\partial \theta} + r\frac{\partial}{\partial r}\left(\frac{w}{r}\right)\right) \qquad (2.11) \\
\tau_{x\theta} &= \tau_{\theta x} = \mu \left(\frac{1}{r}\frac{\partial u}{\partial \theta} + \frac{\partial w}{\partial x}\right) \\
J_{\phi x} &= -\Gamma_\phi \frac{\partial \phi}{\partial x} \\
J_{\phi r} &= -\Gamma_\phi \frac{\partial \phi}{\partial r} \\
J_{\phi\theta} &= -\Gamma_\phi \frac{1}{r}\frac{\partial \phi}{\partial \theta}
\end{aligned}$$

where

$$\mathrm{div}\,\nu = \frac{\partial u}{\partial x} + \frac{1}{r}\frac{\partial}{\partial r}(rv) + \frac{1}{r}\frac{\partial w}{\partial \theta}$$

If isotropy is not assumed, different values of μ and Γ_ϕ may be appropriate to different directions of τ and J_ϕ at the same location. Then, Prandtl, Schmidt and $r\theta$- (and other-) viscosity numbers relate values of other exchange coefficients to the primary component of effective viscosity $\mu \equiv \mu_{rx}$ as discussed in general in the previous section[27].

Sometimes, the turbulent (Reynolds) stress tensor τ_{turb} and the associated turbulent viscosity μ_{turb} are highlighted, and adding these to their laminar counterparts results in the effective quantities highlighted in the present treatment. The two alternative versions are fully consistent, as can be seen by inspection of any of the effective stress terms. For example, consider the xx-effective stress:

$$
\begin{aligned}
\tau_{xx} &= \tau_{xx\,lam} + \tau_{xx\,turb} \\
&= \tau_{xx\,lam} - \rho\overline{u'^2} \\
&= \mu_{lam}\left(2\frac{\partial u}{\partial x} - \frac{2}{3}(\mathrm{div}\,v)\right) \\
&\quad + \mu_{turb}\left(2\frac{\partial u}{\partial x} - \frac{2}{3}(\mathrm{div}\,v)\right) - \frac{2}{3}\rho k \\
&= \mu\left(2\frac{\partial u}{\partial x} - \frac{2}{3}(\mathrm{div}\,v)\right) - \frac{2}{3}\rho k
\end{aligned}
$$

where $\mu = \mu_{1am} + \mu_{turb}$ is the effective viscosity. All the other components may be treated similarly. Notice that the normal components of turbulent (Reynolds) stress contain the term $(-\frac{2}{3}\rho k)$ (which is often omitted in practice) in order that summation of the normal components and application of the continuity equation should be consistent with the definition of $k = (\overline{u^2} + \overline{v'^2} + \overline{w'^2})/2$ for the incompressible flow case. That is:

$$
\begin{aligned}
k &= \frac{1}{2}(\overline{u'^2} + \overline{v'^2} + \overline{w'^2}) \\
&= -\frac{1}{2\rho}(\tau_{xx\,turb} + \tau_{rr\,turb} + \tau_{\theta\theta\,turb}) \\
&= -\frac{1}{2\rho}\Bigg(2\mu_{turb}\underbrace{\left(\frac{\partial u}{\partial x} + \frac{\partial v}{\partial r} + \frac{1}{r}\frac{\partial w}{\partial \theta} + \frac{v}{r}\right)}_{\substack{=\,o \text{ by continuity equation} \\ \text{for incompressible flow}}} - 2\rho k\Bigg) \\
&= k
\end{aligned}
$$

Substitution for the effective τ and J_ϕ components leads to the general form shown in Eqn. (2.8) and Table 2.4. For example, consider the diffusion terms of the equations separately, and apply manipulations so as to isolate the *main* diffusion terms and relegate other parts to the 'catch-all' source term:

u-equation

$$
\frac{\partial}{\partial x}(\tau_{xx}) + \frac{1}{r}\frac{\partial}{\partial r}(r\,\tau_{rx}) + \frac{1}{r}\frac{\partial}{\partial \theta}(\tau_{\theta x})
$$

$$= \frac{\partial}{\partial x}\left(2\mu \frac{\partial u}{\partial x} - \frac{2}{3}[\mu(\text{div } \nu) + \rho k]\right)$$

$$+ \frac{1}{r}\frac{\partial}{\partial r}\left(r\mu\left[\frac{\partial u}{\partial r} + \frac{\partial v}{\partial x}\right]\right)$$

$$+ \frac{1}{r}\frac{\partial}{\partial \theta}\left(\mu\left[\frac{1}{r}\frac{\partial u}{\partial \theta} + \frac{\partial w}{\partial x}\right]\right)$$

$$= \left\{\frac{\partial}{\partial x}\left(\mu \frac{\partial u}{\partial x}\right) + \frac{1}{r}\frac{\partial}{\partial r}\left(r\mu \frac{\partial u}{\partial r}\right) + \frac{1}{r}\frac{\partial}{\partial \theta}\left(\mu \frac{1}{r}\frac{\partial u}{\partial \theta}\right)\right\}$$

$$+ \left\{\frac{\partial}{\partial x}\left(\mu \frac{\partial u}{\partial x}\right) + \frac{1}{r}\frac{\partial}{\partial r}\left(r\mu \frac{\partial v}{\partial x}\right) + \frac{1}{r}\frac{\partial}{\partial \theta}\left(\mu \frac{\partial w}{\partial x}\right)\right.$$

$$\left. - \frac{2}{3}\frac{\partial}{\partial x}[\mu(\text{div } \nu) + \rho k]\right\}$$

and the first braced term is retained as the main diffusion term, and the second one is transferred to the source term.

v-equation

$$\frac{\partial}{\partial x}(\tau_{xr}) + \frac{1}{r}\frac{\partial}{\partial r}(r\,\tau_{rr}) + \frac{1}{r}\frac{\partial}{\partial \theta}(\tau_{\theta r}) - \frac{\tau_{\theta\theta}}{r}$$

$$= \frac{\partial}{\partial x}\left(\mu\left[\frac{\partial u}{\partial r} + \frac{\partial v}{\partial x}\right]\right)$$

$$+ \frac{1}{r}\frac{\partial}{\partial r}\left(r\left[2\mu \frac{\partial v}{\partial r} - \frac{2}{3}\left[\mu(\text{div } \nu) + \rho k\right]\right]\right)$$

$$+ \frac{1}{r}\frac{\partial}{\partial \theta}\left(\mu\left[\frac{1}{r}\frac{\partial v}{\partial \theta} + r\frac{\partial}{\partial r}\left(\frac{w}{r}\right)\right]\right)$$

$$- \frac{2\mu}{r}\left(\frac{1}{r}\frac{\partial w}{\partial \theta} + \frac{v}{r}\right) + \frac{2}{3}\frac{1}{r}\left[\mu(\text{div } \nu) + \rho k\right]$$

$$= \left\{\frac{\partial}{\partial x}\left(\mu \frac{\partial v}{\partial x}\right) + \frac{1}{r}\frac{\partial}{\partial r}\left(r\mu \frac{\partial v}{\partial r}\right) + \frac{1}{r}\frac{\partial}{\partial \theta}\left(\mu \frac{1}{r}\frac{\partial v}{\partial \theta}\right)\right\}$$

$$+ \left\{\frac{\partial}{\partial x}\left(\mu \frac{\partial u}{\partial r}\right) + \frac{1}{r}\frac{\partial}{\partial r}\left(r\mu \frac{\partial v}{\partial r}\right)\right.$$

$$- \frac{2}{3}\frac{1}{r}\frac{\partial}{\partial r}(r\,[\mu(\text{div } \nu) + \rho k])$$

$$+ \frac{1}{r} \frac{\partial}{\partial \theta}\left(\mu r \frac{\partial}{\partial r}\left(\frac{w}{r}\right)\right)$$

$$- \frac{2\mu}{r}\left(\frac{1}{r} \frac{\partial w}{\partial \theta} + \frac{v}{r}\right) + \frac{2}{3} \frac{1}{r} \left[\mu (\operatorname{div} \nu) + \rho k\right]\Big\}$$

and the first braced term is retained as the main diffusion term, and the second one is transferred to the source term with further simplification arising since

$$- \frac{2}{3} \frac{1}{r} \frac{\partial}{\partial r} \left(r \left[\mu (\operatorname{div} \nu) + \rho k\right]\right) + \frac{2}{3} \frac{1}{r} \left[\mu (\operatorname{div} \nu) + \rho k\right]$$

$$= - \frac{2}{3} \frac{\partial}{\partial r} \left[\mu (\operatorname{div} \nu) + \rho k\right]$$

w-equation

$$\frac{\partial}{\partial x} (\tau_{x\theta}) + \frac{1}{r^2} \frac{\partial}{\partial r} (r^2 \tau_{r\theta}) + \frac{1}{r} \frac{\partial}{\partial \theta} (\tau_{\theta\theta})$$

$$= \frac{\partial}{\partial x}\left(\mu \left[\frac{1}{r} \frac{\partial u}{\partial \theta} + \frac{\partial w}{\partial x}\right]\right)$$

$$+ \frac{1}{r^2} \frac{\partial}{\partial r}\left(r^2 \mu \left[\frac{1}{r} \frac{\partial v}{\partial \theta} + r \frac{\partial}{\partial r}\left(\frac{w}{r}\right)\right]\right)$$

$$+ \frac{1}{r} \frac{\partial}{\partial \theta}\left(2\mu \left[\frac{1}{r} \frac{\partial w}{\partial \theta} + \frac{v}{r}\right] - \frac{2}{3} \left[\mu (\operatorname{div} \nu) + \rho k\right]\right)$$

$$= \left\{\frac{\partial}{\partial x}\left(\mu \frac{\partial w}{\partial x}\right) + \frac{1}{r^2} \frac{\partial}{\partial r}\left(r^2 \mu r \frac{\partial}{\partial r}\left(\frac{w}{r}\right)\right) + \frac{1}{r} \frac{\partial}{\partial \theta}\left(\mu \frac{1}{r} \frac{\partial w}{\partial \theta}\right)\right\}$$

$$+ \frac{\partial}{\partial x}\left(\mu \frac{1}{r} \frac{\partial u}{\partial \theta}\right) + \frac{1}{r^2} \frac{\partial}{\partial r}\left(r^2 \mu \frac{1}{r} \frac{\partial v}{\partial \theta}\right)$$

$$+ \left\{\frac{1}{r} \frac{\partial}{\partial \theta}\left(\mu \frac{1}{r} \frac{\partial w}{\partial \theta} + \frac{2\mu v}{r}\right)\right.$$

$$\left. - \frac{2}{3} \frac{1}{r} \frac{\partial}{\partial \theta} \left[\mu (\operatorname{div} \nu) + \rho k\right]\right\}$$

and the r-derivative term in the first braced term is not yet in the standard main diffusion term format. It can, however, be further differentiated out to the form

$$\frac{1}{r^2} \frac{\partial}{\partial r}\left(r^2 \mu r \frac{\partial}{\partial r}\left(\frac{w}{r}\right)\right)$$

$$= \frac{1}{r} \frac{\partial}{\partial r}\left(r\mu \frac{\partial w}{\partial r}\right) - \frac{w}{r^2} \frac{\partial}{\partial r} (r\mu)$$

and the first term on the right is retained as the main r diffusion term and the second term on the right is transferred to the source, that is, transferred to the terms within the second pair of braces. The r-derivative terms of the source are thus

$$-\frac{w}{r^2}\frac{\partial}{\partial r}(r\mu) + \frac{1}{r^2}\frac{\partial}{\partial r}\left(r^2\mu\frac{1}{r}\frac{\partial v}{\partial\theta}\right)$$

and this is the *best version* in which to keep them. Other workers derive an alternative form of these two terms

$$+\frac{1}{r}\frac{\partial}{\partial r}\left(r\mu\left[\frac{1}{r}\frac{\partial v}{\partial\theta} - \frac{w}{r}\right]\right) + \frac{\mu}{r}\left(r\frac{\partial}{\partial r}\left(\frac{w}{r}\right) + \frac{1}{r}\frac{\partial v}{\partial\theta}\right)$$

which, although mathematically equivalent, does *not* isolate the source term in w as well as in the present recommended version; which allows (later) more effective implicit treatment of these source terms and aids the convergence of an iterative solution scheme.

Observation of the expanded forms of the diffusion terms of the u-, v- and w-equations reveals that the main parts are retained in the standard form of Eqn. (2.8) while the other parts are relegated to the source term S_ϕ, as inspection of Table 2.4 reveals. Careful treatment of the latter may encourage convergence of an iterative solution scheme; naive treatment may encourage divergence[53]. Finally, some workers[22-24] simplify the diffusion terms only via application of an assumed incompressibility condition

$$\text{div}\, v = 0$$

then three obvious terms vanish. So also do other parts of the source terms after changing the order of differentiation in two of the three parts of each source term. Further terms vanish if viscosity is assumed constant as well. Although source terms may be so-treated, the simplifying assumption is *not* extended to the compressible continuity equation itself and a variable density is allowed and used in the equations. Another much used simplification is to neglect source terms that contain k, a simplification that is used in the present text from here onward.

Axisymmetric Form with Swirl —— Elliptic Recirculating Flow

Consider now the restricted case where axisymmetry is assumed $\frac{\partial}{\partial\theta} = 0$ although a non-zero swirl velocity w is permitted. The general equation of 2-D axisymmetric cylindrical polar coordinates reduces to[50-52]

$$\frac{\partial}{\partial t}(\rho\phi) + \frac{1}{r}\left[\frac{\partial}{\partial x}(r\rho u\,\phi) + \frac{\partial}{\partial r}(r\rho v\,\phi)\right] \tag{2.12}$$

$$= \frac{1}{r}\left[\frac{\partial}{\partial x}\left(r\Gamma_\phi\frac{\partial\phi}{\partial x}\right) + \frac{\partial}{\partial r}\left(r\Gamma_\phi\frac{\partial\phi}{\partial r}\right)\right] + S_\phi$$

with values of Γ_ϕ and S_ϕ for each variable ϕ being given in Table 2.6. They may also be written out in full as:

$$\frac{\partial \rho}{\partial t} + \frac{\partial}{\partial x}(\rho u) + \frac{1}{r}\frac{\partial}{\partial r}(r\rho v) = 0$$

$$\frac{\partial}{\partial t}(\rho u) + \frac{\partial}{\partial x}(\rho u^2) + \frac{1}{r}\frac{\partial}{\partial r}(r\rho vu)$$

$$= -\frac{\partial p}{\partial x} + \frac{\partial}{\partial x}(\tau_{xx}) + \frac{1}{r}\frac{\partial}{\partial r}(r\,\tau_{rx})$$

$$\frac{\partial}{\partial t}(\rho v) + \frac{\partial}{\partial x}(\rho uv) + \frac{1}{r}\frac{\partial}{\partial r}(r\rho v^2) - \frac{\rho w^2}{r}$$

$$= -\frac{\partial p}{\partial r} + \frac{\partial}{\partial x}(\tau_{xr}) + \frac{1}{r}\frac{\partial}{\partial r}(r\,\tau_{rr}) - \frac{\tau_{\theta\theta}}{r}$$

$$\frac{\partial}{\partial t}(\rho w) + \frac{\partial}{\partial x}(\rho uw) + \frac{1}{r}\frac{\partial}{\partial r}(r\rho vw) + \frac{\rho vw}{r} \qquad (2.13)$$

$$= \frac{\partial}{\partial x}(\tau_{x\theta}) + \frac{1}{r^2}\frac{\partial}{\partial r}(r^2\,\tau_{r\theta})$$

$$\frac{\partial}{\partial t}(\rho\,\phi) + \frac{\partial}{\partial x}(\rho u\,\phi) + \frac{1}{r}\frac{\partial}{\partial r}(r\rho v\,\phi)$$

$$= -\left[\frac{\partial}{\partial x}(J_{\phi x}) + \frac{1}{r}\frac{\partial}{\partial r}(r\,J_{\phi r})\right] + S_\phi$$

where the relevant constitutive assumptions for the isotropic case are

$$\tau_{xx} = 2\mu\frac{\partial u}{\partial x} - \frac{2}{3}\mu\,(\text{div}\,\nu)$$

$$\tau_{rr} = 2\mu\frac{\partial v}{\partial r} - \frac{2}{3}\mu\,(\text{div}\,\nu)$$

$$\tau_{\theta\theta} = 2\mu\frac{v}{r} - \frac{2}{3}\mu\,(\text{div}\,\nu)$$

$$\tau_{rx} = \tau_{xr} = \mu\left(\frac{\partial u}{\partial r} + \frac{\partial v}{\partial x}\right) \qquad (2.14)$$

$$\tau_{r\theta} = \tau_{\theta r} = \mu\, r\frac{\partial}{\partial r}\left(\frac{w}{r}\right)$$

$$\tau_{x\theta} = \tau_{\theta x} = \mu\frac{\partial w}{\partial x}$$

$$J_{\phi x} = -\Gamma_\phi \frac{\partial \phi}{\partial x}$$

$$J_{\phi r} = -\Gamma_\phi \frac{\partial \phi}{\partial r}$$

where

$$\text{div}\ \nu = \frac{\partial u}{\partial x} + \frac{1}{r}\frac{\partial}{\partial r}(rv)$$

Substitution for the $\underline{\underline{\tau}}$ and J_ϕ components leads to the general form shown in Eqn. (2.12) and Table 2.6, where the div $\nu = 0$ condition has been applied to reduce part of the source term. If isotropy is not assumed, different values of μ and Γ_ϕ may be appropriate to different directions under consideration[39].

TABLE 2.6

Governing differential equations – swirling axisymmetric form.

ϕ	Γ_ϕ	S_ϕ
1	0	0
u	μ	$-\frac{\partial p}{\partial x} + \frac{\partial}{\partial x}\left(\mu \frac{\partial u}{\partial x}\right) + \frac{1}{r}\frac{\partial}{\partial r}\left(r\mu \frac{\partial v}{\partial x}\right)$
v	μ	$-\frac{\partial p}{\partial r} + \frac{\partial}{\partial x}\left(\mu \frac{\partial u}{\partial r}\right) + \frac{1}{r}\frac{\partial}{\partial r}\left(r\mu \frac{\partial v}{\partial r}\right) - 2\mu \frac{v}{r} + \rho \frac{w^2}{r}$
w	μ	$-\frac{w}{r^2}\frac{\partial}{\partial r}(r\mu) - \rho \frac{vw}{r}$
h	μ/σ_h	0
m_{fu}	μ/σ_{fu}	R_{fu}
f	μ/σ_f	0
g	μ/σ_g	$G_g - C_{g2}\,\rho\epsilon g/k$
k	μ/σ_k	$G_k - \rho\epsilon$
ϵ	μ/σ_ϵ	$C_1 \epsilon G_k/k - C_2 \rho\epsilon^2/k$

where

$$G_g = C_{g1}\,\mu \left[\left(\frac{\partial f}{\partial x}\right)^2 + \left(\frac{\partial f}{\partial r}\right)^2\right]$$

$$G_k = \mu\left[2\left\{\left(\frac{\partial u}{\partial x}\right)^2 + \left(\frac{\partial v}{\partial r}\right)^2 + \left(\frac{v}{r}\right)^2\right\} + \left(\frac{\partial u}{\partial r} + \frac{\partial v}{\partial x}\right)^2 + \left(r\frac{\partial}{\partial r}\left(\frac{w}{r}\right)\right)^2 + \left(\frac{\partial w}{\partial x}\right)^2\right]$$

and C_1, C_2, C_{g1} and C_{g2} are constants discussed earlier.

Axisymmetric Form with Swirl—Parabolic Boundary Layer Flow

The full elliptic equations just discussed have many terms, and many effective stress and flux components whose specification in turbulent flows is error prone. Recirculating flows also have to be solved iteratively, demanding a somewhat lengthy numerical relaxation procedure. Some physical flows may be simulated by a simplified form of these equations without much loss in accuracy. Such flows are called boundary layer flows and the application of boundary layer approximations results in truncation of the elliptic equations to parabolic form. Fewer terms and unknown fluxes are left in the equations and a simpler, quicker, forward-marching solution procedure can be applied. To qualify for this simplification, a flow must have a single predominant direction of flow and the flux components must be significant only in directions at right angles to this predominant direction. In particular, streamlines are not closed (there are no recirculation regions) and pressure variations should not allow downstream changes to influence upstream events[27]. Some flows fall into the category of partially-parabolic, in which case the pressure field is considered to be an elliptic problem, but the other equations are handled in their boundary layer form. A march downstream using an approximate pressure field allows an updated pressure field to be evaluated, from which repeated downstream marches and pressure update lead to complete solution.

Free, non-swirling jet flows qualify for boundary layer treatment; so do flows with weak swirl if the axial pressure gradient is still small and is well below that sufficient to cause recirculation. A strongly swirling jet flow with recirculation cannot be satisfactorily treated using reduced boundary layer equations and the full elliptic equations must be solved. Boundary layer approximations are applied to weakly swirling flows by considering the relative order to magnitude of terms in the governing equations, assuming that

$$u, w \approx O(1)$$

$$\frac{\partial}{\partial r} \approx O\left(\frac{1}{\epsilon}\right)$$

$$\frac{\partial}{\partial x} \approx O(1)$$

where $\epsilon << 1$. The continuity equation then gives

$$v \approx O(\epsilon)$$

Turbulence fluctuations u', v', w', ϕ' are generally assumed to be $O(\epsilon)$ also, and the approximate order of magnitude of all terms in the equations can be evaluated. Although there is some deliberation regarding the magnitude of the turbulence terms, deleting terms of lowest order in each equation reduces the governing equation set to the form[27,36]:

$$\frac{\partial \rho}{\partial t} + \frac{\partial}{\partial x}(\rho u) + \frac{1}{r}\frac{\partial}{\partial r}(r\rho v) = 0$$

$$\frac{\partial}{\partial t}(\rho u) + \frac{\partial}{\partial x}(\rho u^2) + \frac{1}{r}\frac{\partial}{\partial r}(r\rho vu)$$

$$= -\frac{\partial p}{\partial x} + \frac{1}{r}\frac{\partial}{\partial r}(r\,\tau_{rx}) \qquad (2.15)$$

$$-\frac{\rho w^2}{r} = -\frac{\partial p}{\partial r}$$

$$\frac{\partial}{\partial t}(\rho w) + \frac{\partial}{\partial x}(\rho uw) + \frac{1}{r}\frac{\partial}{\partial r}(r\rho vw) + \frac{\rho vw}{r}$$

$$= \frac{1}{r^2}\frac{\partial}{\partial r}(r^2\,\tau_{r\theta})$$

$$\frac{\partial}{\partial t}(\rho\phi) + \frac{\partial}{\partial x}(\rho u\phi) + \frac{1}{r}\frac{\partial}{\partial r}(r\rho v\phi)$$

$$= -\frac{1}{r}\frac{\partial}{\partial r}(r\,J_{\phi r}) + S_\phi$$

where, in common with most analyses, the centripetal and pressure forces are assumed to *dominate* in the radial v-equation:

$$\rho\, w^2/r = \partial p/\partial r$$

For a free swirling jet emerging into stagnant surroundings, this shows that pressures in the jet are lower than those of the surroundings at $r = r_{max}$ where $p = p_{max}$ and $w = 0$. Radial integration gives

$$p = p_{max} - \int_r^{r_{max}} \frac{\rho w^2}{r}\, dr$$

There are now only two components of shear stress, τ_{rx} and $\tau_{r\theta}$, and no normal stress components, together with $J_{\phi r}$, the r-component of J_ϕ flux. The relevant constitutive assumptions are, with boundary layer assumptions,

$$\tau_{rx} = \mu\frac{\partial u}{\partial r}$$

$$\tau_{r\theta} = \mu\, r\frac{\partial}{\partial r}\left(\frac{w}{r}\right) \qquad (2.16)$$

$$J_{\phi r} = -\Gamma_\phi\frac{\partial \phi}{\partial r}$$

and if isotropy is not assumed, the viscosity need not be the same in these two different directions[36]. By analogy with Prandtl-Schmidt numbers, $r\theta$- (and other-) viscosity numbers relate values to the primary component $\mu = \mu_{rx}$ of viscosity via

$$\sigma_{r\phi} = \mu_{rx}/\mu_{r\theta} \equiv \mu/\mu_{r\theta}$$

and for r-direction ϕ-transport

$$\sigma_{\phi r} = \mu_{rx} / \Gamma_{\phi r} \equiv \mu / \Gamma_{\phi r}$$

When the additional stress terms *are* retained in the radial v-equation, the equation is taken as

$$-\frac{\rho w^2}{r} = -\frac{\partial p}{\partial r} + \frac{1}{r}\frac{\partial}{\partial r}(r\,\tau_{rr}) - \frac{\tau_{\theta\theta}}{r}$$

and further stress terms remain:

$$\tau_{rr} = 2\mu\frac{\partial v}{\partial r} - \frac{2}{3}\mu\,(\text{div}\,\nu)$$

$$\tau_{\theta\theta} = 2\,\mu\frac{v}{r} - \frac{2}{3}\mu\,(\text{div}\,\nu)$$

In fact it is the turbulent contribution to these effective stresses that gives rise to these terms being retained. Recalling that

$$\tau_{rr} = \tau_{rr\ lam} - \rho\,\overline{v'^2}$$

$$\tau_{\theta\theta} = \tau_{\theta\theta\ lam} - \rho\,\overline{w'^2}$$

and neglecting the laminar contributions it may be seen that the extended ν-equation is

$$-\frac{\rho w^2}{r} = -\frac{\partial p}{\partial r} - \frac{1}{r}\frac{\partial}{\partial r}(r\rho\,\overline{v'^2}) + \frac{\rho\,\overline{w'^2}}{r}$$

which rearranges to

$$-\frac{\rho w^2}{r} = -\frac{\partial p}{\partial r} - \frac{\partial}{\partial r}(\rho\overline{v'^2}) - \left[\frac{\rho\overline{v'^2} - \rho\overline{w'^2}}{r}\right]$$

where the last term in square brackets is often neglected since $\overline{v'^2} \simeq \overline{w'^2}$. Neglecting the last bracketed term, radial integration gives

$$p + \rho\overline{v'^2} + \int_r^{r_{max}} \frac{\rho w^2}{r}\,dr = \left[p + \rho\overline{v'^2}\right]_{r = r_{max}}$$

For a free swirling turbulent jet emerging into stagnant surroundings, this shows that sub-pressures in the jet (as compared with jet edge pressures) may be obtained from

$$p = p_{max} - \rho\overline{v'^2} - \int_r^{r_{max}} \frac{\rho w^2}{r}\,dr \tag{2.17}$$

where p_{max} is the pressure at the edge $r = r_{max}$ of the jet at the axial station in question.

The usual swirling boundary layer equations in 2-D axisymmetric cylindrical polar coordinates may be taken in the common form[29, 36]

TABLE 2.7

Governing differential equations — swirling axisymmetric boundary layer form.

ϕ	Γ_ϕ	S_ϕ
1	0	0
u	μ	$-\dfrac{\partial p}{\partial x}$
v	0	$-\dfrac{\partial p}{\partial r} + \rho\dfrac{w^2}{r}$ [Neglect transient and convection terms]
w	μ	$-\dfrac{w}{r^2}\dfrac{\partial}{\partial r}(r\mu) - \rho\dfrac{vw}{r}$
h	μ/σ_h	0
m_{fu}	μ/σ_{fu}	R_{fu}
f	μ/σ_f	0
g	μ/σ_g	$G_g - C_{g2}\rho\epsilon g/k$
k	μ/σ_k	$G_k - \rho\epsilon$
ϵ	μ/σ_ϵ	$C_1\epsilon G_k/k - C_2\rho\epsilon^2/k$

where

$$G_g = C_{g1}\,\mu\left(\frac{\partial f}{\partial r}\right)^2$$

$$G_k = \mu\left[\left(\frac{\partial u}{\partial r}\right)^2 + \left(r\frac{\partial}{\partial r}\left(\frac{w}{r}\right)\right)^2\right]$$

and C_1, C_2, C_{g1} and C_{g2} are constants discussed earlier.

$$\frac{\partial}{\partial t}(\rho\phi) + \frac{1}{r}\left[\frac{\partial}{\partial x}(r\rho u\phi) + \frac{\partial}{\partial r}(r\rho v\phi)\right] = \frac{1}{r}\frac{\partial}{\partial r}\left(r\,\Gamma_\phi\frac{\partial\phi}{\partial r}\right) + S_\phi \tag{2.18}$$

with values of Γ_ϕ and S_ϕ as given in Table 2.7.

Although the swirl equation looks fine in the form given it has been found better to use a rearranged version[36] in computational solution schemes, for reasons of accuracy (see Section 3.4).

Nonswirling Free Jet—Axisymmetric Boundary-layer Flow

For completeness, the most degenerate case may be deduced in which axisymmetric boundary layer flow possesses no swirl. The θ-equation is no longer needed and the r-equation reduces even more. The equations take the form [after deleting appropriate terms from Eqn. (2.15)]

$$\frac{\partial \rho}{\partial t} + \frac{\partial}{\partial x}(\rho u) + \frac{1}{r}\frac{\partial}{\partial r}(r\rho v) = 0$$

$$\frac{\partial}{\partial t}(\rho u) + \frac{\partial}{\partial x}(\rho u^2) + \frac{1}{r}\frac{\partial}{\partial r}(r\rho v u) = -\frac{\partial p}{\partial x} + \frac{1}{r}\frac{\partial}{\partial r}(r\,\tau_{rx}) \tag{2.19}$$

$$0 = -\frac{\partial p}{\partial r}$$

$$\frac{\partial}{\partial t}(\rho\,\phi) + \frac{\partial}{\partial x}(\rho u\,\phi) + \frac{1}{r}\frac{\partial}{\partial r}(r\rho v\,\phi) = -\frac{1}{r}\frac{\partial}{\partial r}(r\,J_{\phi r}) + S_\phi$$

where the radial equation now indicates that pressure is *not* a function of cross-stream distance. Pressure is imposed from the free-stream on the boundary layer mixing region. In a round free jet with constant external free-stream pressure, it follows that

$$p = \text{constant}$$

throughout the region of interest: both $\frac{\partial p}{\partial r}$ and $\frac{\partial p}{\partial r}$ are zero.

Only one component of shear stress τ_{rx} now occurs, together with one component of ϕ-flux, $J_{\phi r}$:

$$\tau_{rx} = \mu\,\frac{\partial u}{\partial r}$$

$$J_{\phi r} = -\Gamma_\phi\,\frac{\partial \phi}{\partial r}$$

The governing equations are simply

$$\frac{\partial \rho}{\partial t} + \frac{\partial}{\partial x}(\rho u) + \frac{1}{r}\frac{\partial}{\partial r}(r\rho v) = 0$$

$$\frac{\partial}{\partial t}(\rho u) + \frac{\partial}{\partial x}(\rho u^2) + \frac{1}{r}\frac{\partial}{\partial r}(r\rho v u) = \frac{1}{r}\frac{\partial}{\partial r}\left(r\mu\,\frac{\partial u}{\partial r}\right)$$

$$p = \text{constant} \tag{2.21}$$

$$\frac{\partial}{\partial t}(\rho\,\phi) + \frac{\partial}{\partial x}(\rho u\,\phi) + \frac{1}{r}\frac{\partial}{\partial r}(r\rho v\,\phi) = \frac{1}{r}\frac{\partial}{\partial r}\left(r\Gamma_\phi\frac{\partial\phi}{\partial r}\right) + S_\phi$$

with source terms for the general ϕ-equation given in Table 2.7.

If the additional stress terms are retained in the radial equation (a possibility discussed in the last section), the cross-stream pressure is given by

$$O = -\frac{\partial p}{\partial r} - \frac{\partial}{\partial r}(\rho\overline{v'^2}) - \left[\frac{\rho\overline{v'^2} - \rho\overline{w'^2}}{r}\right]$$

Neglecting the last bracketed term for the reasons given earlier, radial integration gives

$$p + \rho\overline{v'^2} = [p + \rho\overline{v'^2}\,]_{r = r_{max}}$$

which is constant across the mixing region and may be evaluated at the outer edge by the free-stream boundary. For a free turbulent jet emerging into stagnant surroundings, this equation takes the form:

$$p = p_{max} - \rho\overline{v'^2}$$

where p_{max} is the pressure at the edge $r = r_{max}$ of the jet at the axial station in question. This deduced equation for $p = p(r)$ at some axial station of a free round-jet flow is consistent with standard texts,[4] and may be compared with the extended version given in Eqn. (2.17) which is valid for weakly-swirling free round-jet flows.

2.3 INTEGRAL PROPERTIES AND THE SWIRL STRENGTH

Integral Properties

Consider the time-steady axisymmetric *free* swirling flows governed by the equations of Section 2.2. First look at the continuity, axial momentum and swirl momentum equations, that is, Eqn. (2.13). Gross transport integrals across a section of the jet lead to[27]

$$\frac{d}{dx}\int_0^\infty \rho u r\,dr = -r\rho v|_{r\to\infty}$$

$$\frac{d}{dx}\int_0^\infty (\rho u^2 - \tau_{xx} + (p - p_\infty))\;r\,dr = -r\rho v u\,|_{r\to\infty}$$

$$\frac{d}{dx}\int_0^\infty (\rho u w - \tau_{x\theta})\,r^2\,dr = -r^2\rho v w/r\to\infty$$

where certain terms vanish at lower (r=0) and upper ($r \to \infty$) limits of integration. The following free jet boundary conditions apply:

$$r = 0 : \text{ u finite, } \frac{\partial u}{\partial r} = v = w = 0$$

$$p \text{ finite, } \frac{\partial p}{\partial r} = 0 \text{ and } \tau \text{ bounded}$$

$$r \to \infty : \quad u, v, w, p, \; r^2 \, \tau_{r\theta} \text{ and } \tau_{rx} \to 0$$

The first equation shows that the rate of increase of mass flux with axial distance is equal to the rate of mass entrainment (or radial inflow from large distances). The mass flow rate

$$\dot{m} = \int_0^\infty \rho u r dr \tag{2.23}$$

increases with x as the flow entrains mass.

Inspection of the term on the right-hand side of the second equation reveals its value to be zero, since rv is finite and u is zero at infinity. Then integration with respect to x shows that

$$G_x = \int_0^\infty (\rho u^2 + \rho \overline{u'^2} + (p - p_\infty)) \, r dr \tag{2.24}$$

is independent of distance x; it is the constant *axial flux of axial momentum*, comprised of momentum and pressure terms. Notice that the effective τ_{xx} has been replaced by its laminar and turbulent parts, and the negligibly small laminar contribution has been deleted.

The term on the right of the third equation is proportional to the product of the finite entrainment flux $-2\pi r \rho v|_{r \to \infty}$ per unit length of jet and the circulation $2\pi r w|_{r \to \infty}$ measured around the jet. In free surroundings this is zero, and for a swirling jet emerging into otherwise-undisturbed surroundings, a further integration reveals that

$$G_\theta = \int_0^\infty (\rho u w + \rho \overline{u'w'}) \, r^2 \, dr \tag{2.25}$$

is independent of x, it is the constant *axial flux of swirl momentum*.

Gross transport integrals may also be found for other useful quantities. For example

$$\dot{\phi} = \int_0^\infty \rho u \phi \, r dr \tag{2.26}$$

represents the *axial flux of* ϕ at a particular axial station x. Source-free ϕ have constant axial fluxes, like for example $\phi = h$ or f:

$$h = \int_0^\infty \rho uh \, rdr = \text{constant}$$

$$f = \int_0^\infty \rho uf \, rdr = \text{constant}$$

Negative-source ϕ have reducing axial fluxes as x increases, similar to, for example, $\phi = m_{fu}$:

$$\dot{m}_{fu} = \int_0^\infty \rho u \, m_{fu} \, rdr \tag{2.27}$$

This is the *unburned fuel flow rate* passing a particular axial station, which decreases with axial distance x as chemical reaction proceeds, R_{fu} being the negative source in the fuel equation.

The Swirl Number

Since G_x and G_θ are invariants in a free swirling jet with zero circulation, they can be used to characterize the rotational aspects of the jet by defining a strength, which depends also on the thickness of the mixing layer over which axial fluxes of axial and swirl momenta operate. A local nondimensional parameter called the *local swirl number* may be taken as[36]

$$S_x = \frac{G_\theta}{G_x \cdot r_{edge}} \tag{2.28}$$

where r_{edge} is the radial distance from the axis to the edge (near the free-stream boundary), and at any axial position it characterizes the effect of rotation on the flow. It has been used extensively in modifying simple turbulence models in order to account for rotational effects[36, 39]. So also has the swirl flow Richardson number Ri:

$$Ri = \frac{2 \, w \, \partial (rw)/\partial r}{r^2 \, [(\partial u/\partial r)^2 + (r \, \partial (w/r)/\partial r)^2]} \tag{2.29}$$

which may be evaluated at all point positions in the flow. As the jet width r_{edge} increases with axial distance, the local swirl number decreases from its initial nozzle value of

$$S = \frac{G_\theta}{G_x \cdot d/2}$$

where d is the diameter of the nozzle. This jet-constant S is called the *swirl number* of the flow.[6] It does not completely characterize a swirl jet flow, and the precise effect of swirl on the subsequent flowfield is found to depend on many factors as well as the swirl number: for example, nozzle geometry (the presence of a central hub encourages a larger recirculation zone, as does the addition of a divergent nozzle), size of enclosure if any (central recirculation zones are much more pronounced in enclosures than those of comparable freejets), and the particular exit velocity profiles (recirculation zones tend to the larger when the flow is produced via swirl vanes as opposed to an axial-and-tangential entry swirl generator). These effects are discussed later.[9-12]

Sometimes it is inconvenient to deduce the swirl number S of a jet flow from its definition, and more practically useful ideas are useful. The turbulent fluctuating contributions and the pressure terms are sometimes omitted. If the flow is produced from an axial-plus-tangential entry swirl generator the exit flow through the nozzle is likely to be plug flow with solid body rotation at low and medium swirl strengths. [At very high swirl strengths this is not so and much of the axial flow leaves near to the outer edge of the flow domain.] When plug flow solid body rotation is the case, the ratio of the maximum axial and swirl velocities measured at the exit plane suffices to determine the degree of swirl S via[6]

$$\mathrm{S} = \frac{\mathrm{G}/2}{1 - (\mathrm{G}/2)^2}$$

or, because of deviations from the assumptions in practical cases,

$$S = \frac{G/2}{1 - G/2} \tag{2.30}$$

where $G = w_{mo}/u_{mo}$. When swirl is produced via a vane swirler with flat vanes at angle ϕ to the main-stream direction, S and ϕ are related approximately by[6]

$$S = \frac{2}{3}\left[\frac{1 - (d_h/d)^3}{1 - (d_h/d)^2}\right] \tan\phi \tag{2.31}$$

where d_h is the diameter of the central hub of the vane pack. When $d_h << \mathrm{d}$ this reduces to[10]

$$S \approx \frac{2}{3} \tan\phi \tag{2.32}$$

so that vane angles of 15, 30, 45, 60, 70 and 80 degrees, for example, correspond to S values of 0.2, 0.4, 0.7, 1.2, 2.0 and 4.0. Here 100 per cent efficiency is assumed for the swirl vanes, even though in reality this deteriorates as the vane angle increases.

Flow Types

What about the type of flow regime that results because of a given degree of swirl applied to a jet flow? Clearly, with nonswirling ($S = 0$) jet flows, analyses have legitimately used boundary layer assumptions and neglected pressure variations. Many texts on fluid dynamics deal with these cases[4]. As S increases, the cases of weak, moderate and strong swirling jets present themselves. For weak swirl (approximately $0 \leqslant S \leqslant 0.2$) the boundary layer equations can still be assumed to hold, the pressure variations being small and even neglected, and the coupling in the equations being weak. For moderate swirl (approximately $0.2 \leqslant S \leqslant 0.5$) these equations, including nonzero pressure variations, are somewhat questionable but are still used, for present-day knowledge of turbulence necessitates similar approximation elsewhere in any analysis. A strongly swirling jet ($S \geqslant 0.5$) possesses strong radial and axial pressure gradients in the region near the orifice. Evidently the reduced boundary layer equations will not be valid and simplifying assumptions will not be applicable: the full elliptic equations must be used[10].

2.4 TURBULENCE MODELS AND THE EFFECT OF SWIRL

Practical flows are almost invariably turbulent and, even in the absence of chemical reaction, there are considerable difficulties in their simulation[28]. One such difficulty is scale disparity: important things such as eddy decay take place on a much smaller scale than typical physical dimensions. Current computer technology and computer codes do not allow solution for the true and extremely rapid time-dependent details, because of storage and time requirements, and the time-average approach is favored. That is, when the gross effects of turbulence on a time-mean flow are of interest and the detailed structure of the turbulence is of little concern, solution is usually obtained via time-averaging the Navier-Stokes equations to yield equations (called Reynolds equations) of the same form for the mean variables, provided the stress tensor is augmented by the addition of a symmetric turbulent (Reynolds) stress tensor $\underline{\underline{\tau}}_{turb} = -\rho\overline{v'v'}$. In fully turbulent flow this is considerably greater than the molecular viscous stress tensor which, therefore, is usually omitted except in near wall regions. A difficulty now is that the equations do not form a closed set, the six different unknown components of $\underline{\underline{\tau}}$ being correlations of velocity fluctuation components, as presented in cylindrical polar coordinates in Section 2.2. Similarly, in the ϕ-equation, the turbulent ϕ-diffusive flux vector $J_\phi = +\rho\overline{v'\phi'}$ arises, with three unknown components. The basic turbulence hypothesis is that time-mean values obey the same equations as a general fluid, except that: time-averaged fluid properties (v and ϕ) appear in place of instantaneous ones, transport properties (μ_{lam} and $\Gamma_{\phi lam}$) are augmented to account for the effects of turbulent or eddy transport (and become effective values $\mu = \mu_{lam} + \mu_{turb}$ and $\Gamma_\phi = \Gamma_{\phi\,lam} + \Gamma_{\phi\,turb}$); and finally source terms may require modification (since, in general, the time-average of an expression with time-varying quantities will not be equal to the same expression evaluated with time-average quantities).

Increasingly complex flowfields are governed by increasingly complicated equations for the time-mean properties, which contain increasingly more components of the turbulent (Reynolds) stress tensor; for example, the increasing number of components required are:

1. Nonswirling boundary layer flow NBLF – rx-component only.
2. Swirling boundary layer flow SBLF – rx and rθ components.
3. Nonswirling axisymmetric recirculating flow NARF – rx, xx, rr and $\theta\theta$ components.
4. Swirling axisymmetric recirculating flow SARF – rx, rθ, xθ, xx, rr and $\theta\theta$ components.

with more complex flows requiring, again, all six components. Components of turbulent viscosity need not be equal and its nonisotropy is accounted for via specification of viscosity numbers (by analogy with Prandtl-Schmidt numbers) – these are merely ratios of viscosity components with the primary component of turbulent viscosity $\mu = \mu_{rx}$. For example, the $r\theta$ viscosity number is $\sigma_{r\theta}=\mu/\mu_{r\theta}$. There is some evidence that these values are *not* unity[32,39], but general recommendations are not available[34-51]. The remaining problem is how the main component of turbulent viscosity is to be specified by a turbulence model. Or, rather, the more complete question of how are all the components of turbulent (Reynolds) stress to be specified, either directly (advanced differential or algebraic stress modeling) or indirectly (via the turbulent viscosity concept).

A turbulence model is a set of differential and/or algebraic equations for things like $\overline{u'^2}$, $\overline{u'v'}$, $\overline{u'\phi'}$, k, ϵ, etc. which connect statistical properties of turbulence (correlations) with each other and with terms appearing in the time-averaged equations of conservation of mass, momentum, energy and chemical species. These auxiliary equations allow closure of the conservation equations, and, hence, permit the calculation of the time-mean behavior of the system. Developments have proceeded via theoretical arguments, intuition and empiricism: experimental evidence is demanded. By analogy with a Newtonian fluid a constitutive equation[39]

$$-\rho\overline{v'v'} = \tau_{turb} = 2\mu_{turb}\,\underline{\underline{\Delta}} - \frac{2}{3}\mu_{turb}\,(\text{div}\,v)\,\underline{\underline{I}} - \frac{2}{3}\rho k\underline{\underline{I}} \qquad (2.33)$$

is sometimes assumed with a variable turbulent viscosity μ_{turb}. Often, only the first term on the right of this expression is retained. The second and third terms contribute to the normal stresses (which in any case are not directly required in the governing equations of a boundary layer flow) and the second term is zero in an incompressible fluid. In the past, isotropic turbulence has generally been assumed and the same μ_{turb} has been used for each of the components of this equation. Various hypotheses (turbulence models) have been suggested and used in the past for calculating either τ_{turb} or μ_{turb} prior to solving the Reynolds equations; the more recent hypothesis being evolved in attempts toward universality[28]. In the scalar ϕ-equation the analogy extends to

$$+\rho\overline{v'\phi'} = J_{\phi turb} = -\frac{\mu_{turb}}{\sigma_{\phi\,turb}}\,\text{grad}\,\phi \qquad (2.34)$$

where $\sigma_{\phi turb}$ is the turbulent Schmidt number for the particular ϕ in question.

Since laminar stress tensor and laminar ϕ-flux diffusion vector are similarly connected with gradients of time-mean values (using laminar viscosity μ_{lam} and laminar exchange coefficient $\Gamma_{\phi lam} = \mu_{lam}/\sigma_{\phi lam}$) via the equations

$$\underline{\underline{\tau}}_{lam} = 2\mu_{lam}\,\underline{\underline{\Delta}} - \frac{2}{3}\mu_{lam}\,(\text{div}\,v)\,\underline{\underline{I}}$$

$$J_{\phi\,lam} = -\frac{\mu_{lam}}{\sigma_{\phi lam}}\,\text{grad}\,\phi$$

it follows that effective stress tensor $\underline{\underline{\tau}}$ and effective ϕ-flux diffusion vector J_ϕ are connected with gradients of time-mean values (using effective viscosity μ and effective exchange coefficient $\Gamma_\phi = \mu/\sigma_\phi$) via the equations

$$\underline{\underline{\tau}} = 2\,\mu\,\underline{\underline{\Delta}} - \frac{2}{3}\,\mu\,(\text{div}\,v)\,\mathrm{I} - \frac{2}{3}\,\rho\,\mathrm{k}\,\underline{\underline{\mathrm{I}}}$$

$$J_\phi = -\frac{\mu}{\sigma_\phi}\,\text{grad}\,\phi \qquad (2.35)$$

All these ideas were introduced earlier, where it was convenient to exhibit different levels of complexity of these general equations, and incorporate them into the governing PDEs of conservation (*see* Section 2.1).

Moreover in the ϕ-equation

$$\Gamma_\phi = \Gamma_{\phi\,\text{lam}} + \Gamma_{\phi\,\text{turb}} = \frac{\mu_{\text{lam}}}{\sigma_{\phi\text{lam}}} + \frac{\mu_{\text{turb}}}{\sigma_{\phi\,\text{turb}}}$$

also

$$\Gamma_\phi = \frac{\mu}{\sigma_\phi} = \frac{\mu_{\text{lam}} + \mu_{\text{turb}}}{\sigma_\phi}$$

and it follows that the effective Prandtl/Schmidt number σ_ϕ is linked to laminar and turbulent Prandtl/Schmidt numbers via

$$\sigma_\phi = \frac{1}{\mu_{\text{lam}} + \mu_{\text{turb}}} \cdot \left[\frac{\mu_{\text{lam}}}{\sigma_{\phi\,\text{lam}}} + \frac{\mu_{\text{turb}}}{\sigma_{\phi\,\text{turb}}}\right]^{-1}$$

In general when a model, specifying τ_{turb} directly or indirectly via μ_{turb}, is incorporated into the governing equations, flowfield predictions may be made. Several solution procedures are now available[54] for parabolic boundary layer flows and more general elliptic recirculation flows, each of these being equipped or in principle extendable to predict the properties of weakly or strongly swirling flows, respectively. Essential for these procedures is a realistic turbulence model, for τ or μ, to close the equation set. For a nonswirling free jet with boundary layer assumptions, only *one* component τ_{rx} of $\underline{\underline{\tau}}$ is significant and a simple turbulence hypothesis of the Prandtl mixing length type is sufficient for good predictions to be made. Nevertheless, for a weakly swirling jet, again with boundary layer assumptions, *two* components τ_{rx} and $\tau_{r\theta}$ are significant. The more general case, for example a strongly swirling jet with recirculation where boundary layer assumptions cannot be invoked, requires all nine components (*six* different – not nine – because of symmetry) of $\underline{\underline{\tau}}$ to be specified. Moreover, recent experimental, inverse and prediction works have disputed isotropy assumptions for turbulent swirling flows[39].

The extent to which simple turbulence models may be modified to cater for these flows is of prime concern, though requirements of accuracy and universality have recently encouraged the development of more complex models.

This section describes recent advances in the area of turbulence modeling with emphasis on swirl flows.

The Turbulence Model Choice

Closure of the time-mean equation system is effected by means of a turbulence model, and models are generally classified according to the shear-stress hypothesis (whether or not turbulent viscosities are introduced) and the number of extra differential equations to be solved. Reviews of previous and current work are available with assessments[28].

Until recently, exchange coefficients, if introduced, have generally been assumed isotropic, even in flows with swirl, but recent experimental, inverse and prediction works have disputed this for swirling flows[39]. Briefly, the choice available is:

$$\text{Prandtl mixing length } \mu_{rx\,turb} = \rho l^2 \, (2\underline{\underline{\Delta}}:\underline{\underline{\Delta}})^{1/2}$$

$$\text{Energy-length } \mu_{rxturb} = C_\mu \rho k^2/\epsilon \text{ or } \mu_{rxturb} = C_\mu \rho k^{1/2} \ell \text{ etc.} \qquad (2.36)$$

$$\text{Differential stress modeling } D\,\tau_{rxturb}/Dt = P_{rx} + D_{rx} + R_{rx} + \epsilon_{rx}$$

$$\text{Algebraic stress modeling } \tau_{rxturb} = f\,(\text{other } \tau\text{'s}, k, \epsilon, \underline{\underline{\Delta}})$$

Here $\underline{\underline{\Delta}}$ is the time-mean flow rate of strain tensor, k and ϵ are turbulent kinetic energy and dissipation rate, and P, D, R and ϵ stand for production, diffusion, redistribution and dissipation in the turbulent stress equation. The first two choices are examples of theories of the exchange coefficient type; the second two are of direct stress specification type. The choice will be clarified in subsequent discussion.

Constitutive Equations

In terms of effective stresses the basic Reynolds equations of mass and momentum may be solved for pressure and velocity (via these primitive variables or the associated stream function and vorticity) in the flowfield following their closure by means of a turbulence model. Often, use is made of Eqn. (2.33) so that closure is effected indirectly via components of effective viscosity. For general swirl flows in cyclindrical polar coordinates the component forms of the constitutive assumptions are given in Eqn. (2.11). If isotropy is not assumed, different values of the components of μ may be appropriate to different equations of this set. This may be obtained by the use of variable $r\theta$- (and other-) viscosity numbers defined by the $r\theta$-component [which is stressed here because it turns out to be the most important of the components, and indeed is the only other component of μ in weakly swirling flows]

$$\sigma_{r\theta} = \mu/\mu_{r\theta}$$

and these relate other viscosity components to the primary component of effective viscosity $\mu \equiv \mu_{rx}$. If isotropy is assumed, all the components of μ are considered to be equal, corresponding to taking all viscosity numbers to be unity.

In general, all six different components of $\underline{\underline{\tau}}$ and three different components of J_ϕ need to be specified. All these equations are required in the simulation of general strongly swirling flows, perhaps with recirculation, where the governing conservation equations are elliptic in character and solution is via a lengthy relaxation procedure.

Weakly swirling flows, with a single predominant direction and no recirculation regions, may be simulated by the simplified boundary layer form of the governing equations without much loss in accuracy. This results in truncation of the elliptic equations to parabolic form; fewer terms, and unknown turbulent stresses are left in the equations; and a simpler forward-marching solution procedure can be applied. With these approximations only two turbulent stress components are of interest,—τ_{rx} and $\tau_{r\theta}$—and the non-isotropic boundary layer equivalents of the constitutive assumptions become

$$\tau_{rx} = \tau_{xr} = \mu_{rx} \frac{\partial u}{\partial r}$$

$$\tau_{r\theta} = \tau_{\theta r} = \mu_{r\theta}\, r \frac{\partial}{\partial r}\left(\frac{w}{r}\right) \tag{2.37}$$

Only the first of these remains in the simulation of nonswirling free jet flow and it is immediately recognized as the most important of the constitutive equations upon which much research has been undertaken in the past. The discussion continues with emphasis on $\mu \equiv \mu_{rx}$, the effect of swirl on it and specification of the $r\theta$-viscosity number.

Prandtl Mixing Length Model [PML]

For nonswirling flow the familiar Prandtl model is the simplified form of the first of Eqn. (2.37)

$$\mu = \rho\, l^2 \left|\frac{\partial u}{\partial r}\right|$$

$$l = \lambda \circ r_{edge} \tag{2.38}$$

$$\lambda = \text{constant}$$

Various extensions of Prandtl's mixing length theory to flows with swirl have been proposed[36, 38, 39], the task being to link the $r\theta$-shear with the rx-viscosity of the axial equation and to allow for the nonisotropy of the viscosity. Here the former task is accomplished by taking the *rx*-viscosity proportional to the second invariant of the mean flow rate of deformation tensor and the latter by use of a variable $r\theta$-viscosity number. Thus,

$$\mu = \rho\, l^2 \left\{(\partial u/\partial r)^2 + (r\partial\, (w/r)\, /\, \partial r)^2\right\}^{1/2}$$

$$\mu_{r\theta} = \mu/\sigma_{r\theta} \tag{2.39}$$

$$l = \lambda \cdot r_{edge}$$

$$\lambda = 0.08\,(1 + \lambda_s S_x)$$

where $\sigma_{r\theta}$ and λ_s are constant or functions of S_x. Computer predictions and optimization against experimental data reveal the recommendations[36]

$$\lambda_s = 0.6$$

$$\sigma_{r\theta} = 1 + 5\ S\ \text{(jet constant)}$$

or

$$1 + 5\,S_x^{1/3}\ \text{(station constant)}$$

The factor $(1 + \lambda_S S_X)$ accounts for the change in the length scale due to swirl and is analogous to the Monin-Oboukhov formula

$$l = l_o\,(1 - \beta \text{Ri})$$

which has been suggested[55] as a simple approximate means of correlating the effect of streamline curvature and centripetal accelerations on the mixing length. β is an adjustable parameter and Ri the swirl flow Richardson number which can be regarded as

$$\text{Ri} = \frac{(2w/r^2)\ \partial/\partial r(rw)}{(\partial u/\partial r)^2 + [r\,(\partial/\partial r)\,(w/r)]^2} \qquad (2.40)$$

Energy-Length Models [k – ε]

More recent work[28] on calculating turbulent flows has postulated that the turbulence may be adequately described by two quantities: the kinetic energy k and the length scale ℓ. The second of Eqn. (2.37) is used and two extra differential equations are required, one for k itself and the other for any variable

$$Z = k^m \ell^n$$

For flows *without swirl* it is known that these models exhibit greater universality than the mixing length model; transport effects on turbulent viscosity can be accounted for and the length scale, being the outcome of a differential equation, does not have to be given an *ad hoc* distribution. The differential equations for k and Z are developed by a combination of physical reasoning and intuitive guess work. Following previous work in boundary layer *weakly swirling flows*, the Z equation is taken for $Z = k\ell$. Fully modeled equations for k and Z in weakly swirling boundary layer flows are taken in the form[36]

$$\rho u \frac{\partial k}{\partial x} + \rho v \frac{\partial k}{\partial r} = \frac{1}{r}\frac{\partial}{\partial r}\left(r \frac{\mu}{\sigma_k}\frac{\partial k}{\partial r}\right) + \mu G_k - C_D \rho \epsilon \qquad (2.41)$$

$$\rho u \frac{\partial Z}{\partial x} + \rho v \frac{\partial Z}{\partial r} = \frac{1}{r}\frac{\partial}{\partial r}\left(r \frac{\mu}{\sigma_Z}\frac{\partial Z}{\partial r}\right) + C_B \ell \mu G_k$$

$$- C_s \rho k^{1.5} + C_R \rho \, Ri \, k^{1.5}$$

where $\mu \equiv \mu_{rx}$

$\sigma_{r\theta} = \mu/\mu_{r\theta}$

$$G_k = \left(\frac{\partial u}{\partial r}\right)^2 + \frac{1}{\sigma_{r\theta}}\left(r \frac{\partial}{\partial r}\left(\frac{w}{r}\right)\right)^2$$

Ri = Richardson number as previously defined

$C_D = 0.055$,. $C_B = 0.98$ and $C_S = 0.0397$

$\sigma_k = 1.0$ and $\sigma_Z = 1.0$

$Z = k\ell$ and $C_\mu = 1.0$ (in this model).

These equations resemble those of the current recommendations of Table 2.7. The body force, the last term in the Z-equation, characterizes the effect of rotation on the turbulence structure, extra Z being generated, and hence, higher turbulent viscosity and more rapid mixing properties. The parameter C_R and nonisotropy via $\sigma_{r\theta}$ are chosen via computer optimization of predictions against time-mean experimental data, recommended values being[36]

$$C_R = 0.06$$

$$\sigma_{r\theta} - 1 + 3\,S \text{ (jet constant)}$$

or

$$1 + 2\,S_x^{1/3} \text{ (station constant)}$$

Observe that neglect of convection and diffusion in the k-equation and elimination of k with the second of Eqn. (2.36) yields Eqn. (2.39) except for a factor $1/\sigma_{r\theta}$ multiplying the second term in the brackets and $1 = \ell/C_D^{1/4}$. This gives weight to the extended form of Prandtl's local equilibrium model given in Eqn. (2.39). In this case

$$k = 1\left[\left(\frac{\partial u}{\partial r}\right)^2 + \left(r \frac{\partial}{\partial r}\left(\frac{w}{r}\right)\right)^2\right] / C_D^{1/2}$$

$$\ell = 1\, C_D^{1/4}$$

Recently, engineering emphasis for *strongly swirling flow* with recirculation has been placed on a Z-equation with $m = 1.5$ and $n = -1$, and the combined quantity is called ϵ:

$$\epsilon = k^{1.5}/\ell \tag{2.42}$$

and is governed by a PDE as described earlier, the appropriate boundary layer form being documented in Table 2.7. Indications are that ϵ is preferable as the subject of the second equation to accompany the k-equation in a two-equation turbulence model, though for boundary layer flows the other Z-possibilities are suitable. Notice that ϵ appears directly in the k-equation in the dissipation term. The $k - \epsilon$ turbulence model is moderate in complexity and is considered to be superior to other models having a similar degree of complexity. This model has been extensively used by many investigators[11, 22-24, 50-52] and has proved to be adequate in a wide range of flow conditions. Further details concerning the development of the k and ϵ equation may be found[28]. Values of the constants given in Table 2.5 are typical, but 'computer optimization' for a large number of experiments often leads to slightly different values being quoted.

Differential Stress Modeling

The preceding models are all of the turbulent viscosity type, and interest centers on the specification of μ_{rx}. More advanced alternatives never introduce μ_{rx}, and specification of the stresses is direct from solution of the stress transport equations. General axisymmetric swirl flows contain all six different components of the turbulent (Reynolds) stress tensor. These PDEs contain other second and third order turbulence correlations. Rather than solve additional PDEs for higher-order correlations, modeling of the correlations is preferred (second-order closure), involving k and ℓ terms (or, equivalently k and ϵ). For *general axisymmetric swirl flows* the appropriate modeled PDEs for the *six* stresses $\overline{u'^2}$, $\overline{v'^2}$, $\overline{w'^2}$, $\overline{u'v'}$, $\overline{u'w'}$ and $\overline{v'w'}$ are rather complicated. The details may be found elsewhere[47].

All the equations are of the common form:

$$
\begin{aligned}
\text{Convection} \quad = \quad & \text{Diffusion} \\
& + \text{Normal stress Production} + \text{Shear Stress Production} \\
& + \text{Re-distribution} + \text{Dissipation}
\end{aligned} \tag{2.43}
$$

A model suitable for 2-D cartesian boundary layer flow (no swirl) requires only *one* stress $\overline{u'v'}$ to be successfully modeled, in terms of other quantities, and such a model for k-ϵ-$\overline{u'v'}$ exists[48]. The stress equation is taken as

$$
\rho u \frac{\partial}{\partial x} (\overline{u'v'}) + \rho v \frac{\partial}{\partial y} (\overline{u'v'})
$$

$$
= \frac{\partial}{\partial y} \left(\frac{\mu}{\sigma_t} \frac{\partial}{\partial y} (\overline{u'v'}) \right) - C\rho \left[k \frac{\partial u}{\partial y} + \frac{k^{1/2}}{\ell} \overline{u'v'} \right]
$$

and the constants given the values

$$\sigma_t = 0.9$$

$$C = 2.8$$

In more general cases, the problem of optimizing values of constants appearing is quite formidable; these models are of little immediate use in practical engineering calculations.

Algebraic Stress Modeling

On the assumption of local equilibrium, convection and diffusion of shear stress are neglected and the shear stress differential equations reduce to algebraic equations. The relevant *two* shear stresses in weakly swirling boundary layers become[49]:

$$\overline{u'v'} = -C\frac{k}{\epsilon}\left(\overline{v'^2}\frac{\partial u}{\partial r}\right)$$

$$\overline{v'w'} = -C\frac{k}{\epsilon}\left[\overline{v'^2}\, r\frac{\partial}{\partial r}\left(\frac{w}{r}\right) - D\frac{w}{r}\left(\overline{w'^2} - \overline{v'^2}\right)\right]$$

where C and D are constants. After introducing the notion of turbulent viscosity (for convenience, only)

$$-\rho\overline{u'v'} = \mu_{rx}\frac{\partial u}{\partial r} \equiv \mu\frac{\partial u}{\partial r}$$

$$-\rho\overline{v'w'} = \mu_{r\theta}\, r\frac{\partial}{\partial r}\left(\frac{w}{r}\right)$$

one obtains

$$\mu \equiv \mu_{rx} = C\frac{k}{\epsilon}\overline{v'^2}$$

$$\mu_{r\theta} = C\frac{k}{\epsilon}\overline{v'^2}\,(1 - \beta\,\mathrm{Ri})$$

where

$$\beta = D\left(\frac{\overline{w'^2}}{\overline{v'^2}} - 1\right) \quad \text{is a parameter}$$

and

$$\mathrm{Ri} = \frac{w/r}{r\,\partial(w/r)/\partial r} \quad \text{is a Richardson number.}$$

If the assumption:

$$\overline{v'^2} \propto k$$

is made,

$$\mu \equiv \mu_{rx} \propto \rho k^2/\epsilon$$

so that the theory provides a nonisotropic extension of the usual energy-length model. The function $(1 - \beta Ri)$, a natural outcome of the analysis, is the Monin-Oboukhov proposal as cited earlier. Experimental data for the ratio $\overline{w'^2}/\overline{v'^2}$ vary with swirl number, axial and radial position. Pratte and Keffer[56] reports values of order unity for $S = 0.3$, whereas Allan[57] reports values between 2 and 10 for $S = 0.6$.

This analysis of the modeled equations for the shear stresses in a swirling boundary layer reveals directly the nonisotropic nature of turbulent viscosity. The resulting algebraic equations for $\overline{u'v'}$ and $\overline{v'w'}$ combined with differential equations for k, $k\ell$ (or alternatively ϵ), $\overline{v'^2}$, and $\overline{w'^2}$ form a four-equation turbulence model which has yet to be developed.

Present Advice

Currently, two-equation energy-length models are to be recommended for application in practical engineering situations; in particular, the k-ϵ model where $\epsilon = k^{1.5}/\ell$ and ℓ is the macrolength scale of turbulence. Models of this type have been successfully modified and applied to swirling flows, even with nonisotropic assumptions[39]. Recent relevant work is discussed elsewhere[34-51]. Numerical and analytical inverse solution of the turbulent swirl flow boundary layer equations (which allow turbulence model development directly from time-mean experimental data) have been useful for this purpose. Details of the general turbulence model development in both nonreacting and reacting flows are available via recent conferences[29-31].

The advantage of a turbulent kinetic energy TKE model over a simple algebraic 'local' model is that solution of a PDE for k allows upstream 'historical' influence to assert itself on the subsequent flowfield. Application of several such models to flowfields of interest in sudden expansion burners have been reviewed elsewhere[44]. For high speed turbulent reacting flows, two models show significant promise: the Harsha one-equation model[45] and the Rodi two-equation k-ϵ model[28]. Applications to reacting jet flows show that both appear to be suitable[46]. More advanced turbulence models, such as those based upon the Reynolds-stress modeling approach, are not yet fully developed to warrant their use in recirculating flowfield problems as encountered in gas-turbine combustors. In addition, such an approach will appreciably increase the computation effort.

Recent recognition of coherent structures in turbulent flows[58] is now being complemented by research on the development of numerical simulations. One approach[59] has the basic idea that large eddies cannot and should not be modeled, but the small eddies might be modeled successfully, perhaps by methods akin to previous turbulence modeling based on the usual Reynolds time-average equations. An averaging procedure that separates the large and small-scale structures is introduced, the former being computed explicitly, the latter modeled. The approach requires considerably more computation than conventional methods, but arguments for believing this method to be superior and more universal are given, together with details of the basis of the method and the presentation of typical results. Although enormous promise is revealed, it is clear that much further development is required before these concepts are refined enough for them to be amenable for application in practical engineering problems.

Wall Functions

General ideas about effective exchange coefficients Γ_ϕ for typical variables ϕ are not valid in the proximity of a boundary. The local Reynolds number becomes extremely small, and turbulent fluctuations are damped considerably; the laminar viscosity starts to play a significant role in local diffusion processes. Furthermore, rates of change of variables are large in these locations. One remedy is to use a low Reynolds number turbulence model with an extremely fine grid near walls, but an alternative more efficient technique is most popular[28]. It is based on an extended Couette flow analysis and allows algebraic relations to be derived for the so-called 'logarithmic' region. These are then used directly in a prediction code with relatively coarse grid.

Wall functions are derived by hypothesizing:

1. The presence of a near-wall layer across which the shear stress is uniform.
2. The existence of local equilibrium between production and dissipation of kinetic energy of turbulence k.
3. A linear variation with distance of the length scale of turbulence ℓ.

The nondimensional profiles of time-mean and turbulence quantities become nearly universal functions of the normal distance Reynolds number $(y\sqrt{\tau\rho}\ /u)$. There is now no need to perform detailed calculations in the near-wall regions and values at a near-wall point P are related to values on the wall W by:

$$\frac{V_p\ \rho_w\ (C_\mu{}^{1/4} kp^{1/2})}{\tau_w} = \frac{1}{x}\ \frac{\ell n\ (E\ C_\mu{}^{1/4}\ k_p{}^{1/2}\ y_p)}{\nu}$$

$$k_p = \frac{\tau_w}{\rho_w C_\mu{}^{1/2}}$$

$$E_p \quad \frac{y_p}{k_p{}^{3/2}} = \frac{C_\mu{}^{3/4}}{\chi}$$

Where:

V_p = tangential velocity parallel to the wall at P

τ = shear stress

ν = kinematic viscosity

χ = vonKarman's constant (=0.4)

E = constant depending on surface roughness (=9.0 for a smooth wall)

The last two values, χ and E, are constants derived from the 'logarithmic law of the wall'. Similar expressions may also be derived for other variables, for example, in the case of the enthalpy equation:

$$\frac{(T_w - T_p)\ (c\,\rho_w\, C_\mu^{1/4}\, k_p^{1/2})}{q_w} = \frac{\sigma_{h,\,turb}}{\chi}\ \frac{\ell n\,(E\, C_\mu^{1/4}\, k_p^{1/2}\, y_p)}{\nu} + 9.24\,\sigma_h\left(\frac{\sigma_h}{\sigma_{h,\,turb}} - 1\right)\left(\frac{\sigma_{h,\,turb}}{\sigma_h}\right)^{1/4}$$

where:

cp = mean mixture specific heat at constant pressure

q_w = heat flux to the wall

These ideas are generally used in practical turbulent flow prediction codes[11, 22-24, 50-52].

2.5 COMBUSTION SIMULATION

The Simple Chemically-reacting System SCRS

The concern now is with multicomponent chemically-reacting flow simulation of physically-controlled diffusion flames and kinetically-controlled (or rather, kinetically-influenced) premixed flames. A motivation for seeking a simplified approach is the complexity of real combustion processes: most fuels proceed to their final oxidized state by way of many intermediates; for full computation, each concentration of intermediate species must be calculated at all points; and the associated computer time and storage are very large (for 3-D problems they may be prohibitive). In reality, it is, often, only the major features that are of interest (outlet temperature, heat flux to walls, etc.) and knowledge of full details is relatively unimportant. The SCRS is defined by[5]:

1. The multiple paths, reaction products and combining ratios are replaced by the simple exothermic chemical reaction:

   $$1 \text{ kg fuel} + s \text{ kg oxygen} \rightarrow (1+s) \text{ kg product} + H_{fu}$$

   where s (= *Stoichiometric ratio*) is a constant, and H_{fu} (= *Heat of Combustion* of the fuel) is the energy released in Joules on burning 1 kg of fuel.
2. The exchange coefficients (Γ_{fu}, Γ_{ox}, Γ_{pr}) are equal to each other, and to Γ_h, at each point.
3. The specific heats c_p of all species are equal to each other, and independent of T.

Nevertheless, with little loss of convenience, c_p can be allowed to depend on T alone.

These ideas were all introduced in Section 2.1 where, in addition to the fluid dynamic simulation, it was illustrated that knowledge of local values of

m_{fu} mass fraction of fuel

m_{ox} mass fraction of oxidant

m_{pr} mass fraction of product

T temperature

could be obtained best from the solution of PDEs for

m_{fu} with a source term R_{fu}

f with a zero source term

h with a zero source term unless radiation effects are to be included (later)

together with additional algebraic equations. Given values of p, u, v, w, k, ϵ, m_{fu}, f and h at any point in the flowfield, the other properties may be deduced from the use of, successively,

$$m_{ox} = (m_{fu} - f)s$$

$$m_{pr} = 1 - m_{ox} - m_{fu}$$

$$T = (h - H_{fu}\, m_{fu} - v^2/2)/c_p$$

$$\rho = pM/(RT) \text{ where } 1/M = \sum_j (m_j/M_j)$$

$$\mu_{turb} = C_\mu\, \rho k^2/\epsilon$$

The simple exothermic hydrocarbon chemical reaction is characterized by the molar equation[1]

$$C_xH_y + (x + \frac{1}{4}y)\,O_2 \rightarrow xCO_2 + \frac{1}{2}yH_2O + \text{Energy.} \tag{2.45}$$

and hence the corresponding mass equation

$$(12x + y) + (32x + 8y) \rightarrow (44x) + (9y) + \text{Energy.}$$

This leads to the equation

$$1\text{ kg. } C_xH_y + \frac{32x + 8y}{12x + y}\text{ kg. } O_2 \rightarrow \frac{44x + 9y}{12x + y}\text{ kg. products} + H_{C_xH_y}$$

so that, comparing with Eqn. (2.5), the stoichiometric ratio 5 is given by

$$s = \frac{32x + 8y}{12x + y}\text{ kg } O_2/\text{kg } C_xH_y \tag{2.46}$$

Both s and $H_{fu} = H_{C_xH_y}$ depend on the particular fuel under discussion but for most hydrocarbons

$$s \simeq 3.5 \text{ kg } O_2/\text{kg } C_xH_y$$

$$H_{fu} \simeq 4.5 \times 10^7 \text{ J/kg } C_xH_y$$

Since oxygen represents only 23.2 per cent by mass of air, the stoichiometric Air/Fuel ratio AFR is

$$\begin{aligned} AFR_s &= \left(\frac{32x + 8y}{12x + y}\right)/0.232 \\ &\simeq 3.5/0.232 \\ &= 15.09 \text{ kg air/kg } C_xH_y \end{aligned}$$

Also the lower (net) value of H_{fu} is used, since in general the products are in a gaseous state. Values for typical hydrocarbon fuels are given in Table 2.8 where the following notation is used:

C/H Mass	carbon/hydrogen mass ratio of hydrocarbon fuel
RMM	relative molecular mass (or molecular weight)
m_s	moles of oxygen per mole of fuel under stoichiometric conditions (or volume per volume)
$(F/A)_s$	stoichiometric fuel/air mass ratio
ΔH_f^o	enthalpy (or heat) of formation of fuel at standard conditions
$-\Delta H_r^o$ Dissociated	enthalpy (or heat) of reaction (or combustion) of fuel at standard conditions [lower (net) value]
n_5/n_T	mole fraction (or volume fraction) of oxygen O_2 in product stream of fuel-air reaction
STOIC. T_p ad K	adiabatic flame temperature of stoichiometric fuel-air mixture burning at constant pressure [both nondissociated and dissociated values quoted in degrees Kelvin]

Further simplifications may be possible associated with diffusion and premixed combustion, to which attention is now directed.

Kinetically-influenced Premixed Flames

With only the assumptions of the SCRs, the reaction is chemical kinetically-influenced. In particular, both m_{fu} and m_{ox} can have nonzero values at the same point at the same time, and (apart from the hydrodynamic equations) the three PDEs for m_{fu}, f and h must be solved[5]. [In some cases f and h are linearly related and one needs to solve a PDE for only one of them. Such a situation arises if their inlet boundary conditions are linearly related and the combustion zone is impervious and adiabatic, thereby providing zero normal gradient boundary conditions for f and h. Since their PDEs are identical – equal exchange coefficients and no source terms – their solutions are linearly related.] In solving the PDE for m_{fu}, its source term R_{fu} (generation rate of fuel) must be specified. This effect of turbulence structure on time-mean chemical reaction rates is a problem receiving well-deserved attention[61-65]. One such model involves the eddy-breakup expression

$$R_{fu} = -C_{EBU}\,\rho g \epsilon k^{-1}$$

TABLE 2.8

Some Hydrocarbon Fuel Data[60]

C_xH_y	Name	C/H Mass (approx)	RMM	m_s	$(F/A)_s$	ΔH_f^o kJ/mol	$-\Delta H_r^o$ MJ/mol	$-\Delta H_r^o$ MJ/kg	Dissociated n_5/n_T	STOIC. T_p ad K Non. diss.	STOIC. T_p ad K Diss.
	PARAFFINS (Alkanes)										
CH_4	Methane	3	16.042	2	0.05817	−74.8977	0:8029	50.0471	0.00643	2330	2247
C_2H_6	Ethane	4	30.068	3.5	0.06231	−84.7241	1.4288	47.5187	0.00775	2383	2282
C_3H_8	Propane	4.5	44.094	5	0.06396	−103.9164	2.0454	46.3865	0.00814	2396	2289
C_4H_{10}	Butane	4.8	58.120	6.5	0.06485	−124.8169	2.6602	45.7713	0.00832	2402	2293
C_5H_{12}	Pentane	5	72.146	8	0.06541	−146.5380	3.2743	45.3840	0.00842	2405	2295
C_6H_{14}	Hexane	5.14	86.172	9.5	0.06579	−167.3045	3.8893	45.1338	0.00851	2408	2296
C_7H_{16}	Heptane	5.25	100.198	11	0.06606	−187.9455	4.5044	44.9549		2410	
C_8H_{18}	Octane	5.33	114.224	12.5	0.06627	−208.5864	5.1195	44.8200	0.00849	2411	2299
C_9H_{20}	Nonane	5.4	128.250	14	0.06644	−229.1854	5.7347	44.7149		2413	
$C_{10}H_{22}$	Decane	5.45	142.276	15.5	0.06657	−249.8264	6.3498	44.6302	0.00868	2414	2300
$C_{11}H_{24}$	Undecane	5.5	156.302	17	0.06668	−274.6541	6.9607	44.5339		2413	
	NAPHTHENES (Cyclanes)										
C_3H_6	Cyclopropane	6	42.078	4.5	0.06782				0.01116		
C_4H_8	Cyclobutane	6	56.104	6	0.06782				0.01065		
C_5H_{10}	Cyclopentane	6	70.130	7.5	0.06782	−77.2883	3.1015	44.2255	0.00940	2439	2310
C_6H_{12}	Cyclohexane	6	84.156	9	0.06782	−123.2175	3.6914	43.8634	0.00899	2423	2305
C_7H_{14}	Cycloheptane	6	98.182	10.5	0.06782						
	OLEFINS (Alkenes)										
C_2H_4	Ethylene (Ethene)	6	28.052	3	0.06782	52.3183	1.3238	47.1926	0.01270	2568	2420

TABLE 2.8 (Continued)

C_xH_y	Name	C/H Mass (approx)	RMM	m_s	$(F/A)_s$	ΔH_f^o kJ/mol	$-\Delta H_r^o$ MJ/mol	$-\Delta H_r^o$ MJ/kg	Dissociated n_5/n_T	STOIC. T_p ad K Non. diss.	STOIC. T_p ad K Diss.
C_3H_6	Propene	6	42.078	4.5	0.06782	20.4274	1.9277	45.8130	0.01116	2508	2362
C_4H_8	1–Butene	6	56.104	6	0.06782	1.1723	2.5442	45.3485	0.01065	2480	2348
C_5H_{10}	1–Pentene	6	70.130	7.5	0.06782	–20.9340	3.1579	45.0291	0.00940	2471	2339
C_6H_{12}	1–Hexene	6	84.156	9	0.06782	–41.7005	3.7729	44.8320	0.00899	2465	2333
C_7H_{14}	1–Heptene	6	98.182	10.5	0.06782	–62.1740	4.3882	44.6943	0.00992	2459	2329
C_8H_{16}	1–Octene	6	112.208	12	0.06782	–82.9824	5.0031	44.5880	0.00980	2455	2326
C_9H_{18}	1–Nonene	6	126.234	13.5	0.06782	–103.5814	5.6183	44.5070		2451	
$C_{10}H_{20}$	1–Decene	6	140.260	15	0.06782	–124.2224	6.2334	44.4419	0.00964	2448	2322
$C_{11}H_{22}$	1–Undecene	6	154.286	16.5	0.06782	–144.8633	6.8485	44.3886		2446	
$C_{12}H_{24}$	1–Dodecene	6	168.312	18	0.06782	–165.4623	7.4637	44.3445	0.00953	2444	2319
	ACETYLENES (Alkynes)										
C_2H_2	Acetylene (Ethyne)	12	26.036	2.5	0.07553	226.8994	1.2564	48.2578	0.02477	2909	2583
C_3H_4	Propyne	9	40.062	4	0.07264	185.5548	1.8509	46.1999	0.01704	2700	2476
C_4H_6	1–Butyne	8	54.088	5.5	0.07132	166.2160	2.4673	45.6161	0.01466	2611	2432
C_5H_8	1–Pentyne	7.5	68.114	7	0.07057	144.4446	3.0813	45.2371	0.01328	2573	2406
C_6H_{10}	1–Hexyne	7.2	82.140	8.5	0.07009	123.7199	3.6963	45.0002	0.01271	2552	2394
C_7H_{12}	1–Heptyne	7	96.166	10	0.06955	103.0790	4.3114	44.8333		2533	
C_8H_{14}	1–Octyne	6.86	110.192	11.5	0.06949	82.4800	4.9266	44.7093	0.01156	2518	2366
C_9H_{16}	1–Nonyne	6.75	124.218	13	0.06930	61.8390	5.5417	44.6129		2507	
$C_{10}H_{18}$	1–Decyne	6.67	138.244	14.5	0.06915	41.2400	6.1569	44.5364	0.01102	2498	2354

TABLE 2.8 (Continued)

C_xH_y	Name	C/H Mass (approx)	RMM	m_s	$(F/A)_s$	ΔH_f^o kJ/mol	$-\Delta H_r^o$ MJ/mol	$-\Delta H_r^o$ MJ/kg	Dissociated n_5/n_T	STOIC. T_p ad K Non. diss.	STOIC. T_p ad K Diss.
	AROMATICS										
C_6H_6	Benzene	12	78.108	7.5	0.07553	82.9824	3.1716	40.6054	0.01233	2529	2366
C_7H_8	Toluene	10.5	92.134	9	0.07425	50.0323	3.7744	40.9666	0.01157	2504	2348
C_8H_{10}	Xylene (average)	9.6	106.160	10.5	0.07333	18.0591	4.3780	41.2757	0.01104	2487	2342
$C_{10}H_8$	Naphthalene	15	128.164	12	0.07745	150.9341	5.0566	39.4545	0.01261	2534	2367
	ALIPHATIC ALCOHOLS										
CH_3OH	Methanol	3	32.042	1.5	0.15493	−201.3013	0.6765	21.1114	0.00725	2335	2243
C_2H_5OH	Ethanol	4	46.068	3	0.11137	−235.4656	1.2781	27.7427	0.00762	2356	2258
C_3H_7OH	Propanol	4.5	60.094	4.5	0.09685	−235.1066	1.8932	31.5036	0.00804	2377	2273
	MISCELLANEOUS										
H_2 (g)	Hydrogen (gas)	0	2.016	0.5	0.02924	0	0.2420	120.0338	0.01131	2534	2444
C(gr)	Carbon (graphite)	∞	12.010	1	0.08710	0	0.3938	32.7873	0.01120	2458	2309
CO	Carbon monoxide	∞	28.011	0.5	0.40640	−110.529	0.2830	10.1029	0.02124	2663	2399

as opposed to the time-averaged Arrhenius expression

$$R_{fu} = -A\,p^2 m_{fu}\, m_{ox}\, \exp\,(-B/RT)$$

and both these models were possibilities discussed earlier. Generally, one uses the smaller of these two expressions at a given point in the flowfield, the eddy dissipation rate often slowing chemical reaction. This basic model has had several refinements, culminating in the recent Eulerian-Lagrangian ESCIMO (Engulfment, Stretching, Coherence, Inter-diffusion, Moving Observer) theory of turbulent combustion[66-70]. Realistic simulation of complex chemistry in turbulent reacting flows is probably the area in combustor modeling that will prove to be most useful to study, and the results of which will be most fruitful to apply in practical design situations.

When one's interest is being directed toward pollution problems, other complexities arise[71-81]. In the prediction of oxides of nitrogen NO_x several more reactions need to be considered. Knowledge and expertise about soot-forming reactions are, unfortunately, less satisfactory. Major pollutants include carbon monoxide, total hydrocarbons, nitric oxide(s), smoke (carbon) and sulfur dioxide. The problem of combustion-generated air pollution has spurred a new interest in modeling the details of the combustion process, because the formation of pollutant species is strongly related to the time-temperature history of the combustion gases and the chemical kinetics of the species. In many cases the formation of pollutants can be considered as a perturbation on the model of the combustion process; once the main combustion has been modeled the chemical-kinetics of the pollutants can be simply computed using the established temperatures, pressures and concentrations. In other cases, for example, exhaust hydrocarbons, the model must consider the interaction between the formation of pollutants and the main combustion process[18-19].

Many chemical reaction phenomena possess 'stiff kinetics'; that is, they involve a multitude of species with widely-differing reaction rate coefficients. Their equations have to be solved along with the more usual fluid dynamic equations[82-90]. Special computational techniques for handling the source terms are required, one often solving the associated time-dependent problem even when one is merely seeking the steady state solution. Of course, different time-steps are chosen for the fluid dynamic and chemical-kinetic portions of the problem, which are amalgamated in the solution procedure. Special ordinary differential equation solvers, as, for example, the GEAR package[87] and its simpler variants[88], are used in these transient simulations. A more efficient technique for steady state solution of stiff kinetic problems has recently been developed and shows considerable promise for practical engineering situations[85].

An important problem in finite rate chemistry is choosing an appropriate level of complexity, in view of the large number of species and chemical reactions taking place. One solution to this problem is the use of the quasi-global reaction scheme[19], whose key element is the sub-global oxidation step:

$$C_xH_y + \frac{x}{2}O_2 \rightarrow \frac{y}{2}H_2 + x\,CO \qquad (2.47)$$

which is unidirectional. Coupled with this are a number of intermediate reversible reactions involving H, H_2, O, O_2, OH, N, N_2, NO, NO_2, CO and CO_2. The model affords a useful computer time-saving as compared to a full finite-rate chemical kinetics formulation, and it has been successfully used in a variety of flow configurations, including stirred reactors, plug flows and turbulent diffusion swirling flames[19,46].

Extensions of this quasi-global concept have been made to include fuel-bound nitrogen and other possible species and fuels. Sensitivity studies to ascertain which species and reactions are significant have also been performed. Kinetic modeling problems become more critical with fuels derived from nonpetroleum sources, such as low H/C ratio hydrocarbon fuels derivable from coal and oil shale. Concerns include fuel bound nitrogen and soot, but questions of ignition, flame stabilization and efficiency abound[13-19].

Physically-controlled Diffusion Flames

Most furnace and engine flames are physically-controlled diffusion flames, which means that their outward characteristics, such as temperature distribution, can be computed without knowledge of the detailed reaction-kinetic constants. This is because when fuel and air are injected separately, their rate of mixing is slow (and is therefore the total rate controlling process) in comparison to the rate of reaction which the chemical-kinetic processes can achieve as the completion of the reaction process. Thermodynamic equilibrium now prevails throughout and a further simplification to the mathematical problem is possible. This is because unburnt fuel and oxidant *cannot* both exist at the same place at the same time, and so at any position in the flowfield the mixture is composed of *either* fuel and products *or* oxidant and products[5].

The phenomenon is characterized mathematically by noting that whenever f is positive it is equal to m_{fu} and $m_{ox} = 0$ and whenever it is negative it is equal to $-m_{ox}/s$ and $m_{fu} = 0$. Outlining this

$$f \geqslant 0 \quad \text{implies } m_{ox} = 0 \text{ and } m_{fu} = f$$
$$f < 0 \quad \text{implies } m_{fu} = 0 \text{ and } m_{ox} = -sf$$

The flame region is infinitesimally thin and occurs over the surface where $f = 0$. The reaction problem is now essentially a two-component system and hence solution of just two PDEs for f and h characterizes the problem. That is

$$\left.\begin{matrix} m_{ox} \\ m_{fu} \end{matrix}\right\} \quad \text{deduced from } f$$
$$m_{pr} = 1 - m_{ox} - m_{fu}$$
$$T = (h - H_{fu}m_{fu} - v^2/2)/c_p$$
$$\rho = pM/(RT) \text{ where } 1/M = \sum_j (m_j/M_j)$$
$$\mu_{turb} = C_\mu \rho k^2/\epsilon$$

Consider now the case of a fast-reacting (that is, diffusion controlled) SCRS in a simple steady flow process in which fuel and oxidant enter via separate inlets, then mix and react in an adiabatic impervious combustor, the proceeds exiting via a common outlet. Let F and O denote conditions at the fuel and oxidant inlets, respectively. Then (if the kinetic energy contribution to h is neglected) a consequence of the assumptions is that m_{fu}, m_{ox}, m_{pr}, h and T are all linearly related to the single variable f. Inlet and outlet values are derived as:

Inlet F (fuel)

$$m_{fu} = 1$$
$$m_{ox} = 0$$
$$m_{pr} = 0$$
$$T = T_F$$
$$h = h_F = c_p T_F + H_{fu}$$
$$f = f_F = m_{fu} = 1$$
$$e = 1$$

Inlet O (oxidant)

$$m_{fu} = 0$$
$$m_{ox} = 1$$
$$m_{pr} = 0$$
$$T = T_O$$
$$h = h_O = c_p T_O$$
$$f = f_O = -m_{ox}/s = -1/s$$
$$e = 0$$

where it has also been found convenient to define the *mixture fraction* e as the normalized value of f via

$$e = \frac{f - f_0}{f_F - f_0}$$

so that its value is zero in the oxidant 0 stream, and unity is the fuel F stream. By previous discussion of linearity between f and h in these circumstances, e is also related to h, via

$$e = \frac{h - h_0}{h_F - h_0}$$

The e_{st} value corresponding to the stoichiometric $f = 0$ value is simply

$$e = \frac{0 - f_0}{f_F - f_0}$$

$$= \frac{-(-1/s)}{1 - (-1/s)}$$

$$= \frac{1}{1 + s}$$

where s is the stoichiometric oxidant/fuel mass ratio. Corresponding h_{st} and T_{st} values at the stoichiometric $f = 0$ value are then derived as

$$\frac{h_{st} - h_0}{h_F - h_0} = \frac{1}{1 + s}$$

from which

$$h_{st} = h_0 + \frac{1}{1 + s}(h_F - h_0)$$

$$= c_p T_0 + \frac{1}{1 + s}(c_p T_F + H_{fu} - c_p T_0)$$

$$= \frac{1}{1 + s}(c_p T_F + H_{fu} + c_p s T_0)$$

and hence

$$T_{st} = \frac{1}{1 + s}(T_F + sT_0 + H_{fu}/c_p)$$

which is an expression for the adiabatic flame temperature. Figure 2.1 illustrates all the linear dependences of interest, which are, mathematically,

$e \leqslant e_{st}$ implies

$$m_{fu} = 0$$

$$m_{ox} = (e_{st} - e)/e_{st}$$

$$T = [T_0 (e_{st} - e) + T_{st}\, e]/e_{st}$$

ρ = usual formula with this value of T

$e \geqslant e_{st}$ implies

$$m_{fu} = (e - e_{st}) / (1 - e_{st})$$

$$m_{ox} = 0$$

$$T = [T_F (e - e_{st}) + T_{st} (1 - e)]/(1 - e_{st})$$

ρ = usual formula with this value of T

2.6 MORE REALISTIC SIMULATION

Radiative Heat Transfer

The 'mean free path' of radiative transfer is normally very great (as compared, for example, with typical turbulence eddy sizes) and the penetration is such that all points in the

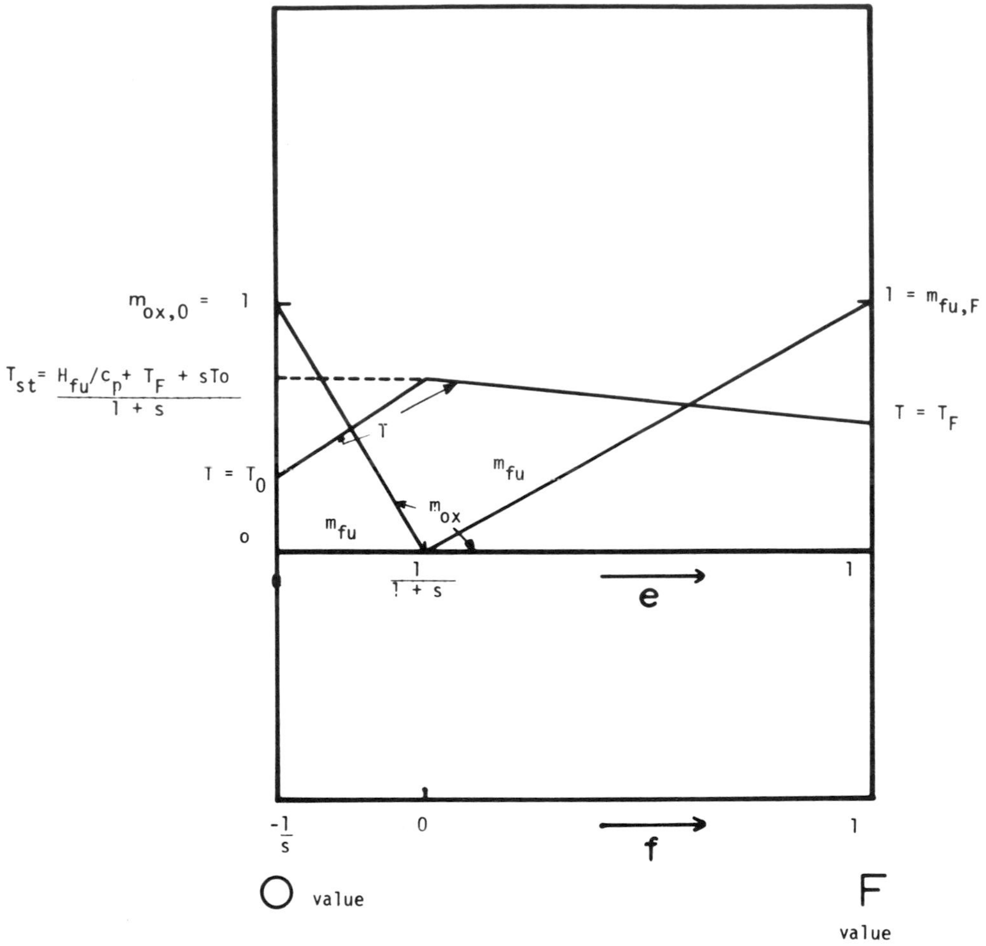

Figure 2.1 Linear relationships in the SCRS physically-controlled diffusion flame

field can 'see' each other participate in interactions. The mathematical formulation that allows for this communication is an 'integro-differential' one, which is especially difficult to solve.

The numerical form of the integro-differential equation is provided by Hottel's 'zone method' of radiative transfer analysis—full matrix equations for interzone transfer must be solved[91-93]. With a large number of zones the method is rigorously correct, but the full matrix must be calculated repeatedly as the estimated composition distribution of the gases changes. Thus, combination of the zone method with hydrodynamic calculation is a very complex task. The basic assumption of the original zone method is the separability of the evaluation of total exchange areas from the solution of energy balance equations, that is, the grey gas hypothesis. This restriction can be removed by assuming a pseudo-grey approximation for the local emissivity of a real gas[92]. With *a priori* knowledge of the flow, heat release and absorption coefficients, it can be shown that the zone method can be used reliably[94].

An alternative method for radiation heat transfer calculations is available via the Monte-Carlo technique. Here, bundles of energy simulate the actual physical processes of radiant emission and absorption, and these are assumed to be similar to photons in behavior. Predictions of temperature profiles and heat flux distributions[95] in a cylindrical furnace identical to Hottel and Sarofim[93] indicate favorable credibility to the technique. It is also flexible in being able to treat local concentration nonuniformities.

Nevertheless, the most popular radiation models to be employed widely in finite difference calculations of the flowfield are the flux methods. This alternative simplified approach is to separate the wavelength and angle dimensions of radiation and use the 'flux method'—sparse matrix equations for 1, 2 and 3 flux sums (so-called two-flux, four-flux and six-flux methods). It is less rigorous than the zone methods but is simple enough to be employed along with fluid dynamic calculations. A detailed derivation of the commonly employed flux methods is available[96-98]. A two-flux method with slug flow,[99] a four-flux method in a cylindrical furnace[100] and a six-flux method in a segment of an annular combustor and a cylindrical can combustor are all examples of flux model usage. Recently, an indication of how the grey-gas restriction may be removed has been presented[101] and used in a comprehensive 3-D furnace flow calculation[102] with good results.

Consider some details about the flux methods. A problem is the fact that because of the variation with angle, radiation intensity varies with six independent variables (3 space dimensions; wavelength; two direction cosines). Allowance for the last two overburdens the computational procedure. One solution is the flux method: the angular space is subdivided, but even more drastically than the other dimensions (distance; wavelength). Specifically, attention is focused on: radiation fluxes *I, J* crossing the $y \sim z$ plane, *K,L* crossing the $y \sim z$ plane, etc. There are three basic levels of subdivision of space: the so-called two-, four- and six-flux methods[103].

In the axisymmetric two-flux method, one starts with the differential equations

$$\frac{1}{r}\frac{d}{dr}(rI) = -(a+s)I + aE + \frac{s}{2}(I+J) + J/r$$

$$\frac{1}{r}\frac{d}{dr}(rJ) = (a+s)J - aE - \frac{s}{2}(I+J) + J/r \qquad (2.48)$$

with the nomenclature:

a	=	Absortivity per unit length
s	=	Scattering coefficient per unit length
E	=	Black body emissive power in the given wavelength interval
r	=	Radius
I	=	Outward-directed flux
J	=	Inward-directed flux

Nevertheless, the asymmetry of the relations is surprising, but correct. Some of J enters I, but not vice versa.

In computational work a single second-order equation is preferable. Addition leads to:

$$\frac{1}{r}\frac{d}{dr}[r(I+J)] = -(a+s)(I-J) + \frac{I+J}{r} - \frac{(I-J)}{r}$$

That is
$$\frac{d}{dr}(I+J) = -(a+s+1/r)(I-J)$$

Subtraction leads to:

$$\frac{1}{r}\frac{d}{dr}\{r(I-J)\} = -a(I+J) + 2aE$$

Combination leads to: (2.49)

$$\frac{1}{r}\frac{d}{dr}\left\{\frac{r}{(a+s+1/r)}\frac{d(I+J)}{dr}\right\} = a(I+J-2E)$$

Here $(I-J)$ is the energy flux, $(I+J)$ is the only term containing I or J, $1/(a+s+1/r)$ occupies the exchange-coefficient position, and the equation remains of standard form with many terms absent.

More realism is portrayed in the axisymmetric four-flux method. Following similar ideas we have the differential equations:

$$\frac{1}{r}\frac{d}{dr}(rI) = -(a+s)I + aE + \frac{s}{4}(I+J+K+L) + J/r$$

$$\frac{1}{r}\frac{d}{dr}(rJ) = (a+s)J - aE - \frac{s}{4}(I+J+K+L) + J/r$$

(2.50)

$$\frac{d}{dz}K = -(a+s)K + aE + \frac{s}{4}(I+J+K+L)$$

$$\frac{d}{dz}L = (a+s)L - aE - \frac{s}{4}(I+J+K+L)$$

with the nomenclature:

r = radial distance
z = axial distance

I, J are fluxes in $+, -\ r$ direction
K, L are fluxed in $+, -\ z$ direction

As previously, one can form second-order equations with the result:

$$\frac{1}{r}\frac{d}{dr}\left[\frac{r}{(a+s+1/r)}\frac{d(I+J)}{dr}\right] = a(I+J-2E) + s(I+J-K-L)$$

$$\frac{d}{dz}\left[\frac{1}{(a+s)}\frac{d(K+L)}{dz}\right] = a(K+L-2E) + s(K+L-I-J) \qquad (2.51)$$

Now, the term $s\ (I + J - K - L)$ represents the transfer of radiation from the radial to the axial direction by scattering. The fluxes again appear only in the paired forms: $I + J,\ K + L$, and the conduction approximation is valid where ar is large (not near center).

Even more realistic is the six-flux method which may be combined with a fully 3-D calculation procedure. Now there are six differential equations:

$$\frac{1}{r}\frac{d}{dr}(rI) = -(a+s)I + aE + \frac{s}{6}(I+J+K+L+M+N) + J/r$$

$$\frac{1}{r}\frac{d}{dr}(rJ) = (a+s)J - aE - \frac{s}{6}(I+J+K+L+M+N) + J/r$$

$$\frac{dK}{dz} = -(a+s)K + aE + \frac{s}{6}(I+J+K+L+M+N)$$

$$\frac{dL}{dz} = (a+s)L - aE - \frac{s}{6}(I+J+K+L-M+N) \qquad (2.52)$$

$$\frac{1}{r}\frac{DM}{d\theta} = -(a+s)M + aE + \frac{s}{6}(I+J+K+L+M+N)$$

$$\frac{1}{r}\frac{dN}{d\theta} = (a+s)N - aE - \frac{s}{6}(I+J+K+L+M+N)$$

where M and N are intensities in the +and $-\ \theta$ directions.

The result of manipulation is:

$$\frac{1}{r}\frac{d}{dr}\left\{\frac{r}{(a+s+1/r)}\frac{d(I+J)}{dr}\right\} = a(I+J-2E) + \frac{s}{r}\{2(I+J)-(K+L)-(M+N)\}$$

$$\frac{d}{dz}\left\{\frac{1}{(a+s)}\frac{d(K+L)}{dz}\right\} = a(K+L-2E) + \frac{s}{3}\{2(K+L)-(I+J)-(M+N)\}$$

$$\frac{1}{r}\frac{d}{d\theta}\left\{\frac{1}{(a+s)r}\frac{d(M+N)}{d\theta}\right\} = a(M+N-2E) + \frac{s}{3}\{2(M+N)-(I+J)-(K+L)\} \qquad (2.53)$$

Now radiation is transferred by scattering between all three flux pairs, the equations are easy to solve numerically, and apart from E, they are linear.

Droplet Sprays, Evaporation and Combustion

Two-phase effects also require to be modeled, because in combustion systems fuel is often injected in the form of a spray of small liquid droplets. Products of combustion such as soot are present as solid particles as well. Spray combustion, and droplet evaporation and combustion, present an almost formidable problem, as inspection of their relevant conservation equations reveals. More realistic approaches are sought. One such approach relates the characteristics of the nozzle to the jet penetration distance, droplet size and number density distribution[104]. Simplified approaches to determining the rate of change of droplet density and size distribution need to account for the time rate of change of droplet size, particle formation and destruction[105]. Because of turbulence, statistical analysis of particle behavior is required and attention is focused on the density of particle population in given intervals of particle size, velocity, temperature, etc. Computer size restricts the depth of detail that can be accommodated. One practice, valid for small particles, is the infinite drag assumption that particles at all times possess the local gas velocity. Then, differential equations are solved for the distribution of solid material in particle-size space, in discrete ranges[5, 23-26]. Thus, if f_i is the mass fraction of the ith size interval, the appropriate differential equation is the Eqn. (2.1) with ϕ replaced by f_i. Knowledge of particle physics is now concentrated into the source term via equations such as

$$S_{f_i} = \rho V_i \; \partial f_i / \partial s \tag{2.54}$$

where V_i stands for the rate of increase of particle size s with time; unfortunately, how this may be specified in terms of local conditions is not well-established, although an approximation for the interaction may be obtained via single-droplet theory[106-108]. Typical simplifying assumptions made by various authors in the derivation of a droplet-burning model include[109].

1. The ratio of flame radius to droplet radius remains constant.
2. Fuel vapor reacts with oxidant stoichiometrically at the flame surface.
3. Chemical reaction is instantaneous.
4. The prevailing temperature within the droplet corresponds to that of the boiling point.
5. The mode of heat transfer is conduction at the droplet surface. The effects of fuel volatility on the burning rate are negligible.
6. Radiation and natural convection influences are negligible.

The mathematical simulation of the presence of a fuel spray in a combustion environment must account for mass, momentum and energy exchange between the separate phases. Physical models treat the effects of particle growth, disappearance, drag and turbulence, and particle interaction.

Larger particles do not follow the streamlines; also fuel droplets which are sprayed into the combustor across the airstream come into this category as well. The problem is then even more complicated. As well as particle-size range computation, one has to compute droplet trajectories via ordinary differential equations, and these differ according to droplet size: large droplets are less affected by the flowfield. The effect of the aerodynamics on the trajectories and the reverse effect must be considered. A rigorous development of the gas-droplet flow equations utilizing a control volume approach in conjunction with the transport theorem is quite complicated[110, 111]. Studies on the rates of burning of droplets, clouds and sprays are also proving to be extremely worthwhile. A statistical analysis yielding a distribution function is generally required, and various levels of approximation are possible[112]. In practical computation, the smooth distribution function is frequently replaced by a discrete one. Westbrook[113] solves the general spray equation in a 7-D phase space. A related study develops a comprehensive model for the solution of subsonic 2-D gas-laden flows in an axial inlet peripheral-discharge cyclone separator[114], and an axisymmetric sudden expansion[115]. A similar model has been applied to a combustor configuration[116]. Typical techniques[23, 24, 117] for the inclusion of a fuel droplet spray in finite difference flowfield calculations follow the technique which is now outlined. The analysis begins with the assumptions:

1. In the course of diminution of size by vaporization, the heat absorbed is proportional to the mass of material changing phase.
2. The specific heat of the liquid phase fuel is taken as identical with that of the vapor-phase.
3. It is presumed that the droplets are small enough in size for Reynolds number of relative motion between phases to be negligible (N.B. see later discussion).
4. Under turbulent conditions, the mode of diffusion for droplets is taken to be identical to that of the gaseous phase.
5. The temperature and concentration fields surrounding the droplets are spherically symmetric (forced convection effects are neglected in this analysis).
6. The droplets are of uniform density, and spherical in shape.
7. The mode of mass transfer depends on either:

The driving force due to a temperature difference between the local gas mixture and the presumed droplet surface temperature.

or:

The oxygen concentration in the local mixture.

Defining:

S = square of the particle radius
n = number of particles per unit volume per unit size increment (S to $S + ds$)
M = mass of a single droplet in this size range
m = mass of droplets in this size range per unit volume in space.
f_J = mass of particles in the size range S_{J+1} to a larger size S_J per unit mass of gas-droplet mixture [J = 1, 2, . . . , K ranges over the particle sizes from large to small]
ρ = local mixture density

it follows that

$$m = M_n$$

$$\rho f_J = \int_{S_{J+1}}^{S_J} m ds$$

A control volume analysis for the balance of droplets entering, leaving and changing size yields the PDE for *m*.

$$\frac{\partial m}{\partial t} + \dot{S}\left[\frac{\partial m}{\partial S} - \frac{m}{M}\frac{\partial M}{\partial S}\right] = 0$$

and integration over a size range yields

$$\frac{d}{dt}(\rho f_J) + \int_{S_{J+1}}^{S_J} \dot{S}\left[\frac{\partial m}{\partial S} - \frac{m}{M}\frac{\partial M}{\partial S} dS\right] = 0$$

To proceed further it is necessary to model the terms $\dot{S}$ and $\partial m/\partial S$ via suitable hypotheses. A droplet-size-change law for mass transfer rate from the condensed phase to the gaseous phase, per unit surface area, is expressible as:

$$\dot{m}'' = \frac{\Gamma}{r} \ln (1 + B)$$

where

$\dot{M}''$ = mass transfer rate
Γ = gas phase transport property
r = instantaneous drop radius
B = dimensionless driving force for mass transfer

B may be evaluated via considerations of vaporization only, direct oxidation or a combination of both. The finally evolved general equation is

$$\frac{d}{dt}(\rho f_J) = -\dot{S}\left\{m_J - m_{J+1}\right) - \int_{S_{J+1}}^{S_J} 3/2 \frac{m}{S} dS\right\}$$

The $m \sim S$ variation is approximated as a series of finite steps with droplets in size-ranges $J=1$ (largest particles) to $J=K$ (smallest particles). The above equation is amended to the form

$$\frac{d}{dt}(\rho f_J) = \frac{\rho\Gamma}{\rho_p} \ln (1 + B)\left\{\frac{f_{J-1}}{S_{J-1} - S_J} - \frac{f_J}{S_J - S_{J+1}} - \frac{3}{2}\frac{f_J}{S_J}\right\} \qquad \text{for } J < K$$

$$\frac{d}{dt}(\rho f_1) = \frac{\rho\Gamma}{\rho_p}\,\ell n\,(1+B)\left\{\frac{f_1}{S_1 - S_2} + \frac{3}{2}\frac{f_1}{S_1}\right\} \quad \text{for } J = 1$$

$$\tag{2.55}$$

$$\frac{d}{dt}(\rho f_K) = \frac{\rho\Gamma}{\rho_p}\,\ell n\,(1+B)\left\{\frac{S_{K-1}}{S_{K-1} - S_K} - \frac{3}{2}\frac{f_K}{S_K}\right\} \quad \text{for } J = K$$

covering all size categories. Notice that these equations conform to the general pattern

$$\partial(\rho\phi)/\partial t + \text{div}\,(\rho\,\phi) = \text{div}\,(\Gamma_\phi\,\text{grad}\,\phi) + S_\phi$$

as presented in Section 2.1 for a general variable ϕ. Thus, the relevant droplet size categories may be calculated in the same manner as the other variables.

Two-step Chemical Reaction Model

The one-step reaction model of Section 2.5 (popular in the simulation of heat release) may be replaced by a slightly more sophisticated kinetics model which allows prediction of local mass fractions of hydrocarbon fuel C_xH_y, carbon dioxide CO_2, and nitrogen N_2. In the case of the hydrocarbon fuel kerosine (taken as $C_{12}H_{24}$) the appropriate two reaction steps are:

$$C_{12}H_{24} + 12\ O_2 \rightarrow 12\ CO + 12\ H_2O$$

$$12\ CO + 6\ O_2 \rightarrow 12\ CO_2 \tag{2.56}$$

Following a partial equilibrium model for CO concentration[118], it is necessary to solve three PDEs for f (or e), m_{fu} and m_{CO}. Then three algebraic equations for atomic balances of C, H and O.

$$m_C = \frac{144}{168}m_{fu} + \frac{12}{28}m_{CO} + \frac{12}{44}m_{CO_2}$$

$$m_H = \frac{24}{168}m_{fu} + \frac{2}{18}m_{H_2O}$$

$$m_O = m_{Ox} + \frac{16}{28}m_{CO} + \frac{16}{18}m_{H_2O} + \frac{32}{44}m_{CO_2}$$

are used with the total sum of species mass fractions being equal to unity.

$$m_{fu} + m_{CO} + m_{CO_2} + m_{H_2O} + m_{Ox} + m_{N_2} + \sum_{j=1}^{K} m_{d,j} = 1 \tag{2.57}$$

The last term on the left represents summation of mass fractions in fuel droplets over their specified size ranges j = 1, . . . , K (see previous section). The reaction rates for the two reaction steps are specified via expressions of the Arrhenius type, or the influence of turbulence on reaction rates may be included. One way is to utilize the eddy-breakup model and take the reaction rates to be the smaller of the two expressions, Arrhenius and eddy-breaking.

The problem is then closed mathematically, and simple algebraic manipulation yields:

$$m_C = \frac{144}{168} e$$

$$m_H = \frac{24}{168} e$$

$$m_O = 0.232\ (1 - e) - \sum_{j=1}^{K} m_{d,j}$$

and finally equations for mass fractions of O_2, H_2O and CO_2:

$$m_{O_2} = \frac{576}{168} m_{fu} + \frac{16}{28} m_{CO} + 0.232 - \left[0.232 + \frac{576}{168} \right] e - 0.232 \sum_{j=1}^{K} m_{d,j}$$

$$m_{H_2O} = \frac{216}{168} (e - m_{fu})$$

$$m_{CO_2} = \frac{22}{7} (e - m_{fu}) - \frac{44}{28} m_{CO}$$

Then, m_{N_2} follows from Eqn. (2.57) directly.

Thus, the solution of three PDEs for f (or e), m_{fu} and m_{CO} allows mass fractions of all the species fuel C_xH_y, CO, CO_2, H_2O, O_2 and N_2 to be deduced at all points in the flowfield. One is now in a position to deduce, from these species concentrations, velocities and temperature distributions, further desirable information. For example, nitric oxide NO may be calculated via the simple Zeldovich[119] mechanism:

$$\begin{aligned} O + N_2 &= NO + N \\ N + O_2 &= NO + O \\ N + OH &= NO + H \end{aligned} \qquad (2.58)$$

or other techniques given in the next section.

Probability Density Function PDF Combustion Models

Recent conferences have highlighted turbulent reacting flow simulation and solution problems[156-159]. A cohesive overview of the field is provided by three recent review papers[159] on the modeling of turbulent reacting flows in practical systems from the points of view of the chemical kineticist [Westbrook and Dryer], the turbulence fluid dynamic modeler [Jones and Whitelaw], and the user [Harsha]. The differential equations of turbulent reacting flow may be manipulated via conventional (that is, unweighted) or density-weighted averaging. Jones and Whitelaw[160] conclude, in general, that the latter technique is superior, and point out that the interpretation of measurements requires special care to distinguish between conventionally averaged and density-weighted properties. Various recent methods proposed to represent reaction in turbulent flames are reviewed in relation to diffusion and premixed flames and to flames in which an element of both is present. The application of laminar flame sheet models, chemical equilibrium assumptions, probability density functions of different forms and truncated series expansion of reaction rate expressions are considered together with the use of probability density function transport equations and their (Monte-Carlo) solution. The appraisal is made in relation to presently available results and future requirements and possibilities.

Combusting flows in general comprise many chemical species in which reaction may occur between certain ones via a large number of finite rate reaction steps. A conservation equation with mean formation rate can be set up for each species. Nevertheless, the formation rates are inevitably highly nonlinear functions of temperature and species concentrations and thus knowledge of the mean values of these latter quantities is *insufficient* to allow the evaluation of mean formation rates. In fact, the determination of mean formation rates represents a major difficulty in the development of prediction methods for combusting flows. The importance of fluctuations in turbulent flows is well known and must be represented in the evaluation of mean formation rates, density and temperature. Clearly, the use of time mean quantities in the simple three-component one-step Arrhenius reaction expression can lead to serious errors, and this fact led to eddy-breakup type mean reaction rate expressions which allow turbulence effects to reveal themselves, as discussed earlier in Section 2.5.

The most convenient way to represent the necessary scalar fluctuations is with a probability density function PDF. Other approaches are possible and can be described in terms of PDF procedures. At the present time it appears that only PDF transport equation formulations offer the possibility of handling large numbers of reacting species. But in view of the multi-dimensionality of the approach, computer storage requirements and run times can be expected to be very large, and their viability remains to be demonstrated. For hydrocarbon fuels there is an additional problem that the detailed reaction mechanism whereby oxidation occurs is known only for a few of the simpler hydrocarbons. In practice, however, this is not likely to present a problem since only a small number of finite rate reactions are likely to be handled and approximate semi-global-type reaction hypotheses predominate. Also, in practice the chemistry is 'fast' compared to the mixing, and this assumption provides a useful simulation in many cases. Of course it is not appropriate under all circumstances. In particular, the calculation of the formation and emissions of pollutants such as carbon monoxide, unburnt fuel and nitric oxide all require consideration of finite rate chemistry as do ignition and extinction (blow-out) phenomena.

Diffusion Flames. When fuel and oxidant enter the combustion system in separate streams, often the 'fast' chemistry assumption is invoked with all reactions going to completion (or equilibrium) as soon as they are mixed. Mean reaction rates are not specified; they are infinitely fast. Then the thermochemical state of the resulting mixture may be determined purely in terms of strictly conserved scalar variations as discussed in Section 2.5. The need to evaluate mean reaction rates is thereby removed, and all strictly conserved scalar variables (with zero source expressions) are *linearly related* to the mixture fraction

f. Fig. 2.1 is appropriate for a three-component mixture undergoing a simple one-step reaction.

The instantaneous thermochemical state is related to the instantaneous value of the mixture fraction at all points in the flowfield. But it is necessary to take account of the fluctuations in mixture fraction that arise in all turbulent diffusion flames. The most convenient way of achieving this is via the introduction of the probability density function for mixture fraction, $P(f, x_i)$. The simplest and most popular approach is to specify a two-parameter form of the probability density function in terms of the mean and variance of f. If Favre averaging is used then the values of these quantities is obtained from the solution of the equations: –

$$\bar{\rho}\,\tilde{U}_j \frac{\partial \tilde{f}}{\partial x_j} = \frac{\partial}{\partial x_j}\left\{\frac{\mu_t}{\sigma_t}\frac{\partial \tilde{f}}{\partial x_j}\right\}$$

$$\bar{\rho}\,\tilde{U} \frac{\partial \widetilde{f''^2}}{\partial x_j} = \frac{\partial}{\partial x_j}\left\{\frac{\mu_t}{\sigma_t}\frac{\partial \widetilde{f''^2}}{\partial x_j}\right\} + 2\frac{\mu_t}{\sigma_t}\left(\frac{\partial \tilde{f}}{\partial x_j}\right)^2 - 2\frac{\bar{\rho}\epsilon}{k}\widetilde{f''^2}$$

The PDF to be constructed is now a density weighted function which allows evaluation of both density weighted and unweighted mean values. Density weight mean values are given by: —

$$\tilde{\phi} = \int_0^1 \phi(f)\,P(f, x_i)\,df$$

and unweighted values by: —

$$\tilde{\phi} = \bar{\rho}\int_0^1 \frac{\phi(f)}{\rho(f)}\,P(f, x_i)\,df$$

where x_i is the ith coordinate direction and ϕ stands for any quantity which may be uniquely related to f [including temperature and species mass fractions]. Also in these equations the prime denotes unweighted fluctuating component and the double prime denotes density-weighted fluctuating component. The density can be obtained from: —

$$\bar{\rho} = \left[\int_0^1 \frac{P(f, x_i)}{\rho(f)}\,df\right]^{-1}$$

Not all authors use Favre averaging and sometimes certain correlations involving fluctuating density are ignored.

A number of assumed forms for the PDFs have been made. Spalding[161] suggests the rectangular wave variation of f with time, corresponding to two δ-functions located at f^+ and f^- :

$$P(f, x_i) = a\delta(f - f^+) + (1 - a)\,\delta(f - f^-)$$

where a, f^+ and f^- are determined from the values of $\tilde{f}$ and $\widetilde{f''^2}$. Clipped Gaussian distributions provide more realistic specifications. Naguib[162] proposes

$$P(f, x_i) = \frac{1}{2}\,\mathrm{erfc}\left\{\frac{f_o}{\sqrt{2}\sigma_o}\right\}\delta(f) + \frac{1}{2}\,\mathrm{erfc}\left\{\frac{1-f_o}{\sqrt{2}\sigma_o}\right\}\delta(1-f)$$

$$+\left[H(f) - H(f-1)\right]\frac{1}{\sqrt{2}\sigma_o}\exp\left\{-\frac{(f-f_o)^2}{2\sigma_o^2}\right\}$$

where H ( ) is the Heaviside function and where again the parameters f_o and σ_o are obtained from the values of $\tilde{f}$ and $\widetilde{f''^2}$. In this case explicit expressions for f_o and σ_o cannot be obtained and their values must be obtained iteratively; for computational purposes this is often done 'once and for all'-and the results stored in tabular form. Kent and Bilger[163] utilize intermittency to get an alternative formulation, writing

$$P(f, x_i) = (1 - I)\,\delta(f) + IP_1(f, x_i)$$

with intermittency $I(x_i)$ estimated from an empirical correlation in jet diffusion flames and P_1 ( ) being the probability function for the turbulent fluid for which a clipped Gaussian distribution is used. A distribution that is free from the arbitrary and unappealing 'clipping' is the β-probability density function which can be written

$$P(f, x_i) = \frac{f^{a-1}(1-f)^{b-1}}{\int_0^1 f^{a-1}(1-f)^{b-1}\,df} \qquad (0 < f < 1)$$

where a and b can be determined explicitly from the values of $\tilde{f}$ and $\widetilde{f''^2}$. (see Refs. 164-166). With the measurements of Kent and Bilger[167], a comparison of calculations using density-weighted averaged equations was performed by Jones[168]. The general result is that the double δ-function PDF is unsatisfactory and that there is little to choose between the 'clipped' Gaussian and β-PDFs. Major species and temperature are relatively insensitive to precise shape of PDF provided it is continuous with pre-determined mean and variance.

Premixed Flames. In contrast to diffusion flames, premixed turbulent flames *require* the evaluation of mean reaction rates. In terms of the three-component mixture undergoing a simple-one step reaction, partial differential equations are set up for m_{fu}, f [$= m_{ox} - sm_{fu}$] and h, with the first of these for mass fraction of fuel requiring the specification of its source R_{fu}, the mean formation rate of fuel. In Section 2.5 and earlier the Arrhenius expression was introduced, but clearly its mean (time-averaged) value should not be calculated merely from mean values of components (like mass fractions, pressure and temperature) in its expression. In practice, experimental results for premixed turbulent flames are only weakly dependent on mass fractions, pressure and temperature. This fact led to the turbulence dominated mean reaction expression called the eddy-breakup reaction model[5,63-70], also described earlier. It is based on the idea that the mean reaction rate is determined solely by the rate of scale reduction via a process of turbulence vortex stretching. The model, thus takes no explicit account of chemical kinetics and relates to combustion which is entirely mixing controlled. In this situation it has been shown to be in good accord with the available evidence for premixed flames. The model has also been used occasionally for nonpremixed flames, but it is generally inappropriate in this situation. Several practical prediction procedures simply take the minimum value from between the time-averaged Arrhenius expression (with certain pre-exponential and activation energy constants) and eddy-breakup expression.

A more logical basis for expressions of the eddy-breakup type is provided by the Bray-Moss model[169,170] for premixed flames. For reaction via a single global step and adiabatic flow a single reaction progress variable, defined as the ratio of product mass fraction to its fully burnt value, is introduced and is sufficient to determine the (instantaneous) composition, temperature and density of the mixture. The probability density function for the reaction progress variable, r, is then assumed to have the form

$$P(r, x_j) = \alpha(x_j)\,\delta(r) + \beta(x_j)\,\delta(1-r) + [H(r) - H(r-1)]\,\gamma(x_j)\,F(r, x_j)$$

In the limit of large Damkohler and Reynolds numbers, that is $\gamma \gg 1$, the mean product formation rate is deduced to be like the previous eddy-breakup expression with $g^{1/2}$ replaced by $\tilde{r}\,(1-\tilde{r})$ and whose initial constant is dependent on the continuous part F ( ) of the PDF. This expression may be compared with the earlier eddy-breakup expression. The burning mode part of the PDF, F( ), can be determined from a laminar flamelet description though steady results are found to be relatively insensitive to the shape chosen[170]. The model has also been extended to cover more complex reaction mechanisms though the assumption invoked here is that the reaction steps proceed sequentially. A laminar flamelet description has also been used in conjunction with the Bray-Moss model by Libby and Bray[171] to construct models for turbulent transport and scalar dissipation.

Premixed and Diffusion Flames. A desirable development is the availability of general methods for both premixed and diffusion flames in which finite rate reactions (both fast and slow) occur. A simple approach is the moment closure method of Borghi[172], in which the mean reaction rate is obtained by decomposing the temperature, density and mass fractions appearing therein into mean and fluctuating components, expanding the term via a Taylor series expansion and then averaging. The resulting infinite series involving moments of all orders is then truncated through the neglect of moments higher than second order. This neglect is, however, generally inappropriate for most flame reactions, and, on the other hand, retention of these terms renders the approach intractable. Another approach is to presume a form for the joint probability density function for the appropriate number of scalars in terms of their means and covariances. The values of these latter quantities then have to be obtained from solution of transport equations for which closure assumptions are required. Donaldson[137] developed a 'typical eddy' model as an attempt to construct a joint PDF from Dirac delta functions at fixed locations in composition space. There exists some arbitrations in specifying the locations of the delta functions and it is likely that this will be reflected in predictions: mean reaction rates are likely to be sensitive to the precise 'typical eddy' treatment, particularly where the chemistry is fast. One complex method of overcoming this is the construction of joint PDFs from continuous functions: Jones[168] suggests the use of exponential functions, for example, but the presumed shape joint PDF formalism suffers from the disadvantage that the number of moment equations increases very rapidly with the number of independent species present, and the approach is thus only practicable for simple kinetic schemes involving only a small number (up to three) of independent scalars. Alternatively, rather than specify or construct a PDF, a potentially more powerful technique is to obtain the joint PDF from its transport equation. Jones and Whitelaw[160] give a good overview of the possibilities of this.

Summary

Turbulent premixed chemically reacting multicomponent mixtures are governed by PDEs for ρ-u-v-w-k-ϵ-h-m_{fu}-f as illustrated in Section 2.1, together with the application of several algebraic equations. With the more realistic simulation of radiative heat transfer, two-step chemistry and the evaporation and combustion of a fuel droplet spray, further PDEs need to be solved. Table 2.9 gives a summary of a typical set of many such equations[24].

2.7 ALTERNATIVE FUELS

The fuel characteristics of significant importance for the design of a combustor are fuel C/H ratio, viscosity, nitrogen and sulfur content, ignition and thermal stability. High fuel-bound nitrogen, high C/H atomic ratio and high aromatic content in alternative fuels lead to the problems of high NO_x emission levels, increased rates of soot and carbon particle formation, and poor ignition and stability limits. Low volatility and high viscosity affect droplet life times and atomization (size distribution) respectively. Volatility affects the rate at which the fuel can vaporize and, hence, the droplet life time. Carbon particle formation is aided by the formation and maintenance of fuel rich pockets in the hot combustion zone[138-140]. The desired formation of a finely dispersed spray of fine droplets is adversely affected by viscosity. Consequently, the reduced time for gas phase combustion reactions and prolonging of fuel-rich pockets experienced with low volatility can also occur with increased viscosity. Ignition, stability, emissions, and smoke problems also increase for higher viscosity fuels.

Many studies of soot formation have been carried out, but very few lead to quantitative predictions of soot production, and there is little agreement as to the details of the mechanism. Nevertheless, there seems to be general agreement that the overall soot formation reaction is triggered by hydrocarbon pyrolysis and involves subsequent soot nuclei formation, soot particle formation, and particle growth and coagulation. A model that treats these in some details has been considered in reference 123. Applications of the model to a methane flame has led to qualitative agreement with experimental observations. Although this approach represents an attempt to deal with the problem at a mechanistic level, the uncertainty of intermediate species, reactions and rates requires long-term development to provide quantitative predictions. Tesner, *et al.*[124] have proposed a model in which soot formation is characterized by three rate equations. The feature of the model is that all the complex elementary steps associated with pyrolysis, nuclei formation and soot formation are grouped into three subglobal steps which are characterized by three

TABLE 2.9
Summary of Equations Solved

Equation	ϕ	β	Γ	S_ϕ
Continuity	1	ρ	0	0
x-momentum	u	ρ	μ	$-\frac{\partial p}{\partial x} + \frac{\partial}{\partial x}(\mu \frac{\partial u}{\partial x}) + \frac{1}{r}\frac{\partial}{\partial r}(r\mu \frac{\partial v}{\partial x}) + \frac{\partial}{r\partial\theta}(\mu \frac{\partial w}{\partial x})$
r-momentum	v	ρ	μ	$-\frac{\partial p}{\partial r} + \frac{\partial}{\partial x}(\mu \frac{\partial u}{\partial r}) + \frac{1}{r}\frac{\partial}{\partial r}(r\mu \frac{\partial v}{r}) + \frac{1}{r}\frac{\partial}{\partial\theta}\left[\mu \frac{\partial w}{r} - \frac{w}{r}\right] + \frac{\rho w^2}{r} - \frac{2\mu}{r}(\frac{\partial w}{r\partial\theta} + \frac{v}{r})$
θ-momentum	w	ρ	μ	$-\frac{\partial p}{r\partial\theta} + \frac{\partial}{\partial x}(\frac{\mu}{r}\frac{\partial u}{\partial\theta}) + \frac{1}{r}\frac{\partial}{\partial r}\left[\mu r(\frac{1}{r}\frac{\partial v}{\partial\theta} - \frac{w}{r})\right] - \frac{\rho w}{r} + \frac{\partial}{r\partial\theta}\left[\frac{\mu}{r}(\frac{\partial w}{\partial\theta} + 2v)\right] + \frac{\mu}{r}(\frac{\partial w}{\partial r} + \frac{\partial v}{r\partial\theta} - \frac{w}{r})$
Turbulence energy	k	ρ	$\frac{\mu_{eff}}{\delta_{k,eff}}$	$G_K - C_D\,\rho\epsilon$
Energy dissipation rate	ϵ	ρ	$\frac{\mu_{eff}}{\sigma_{\epsilon,eff}}$	$(C_1 G_K - C_2\,\rho\epsilon)\,\epsilon/k$
Fuel Mass fraction	m_{fu}	ρ	$\frac{\mu_{eff}}{\sigma_{fu,eff}}$	R_{fu} depends on the case considered.
Composite mass fraction	f	ρ	$\frac{\mu_{eff}}{\sigma_{f,eff}}$	0
Stagnation enthalpy	$\tilde{h}$	ρ	$\frac{\mu_{eff}}{\sigma_{h,eff}}$	1) 0, if no radiation; 2) $2a(R^x + R^y + R^z - 3E)$ if radiation is included

separate equations. The model includes a first order (with respect to hydrocarbon concentration) pyrolysis rate, a chain branching and chain termination rate, and a soot formation rate:

$$\text{Pyrolysis:} \quad N_o = 10^{13} N_o e^{-170{,}000/RT} \tag{R1}$$

$$\text{Nuclei Formation} \quad \frac{dn}{dt} = N_o + (f-g)\,n - g_o Nn \tag{R2}$$

$$\text{Soot Formation} \quad \frac{dN}{dt} = (a - bN)\,n \tag{R3}$$

Values of the kinetic parameters (f, g, g_o, a, b) for acetylene and toluene are available, so that the model can be evaluated through comparison with experimental data. Greeves, *et al.*[125] developed a model using diesel engine data obtained under high pressures. The model consists of a single global Arrhenius type equation:

$$\frac{dS}{dt} = 4.68 \times 10^5 \; p_{HC} \; \phi^3 \; e^{-40{,}000/RT} \qquad \text{(R4)}$$

where p_{HC} and ϕ are the local partial pressure of the unburnt hydrocarbon and the local equivalence ratio, respectively. This type of one-step model lumps all intermediate reactions associated with nuclei formation and soot formation into one rate equation, and the application of the model requires knowledge of the local hydrocarbon concentration and the unburnt equivalence ratio.

The Greeves and Tesner models represent the essential state-of-the-art of practical soot prediction methods. Nevertheless, the process requires information on certain intermediates that must be assumed in order to implement these models in a strictly predictive mode. This information includes, for example, the local hydrocarbon and oxygen concentrations as well as the temperature. In addition, net soot generation requires not only consideration of soot formation but its oxidation as well. These factors are included in the following quasiglobal model[122].

The essential feature of the quasiglobal concept is the coupling of a set of subglobal steps to a set of detailed steps for those reaction chains for which sufficient information to describe their kinetics and mechanisms accurately exists. The basic quasiglobal model is described in reference 126. In addition to having demonstrated the ability of the quasiglobal model to predict experimental observations it has been shown to be ideally structured to account for the variation in fuel type; that is, aliphatic vs. cyclic, etc. Of particular interest here is the current work on fuel-rich systems for which this basic model is being extended. The model of Edelman *et al.*[122] includes the following additional subglobal finite rate reaction steps:

Pyrolysis: $C_nH_mBN + M \rightarrow C_xH_y + M + BN$ ($M \equiv$ third body) (R5)

Partial Oxidation: $C_nH_m + O_2 \rightarrow CO + H_2$ (R6)

$C_xH_y + O_2 \rightarrow CO + H_2$ (R7)

Soot Formation: $C_nH_m \rightarrow C_{(s)} + H_2$ (R8)

$C_xH_y \rightarrow C_{(s)} + H_2$ (R9)

Soot oxidation: $C_{(s)} + O_2 \rightarrow CO + CO_2$ (R10)

where BN represents the bound nitrogen. Reactions 5-10 are coupled to detailed mechanisms describing the rate at which H_2, CO and BN are converted to H_2O, CO_2, and NO_x. The rate constants for the subglobal steps are expressed in modified Arrhenius form and the rate of production (or consumption) is given by expression of the type:

$$C_1 = A\,T^a\,C_1^b\,\exp(-E/RT) \qquad \text{(R11)}$$

where the constants A, a, b, c, and E are determined through controlled experiments.

The reactions and rates associated with the detailed steps are based upon the available information.

The quasiglobal model, described in reference 122, is for high energy fuels, such as shelldyne-H and H-methylcyclopentadiene, as well as for conventional fuels such as propane and JP-types. The versatility of this approach has been demonstrated by comparisons with experimentally determined combustion characteristics including ignition delay times for both long chain and cyclic type hydrocarbons reacting in air.

For the prediction of net soot generation, additional information related to reactions R8, R9, and R10 is required. The soot model is constructed in terms of two steps reflecting the dependence of net soot generation on the simultaneous formation and oxidation of soot particles. The soot formation rate is assumed to be a function of the hydrocarbon concentration, the oxygen concentration and the temperature, namely:

$$\dot{R}^{+}_{c(s)} = A\,T^{a}\,C^{b}_{HC}\,C_{O_2}^{-\alpha}\,e^{-E/RT} \qquad \text{(R12)}$$

where A, B, α and E are constants. The oxidation step is based upon data involving the consumption of soot (and carbon) particles in oxidizing environments.

Lee, *et al.*[127] model the rate of consumption per unit surface area according to:

$$\dot{R}^{-}_{c(s)} = 1.085 \times 10^{4}\,\frac{p_{O_2}}{T^{1/2}}\,\exp\frac{(-39{,}300)}{RT} \qquad \text{(R13)}$$

where p_{O_2} is the partial pressure of oxygen in the mixture. Reactions R12 and R13 are combined to yield the net rate of soot production as a function of hydrocarbon and oxygen concentrations and temperature. The constants A, a, b, α, and E have been determined from experimental data, and it is interesting to note that net soot production is more strongly dependent upon the hydrocarbon concentrations than on the temperature.

The values of these parameters can be taken as:

$$A = 5.0 \times 10^{13} \qquad \alpha = 0.5$$

$$a = -2 \qquad E = 32{,}000 \text{ cal./mole.}$$

$$b = 1.75$$

The equations (R12) and **(R13)** can be combined to give net soot production from a perfectly stirred reactor according to[122]:

$$s = \frac{A\,T^{a}\,|HC|^{b}\,|O_2|^{-\alpha}\,e^{-E/RT}}{\dfrac{\dot{m}}{\rho V} + \dfrac{6}{\rho_s d}\cdot\dfrac{1.085 \times 10^{4}\,P_{O_{2e}}\;{-39{,}300/RT}}{T^{1/2}}} \left(\frac{gm}{cm^{3}}\right) \qquad \text{(R14)}$$

where $|HC|$ and $|O_2$ are the molar concentrations of the hydrocarbon and molecular oxygen, ρ is the mixture density, ρ_s is the soot density, m is input flow rate, V is the reactor volume and d is the soot particle diameter.

The effect of flame radiation to the combustor walls, in particular gas turbine combustor liners, can be considered due to luminous and nonluminous radiation. The nonluminous infrared emission is due to CO_2 and water band radiation, whereas the luminous component is due to radiation from carbon particles from within the flame. The nonluminous contribution of the flame emissivity can be calculated from[128]:

$$\epsilon_{nl} = 1 - \exp\left[-2.86 \times 10^2 p\ (\phi_m \ell)^{1/2}\ T_f - 1.5\right]$$

where

p = combustor pressure, KN/m^2

ϕ_m = fuel-air mass ratio

ℓ = radiation path length, m

T_f = flame temperature, K

A simplified heat-transfer analysis of the combustor linear temperature data can yield a relationship between particulate concentration in the primary zone (which increases the luminous portion of radiation) and the fuel hydrogen content as:

$$p_c/(p_c)_o = 1 + c_1\ (\Delta H)^n$$

where:

p_c = particulate concentration

$(p_c)_o$ = reference particulate concentration

c_1 = constant

ΔH = hydrogen content with respect to some reference fuel

n = 0, 1, 2, etc.

Increases in luminous emissivity resulting from the use of a low H/C ratio fuel can have substantial effect upon heat transfer.

In order to have good ignition and flame-stabilization, recirculation of the burned gases, to provide a continuous source of ignition to the fresh reactants it is necessary (for example, by using swirl). The homogeneous induction kinetics of the fuel are also important, but these are rather poorly understood by alternative fuels, which are blends of many compounds. The ignition delay time for long chain hydrocarbons can be estimated from the following rate equation derived from experimental plug flow reaction data[128]:

$$\frac{d\,(C_nH_m)}{dt} = -\frac{5.52 \times 10^8}{p^{0.825}}\ T\,(C_nH_m)^{1/2}\ (O_2)\ e^{-12,200/T}$$

where parenthesis denote concentration (mole/cc) and p the pressure (atm).

The effect of fuel properties upon droplet particle size (SMD), droplet life time, etc. can be calculated by some empirical or semi-empirical relationships given in reference[129]

In order to develop strategies for controlling emission of NO_x by combustion process modification from alternative fuels, it is necessary to understand the rate of evolution of organically bound nitrogen from the fuel (which is strongly dependent upon temperature). The optimum strategy for secondary air addition in a staged combustor is to delay completion of the air addition until most of the bound nitrogen has been evolved and converted to molecular nitrogen. Fuel nitrogen conversion to NO_x, also depends upon mixing and heat transfer.

There is a lack of understanding of the processes of multicomponent vaporization, gas and liquid phase pyrolysis and oxidation which play important roles in the conversion of organically bound nitrogen to NO_x. When a droplet of fuel oil is introduced into a hot oxygen deficient environment, the droplet will heat up until its surface attains the initial boiling point of the fuel. Internally, to a lesser or greater extent, depending upon the droplet size, a thermal gradient will be established. At the droplet surface, the more volatile compounds are evolved. This causes several effects. In the gas phase the radial convective flux thickens the boundary layer surrounding the droplet which causes reduced rates of heat transfer, and a reduction in drag experienced by the droplet. As the droplets start to vaporize, the temperature profile in the boundary layer adjusts to provide the enthalpy flux to the surface needed for vaporization. A transient persists through the vaporization of a multicomponent fuel, since the surface temperature is always rising with the changing surface composition. In the liquid phase, the loss of light (more volatile) species from the surface causes a concentration profile to be established for each compound. The lighter compounds, being deficient at the surface, diffuse to the surface and the heavier compounds, being concentrated at the surface, diffuse to the center of the droplet. The combined effects of vaporization and diffusion determine the surface composition and thereby the surface temperature. This combination of temperature and composition determines the relative volatilities of the species present at the surface, and hence the vapor phase composition. Nevertheless, the process, although linear in composition, is highly non-linear in temperature. The net result of the vaporization is a reduction in drop size, and it is the rate at which this takes place, relative to the rate of diffusion coupled with the changing relative volatilities, that controls the behavior of the droplet[121].

In an oxidizing atmosphere, the volatiles will interdiffuse with oxygen, and eventually ignite. Heat transfer from the flame front to the particle will augment the vaporization rate and, under extreme conditions, heat the liquid to temperatures at which cracking and polymerization reactions become significant, and char may be formed.

Due to the non linearity of the processes involved, the behavior of a vaporizing-burning fuel droplet is strongly influenced by the initial conditions of drop size and ambient temperature as well as fuel composition.

Certain kinds of fuels swell upon rapid heating (for example, raw Paraho Shale Oil), and under such conditions most of the alternative fuel chemical composition depart from that found under equilibrium distillation, which suggests that these processes have a profound influence on the distribution of nitrogen compounds during combustion of residual oils[121].

2.8 POLLUTANT PREDICTION

General Ideas

An appropriate level of complexity of the simulation must be chosen, with judicious matching of physical detail and mathematical tractability, the combustion designer is tempted to fall back on past experience and obtain improvements in efficiency and intensity by redesign of existing systems and scale-up of laboratory experiments, but in order to meet recent goals on pollutant control, involving reducing species (hydrocarbons and carbon monoxide) and oxidizing species (nitrogen oxides), a better understanding of the combustion process is required.

A common feature of many models is the prediction of trends; that is, the prediction of the relative change of some performance parameter caused by a relative change in some operating parameter. Basic chemical mechanisms are concentrated upon, so that models recommended for pressure and temperature conditions in some device may be completely inadequate when applied to a different device. A basic practice in the formation of a model is the identification of the critical rate-limiting steps, which must be modeled very carefully: effects of processes that are very fast compared with these rate-limiting steps can be estimated from equilibrium considerations (mechanical, thermal, or chemical); effects of processes that are too slow to have a significant effect can be ignored.

It is in this spirit that simplifications to chemical-kinetics, and simple flow models for application, have evolved. Excellent reviews are available[20], with emphasis on pollution modeling (Caretto, Bowman), mixing theories (Pratt), spark-ignition internal combustion (IC) engines (Heywood), diesel engines (Henein), furnaces (Godridge and Read), and gas turbines (Mellor, Jones). It may be noted that the most common simplified models of mixing processes in common use are as follows[21]: 1) piston- and combustion-induced compression and expansion in piston engines, 2) perfectly stirred reactor (PSR) analysis for recirculation regions of combustor and 3) plug flow analysis for furnaces and dilution zones of gas turbine combustors.

The Choice

At the present time, most of the models employ methane as the fuel, since the kinetics of methane oxidation are relatively well understood. For other hydrocarbons, the breakdown is assumed to be infinitely fast, followed by the combustion of carbon monoxide and hydrogen, as described by their relevant kinetics[130]. Table 2.10 gives a typical system of reactions[131] involving the quasi-global reaction step [*see* Section 2.6]. The model is supposed to be applicable to any hydrocarbon/air reaction. One restriction is that the kinetics used to estimate the nitric oxide imply that there is a temperature limitation of not less than 2000°K in the combustion region; (that is, a high combustion efficiency in the primary zone). All the rate constants are expressed in the modified Arrhenius form:

$$k_i = A_i T^{\delta i} \exp\,(-E_i RT) \tag{2.59}$$

The above kinetic system was used in conjunction with a model of flow conditions within the combustor. This model consisted of a two-reactor primary zone with fuel admittance to each part, followed by a secondary combustion zone modeled as a sequence of perfectly stirred reactors of finite and equal volume. The computations were carried out on a CDC 6500 machine. Trend directions correspond to those anticipated for the combustor modeled.

TABLE 2.10
Reaction Mechanisms Used by Hammond and Mellor[131] to Model a Gas Turbine Combustion Chamber

Reaction*	A_i	δ_i	E_i	
$C_aH_b + (a/2 + b/4)\,O_2 \rightleftharpoons aCO + b/2H_2O$	Assumed infinitely fast forward			
$CO + OH \rightleftharpoons CO_2 + H$	5.600X10^{11}	0	1 080	Forward
	1.455X10^{18}	−1.19	27 047	Reverse
$O_2 + H_2 \rightleftharpoons OH + OH$	8.000X10^{14}	0	45 000	Forward
	1.071X10^{12}	0.39	25 751	Reverse
$OH + H_2 \rightleftharpoons H_2O + H$	2.190X10^{13}	0	5 150	Forward
	4.858X10^{14}	−0.20	20 727	Reverse
$O_2 + H \rightleftharpoons OH + O$	2.240X10^{14}	0	16 800	Forward
	6.647X10^{11}	0.39	−469	Reverse
$O + H_2 \rightleftharpoons OH + H$	1.740X10^{13}	0	19 450	Forward
	7.737X10^{12}	0	7 467	Reverse
$O + H_2O \rightleftharpoons OH + OH$	5.750X10^{13}	0	18 000	Forward
	1.169X10^{12}	0.2	444	Reverse
$H + H + M \rightleftharpoons H_2 + M$	5.000X10^{18}	0	0	Forward
	1.662X10^{19}	−1.14	103 988	Reverse
$O + O + M \rightleftharpoons O_2 + M$	4.700X10^{15}	0	0	Forward
	2.375X10^{18}	0.66	119 279	Reverse
$O + H + M \rightleftharpoons OH + M$	5.300X10^{15}	0	−2 780	Forward
	8.477X10^{15}	0	99 246	Reverse
$H + OH + M \rightleftharpoons H_2O + M$	1.170X10^{17}	0	0	Forward
	8.629X10^{18}	−0.19	119 565	Reverse
$N + O_2 \rightleftharpoons NO + O$	6.430X10^{9}	1.00	6 250	Forward
	3.661X10^{8}	1.16	37 847	Reverse
$N_2 + O \rightleftharpoons NO + N$	6.192X10^{13}	0.10	75 241	Forward
	3.100X10^{13}	0	334	Reverse
$N + O + M \rightleftharpoons NO + M$	6.450X10^{14}	−0.50	0	Forward
	1.856X10^{16}	−0.72	150 876	Reverse

*Units, g mol, cm^3, K, cal.

There is still uncertainty about the number of representative reactions to include in reactor models, as inspection of Table 2.11 reveals[130]. Some of these multi-step kinetic systems are not representative of the real conditions within the combustor, although most of them show sensible agreement at the exhaust plane. Most models exhibit large errors of prediction when applied to other experimental environments. Such errors may be due to one or more of the following: (a) inadequate modeling; (b) a change in kinetic route; (c) a change in mixing characteristics; (d) a change in droplet evaporation characteristics.

With this insensitivity to reaction rate, possibly it might be better to concentrate more on the mixing problem, using simple kinetics. To the engineer, a model's use depends on its predictive accuracy and not necessarily on its portrayal of the true detailed physics, and among the choices, the simpler the model the better.

TABLE 2.11

Some Multi-Step Kinetic Systems[130]

Ref.	Fuel/oxidant	ϕ	P atm	T°K	t ms	Number of reactions
131	H_2/air	0.2–3	2.2	2150–2800	0–10	10
132	H_2/O_2	Lean to rich	N.A.	N.A.	N.A.	12
133	$H_2/CO/O_2/N_2$	0.33–1.33	1.0	750–3000	0.1–100	22
134	CH_4/air	0.8–1.2	0.25–1.0	1500–2080	1–10	24
135	CH_4/air	0.8–1.0	1.15	Inlet T = 700	0.2–2000	10
136	CH_4/air	0.8–1.25	1–10	1000–3079	10^{-4}–10	12 and 15
137	CH_4/O_2	0.2–5.0	1.5–4.0	1350–1900	0–1.0	7
138	CH_4/Ar	–	N.A.	2000–2600	10^{-3}–0.05	6
	CH_4/O_2/Ar	0.5–12				7
139	JP5/air	Overall engine 0.004–0.02	N.A.	600–2400	N.A.	21
140	JP5/air	1.0–1.5	2 to 20	Inlet T = 400	0.6–6.0	19
141	Gasoline/air	0.8–1.2	N.A.	2000–2700	N.A.	20
142	Hydrocarbon/air	N.A.	N.A.	800–2500	N.A.	15
143	C_3H_8/air	0.15–1.3	1–10	1200–2750	0–14	12

Hydrogen/Oxygen Combustion System

In the integration of chemically reacting flows, the species, and energy equations present stability difficulties in their numerical solutions because of their coupling with the kinetic source terms. Such equations are termed stiff. Two methods for handling these equations for multidimensional flow problems are examined and applied to an H_2O_2 reaction in a two-dimensional flow, in a recent paper[145]. The two techniques are relaxation and quasi-linearization of the species production rates [*see* Chapter 3 for solution technique discussion]. The latter method, based on Moretti's work[146], was found to be superior to the relaxation approach. This conclusion was reached on the basis of a stream function-vorticity approach to the fluid dynamics, amalgamated with a hydrogen/oxygen H_2O_2 flame. For this reaction, six different species will be involved: H, O, H_2O, OH, O_2, and H_2 (these species will be referred respectively, as 1, 2, 3, 4, 5, 6). Based upon Pergament's work[147] eight reaction mechanisms will be assumed

1) $H + O_2 = OH + O$

2) $O + H_2 = OH + H$

3) $H_2 + OH = H + H_2O$

4) $2OH = O + H_2O$

5) $H_2 + X = 2H + X$

6) $H_2O + X = OH + H + X$

7) $OH + X = O + H + X$

8) $O_2 + X = 2O + X$

where X is a catalyst.

Global Hydrocarbon Combustion System

Kennedy and Scaccia[148] extended their work to a global hydrocarbon combustion system, where the complete kinetic model is a composite of two separate models for the basic reaction systems involved. These kinetic sub-models are: (1) the C-H-O system which controls the energy release and the concentrations of carbon monoxide and unburnt hydrocarbons; and (2) the N-O system which controls the nitric oxide concentrations. Their approach is to use the quasi-global reaction technique[142], which accounts for partial oxidation of the hydrocarbon, and the remaining kinetic processes are assumed to follow the CO oxidation mechanisms. These latter mechanisms provide the kinetic link between the nitric oxide and the hydrocarbon combustion reactions through their influence on the concentration of hydroxyl radicals and monatomic species. The equation

$$C_nH_m + \left(\frac{1}{2}n + \frac{1}{4}a_1\right) O_2 = \left(\frac{1}{2}n\right) CO + a_1 H_2O + \left(\frac{1}{2}m - a_1\right) H_2 \tag{2.60}$$

is used with appropriate finite rate, as recommended[142] to give good agreement for lean mixtures at high temperature and pressure.

The oxidation of carbon monoxide in mixtures containing hydrogen can be represented by the simple reaction

$$\begin{aligned} CO + OH &= CO_2 + H \\ CO + O_2 &= CO_2 + O \\ CO + O + M &= CO_2 + M \end{aligned} \tag{2.61}$$

along with the fast branching reactions

$$\begin{aligned} H + O_2 &= OH + O \\ O + H_2 &= OH + H \\ O + H_2O &= OH + OH \\ OH + H_2 &= H_2O + H \end{aligned} \tag{2.62}$$

and the thermolecular recombination reactions

$$H + O + M = OH + M$$

$$H + OH + M = H_2O + M \qquad (2.63)$$
$$H + H + M = H_2 + M$$
$$O + O + M = O_2 + M$$

Table 2.12 provides appropriate rate parameters. Notice that the first four reactions are so fast that they can be considered to be in a state of partial equilibrium. This assumption then offers a set of algebraic equations which are used to reduce the number of kinetic rate equations that must be integrated to obtain the overall composition of the system.

TABLE 2.12

Rate Parameters for Kinetic Model

$k_f = AT^b \exp(-E/RT)$ (cm^3/sec)

Reaction	A	b	E/R
Hydrogen Reactions			
$OH + H_2 = H_2O + H$	2.19×10^{13}	0	2590
$OH + OH = O + H_2O$	5.75×10^{12}	0	393
$O + H_2 = H + OH$	1.74×10^{13}	0	4750
$H + O_2 = O + OH$	2.24×10^{14}	0	8450
$O + H + M = OH + M$	1×10^{16}	0	0
$O + O + M = O_2 + M$	9.38×10^{14}	0	0
$H + H + M = H_2 + M$	5×10^{15}	0	0
$H + OH + M = H_2O + M$	1×10^{17}	0	0
Carbon Monoxide Reactions			
$CO + OH = H + CO_2$	5.6×10^{11}	0	543
$CO + O_2 = CO_2 + O$	3×10^{12}	0	25000
$CO + O + M = CO_2 + M$	1.8×10^{19}	-1	2000
Nitric Oxide Reactions			
$N + NO = N_2 + O$	2×10^{-11}	0	0
$N + O_2 = NO + O$	2×10^{-11}	0	7100
$N + OH = NO + H$	7×10^{-11}	0	0

Reverse reaction rate, k_r, is obtained from k_f and the equilibrium constant, K_c.

Zeldovich Nitric Oxide Formation Mechanism

Zeldovich proposed the following two kinetic reaction equations for nitric oxide NO formation in typical temperature-pressure ranges of interest:

$$O + N_2 = NO + N - 75.0 \text{ K cal} \qquad (2.64)$$
$$N + O_2 = NO + O + 31.8 \text{ K cal}$$

with the additionally important equation

$$N + OM = NO + M + 39.0 \text{ K cal} \tag{2.65}$$

The rate data are also given in Table 2.12.

Results of application of this chemistry model [Table 2.12] to a swirl flow in a furnace with methane/air coaxial inlets and backward and forward facing stops are presented in Ref. 142. The stream function-vorticity approach with upstream differencing and modified Gauss-Seidel iteration procedure was used, and parameter tests established the influence of the inlet conditions on the interior recirculation flow.

Caretto[20,21] discusses detailed pollutant formation modeling and its amalgamation with fluid dynamic calculations. He considers[21] the formation rate of nitric oxide to be[149]

$$\frac{d[NO]}{dt} \doteq 2\,[O] \cdot \left[\frac{k_{F1}\,[N_2] - k_{R1}\,k_{R2}\,[NO]^2/k_{F2}\,[O_2]}{1 + k_{F1}\,[NO]/(k_{F2}\,[O_2] + k_{F3}\,[OH])} \right] \tag{2.66}$$

where the only assumptions are that the nitrogen atom concentration has its steady-state value, and the $H+O_2 \rightleftharpoons OH+O$ reaction is equilibrated. Both these assumptions are generally satisfied in practical combustion systems. Here, the forward and backward rates labeled 1, 2 and 3 refer to the Zeldovich equations. Various simplifications are considered, the simplest being in the early stages of the reaction, where $[NO] \simeq O$ and oxygen dissociation is assumed to be in equilibrium with $[O] = K_o[O_2]^{1/2}$. Then the expression simplifies to:

$$\frac{d\,[NO]}{dt} = 2\,k_{F1}\,K_o\,[N_2]\,[O_2]^{1/2} \tag{2.67}$$

This equation can be used as an estimate for the formation of small amounts of nitric oxide.

As an example, a 3-D boundary layer laminar flow of carbon monoxide and air enters a square-sectioned duct[21]. The combustion is assumed to be an instantaneous reaction of fuel plus oxidizer to products. At a given node in the computational grid there is either fuel and products or oxidizer and products. This model is called the simple chemically reacting system. As the flow proceeds down the duct, the buoyant forces lift the flame above the centerline. This problem was initially solved to obtain the velocity, temperature, and mass fraction fields. Once this was done, a C-H-O model of NO formation was used to compute the NO concentrations down the duct. Predictions of mean concentration, averaged over each station cross-section, are discussed. As expected, the main formation takes place at the high-temperature, near-stoichiometric region about the flame front. The NO-concentration profiles at a cross section tend to even out, however, because of the rapid mixing in the cross-stream plane. This recirculation in the cross-stream plane is largely induced by the buoyancy of the flame.

This calculation is not intended as a highly accurate solution of the convective balance equations. Rather, it is offered in the spirit of the models presented. This computation simply shows that it is possible to obtain a more accurate representation of the fluid mechanics in the modeling of combustion processes. Very accurate solutions of the problem would require a much finer grid than the one used.

More Complex Kinetic Modeling

Edelman and Harsha[7] introduce a basic quasi-global scheme which has been applied to a variety of hydrocarbon combustion problems. It consists of a single 'sub-global' step coupled to the 'wet CO' mechanism, as given in Table 2.13. Note some observations. First, it is generally agreed that in hydrogen-bearing systems carbon monoxide is rapidly oxidized to CO_2 via the reaction

$$CO + OH = CO_2 + H$$

They have, however, included other reactions involving CO and oxygen for completeness including,

$$CO + O_2 = CO_2 + O$$

Table 2.13 Extended C-H-O Chemical Kinetic Reaction Mechanism

$k_f = A T^b \exp(-E/RT)$

Reaction	*A* Long chain	*A* Cyclic	Forward *b*	*ER* Long chain	*ER* Cyclic
1. $C_nH_m + \frac{n}{2} O_2 \rightarrow \frac{m}{2} H_2 + nCO$*	6.0×10^4	2.8×10^7	1	12.2×10^3	19.65×10^3
2. $CO + OH = H + CO_2$	5.6×10^{11}		0	0.543×10^3	
3. $CO + O_2 = CO_2 + O$	3×10^{12}		0	25.0×10^3	
4. $CO + O + M = CO_2 + M$	1.8×10^{19}		−1	2×10^3	
5. $H_2 + O_2 = OH + OH$	1.7×10^{13}		0	24.7×10^3	
6. $OH + H_2 = H_2O + H$	2.19×10^{13}		0	2.59×10^3	
7. $OH + OH = O + H_2O$	$5.75X10^{12}$		0	0.393×10^3	
8. $O + H_2 = H + OH$	1.74×10^{13}		0	4.75×10^3	
9. $H + O_2 = O + OH$	2.24×10^{14}		0	8.45×10^3	
10. $M + O + H = OH + M$	1×10^{16}		0	0	
11. $M + O + O = O_2 + M$	9.38×10^{14}		0	0	
12. $M + H + H = H_2 + M$	5×10^{15}		0	0	
13. $M + H + OH = H_2O + M$	1×10^{17}		0	0	
14. $O + N_2 = N + NO$	1.36×10^{14}		0	3.775×10^4	
15. $N_2 + O_2 = N + NO_2$	2.7×10^{14}		−1.0	6.06×10^4	
16. $N_2 + O_2 = NO + NO$	9.1×10^{24}		−2.5	6.46×10^4	
17. $NO + NO = N + NO_2$	1.0×10^{10}		0	4.43×10^4	
18. $NO + O = O_2 + N$	1.55×10^9		1.0	1.945×10^4	
19. $M + NO = O + N + M$	2.27×10^{17}		−0.5	7.49×10^4	
20. $M + NO_2 = O + NO + M$	1.1×10^{16}		0	3.30×10^4	
21. $M + NO_2 = O_2 + N + M$	6.0×10^{14}		−1.5	5.26×10^4	
22. $NO + O_2 = NO_2 + O$	1×10^{12}		0	2.29×10^4	
23. $N + OH = NO + H$	4×10^{13}		0	0	
24. $H + NO_2 = NO + OH$	3×10^{13}		0	0	
25. $CO_2 + N = CO + NO$	2×10^{11}		−½	4×10^3	
26. $CO + NO_2 = CO_2 + NO$	2×10^{11}		−½	2.5×10^3	

*$-(dC_{CnHm}/dt) = A T^b P^3 C_{CnHm}^{1/2} C_{O_2} \exp[-E/RT]$ [C] = g moles/cc, [T] = °K, [P] = atm [E] = k cal/mole. Reverse reaction rate, k_r is obtained from k_f and the equilibrium constant. K_e

and

$$CO + O + M = CO_2 + M$$

where M is the general third body. The latter two reactions are much slower than the first reaction, but their inclusion was necessary for basic studies performed on systems including the CO/air system reported in Ref. 150. In addition, a number of reactions involving NO_x are included. They represent a necessary extension of the basic Zeldovich mechanism to account for certain of the ambient long time NO-NO_2 conversion reactions which occur in the atmosphere, particularly when coupled with appropriate daylight photochemical mechanisms. These reactions have proved to be relatively unimportant in combustion processes.

There are, however, many other species that can play an important role in the hydrocarbon oxidation process, especially fuel rich cases, as discussed at length elsewhere[7]. Methane oxidation has proved to be a valuable testground, with typical alternative schemes given in Table 2.14 and 2.15. Clearly, since many pollutants are at trace concentrations, it is a perplexing task to simulate adequately their production and consumption. A basic understanding needs well-controlled laboratory experiments, and it must be noted that Ref. 150 details the first such experiments and theory for NO_x emissions from H_2/air and CO/air chemical reactions.

TABLE 2.14

CH_4/O/N System[151]

$$k_f = A T^b \exp(-E/RT)$$

Reaction	A	Forward B	E/R
1. $CH_4 + M = CH_3 + H + M$	2×10^{17}	0	44.5×10^3
2. $CH_4 + OH = CH_3 + H_2O$	2.8×10^{13}	0	2.5×10^3
3. $CH_4 + O = CH_3 + OH$	2×10^{13}	0	4.64×10^3
4. $CH_4 + H = CH_3 + H_2$	6.9×10^{13}	0	5.95×10^3
5. $CH_3 + O_2 = H_2O + CHO$	2×10^{10}	0	0
6. $CH_3 + O = CHO + H_2$	1×10^{14}	0	0
7. $CHO + OH = CO + H_2O$	1×10^{14}	0	0
8. $CHO + M = H + CO + M$	2×10^{12}	½	14.4×10^3
9. $O + N_2 = NO + N$	1.4×10^{14}	0	3.79×10^3
10. $N + O_2 = NO + O$	6.4×10^9	1	3.14×10^3
11. $N + OH = NO + H$	4×10^{13}	0	0

Extensions of the quasi-global concept have been proposed. For example, Caretto[153] extended the model to include fuel bound nitrogen by allowing some nitrogen-containing intermediate compounds to be a product of the initial subglobal fuel decomposition step.

TABLE 2.15

$CH_4/O/N$ System[152]

$k_f = AT^b \exp(-E/RT)$

Reaction	Forward A	b	E/R
1. $CH_4 + M = CH_3 + H + M$	2×10^{17}	0	44.5×10^3
2. $CH_4 + OH = CH_3 + H_2O$	3.5×10^{14}	0	4.5×10^3
3. $CH_4 + O = CH_3 + OH$	2×10^{13}	0	3.45×10^3
4. $CH_4 + H = CH_3 + H_2$	2×10^{14}	0	5.95×10^3
5. $CH_3 + O = HCHO + H$	1.9×10^{13}	0	0
6.* $CH_3 + O_2 = CHO + H_2O$	2×10^{10}	0	0
7. $CH_3 + O_2 = HCHO + OH$	1×10^{14}	0	0.75×10^3
8.* $CH_3 + O = CHO + H_2$	1×10^{14}	0	0
9. $HCHO + OH = CHO + H_2O$	3×10^{13}	0	0
10. $HCHO + H = CHO + H_2$	1.7×10^{13}	0	1.5×10^3
11. $HCHO + CH_3 = CHO + CH_4$	2.5×10^{10}	½	2.65×10^3
12. $HCHO + O = CHO + OH$	3×10^{13}	0	0
13. $HCHO + O_2 = CO_2 + H_2O$	7.3×10^{10}	½	0
14. $CHO + O_2 = CO_2 + OH$	7.4×10^{11}	½	0
15. $CHO + O = CO_2 + H$	5.4×10^{11}	½	0
16. $CHO + O = CO + OH$	5.4×10^{11}	½	0
17. $CHO + CH_3 = CH_4 + CO$	2.5×10^{11}	½	0
18. $CHO + OH = CO + H_2O$	3×10^{13}	0	0
19.* $HCO + M = H + CO + M$	2×10^{12}	½	14.4×10^3
Plus reactions in Table 2.13			

*These reactions are retained for purposes of comparing with the mechanisms of Table 2.12.

Caretto's results, although limited, indicate the feasibility of such an approach. The other alternative is to formulate the kinetics scheme in terms of all possible species and reactions that could appear during the oxidation of any particular fuel. This is the approach adopted by Engleman[154] in his study on the methane-air system. As many as thirty-nine species entering into over 1000 reactions are presented although this scheme was narrowed down to twenty-five species and 322 reactions. The reduction of the system is based largely on estimates for steric factors and activation energies.

Development and refinement of these concepts is an important task being undertaken[19], with typical intermediates including those shown in Table 2.16. Finally, a list of 55 reaction equations for the CHON system is given in Table 2.17 with appropriate reactions rates, which are discussed at length elsewhere[28].

TABLE 2.16

Potentially Important Species to be Considered in the Detailed Mechanism for the Oxidation of Hydrocarbons

Species No.	Species	Species No.	Species
1	H	20	C_2H_4
2	H_2	21	C_2H_2
3	O	22	C_2H
4	O_2	23	C_2H_5O
5	OH	24	C_2H_5OH
6	H_2O	25	CH_3CO
7	HO_2	26	CH_3CHO
8	H_2O_2	27	C_3H_3
9	CO	28	C_2H_7
10	CHO	29	C_3H_6
11	HCHO	30	C_2H_5CHO
12	CH_3	31	C_2H_5CO
13	CH_4	32	C_3H_4
14	CH	33	N_2
15	CH_3O	34	HCN
16	CH_3O	35	CN
17	CH_3OH	36	NO
18	C_2H_6	37	NO_2
19	C_2H_5	38	N

Recent developments in the acquisition and use of alternative fuels have their impact. The problem of modeling the kinetics of the oxidation process becomes more critical in terms of fuels derived from nonpetroleum sources. The problem(s) arise in connection with the economically attractive utilization of the low H/C hydrocarbon fuels more directly derivable from coal and oil shale. The production, utilization and combustion problems of such fuels have been discussed by Longwell[155]. Fuel-bound nitrogen and soot appear to be the principal concerns in the use of these fuels in conventional combustion equipment. Beyond the NO_x, and soot problems are questions relevant to the ignition, flame stabilization and combustion efficiency of low H/C fuels. Some of these questions have been addressed in the foregoing discussions with the exception of the soot problem. Soot formation and oxidation involve complex physico-chemical processes. Some of what is known and required to characterize these processes are discussed at length in Ref. 19.

TABLE 2.17

Chemical Reactions in the C/N/H/O System[28]

Reaction	Reaction Rate A	n	E	Ref.
1. $H + CO_2 = CO + OH$	5.6×10^{13}	0	23,500	106
2. $O + N_2 = NO + N$	1.44×10^{14}	0	75,580	107
3. $O + NO = N + O_2$	4.1×10^{9}	1	38,340	107
4. $N + OH = NO + H$	4.21×10^{13}	0	0	108
5. $OH + H_2 = H_2O + H$	2.2×10^{13}	0	5,150	106
6. $OH + OH = O + H_2O$	5.75×10^{12}	0	780	106
7. $O + H_3 = H + OH$	1.74×10^{13}	0	9,450	106
8. $H + O_2 = O + OH$	1.56×10^{14}	0	16,633	109
9. $O + H + M = OH + M$	3.6×10^{17}	−1	0	110
10. $O + O + M = O_2 + M$	3.6×10^{17}	−1	0	109
11. $H + H + M = H_2 + M$	1.81×10^{18}	−1	0	109
12. $H + OH + M = H_2O + M$	7.3×10^{18}	−1		109
13. $O + CO_2 = CO + O_2$	1.9×10^{13}	0	54,150	106
14. $CO + O + M = CO_2 + M$	6.0×10^{17}	−1	2,484	110
15. $N_2 + O_2 = N + NO_2$	2.7×10^{14}	−1	120,428	56
16. $N_2 + O_2 = NO + NO$	4.2×10^{14}	0	119,100	106
17. $NO + NO = N + NO_2$	3.0×10^{11}	0	0	106
18. $NO + M = O + NO + M$	2.27×10^{17}	−0.5	148,846	56
19. $O + NO + M = NO_2 + M$	1.05×10^{15}	0	−1,870	105
20. $N + O_2 + M = NO_2 + M$	7.0×10^{11}	−1		56
21. $O + NO_2 = NO + O_2$	1.0×10^{13}	0	600	106
22. $H + NO_2 = NO + OH$	7.25×10^{14}	0	1,930	*
23. $N + CO_2 = CO + NO$	2.0×10^{11}	−0.5	7,950	*
24. $CO + NO_2 = NO + CO_2$	2.0×10^{11}	−0.5	4,968	*
25. $H + N_2O = OH + N_2$	3.01×10^{13}	0	10,800	108
26. $O + N_2O = O_2 + N_2$	3.61×10^{13}	0	24,800	107
27. $N_2 + NO_2 = NO + N_2O$	1.41×10^{14}	0	83,000	107
28. $NO + HO_2 = OH + NO_2$	6.0×10^{11}	0	0	106
29. $O + N_2 + M = N_2O + M$	6.3×10^{14}	0	56,800	107
30. $H + O_2 + M = HO_2 + M$	1.5×10^{15}	0	−1,000	106
31. $H + HO_2 = OH + OH$	2.5×10^{14}	0	1,900	106
32. $OH + HO_2 = H_2O + O_2$	1.2×10^{13}	0	1,000	106
33. $O + HO_2 = OH + O_2$	5.0×10^{13}	0	1,000	106
34. $H + HO_2 = H_2 + O_2$	2.5×10^{13}	0	700	106
35. $H + HO_2 = O + H_2O$	1.0×10^{13}	0	1,000	106
36. $H_2 + HO_2 = H + H_2O_2$	1.9×10^{13}	0	24,000	106
37. $H_2O_2 + M = 2OH + M$	7.1×10^{14}	0	−5,100	106
38. $CH_4 + M \rightarrow CH_3 + H + M$	1.5×10^{19}	0	99,960	72
39. $CH_4 + H = CH_3 + H_2$	5.1×10^{13}	0	12,900	109
40. $CH_4 + OH = CH_3 + H_2O$	2.85×10^{13}	0	4,968	72

TABLE 2.15 (Continued)

Reaction	Reaction Rate A	n	E	Ref.
41. $CH_4 + O = CH_3 + OH$	1.7×10^{13}	0	8,700	72
42. $CH_3 + O_2 = HCO + H_2O$	1.0×10^{11}	0	0	72
43. $HCO + OH = CO + H_2O$	3.0×10^{13}	0	0	111
44. $H + CO + M = HCO + M$	1.0×10^{17}	1	0	111
45. $HO_2 + HO_2 = H_2O_2 + O_2$	6.5×10^{13}	0	0	106
46. $H_2O_2 + H = H_2O + OH$	3.18×10^{14}		9,000	106
47. $CH_2 + \frac{1}{2} O_2 \rightarrow CO + H_2^{+}$	$5.52 \times 10^{8}\ p^{-0.825}$	1	24,642	79
48. $H + NO + M = HNO + M$	4.8×10^{15}		0	112
49. $HNO + H + M = H_2NO + M$				
50. $HNO + HNO + M \rightarrow H_2O + N_2O + M$				
51. $R + NO + M \rightarrow RNO + M$				
52. $R + RNO + M \rightarrow R_2NO + M$				
53. $R + R_2NO + M \rightarrow R_2NOR + M$				
54. $H + HNO = H_2 + NO$	1.4×10^{11}	0.5		113
55. $H + HCO = H_2 + CO$	2.0×10^{13}	0	0	111

Reaction Rate Constant $k = AT^n \exp(-E/RT)$
Reverse Reaction Rate Constant Obtained from k and the Equilibrium Constant
*Recommended by R. B. Edelman
+Any C_nH_m hydrocarbon is given this rate, however, with n CO molecules and m/2 H_2 molecules produced at this rate.

References to Chapter 2

1. Spalding, D. B.: *Some Fundamentals of Combustion,* Butterworths, London, 1954.
2. Williams, F. A.: *Combustion Theory,* Addison-Wesley, New York, 1965.
3. Bird, R. B., Stewart, W. E. and Lightfoot, E. N.: *Transport Phenomena,* Wiley, New York, 1960.
4. Streeter, V. L. (Ed.): *Handbook of Fluid Dynamics,* McGraw-Hill, New York, 1961.
5. Spalding, D. B.: *Combustion and Mass Transfer,* Pergamon Press, London, 1979.
6. Beér, J. M. and Chigier, N. A.: *Combustion Aerodynamics,* Halsted-Wiley Int., New York, 1972.
7. Fletcher, R. S. (course organizer): *Gas Turbine Combustion,* Short course at Cranfield Inst. of Tech., Bedford, England, May 14-18, 1973. Revised and repeated annually.
8. Boni, A. A., Gelinas, R. J. and Ludwig, C. B.: National Combustion Applied Research and Development Plan, *SAI-75-637-LJ,* Science Applications Inc., La Jolla, California, August 1975, revised March 1976.
9. Syred, N. and Beér, J. M.: *Comb. and Flame,* **23**, 1974, p. 143.
10. Lilley, D. G.: *AIAA Journal,* **15**, 8, August 1977, p. 1063.
11. Lilley, D. G.: *J. of Energy,* **3**, 4, July-August, 1979, p. 193.
12. Lilley, D. G.: *AIAA Paper 80-1189,* Hartford, Connecticut, June 30-July 2, 1980.
13. Edelman, R. B., and Harsha, P. T.: Analytical Modeling of Sudden Explosion Burners, *CPIA Publication 287,* Chemical Propulsion Information Agency, the Johns Hopkins University, Laurel, Maryland, June 1977.
14. Oates, G. C.: The Aerothermodynamics of Aircraft Gas Turbine Engines. *AFAPL-TR-78-52,* 1978.

15. Chigier, N. A. (Ed.): Progress in Energy and Combustion Science, Pergamon Press, New York, 1976+.
16. Palmer, H. B., and Beér, J. M. (Eds.): *Combustion Technology: Some Modern Developments.* Academic Press, New York, 1974.
17. Afgan, N. H. and Beér, J. M. (Eds.): *Heat Transfer in Flames,* Scripta Book Company (Hemisphere-Wiley), Washington, D.C., 1974.
18. Caretto, L. S.: *Prog. in Energy and Comb. Sci.,* **1**, 1976, p. 47.
19. Edelman, R. B., and Harsha, P. T.: *Prog. in Energy and Comb. Sci.,* **4**, 1978, p. 1.
20. Beér, J. M.: *J. Inst. Fuel,* **45**, July 1972, p. 370.
21. Lilley, D. G.: *Acta Astro.,* **1**, 9, Sept. 1974, p. 1129. Also Lilley, D. G., *AIAA Paper No. 74-527,* Palo Alto, Ca., June 17-19, 1974.
22. Serag-Eldin, M. A., and Spalding, D. B.: Trans ASME, *J. of Eng. Power,* **101**, July 1979, p. 326.
23. Mongia, H. C., and Reynolds, R. S.: Combustor Design Criteria Validation, III – User's Manual, Report *USARTL-TR-78-55C,* US Army Res. & Tech. Lab., Fort Eustis, Virginia, February 1979 [see also **I** and **II**].
24. Swithenbank, J., Turan, A., and Felton, P. G.: Paper in *Gas Turbine Combustor Design Problems* [A. H. Lefebre, (Ed.)], Hemisphere – McGraw Hill, New York, 1980.
25. Spalding, D. B.: Numerical Computation of Practical Combustion Chamber Flows, Paper presented at AGARD Propulsion and Energetics Panel, Liege, Belgium, April 1-2, 1974. *AGARD-CP-164,* 1974.
26. Patankar, S. V., and Spalding, D. B.: Paper in *Heat Transfer and Flames* [Afgan, N. H., and Beér, J. M., (Eds.)], Scripta Book Company (Hemisphere-Wiley), Washington, D. C., 1974.
27. Lilley, D. G.: Theoretical Study of Turbulent Swirling Boundary Layer Flow with Combustion, Ph.D. Thesis, Sheffield University, England, 1970.
28. Launder, B. E. and Spalding, D. B.: *Mathematical Models of Turbulence,* Academic Press, London, 1972.
29. Murthy, S.N.B. (Ed.): *Turbulent Mixing in Nonreactive and Reactive Flow* (A Project SQUID Workshop), Plenum Press, New York, 1975.
30. Combustion Institute/Central States Section, Fluid Mechanics of Combustion Processes, Meeting held at NASA Lewis Research Center, Cleveland, Ohio, March 28-30, 1977.
31. ASME/Pennsylvania State University Symposium on Turbulent Shear Flows, held at University Park, Pennsylvania, April 18-20, 1977.
32. Syred, N., Beér, J. M., and Chigier, N. A.: Proc. of Salford Symp. on Int. Flows, Inst. of Mech. Engr., London, 1971, p. 739.
33. Pratte, B. D., and Keffer, J. R.: *J. of Basic Eng.,* **94**, Dec. 1972, p. 739.
34. Davies, T. W., and Snell, D. J.: Turbulent Flow Over a Two-Dimensional Step and its Dependence upon Upstream Flow Conditions, Ref. 31, p. 13.29.
35. Launder, B. E., Morse, A., Rodi, W., and Spalding, D. B.: The Prediction of Free Shear Flows – A Comparison of the Performance of Six Turbulence Models, Proc. of NASA Conf on Free Shear Flows, NASA Langley Research Center, Hampton, Virginia, 1972.
36. Lilley, D. G.: *AIAA Journal,* **11**, July 1973, p. 955.
37. Launder, B. E., and Spalding, D. B.: *Comp. Methods in Appl. Mech. and Eng.,* **3**, March 1974, p. 269.
38. Koosinlin, M. L., and Lockwood, F. C.: The Prediction of Axisymmetric Turbulent Swirling Boundary-Layers, *AIAA Journal.*
39. Lilley, D. G.: *Acta Astro.,* **3**, 1977, p. 919.
40. Peck, R. E., and Samuelsen, G. S.: *16th Symp. (Intl.) on Comb., The Comb. Inst.,* 1977, p. 1675.
41. Coakley, T. J., and Viegas, J. R.: Turbulence Modeling of Shock Separated Boundary-Layer Flows, Paper in Ref. 31, p. 13.19.
42. Tennankore, K.N., and Steward, F. R.: Comparison of Several Turbulence Models for Predicting Flow Patterns within Confined Jets, Paper in Ref. 31, p. 10.9.
43. Durst, F., and Rastogi, A. K.: Theoretical and Experimental Investigations of Turbulent Flows with Separation, Paper in Ref. 31, p. 18.1.
44. Harsha, P. T.: *Kinetic Energy Methods, in Handbook of Turbulence* [W. Frost and T. Moulden, (Eds.)], Plenum Press, 1977.
45. Harsha, P. T.: A General Analysis of Free Turbulent Mixing, TR-73-177, Arnold Engineering Development Center, 1974.
46. Harsha, P. T. and Edelman, R. B.: *AIAA Paper 78-944,* Las Vegas, Nevada, July 25-27, 1978.
47. Rodi, W.: Basic Equations for Turbulent Flow in Cartesian and Cylindrical Co-ordinates, *Rept. BL/TN/A36,* 1970. Dept. of Mech. Eng., Imperial College, London.

48. Hanjalic, K., and Launder, B. E.: A Reynolds Stress Model of Turbulence and its Application to Asymmetric Boundary Layers, *Rept. TM/TN/A/8,* 1971, Dept. of Mech. Eng., Imperial College, London.
49. Koosinlin, M. L.: Anisotropic Turbulence in Axisymmetric Swirling Boundary Layers, *Rept. TM/TN/A/13,* 1971, Dept. of Mech. Eng., Imperial College, London.
50. Lilley, D. G.: *AIAA Journal,* **14**, 6, June 1976, p. 749.
51. Novick, A. S., Miles, G. A., and Lilley, D. G.: *J. of Energy,* **3**, 2, March-April 1979, p. 95.
52. Khalil, E. E., Spalding, D. B., and Whitelaw, J. H.: *Intl. J. of Heat and Mass Transfer,* **18**, 1975, p. 775.
53. Patankar, S. V.: *Numerical Methods in Fluid Flow and Heat Transfer,* Hemisphere—McGraw Hill, New York, 1980.
54. Lilley, D. G.: *Numerical Solution of Turbulent Swirling Flows,* Proc IMA Conf on Comp Methods in Aeronautical Fluid Dynamics, Academic Press, London, 1976, p. 492.
55. Bradshaw, P.: Effects of Streamline Curvature on Turbulent Flow, *AGARD-AG0169,* August 1973.
56. Pratte, B. D., and Keffer, J. R.: *ASME J. of Basic Eng.,* **94**, Dec. 1972, p. 739.
57. Allan, R. A.: Ph.D. Thesis, Sheffield University, England, 1970.
58. Roshko, A.: *AIAA Journal,* **14**, 10, Oct. 1976, p. 1349.
59. Ferziger, J. H.: *AIAA Journal* **15**, 9, Sept. 1977, p. 1261.
60. Goodger, E. M.: *Combustion Calculations,* Macmillan Press, London, 1977.
61. Bracco, F. V. (Ed.): *Comb. Sci. and Tech.,* **13**, 1-6, 1976.
62. Kennedy, L. A. (Ed.): *Turbulent Combustion. Prog. in Astro. and Aero.,* **58**, AIAA, New York, 1978.
63. Mellor, A. M.: *17th Symp. (Intl.) on Comb.* The Comb. Inst., 1979, p. 377.
64. Spalding, D. B.: *17th Symp. (Intl.) on Comb.,* The Comb. Inst., 1979, p. 431.
65. Bray, K. N. C.: *17th Symp. (Intl.) on Comb.,* The Comb. Inst., 1979, p. 223.
66. Spalding, D. B.: Mathematical Models of Turbulent Flames: A Review, *Report No. HTS/75/1,* Dept. of Mech. Eng., IC, London, 1975. Also Ref. 61, 1976, p. 1.
67. Spalding, D. B.: A General Theory of Turbulent Combustion; The Lagrangian Aspects, *AIAA Paper No. 77-98,* Los Angeles, California, January 24-26, 1977.
68. Spalding, D. B.: The Eddy Break-Up Model Applied to Confined Turbulent Steady Flames, *AIAA Paper No. 77-98,* Los Angeles, California, January 24-26, 1977.
69. Spalding, D. B.: *16th Symp. (Intl.) on Comb.,* The Comb. Inst., 1977, p. 1657.
70. Spalding, D. B.: The Escimo Theory of Turbulent Combustion, *Rept. No. HTS/76/13,* Dept. of Mech. Eng., IC, London, 1976 (extension of 16th Symp. (Intl.) on Comb. paper).
71. Edelman, R. B. and Harsha, P. T.: Some Observations on Turbulent Mixing with Chemical Reactions, *AIAA Paper No. 77-142,* Los Angeles, California, January 24-26, 1977.
72. Gouldin, F. C.: *Comb. Sci. & Tech.,* **9**, 1974, p. 17.
73. Chigier, N. A. (Ed.): *Prog. in Energy and Comb. Sci.,* **1**, 1976.
74. Starkman, E. S., Mizutani, Y., Sawyer, R. F., and Teixeira, D. P.: *Trans ASME J. of Eng. for Power,* July 1971, p. 333.
75. Caretto, L. S.: *14th Symp. (Intl.) on Comb.,* The Comb. Inst., 1973, p. 661.
76. Osgerby, I. T.: *AIAA Journal,* **12**, 6, June 1974, p. 743.
77. Odgers, J.: Combustor Modelling within Gas Turbine Engines, *AIAA Paper No. 77-52,* Los Angeles, California, January 24-26, 1977.
78. Boccio, J. L., Weilerstein, G., and Edelman, R. B.: A Mathematical Model for Jet Engine Combustor Pollutant Emissions, *NASA-CR-121208,* March 1973, GASL Inc.
79. Rai, C., and Siegel, R. D. (Eds.): Air: II. Control of NO_x and SO_x Emissions, *AIChE Symposium Series* No. 148, **71, 1975**.
80. Altenkirch, R. A., and Mellor, A. M.: *16th Symp. (Intl.) on Comb.,* The Comb. Inst., 1977.
81. Cernansky, N. P.: Formation of NO and NO_2 in a Turbulent Propane/Air Diffusion Flame, *Rept. No. UCB-ME-74-5,* Dept. of Mech. Eng., University of California, Berkeley, November 1974.
82. Butler, T. D., and O'Rourke, P. J.: *16th Symp. (Intl.) on Comb.,* The Comb. Inst., 1977.
83. Magnussen, B. F., and Hjertager, B. H.: *16th Symp. (Intl.) on Comb.,* The Comb. Inst., 1977.
84. Quan, V., Bodeen, C. A., and Teixeira, D. P.: *Comb. Sci. & Tech.,* **7**, 1973, p. 65.
85. Pratt, D. T.: Calculation of Chemically Reacting Flows with Complex Chemistry, in *Studies in Convection* [Launder, B. E., (Ed.)], **2**, Pergamon Press, Oxford, 1976.
86. Wormeck, J. J., and Pratt, D. T.: *16th Symp. (Intl.) on Comb.,* The Comb. Inst., 1977.
87. Hindmarch, A. C.: GEAR: Ordinary Differential Equation System Solver, *Report No. UCID-30001* Rev 3, Lawrence Livermore Lab, University of California, December 1974.
88. Young, T. R., and Boris, J. R.: A Numerical Technique for Solving Stiff Ordinary Differential

Equations Associated with Reactive Flow Problems, *Memo Report No. 2611*, Naval Research Lab, Washington, D. C., July 1973.
89. Scaccia, C., and Kennedy, L. A.: *AIAA Journal,* **12**, 9, September 1974, p. 1268.
90. Boni, A. A., Chapman, M., Cook, J. L., and Schneyer, G. P.: *16th Symp. (Intl.) on Comb.,* The Comb. Inst., 1977.
91. Hottel, H. C., and Sarofim, A. F.: *Radiative Transfer,* McGraw-Hill, New York, 1967.
92. Hottel, H. C., and Cohen, E. S.: *AIChE Journal,* **4**, 3, 1958.
93. Hottel, H. C., and Sarofim, A. F.: *Int. J. of Heat and Mass Transfer,* 8, 1965, p. 1153.
94. Johnson, T. R., and Beér, J. M.: The Zone Method of Analysis of Radiant Heat Transfer: A Model for Luminous Radiation, 4th Symp. on Flames and Industry, Inst. Fuel, 1972.
95. Stewart, F. R., and Cannon, P.: *Int. J. of Heat and Mass Transfer,* **14**, 1971, p. 245.
96. Siddall, R. G.: Flux Methods for the Analysis of Radiant Heat Transfer, *4th Symp. on Flames and Industry,* 1972.
97. Beér, J. M.: *Heat Transfer in Flames,* [N. H. Afgan and J. M. Beér (Eds.)], Scripta Technica, 29, 1974.
98. Siddall, R. G., and Selçuk, N.: *Heat Transfer in Flames,* [N. H. Afgan and J. M. Beér (Eds.), Scripta Technica, 1974, p. 191.
99. Chen, J. C.: *AIChE Journal,* **10**, 1964, p. 253.
100. Gosman, A. D., and Lockwood, F. C.: *14th (Intl.) Symp. on Comb.,* 1973, p. 661.
101 Lockwood, F. C., and Shah, N. G.: An Improved Flux Model for the Calculation of Radiation Heat Transfer in Combustion Chambers. *ASME Paper No. 76-HT-55,* St. Louis, Missouri, August 9-11, 1976.
102. Abou Ellail, M. M. M., Gosman, A. D., Lockwood, F. C., and Megahed, I. E. A.: *Prog. in Astro. and Aero.,* **58**, AIAA, New York, 1978, p. 163.
103. Spalding, D. B.: Basic Equations of Fluid Dynamics, Heat and Mass Transfer, and Procedures for their Solution.
104. Harrje, D. T. (Ed.): Liquid Propellant Rocket Motor Combustion Stability, *NASA SP-194,* 1972.
105. Cornelius, W., and Agnew, W. G. (Eds.): *Emissions from Continuous Combustion Systems,* Plenum Press, New York, 1972.
106. Boccio, J. L., Weilerstein, G., and Edelman, R. B.: A Mathematical Model for Jet Engine Combustor Pollutant Emissions, *NASA CR1212083,* 1973.
107. Gibson, M. M., and Morgan, B. B.: *J. Inst. Fuel,* **43**, 1970, p. 517.
108. Lilley, D. G., and Wendt, J. O. L.: Modeling Pollutant Formation in Coal Combustion, in *Proc. 25 HTFM Inst.* [McKillop, A. A., Baughn, J. W., and Dwyer, H. A., (Eds.)], Stanford University Press, 1976, p. 196.
109. Vincent, M. W.: Ph.D. Thesis, University of Sheffield, 1973.
110. Crowe, C. T.: Conservation Equations for Vapor-Droplet Flows, in *Proc. 25th HTFM Inst.* (McKillop, A. A., Baughn, J. W., and Dwyer, H. A., Eds.), Stanford University Press, 1976, p. 214.
111. Crowe, C. T.: Vapour-Droplet Flow Equations, Lawrence Livermore Laboratory, *Report No. UCRL-51877,* 1977.
112. Williams, F. A.: *Combustion Theory,* Addison-Wesley, 1965.
113. Westbrook, C. K.: *16th Symp. (Intl.) on Comb.,* The Comb. Inst., 1977.
114. Crowe, C. T., and Pratt, D. T.: *Computers and Fluids,* **2**, 1974, p. 249.
115. Crowe, C. T., and Pratt, D. T.: Two-Dimensional Gas-Particle Flows, Proc. of the Heat Transfer and Fluid Mechanics Inst., 1972.
116. Boysan, F., and Swithenbank, J.: *17th Symp. (Intl.) on Comb.,* 1979, p. 443.
117. Elgobashi, S. E., Pratt, D. T., Spalding, D. B., and Srivatsa, S. K.: *3rd (Intl.) Symp. on Air Breathing Engines,* 1976.
118. Morr, A. R., and Heywood, J. B.: *Acta Astro.,* **1**, 1974, p. 949.
119. Zeldovich, Ya. B., Sadovnikoo, P. Ya., and Frank-Kamenetskii, D. A.: Oxidation of Nitrogen in Combustion, Academy of Sciences of USSR, Inst. of Chem. Phys., Moscow-Leningrad [Trans by M. Shelef], 1947.
120. Beretta, F., Cavaliere, A., Ciajolo, A., D'Alessio, A., DiLorenzo, A., Langella, C., and Noviello, C.: *18th Symp. (Intl.) on Comb.*, August, 1980.
121. Beér, J. M., Jacques, M. T., Hanson, S., Gupta, A. K., and Rovesti, W.: Control of NO_x and Particulates Emission from SRC-II Spray Flames, Paper Presented at the EPA/EPRI Symposium, Denver, Colorado, October 6-9, 1980.
122. Edelman, R., Turan, A., Harsha, P., and Wong, E.: Fundamental Characterization of Alternative Fuel Effects in Continuous Combustion Systems, Science Applications, Inc., Canoga Park, California.

123. Jenson, D. E.: *Proc. Roy. Soc., London,* A., 338, 1974, p. 375.
124. Tesner, P. A., Snegiriova, T. D., and Knorne, V. G.: *Comb. and Flame,* **17**, 1971, p. 253.
125. Khan, I. M. and Greeves, G.: *Heat Transfer for Flames,* [N. H. Afgan and J. M. Beér (Eds.)], Halstead Press, 1974, p. 389.
126. Edelman, R. and Harsha, P.: *Prog. Energy Comb. Sci.,* **4**, 1978, p. 1.
127. Lee, K. B., Thring, M. W., and Beér, J. M.: *Comb. and Flame,* **6**, 1962, p. 137.
128. Edelman, R. and Fortune, O. F.: A Quasiglobal Chemical Kinetic Model for the Finite Rate Combustion of Hydrocarbon Fuels with Application to Turbulent Burning and Mixing in Hypersonic Engines and Nozzles, *AIAA Paper No. 69-86,* January, 1969.
129. Lefebvre, A. H., Mellor, A. M., and Peters, J. E.: *Prog. in Astro. and Aero.,* **62**, 1977, p. 137.
130. Odgers, J.: *15th Symp. (Intl.) on Comb.,* 1974, p. 1321.
131. Hammond, D. C. and Mellor, A. M.: Analytical Calculations for the Performance and Pollutant Emissions for Gas Turbine Combustors, *AIAA Paper No. 71-711,* 1971.
132. Bowman, C. T.: *Comb. Sci. Tech.,* **3**, 37, 1971.
133. Dixon-Lewis, G., Greenberg, J. B., and Goldsworthy, F. A.: *Comb. Inst. European Symp.,* Academic Press, 1973, p. 59.
134. Mohindra, D. G. S.: Unpublished Ph.D. Thesis, Dept. of Mech. Eng., University of Calgary, 1972.
135. Bowman, B. R., Pratt, D. T. and Crowe, C. T.: *14th Symp. (Intl.) on Comb.,* The Comb. Inst., 1973, p. 819.
136. Pratt, D. T., Bowman, B. R., Crowe, C. T., and Sonnichen, T. C.: Prediction of Nitric Oxide Formation in Turbojet Engines, by PSR Analysis, *AIAA Paper No. 71-713,* 1971.
137. Lipfert, F. W.: Correlation of Gas Turbine Emission Data, *ASME Paper No. 72-GT-60,* 1972.
138. Marteney, P. M.: *Comb. Sci. Tech.,* **1**, 1970, p. 461.
139. Seery, D. J., and Bowman, C. T.: *Comb. Flame,* **14**, 1970, p. 101.
140. McLean, W. J., Miller, J. A., Resler, E. L. and Bauer, S. H.: Early Stages in the Mechanism of Methane Pyrolysis and Oxidation, Eastern Section/Comb. Inst., Oct. 1973.
141. Moisier, S. A., Roberts, R., and Henderson, R. E.: Atmospheric Pollution by Aircraft Engines, *AGARD Conf. Proc. No. 125,* April 1973, p. 25-1.
142. Edelman, R. and Economos, C.: A Mathematical Model for Jet Engine Combustor Pollutant Emissions, *AIAA Paper No. 71-714,* 1971.
143. Pischinger, F. and Kleinschmidt: *Combustion Institute European Symposium,* Academic Press, 1973, p. 457.
144. Roberts, R., Aceto, L. D., Kollrack, R., Bonnell, J. M., and Teixeira, D. P.: An Analytical Model for Nitric Oxide Formation in a Gas Turbine Combustion Chamber, *AIAA Paper No. 71-715,* 1971.
145. Scaccia, C. and Kennedy, L. A.: *AIAA Journal,* **12**, Sept., 1974, p. 1268.
146. Moretti, G.: *AIAA Journal,* **3**, Feb. 1965, p. 223.
147. Pergament, H. S.: *AIAA Paper 65-113,* White Oak, Md., 1963.
148. Kennedy, L. A. and Scaccia, C.: *ASME Paper No. 73-HT-22,* Atlanta, GA., Aug. 5-8, 1973.
149. Westenberg, A. A.: *Comb. Sci. and Tech.,* **4**, 1971, p. 59.
150. Engleman, V. S., Edelman, R. B., Bartok, W. and Longwell, J. P.: *14th Symp. (Intl.) on Comb.,* 1973, p. 755.
151. Bowman, C. T. and Seery, D. J.: In Emissions from Continuous Combustion Systems [Cornelius, W. and Agnew, W. G. (Eds.)], Plenum Press, New York, 1972, p. 123.
152. Edelman, R. B., Fortune, O. and Weilerstein, G.: *Ibid.,* p. 55.
153. Caretto, L. S.: Paper at CI/WSS Spring Tech. Meeting, Salt Lake City, Utah, April 19-20, 1976.
154. Engleman, V. S.: *Report No. EPA-600/2-76-003,* 1976.
155. Longwell, J. P.: *16th Symp. (Intl.) on Comb.,* 1977, p. 1.
156. Kennedy, L. A. (Ed.): *Prog. in Astro. and Aero.,* **58**, AIAA, New York, 1978.
157. Combustion Modelling, *AGARD Conf. Proc. No. 275,* Feb. 1980.
158. Morel, T., Lohmann, R. P. and Rackley, J. M. (Eds.): Fluid Mechanics of Combustion Systems, *ASME Conf.* in Boulder, CO, June 22-24, 1981.
159. Morel, T. (Ed.): Prediction of Turbulent Reacting Flows in Practical Systems, *ASME Conf.* in Boulder, CO, June 22-24, 1981.
160. Jones, W. P. and Whitelaw, J. H.: Calculation Methods for Reacting Turbulent Flows, *Ibid.,* 1981, pp. 9-22.
161. Spalding, D. B.: *Chem. Eng. Sci.,* **26**, 1971, p. 95.
162. Naguib, A. S.: Ph.D. Thesis, Imperial College, London, 1975.
163. Kent, J. H. and Bilger, R. W.: *16th Symp. (Intl.) on Comb.,* 1977, p. 1643.
164. Rhodes, R. P., Harsha, P. T. and Peters, C. E.: *Acta Astro.,* **1**, 1974, p. 443.
165. Jones, W. P. and Priddin, C.: *17th Symp. (Intl.) on Comb.,* 1979, p. 399.

166. Jones, W. P. and McGuirk, J.: A Comparison of Two Droplet Models for Gas Turbine Combustion Chamber Flows. *Proc. 5th ISABE,* Bangalore, India, 1981.
167. Kent, J. H. and Bilger, R. W.: Turbulent Diffusion Flames, Univ. of Sydney, Australia, *Report No. 7N F-37.* See also *14th Symp. (Intl.) on Comb.,* 1973, p. 615.
168. Jones, W. P.: Models for Turbulent Flows with Variable Density [VKI Lecture Series 1979-2] in Prediction Methods for Turbulent Flows (W. Kellmann, Ed.), Hemisphere, 1980.
169. Bray, K. N. C. and Moss, J. B.: *Acta Astro.,* **4**, 1977, p. 291.
170. Bray, K. N. C.: *Turbulent Flows with Premixed Reactants in Turbulent Reacting Flows* (P. A. Libby and F. A. Williams, Eds.) [Topics in Applied Physics Series], Springer-Verlag, 1980.
171. Libby, P. A. and Bray, K. N. C.: *Comb. and Flame,* **39**, 1980, p. 33.
172. Borghi, R.: *Adv. Geophysics* 18 B, 1974, p. 349.
173. Donaldson, C. du P.: in *Turbulent Mixing in Nonreactive and Reactive Flows* [S. N. B. Murthy, (Ed.)], Plenum Press, New York, 1975.

CHAPTER 3

PREDICTIVE TECHNIQUES

3.1 THEORETICAL DESIGN AND DEVELOPMENT

Theoretical Studies

Problems and progress in solution techniques for complex turbulent reacting flows are now discussed, with emphasis on swirl flow combustion application. This chapter reviews the difficulties, discusses developments and demonstrates that a useful predictive capability exists to aid the designer. The basic combustor configuration, illustrated in Fig. 3.1, is the so-called sudden-expansion dump combustor. In this type of combustor, liquid fuel is sprayed into the air upstream of the dump station as shown, although it may also be injected directly into the chamber via side-wall inlets. Ignition is achieved by electric spark or hot gas generator piloting. Primary flame stabilization is provided by the flow recirculation regions shown, which may be supplemented, at the expense of total pressure loss, with mechanical flame-holding devices at the air inlet/combustor interface and/or the presence of inlet air swirl, obtained by the using of tangential injection or swirl vanes. The flow throughout is multiphase, subsonic and turbulent and involves large-scale recirculation zones. Corner recirculation zones CRZs are shown in the figure. With strong swirl in the inlet flow a central toroidal recirculation zone CTRZ (a recirculation bubble in the middle of the chamber near the inlet) also presents itself.

The schematic of Fig. 3.1 is actually typical of ramjet combustors[1-4], but this configuration is also taken in many laboratory experiments and computer predictions to be representative of more realistic combustion geometries, as for example, the gasoline engine, the diesel engine, the industrial furnace and the gas turbine combustion chamber. Except for discrete fuel injection locations, the flowfield of the dump combustor of Fig. 3.1 is almost axisymmetrical. Many combustors contain fully 3-D flowfields because of air multi-inlets at discrete circumferential locations. Many of the features found in the simpler axisymmetric flowfields are also present in these more complex cases. Clearly, the general case requires a fully 3-D simulation, together with highly sophisticated techniques in order to gain the resolution required to define adequately the multiple flowfield regions and their interaction. Major problems include flame stabilization, combustion performance and instabilities, as well as the more fundamental aspects of multiphase turbulent reacting flow phenomena with swirl and recirculation. The designer has a form-

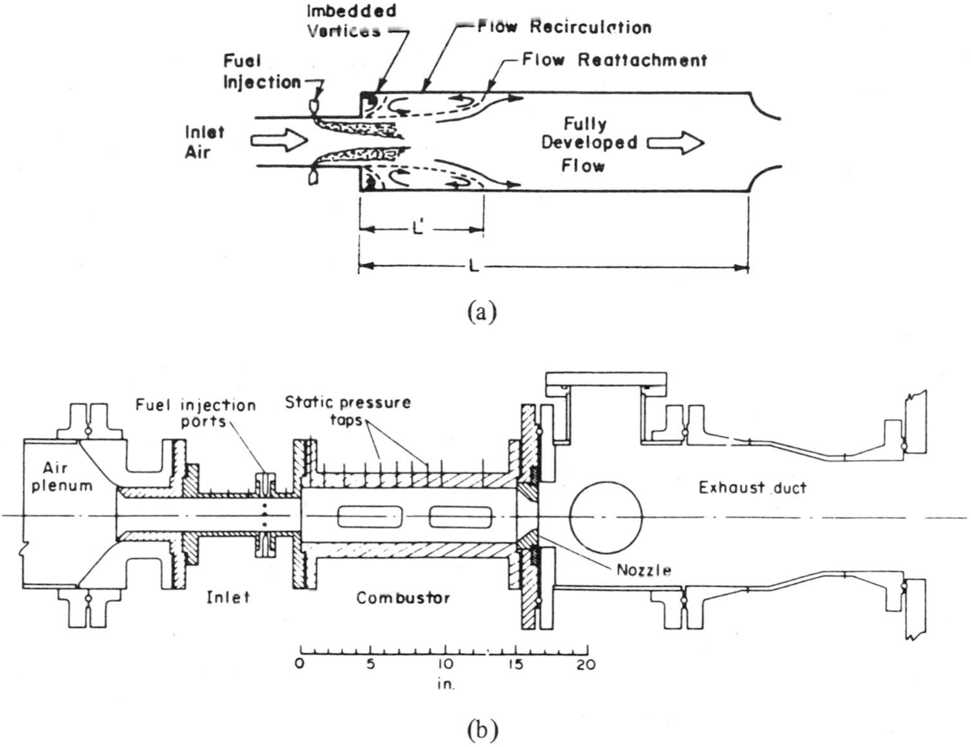

Figure 3.1 (a) Schematic Illustration of Dump Combustor Flowfield[2]
(b) Experimental Arrangement[2]

idable problem in aerothermochemistry, and the modeling task is to provide a route that leads to the accomplishment of design objectives more quickly and less expensively than current practice permits. Some combustor modeling problems are:

1. Physical processes—turbulence, radiation, combustion and multiphase effects.
2. Computer programs—0-, 1-, 2- and 3-D approaches in steady state and transient cases.
3. Unresolved problems—effect of swirl and wall proximity on turbulence turbulence—reaction interaction multiphase simulation.

In design situations, the engineer has to seek an optimum path between irreconcilable alternatives. The general aim of most investigations is to provide information that is useful to designers by 'characterizing' of 'modeling' certain features of the phenomenon in question. Investigations may be theoretical or experimental; the two approaches are complementary. Up to now, designers have relied heavily on the experimental approach. The mathematical modeling approach is now finding favor, is being used to supplement existing design procedures, and, clearly, computer modeling of combustion processes is now an established fact. Recent major reviews of relevant studies are readily available, with emphasis on ramjet combustor modeling[5], combustion modeling[6-8] and swirl flow combustion[9-12]. In particular, one of the present author's previous two review papers[9,10] serve to supplement the present text by their extensive discussion and citations of the literature.

Several recent conferences and workshops of interest in the fluid dynamics of combustion and its application to high intensity combustors are cited as[13-23]. Current combustor design and development *problems*, the *needs* of the combustion engineer in practice and proposed research *tasks* that will assist in the attainment of design objectives are becoming clear. Improvements and new developments (both experimental and theoretical) can and should be made, theoretical modeling being aided by the performance of specific carefully chosen experiments. Numerical procedures for predicting combustion chamber flows (which in practice are complex 3-D turbulent reacting flows) rest on two foundations: mathematical models of physical processes (turbulence, radiation, combustion and two-phase effects) and computer programs for solving the appropriate level of sophistication of the resulting differential equations (0-, 1-, 2- and 3-D approaches). Each of these has particular applications and limitations. In deciding on and justifying the use of a particular procedure, one needs to weigh up all the problems: Does it predict with sufficient accuracy? How much time is needed to obtain a solution? How easy is it to understand the result and its implications? What is the cost?

The objective of the present chapter is to clarify the choice and give appropriate advice, emphasizing computer application where appropriate. Associated computational results are discussed in Chapter 5.

Experimental Studies

Problems in complex turbulent reacting flows of the type found in combustion equipment abound. Additional features of fuel sprays, swirl flow and recirculation make it difficult, either experimentally or theoretically, to characterize the system. Most extensive turbulent fluctuation data obtained to date in complex turbulent flows (perhaps in swirling recirculating flows where the local time-mean velocity vector direction is not known in advance) has been with hot-wire anemometers. The cost advantage over LDA methods is offset by the disadvantage of probe intrusion and restriction to nonburning conditions. Even so, there are difficulties with respect to technique, multimeasurement with different probe orientations at each flowfield location, probe alignment, and analog or digital data reduction techniques. Recent hotwire techniques in complex turbulent flow are discussed elsewhere[24-30].

Concerning combustor flowfields of the type shown in Fig. 3.1 very little in the way of useful experimental data (time-mean or fluctuating) is available in the open literature. It is as if designers have devoted resources almost exclusively to realistic performance tests, and actual internal mean-flow patterns and turbulence details are unknown. Even isothermal flows without swirl have been investigated in abrupt ($\alpha = 90^o$) expansions in most cases. Recent experimental works[31-40], on turbulent flows in expansions is available[31-40], while corresponding citations to reacting flows may be found elsewhere[8-11].

The first two items discuss 2-D Cartesian flow expansions; the others discuss 2-D axisymmetric flow through sudden pipe expansions, while Chaturvedi[33] deals only with gradual expansions. Experiments on abrupt pipe expansions (side wall angle $\alpha = 90^o$) exhibit considerable variation of observed reattachment length with upstream Reynolds number[34-37] and show qualitative agreement with theory[34]. More extensive data (time-mean velocities and various turbulence stress terms) are available via recent hotwire measurements[39], and these are compared with predicted values from eddy viscosity and Reynolds stress turbulence models. Gradual expansion angles $\alpha = 15^o$, 30° and 45° along with a sudden expansion $\alpha = 90^o$ are considered by Chaturvedi[33], all measurements being taken with an upstream Reynolds number of 2×10^5 and an expansion diameter ratio $D/d = 2$. Streamlines, kinetic energy of turbulence k and Reynolds shear stress $u'v'$ data are also given. Detailed measurements via laser anemometry of turbulent recirculating confined jet flows are described in Owen[38].

Recent turbulence modeling efforts for combustor flowfields are discussed[40-51], and assessments, extensions and limitations of the two-equation k-ϵ turbulence model are included. Some authors emphasize swirl[44,50] and nonisotropic effects,[42,45] others compare various models[41,43,47-49] and still others stress the model parameter influences[46-51]. Other turbulence modeling work is included in flowfield prediction efforts outlined later in this and subsequent chapters.

Mathematical Modeling Contribution

Designers are aided by experiments, but as an alternative to them economical design and operation can be greatly facilitated by the availability of prior predictions of the flowfield, obtained via the use of a mathematical model incorporating a numerical prediction procedure. Such work combines the rapidly developing fields of theoretical combustion aerodynamics and computational fluid dynamics; and its improvement and use will significantly reduce the time and cost of the development programs. The model should simulate the flow in all its important respects and quantitatively solve the governing equations. Rapid progress has been made in recent years in the development of mathematical models of combustor swirl flows which simulate the processes of turbulence, combustion, fuel droplet sprays, radiation and pollutant formation, and solve the resulting equations via a computational procedure, which seeks an optimum path to the solution of the governing set of several simultaneous nonlinear partial differential equations. Mathematical models of steadily increasing realism and refinement are being developed, both in the dimensionality of the model (together with the computational procedures) and in problems associated with the simulation of the physical processes that occur. These equations governing combustor flowfields may be parabolic (boundary layer type with no recirculation) but are more often elliptic (recirculating type) and the solution scheme differs according to the category, as described in Chapter 2. Marching methods are often appropriate for the former (flows with weak swirl); relaxation methods for the latter (flows with strong swirl). Many approaches proceed with the following equations of conservation of mass, momentum, stagnation enthalpy, and chemical species may all be taken in the common form

$$\frac{\partial}{\partial t}(\rho\phi) + \text{div}\,(\rho v\phi - \Gamma_\phi \,\text{grad}\,\phi) = S_\phi \qquad (3\text{-}1)$$

where the exchange coefficient assumptions have been invoked. Here ϕ is a general dependent variable, and equations may be solved for ϕ equal to time-mean axial, radial, and swirl velocities, u, v, w, stagnation enthalpy h, fuel mass fraction m_{fu}, mixture fraction f, turbulent kinetic energy k and dissipation rate ϵ, and possibly many of the other variables as well. The equations differ not only in their exchange coefficients Γ_ϕ but also, and primarily, in their final source terms S_ϕ. Specific details about the equations may be found in Chapter 2, and note that more sophistications regarding density fluctuations, radiation effects and equations for certain correlations may also be included.

General Methodology. These equations have to be solved for time-mean pressure p and velocity components u, v and w, and other variables as required. Then other useful designer information such as streamline plots, breakaway and reattachment points, recirculation zones and stagnation points, for example, may be readily deduced. The TEACH code approach is conceptually simple and computationally efficient.

Eulerian finite difference approximations to the steady elliptic governing equations are solved implicitly for the primitive pressure and velocity variables, via the SIMPLE [Semi-Implicit Method for Pressure-Linked Equations] technique using the TDMA [Tri-Diagonal Matrix Algorithm] in columns.

The following features are incorporated into the program:

1. a finite difference procedure is used in which the dependent variables are the velocity components and pressure;
2. the pressure is deduced from an equation that is obtained by the combination of the continuity equation and the momenta equations (yielding a new form of what is known in the literature as the Poisson equation for pressure);
3. the idea is present at each iteration of a first approximation to the solution followed by a succeeding correction;
4. the procedure incorporates displaced grids for the axial and radial velocities u and v, which are placed between the nodes where pressure p and other variables are stored; and
5. an implicit line-by-line relaxation technique is employed in the solution procedure (requiring a tridiagonal matrix to be inverted in order to update a variable at all points along a column).

The incorporation of these enhances the accuracy and rapidity of convergence of the finally developed computer program.

The solution of these differential equations, together with the use of several algebraic equations, allow flowfield parameters of special interest to be deduced. It may be noted, however, that recirculating flowfield computations are particularly sensitive to the initial conditions specified. Closure and completeness of the governing equation set are effected by means of models of the physical processes taking place within the combustion system. Either our knowledge of these processes or computer size limitations restricts the degree of sophistication to be used in any simulation.

Solution Techniques

Some very useful 0-D and 1-D approaches to characterizing combustor flowfield problems are readily available and discussed in Section 3.2. Concerning the application of computational fluid dynamics, research emphasis today is being directed toward 2-D and 3-D simulations of the phenomena in question, with discussion in later sections of Chapter 3. Elliptic problems in 2-D space, implying the possible existence of recirculation zones, proceed with typical equations of the form

$$\sum_{i=1}^{2} a_i \frac{\partial \phi}{\partial x_i} + \sum_{i=1}^{2} b_i \frac{\partial}{\partial x_i} (c_i \frac{\partial \phi}{\partial x_i}) = d \qquad (3\text{-}2)$$

where ϕ is a general dependent variable, $x_1 = x$ and $x_2 = r$ (axial and radial coordinates). Current preference is to solve such problems directly in terms of the primitive p-u-v variables, rather than in terms of the associated stream function-vorticity variables. Moreover, the solution may be via an iterative relaxation method using equations of the type above or via a time-march method heating toward the steady state solution, while making use of the associated transient equations of the form

$$\sum_{i=1}^{3} a_i \frac{\partial \phi}{\partial x_i} + \sum_{i=1}^{2} b_i \frac{\partial}{\partial x_i} (c_i \frac{\partial \phi}{\partial x_i}) = d \qquad (3\text{-}3)$$

where, additionally, $x_3 = t$ (time coordinate).

SOLA[52] (Solution Algorithm) is a computer code of the latter variety from Los Alamos, New Mexico, which utilizes a simple explicit transient treatment. Its algorithm is easy to comprehend. TEACH[53] (Teaching Elliptic Axisymmetric Characteristics Heuristically) is a computer code of the former category from Imperial College, London, which uses a more complex but more accurate and economical solution algorithm based directly on the steady state equations. When accuracy and economy are of prime importance, this is the preferred approach. With either technique, the problem of pressure-velocity coupling must be overcome. Basically, pressure and velocity adjustments are made after each iterative or time-march step, via application of the continuity equation. The details may be found in recent experiences with these codes[50-74] including the earlier ψ-ω methods and more complex codes used for numerical prediction studies of high intensity combustion.

Notice that corresponding fully 3-D versions of eqns. (3-2) and (3-3) are obtained by increasing by one the range of the summations, so as to include a third coordinate, typically the swirl direction θ. On the other hand, parabolic problems, implying boundary layer behavior in the main direction and denying the existence of recirculation zones, are obtained by decreasing by one the range of summation over the diffusion terms (the second terms on the left-hand sides of these equations). The relevant equations have been presented in Chapter 2 and will be recalled, as appropriate, in the present chapter. Attention is now given to solving the differential equations the mathematical models have supplied. Generally, the equations are expressed in finite difference form (using finite difference or finite element techniques for separation) and solved via a suitable algorithm. Problems are classed according to the degree of realism and refinement, as represented by their dimensionality (the number of independent variables from three space dimensions and time) and type (parabolic or elliptic). The flow classification of parabolic (possessing one coordinate direction with first–but without second-order derivatives—boundary layer type with prominent direction(s)) or elliptic (possessing second-order derivatives in all coordinate directions – recirculating type with upstream influence) governs the type of boundary conditions required, and solution method. Marching methods are appropriate for the former, relaxation methods for the latter. The problems, methods and solutions are discussed in recent texts[75-79], AGARD reports[80-83], AIAA Selected Reprint

Series[84-85], as well as AIAA Computational Fluid Dynamics Conferences and Numerical Methods in Fluid Mechanics Conferences.

The essential differences between the various available computer codes (and those that are not available) include: the complexity of the equation set for the simulation of the physical processes, the storage requirements, the location of variables in the grid space system, the method of deriving the finite difference equations that are incorporated, and the solution technique. In primitive pressure-velocity variable formulations a staggered grid system is normally used, as recommended by Los Alamos for its special attributes. In computational fluid dynamics the 'best' representation of the convection and diffusion terms is essential to the accuracy and convergence or stability of the iteration scheme or marching procedure. At high cell Reynolds numbers a certain degree of 'upstream differencing' is essential, using upwind differencing, a hybrid formulation or the Los Alamos zip, donor cell, etc. techniques, for example[86]. Solution procedures vary from Gauss-Seidel GS point methods[87] to more efficient line-by-line LBL SIMPLE (semi-implicit method for pressure-linked equations) methods[88, 89] for steady state problems, with corresponding explicit and SIMPLE methods for associated transient problems. The application of finite element computational methods, to combustor problems with complex boundary geometry and complex boundary conditions to apply, is in its infancy; further work in this fertile area will be most useful.

3.2 SIMPLIFIED APPROACHES

Simple Flowfield Deductions

Consider the simplified axial u and swirl w velocity profiles of Fig. 3.2 as an assumed incompressible flow passing through a sudden expansion in cross-sectional area. The flow is axisymmetric and some simplified deductions will be made on the basis of plug flow axial velocity with (a) flat swirl profile and (b) solid body rotation. Appropriate macroscopic global balances, deducible from conservation laws will be set up and results developed for the changes in velocities from station 1 to 2, using w_m for the station maximum swirl velocity in the latter case and omitting suffixes (except 1 and 2) otherwise.

Global continuity equation is

$$\dot{m} = \int_0^R \rho u r dr = \text{constant}$$

and global axial flux of swirl momentum equation is

$$G_\theta = \int_0^R \rho u w r^2 \, dr = \text{constant}$$

since there is very little torque on the system. The global axial flux of axial momentum may also be written down, but it includes a pressure term [at stations 1 and 2 and the sidewall] which must then be eliminated via knowlege about the total force acting axially on the system. The two equations given above are sufficient for simple deductions to be made.

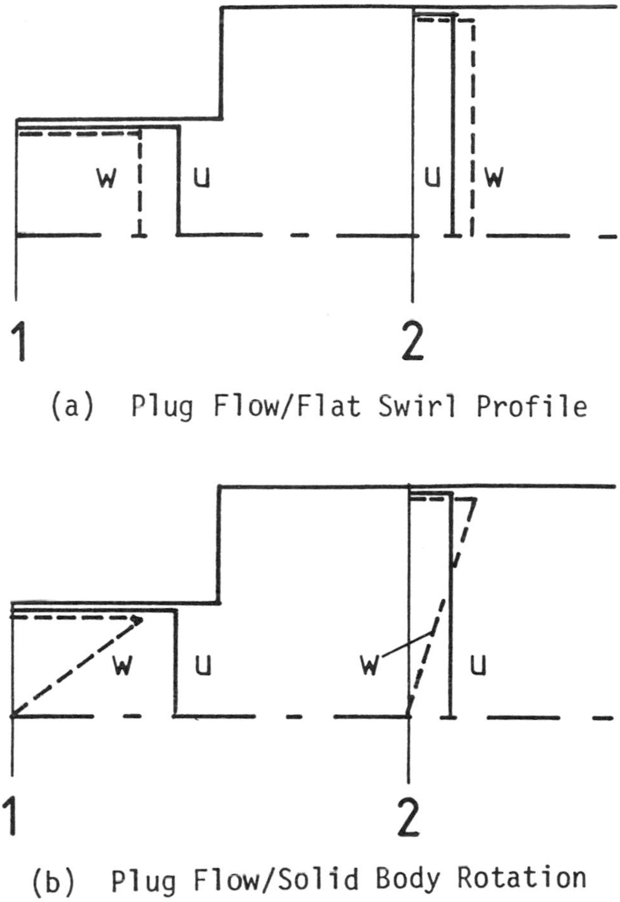

Figure 3.2 Idealized Flow Through a Sudden Expansion:
(a) Flat u and w profiles,
(b) Flat u profile with w solid body rotation.
[——u, – – – –w]

(a) *Plug Flow/Flat Swirl Profile.* Put $u = u_1$ and $w = w_1$ (and similar at station 2) and hence continuity and swirl momentum give:

$$u_1 R_1^2 = u_2 R_2^2$$
$$u_1 w_1 R_1^3 = u_2 w_2 R_2^3.$$

Also, the swirl number S is given in this hubless swirler system by

$$S = \frac{2}{3} \tan \phi$$
$$= \frac{2}{3} w/u$$

where ϕ is the turn angle [equal to $\tan^{-1}(w/u)$] and is independent of radius. Hence

$$\begin{aligned} u_2/u_1 &= R_1^{\,2}/R_2^{\,2} \\ w_2/w_1 &= R_1/R_2 \\ S_2/S_1 &= R_2/R_1 \\ \tan\phi_2/\tan\phi_1 &= R_2/R_1 \end{aligned} \qquad (3.4)$$

and for the case of a 2 to 1 linear expansion [4 to 1 area change] with $R_2 = 2R_1$ these reduce to

$$\begin{aligned} u_2/u_1 &= 1/4 \\ w_2/w_1 &= 1/2 \\ S_2/S_1 &= 2 \\ \tan\phi_2/\tan\phi_1 &= 2 \end{aligned}$$

Hence the swirl number increases through such a sudden expansion, and, since $\tan\phi$ is a monotonically increasing function of ϕ, the turn angle also increases.

(b) *Plug Flow/Solid Body Rotation*

Put $u = u_1$ and $w = w_{M1}\,(r/R_1)$ (and similar at station 2) [swirl velocity is a linearly increasing function of radius] and hence continuity and swirl momentum give:

$$\begin{aligned} u_1 R_1^{\,2} &= u_2 R_2^{\,2} \\ u_1 w_{M1} R_1^{\,3} &= u_2 w_{M2} R_2^{\,3}. \end{aligned}$$

Also, the swirl number S is given in this system as [see Section 2.3]

$$S = \frac{G/2}{1-(G/2)^2}$$

where $G_1 = w_{M1}/u_1$ at station 1 (and similar at station 2). For small values of G this reduces to

$$S = G/2.$$

Hence

$$\begin{aligned} u_2/u_1 &= R_1^{\,2}/R_2^{\,2} \\ w_{M2}/w_{M1} &= R_1/R_2 \\ G_2/G_1 &= R_2/R_1 \end{aligned} \qquad (3.4)$$

and for the case of a 2 to 1 linear expansion [4 to 1 area change] with $R_2 = 2R_1$ these reduce to

$$u_2/u_1 = 1/4$$
$$w_{M2}/w_{M1} = 1/2$$
$$G_2/G_1 = 2.$$

Hence G [$= w_m/u$] increases through such a sudden expansion and, since the S vs G curve monotonically increases [*see* Ref. 12], the swirl number also increases.

Final Remark. It is clear that the degree of swirl increases in both these cases as the flow cross-sectional area increases. Hence, in general, the complexities associated with higher swirl also increase.

Simplified Combustor Models

Because application of the general PDEs is complex, time-consuming and in a development stage, simplified approaches to the problem are extremely popular. The most common models include: perfectly stirred reactors PSRs, well-stirred reactors WSRs and plug flow reactors PFRs. Models differ in the way these are interrelated to simulate various aspects of the mixing/reaction taking place; several well-known models are now discussed.

One approach[90] is to assume that the sudden expansion flowfield is dominated by the jet flow near the centerline, and couple this with an assumed model for the behavior of the recirculation zones. The jet flow calculation is based on an integral model for ducted co-axial turbulent mixing, using boundary layer jet assumptions and a cosine function for the cross-stream velocity profile. Peak reverse flow velocities are overpredicted but the locations of stagnation points are predicted quite well. The method shows promise in the prediction of overall fluid dynamics but would fail to clarify flameholding characteristics, because of the neglect of species transport in the recirculation zones and of the difficulty of including finite-rate chemical kinetics within the integral analysis.

The four modular approaches cited[91-94] differ in their construction and implementation. The first one[91] consists of two PSRs followed by a series of three PFRs, the second one[92] uses a statistical mixing model for the primary zone using the concept of a macromixed stirred reactor, the third one[93] has a series of WSRs and PFRs, and the last one[94] divides the combustor into three PFRs with the initial portion consisting of a central recirculating region surrounded by an outer stream tube of reacting flow and the secondary portion consisting of a single stream tube dilution zone. Figure 3.3 shows a schematic of the Swithenbank *et al.*[93] modular arrangement, which serves to exemplify the concepts. In a recent review of high intensity spray combustion[96], it is asserted that useful correlations of gas turbine emissions may be obtained by a modular approach, a particular technique being recommended[94]. Further testing of this model is warranted in order to extend its range of applicability and establish its limitations in terms of predictions. Only qualitative trend predictions for emissions can be expected from the other modular and finite-difference models investigated. The most important reason cited for this is the inability to model and include turbulence/chemistry/spray interactions with much certainty.

The hybrid methods advance the level of complexity and expected realism. For example, the sudden expansion flowfield of the ramjet dump combustor, shown in Fig.

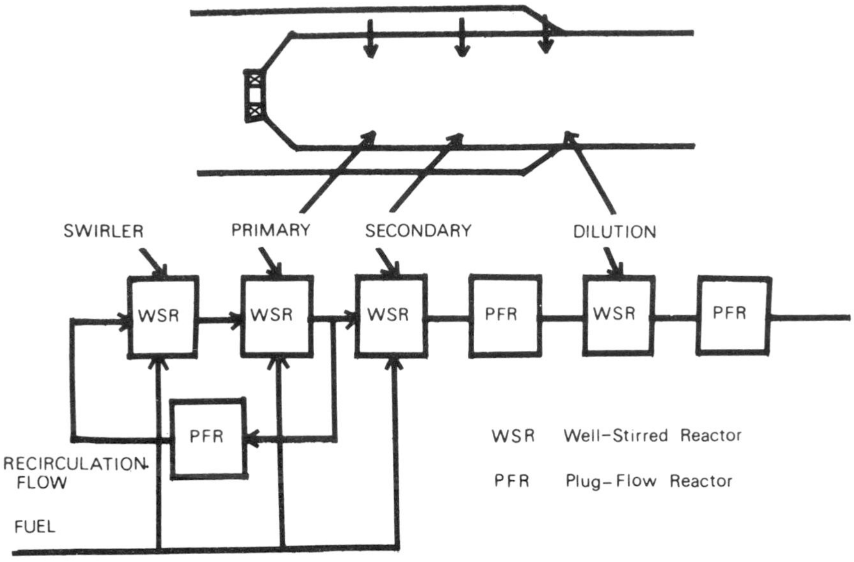

Figure 3.3 Schematic of the Swithenbank et al Modular Model[93]

3.1, has been broken down into the three major regions: a directed flow (treated by a parabolic marching procedure), a corner recirculation zone (treated as a WSR) and a turbulent shear layer region along the dividing streamline between the first two regions[95]. A schematic of the modular interactions appears in Fig. 3.4. Fluxes of species and energy across this dividing streamline form the boundary conditions on the two computational regions. Full finite-rate chemistry is included in both the directed flow and the well-stirred reactor, and particle and droplet effects can also be computed. The directed flow is assumed to be fully turbulent and the shear stress distribution is obtained within this region through the use of a one-equation turbulence model (i.e. the turbulent kinetic energy equation with an algebraic specification of the dissipation length scale distribution). The method, in its development stage, offers a useful technique for parametric

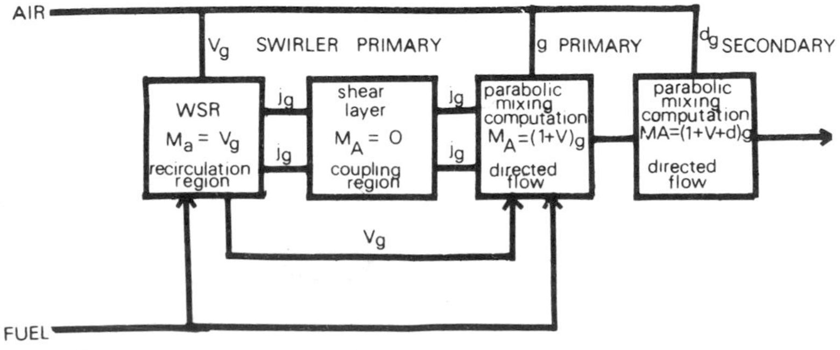

Figure 3.4 Schematic of the Harsha & Edelman Modular Model[95]

investigation and gives commendable predictions. The more advanced hybrid scheme[74] couples a full 3-D finite difference flowfield calculation with the modular approach of Fig. 3.3 and is further discussed in Chapter 5.

3.3 SCALING AND MODELING CRITERIA

General Philosophy

The essential function of a burner is to mix the fuel with the combustion air and introduce the mixture into the furnace/combustor in such a way that the correct flame characteristics and shape are obtained. The desired flame shape for a given combustion process is determined by the furnace geometry and thermal requirement. The use of scaling criteria to predict flame behavior in a given furnace is concerned with the relationship between the geometric and flow variables and the flame characteristics.

Physical modeling generally involves two systems: model and prototype. The prototype is the full-scale system, the model is the small-scale system designed to simulate the operation of the prototype. Measurements are made on the model; the results are then extrapolated to the operation of the prototype. The measure of the success of any model is the validity of the extrapolated results in terms of the prototype. For extrapolation of the experimental results to be valid certain similarities must exist between the model and the prototype.

Spalding[97] has pointed out that complete modeling of combustion systems is not possible. He has compiled a list of 120 parameters; even this listing does not cover the multifarious facts of combustion (for example, fuel properties). Many of the parameters are mutually incompatible. Table 3.1 presents dimensionless parameters that appear to be related to the problems of pulverized coal combustion scaling. In practice, therefore, it is necessary to resort to partial modeling, in which only the dominant processes (relative to the aspects of interest) are modeled. The ideal approach, of course, is to formulate a theory that rigorously describes the physico-chemical processes involved and to check the theory against experiments carried out in a well-determined system. One must therefore make a decision on the important characteristics to be studied (or modeled) and compromise on the criteria to be satisfied. One author suggests that for reliable scaling of results, the model should not be smaller than about one-quarter full-size[98], another suggests one-third[97]. To date, various investigators have studied the importance of scaling-up from the scientific and industrial point of view in order to relate correctly the data produced in one combustion installation to a different combustion installation 'on scale'. The studies are inconclusive. Brown and Thring[99] measured the flame length in marine boilers using 1/3 scale models. Most of the results for equivalence ratio and combustion efficiency were found to agree within 15 per cent; the maximum discrepancy being some 40 per cent. Ball[100] studied heat transfer, combustion and temperature in a 1/3 scale boiler furnace tube model. The model results could not be reproduced on the full-scale plant. Mean temperatures in the model study were found to be higher than in the actual plant and were interpreted as being due to the increase in convective heat transfer from thinner walls. Lane and Morrison[101] measured velocity profiles in burner ports. The model results were found to be within 5 per cent of those obtained on the full-scale system. Stewart[102] reported a comparative study conducted by Rolls Royce on a typical

TABLE 3.1

Similarity Parameters for Combustion in Boilers

Similarity Parameter	Related Characteristics	Relationship
Damkohler I	Homogeneous Reaction/Kinematics	$\frac{ZL}{\rho v}$
Particle Disappearance	Particle Disappearance/Radiation	$\frac{D\rho c}{\sigma T^3 L} \ln (1 + B)$
Entrainment	Entrainment of Secondary Air	$\frac{M_o}{M} \frac{L}{d_o} \left(\frac{\rho_1}{\rho_0}\right)^{1/2}$
Kinetic Flame Propagation	Flame Propagation/Kinematics	$\frac{S_L}{v}$
Furnace Wall Temperature	Slagging	T
Reaction Kinetics	Reaction Rate	$\frac{H'}{RT_f}$
Flame Temperature	Flame Radiation/Heat Generation	$\frac{Svf\ (\epsilon)}{\sigma}$
Radiation/Conduction	Heat Radiation/Heat Conduction	$\frac{\sigma T^3 L}{k}$
Shear/Momentum	Turbulent Shear/Source Momentum	$\frac{L^2}{d^2} c^2 \left(\frac{\rho_f \rho_o}{\rho_a}^2\right)$
Shear/Buoyancy	Turbulent Shear/Buoyancy Force	$\left(\frac{v}{c}^2\right) \frac{1}{L^5} \frac{\rho_a{}^2}{\rho_f \rho_f - \rho_a g}$

TABLE 3.1 (Continued)

Similarity Parameter	Related Characteristics	Relationship
Carbon Dioxide Formation	Rate of Formation of Carbon Dioxide	$\lambda \ \mathrm{Sk} \ \frac{L}{v} \left(1 - \frac{\mathrm{L}}{F_c K_c d_o v} \ ^2 \right)$
Gravitational Effects	Source Momentum/Buoyancy Force	$\frac{v_o^2}{gL}$

where

Z = homogeneous reaction rate
L = length
ρ = density
v = velocity
c = specific heat
σ = Stefan-Boltzmann constant
T = temperature
B = heat transfer number
M = mass flow rate
d = nozzle diameter
S = flame speed
ϵ = flame surface emissivity

re-heat system. A reasonably good agreement was found for combustion efficiency between the $^1/_3$ scale model results and the full-scale system.

From the foregoing it is apparent that the 'scale up' has several advantages and points of weakness. In general, the different variables and the range within which they can be varied are limited, and the results are strictly valid only for the experimental system in which they were obtained. The generalization of results 'on scale' are possible, but only partially. Theoretical and detailed experimental investigations of turbulent flames in geometric confines with flow patterns similar to those in industrial use have been carried out. Model results can give reasonable information on the scale-up effects from basic studies such as chemical kinetics of flame reactions, fluid mechanics of turbulent mixing, heat transfer and pollutant emission from flames. Nevertheless, it is notoriously difficult to predict the degree of corrosion and erosion from the model results. In coal combustion, the mechanism of ash fouling is complex and is not yet fully understood. The most widely accepted concept is that the presence of alkali metals in the ash contributes to formation of ash. The alkali metals volatilize and react with oxygen to form oxides, which then react with SO_2 and SO_3 to form sulphites and sulphates. These compounds have low melting points and thus tend to deposit as fused masses on heat-absorbing surfaces. They also trap ash particles which are then embedded in the deposit.

The design of a new utility boiler relies heavily on engineering calculations and measurements on similar earlier units. Design extrapolation in general tends to be conservative. In combustion research-technology transfer, the basic research studies on the coordination of fundamental information can be done best by means of mathematical and physical modeling. These models serve primarily to describe the process quantitatively and also to assist in highlighting the areas where information is lacking; for example on physical, chemical constants or mathematical computational methods. On the other hand, applied combustion research has the task of bringing results of basic studies to the stage of industrial application wherein several intermediate stages of research are necessary for their proper development.

The first stage involves the close coordination of results of basic studies such as chemical kinetics of flame reactions, fluid mechanics of turbulent mixing, heat transfer and pollutants emission from flames by theoretical and detailed experimental investigations of turbulent flames with involved flow pattern and geometry such as those in industrial use. Because of the need to use advanced nonintrusive optical combustion diagnostic techniques and carrying out detailed measurements in flames, it is preferable that the size of the experimental facility should not exceed that of the pilot plant. On the other hand, meaningful interpretation of data requires a certain minimum size of combustor.

The second stage of the investigations is aimed at providing evidence that results obtained in the pilot plant studies and generalized by mathematical models or dimensionless parameters can be scaled-up with confidence to the industrial size. The size of the experimental facility has to be industrial and equipped to enable experiments to be carried out in detail for testing predictions concerning significant combustion parameters.

The third stage of the development is represented by a demonstration plant. The newly developed and scaled-up combustion device or new pollution control method will have to be tested over extended periods of time (one to three months) to ensure that material problems or those of slagging of heating surfaces can be assessed at this early stage of development. An old utility boiler ($>$ 20 MW thermal capacity) in an industry is ideal in which the energy produced from the boiler during experiments can be utilized efficiently.

Scaling Parameters

Although the theory of modeling requires that all the set-ups and interpretation rules should be obeyed, experience in the past has shown that flouting some of them does not invalidate the prediction. At present, most of the combustion models used, in which only few of the rules are obeyed, are examples of partial modeling. The omission of the others inevitably introduces some uncertainty about how the results of the experiments should be interpreted.

In the modeling of combustion systems there are several areas in which similarity is required; the various categories of similarity are now discussed.

1. *Geometric Similarity.* The shape of the model and the prototype must be the same. All distances (lengths) are proportional and include all boundaries and geometries, for example, the size, shape and position of the flame front.

2. *Kinematic or Flow Similarity.* The individual particles must trace out paths of the same shape in both model and prototype, and the flow velocities at various points of the model must be in a constant ratio with velocities in the prototype.

3. *Dynamic Similarity.* The relative importance of the various-forces acting must be the same in both the model and prototype.

Mathematically, kinematic similarity can be represented as follows. For a Newtonian viscous fluid the fundamental Navier-Stokes equation for isothermal flow can be written as:

$$\underset{\text{(I)}}{\rho \frac{\partial u}{\partial t}} + \underset{\text{(II)}}{\rho \left(u \frac{\partial u}{\partial x} + v \frac{\partial u}{\partial y} + w \frac{\partial u}{\partial z} \right)} = \underset{\text{(III)}}{\rho g \cos \alpha_x} - \underset{\text{(IV)}}{\frac{\partial p}{\partial x}}$$

$$+ \underset{\text{(V)}}{\frac{1}{3} \frac{\partial}{\partial x} \left[\mu \left(\frac{\partial u}{\partial x} + \frac{\partial v}{\partial y} + \frac{\partial w}{\partial z} \right) \right]} + \underset{\text{(VI)}}{\mu \left(\frac{\partial^2 u}{\partial x^2} + \frac{\partial^2 u}{\partial y^2} \frac{\partial^2 u}{\partial z^2} \right)}$$

In the above equation each term has the dimensions of a force per unit volume. Successive terms represent respectively:

(I) = Force required to accelerate unit volume of fluid when the flow is unsteady.
(II) = Transport of momentum by fluid flowing through unit cross-section area.
(III) = Gravitational body force.
(IV) = Static pressure gradient.
(V) = Viscous resistance to change of volume of the fluid (negligible for liquids).
(VI) = Viscous resistance to shear.

The generalized dimensional equation may be written as

$$\underset{\text{(I)}}{\left[\frac{\rho v}{t}\right]} + \underset{\text{(II)}}{\left[\frac{\rho v^2}{L}\right]} = \underset{\text{(III)}}{[\rho g]} - \underset{\text{(V)}}{\left[\frac{\Delta p}{L}\right]} + \underset{\text{(V) (VI)}}{\left[\frac{\mu v}{L^2}\right]}$$

(I) and (II) are dimensionally equivalent; hence there are only three independent dimensionless groups:

$$\frac{(II)}{(V)} \text{ gives } \frac{\rho v L}{\mu} = \text{Reynolds number—ratio of inertial to viscous forces.}$$

$$\frac{(II)}{(III)} \text{ gives } \frac{v}{Lg} = \text{Froude number—ratio of inertial to gravitational forces.}$$

$$\frac{(IV)}{(II)} \text{ gives } \frac{\Delta p}{\rho v^2} = \text{Pressure coefficient—ratio of pressure to inertial forces.}$$

The Kinematic viscosity of hot combustion gases is about 12 times that of cold air and about 120 times that of cold water. A twelfth-size air model would therefore require a cold air velocity equal to hot gas velocity in the actual scale-up, whereas in a twelfth-size water model the water velocity would be only one-tenth of it.

4. *Thermal Similarity.* The heat release rates and temperature differences in different parts of the system must have the same importance in both model and prototype.

The thermal similarity concepts are now illustrated with respect to conduction, convection (free and forced) and radiation.

Conduction in Solids: for isotropic conductors with no internal heat generation the differential equation for conduction of heat is

$$\underset{(I)}{\rho c_p \frac{\partial T}{\partial t}} = \underset{(II)}{k \left(\frac{\partial^2 T}{\partial x^2} + \frac{\partial^2 T}{\partial y^2} + \frac{\partial^2 T}{\partial z^2} \right)}$$

Where (I) = rate of increase in enthalpy per unit volume.
(II) = rate of conduction into unit volume.

The dimensionless form of the equation is

$$\left[\frac{\rho c_p T}{t}\right] = \left[\frac{kT}{L^2}\right]$$

Whence the dimensionless group

$$\phi \left[\frac{\rho c_p L^2}{kt}\right] = \text{Const.}$$

Natural Convection in Fluids: the transfer of heat by mixing one parcel of fluid with another. The generalized equation can be given by:

$$\frac{H}{kL\Delta T} = \phi \left[\frac{\beta g \Delta T L^3 \rho^2}{\mu^2} , \frac{c_p \mu}{k} \right]$$ i.e., a function of Grashof number and Prandtl number,

where β = volumetric coefficient of thermal expansion of fluid.
and ΔT = temperature difference

The requirement for thermal similarity is that Prandtl number and Grashof number in the model and prototype to be equal. In homologous system where the scale ratio is large the temperature difference would have to be impracticably high in the model in order to simulate a reasonable value in the prototype. By choosing a fluid of higher viscosity for the model system and selecting the scale ratios and temperature differences accordingly, ΔT may be brought within a practicable range. Hence in a model, where homologous systems are essential, rates of heating under a thermal regime controlled by natural convection cannot as a rule be strictly simulated.

Forced Convection in Fluids: the heat flow by forced convection in a moving fluid is given by

$$\underset{(I)}{-\rho c_p \left(u \frac{\partial T}{\partial x} + v \frac{\partial T}{\partial y} + w \frac{\partial T}{\partial z}\right)} + \underset{(II)}{k\left(\frac{\partial^2 T}{\partial x^2} + \frac{\partial^2 T}{\partial y^2} + \frac{\partial^2 T}{\partial z^2}\right)} = \underset{(III)}{+\rho c_p \frac{\partial T}{\partial t}}$$

Where (I) = rate of heat loss by convection
(II) = rate of heat loss by conduction
(III) = rate of change of enthalpy

The above equation can be written in the following dimensionless form

$$\underset{(I)}{\left[\frac{\rho c_p v T}{L}\right]} + \underset{(II)}{\left[\frac{kT}{L^2}\right]} = \underset{(III)}{+\left[\frac{hT}{L}\right]}$$

Dividing (I) and (III) by (II) and re-arranging

$$\phi\left[\frac{\rho c_p v L}{k}, \frac{hL}{k}\right] = \text{Const.}$$

The group $\left(\frac{\rho c_p v L}{k}\right)$, the ratio of heat transfer rates by bulk flow of fluid and conduction, is called Peclet group. Equality of Peclet group ensures that the ratios of heat flows by conduction and forced convection across corresponding surfaces in model and prototype are equal (that is, fixed wall thickness independent of the scale ratio). The other condition for thermal similarity is that the fluid flow patterns are similar, that is, kinematic similarity.

Radiation: the modeling for radiation can be somewhat difficult. The net integral rate equation for the radiation of heat is given by:

$$H = \frac{dQ}{dt} = \sigma\epsilon(T_1^4 - T_2^4)$$

where ϵ = combined emissivities of hot and cold surfaces

σ = Stefan – Boltzmann Constant

Dimensionally

$$\left[\frac{Q}{L^2T}\right] = [\sigma\epsilon T_1^4] \left[\frac{T_1^4 - T_2^4}{T_1^4}\right]$$

whence the dimensionless equation including the heat transported by bulk movement of fluid

$$\phi\left[\frac{\rho c_p v}{\sigma\epsilon T^3}, \frac{T_1}{T_2}, \frac{\rho c_p L v}{k}, \frac{H}{kLT}\right] = \text{Const.}$$

$$\text{(I)} \quad \text{(II)} \quad \text{(III)} \quad \text{(IV)}$$

The significance of the terms in the above equation is

(I) = ratio of bulk transport to radiation, also called radiation group
(II) = absolute temperature ratio
(III) = ratio of bulk transport to conduction
(IV) = ratio of total heat transferred to conduction

The above dimensionless equation would apply under conditions in which flow could be taken as streamline and the effects of turbulence neglected.

Under conditions in which there is no radiation-absorbing medium between radiating surfaces, the radiation q_i from a surface S_i that reaches surface S_j, designated as $\overline{S_iS_j}$, equals L^2 times a dimensionless function of the shape of the system and of the emissivities of surfaces forming the enclosure. If all surfaces are grey then the net flux by radiation between zone i and j can be given as

$$q_i = \overline{S_iS_j}\ \sigma(T_i^4 - T_j^4)$$

For a system in which there are only two radiant surfaces (of fairly uniform temperatures), the characteristic for heat transfer by radiation and for other modes of heat transfer can be replaced by $4T_{Av}^3\epsilon_s$

where $T_{Av} = \dfrac{T_1 + T_2}{2}$, and ϵ_s = surface emmissivity

When there is a radiation-absorbing medium (combustion gases with or without solid phase such as soot) the modeling becomes considerably more involved. For an interchange of radiation between a surface element and a gas volume element a similar relationship can be written

$$q_{i=j} = \overline{S_iS_j}\ \sigma(T_1^4 - T_2^4)$$

where $\overline{S_iS_j}$ can be expressed, as before, as L^2 times a dimensionless function ϵ_{s2} of the surface emissivities and of KL where K is the attenuation coefficient of radiation in the radiation-absorbing medium ($\epsilon = 1 - e^{-KL}$). The value of K will be a function of the concentration of the radiation-absorbing medium and of the incident wave length, and for luminous radiation it will depend also on the optical characteristics of the dispersed solid phase.

Homogeneous Chemical Processes

Chemical reactions take place in fluid media and are accompanied by the evolution or absorption of heat. The reaction rate is not only strongly influenced by the temperature but also by the point concentration of reactants and reaction products, and hence by the fluid flow patterns and rates of mass transfer.

An equation connecting heat transfer by conduction and convection with rate of heat evolution is

$$\rho c_p \left(u \frac{\partial T}{\partial x} + v \frac{\partial T}{\partial y} + w \frac{\partial T}{\partial z}\right) - k\left(\frac{\partial^2 T}{\partial x^2} + \frac{\partial^2 T}{\partial y^2} + \frac{\partial^2 T}{\partial z^2}\right) + \rho c_p \frac{\partial T}{\partial t} = qQ$$

where Q = chemical reaction rate expressed as mass of product formed per volume and time

q = heat of reaction per unit mass of product

In dimensionless form the above equation can be expressed as

$$\phi \left[\frac{\rho c_p vL}{k}, \frac{qQL}{\rho c_p vT}\right] = \text{Const.}$$

The mass-transfer equation can be written as

$$\left(u \frac{\partial a}{\partial x} + v \frac{\partial a}{\partial y} + w \frac{\partial a}{\partial z}\right) - D\left(\frac{\partial^2 a}{\partial x^2} + \frac{\partial^2 a}{\partial y^2} + \frac{\partial^2 a}{\partial z^2}\right) + \frac{\partial a}{\partial t} = Q$$

where a = concentration of reacting substance per unit volume

D = diffusion coefficient of reacting substance

Whence the dimensionless equation

$$\phi \left(\frac{vL}{D}, \frac{QL}{av}\right) = \text{Const.}$$

Heat transfer by radiation cannot, in general, be neglected, and therefore must also be taken into account. Then the full dimensionless equation for a homogenous chemical reaction taking place in a moving-fluid medium is given as:

$$\phi \left(\frac{\rho vL}{\mu}, \frac{v^2}{2q}, \frac{\Delta p}{\rho v^2}, \frac{\rho c_p vL}{k}, \frac{qQL}{\rho c_p vT}, \frac{vL}{D}, \frac{QL}{av}, \frac{Q}{\sigma \epsilon L^2 T^4}, \frac{T_1}{T_2}\right) = \text{Const.}$$

which with some re-arrangement becomes

$$\frac{QL}{av} = \phi\left(\frac{\rho vL}{\mu}, \frac{c_p\mu}{k}, \frac{\mu}{\rho D}, \frac{qa}{\rho c_p T}, \frac{qav}{\sigma\epsilon T^4}, \frac{T_1}{T_2}\right)$$
$$\text{(I)} \qquad \text{(II)} \qquad \text{(III)} \qquad \text{(IV)} \qquad \text{(V)} \qquad \text{(VI)} \qquad \text{(VII)}$$

The significance of the terms in the above equation is:

(I) = Ratio of product concentration to reactant concentration after a given time or length of travel.

(II) = Reynolds number, representing the ratio of inertial to viscous forces and governing the flow pattern and hence the statistical distribution of residence times among the reactant molecules.

(III) = Prandtl number, representing the ratio of heat transferred by bulk transport to heat transfer by conduction.

(IV) = Schmidt number, representing the material transferred in ratio of bulk transport to molecular diffusion.

(V) = Ratio of potential to sensible-heat content per unit volume.

(VI) = Ratio of potential chemical heat transferred by bulk transport to heat radiated

(VII) = Ratio of emission rates of hot and cold radiating surfaces.

Reaction Rate

The reaction rate Q depends upon controllable variables such as concentration and temperature. The general equation for the rate of a homogeneous chemical reaction is

$$Q = u_n F\,(a_1 a_2 a_3 \text{-------} a_n)$$

Where u_n = rate constant of nth order reaction and $a_1 a_2 a_3 \text{----} a_n$ = molecular concentration of reactants.

The dimensions of u_n vary with the order of the reaction and its value is strongly influenced by the reaction temperature in accordance with the modified Arrhenius equation (assuming negligible pressure dependence)

$$u_n = AT^{1/2} \exp\left(\frac{-E}{RT}\right)$$

where A = a dimensional constant
R = gas constant
T = absolute temperature
E = activation energy

Heterogeneous Reactions

The rate of heterogeneous chemical reaction depends upon the interfacial area between the phases and can be represented by a generalized equation

$$Q^1 = \phi\,[u_n^1\, F\, \alpha (a_1 a_2 a_3 \text{------} a_n)\,]$$

where u_n = velocity constant for a heterogeneous reaction of nth order; its dimension varies with the order of the reactions.

F = kinetic factor as for homogeneous reactions.

α = dimensionless factor proportional to catalytic activity of interface.

Enthalpy

Enthalpy in a bulk of 1-D flow may be expressed by

$$\underset{\text{(I)}}{\frac{\partial}{\partial x}(\rho u H)} = \underset{\text{(II)}}{\frac{\partial}{\partial x}\Gamma_H \frac{\partial H}{\partial x}} + \underset{\text{(III)}}{a(R_x - \sigma T^4)}$$

where $H = C_p T + \sum_j I_j m_j + \dfrac{u^2}{2}$

$$\Gamma_H = \frac{\mu}{\text{Prandtl number}}$$

Transport of individual species can be described by a similar equation for each m_j in which

$\Gamma_j = \dfrac{\mu}{\text{Schmidt number}}$ and the radiation term is replaced by a net production term for m_j.

$$\frac{\text{(I)}}{\text{(II)}} = \text{Re x Pr} = \text{Peclet number}$$

$$\frac{\text{(I)}}{\text{(III)}} = \text{Thring radiation group.}$$

From the above equations it appears that there is no possibility of getting thermal similarity without first having kinematic similarity.

Entrainment

The ratio of the mass of ambient fluid entrained to the mass of forward flow is given by the expression[103]

$$\frac{M}{M_o} = K\frac{x}{d_o}\left(\frac{\rho_s}{\rho_o}\right)^{1/2} = K\frac{x}{d_o}\left(\frac{T_o}{T_s}\right)^{1/2}$$

For swirling jets[105]

$$K = K(1 + 0.8S)$$

where S, the swirl number is defined as

$$S = \frac{G_\phi}{G_x R}$$

and where G_ϕ = axial flux and angular momentum

G_x = axial flux and linear momentum

R = burner radius

Residence Time Distribution

The problem of residence time distribution in burners and combustors is of great interest mainly because of its potential in predicting the performance and efficiency of reactors[106, 107]. In different systems it is reasonable to assume that kinetic time is fixed and independent of scale. In gas flames, combustion is largely mixing controlled and it is reasonable to assume that kinetic time is not so important. Nevertheless, in temperature-dependent reactions, for example those involved in pulverized fuel and oil combustion, the time-dependent processes such as droplet/particle aerodynamics, heating and evaporation are important and must be taken into consideration. If one assumes that the droplet burning rate is proportional to its diameter then droplet size should be scaled in relation to the ratio of length scale to the velocity scale, that is, in proportion to the residence time[108].

The three following possibilities can therefore be suggested:

1. Constant Reynolds number – Load $\propto$ (burner diameter) leads to large distortions in linear dimension and velocity when scales are widely different. Also for a given reaction an equality in Re is of model and prototype need not be the same[97]. This is also true when the flow is of the jet-mixing type used in furnaces.
2. Constant velocity – Load $\propto$ (burner diameter)^2. This criteria was applied at IFRF on trials with 1MW and 3MW burners. Good agreement was found for gas flames. Nevertheless, for oil flames, poor stability was found and was attributed to the reduced residence time of oil droplets in the flame.
3. Constant mean residence time – Load $\propto$ (burner diameter)^3. In this case it is assumed that the flame volume can be related to the burner dimensions so that burner diameter is proportional to (flow throughput)$^{1/3}$. This results in higher burner velocities in scaled-up burners and proportionally lower velocities in scaled-down burners. Residence time scaling criterion is also applicable if one is to obtain both kinematic and thermal similarity[108]. In 'perfectly-stirred flows' the residence time distribution can be shown to be of the form[107]

$$\phi\ (t) = \frac{1}{\bar{t}}\ \exp\ (\frac{-t}{\bar{t}})$$

where t = time

$\bar{t}$ = mean residence time (reactor volume divided by volume flow rate)

In 'plug-type flows' where the elements of fluid move through at radially uniform velocity, the residence time is equal to $\bar{t}$. The distribution of residence times by a consequence of departure from plug flow, and the degree of this departure can be characterized also by the recirculation patterns. A comparison of the residence time distributions in the 1/10-scale water model and in the furnace showed a reasonably good agreement so long as the swirl number was kept constant. Nevertheless, for stirred part model and furnace some differences in mean residence time were found, suggesting different sizes of the internal recirculation zones in model and furnace.

Combustion Noise

Combustion noise is the unwanted sound associated with the combination process, the oxidation in air of solid, liquid and gaseous fuel to produce heat and light. Noise from a combustion system may come from the vibration of combustors and the rotation, translation, and vibration of ancillary machinery. Combustion noise may come from one or more types of simple source—monopoles, dipoles, or quadrupoles.

Monopole noise arises from the local change in combustion rate.

Dipole noise arises from combustion oscillations, vortex shedding, etc. and its acoustic power increases as u^4.

Quadrupole or aerodynamic noise arises from a jet flow and its acoustic power increases as u^8.

In view of the diversity of combustion noise prediction techniques, and the many results now available, a review is undertaken to clarify the resultant scaling laws for this noise source.

In brief, the following 'laws' can be predicted, to many of the available measured or theoretical predictions for combustion roar sound power output[109, 110]

$$P \propto u^{4-3g} S_L^{r+3g} L^{2+r}$$

where u = flow velocity, S_L = laminar burning velocity, and L = linear dimension (diameter). For the Bragg method[11]:

from [109]: $r + o$, and $g = 1/3$
$r = o$, and $g = 2/3$
from[112]:
$r = 1$, and $g = o$
from[113]:
$r = 0$, and $g = 0$

From the above examples the diversity of results and theories pertaining to combustion roar sound power may be clearly seen.

It must be noted, also, that the above results are taken from measurements and theories relating to open turbulent flames. The principal effect of enclosing the flame in an enclosure; for example, a tunnel or cavity or combustion chamber is to amplify or cancel certain parts of the noise spectrum[114, 115] or to cause a structural damage to the outer shell during prolonged running of the combustor[115]. The decrease in noise levels can also be explained by flame shielding[116] which was investigated on small swirl burners.

In studying several burner sizes in a series, one cannot assume that burners can be 'scaled up' acoustically. The relative effect of dimensionless parameter, swirl number, on the 'scale up' is unknown. Some burners are scaled up on a constant combustion intensity basis, which changes the prediction rules.

Application of Theory

The fundamental information in flames from bench scale experiment can be obtained by a detailed experimental analysis using modern advanced combustion diagnostic techniques. These detailed results are then applied for checking the mathematical models. The results of basic combustion studies are then used in applied combustion studies of domestic and industrial importance, using scaling criteria and generalized by mathematical models or dimensionless parameters. Although the technique of partial modeling can provide reasonable information on pre-selected parameters such as fluid mechanics of turbulent mixing, heat transfer in flames, chemical kinetics, etc., it cannot predict effects due to prolonged running of the combustor upon corrosion, erosion, acid smut, ash fouling, slagging, etc. One cannot even predict with reasonable confidence the pollutants emission levels, in particular noise and instability. In the previous section it was indicated that there is a fewfold difference in the available data and prediction for combustion noise sound power output from simple bench type diffusion or premixed flames. Very little data is available from flames of industrial importance[120]. Furthermore, this data cannot be correlated well with simple flames due to the lack of understanding of shielding of noise from the flame surface, (that is, reflection, transmission and absorption of sound from within the flame). It is therefore recommended that more rigorous detailed data and its analysis should be obtained from flames of industrial importance and their effect upon prolonged running of the combustor.

The Damköhler kinetic parameter is the primary factor in the formation of combustion products[97, 104]. The flame temperature is based on the heat generation from combustion and radiative heat transfer from the flame.

In large boilers, radiation accounts for most of the heat transfer, typically 90 per cent. For small boilers, however, heat conduction assumes a far more significant role. Therefore, it is important to maintain this characteristic of the full-scale system through similarity in the radiation/conduction parameter. Shear/momentum, shear/bouyancy, and gravitational effects relate various flow characteristics of the fuel mixture to its ambient environment. Similarity, in carbon dioxide formation should help insure accuracy in the results for flue gas composition.

The relationships required among scale factors in order to maintain similarity can now be determined. The required scale factors for velocity, nozzle diameter, and wall temperatures for the required similarity as a function of the linear dimension scale factor are shown in Figs. 3.5-3.7 respectively[117].

Most of the functions in these figures tend to diverge as the linear dimension scale-up factor increases; that is, as the model becomes smaller in relation to the prototype, except for temperature and slagging. These results reveal the increasing difficulty in maintaining similarity among a number of system characteristics as scale-up increases in size.

Concerning the noise output from burners/combustors, very little data is available from flames of industrial importance. A comparison of the thermoacoustic efficiencies from pre-mixed and diffusion type flames shows large variations in thermoacoustic efficiency.

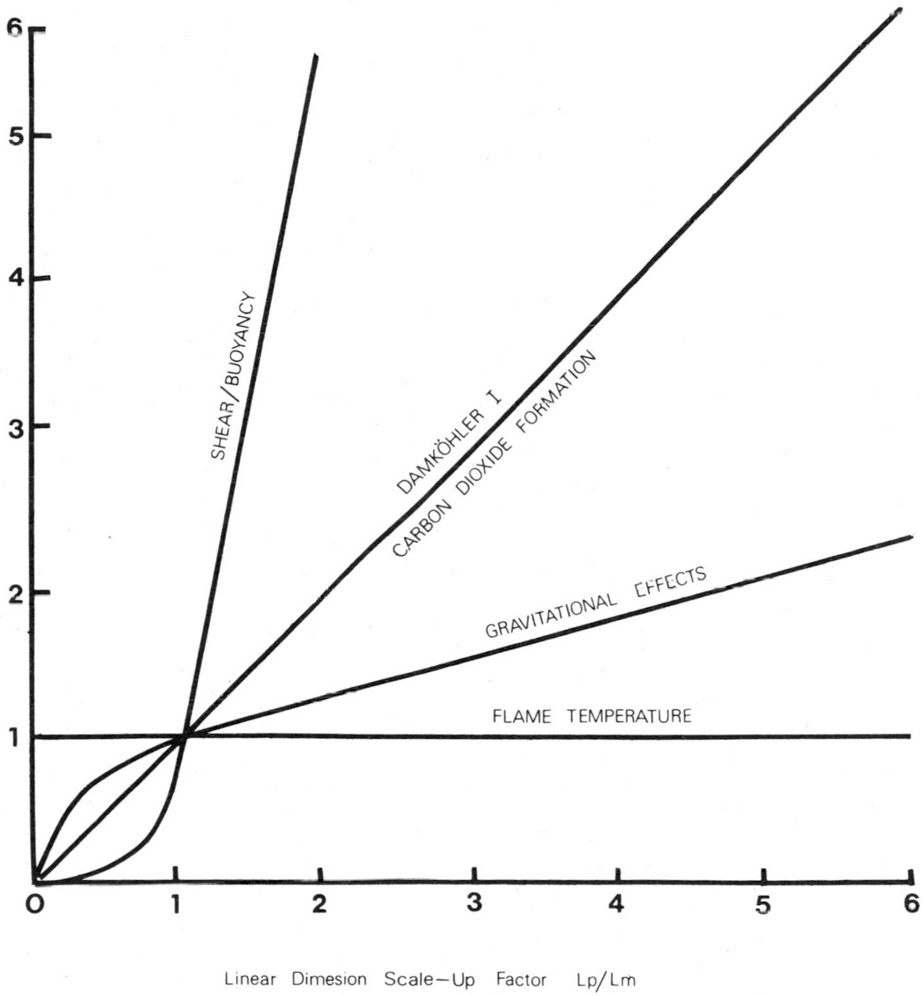

Figure 3.5 Velocity Scale-Up Requirements Related to Size Scale-Up

Long-term effects due to corrosion and erosion in boiler/combustor installation is much more difficult to predict. The reason for corrosion is that the rate of attack depends not only on the chemical composition and temperature of the process fluids and materials of construction, but also on velocity, flow aerodynamics, and geometry of the system. Short duration prototype tests are not sufficient to furnish a reliable information upon corrosion under actual running of the combustor. The diffusion mechanism is complicated by the formation of ferric hydroxide which partly protects the surface from further attack by creating an effective film thickness. In 'scaling up' therefore, the corrosion rates are not those predicted on the assumption of constant average penetration and furnace tube diameter.

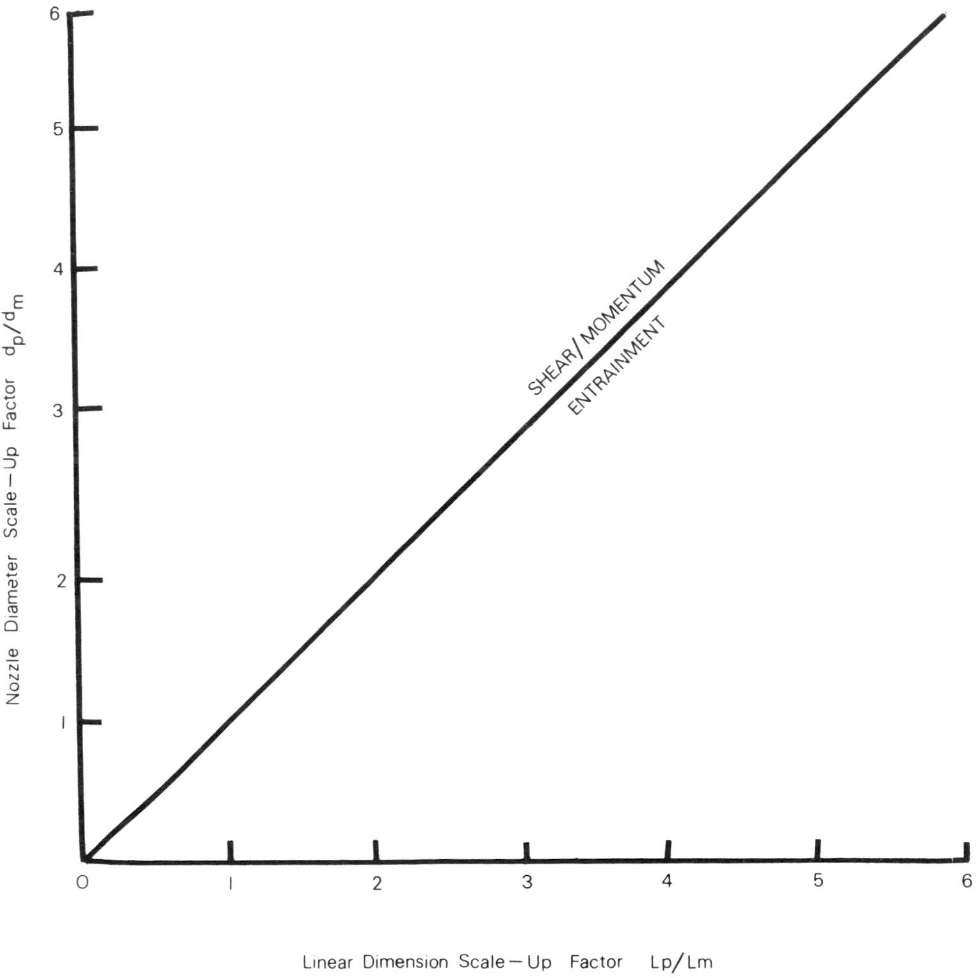

Figure 3.6 Nozzle Diameter Scale-Up Requirements Related to Size Scale-Up

The erosion, in general, is due either to the direct abrasion of metal by solid particles or by the continuous removal of oxide or protective film so that the corrosion is accelerated. Suspended fluid particles can also cause erosion; for example, water droplets in steam or air bubbles in water. It is difficult to give quantitative scale relations for the overall rate of attack by corrosion and erosion[104]. Even under the conditions in which heat and mass transfer coefficients are equal in the model and prototype, although the average corrosion rates are of the same order of magnitude, the localized corrosion and erosion rates are not and, in general, are higher in the prototype. This is also true for new types of coal-derived fuels, coal/oil slurries, high C/H ratio fuels with high nitrogen and aromatic content.

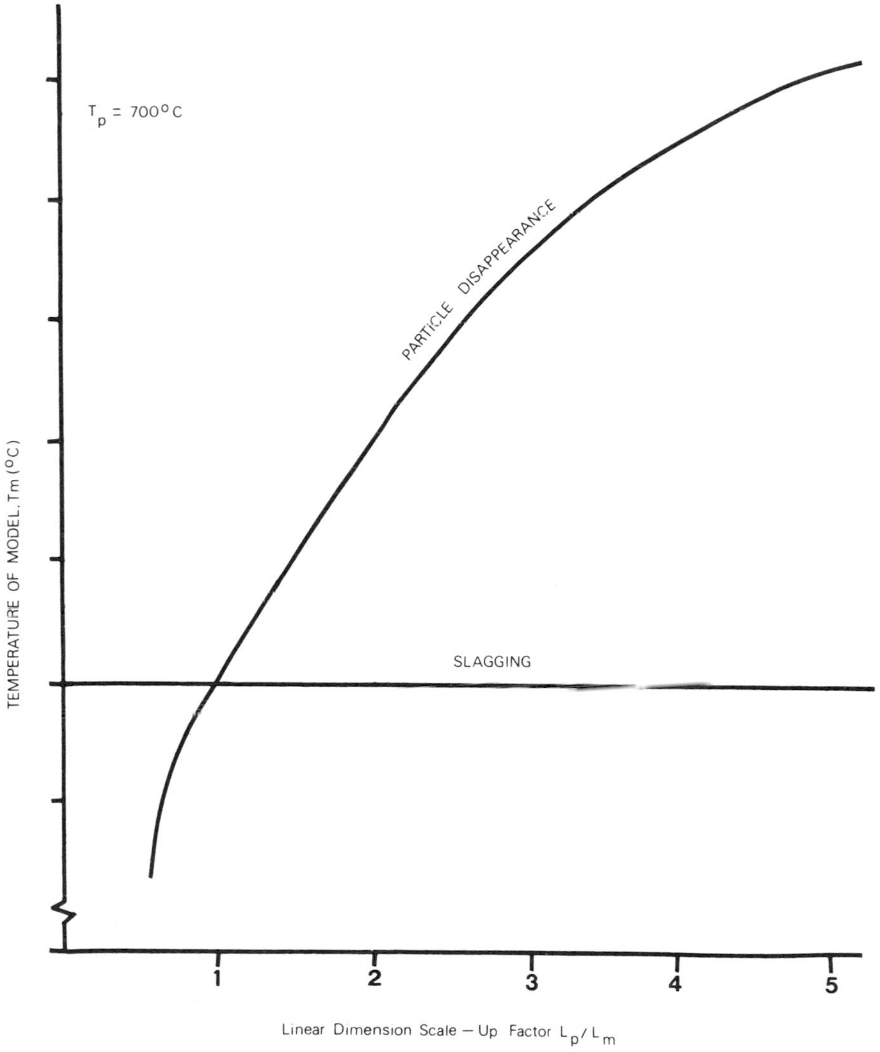

Figure 3.7 Wall Temperature Requirements to Size Scale-Up for Phototype Wall Temperature 700 C

For modeling and scaling criteria for 'scale-up' of burners and combustors, it is therefore appropriate to develop, under sufficiently severe conditions, methods for predicting furnace performance; that is, flame stability and contour, radiative and convective heat flux distributions, and combustion generated pollutant emission. This research will feed back information for the formulation of basic research projects in areas where lack of physical and chemical parameters are hindering the development of mathematical models and will also enable comparisons to be made between various models regarding their accuracy and the relative efforts required to be expended in computation.

3.4 AXISYMMETRIC SWIRLING BOUNDARY LAYER FLOWS

von Mises (x, ψ) Forward Marching Solution Procedure

Typically, 2-D marching methods are used for parabolic boundary layer flows. They involve 1-D storage, automatic expanding grid using nondimensionalized stream function ψ instead of r as the radial coordinate, and implicit solution procedure[122, 123]. A 2-D axisymmetric parabolic flow is simulated by a simplified form of the governing equations, typified by

$$\sum_{i=1}^{2} a_i \frac{\partial \phi}{\partial x_i} + b \frac{\partial}{\partial x_2} \left(c \frac{\partial \phi}{\partial x_2}\right) = d \tag{3.6}$$

Many examples of this type of flow exist in connection with combustion equipment: axisymmetric steady jets, wakes and flames, boundary layers on walls, flows in pipes, diffusers, nozzles, solid-propellant rockets, and after-burner reheat systems. In particular, weakly swirling flows without recirculation are examples of 2-D axisymmetric boundary layer flows. A standard computer program is available for solving this type of problem; some details are shown in Fig. 3.8 which includes an example of a flame computation. The marching integration proceeds on an automatic expanding grid and the finite difference formulation is implicit in character; this combination ensures economy and stability; accuracy is achieved by having a fine grid. Of all the techniques available for this type of flow, this particular one is noteworthy in that the program is generally formulated and includes the novelty of a nondimensional stream function which replaces the

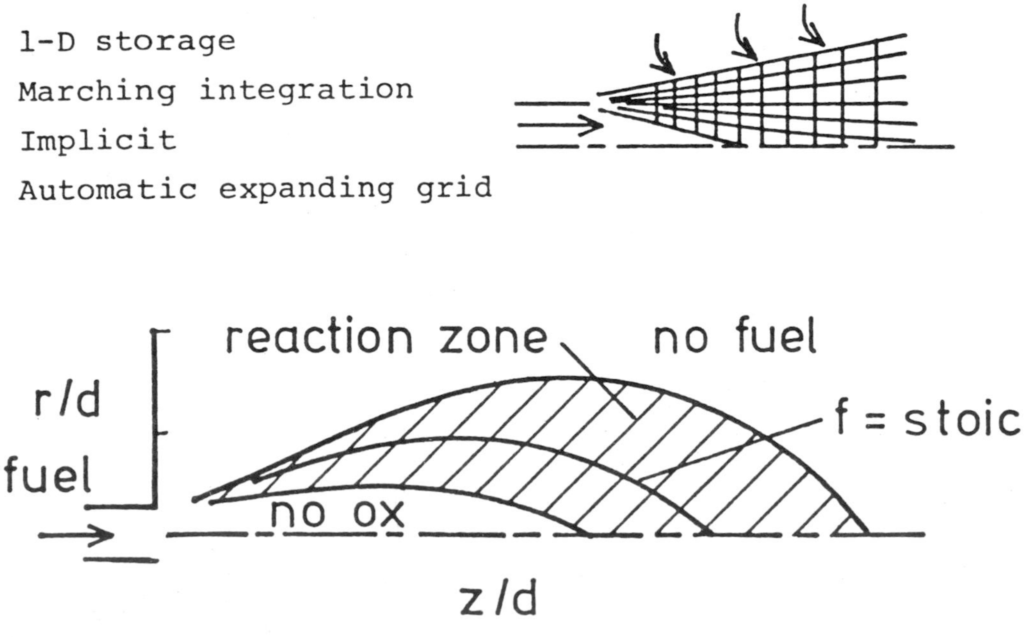

Figure 3.8 Computation Procedure for 2–D Parabolic Flows

radial coordinate. The computation shown concerns a turbulent propane-air diffusion flame and the diagram shows the computed shape of the reaction zone. To make such computations, one has to solve seven simultaneous differential equations for u, k, ℓ, h, m_{fu}, f and g. The last of these is required in order to allow the turbulent diffusion flame zone to have a finite thickness.

Although the main structure of the method[122] proved to be quite satisfactory in subsequent intensive use, some of the details had to be altered for accuracy, simplicity and computational efficiency. These included the satisfaction of the conservation equations throughout the entire layer, a more accurate finite difference representation of first order cross-stream derivatives to allow for high lateral flux and a simpler and more generally applicable entrainment rate calculation. A substantially modified version of the original program is now available[123]. Extensive modifications are required in order to predict swirl flows with the basic code; some details are available for inert[42, 44, 124] and reacting[125, 126] swirl flows, which are now summarized.

Transformed Basic Equations

The parabolic partial differential equation system is first transformed from (x, r)-coordinates to von Mises coordinates (x, ψ) via

$$\psi\ (r) = \int_0^r \rho u r dr \qquad \text{(for fixed } x\text{)}$$

The stream function ψ has the properties

$$r\rho u = \partial\psi/\partial r$$

$$r\rho v = -\partial\psi/\partial x$$

$$d\psi_I/dx = -r_I \dot{m}_I''$$

$$d\psi_E/dx = -r_E \dot{m}_E''$$

where $\dot{m}_I''$ and $\dot{m}_E''$ are the rates of mass transfer across the I (interior) and E (exterior) boundaries. These entrainment rates are related to local turbulent viscosity and local velocity gradients via

$$r_E \dot{m}_E'' = \lim_{r \to r_E} \left[\frac{\partial}{\partial r}\left(r\mu \frac{\partial u}{\partial r}\right) / \frac{\partial u}{\partial r}\right]$$

$$r_I \dot{m}_I'' = 0$$

where the I boundary lies on the axis of symmetry.

The new nondimensional stream function ω, defined by

$$\omega = \frac{\psi - \psi_I}{\psi_E - \psi_I}$$

where ψ_I and ψ_E represents values of ψ at the interior and exterior edges of the boundary layer, allows further transformation to (x,ω)-coordinates, with the property that regardless of the width of the layer the value of ω always lies between 0 and 1. Thus, the whole of the interesting region is confined between these values of ω. The continuity equation is now redundant, ν having been deleted and ψ introduced via

$$\nu = \frac{-1}{r\rho}\left\{(1-\omega)\frac{d\psi_I}{dx} + \omega\frac{d\psi_E}{dx}\right\}.$$

Applying these transformations to the relevant boundary layer equation from Chapter 2 yields the system

$$\frac{\partial\phi}{\partial x} + (a + b\omega)\frac{\partial\phi}{\partial\omega} = \frac{\partial}{\partial\omega}\left(c\frac{\partial\phi}{\partial\omega}\right) + d \tag{3.7}$$

where

$$a = r_I\dot{m}_I''/(\psi_E - \psi_I) = -\frac{1}{\psi_E - \psi_I}\frac{d\psi_I}{dx},$$

$$b = (r_E\dot{m}_E'' - r_I\dot{m}_I'')/(\psi_E - \psi_I) = -\frac{1}{\psi_E - \psi_I}\left(\frac{d\psi_E}{dx} - \frac{d\psi_I}{dx}\right),$$

c and d depend on the ϕ in question and are given in Table 3.2 which includes enthalpy, fuel and mixture fraction.

TABLE 3.2

Coefficients c and d in (x, ω) equation set

ϕ	c	d
u	$r^2\rho u\mu/(\psi_E - \psi_I)^2$	$-\frac{1}{\rho u}\frac{dp}{dx}$
rw	$r^2\rho u\frac{\mu}{\sigma_{r\theta}}/(\psi_E - \psi_I)^2$	$-\frac{2}{(\psi_E - \psi_I)}\frac{\partial}{\partial\omega}\left(rw\frac{\mu}{\sigma_{r\theta}}\right) - \frac{2vw}{u}$
h	$r^2\rho u\frac{\mu}{\sigma_h}/(\psi_E - \psi_I)^2$	0
m_{fu}	$r^2\rho u\frac{\mu}{\sigma_{fu}}/(\psi_E - \psi_I)^2$	$R_{fu}/(\rho u)$
f	$r^2\rho u\frac{\mu}{\sigma_f}/(\psi_E - \psi_I)^2$	0

The radial momentum equation transforms to the auxiliary pressure equation

$$(\psi_E - \psi_I)\, w^2 / (r^2 u) = \frac{\partial p}{\partial \omega}$$

Rather than solve the swirl equation as given in the table the swirl equation may be rewritten to yield the form

$$\frac{\partial}{\partial x}(rw) + (a + b\omega)\frac{\partial}{\partial \omega}(rw) = \frac{\partial}{\partial \omega}\left(cr^2 \frac{\partial}{\partial \omega}(w/r)\right) \qquad (3.8)$$

Here there is no source term but the form of the equation differs from the standard one: *rw* is the operand on the left and *w/r* on the right. This equation possesses the desirable quality of having no source term and is needed for accuracy purposes, but its incorporation into the general procedure necessitates some detailed changes in the finite difference formulation and associated changes to the program. The swirl equation and subsequent equations are solved in turn so that a more accurate downstream pressure gradient can be used in the source term of the axial equation.

The Finite Difference Equations

The (x, ω)-grid system, shown in Fig. 3.9 covers a physical (x,r) domain which diverges with the streamlines. To ensure conservation, rather than use the usual Taylor series method, a micro-integral method is used and each differential equation is integrated over a small control volume formed around each node, as shown in Fig. 3.10. On the assump-

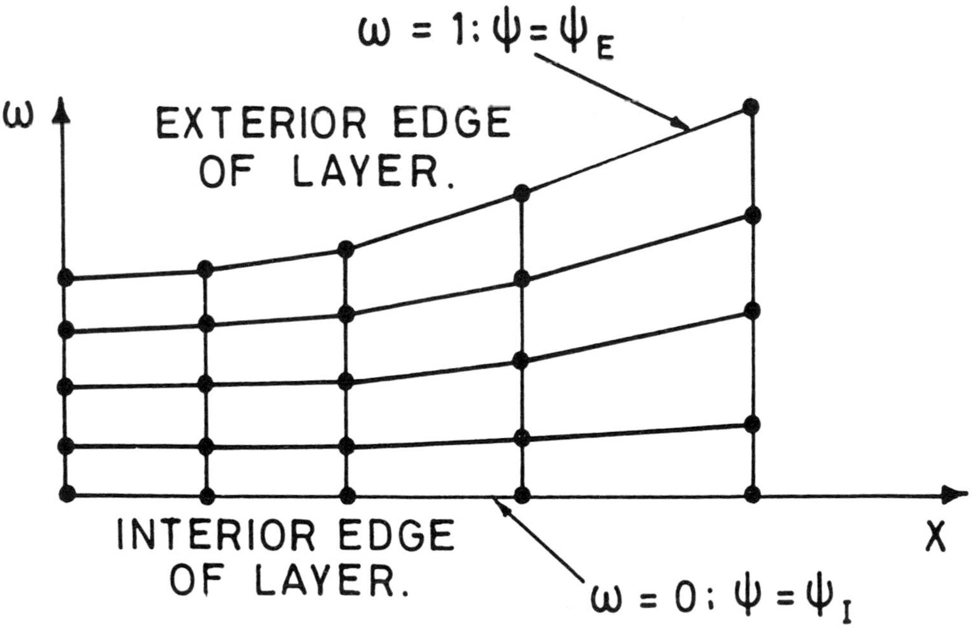

Figure 3.9 (x,ω) – Grid System[125]

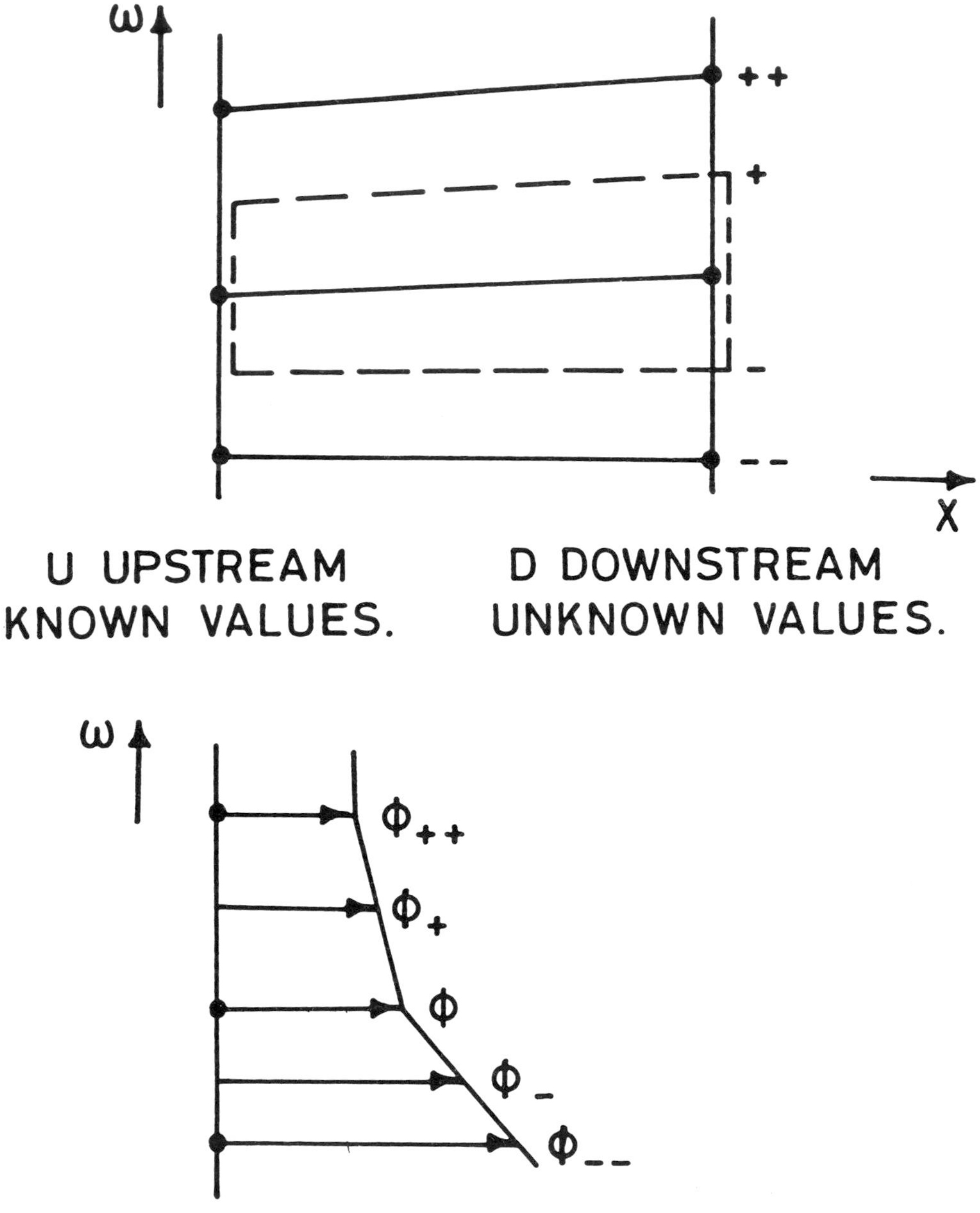

Figure 3.10 Micro-integral Method Applied to Control Volume [122]

tion that in the ω-direction ϕ varies linearly with ω between grid nodes, each term appears as an integrated average over the small control volume. For stability a fully implicit form, using downstream unknown values, is used. Iteration is avoided; linearization is effected by using upstream values for *a, b* and *c*, but accuracy demands that a forward extrapolation

$$d_D = d_U + \left[\frac{\partial d}{\partial \phi}\right]_U (\phi_D - \phi_U)$$

be used in the representation of the more important source term *d*. The variation of ϕ with *x* is supposed stepwise; for each ω the value of ϕ within the small control volume is equated to its value at the downstream edge. There is some modification for the half intervals near the boundaries involving the use of 'slip' values.

Introduction of the ϕ-ω profile assumption yields, after a little algebraic manipulation the finite difference equation

$$\phi = A\phi_{++} + B\phi_{--} + C$$

in which A, B and C are functions of the ω-differences, the values of the ϕ's at the upstream edge and the coefficients *a, b, c* and *d*. A, B and C are thus known when the entrainment rate is expressed in finite difference form. A reduced form of the equation is

$$r_E \dot{m}''_E = \frac{-2\mu}{r_{N+2} - r_{N+1}}$$

where N+2 is the slip grid-line and N+1 is the first interior grid-line near the E boundary. The procedure is applied to each grid node in the (x, ω)-grid system in turn and the result is a set of FDEs (one for each ϕ) valid at each node.

These equations are then solved for all the values of the dependent variables, in turn, at each successive down stream grid location. Because, for each forward step, the equations contain only three unknowns in a particular order and the grid edge values are known, matrix inversion difficulties are avoided by use of a simple successive-substitution technique in the form of the TriDiagonal Matrix Algorithm TDMA. In this way the solution is marched downstream as far as required, beginning with known profiles at the jet orifice. The standard code uses a form of Prandtl's mixing length hypothesis to specify the turbulent viscosity. Later studies have shown how it can be replaced by an appropriate two-equation or multi-equation turbulence model with considerable success[42, 44].

Analytic Inverse Analysis

In the development of turbulence models for complex flow systems, turbulent swirling boundary layers provide a convenient testground. Their equations contain two components of turbulent stress τ_{rx} and $\tau_{r\theta}$, which may be replaced in terms of their associated components of turbulent viscosity μ_{rx} and $\mu_{r\theta}$. These must be specified by a turbulence model prior to the prediction of time-mean velocity and pressure in the flowfield. Recent experimental, inverse, and prediction studies have tried to assess the effect of swirl on these components, and have disputed the isotropy assumption that the $r\theta$-viscosity number $\sigma_{r\theta} = \mu_{rx}/\mu_{r\theta}$, is equal to unity[42,44,45,127,129]. The present work obtains expressions for these components directly from analytical operations being performed on fitted-curve spatial distributions of time-mean values in swirling jet flows, so paralleling an associated numerical inverse technique, which is described in the next section[127,128].

Research experiments have been conducted concerning time-mean measurements on weakly swirling turbulent jet flows[130,132]. So that the variation of values with position in the flowfield and degree of swirl is easily calculable, curves have been fitted to the spatial distributions of time-mean values of u, v, w, and p (time-mean axial, radial and swirl velocity in x, r, θ-cylindrical polar coordinates and pressure). How these curvefit parameters vary, based on the sparse amount of experimental data available, with the swirl number S of the jet, is described in Chapters 1 and 3 (Ref. 12) and elsewhere[133,134]

The axial and swirl momentum equations (for quasi-steady axisymmetric boundary-layer flow neglecting laminar viscosity) may be taken in integral form to isolate the two turbulent stress components, so expressing them directly as functions of the other terms. The equations become

$$\frac{\partial}{\partial x}(r\rho u) + \frac{\partial}{\partial r}(r\rho v) = 0$$

$$\frac{\partial}{\partial r}(r\tau_{rx}) = r\rho\left[u\frac{\partial u}{\partial x} + v\frac{\partial u}{\partial r}\right] + r\frac{\partial p}{\partial x} \tag{3.9}$$

$$\frac{\partial}{\partial r}(r^2\tau_{r\theta}) = r^2\rho\left[u\frac{\partial w}{\partial x} + v\frac{\partial w}{\partial r}\right] + r\rho v w$$

$$\frac{\rho w^2}{r} = \frac{\partial p}{\partial r}$$

Substitution of the fitted-curve functions, and carrying out the appropriate analytic differentiation and integration operations yields simple expressions for the two stress components at any point in the flowfield, in terms of the curvefit parameters

$$r\tau_{rx} = -r\rho\xi u^2 + r\rho u v + P \tag{3.10}$$

$$r^2\tau_{r\theta} = -r^2\rho\xi u w + r^2\rho u w$$

where P is the pressure term considered in detail in the paper[132], and $\xi = r/(x+a)$ where a is apparent origin distance upstream from nozzle. Invoking stress-strain constitutive assumptions gives expressions for the two associated components of turbulent viscosity. Then $r\theta$-viscosity number $\sigma_{r\theta}$, mixing lengths L and l, and mixing length parameter λ may be calculated from

$$\sigma_{r\theta} = \mu_{rx}/\mu_{r\theta}$$

$$\mu_{rx} = \rho L r_{0.01} u_m$$
$$\mu_{rx} = \rho l^2 \left[(\partial u/\partial r)^2 + (r\partial(w/r)/\partial r)^2 \right]^{1/2}$$
$$l = \lambda r_{0.01}$$

where u_m is the station maximum axial velocity and the suffix 0.01 refers to the position where $u/u_m = 0.01$. From the calculated values of these, and possibly other, turbulence quantities in swirling systems, modification to turbulence models may be deduced. Hence a direct link is established between experimental *time-mean* values and certain *turbulence* quantities.

Numerical Inverse Analysis

Inversion of the equations must be done numerically if the experimenter's curve-fits cannot be handled analytically as in the last section. Again, this is an intermediate step that has been used on both swirling isothermal and combustion[129] systems. The method utilizes the grid system shown in Figs. 3.11 and 3.12 and allows distributions of τ_{rx}, $\tau_{r\theta}$, $(J_h)_r$ and $(J_j)_r$ and associated exchange coefficients (isotropy is not assumed) to be determined from the experimental mean distributions of u, w, T and m_j. It thus provides a link between mean measurements and certain correlations of turbulent fluctuation components and throws light on the appropriateness or otherwise of any given turbulence model for the flow under consideration. From the calculated valued of turbulence quantities in swirling systems, modifications to turbulence models may be deduced.

The calculation procedure[128] starts from the assumption that curves have been fitted to experimentally-observed time-mean u, w, T and m_j so that for given S, x and r their values are easily calculated. The unknowns p, ρ, v and the turbulent fluxes cannot be calculated at all points P of the flowfield, which are in the set [(4,J,4) $(1 \leqslant J \leqslant N$, J odd)] for some choice of axial station x and number of J values N:

In order to allow the outward sweep calculation, as mentioned above, the axis subpressures at the nodes (I, 1, 1) $(1 \leqslant I \leqslant 7)$ are first calculated from the radial momentum equation by inward integration using the trapezoidal rule with $h = \delta r$. Let P be one of the points (4,J,4) at the center of a small 7x7 rectangular subgrid. Since values of u, w, T and m_j (and hence h and ρu) are obtained at any of the nodes (I,J,K) $(1 \leqslant I \leqslant 7)$, respectively. Not all of these are required and thus not all of them are calculated. Most are calculated only at the center node (4,J,4).

The procedure for calculating the unknowns successively at P (The node (J,J,4) (J fixed)) is as follows:

1. The density ρ is calculated at the nodes (I,J,K) $(1 \leqslant I, K \leqslant 7)$ from the ideal gas law and knowledge of T at these nodes and disregard of density change due to pressure. Hence, ρu is calculated at these nodes and $\partial(\rho u)/dx$ at (4,J,K) $(1 \leqslant K \leqslant 7)$.
2. The pressure p is calculated at the nodes (I,J,K) $(1 \leqslant I, K \leqslant 7)$ from the radial momentum equation trapezoidal integration with stepsize δr, using the axis subpressures as boundary conditions. This exactly reverses the initial axis subpressure calculation. Hence $\partial p/\partial x$ is obtained at P.
3. The radial velocity v is calculated at P from the continuity equation using outward Simpson integration with stepsize δr.

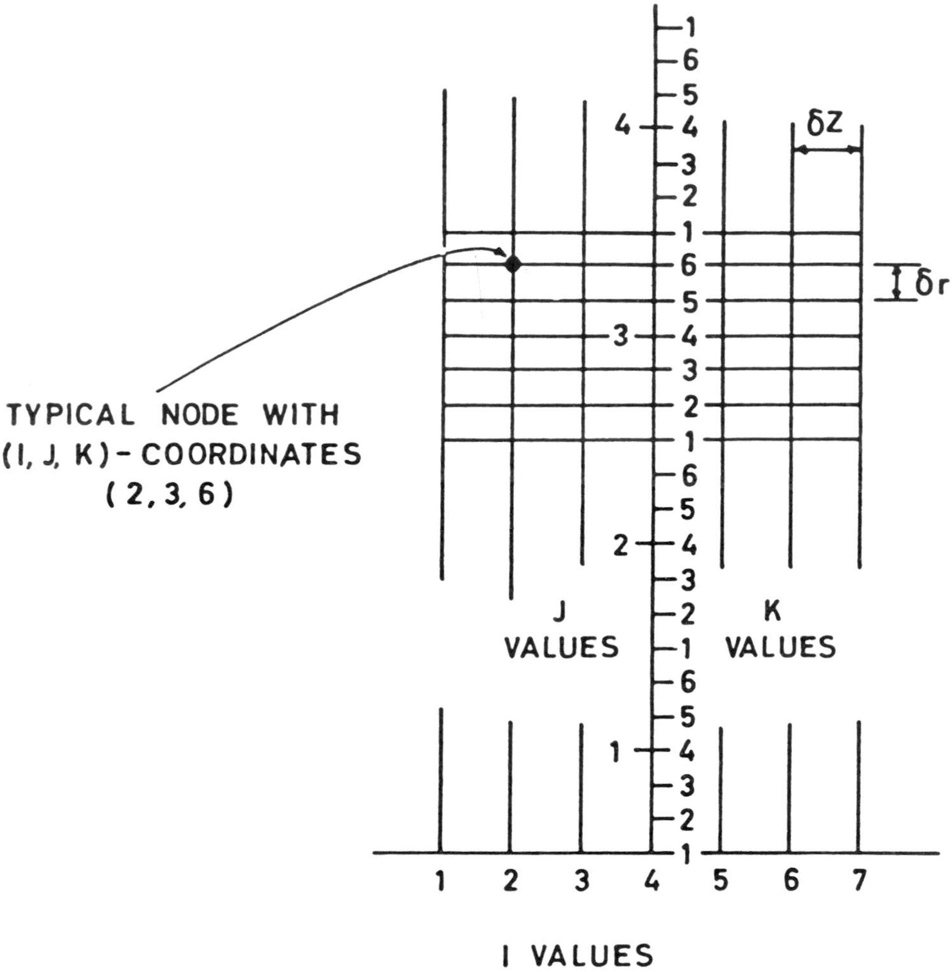

Figure 3.11 The Grid System for Each Axial Station, Used with the Inverse Computational Procedure.[128]

4. The values of all terms on the right-hand sides of the momentum and other conservations equations are calculated at P and values appropriate to the left-hand sides are deduced.
5. If J is odd and greater than unity, Simpson integration of these values over the three points (4,J-2,4), (4,J-1,4) and (4,J,4) with stepsize $6\delta r$, together with values of $r\tau_{rx}$, $r^2\tau_{r\theta}$, $r(J_h)$ and $r(J_j)_r$ at (4,J-2,4), enables the fluxes τ_{rx}, $\tau_{r\theta}$, $(J_h)_r$, and $(J_j)_r$ to be calculated at (4,J,4). If J is unity or even, the values of the right-hand sides are stored and no integration is performed until the next odd J value is reached.

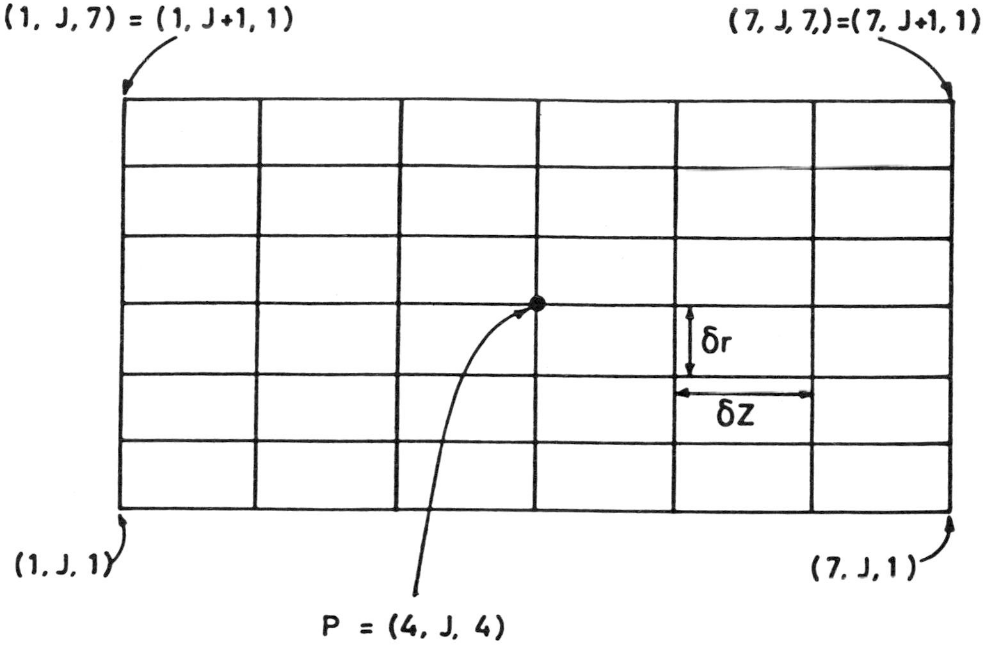

Figure 3.12 The Subgrid Associated With Points P = (4,J,4) ($1 \leqslant J \leqslant N$) [Ref. 128]

6. If J is odd and output is required here, calculation and output are made of the flux, exchange coefficients, Prandtl, Schmidt and $r\theta$-viscosity numbers and mixing length parameter.

Repetition of this process for higher values of J allows cross-stream results at some axial station to be deduced. If experimental mean measurements of p and/or ν are available, step (ii) and/or (iii) may be omitted. Boundary conditions are required for the integration stages; these are

$$p = P_\infty \text{ at } r = \infty ,$$

$$\text{v} = \tau_{rx} = \tau_{r\theta} = (J_h)_r = 0 \text{ at } r = 0.$$

Repetition of the procedure at other axial stations x and other swirl number S enables full spatial and swirl distributions to be obtained.

3.5 AXISYMMETRIC SWIRLING RECIRCULATING FLOWS

Basic Ideas

Axisymmetric 2-D elliptic recirculating flows require relaxation solution techniques. They involve 2-D storage, stream function-vorticity ψ-ω or primitive pressure-velocity p-u-v formulation, and Gauss-Seidel or line-by-line SIMPLE solution procedure[87,88]. Most combustion systems exhibit recirculation. They are therefore not amenable to the kind of marching integration process that has just been mentioned in Section 3.4; instead, iterative procedures are essential, unless, of course, the equations are time-dependent as well, in which case they are parabolic in the time-direction and a time-march is appropriate. The typical equation is now

$$\sum_{i=1}^{2} a_i \frac{\partial \phi}{\partial x_i} + \sum_{i=1}^{2} b_i \frac{\partial}{\partial x_i}\left(c_i \frac{\partial \phi}{\partial x_i}\right) = d \tag{3.11}$$

which exemplifies axisymmetric steady flows with recirculation, flame stabilization, rocket-base flow, and swirling flow in a cylindrical chamber. In particular, strongly swirling flames with recirculation fall into this category. The equations now possess second-order derivatives with respect to both x_1 and x_2 directions, and a greater number of coefficients occur than was the case in Section 3.4. The equations are elliptic and together with this simulation problem it is the necessity to solve the equations; a more lengthy numerical relaxation method is appropriate. The solution may be obtained using the pressure-velocity[88] or stream function-vorticity[87] approach (which reduces the number of equations to be solved and eliminates the troublesome pressure at the expense of trouble with the vorticity equation). General methods are available for these problems and some details are shown in Fig. 3.13 together with an example computation obtained by use of the latter approach. The iteration proceeds by Gauss-Seidel relaxation on a predetermined variable size grid which is made fine in regions of great activity. The programs are generally formulated and recent developments include a line-by-line SIMPLE relaxation method to speed convergence. All values of dependent variables at grid points must

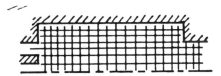

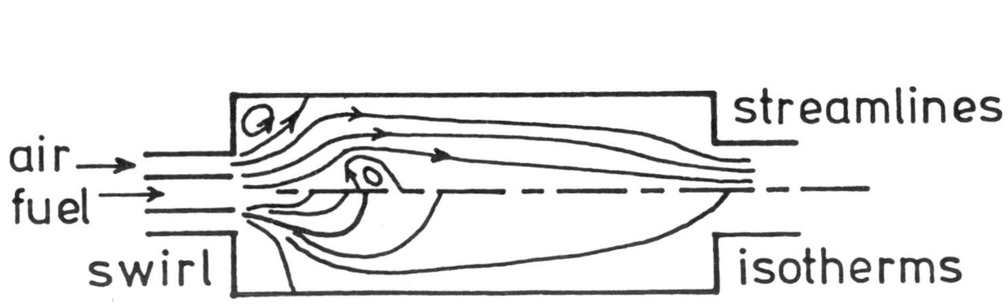

Figure 3.13 Computational Procedure for 2-D Elliptic Flows

be simultaneously in store and memory requirements are therefore greater than those of the previous section.

The example shows early computations with simple simulations of the processes involved[87]. It shows streamline patterns and constant temperature contours in an axisymmetric chamber supplied with gaseous fuel in a jet along the axis and with an annular swirling stream of oxidant gas. To make such computations equations are solved for ω, ψ, w and f. Similar computations can now be made via the primitive variables, in which case equations are solved for p-u-v-w and f. Chapter 5 cites sample computations of strongly swirling flows obtained using both of these techniques, which are now discussed more fully.

Stream Function ∿ Vorticity (ψ, ω) Iterative Solution Procedure

In this technique[87] the equations are reduced to the general form, in cylindrical polar coordinates:

$$a\left\{\frac{\partial\psi}{\partial x}\left(\phi\,\frac{\partial\psi}{\partial r}\right)-\frac{\partial}{\partial r}\left(\phi\,\frac{\partial\psi}{\partial x}\right)\right\}-\frac{\partial}{\partial x}\left\{br\,\frac{d}{dx}(c\phi)\right\}$$

$$-\frac{\partial}{\partial r}\left[br\,\frac{\partial}{\partial r}(c\phi)\right]+rd=0 \qquad (3.12)$$

where ϕ represents a general dependent variable and, again, the equations differ primarily in their final source terms d. The forms of the coefficients a, b, c and d are given in Table 3.3 for a typical set of variables. These equations involve ψ and ω, which are defined by

$$r\rho u = \partial\psi/\partial r$$

$$r\rho v = -\partial\psi/\partial x$$

$$\omega = \partial v/\partial x - \partial u/\partial r$$

A tank and tube micro-integral method is used to obtain the corresponding finite difference equation FDE

$$\phi_P = \sum_j c_j\phi_j + D_F \qquad (3.13)$$

relating the value of a dependent variable at a node point P to its values at its four neighboring points of a variable size rectangular grid, which is made fine in regions of a great activity, for accuracy and economy reasons.

In obtaining these FDEs a certain degree of upwind-differencing is employed to enhance the iterative stability[87]. The scheme has a first order accuracy, but its use for the first order terms of the equation causes the stability of the solution procedure to be far greater than could be obtained by using a central-differencing method, which has a second order accuracy. This is true especially for high Reynolds number flows. Nevertheless, it has been found that upwind-differencing (as well as all schemes associated with

TABLE 3.3

Coefficients a, b, c and d in (ψ, ω) Equation Set*

ϕ	a	b	c	d
ψ	0	$\frac{1}{\rho r}$	1	$-\omega$
ω/r	r^2	r^3	μ	$-\frac{\partial}{\partial x}(\rho w^2) - r\left[\frac{\partial}{\partial x}\left(\frac{u^2+v^2}{2}\right)\frac{\partial \rho}{\partial r} - \frac{\partial}{\partial r}\left(\frac{u^2+v^2}{2}\right)\frac{\partial \rho}{\partial x}\right] + S_\omega$
rw	1	$r^3\mu$	$\frac{1}{r^2}$	0
h	1	$r\frac{\mu}{\sigma_h}$	1	0
m_{fu}	1	$r\frac{\mu}{\sigma_{fu}}$	1	R_{fu}
f	1	$r\frac{\mu}{\sigma_f}$	1	0

*S_ω in the ω/r equation is rather complex and defined in Gosman *et al.*[87] Nevertheless, it may often be taken simply as zero.

one-sided differencing) gives rise to a false diffusion of ϕ. The importance of this false diffusion is related to the ratio of Γ_{false} to Γ_{eff}, which is given as

$$\frac{\Gamma_{false}}{\Gamma_{eff}} = 0.36R_{loc}\,\sigma_{eff}\left(\frac{\mu_{lam}}{\mu_{eff}}\right)\left(\frac{h}{L}\right)\sin(2\alpha)$$

where R_{loc} is the Reynolds number ($\rho VL/\mu$) based on a typical length L. These equations are then solved iteratively (by the Gauss-Seidel point by-point technique) using under-relaxation (to produce convergence) or over-relaxation (to speed convergence) as required.

From the finally converged solution, it is necessary to deduce values of further interest in the flowfield; namely the axial and radial velocities and pressure. The velocity components are readily deducible from the stream function defining equation given earlier. Pressure may be obtained from its Poisson equation, obtained by appropriately differentiating the axial and radial momentum equations, and adding to yield.

$$\nabla^2 p = f(\rho, \mu, u, v, w) \tag{3.14}$$

where, of course, u and v on the right may be written in terms of stream function[75].

Examples of relevant calculations made via this technique may be found in Ref. 61-65, with additional information being given in Chapter 5 of the present text. Whereas this technique has given good service, it is now somewhat dated and being superseded by primitive variable solution procedures, which are now described at rather greater length.

Primitive Variable (p, u, v) TEACH Iterative Solution Procedure

The technique described[50-54] solves directly for the primitive pressure and velocity variables, unlike the one just described which obtains these by way of stream function and vorticity. There is now increasing evidence that this approach possesses several advantages: It can be used for 3-D as well as 2-D problems, it can handle compressible and time-dependent problems as well as incompressible steady ones; and boundary conditions and variable properties are more accurately and realistically handled. The u and v velocities are positioned between the nodes where p and other variables are stored and the combination of staggered grid and a line relaxation method leads to rapid solution. The equations are reduced to the form

$$\frac{\partial}{\partial x}(r\rho u\phi) + \frac{\partial}{\partial r}(r\rho v\phi) - \left(\frac{\partial}{\partial x}\frac{r\mu}{\sigma_\phi}\frac{\partial\phi}{\partial x}\right) - \frac{\partial}{\partial r}\left(\frac{r\mu}{\sigma_\phi}\frac{\partial\phi}{\partial r}\right) = rS^\phi \tag{3.15}$$

as shown in Chapter 2, where ϕ is a general variable equal to l, u, v, w, h, m_{fu}, f, k and ϵ. Here a general turbulent reacting swirling flow is being considered with three equations for a simple chemical reaction and two equations for the k-ϵ turbulence model. The corresponding values of the source term S^ϕ have also been given for this equation set in Chapter 2.

The mesh system of staggered grids is shown in Fig. 3.14. All variables except u-and v-velocities are stored at grid point P, while these velocities are stored at locations corresponding to the arrows shown midway between grid points. Thus, three staggered mesh systems produce a triad of points encompassed by a boomerang-shaped envelope associated with each grid point P. Hence u_{ij} is the axial velocity associated with location (i,j), although its true location is $(i,-1/2, j)$. Boundaries are positioned midway between grid points so that they coincide with normal velocities as shown for a typical grid in Fig. 3.15. A recent modification[66] has been to position the u-and v-cell boundaries to be either exactly on or exactly halfway between the grid intersection points P. This improves the accuracy of calculating pressure gradient effects on the u and v velocities [as pressure values now lie directly on appropriate cell faces] and of calculating certain cell boundary fluxes.

The finite difference equations for each ϕ are obtained by integrating the basic equation over the appropriate control volume (centered about the location of ϕ) and expressing the result in terms of neighboring grid point values. The convection and diffusion terms become surface integrals of the convection and diffusive fluxes. For these, a hybrid scheme is used[53], which is a combination of the so-called central and upwind differencing approaches. The source term is linearized in the form

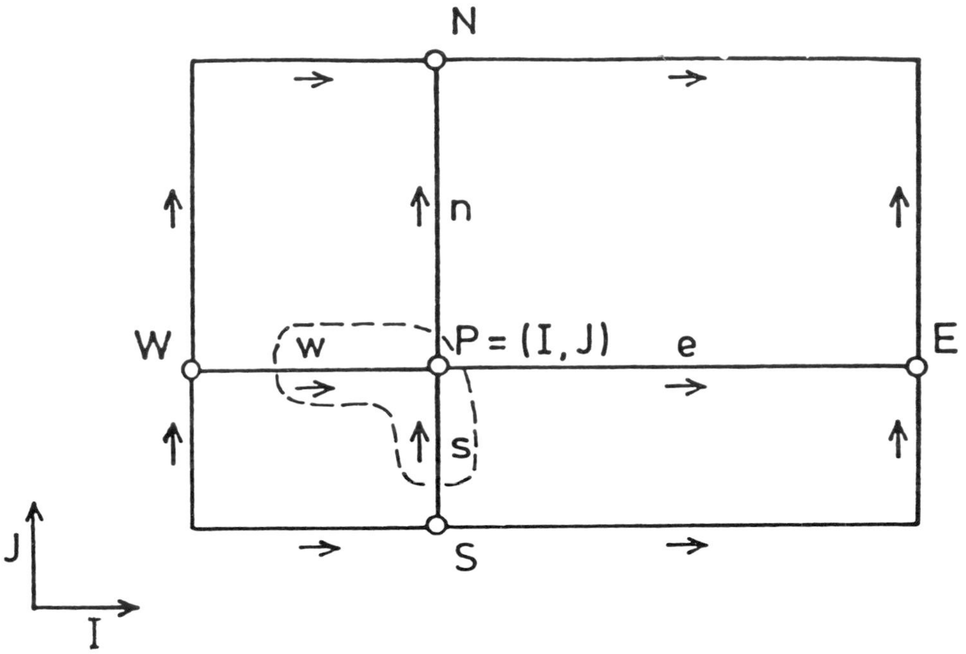

Figure 3.14 Staggered Grid System and Notation

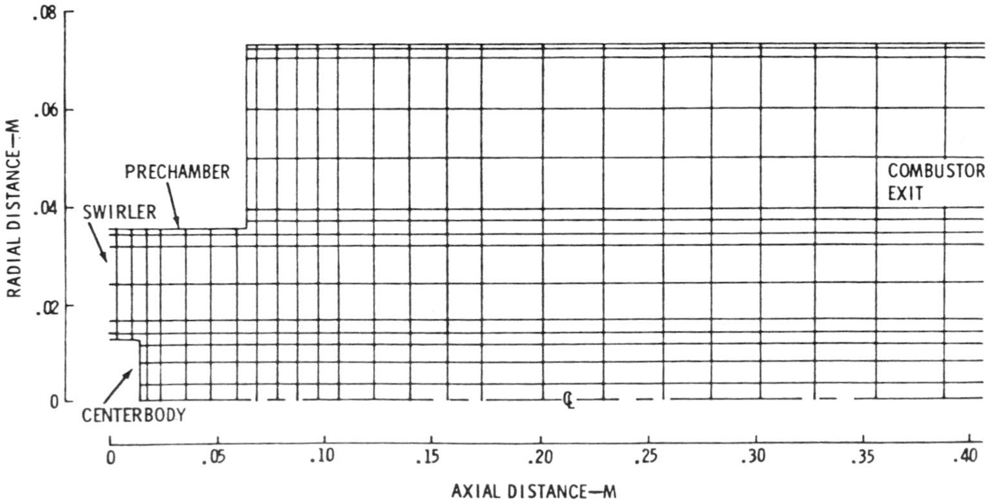

Figure 3.15 Schematic of Typical Nonuniform Rectangular Grid System[50]

$$\int_V S_\phi dV = S_p^\phi \phi_P + S_u^\phi$$

where S_p^ϕ and S_u^ϕ are tabulated in Table 3.4. The general finite difference equation becomes

$$\sum_j a_j^\phi (\phi_P - \phi_j) = S_p^\phi \phi_p + S_u^\phi \tag{3.16}$$

which is reduced to

$$a_P^\phi \phi_P = \sum_j a_j^\phi \phi_j + S_u^\phi$$

where

$$a_p^\phi = \sum_j a_j^\phi - S_p^\phi$$

and

$$\sum_j = \text{sum over N, S, E, and W neighbors}$$

TABLE 3.4

Components of the Linearized Source Term*

ϕ	S_P^ϕ / V	S_U^ϕ / V
u	0	$S^u - \dfrac{\partial p}{\partial x}$
v	$-\dfrac{2\mu}{r^2}$	$S^v - \dfrac{\partial p}{\partial r} + \dfrac{\rho w^2}{r}$
w	$-\rho \dfrac{v}{r} - \dfrac{1}{r^2} \dfrac{\partial}{\partial r} (r\mu)$	S^w
h	0	S^h
m_{fu}	R_{fu}/m_{fu}	0
f	0	0
k	$-c_\mu c_D \rho^2 k/\mu$	G
ϵ	$-c_2 \rho \epsilon / k$	$c_1 G\epsilon/k$

*In this table, V stands for the cell control volume

The source terms of the difference equations for u and v contain pressure values of the neighboring grid points. Velocities (u^* and v^*) and pressure (p^*) are only estimates prior to convergence and, for example, the equation for u_p^* is

$$a_P^u u_P^* = \sum_j a_j^u u_j^* + S_u^u + A_w (p_W^* - p_P^*)$$

The true pressure p is taken as

$$p = p^* \; p'$$

and true velocity, e.g., u_p as

$$u_P = u_P^* + D^u (p'_W - p'_P)$$

where p' is the pressure correction and $D^u = A_w/a_p^u$. This pressure adjustment is imposed on the estimate velocities to subject them to the continuity constraint, and p' is obtained from

$$a_P^p p'_P = \sum_j a_j^p p'_j + S_u^p \qquad (3.17)$$

which is a form of the Poisson equation for pressure.

Boundary Conditions. The earlier Fig. 3.15 shows an example of grid specification for a sudden expansion geometry. The flowfield is covered with a non-uniform rectangular grid system; typically the boundary of the solution domain falls halfway between its immediate nearly parallel gridlines; and clearly specification of the x and r coordinates of the gridlines, together with information concerned with the position of the boundaries is sufficient to determine the flowfield of interest. A sloping boundary may be simulated by means of a stairstep approach, or a more advanced technique[79].

Difference equations for grid points adjacent to a western boundary, for example, are modified for boundary condition implementation by usually setting $a_W^\phi = 0$ and inserting the necessary expression as a false source by altering S_u^ϕ and S_p^ϕ values. Velocities or pressures are typically known along the boundaries. Implementation of the former is straightforward: velocity values are known and $\partial p'/\partial n = 0$ at the boundary. In the latter case pressure is specified and one sets $p = p^*$ and $p' = 0$ at the boundary. For an outflow boundary, velocities may be adjusted to enforce global mass continuity. At the inflow boundary, variables are given definite fixed values associated with known conditions.

A final observation concerns velocities, k and ϵ at wall boundaries. To avoid the need for detailed calculations in the nearwall regions, equations are introduced to link the dependent variables on the wall to those in the logarithmic region. This one-dimensional Couette flow characterization of the flow (diffusion perpendicular to the wall is dominant) is extremely useful and provides a way around this region of steep nonlinear variations of the variables and the fact that laminar and turbulent effects become of the same order of magnitude. The new equations introduced are called wall functions and are described fully in the references. They follow from the fact that in 1-D Couette flow near a solid boundary the drag coefficient is a function of Reynolds number, k, ϵ, . . . ; the function may be obtained by analysis or experiment and expressed as algebraic formulas called wall functions, which are then used in the finite difference calculations in place of the usual τ_B expression. They occur in the momenta equations and k-generation terms, and their implementation is discussed elsewhere[43, 135], together with appropriate near-wall ϵ specification.

The effect of swirl on wall function specification is handled as follows. The previous ideas are extended to find *total* tangential wall shear stress near boundaries [involving $x\theta$ for an $r =$ constant wall, and $r\theta$ for an $x =$ constant wall]. Then appropriate *components* are deduced directly [for the u and w velocities which are tangential to an $r =$ constant wall, and v and w velocities which are tangential to an $x =$ constant wall]. The effects on u, v and w momentum equations are incorporated via the usual linearized source technique[66].

Two points clarify the stairstep sloping boundary technique. First, interior points adjacent to the boundary must 'feel' the boundary in the usual way. Thus, values in the external field must not be inadvertently picked up at these points. Usually the standard coupling coefficient of interest is set to zero and the wall effect given by way of a false source, according to the previous description. Secondly, if the TDMA is applied in columns over the entire 2-D array of points, the solution at external points can be automatically set to zero by giving S_p^ϕ a very large negative value at these locations. This term then dominates in its finite difference equation at P with solution $\phi = 0$. Alternatively, the domain of TDMA execution can be restricted to the interesting part of the 2-D array of points.

Iteration Scheme. Numerical solution proceeds by iterating the following steps:

1. guess values of all variables and hence calculate auxiliary variables such as density;
2. calculate u^* and v^* from the momentum difference equations;
3. solve the pressure correction equation for p';
4. obtain pressure p and corrected velocities u and v from their simple algebraic corrector equations;
5. solve for other ϕ variables successively; and
6. return to (1) using the new values as improved guesses.

The numerical scheme considers variables at points along a vertical line as unknowns (e.g., N, P, and S for each point P), whereas the latest values of each E and W neighbor are treated as known. The tridiagonal matrix algorithm (TDMA) is employed to sequentially solve the system of algebraic equations resulting for each vertical line, sweeping from left to right. Some underrelaxation is used and final convergence is attained when the residual source R_p^ϕ, which is defined by

$$R_p^\phi = a_p^\phi \phi_p - \sum_j a_j^\phi \phi_j - S_u^\phi$$

becomes smaller than some reference value for each variable at each point in the flow domain. Several techniques are incorporated in later versions of the computer programs to enhance accuracy and efficiency[66].

Primitive Variable (p, u, v) SOLA Time-March Solution Procedure

General Methodology. Existing flowfield prediction packages, although incorporating many complexities and being efficient in their solution algorithms, present a major struggle to the practical designer who is faced with the task of understanding, amending and utilizing the available codes. There is a need for simplified techniques for persons with little or no experience in computational fluid dynamics CFD, and into which user-oriented complexities can easily be added. Here is presented the basics of such a method which, in a computer program of approximately 350 cards, solves the 2-D axisymmetric swirling transient flow in the context of a cyclone chamber.

Mathematically the governing equations are elliptic in character and a relaxation method of solution is appropriate (if solving directly for the steady-state); they are parabolic (in time) and a marching method of solution is appropriate (if solving for the steady-state via the time evolution of the transient state flow process).

The technique used here is based on the latter approach and incorporates the following:

1. A finite difference procedure is used in which the dependent variables are the velocity components and pressure, formulated in cylindrical polar coordinates.
2. The pressure is deduced from the continuity equation and the latest velocity field, using a guess-and-correct iterative procedure after each forward time-step to adjust sequentially the pressure and velocity fields.
3. the procedure incorporates displaced grids for the two velocity components, which are placed between the nodes where pressure and swirl velocity are stored.

A 2-D version of this simplified Marker and Cell MAC Los Alamos technique is described[52], upon which the present approach is based.

An Eulerian finite difference formulation is used with pressure and velocity as the main dependent variables. In addition the velocity components are positioned between the nodes where pressure and other variables are stored. At each time step, the time-advanced expressions for u, v and w are substituted into the finite difference form of the continuity equation for each cell, and the guess-and-correct iterative process on pressure and velocity corrections is done until the continuity equation is sufficiently well satisfied.

For incompressible laminar flow the partial differential equation (PDEs) of conservation of mass (continuity equation) and momentum may be taken in conservative form as[75]

$$\frac{\partial u}{\partial x} + \frac{\partial v}{\partial y} + \frac{u}{x} = 0$$

$$\frac{\partial u}{\partial t} + \frac{\partial}{\partial x}(u^2) + \frac{\partial}{\partial y}(vu) + \frac{(u^2 - w^2)}{x} = -\frac{\partial p}{\partial x} + \nu\left(\nabla^2 u - \frac{u}{x^2}\right)$$

$$\frac{\partial v}{\partial t} + \frac{\partial}{\partial x}(uv) + \frac{\partial}{\partial y}(v^2) + \frac{uv}{x} = -\frac{\partial p}{\partial y} + \nu\nabla^2 v \tag{3.18}$$

$$\frac{\partial w}{\partial t} + \frac{\partial}{\partial x}(uw) + \frac{\partial}{\partial y}(vw) + \frac{2uw}{x} = \nu\left(\nabla^2 w - \frac{w}{x^2}\right)$$

where

$$\nabla^2 \phi = \frac{\partial^2 \phi}{\partial x^2} + \frac{\partial^2 \phi}{\partial y^2} + \frac{1}{x}\frac{\partial \phi}{\partial x}$$

u, v, w are velocity components in $x(=r)$, y, θ directions,
p is the ratio of pressure to constant density,
ν is the kinematic viscosity,

Figure 3.16 shows a schematic of the physical problem and the orientation of the cylindrical polar coordinate system used. Notice that the axis of symmetry is the y-axis and that x represents the radius direction. Thus v is the axial velocity, and u is the radial velocity. The region is divided into equal sized rectangular cell divisions. This solution domain is complemented by a layer of cells on all sides, so as to allow easy simulation of the required boundary conditions (BCs). A single cell of this mesh is enlarged in Fig. 3.17 which shows the location of each field variable *p,u,v and w* relative to this (I,J)-cell. The pressure and swirl velocity w are located at the center of each cell and the radial and axial velocities are on the right and top boundaries, respectively. Thus normal velocities lie directly on the physical boundaries of the solution domain, while the tangential velocities and pressure are *displaced half a cell interval* inside the flowfield. In this way the exterior fictitious cells are particularly convenient when applying the BCs.

Boundary Conditions. In Section 3 finite difference equations (FDEs) simulating the PDEs of Eqn. 3.18 are set up and solved by way of a time-march process applied to cells within the flow domain of interest. Cells touching the boundary thus utilize the value on the boundary (in the case of tangential velocities).

Interior normal velocity calculations take the zero normal wall values, the given normal inlet values, or the yet-to-be-determined outlet values as appropriate BCs during their calculations.

Interior tangential velocity calculations use the fictitious values which are placed in the surrounding layer of complementary cells. Specification of these is after each time-step *and* after each sweep of the cells during the pressure iteration. With a course grid, *free-slip* BCs are appropriate for tangential velocities, and external values are set *equal* to their associated immediately interior values. On the other hand, with a fine grid computing through the boundary layer, *no-slip* BCs are appropriate for tangential velocities and external values are set equal to the *negative* of their associated immediately interior values.

Specification of normal velocities at an outflow boundary often poses a problem, as it can have detrimental upstream influence. One might merely impose the zero-normal gradient of continuative condition and set these values equal to their immediately upstream values[52]. When primary interest is being focused on the final steady-state solution, it has been found[53] that a suitable constant may be added to each such extrapolated value, with advantage to the rapidity of convergence. This constant value is chosen so as to make the total outlet flux equal to the total inlet flux, thus ensuring the requirement of a macroscopic mass balance. Outlet boundary specification is imposed *only* after each

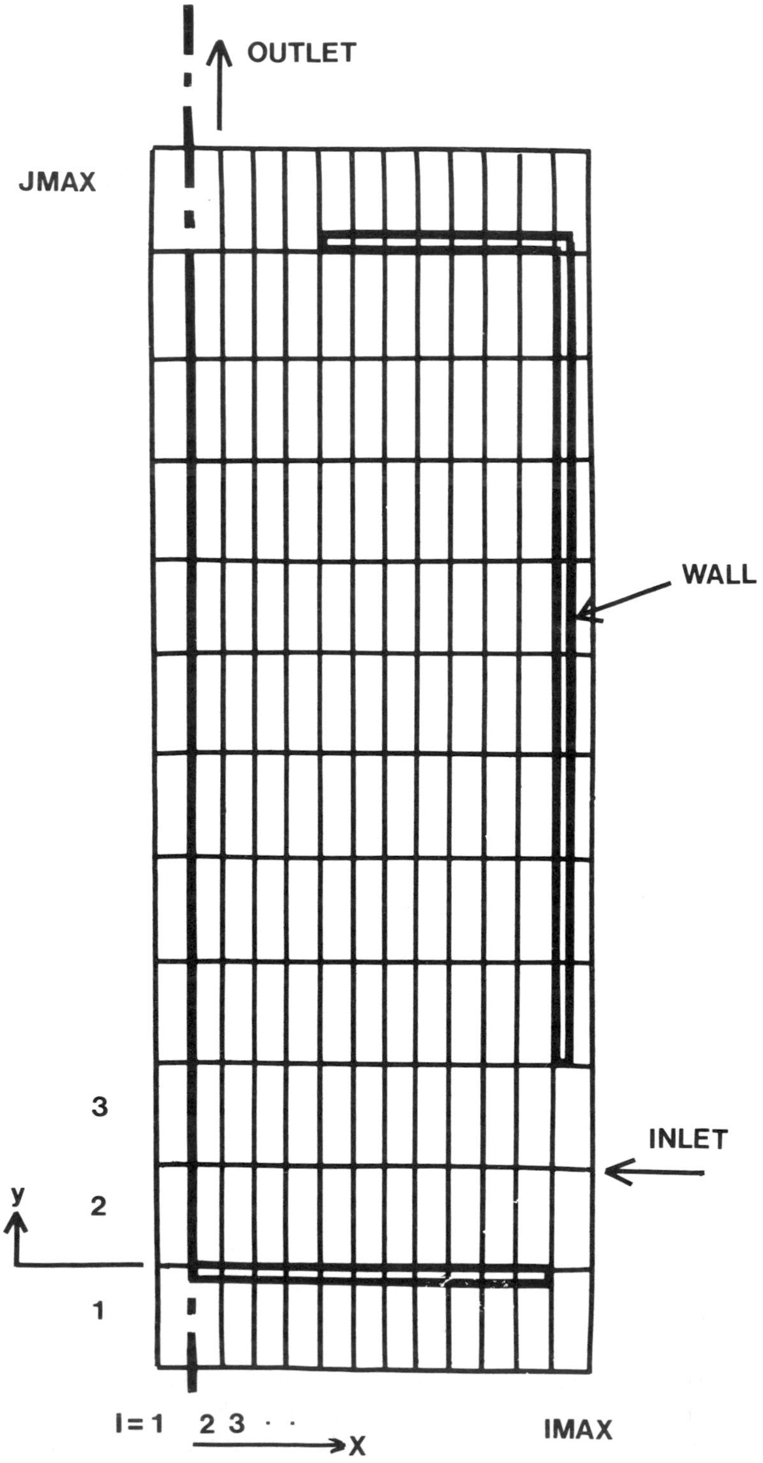

Figure 3.16 General Mesh System for Cyclone Calculations

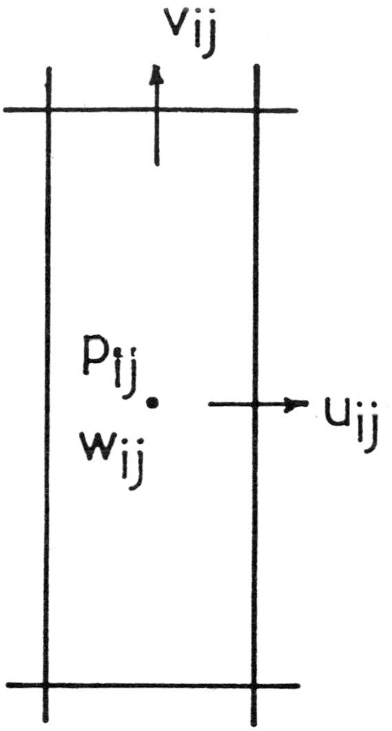

Figure 3.17 Arrangement of Finite Difference Variables in a Typical Cell[55]

time-step as computed via the momentum equations, and *not* after each pass through the mesh during the pressure iteration.

On the axis of symmetry the usual zero normal velocity and free-slip axial velocity specification are applicable; the swirl velocity is given a definite zero value via a no-slip condition.

The Finite Difference Equations and Solution Scheme. Finite difference representations are required of the governing PDEs. The usual intuitive estimates of one-sided first-derivatives, centered first-derivatives and centered second-derivatives are used in representing these equations. With nonuniform mesh layouts appropriate modifications are required. Superscripts n and (blank) are used to denote values at time-level t and $t + \Delta t$, respectively. Portrayed now are equations enabling one such forward time-step to be accomplished; thus, starting from initial field values throughout the domain of interest, a time-march process is used so as to advance toward the final steady-state solution, which is of special interest to combustion engineers investigating continuous processes. The time-derivatives are approximated by forward one-sided derivatives: most spatial derivatives are approximated by central differences based on values at time-level t. Special techniques are required in computational fluid dynamics, however, in the representation of the convection terms, and a certain amount of upstream differencing is required. The difference equations representing the conservation of momentum in direction x and y may be written and used to accomplish one forward time-step as follows:

$$u_{ij} = u_{ij}^{n} + \Delta t \left\{ \frac{1}{\Delta x}(p_{ij}^{n} - p_{i+1,j}^{n}) - FUX - FUY - FUC + VISX \right\}$$

$$v_{ij} = v_{ij}^{n} + \Delta t \left\{ \frac{1}{\Delta y}(p_{ij}^{n} - p_{i,j+1}^{n}) - FVX - FVY - FVX + VISY \right\}$$

$$w_{ij} = v_{ij}^{n} + \Delta t \left\{ - FWX - FWY - FWC + VISZ \right\} \qquad (3.19)$$

where the 4 terms on the right of each of these equations are defined with obvious analogy with the PDEs, and represent, for example, flux of u in x and y directions (FUX and FUY), viscous term in x-equation (VISX) and other terms (FUC). Further exemplifying, in the first equation these terms are:

$$FUX = \frac{1}{4\Delta x}\Big[(u_{i,j} + u_{i+1,j})^2 + \alpha \left| u_{i,j} + u_{i+1,j} \right| (u_{i,j} - u_{i+1,j})$$
$$- (u_{i-1,j} + u_{i,j})^2 - \alpha \left| u_{i-1,j} + u_{i,j} \right| (u_{i-1,j} - u_{i,j}) \Big]$$

$$FUY = \frac{1}{4\Delta y}\Big[(v_{i,j} + v_{i+1,j})(u_{i,j} + u_{i,j+1})$$
$$+ \alpha \left| v_{i,j} + v_{i+1,j} \right| (u_{i,j} - u_{i,j+1})$$
$$- (v_{i,j-1} + v_{i+1,j-1})(u_{i,j-1} + u_{i,j})$$
$$- \alpha \left| v_{i,j-1} + v_{i+1,j-1} \right| (u_{i,j-1} - u_{i,j}) \Big]$$

$$FUC = \frac{1}{8\Delta x\,(i-l)}\Big[(u_{i,j} + u_{i+1,j})^2 + (u_{i-1,j} + u_{i,j})^2$$
$$+ \alpha \left| u_{i,j} + u_{i+1,j} \right| (u_{i,j} - u_{i+1,j})$$
$$+ \alpha \left| u_{i-1,j} + u_{i,j} \right| (u_{i-1,j} - u_{i,j}) - \frac{1}{4\Delta x(i-l)} (w_{i,j} + w_{i+1,j})^2 \Big]$$

$$VISX = \nu \Big[\frac{1}{\Delta x^2}(u_{i+1,j} - 2u_{i,j} + u_{i-1,j})$$
$$+ \frac{1}{\Delta x^2}(u_{i,j+1} - 2u_{i,j} + u_{i,j-1})$$
$$+ \frac{1}{2\Delta x^2\,(i-l)}(u_{i+1,j} - u_{i-1,j}) - \frac{u_{i,j}}{\Delta x^2\,(i-l)^2} \Big]$$

using old-time values on the right. All the other terms are similarly expressed as given in Ref. 55. The coefficient α in these equations is a constant taking a value between 0 and 1, and so giving the desired amount of upstream (donor cell) differencing in the convection terms. A value of 0 gives merely central differencing code and numerical instability problems arise; a value of 1 gives the full upstream or donor cell form which, though introducing errors, is stable provided the fluid is not allowed to pass through more than one cell in one time-step, see the stability criterion given later.

Although these equations accomplish one forward time-step based on conservation of momentum principles, the newly calculated velocities will not, in general, satisfy the continuity requirement, as expressed by the central finite difference form of the continuity equation

$$D = \frac{1}{\Delta x}(u_{ij} - u_{i-1,j}) + \frac{1}{\Delta y}(v_{ij} - v_{i,j-1}) + \frac{1}{2\,\Delta x\,(i-1.5)}(u_{ij} + u_{i-1,j}) = 0 \tag{3.20}$$

Terms here are evaluated at time-level $t + \Delta t$. This incompressibility condition is imposed by iteratively adjusting the cell pressure. That is, if the divergence D of a cell is positive (the left hand side of this equation is positive) there is a net mass outflow from that cell. This is corrected by reducing the cell pressure. If the divergence is negative, an increase in cell pressure is appropriate.

When a cell pressure changes from p to $p + \Delta p$, the velocity components on the 4 faces of that cell change, given from a linear analysis from their forward stepping FDEs, by an amount:

$$\begin{aligned} u_{i,j} &= u_{i,j} + \Delta t\ \Delta p/\Delta x \\ u_{i-l,j} &= u_{i-1,j} - \Delta t\ \Delta p/\Delta x \\ v_{i,j} &= v_{i,j} + \Delta t\ \Delta p/\Delta y \\ v_{i,j-l} &= v_{i,j-l} - \Delta t\ \Delta p/\Delta y \end{aligned} \tag{3.21}$$

Substitution of these in the continuity requirement yields the amount of correction to p required as:

$$\Delta p = -D/(2\ \Delta t\ (1/\Delta x^2 + 1/\Delta y^2)) \tag{3.22}$$

where D is the current (nonzero) value of the left-hand side. Pressure update iterates until the Ds of *all* the cells are less than some prescribed small positive equantity ϵ. The p,u and v corrections are applied with an over-relaxation factor ω between 1 and 2, in order to speed up the convergence of the pressure iteration process.

In order to converge on the steady-state solution of the FDEs, many forward time steps must be taken, a recommendation being at least twice the average residence time of a typical particle passing through the flow domain, based on a simple 1-D flow analysis. Accuracy is enhanced by using small spatial and time intervals, at the expense of large computer time. When total time requirements necessitate a large grid size, it is not possible to resolve thin boundary layers along confining walls and free-slip BCs for tangential velocities are more appropriate than the no-slip BCs. Having chosen the spatial subdivision, the time increment must be restricted in two ways and a suitable amount of upstream differencing must be effected. Thus:

1. Δt must be less than (typically equal to 0.25 to 0.33 times) the minimum cell transit time taken over all cells:

$$\Delta t < \min \left(\left| \frac{\Delta x}{u} \right| , \left| \frac{\Delta y}{y} \right| \right)$$

2. When the kinematic viscosity is nonzero, momentum must not diffuse more than approximately one cell in one time-step, for which a linear analysis shows

$$\upsilon \, \Delta t < \frac{1}{2} \min \left\{ (\Delta x)^2 \, , \, (\Delta y)^2 \right\}$$

3. When the time-step is so restricted, the required amount of upstream (donor cell) differencing must be achieved by choosing α slightly larger than (typically 1.2 to 1.5 times) the larger of the right hand side members of

$$1 \geqslant \alpha > \max \left(\left| \frac{u \, \Delta t}{\Delta x} \right| , \left| \frac{v \, \Delta t}{\Delta y} \right| \right)$$

where the maximum is taken over all cells. If α is chosen to be too large, stability is being achieved at the introduction of an unnecessarily large amount of diffusion-like truncation errors (called numerical smoothing).

3.6 FULLY THREE-DIMENSIONAL FLOWS

Only recently have fully 3-D flows become amenable to prediction. The methods are not yet seriously used in typical practical design processes. But the methods are available and will become everyday tools in the design and development phase in the future[9]. The flow may or may not exhibit transient features of interest. If it does, then a time-march solution procedure is needed, since the governing equations are parabolic in the time direction. If not, one considers whether or not the flow in three space dimensions has a predominant direction. If it does, then simplifying boundary layer approximations may be applied to reduce the complexity of the governing equations and a forward-marching solution procedure may be applied in the appropriate direction. If not, a fully 3-D iterative procedure is needed. These ideas are now further clarified.

Three-dimensional Boundary-layer Flows

Three-dimensional parabolic boundary layer flows may be solved by marching methods, which use 2-D storage, primitive formulation, and explicit or a semi-implicit SIMPLE solution procedures[59, 89]. If a steady 3-D flow possesses a predominant direction, the equations become parabolic and have merely a first-order derivative in this predominant direction. However, it is not only these types of 3-D flows that fall into this category: the unsteady behavior of 2-D problems possess a similar character, a third first-order derivative being introduced, this time in the time-direction. The SOLA technique of Section 3.5 is an applicable solution scheme. This type of 3-D flow with a single predominant direction and no recirculation is illustrated in Fig. 3.18. Besides transient versions of the examples given in Section 3.5, other examples are steady flows with one prominent direction, like steady flow in ducts of non-circular cross-section and/or non-axisymmetric boundary conditions. In practice there are many phenomena of this kind in furnace and process technology, axisymmetric transient reciprocating engines, and gas turbine combustors, downstream of the primary zone. Now the typical governing equation is

$$\sum_{i=1}^{3} a_i \frac{\partial \phi}{\partial x_i} + \sum_{i=1}^{2} b_i \frac{\partial}{\partial x_i} \left(c_i \frac{\partial \phi}{\partial x_i} \right) = d \tag{3.23}$$

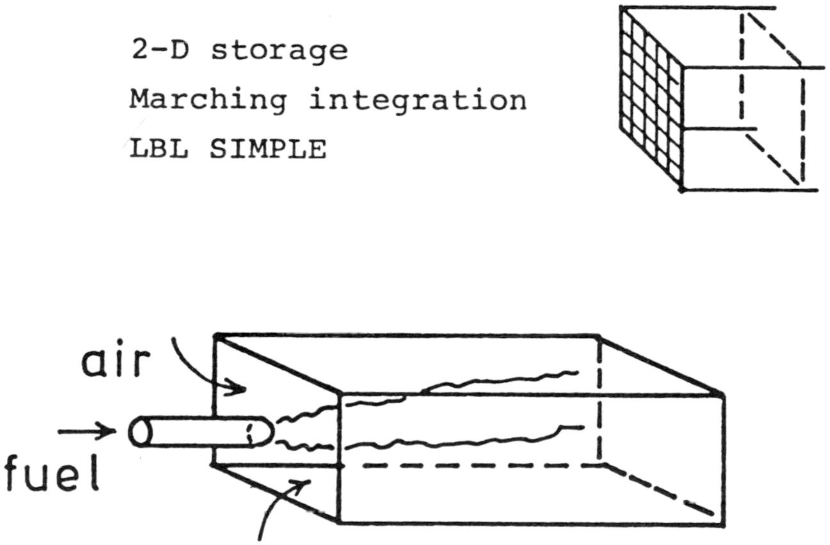

Figure 3.18 Computational Procedure for 3-D Parabolic Flows

Since the main direction velocity is always positive, it allows the deduction of downstream grid-point values from those at the next section upstream. This means it is possible to make a marching integration in the main direction and only 2-D storage is needed, for upstream values are overwritten as soon as downstream ones are calculated. A line-by-line method using the SIMPLE algorithm is used during each implicit step of the march[89]. The sample calculation concerns fuel being injected into a furnace of rectangular cross-section resulting in a diffusion flame. Of course, refinements can allow for a premixed flame and other complications, but these complexities are of a modeling nature and not so much of a computational nature. Other sample results are given in Chapter 5.

Three-dimensional Recirculating Flows

Relaxation methods are used for 3-D elliptic recirculating flows, associated with general non-axisymmetric problems. Typically, they make use of 3-D storage, primitive formulation, and Gauss-Seidel or SIMPLE solution procedure. Procedures have been developed specifically for the gas turbine[67-74] and furnace[136-140] industries. Brave attempts at 3-D time-dependent flow prediction, as found in internal combustion engines, for example, are discussed in Refs. 9 and 12. Griffin *et al.*[141] exhibits such a prediction procedure. In the most general case, one has first- and second-order derivatives in three space directions, plus an additional first-order derivative if the flow is transient. They are parabolic if transient (requiring a time-march with a 3-D frame) and elliptic if steady (requiring relaxation with a 3-D frame). Typical equations which must be solved when there are positive and negative velocities in all three directions are like

$$\sum_{i=1}^{4} a_i \frac{\partial \phi}{\partial x_i} + \sum_{i=1}^{3} b_i \frac{\partial}{\partial x_i}\left(c_i \frac{\partial \phi}{\partial x_i}\right) = d \qquad (3.24)$$

where the summation over the first term in replaced by $i = 1, 3$ under steady conditions. Most interesting practical combustion phenomena are in this category including furnaces, combustion chambers, stalled diffusers, elbows, rocket motors, compressor cascades, and automotive reciprocating engines. The flow is fully 3-D and 3-D storage is required. Relaxation proceeds via a line method and storage and time requirements are very large. Figure 3.19 displays some of the ideas, together with an example of a typical problem of the flow and reaction inside a segment of an annular combustion chamber[67, 68], which is idealized as a rectangular box shape. This particular example is steady; but it is fully 3-D with axial recirculation due in part to the laterally-induced additional air supply. Computational results obtained in this and associated problems are discussed in Chapter 5.

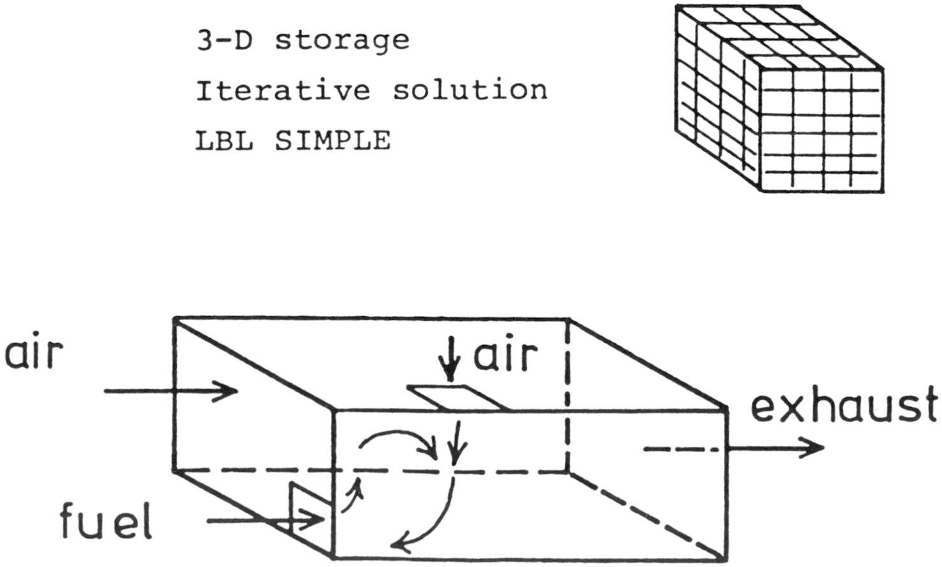

Figure 3.19 Computational Procedure for 3-D Elliptic Flows

Basic Concepts for Numerical Prediction of Fully Three-dimentional Flowfields

The Simulation. Described now is a fully 3-D version of the primitive variable (p,u,v,w) SOLA solution procedure for time-dependent flow in cylindrical polar coordinates[60]. Low speed compressible flow is presumed to include also the simulation of a single one-step premixed chemical-reaction. Multicomponent chemically-reacting turbulent flows are characterized by partial differential equations PDEs for the hydrodynamics (p,u,v and w), combustion (h, m_{fu} and $f = m_{ox} - sm_{fu}$) and possibly turbulence (k and ϵ, for example). Firstly, the hydrodynamics is characterized by the conservation equations in 3-D cylindrical polar coordinates for compressible constant viscosity fluid flow

$$\frac{\partial \rho}{\partial t} + \frac{\partial}{\partial x}(\rho u) + \frac{1}{r}\frac{\partial}{\partial r}(r\rho v) + \frac{1}{r}\frac{\partial}{\partial \theta}(\rho w) = 0$$

$$\frac{\partial}{\partial t}(\rho u) + \frac{\partial}{\partial x}(\rho u^2) + \frac{1}{r}\frac{\partial}{\partial r}(r\rho vu) + \frac{1}{r}\frac{\partial}{\partial \theta}(\rho wu) = \frac{\partial p}{\partial x} + \mu\nabla^2 u$$

$$\frac{\partial}{\partial t}(\rho v) + \frac{\partial}{\partial x}(\rho uv) + \frac{1}{r}\frac{\partial}{\partial r}(r\rho v^2) + \frac{1}{r}\frac{\partial}{\partial \theta}(\rho wv) - \frac{\rho w^2}{r} = -\frac{\partial p}{\partial r} + \mu[\nabla^2 v - \frac{v}{r^2} - \frac{2}{r^2}\frac{\partial w}{\partial \theta}] \tag{3.25}$$

$$\frac{\partial}{\partial t}(\rho w) + \frac{\partial}{\partial x}(\rho uw) + \frac{1}{r}\frac{\partial}{\partial r}(r\rho vw) + \frac{1}{r}\frac{\partial}{\partial \theta}(\rho w^2) + \frac{vw}{r} = -\frac{1}{r}\frac{\partial p}{\partial \theta} + \mu[\nabla^2 w - \frac{w}{r^2} + \frac{2}{r^2}\frac{\partial v}{\partial \theta}]$$

where $\nabla^2\phi = \frac{\partial^2\phi}{\partial r^2} + \frac{1}{r}\frac{\partial\phi}{\partial r} + \frac{1}{r^2}\frac{\partial^2\phi}{\partial\theta^2} + \frac{\partial^2\phi}{\partial x^2}$

u, v, w are velocities in x, r, θ directions,
p is the pressure,
μ is the laminar viscosity.

These 4 equations are sufficient to determine p,u,v and w once ρ is specified. Typical boundary condition BC specification includes known values at the inlet(s), and no slip or free slip values elsewhere.

Secondly, the simple one-step combustion process

$$1 \text{ kg fuel} + s \text{ kg oxygen} \rightarrow (1+s) \text{ kg products} + H_{fu}$$

may be characterized by 3 PDEs for h, m_{fu} and $f = m_{ox} - sm_{fu}$, where s is the stoichiometric (ox/fu) ratio. Again BC specification includes definite known values at the inlet(s) and usually zero gradients elsewhere, although nonadiabatic boundaries possess obvious changes, for example. Notice that a PDE for f is used instead of one for m_{ox} since it possesses no source term, and is thus more easily and more accurately solved. Immediately m_{fu} and f values allow m_{fu} and m_{ox} values to be retrieved at any point in the flowfield. Then the algebraic equations

$$m_{fu} + m_{ox} + m_{Pr} = 1$$
$$h = c_pT + H_{fu}m_{fu} + (u^2 + v^2 + w^2)/2$$
$$p = \rho RT/M \text{ where } 1/M = \sum_j m_j/M_j$$

enable the other flowfield variables of special interest (m_{pr}, T and ρ) to be successively deduced and ρ now feeds back into the hydrodynamics. All these details are applicable readily to kinetically-controlled premixed flames.

In physically-controlled diffusion flames, the above equations also hold but a remarkable simplification follows from the infinitely thin flame zone assumption that fuel and oxygen do not pass through from their respective sides. The extra algebraic equations are

$$f \geqslant 0 \Rightarrow m_{ox} = f \text{ and } m_{fu} = 0$$
$$f \leqslant 0 \Rightarrow m_{fu} = -f/s \text{ and } m_{ox} = 0$$

and so the PDE for m_{fu} is no longer required, both m_{fu} and m_{ox} now being simply deducible from f. The chemical reaction rate source term R_{fu} no longer appears in the governing equation set. Now just 2 PDEs for h and f allow combustion to be characterized, and in some cases they are linearly related and one need solve for only one of them, f.

Thirdly, turbulence may be simulated via a simple algebraic equation or the popular k-ϵ model, where 2 PDEs are solved from which the turbulent viscosity can be specified. These PDEs are similar to the others, with terms for the generation and dissipation appearing in the source expressions. The standard models are easy to incorporate; however the right hand sides of the conservation equations must now reflect the variable viscosity possibility.

Solution Technique. Following Los Alamos MAC techniques[52,58-60], the solution domain is covered with a grid system as illustrated in Fig. 3.20 where normal velocities are located on cell boundaries and pressure and other variables are located at cell centers. This grid system arrangement has special merits. Except for the continuity equation, explicit finite difference equations FDEs are set up for forward time-stepping solution of the PDEs. Those for momentum take the form (where the superscript n denotes old-time value)

$$u_{ijk} = u^n_{ijk} + \frac{\Delta t}{\rho}\left\{\frac{1}{\Delta x}[P^n_{ijk} - P^n_{i+1,j,k}] \begin{array}{l} - FUX - FUR \\ - FUT + VISX \end{array}\right\}$$

$$v_{ijk} = v^n_{ijk} + \frac{\Delta t}{\rho}\left\{\frac{1}{\Delta r}[P^n_{ijk} - P^n_{i,j+1,k}] \begin{array}{l} - FVX - FVR \\ - FVT + VISR \end{array}\right\} \quad (3.26)$$

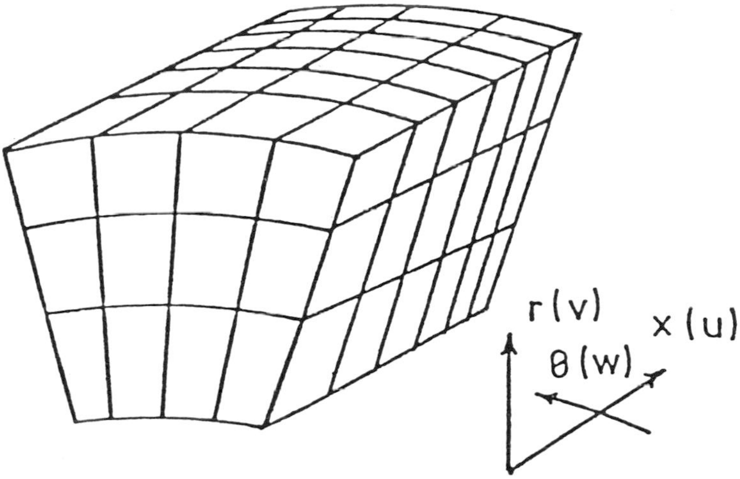

Figure 3.20 The Grid System for 3-D Cylindrical Polar Coordinate Flow Prediction[60]

$$W_{ijk} = \overset{n}{w}_{ijk} + \frac{\Delta t}{\rho} \left\{ \frac{1}{r\Delta\theta} [\overset{n}{P}_{ijk} - \overset{n}{P}_{i,j,k+1}] \begin{array}{l} - \text{FWX} - \text{FWR} \\ - \text{FWT} + \text{VIST} \end{array} \right\}$$

and similar equations represent all the other PDEs. Except for pressure and velocities, these new-time values are accepted: this allows the new densities to be calculated (but better estimates can be made after the pressures have been adjusted if pressure changes are large enough to make density changes significantly different from the first estimates). The first-estimate new-time velocities are then accompanied by a pressure-velocity corection iteration

$$\begin{aligned} D = {} & \frac{1}{\Delta t}(\rho_{ijk} - \overset{n}{\rho}_{ijk}) + \frac{1}{\Delta x}\left\{(\rho u)_{ijk} - (\rho u)_{i-1,j,k}\right\} \\ & + \frac{1}{r\Delta r}\left\{(r\rho v)_{ijk} - (r\rho v)_{i,j-1,k}\right\} \\ & + \frac{1}{r\Delta\theta}\left\{(\rho w)_{ijk} - (\rho w)_{i,j,k-1}\right\} \\ = {} & 0 \end{aligned} \tag{3.27}$$

The iteration of several sweeps over the solution domain drives D towards zero, with corresponding pressure adjustment

$$\Delta p = -D/\left\{2\Delta t \left(\frac{1}{\Delta x^2} + \frac{1}{\Delta y^2} + \frac{1}{(r\Delta\theta)^2}\right)\right\} \tag{3.28}$$

and velocity adjustment

$$
\begin{aligned}
u_{i,j,k} &= u_{i,j,j} + \Delta t\ \Delta p/\Delta x.\rho \\
u_{i,-1,j,k} &= u_{i-1,j,k} - \Delta t\ \Delta p/\Delta x.\rho \\
v_{i,j,k} &= v_{i,j,k} + \Delta t\ \Delta p/\Delta r.\rho \\
v_{i,j-1,k} &= v_{i,j-1,k} - \Delta t\ \Delta p/\Delta r.\rho \\
w_{i,j,k} &= w_{i,j,k} + \Delta t\ \Delta p/r\Delta\theta.\rho \\
w_{i,j,k-1} &= w_{i,j,k-1} - \Delta t\ \Delta p/r\Delta\theta.\rho
\end{aligned} \tag{3.29}
$$

applied to all cells in turn. Before, or possibly during, the pressure-velocity adjustment phase, the BCs must be set. These are particularly simple to incorporate via setting values to variables in the exterior cells which surround the solution domain. Of course, there are stability and accuracy criteria which restrict the forward time-step and promote upstream differencing practices:

Cell Transit Time

$$\Delta t < \min \left\{ \frac{\Delta x}{u}, \frac{\Delta y}{v}, \frac{\Delta z}{w} \right\}$$

Cell Diffusion Time

$$\upsilon\ \Delta t < \tfrac{1}{2} \min \left\{ \Delta x^2, \Delta r^2, (r\Delta\theta)^2 \right\}$$

Upstream (Donor Cell) Convection Representation

$$1 \geqslant \alpha > \max \left(\frac{u\Delta t}{\Delta x}, \frac{v\,\Delta t}{\Delta y}, \frac{w\,\Delta t}{\Delta z} \right)$$

Most of the above ideas for this 3-D simulation and solution follow directly from corresponding 2-D work exhibited in Section 3.5. Simple ideas characterize the 3-D cylindrical chemically-reacting flowfield prediction code, to which special user-oriented complexities and sophistications can easily be added as required. As such, it represents a useful and versatile starting point for the solution of many more difficult practical problems.

Some Complexities

It is necessary to be forewarned about some of the complexities, which hitherto have been passed over lightly, in order to convey the main ideas. Proponents of the mathematical modeling approach tend to be overly optimistic, not only about the quality and accuracy of their work, but also its relevance in the practical design situation. For example, Serag-Eldin and Spalding[72] present a recent step in the evolution of an advanced 3-D mathematical modeling design aid. Cylindrical polar coordinates are now introduced in the context of a conventional can-type combustor, and the solution domain consists of a 60° segment of the cylindrical geometry, with one lateral injection port for additional air supply. Again, gaseous phase diffusion-controlled combustion is assumed, with significant swirl and negligible radiation heat transfer. The two-equation k-ϵ turbulence model is used, and a thick diffusion flame region is simulated via solving a conservation equation for the mean square of concentration fluctuations and employing a battlement-shape probability distribution function for the mixture fraction. Nine partial differential equations are now solved. The technique appears deceptively simple, though in practice these are problems concerned with large unbalanced centrifugal forces under strong swirl conditions, values at nodes near the centerline, and the use of CTDMA [Cyclic TriDiagonal Matrix Algorithm]. Only after a certain maturity in the field and broad reading around the subject[75-85] does one really develop the confidence to pursue and succeed in this area.

One key area in need of further development and generalization is the representation of irregular boundaries. Considerations of accuracy and economy in regions with irregular-shaped boundaries are not well addressed. Yet flows of this type, with the added complexity of the simulation of turbulent reacting flowfields, are of prime concern in the application of numerical methods to the design and development of gas turbine combustion systems. Most combustor flowfield prediction treatments to date have been based on rectangular boundaries; sloping wall boundaries, if present, are simulated by a series of staircase-like steps. This constitutes a preliminary, coarse attack on a complicated problem. Specification of boundary conditions greatly affects the accuracy of solution. Moreover, errors arising from approximations along irregular boundaries occur precisely in regions of greatest sensitivity, since large gradients and rates of change for gradients occur in these regions. Clearly there is a definite need for more accurate methods.

Complexities of irregular boundaries (sloping or curved side-wall, for example) may be handled via a variety of possible ways:

1. Nonuniform Rectangular Mesh
2. Uniform Rectangular Mesh
3. Finite Element Method
4. Simplify the Problem
5. Hybrid Mesh
6. Analytical Transformations
7. Numerical Transformations

The last two methods offer useful possibilities, and they are conceptually the same, being distinguishable primarily in their implementation schemes. Thus, both approaches solve transformed conservation PDEs and BCs in a more convenient rectangularized computational domain where the boundaries coincide with coordinate lines and greater overall accuracy results. Either type of transformation may be orthogonal or nonorthogonal. Some relevant studies include analytical[142-146] and numerical[147-154] transformation methods.

Finite element techniques offer several advantages over the more widely used finite difference techniques, the most important being in the more accurate simulation of irregular boundaries. The COMOC code[155] is one of the more extensively reported finite element techniques applied to fluid dynamics problems. Although design for 3-D boundary layer flows, it can also be used for axisymmetric 2-D recirculating flows.

3.7 CLOSURE

Studies presented at recent conferences on the fluid dynamics of combustion have helped to clarify the current status and highlight future prospects[13-23]. Practical problems almost always involve complex geometries, and so numerical modeling must of necessity be of multi-dimensional nature. Handling of multi-dimensional calculations, solving the Navier-Stokes equations, is a formidable task, especially when complicated geometries are involved. Nevertheless, the past decade has witnessed an impressive steady progress in this area. Great advances have been made in numerical algorithms for solutions of multi-dimensional partial differential equations, in handling of nonrectangular solution domains, and in the speed and capacity of computers available on a fairly wide basis. As a result, the state-of-the-art in fluid mechanical calculations has advanced to the point where useful predictions of nonreacting flows may be made in many instances. These successes opened the door to consideration of calculations of reacting flows. The presence of chemical reactions in these flows introduces considerable additional challenges the modelers have to tackle. One challenge is the description of kinetics of a wide variety of fuels, valid over wide range of temperatures and pressures. Another is that the list of all possible reactions that describe the processes taking place during combustion of even simple fuels is much too long for computers to handle. One has to result to judicious selection of those that may be expected to dominate, reducing the list to two or three reactions – but that is still more art than science. When the flow is turbulent, as it usually is, there is the additional complication of how to represent the effect of fluctuations of temperature and species concentrations on the mean reaction rates; simply using mean values of fluid properties in the reaction rate equations is generally grossly incorrect, because of the highly nonlinear nature of these equations. Finally, a cohesive overview of the field is provided by these recent review papers[23] on the modeling of turbulent reacting flows in practical systems from the points of view of the chemical kineticist [Westbrook and Dryer], the turbulence fluid dynamic modeler [Jones and Whitelaw], and the user [Harsha]. Clearly, the field is still evolving rapidly and, although each success seems to raise more questions than answers, continued progress is assured.

References to Chapter 3

1. Dugger, G. L. (Ed.): Ramjets, *AIAA Selected Reprints* **VI**, 1969.
2. Drewry, J.E.: *AIAA Journal,* **16**, 4, April 1978, pp. 313.
3. Choudhury, P. R.: *AIAA Journal,* **18**, 4, April 1980, pp. 450-454.
4. Lilley, D. G.: Prospects for Computer Modeling in Ramjet Combustors. *AIAA Paper No. 80-1189,* Hartford, CT, June 30-July 2, 1980.
5. Edelman, R. B., and Harsha, P. T.: Analytical Modeling of Sudden Expansion Burners. *CPIA Publication 287,* Chemical Propulsion Information Agency, The Johns Hopkins Univ., Laurel, MD., June 1977.
6. Oates, G. C.: The Aerothermodynamics of Aircraft Gas Turbine Engines, *AFAPL-TR-78-52,* 1978.
7. Chigier, N. A., (Ed.): *Progress in Energy and Combustion Science,* Pergamon Press, New York, 1976+.
8. Edelman, R. B., and Harsha, P. T.: *Prog. in Energy and Comb. Sci.,* **4**, 1978, p. 1.
9. Lilley, D. G.: *J. of Energy,* **3**, 4, July-August, 1979, p. 193.
10. Lilley, D. G.: *AIAA Journal,* **15**, Aug. 1977, p. 1063.
11. Syred, N., and Beér, J. M.: *Combustion and Flame,* **23**, 1974, p. 143.
12. Gupta, A. K., Lilley, D. G., and Syred, N.: *Swirl Flows,* Abacus Press, Tunbridge Wells, England, 1984.
13. Cornelius, W., and Agnew, W. G. (Ed.): *Emissions from Continuous Combustion Systems,* Plenum Press, New York, 1972.
14. British Flame Res. Comm. and Inst. of Fuel, Predictive Methods for Industrial Flames, *Proc. of 4th Symp. of Flames and Industry,* held at I.C., London, Sept. 19-20. 1972.

15. Dussourd, J. L., Lohmann, R. P., and Uram, E. M. (Ed.): Fluid Mechanics of Combustion (Papers presented at Conference held in Montreal, Canada, May 13-15, 1974) *ASME Book No. I00034,* 1974.
16. Murthy, S. N. B. (Ed.): *Turbulent Mixing in Nonreactive and Reactive Flow* (A Project SQUID Workshop), Plenum Press, New York, 1975.
17. Combustion Institute/Central States Section, Fluid Mechanics of Combustion Processes, Meeting held at NASA Lewis Research Center, Cleveland, Ohio, March 28-30, 1977.
18. ASME/Pennsylvania State Univ. Symposium on Turbulent Shear Flows, University Park, PA, April 18-20, 1977.
19. Lefebvre, A. H. (Ed.): *Gas Turbine Combustor Design Problems* (A Project SQUID Workshop), Hemisphere-McGraw-Hill, New York, 1980.
20. Kennedy, L. A. (Ed.): *Prog. in Astro. and Aero.*, **58**, AIAA, New York, 1978.
21. Combustion Modelling, *AGARD Conf. Proc., No. 275,* Feb. 1980.
22. Maltavi, J. N. and Amann, C. A. (Eds.): *Combustion Modeling in Reciprocating Engines,* Plenum Press, New York, 1980.
23. Morel, T., Lohmann, R. P. and Rackley, J. M. (Ed.): Fluid Mechanics of Combustion Systems, *ASME Conf.* in Boulder, CO, June 22-24, 1981.
    See also Morel, T. (Ed.): Prediction of Turbulent Reacting Flows in Practical Systems. *ASME Conf.* in Boulder, CO, June 22-24, 1981.
24. Champagne, F. H., Sleicher, C. A., and Wehrmann, O. H.: *J. of Fluid Mechanics,* **28** Part 1, 1967, p. 153.
25. Fejer, A., Lavan, Z., and Wolf, L.: Study of Swirling Fluid Flows. *ARL 68-0173,* 1968.
26. Wygnanski, I., and Fiedler, H. E., *Some Measurements in the Self Preserving Jet.* Boeing Sci. Labs, Doc. D1-82-0712, Seattle, Wa., 1968.
27. Razinsky, E., and Brighton, J. A., *ASME* Paper 70-WA/FE-2, 1970.
28. Syred, N., Beér, J. M., and Chigier, N. A., *Proc. of Salford Symp. on Internal Flows.* Inst. of Mech. Engr., London, 1971, p. B27.
29. Pratte, B. D., and Keffer, J. R., *J. of Basic Engrg.,* Vol. 94, Dec. 1972, p. 739.
30. Yavuzkurt, S., Crawford, M. E., and Moffat, R. J., Real-Time Hot-Wire Measurements in Three-Dimensional Flows. *Proc. of 5th Biennial Symp. on Turb.,* Univ. of Missouri, Rolla, Missouri, 1977, p. 265.
31. Tani, I., Inchi, M., and Komoda, H., Experimental Investigation of Flow Separation Associated with a Step or a Groove. *Report No. 364, ARI,* Univ. of Tokyo, Japan, 1961.
32. Abbott, D. E., and Kline, S. J., J. of Basic Engr., *ASME,* Vol. D84 (1962), p. 317.
33. Chaturvedi, M. C., *J. Hydraulic Division, ASCE,* Vol. 89, No. HY3 (1963), p. 61.
34. Macagno, E. O., and Hung, T. K., *J. Fluid Mech.,* Vol. 28 (1967), p. 43.
35. Back, L. H., and Roschke, E. J., *J. of Appl. Mech.,* ASME, Vol. E94 (1972), p. 678.
36. Iribarne, A., Frantisak, F., Hummel, R., and Smith, J., *AIChE J.,* Vol. 18, No. 4 (1972), p. 689.
37. Roschke, E. J., and Back, L. H., *J. Biomech.,* Vol. 9 (1976), p. 481.
38. Owen, F. K., *AIAA Journal,* Vol. 14, No. 11, Nov. 1976, p. 1556.
39. Ha Minh, H., and Chassaing, P., Perturbations of Turbulent Pipe Flow, *Symposium on Turbulent Shear Flows,* Pennsylvania State University, April, 1977, p. 13.9.
40. Davies, T. W., and Snell, D. J., *Turbulent Flow Over a Two-Dimensional Step and its Dependence upon Upstream Flow Conditions,* Ref. 18, p. 13-29.
41. Launder, B. E., Morse, A., Rodi, W., and Spalding, D. B., The Prediction of Free Shear Flows – A Comparison of the Performance of Six Turbulence Models, *Proc. of NASA Conf. on Free Shear Flows,* NASA Langley Research Center, Hampton, Va., 1972.
42. Lilley, D. G., *AIAA Journal,* Vol. 11, July 1973, p. 955.
43. Launder, B. E., and Spalding, D. B., *Comp. Methods in Appl. Mech. and Engrg.,* Vol. 3, March 1974, p. 269.
44. Koosinlin, M. L., and Lockwood, F. C., *AIAA Journal,* Vol. 12, No. 4, April 1974, p. 547.
45. Lilley, D. G., *Acta Astronautica,* Vol. 3, 1977, p. 919.
46. Peck, R. E., and Samuelsen, G. S., Eddy Viscosity Modeling in the Prediction of Turbulent Backmix Combustion Performance, *16th Symp. (Int.) on Comb.*, The Comb. Inst., Pittsburgh, Pa., 1977, p. 1675.
47. Coakley, T. J., and Viegas, J. R., Turbulence Modeling of Shock Separated Boundary-Layer Flows, *Paper in Ref. 18,* p. 13.19.
48. Tennankore, K. N., and Steward, F. R., Comparison of Several Turbulence Models for Predicting Flow Patterns within Confined Jets, *Paper in Ref. 18,* p. 10.6.
49. Durst, F., and Rastogi, A. K., Theoretical and Experimental Investigations of Turbulent Flows with Separation, *Paper in Ref. 18,* p. 18.1.

50. Novick, A. S., Miles, G. A. and Lilley, D. G. *J. of Energy,* Vol. 3, No. 2, March-April, 1979, p. 95.
51. Wuerer, J. E. and Samuelsen, G. S. Predictive Modeling of Backmixed Combustor Flows: Mass and Momentum Transport. *AIAA Paper* 79-0215, New Orleans, LA., Jan. 15-17, 1979.
52. Hirt, C. W., Nichols, B. D., and Romero, N. C., SOLA – A Numerical Solution Algorithm for Transient Fluid Flows, *Report LA-5852,* Los Alamos Scientific Laboratory, Los Alamos, N. Mex., 1975.
53. Gosman, A. D., and Pun, W. M., Calculation of Recirculating Flows, *Report No. HTS/74/2,* Dept. of Mech. Eng., I.C., London, 1974.
54. Lilley, D. G., *AIAA Journal,* Vol. 14, No. 6, June 1976, p. 749.
55. Busnaina, A. A. and Lilley, D. G., Numerical Simulation of Swirling Flow in a Cyclone Chamber. *Chem. Eng. Comm.*, 1984.
56. Balbul, S., and Lilley, D. G., A Basic Computational Procedure for Fully Three-Dimensional Flowfields. *Paper presented at Comb. Inst./Canadian Section* Meeting, held in Ottawa, Canada, May 4-5, 1978.
57. Novick, A. S., Miles, G. A., and Lilley, D. G., *J. of Energy,* Vol. 3, No. 5, Sept.-Oct. 1979, p. 257.
58. Harlow, F. H. and Welch, J. E. *Physics of Fluids,* Vol. 8, 1965, p. 2182.
59. Amsden, A. A. and Harlow, F. H. The SMAC Method: A Numerical Technique for Calculating Incompressible Fluid Flows. *Report No. LA-4370,* Los Alamos Scientific Laboratory, Los Alamos, N. Mex., 1970.
60. Vatistas, G. H., Lilley, D. G., and Rhode, D. L., Basic Concepts for Numerical Prediction of Fully Three-Dimensional Chemically-Reacting Flowfields. *Paper No. 24 presented at Comb. Inst./Canadian Section* Meeting, held in Kingston, Ont., Canada, May 3-4, 1979.
61. Schorr, C. J., Worner, G. A., and Schimke, J., The Analytical Modeling of a Spherical Combustor Including Recirculation, *14th Symp. (Int.) on Comb.*, The Comb. Inst., Pittsburgh, Pa., 1973, p. 567.
62. Lilley, D. G., Swirl Flow Modeling for Combustors, *AIAA Paper 74-527,* Palo Alto, CA, June 17-19, 1974.
63. Scaccia, C., and Kennedy, L. A., *AIAA Journal,* Vol. 12, No. 9, Sept. 1974, p. 1268.
64. Anasoulis, R. F., McDonald, H., and Buggeln, R. C., Development of a Combustor Flow Analysis, Part 1: Theoretical Studies," *Tech. Report No. AFAPL-TR-73-98,* Part 1, Air Force Aero Prop. Lab., Air Force Systems Command, Wright-Patterson AFB, Ohio, Jan. 1974. (See also Parts 2 and 3.)
65. Kubo, I., and Gouldin, F. C., *J. of Fluids Engineering,* Sept., 1975, p. 310.
66. Rhode, D. L., Lilley, D. G. and McLaughlin, D. K. *ASME J. of Fluids Engineering,* Vol. 104, Sept. 1982, p. 378.
67. Patankar, S. V. and Spalding, D. B: Simultaneous Predictions of Flow Pattern and Radiation for Three-Dimensional Flames, paper in *Heat Transfer and Flames,* [N. H. Afgan and J. M. Beér (Ed.)] Scripta Book Co. (Hemisphere-Wiley), Washington, D.C., 1974.
68. Patankar, S. V.: *Studies in Convection* [Launder, B. E., (Ed.)] 1, Academic Press, London, 1975, p. 1.
69. Gibeling, H. J., McDonald, H., and Briley, W. R.: Development of a Three-Dimensional Combustor Flow Analysis, **II**, Theoretical Studies. United Technologies Research Center, *Report AFAPL-TR-75-59* **II**, East Hartford, Conn., Oct., 1976.
70. Mongia, H. C., and Smith, K. F.: An Empirical/Analytical Design Methodology for Gas Turbine Combustors. *AIAA Paper 78-998,* Las Vegas, Nev., July 25-27, 1978.
71. Jones, W. P., and Priddin, C. H.: Predictions of the Flowfield and Local Gas Composition in Gas Turbine Combustors, *17th Symp. (Intl.) on Comb.,* The Comb. Inst., 1979.
72. Serag-Eldin, M. A., and Spalding, D. B.: *J. of Eng. for Power,* **101**, July 1979, p. 326.
73. Mongia, H. C., and Reynolds, R. S.: Combustor Design Criteria Validation **III** – User's Manual, *Report USARTL-TR-78-55C,* US Army Res. & Tech. Lab., Ft. Eustis, Va., Feb. 1979. [See also **I** and **II**]
74. Swithenbank, J., Turan, A., and Felton, P. G.: 3-Dimensional 2-Phase Mathematical Modeling of Gas Turbine Combustors, Paper in Ref. 19, p. 249.
75. Roache, P. J.: *Computational Fluid Dynamics.* Hermosa, Albuquerque, N. Mex., 1972.
76. Potter, D.: *Computational Physics.* Wiley, London, 1973.
77. Croft, D. R. and Lilley, D. G.: *Heat Transfer Calculations using Finite Difference Equations. Applied Science,* London, 1977.
78. Chow, C.-Y.: *An Introduction to Computational Fluid Mechanics.* Wiley, New York, 1979.
79. Patankar, S. V.: *Numerical Heat Transfer and Fluid Flow.* Hemisphere-McGraw-Hill, New York, 1980.

80. Taylor, T. D.: Numerical Methods for Predicting Subsonic, Transonic and Supersonic Flow. *AGARD-AG-187*, 1974.
81. Peyret, R. and Viviand, H.: Computation of Viscous Compressible Flows Based on the Navier-Stokes Equations. *AGARD-AG-212,* 1975.
82. Krause, E. (Lecture Series Ed.).: Advances in Numerical Fluid Dynamics. *AGARD-LS-64,* 1973.
83. Krause, E. (Lecture Series Ed.): Computational Methods for Inviscid and Viscous Two- and Three-Dimensional Flow Fields. *AGARD-LS-73,* 1975. [See also, Computational Fluid Dynamics, *AGARD-LS-86,* 1977].
84. Chu, C. K. (Ed.): Computational Fluid Dynamics. *AIAA Selected Reprints,* **4**, AIAA, New York, 1968.
85. Harlow, F. H.: Computational Fluid Dynamics – Recent Advances. *AIAA Selected Reprints,* **15**, AIAA, New York, 1973.
86. Patankar, S. V.: *Numerical Prediction of Three-Dimensional Flows, in Studies in Convection,* [B. E. Launder (Ed.)] **1**, Academic Press, London, 1975, p. 1.
87. Gosman, A. D., Pun, W. M., Runchal, A. K., Spalding, D. B. and Wolfshtein, M. W.: *Heat and Mass Transfer in Recirculating Flows.* Academic Press, London, 1969.
88. Gosman, A. D. and Pun, W. M.: Calculation of Recirculating Flows. *Report No. HTS/74/2,* Dept. of Mech. Eng., I.C., London, 1974.
89. Patankar, S. V., and Spalding, D. B.: *Int. J. of Heat and Mass Transfer,* **15**, 1972, p. 1787.
90. Peters, C. E.: Turbulent Mixing and Burning of Coaxial Streams Inside a Duct of Arbitrary Shape, *TR-68-270,* Arnold Engineering Development Center, Jan. 1969.
91. Hammond, D. C., Jr., and Mellor, A. M.: *Comb. Sc. and Tech.*, **2**, 1970, p. 67.
92. Fletcher, R. S., and Heywood, J. B.: A Model for Nitric Oxide Emissions from Gas Turbine Engines. *AIAA Paper 71-123,* 1971.
93. Swithenbank, J., Poll, I., Vincent, M. W., and Wright, D. D.: *14th Symp. (Int.) on Comb.,* The Comb. Inst., p. 627.
94. Mosier, S. A., and Roberts, R.: Low-Power Turbo-Propulsion Combustor Exhaust Emissions, III Analysis, *AFAPL-TR-73-36*, **III**, 1974. [See also I and II].
95. Harsha, P. T. and Edelman, R. B.: Application of Modular Modeling to Ramjet Performance Prediction. *AIAA Paper 78-944,* Las Vegas, Nev., July 25-27, 1978.
96. Mellor, A. M.: *17th Symp. (Int.) on Comb.,* The Comb. Inst., 1979, p. 377.
97. Spalding, D. B.: *9th Symp., (Int.) on Comb.,* The Comb. Inst. 1963, p. 833.
98. Evans, D. C. and Patrick, M.A.: *J. Inst. Fuel,* Oct., 1966, p. 414.
99. Brown, A. M. and Thring, M. W.: *10th Symp. (Intl.) on Comb.,* 1965, p. 1203.
100. Ball, C.: *J. Inst. Fuel,* March, 1965, p. 115.
101. Lane, R. A. and Morrison, E. L.: Southwark Station Boiler Air-Flow Model Tests and Operation Results, *ASME Annual Conference, 48-A-26,* 1948.
102. Stewart, D. C.: *Selected Combustion Problems,* **2**, AGARD, Butterworths, London, 1955, p. 384.
103. Beér, J. M.: *J. Inst. Fuel,* Nov., 1966, p. 466.
104. Johnstone, R. E. and Thring, M. W.: *Pilot Plants, Models, and Scale-up Methods in Chemical Engineering,* McGraw-Hill, New York, 1957.
105. Kerr, N. M., and Fraser, D. : *J. Inst. Fuel,* **33**, 1965, p. 527.
106. Drake, P. E. and Hubbard, E. H.: *J. Inst. Fuel,* March, 1966, p. 98.
107. Beér, J. M. and Le, K. B.: *10th Symp. (Intl.) on Comb.*, The Comb. Inst., 1965, p. 1187.
108. International Flame Research Foundation, Ijmuiden, Holland, *Doc. nr. A33/a/55,* April, 1977.
109. Smith, T. and Kilham, J.: *J. Acons. Soc. Am.* **35**, 5, 1963, p. 715.
110. Strahle, W. C.: *J. Fluid Mech.* **49**, 2, Sept. 1971, p. 399.
111. Bragg, S. L.: *J. Inst. E.,* 1963, p. 12.
112. Kotake, S. and Hatta, K.: *Bulletin J.S.M.E., Japan,* 8, 30, 1965, p. 261.
113. Smithson, R. N. and Foster, P. J.: *Combustion and Flame*, 9, 1965, p. 426.
114. Giammer, R. D. and Putnam, A. A.: *A.G.A. Report No. BR-3-5,* 1971.
115. Syred, N., Hanby, V. I., and Gupta, A. K.: *J. Inst. Fuel,* Dec., 1973, p. 402.
116. Gupta, A. K., Syred, N., and Beér, J. M.: *15th Symp. (Intl.) on Comb.,* The Comb. Inst., 1975, p. 1367.
117. Barrett, M. J. *et al.:* Direct Needs for Direct Combustion of Coal, *MRI*, April, 1977.
118. Smithson, R. N., and Foster, P. J.: *Comb. and Flame,* 9, 1965, p. 426.
119. Gupta, A. K., Syred, N., and Beér, J. M.: *Applied Acoustics,* 9, 1976, p. 151.
120. Bertrand, C. and Michelfelder, S.: *16th Symp. (Intl.) on Comb.,* MIT, 1976, p. 1757.
121. Speller, F. N. and Kendall, V. V.: *Ind. Eng. Chem.,* **15**, 134, 1923.

122. Patankar, S. V. and Spalding, D. B.: *Heat and Mass Transfer in Boundary Layers,* 2nd ed. Intertext, London, 1970.
123. Spalding, D. B.: *GENMIX, A General Computêr Program for Two-Dimensional Parabolic Phenomena,* Pergamon Press, Oxford, 1977.
124. Siddhartha, V.: Ph.D. thesis, 1971, Dept. of Mechanical Engineering, Imperial College, London.
125. Lilley, D. G.: Ph.D. thesis, 1970, Dept. of Chemical Engineering and Fuel Technology, Sheffield University, England.
126. Lilley, D. G.: *AIAA Journal,* **12**, Feb., 1974, p. 219.
127. Lilley, D. G. and Chigier, N. A.: *Int. J. of Heat Mass Transfer,* **14**, 1971, p. 57.
128. Lilley, D. G.: *Int. J. of Comp. and Fluids,* **4**, 1976, p. 45.
129. Lilley, D. G. and Chigier, N. A.: *Combustion and Flame,* **16**, 1971, p. 171.
130. Chigier, N. A. and Chervinsky, A.: *J. of Appl. Mech.* **34**, 1967, p. 443.
131. Chervinsky, A.: *AIAA Journal,* **6**, May 1968, p. 912.
132. Pratte, B. D. and Keffer, J. R.: *J. of Basic Engineering,* **94**, Dec. 1972, p. 739.
133. Lilley. D. G.: *AIAA Journal,* **14**, 5, 1976, p. 54.
134. Lilley, D. G.: Analytic Inverse of the Turbulent Swirl Flow Boundary Layer Equations, *AIAA Paper No. 75-856,* Hartford, Conn., June 16-18, 1975.
135. Launder, B. E. and Spalding, D. B.: *Mathematical Models of Turbulence,* Academic Press, London, 1972.
136. Zuber, I. and Konecny, V.: *Proc. of 4th Symp. of Flames and Industry:* Predictive Methods for Industrial Flames (organized by British Flame Research Committee and Institute of Fuel), Imperial College, London, Sept. 19-20, 1972, p. 19.
137. Patankar, S. V., and Spalding, D. B.: *Proc. of 4th Symp. of Flames and Industry:* Predictive Methods for Industrial Flames, organized by British Flame Research Committee and Institute of Fuel, Imperial College, London, Sept. 19-20, 1972, p. 13.
138. Patankar, S. V., and Spalding, D. B.: *14th Symp. (Intl.) on Comb.,* The Comb. Inst., 1973 p. 604.
139. Abou Ellail, M. M. M., Gosman, A. D., Lockwood, F. C., and Megahed, I. E. A.: *Progress in Astro. and Aero.,* **58**, AIAA, New York, 1978, p. 163.
140. Pai, B. R., Michelfelder, S., and Spalding, D. B.: *Intl. J. of Heat Mass Transfer,* **21** 1978, p. 571.
141. Griffin M. D., Diwaker, R., Anderson, J. D., Jr., and Jones, E.: Computational Fluid Dynamics Applied to Flows in an Internal Combustion Engine. *AIAA Paper 78-57,* Huntsville, Alabama, Jan. 16-18, 1978.
142. Lee, J . S., and Fung, Y. C.: ASME *J. of Appl. Mech.,* **E37**, 1, 1970, p. 9.
143. Oberkampf, W. L., and Goh, S. C.: *Proc. Inst. Conf. Comput. Methods Nonlinear Mech.,* University of Texas, Austin, TX, 1974, p. 569.
144. Chien, J. C.: Numerical Analysis of Turbulent Separated Subsonic Diffuser Flow, Ref. 18, p. 18.
145. Markatos, N. C., Spalding, D. B., and Tatchell, D. G.: Combustion of Hydrogen Injected into a Supersonic Airstream (The SHIP Computer Program), *NASA CR-2802,* April, 1977.
146. Ghia, K. N.: *AIAA 3rd Comp. Fluid Dynamics Conference,* Albuquerque, NM, June 27-28, 1977, p. 156.
147. Viecelli, J. A.: *J. of Comp. Physics,* **4**, 1969, p. 543.
148. Chu, W. H.: *J. of Comp. Physics,* **8**, 1971, p. 392.
149. Amsden, A. A., and Hirt, C. W.: *J. of Comp. Physics,* **11**, 1973, p. 348.
150. Thompson, J. F., *et al.: AIAA 2nd Comput. Fluid Dyn. Conf.,* Hartford, Conn., June 19-20, 1975, p. 68.
151. Hung, T. K., and Brown, T. D.: *J. of Comp. Physics,* **23**, 1977, p. 343.
152. Pope, S. B.: *J. of Comp. Physics,* **26**, 1978, p. 197.
153. Davis, R. T., Paper 79-1463, AIAA *4th Computational Fluid Dynamics Conf.,* Williamsburg, Va., July 23-25, 1979, p. 180.
154. Anderson, O. L.: Calculation of Internal Viscous Flows in Axisymmetric Ducts at Moderate to High Reynolds Numbers. *Intl. J. of Computers and Fluids*, 1980.
155. Baker, A. J., and Zelazny, S. W.: COMOC: Three-Dimensional Boundary Region Variant, Theoretical Manual and Users Guide, *NASA CR-132450,* 1974.

CHAPTER 4

EXPERIMENTAL DIAGNOSTIC TECHNIQUES

In this chapter the experimental diagnostic techniques, applicable to swirl flows, are discussed in the following groups: (i) velocity, (ii) temperature, (iii) pressure, (iv) density, (v) species concentration, (vi) particle/droplet size distribution. Various possible perturbing and non-perturbing optical diagnostic techniques currently used in the university research laboratory or industry, are shown in Table 4.1.

In evaluating a particular technique, one must always keep in mind several criteria that determine an effective measurement. Some of the criteria to consider in evaluating a particular technique for flow diagnostics are: (a) intrusiveness or nonintrusiveness; (b) mechanical handling; (c) sensitivity; (d) signal to noise ratio and relative error; (e) accuracy; (f) resolution both in time and space; (g) calibration methods available; (h) degree of difficulty of the technique; and (i) the cost effectiveness. Depending on the flow situation some of the above criteria may be of major or minor importance.

4.1 VELOCITY MEASUREMENT

Pressure Probes

Pitot Probe. This method involves transfer of kinetic energy into pressure energy. The standard pitot tube, Fig. 4.1, is made up of a central tube in which the total pressure is measured by the flow impact into the tube forcing the oncoming stream. The static pressure is measured through circumferential holes normal (or nearly so) to the flow stream direction. Flow velocity is calculated from the measured total and static pressure differential and the mean gas density according to the relation

$$p_t - p_s = \frac{1}{2} \rho u^2$$

Where ρ is the mean gas density within the measurement volume that can be measured from the local temperature and species concentration levels using the equation

TABLE 4.1

Experimental Diagnostic Techniques

Velocity	Pitot probe, Hot wire, Hot film, LV, Photon correlation, Two-spot method, Real time LV, Transient recorders, Image photography and Holography
Temperature	Bare wire thermocouple (without and with thermal inertia compensation), Computer compensated thermocouple, suction pyrometer, Laser schlieren, Two-color optical pyrometer, Laser Raman spectroscopy, and Coherent anti-stokes Raman scattering (CARS)
Pressure	Probe, Transducer, and Probe microphone
Density	Schlieren system, Knife edge, Shadow method, and Interference method
Species Concentration	Separation of particles and gas, Physical and chemical analysis of particles, Species concentration measurement by gas phase chromatography, Chemiluminescence, Flame ionization, Flourescence, and Laser Raman
Particle/Droplet Size Distribution	Mechanical methods – Frozen drop and wax methods, Cascade impactor, Pulse counting technique, and Coated slide system
	Optical methods – Single and double spark photography, Laser diffraction, Holography, and Light scattering (LV and others)
Flow Visualization	Water model study, Tracer techniques (e.g. dye, smoke), High speed photography, Schlieren method, Color Schlieren system, and Holography

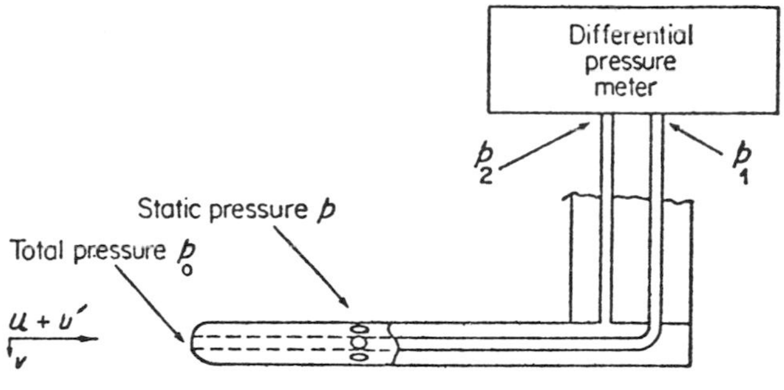

Figure 4.1 The Pitot-static probe.

Where p is pressure (atm), T is temperature (K), and R is a constant related to the molar ideal-gas constant (universal gas constant) $\bar{R}$ by

$$R = \frac{\bar{R}}{\bar{M}}$$

Where $\bar{M}$ is the average molecular weight, and the currently accepted value of $\bar{R}$ is 8.31433 KJ/kg mole K.

In small laboratory size flames, mean flow velocity can be measured using uncooled quartz or water-cooled stainless steel pitot probe.[1-5]

The above Bernoulli theory cannot be applied when the conditions in the gas can no longer be considered as incompressible. For measurements at high velocities the readings must be corrected[6]. In small laboratory size or large industrial flames, velocities are rarely higher than about 100 m/sec and therefore this problem will not be considered here.

When the flow is turbulent the pressures at the sensing points in the probe will fluctuate with the local flow direction, velocity and pressure. Nevertheless, if the damping in the pressure lines is high enough, then the recorded differential will be nearly steady. It is not possible to predict the instantaneous pressures just inside the sensing holes for a specified structure of ambient turbulence, but a plausible assessment of the effect of fluctuations can be obtained by assuming that the fluctuating pressure differential has the form

$$p_t - p_s = \frac{1}{2} \rho \, [u^2 + k_1 u'^2 + k_2 (v'^2 + w'^2)]$$

Where u', v', w' are components of fluctuating axial, radial and tangential velocity respectively around the probe, and the constants k_1 and k_2 are of the order of magnitude unity. The steady measured differential will be something like

$$p_t - p_s = \frac{1}{2} \rho \, [u^2 + k_1 \overline{u'^2} + k_2 (\overline{v'^2} + \overline{w'^2})]$$

with the constants modified to account for distortions introduced within the pressure lines.

One can also expect similar difficulties for instruments with low frequency response.

Becker and Brown[7] investigated the response of pitot probes in turbulent streams and suggested that, if stated conditions are satisfied, the response can be given by an expression of the form

$$p_t = \bar{p}_s + \frac{1}{2}\rho u^2 - \frac{1}{2} k\rho \overline{u^{2\,(1-m)}\, u_n^{\,2m}} \tag{4.1}$$

Where p_t is the mean pressure sensed by the probe, $\bar{p}_s$ is the local mean static pressure in the turbulent stream, u is the flow velocity, $u_n \equiv u \sin\theta$ and θ is the angle between the velocity vector and the probe axis. The probe is considered to be orientated with its axis parallel to the mean velocity vector. The parameter m and k in eqn. 4.1 are constants for a probe which are evaluated by calibrating the probe in a steady, uniform, laminar flow. Correlations for predicting the values of m and k are given by Becker and Brown[8] for sphere-nosed, round-nosed and square-nosed probes.

The principal difficulty in the application of eqn. 4.1 is the evaluation of the quantity $\overline{u^{2\,(1-m)}\, u_n^{\,2m}}$. The scheme for solving this problem and the computed results are given by Becker[8] and Brown[7].

Ebrahimi[9] and Lenze[10] used a condenser microphone probe to measure the local distribution of velocity fluctuations and turbulence intensities in diffusion flames, Fig. 4.2. A condenser microphone having a sensitivity of 2.2 mv/μbar at 1000 Hz was chosen as the measuring instrument. When the flow direction is perpendicular to the microphone diaphragm, the pressure registered on the diaphragm is the stagnant pressure given by (assuming static pressure to be negligible)

$$p_t = \frac{1}{2}\rho u^2$$

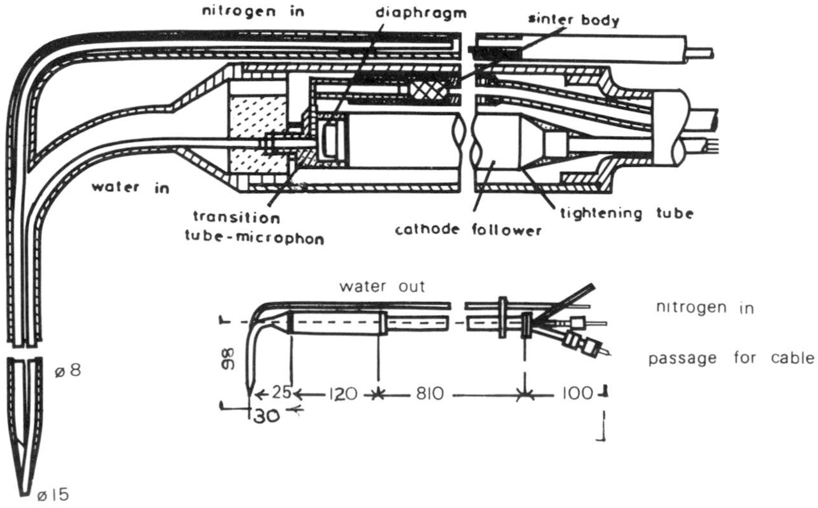

Figure 4.2 Water-cooled condenser microphone probe[9]

The term u in the above equation can be substituted in terms of $\bar{u}$, the time averaged velocity component and u' the fluctuating velocity component as follows:

$$p_t = \frac{1}{2}\rho(\bar{u} + u')^2 = \frac{1}{2}\rho\bar{u}^2 + \frac{1}{2}\rho u'^2 + \rho\bar{u}u'$$

The condenser microphone is sensitive to the fluctuating component only. The presure due to the fluctuating component p'_t is

$$p'_t = \frac{1}{2}\rho u'^2 + \rho\bar{u}u'$$

or

$$\frac{1}{2}\rho u'^2 + \rho\bar{u}u' - p'_t = 0 \qquad (4.2)$$

From eqn. 4.2 an instantaneous fluctuation at a particular time t can be calculated as follows:

$$u'_{(t)} = [-\rho\bar{u} \pm (\rho^2\bar{u}^2 + 2\rho p'_{t(t)})^{1/2} \; / \rho$$

$$u'_{(t)} = \bar{u} \pm [\bar{u}^2 + (2/\rho)p_{t(t)}]^{1/2} \qquad (4.3)$$

The term $(\overline{u'^2})^{1/2}$ can be found from eqn. 4.3 by introducing $(\overline{p_t'^2})^{1/2}$ in place of p'_t so that

$$(\overline{u'^2})^{1/2} = -\bar{u} \pm [\bar{u}^2 + (2/\rho)\,(\overline{p_t'^2})^{1/2}\,]^{1/2}$$

In the above equation $\bar{u}^2$ can be substituted by $(2/\rho)\bar{p}_t$. Further, as can be readily seen, the negative sign before the root yields only negative values of u' that are greater than $\bar{u}$. Hence, taking the positive sign only, we have

$$(\overline{u'^2})^{1/2} = [(2/\rho)\{(\overline{p_t'^2})^{1/2} + \bar{p}_t\}\,]^{1/2} - \bar{u}$$

The intensity of turbulence is then given by

$$\frac{(\overline{u'^2})^{1/2}}{\bar{u}} = \left[1 + \frac{(\overline{p_t'^2})^{1/2}}{\bar{p}_t}\right] - 1 \qquad (4.4)$$

in Eqn. 4.4 the term $(\overline{p_t'^2})^{1/2}$ can be measured with the condenser microphone and $\bar{p}_t$ with a pitot probe. Nevertheless, it must be borne in mind that the pressure measured with the pitot probe does not correspond exactly to $\bar{p}_t$ and the above simplified analysis is true only for 1-D flows.

Eickhoff[11] used a water-cooled disc static probe for turbulence measurements; the reader is referred to the reference for details.

Five-hole Pressure Probe. In systems with three dimensional flow such as swirl flows or those involving recirculation (for example, flow behind a bluff body stabilizer), it is necessary to measure both the magnitude and direction of the velocity. For the measurement of velocity head the conventional pitot-static probe is unsuitable since the total head and static tappings are not close enough to measure the local flow conditions. It is also inadmissible to make local measurements of total head pressure and to rely on wall static tappings, since where swirl is present there is a considerable radial pressure gradient. The use of standard yaw and pitch meters requires rotation of the probe and in many flow systems it is not possible, or it is inconvenient.

Fechheimer[12] showed that, in two-dimensional flows, if a cylinder is placed with its axis normal to a fluid stream, the pressure on the surface of the cylinder at a point distant approximately 40 degrees from the stagnation point is equal to the static pressure of the stream. Therefore, a tube having two radial holes 40 degrees apart, separately connected to the two legs of a manometer, will give a direct measurement of velocity head in a stream normal to the tube axis if the tube is positioned so that one of the holes is at the stagnation point. The direction of flow (yaw angle) is determined by a second static tapping sited at 40 degrees on the opposite side of the pitot tapping. The flow direction is determined by rotating the tube to a position where the two static pressures balance. The precise angle between the pitot and static tappings to indicate true velocity head is dependent on the diameter of the tube and the size of the tapping holes. In practice, it is most convenient to select an arbitrary angle and to calibrate the instrument in a stream of known velocity; a constant factor relating the indicated to the true velocity head is thus established.

Measurements of velocity magnitude and direction as well as the static pressure in swirl flows can be made with a modified (three dimensional) version of the Fechheimer probe. The principle of this five-hole pressure probe is based upon the measured pressure distribution around a sphere introduced into a flowing stream. Hiett and Powell[13], and Lee and Ash[14] have shown that with five holes on the circumference of a sphere the instrument can be calibrated so that from a measurement of three differential pressures the magnitude and direction of the velocity vector can be determined.

In order to reduce the dimensions of the sensing head to a minimum and still allow for water cooling of the probe, a hemispherical head probe, similar to that shown in Fig. 4.3 is adopted for measurements in flames. Five holes are drilled into the stainless-steel head – a central hole surrounded by four others at an angle of 45 degrees to the axis. Water cooling of the probe head can be avoided by constructing the head from platinum or platinum-irridium alloy. A platinum five-hole pressure probe has been used in flames by MacPharlane[15] and Gupta[15].

In flames when particles of coal, soot and/or liquid fuel droplets are present the holes of the pitot probe become blocked. Provision needs to be made so that the holes can be blown out frequently with an inert gas or nitrogen. Calibration of the probe can be carried out in a wind tunnel or in the potential core region of an air jet. Calibration is carried out by progressively changing the yaw and pitch angles and measuring three differential pressures. Details of calibration charts[16] and the method of converting the pressure information into velocity[13] are given.

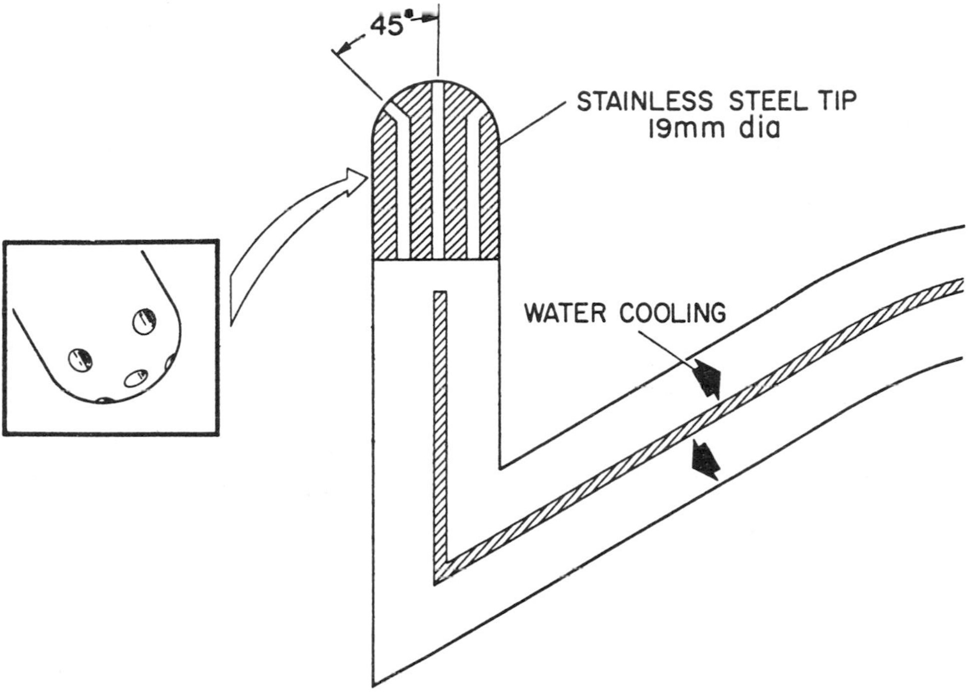

Figure 4.3 Water-cooled five-hole probe for the measurement of velocity magnitude and direction.[14]

The three-dimensional five-hole pressure probe developed by Hiett and Powell[13] has been successfully used by Poulston and Winter[17] for the investigation of flow patterns in combustion chambers.

Pressure probes have many limitations, particularly when they are intended for use in swirl flames. When five-hole probes are placed in regions of high velocity gradient the stagnation point is displaced towards the region of highest velocity and errors then become dependent upon the dimension of the instrument[18]. The large physical size of the probe causes considerable disturbance to the flow. Velocity levels in flames can vary from a few m/sec to about 100 m/sec and because of the low density of gases it is usually required to measure pressures of less than 1 mm of water gauge. In swirl flows, static pressures on the jet axis or within the recirculation zone are sub-atmospheric and a separate traverse is necessary to measure static pressure. Little information is available for the effect of turbulence intensities in swirl flows on the pitot probe—which can no doubt be considerable for turbulence intensities greater than about 20 per cent. An indication of the degree of error is given by

$$p_m = p_{si} + c_i \rho \overline{u'^2}$$

Where p_m is the measured pressure; p_{si} is the true pressure; $\overline{u'^2}$ is the fluctuating mean velocity component; and the c_i constant varies between 0 and 0.33.

There are three such equations and if the turbulence intensity in all three directions is larger than 20 per cent these simple expressions do not hold. The procedure for making corrections for turbulence levels is long and tedious and even then the confidence to their applicability is unknown. In general, pitot probes do not give high sensitivity and have poor frequency response. Significant errors can also arise when there are large density gradients across the probe head.

Hot-wire Anemometry

The hot-wire anemometer operates on the principle of the rate of heat loss from a wire whose temperature is deduced from its resistance. The sensing element of the hot-wire anemometer is a small diameter wire (about 5μm or less) made of tungsten, platinum, or platinum alloy (10 to 20 per cent irridium or rhodium) and is usually between 0.5 and 3 mm long. The ends of the wire are welded or soldered by sleeves of gold or copper plating (diameter $\simeq$ 25 μm) to the supporting steel prongs. Typical electrical resistance of the wires is about 2 ohm at ambient temperature and about 6–8 ohm when heated. It is always preferable to use pure metal in constructing the hot wire since they have higher temperature coefficients of resistance. Platinum is widely used mainly because it can be conveniently obtained in the form of Wollaston wire. In the Wollaston process the thin platinum rod to be drawn is covered by a thick sheath of silver or with some other metal with about the same Young's modulus and yield stress and the above combination is drawn like a solid billet down to the smallest practicable outside diameter so that the diameter of the platinum core is a small fraction of that otherwise attainable. An additional advantage of the Wollaston wire is that most of the manipulation can be done before etching the silver sheath from the wire and exposing the small and fragile platinum core. Platinum alloys are also available in Wollaston wire which are stronger than platinum, hence their suitability in high velocity flows but it has a smaller coefficient of resistance. There is no suitable material for sheathing tungsten, therefore, small diameters can only be obtained by etching. Platinum-plated tungsten is less liable to oxidation than pure tungsten and is also easier to solder or weld.

Hot-wire anemometry is now a well-known and well-understood technique for fluid flow measurement[19-41]. A typical hot-wire probe together with the wire-orientated coordinate system is shown in Fig. 4.4.

A hot wire placed perpendicular to a constant pressure air stream will be sensitive to the mean velocity and the stream wise component of the turbulent fluctuations. The hot wire is also sensitive to temperature, density, and composition fluctuation of the air stream.

The rate of heat transfer per unit length $(\frac{\dot{Q}}{L})$ from a long fine wire placed normal to a flow stream of velocity U depends upon:

wire diameter, d

absolute temperatures of wire and free-stream fluid, T_w, T_f

fluid thermal conductivity, and diffusivities of momentum and heat at free-stream temperature, k, ν, k

mean free path of the gas molecules, λ

In dimensionless form the heat transfer may be written as:

$$N_u = f(\mathrm{Re}, Pr, \frac{T_w}{T_f}, \mathrm{Kn}) \tag{4.5}$$

where Nu $= (\frac{\dot{Q}}{L})/\pi\, k\, (T_w - T_f)$ – Nusselt number based on wire diameter and surface area.

R_e = Reynolds number based on wire diameter

P_r = Prandtl number of the fluid $= \frac{\nu}{\kappa}$

$\frac{T_w}{T_f}$ = Temperature ratio which can be used to take partial account of variations in fluid properties around wire.

K_n = Knudsen number to indicate whether continuum flow is established around the wire.

Nevertheless, it is usually found that all the above need not be included in the heat transfer law. Prandtl number is nearly constant for air ($\simeq$0.7) or for any gas over the normal range of operating temperatures. Furthermore, it is taken into account by calibrating it in the fluid in which measurements are to be made. For gases, continuum flow is estabished for $Kn<0.015$; and when it is, the role of Knudsen number is negligible. Normal operating conditions lie near this limit, but so long as the gas density does not change much between the calibration and the measurement, the calibration will absorb non-continuum effects.

Density Effects

Gas density changes associated with high velocity flows have been neglected in eqn. 4.5; had this not been done, the Mach number would have appeared in the law (eqn. 4.5). Effects of free convection have also been eliminated by not including some measure of fluid buoyancy. Convection (free) effects are in fact only significant for velocities smaller than about 0.05 m/sec and a criterion for its neglect is that the Reynolds number should be greater than twice the cube root of the Grashof number[42]

$$Gr = \frac{g\, d\, (T_w - T_f)}{\nu^2\, T_f}$$

For a typical wire, the Grashof number is about $6\text{x}10^{-6}$ so that buoyant convection can be neglected for fluid speeds greater than 0.05 m/sec. For most purposes, we can neglect radiation, buoyant convection and also the various small thermoelectric effects that occur; the main contributions to heat transfer from the wire are conduction to the supports and forced convection to the fluid flow.

According to Collins and Williams[42], remaining parameters of eqn. 4.5 can be related by

$$Nu\left(\frac{T_f}{T_m}\right)^{0.17} = 0.24 + 0.56\, Re^{0.45} \quad \text{for } 0.02<Re<44$$

$$= 0.48 Re^{0.51} \quad \text{for } 44<Re<140$$

Where the mean film temperature, $T_m = (T_w + T_f)/2$.

If the free stream temperature and temperature dependent transport properties remain constant, and if, in addition, the pressure is uniform and the temperature loading factor does not vary significantly, the relationship suggested between heat transfer and velocity is

$$\frac{\dot{Q}}{T_w - T_f} = A + B\,U^{0.45}$$

Where A and B are constants.

An earlier, much quoted result – King's law[21]—gave

$$Nu = A + B\,U^{1/2}\ .$$

The heat transfer from the sensor of a hot-wire anemometer is influenced by some of the following factors, several of which are not considered in the above derivation.

(i) Non-uniformities in temperature, and flow pattern near the ends of the sensor.
(ii) The accumulation of dirt during operation—dust, lint and oil in gases; particles, slime, and bubbles in liquids.
(iii) Variation in temperature, density, and concentration of the ambient fluid.
(iv) Aging—the physical and geometric changes occuring during prolonged use at high velocities and temperatures.
(v) Rapid variations in the direction and turbulence intensity around the wire.
(vi) Inclination of the wire to the mean flow direction.

Modes of Operation

The hot-wire anemometer may be operated in either of the following two modes:
(a) Constant current mode
(b) Constant temperature (or resistance) mode

In the constant current mode the heating current I is maintained sensibly constant and the wire temperature T_w and the resistance R_w fluctuate with local changes in the fluid velocity. Nevertheless, in the constant temperature mode the wire temperature or resistance is maintained constant by an amplifier in wheatstone bridge type feed back loop which has the effect of compensating for the thermal inertia of the wire. In turbulent flows it is often found necessary to investigate turbulent fluctuations with much higher frequencies; for example, to pick up a length scale of 2 mm convected at 50 m/sec one must measure up to $\omega = 50/.002 = 25{,}000$ Hz. Frequencies of this order, and beyond 100 k Hz, can be retained by passing the output from the constant current operational mode of the hot wire through a compensator. The compensator attenuates amplitude response to high frequency fluctuations by an amount equal to $1/(1+\omega^2\tau^2)^{0.5}$ where τ is the 'time constant'. The amplitude attenuation is set by feeding the hot wire output through an amplifier whose gain rises with frequency as $(1+\omega^2\tau^2)^{0.5}$ up to the limit set by the amplifier components so that the effective time constant ($\equiv 1/$ bandwidth in radians/sec) is approximately equal to the hot wire time constant divided by the 'intrinsic' gain of the amplifier. Since the time constant depends somewhat upon the operating conditions of the wire, the compensator gain has to be adjusted manually during the course of the experiment. Hot films do not have simple time constant and are very rarely operated in the constant current mode. In brief, the essential difference between the constant current and constant temperature is, therefore, whether the compensation for thermal inertia is performed manually or automatically. Constant current anemometers are less convenient to operate than the constant temperature anemometers. The only advantage of the constant current anemometer is that it is straightforward to couple the wire to the amplifier by a transformer—which is ideally an amplifier with practically no noise and thus increasing the signal to noise ratio.

In swirl flows with large turbulence intensities, the constant temperature mode is to be preferred because the time constant of a hot wire depends on the operating conditions or, for a given wire, on the speed of flow past the wire (an operation that is controlled automatically by the amplifier). Compensation for modulation of time constant in the constant current mode would require a parametric amplifier whose high frequency gain is controlled by the wire voltage itself. Constant current anemometers are generally used for studying flows with low turbulence intensities, of the order of 0.1 per cent or less and in very high-speed flows. Nevertheless, in flows with large temperature fluctuations and/or velocity fluctuations it is necessary to operate the wire at several different temperatures; that is, several different ratios of velocity/temperature sensitivity so that the statistical properties of the velocity and temperature fluctuation fields can be deduced. This is somewhat easier to do with a constant current anemometer than with a constant temperature anemometer because the overall frequency response and stability of the latter depend upon the wire temperature, partly because the time constant τ of the wire varies and partly because the amplifier gain depends on the output current.

So far we have said a great deal about the frequency response of the hot wires but little about their spatial resolution. In turbulent shear flows or flows near to a wall the latter often provides a more stringent limit than does frequency response. Consider a flow near to a wall with u=10 m/sec, and with the smallest scale of turbulence around 1mm corresponding to ω=10/0.001 = 100,000 Hz. But for a sensor length of 1 mm, the smallest disturbance that will be faithfully recorded has a length scale around 5 mm, corresponding to 2000 Hz.

Response Equations for Hot Wire

The hot wire has different sensitivity to each of its three planes. Various expressions have been derived and used for calibration purposes, the usual one being

$$E^2 = A + B u^n \tag{4.6}$$

Where E is the DC voltage output and u is the mean velocity and n is a constant having value between 0.5 and 0.7. For mean velocity measurements the above expression is only satisfactory over a restricted velocity range. Dynamic calibration techniques have also shown that eqn. 4.6 is unsatisfactory for all except low turbulence flows.

The six-orientation hot-wire technique requires a single, straight, hot-wire to be calibrated for three different probe directions in order to determine the directional sensitivity of such a probe. The three directions and the three calibration curves are shown in Fig. 4.4. Each of the three calibration curves is obtained with zero velocity in the other two directions. The calibration curves demonstrate that the hot-wire is most efficiently cooled when the flow is in the û direction. Whereas, the wire is most inefficiently cooled for the flow in $\hat{w}$ direction. Each of the calibration curves follows a second order, least square fit, of the form:

$$E^2 = A + BZ^{1/2} + CZ \tag{4.7}$$

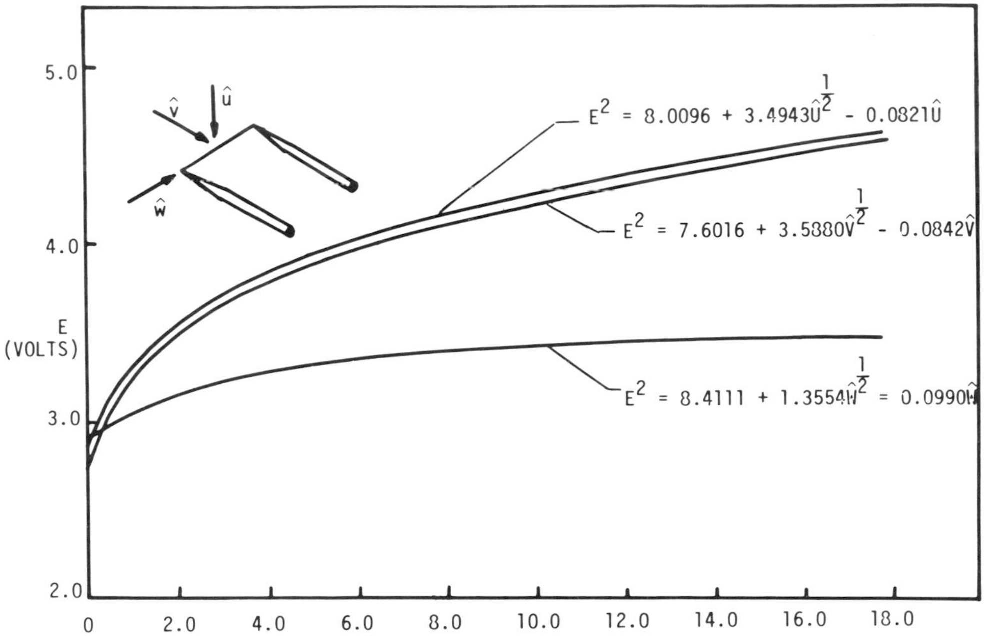

Figure 4.4 The calibration of hot wire in three directions

where A, B, and C are the calibration constants and Z can take a value of $\hat{u}$, $\hat{v}$, and $\hat{w}$ for the three calibration curves, respectively. The cooling velocity, z, equals the velocity perpendicular to the wire in the plane of the support and corresponds to the heating voltage E applied across the terminals of the wire. The exponent n varies between 0.5 and 0.9. Coefficient A equals to $E_o{}^2$, where E_o is the voltage across the terminals of the wire at zero flow velocity (owing to free convection effects). Typical values of A obtained from measurement is about 8.5.

When the wire is placed in a 3-dimensional flowfield, the effective cooling velocity experienced by the hot-wire, in terms of the probe coordinator and pitch and yaw factors (G and K) as defined by:

$$Z^2 = \hat{v}^2 + G^2\hat{u}^2 + K^2\hat{w}^2$$

where
$$G = \frac{\hat{v}\ (\hat{w}, \hat{u}\ =\ 0)}{\hat{u}\ (\hat{w}, \hat{v}\ =\ 0)}\ ,$$

$$K = \frac{\hat{v}\ (\hat{w}, \hat{u}\ =\ 0)}{\hat{w}\ (\hat{v}, \hat{u}\ =\ 0)}\ ,$$

evaluated from the three calibration curves for a constant value of E^2.

To carry out measurements in the combustor flowfield, the wire is aligned in the flow in such a way that in the first orientation, the wire is normal to the flow in the axial direction and the probe coordinates coincide with the coordinates of the experimental facility. Thus, the six equations for the instantaneous cooling velocities at the six orientations, as given by King[21], are:

$$Z_1^2 = v^2 + G^2 u^2 + K^2 w^2$$

$$Z_2^2 = v^2 + G^2 (u \cos 30° + w \sin 30°)^2 + K^2 (w \cos 30° - u \sin 30°)^2$$

$$Z_3^2 = v^2 + G^2 (u \cos 60° + w \sin 60°)^2 + K^2 (w \cos 60° - u \sin 60°)^2$$

$$Z_4^2 = v^2 + G^2 w^2 + K^2 u^2$$

$$Z_5^2 = v^2 + G^2 (w \sin 120° + u \cos 120°)^2 + K^2 (u \sin 120° - w \cos 120°)^2$$

$$Z_6^2 = v^2 + G^2 (w \sin 150° + u \cos 150°)^2 + K^2 (u \sin 150° - w \cos 150°)^2$$

Replacing the sines and cosines and expanding the square brackets:

$$Z_1^2 = v^2 + G^2 u^2 + K^2 w^2$$

$$Z_2^2 = v^2 + G^2 \left(u^2 \frac{3}{4} + \frac{w^2}{4} + uw \sqrt{\frac{3}{2}}\right) + K^2 \left(w^2 \frac{3}{4} + \frac{u^2}{4} - uw \sqrt{\frac{3}{2}}\right)$$

$$Z_3^2 = \nu^2 + G^2 \left(\frac{u^2}{4} + w^2 \frac{3}{4} + uw \sqrt{\frac{3}{2}}\right) + K^2 \left(\frac{w^2}{4} + u^2 \frac{3}{4} - uw \sqrt{\frac{3}{2}}\right)$$

$$Z_4^2 = v^2 + G^2 w^2 + K^2 u^2$$

$$Z_5^2 = \nu^2 + G^2 \left(\frac{u^2}{4} + w^2 \frac{3}{4} - uw \sqrt{\frac{3}{2}}\right) + K^2 \left(\frac{w^2}{4} + u^2 \frac{3}{4} + uw \sqrt{\frac{3}{2}}\right)$$

$$Z_6^2 = v^2 + G^2 \left(u^2 \frac{3}{4} + \frac{w^2}{4}\ uw \sqrt{\frac{3}{2}}\right) + K^2 \left(w^2 \frac{3}{4} + \frac{u^2}{4} + uw \sqrt{\frac{3}{2}}\right)$$

Solving simultaneously any three adjacent equations provides expressions for the instantaneous values of the three velocity components, u, w, and v, in terms of the equivalent cooling velocities (Z_1, Z_2, and Z_3 for example, when the first three equations are chosen). King refers to these instantaneous velocity components as F1, F2, and F3 as follows:

$$F1 = \left[\left\{ AO + \left(AO^2 + \frac{BO^2}{3}\right)^{1/2} \right\} \frac{1}{(G^2 - K^2)} \right]^{1/2} \quad (4.8)$$

$$F2 = \left[\left\{ -AO + \left(AO^2 + \frac{BO^2}{3}\right)^{1/2} \right\} \frac{1}{(G^2 - K^2)} \right]^{1/2} \quad (4.9)$$

$$F3 = \left[CO - \frac{(G^2 + K^2)}{(G^2 - K^2)} \left(AO^2 + \frac{BO^2}{3}\right)^{1/2} \right]^{1/2} \quad (4.10)$$

The values of AO, BO, and CO depend on the set of the three equations chosen and are given in Fig. 4.5. Nevertheless, these equations cannot be used directly because it is impossible to obtain Z_1, Z_2, and Z_3 at a single instance in time. Therefore Equation 4.8 through 4.10 must be expressed in terms of mean and root-mean-square values. Equation 4.7 can be written as:

$$\phi(E_i) = Z_i = \left[\left[-B + \left\{ B^2 - 4C(A - E_i^2) \right\}^{1/2} \right] / 2C \right]^{1/2} \quad (4.11)$$

The above equation is in terms of instantaneous velocity Z_i and instantaneous voltage E_i. In order to obtain an expression for time-mean velocity as a function of time-mean voltage, a Taylor series expansion of Eqn. 4.11 can be carried out.

$$\text{Since } Z_1 = \phi(\bar{E}_i + E_i')$$

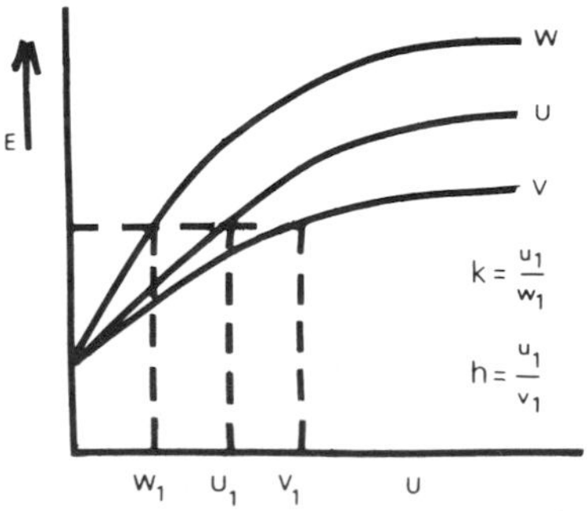

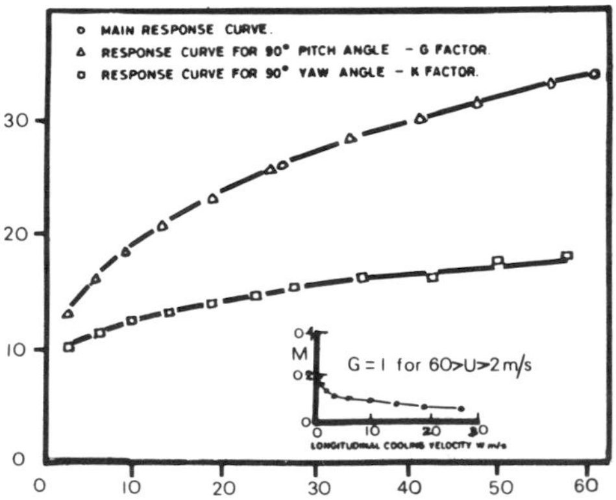

Typical Response Characteristics for Disa Type 55 F11 Hot Wire Probe

Figure 4.5 (Left) Calibration curves for three different directions (Right) Typical response curve for a hot-wire probe

$$Z_i = \phi(\bar{E}_i + E_i') = \phi(\bar{E}_i) + \frac{E_i'}{1!}\frac{\partial\phi}{\partial E_i} + \frac{E_i'^2}{2!}\frac{\partial^2\phi}{\partial E_i^2} \quad (13)$$

The Taylor series is truncated after second order terms assuming the higher order terms to be relatively small. Time averaging both sides of the above equation and employing the fact that $\bar{E}' = 0$, yields:

$$\bar{Z}_i = \bar{\phi} + \tfrac{1}{2}\frac{\partial^2\phi}{\partial \bar{E}_i^2}\sigma_{E_i}^2 \quad (4.12)$$

where $\bar{\phi}$ indicates that the function is evaluated for $\bar{E}_i$. To obtain $\overline{Z_i'^2} = \sigma_{Z_i}^2$, the relationship is given by Hinze[29] is:

$$\overline{Z_i'^2} = \sigma_{Z_i}^2 = \text{Expec}\,[Z_i^2] - (\text{Expec}\,[Z_i])^2 \quad (4.13)$$

$$\text{Since Expec}\,[Z_i^2] \simeq \bar{\phi} + \tfrac{1}{2}\frac{\partial^2\phi}{\partial \bar{E}_i^2}\sigma_{E_i}^2, \quad (4.14)$$

the differential in Eqn. 4.14 can be evaluated as:

$$\frac{\partial^2 \overline{\phi^2}}{\partial E_i^2} = 2\left(\frac{\partial \bar{\phi}}{\partial E_i}\right)^2 + 2\bar{\phi}\frac{\partial^2 \bar{\phi}}{\partial E_i^2} \quad (4.15)$$

Then Eqn. 4.12 becomes:

$$\text{Expec}\,[Z_i^2] \simeq \bar{\phi}^2 + \left(\frac{\partial\bar{\phi}}{\partial E_i}\right)^2\sigma_{E_i}^2 + \phi\frac{\partial^2\bar{\phi}}{\partial E_i^2}\sigma_{E_i}^2 \quad (4.16)$$

Squaring Eqn. 4.12 and substituting with Eqn. 4.16 into Eqn. 4.13 gives:

$$\overline{Z_i'^2} = \sigma_{Z_i}^2 \simeq \frac{\partial\bar{\phi}}{\partial \bar{E}_i}^2 \sigma_{E_i}^2 - \left(1/2\,\frac{\partial^2\bar{\phi}}{\partial \bar{E}_i^2}\sigma_{E_i}^2\right)^2 \quad (4.17)$$

Thus, Equations 4.12 and 4.17 give the mean and variance of individual cooling velocities in terms of the mean and variance of the appropriate voltage.

In a 3-dimensional flow, usually one wishes to obtain the mean and variance for the individual velocity components in axial, azimuthal, and radial directions, and also their cross correlations.

The procedure to obtain the mean and variance of the individual velocity components is the same as for the effective cooling velocities except that *u*, *w*, and *v* are functions of three random variables and there are extra terms in the Taylor expansion to account for the covariances of the cooling velocities. Thus, the three mean velocities as given by Dvorak and Syred[37] and King[21] are:

$$\bar{u} = F1(Z_P, Z_Q, Z_R) + \frac{1}{2}\sum_{i=1}^{3} \frac{\partial^2 F1}{\partial Z_i^2} \sigma_{Z_i}^2 + \sum_{i<j}^{3} \frac{\partial^2 F1}{\partial Z_i \partial Z_j} K_{Z_i Z_j},$$

where time-mean values are to be understood on the right side of this and subsequent equations.

$$\bar{w} = F2(Z_P, Z_Q, Z_R) + \frac{1}{2}\sum_{i=1}^{3} \frac{\partial^2 F2}{\partial Z_i^2} \sigma_{Z_i}^2 + \sum_{i<j}^{3} \frac{\partial^2 F2}{\partial Z_i \partial Z_j} K_{Z_i Z_j},$$

and

$$\bar{v} = F3(Z_P, Z_Q, Z_R) + \frac{1}{2}\sum_{i=1}^{3} \frac{\partial^2 F3}{\partial Z_i^2} \sigma_{Z_i}^2 + \sum_{i<j}^{3} \frac{\partial^2 F3}{\partial Z_i \partial Z_j} K_{Z_i Z_j}$$

where $K_{Z_i Z_j}$ is the covariance of the cooling velocity fluctuations and is defined as[29, 30]:

$$K_{Z_i Z_j} = \frac{1}{T}\int_{0}^{T} (Z_i - \bar{Z}_i)(Z_j - \bar{Z}_j)\,dt$$

Also the normal stresses are given as:

$$\overline{u'^2} = \sum_{i=1}^{3} \left(\frac{\partial F1}{\partial Z_i}\right)^2 \sigma_{Z_i}^2 + \sum_{i}^{3}\sum_{\substack{j \\ i \neq j}}^{3} \frac{\partial F1}{\partial Z_i} \cdot \frac{\partial F1}{\partial Z_j} - \left[\frac{1}{2}\sum_{i=1}^{3} \frac{\partial^2 F1}{\partial Z_i^2} \sigma_{Z_i}^2 + \sum_{i<j}^{3} \frac{\partial^2 F1}{\partial Z_i \partial Z_j} K_{Z_i Z_j}\right]^2,$$

$$\overline{w'^2} = \sum_{i=1}^{3} \left(\frac{\partial F2}{\partial Z_i}\right)^2 \sigma_{Z_i}^2 + \sum_{i}^{3}\sum_{\substack{j \\ i \neq j}}^{3} \frac{\partial F2}{\partial Z_i} \frac{\partial F2}{\partial Z_j} - \left[\frac{1}{2}\sum_{i=1}^{3} \frac{\partial^2 F2}{\partial Z_i^2} \sigma_{Z_i}^2 + \sum_{i<j}^{3} \frac{\partial^2 F2}{\partial Z_i \partial Z_j} K_{Z_i Z_j}\right]^2,$$

and

$$\overline{v'^2} = \sum_{i=1}^{3} \left(\frac{\partial F3}{\partial Z_i}\right)^2 \sigma Z_i^2 + \sum_{i}^{3}\sum_{\substack{j \\ i \neq j}}^{3} \frac{\partial F3}{\partial Z_i} \frac{\partial F3}{\partial Z_j} - \left[\frac{1}{2}\sum_{i=1}^{3} \frac{\partial^2 F3}{\partial Z_i^2} \sigma_{Z_i}^2 + \right.$$

$$\left.\sum_{i<j}^{3} \frac{\partial^2 F3}{\partial Z_i \partial Z_j} K_{Z_i Z_j}\right]^2,$$

Also the shear stresses as given by Dvorak and Syred[19] are:

$$\overline{u'w'} = \sum_{i=1}^{3} \frac{\partial F1}{\partial Z_i} \frac{\partial F2}{\partial Z_i} \sigma_{Z_i}{}^2 + \sum_{\substack{i \\ i \neq j}}^{3} \sum_{j}^{3} \frac{\partial F1}{\partial Z_i} \frac{\partial F2}{\partial Z_j} K_{Z_i Z_j} - \left[\frac{1}{2} \sum_{i=1}^{3} \frac{\partial^2 F1}{\partial Z_i{}^2} \sigma_{Z_i}{}^2\right.$$

$$\left.+ \sum_{\substack{i \\ i<j}}^{3} \sum_{j}^{3} \frac{\partial^2 F1}{\partial Z_i \partial Z_j} K_{Z_i Z_j}\right] \left[\frac{1}{2} \sum_{i=1}^{3} \frac{\partial^2 F2}{\partial Z_i{}^2} \sigma_{Z_i}{}^2 + \sum_{\substack{i \\ i<j}}^{3} \sum_{j}^{3} \frac{\partial^2 F2}{\partial Z_i \partial Z_j} K_{Z_i Z_j}\right]$$

$$\overline{u'v'} = \sum_{i=1}^{3} \frac{\partial F1}{\partial Z_i} \frac{\partial F3}{\partial Z_i} \sigma_{Z_i}{}^2 + \sum_{\substack{i \\ i \neq j}}^{3} \sum_{j}^{3} \frac{\partial F1}{\partial Z_i} \frac{\partial F3}{\partial Z_i} K_{Z_i Z_j} - \left]\frac{1}{2} \sum_{i=1}^{3} \frac{\partial^2 F1}{\partial Z_i{}^2} \sigma_{Z_i}{}^2\right.$$

$$\left.+ \sum_{\substack{i \\ i<j}}^{3} \sum_{j}^{3} \frac{\partial^2 F1}{\partial Z_i \partial Z_j} K_{Z_i Z_j}\right] \left[\frac{1}{2} \sum_{i=1}^{3} \frac{\partial^2 F3}{\partial Z_i{}^2} \sigma_{Z_i}{}^2 + \sum_{\substack{i \\ i<j}}^{3} \sum_{j}^{3} \frac{\partial^2 F3}{\partial Z_i \partial Z_j} K_{Z_i Z_j}\right]$$

and finally,

$$\overline{w'v'} = \sum_{i=1}^{3} \frac{\partial F2}{\partial Z_i} \frac{\partial F3}{\partial Z_i} \sigma_{Z_i}{}^2 + \sum_{\substack{i \\ i \neq j}}^{3} \sum_{j}^{3} \frac{\partial F2}{\partial Z_i} \frac{\partial F3}{\partial Z_j} K_{Z_i} - \left[\frac{1}{2} \sum_{i=1}^{3} \frac{\partial^2 F2}{\partial Z_i{}^2} \sigma_{Z_i}{}^2 +\right.$$

$$\left.\sum_{\substack{i \\ i<j}}^{3} \sum_{j}^{3} \frac{\partial^2 F2}{\partial Z_i \partial Z_j} K_{Z_i Z_j}\right] \left[\frac{1}{2} \sum_{i=1}^{3} \frac{\partial^2 F3}{\partial Z_1{}^2} \sigma_{Z_i}{}^2 + \sum_{\substack{i \\ i<j}}^{3} \sum_{j}^{3} \frac{\partial^2 F3}{\partial Z_i \partial Z_j} K_{Z_i Z_j}\right]$$

Nevertheless, the limitation of the hot-wire anemometer is that it is not sensitive to local flow reversals, commonly encountered in turbulent flows (for example, swirl flows), and can only be applied to non burning (isothermal) conditions. The relative error in velocity measured by a hot-wire anemometer is about 1 per cent with 1°C change in fluid temperature. The region or onset of flow recirculation can be found by a directional sensitive pulsed-wire technique or a laser velocimeter.

Pulsed Wire Technique

In highly turbulent swirl flows, velocity measurement by pitot probe or hot-wire anemometer can be subjected to serious errors due to their ambiguous response to variations in the direction of the velocity vector. Thus, the results of measurements in swirl flows with reverse flow region have to be treated with great care, and in cases where apparent anomalies in measurement arise, it is not generally possible to decide whether these are due to the instruments used or whether they are genuine characteristics of the flow.

The pulsed-wire technique was first described by Bauer[44] in 1965. He used two fine platinum wires of 0.0001 inch diameter mounted on hot-wire probes and placed parallel to one another with one wire downstream of the other. A 'tracer' of heated air was introduced into the flow by pulsing the upstream wire with a voltage pulse of about 1μsec duration and the time taken for this 'tracer' to reach the downstream wire was measured by using the downstream wire as a detector (that is as a resistance thermometer). This parallel wire arrangement is very sensitive to flow direction, and in turbulent flow, many of the heat pulses would miss the resistance wire altogether.

Bradbury[40] modified the above technique by placing the pick-up at right angles to the pulsed wire; the resultant instrument had a very wide yaw response. His probe consisted of three wires, Fig. 4.6. The central wire was the pulsed wire and at either side of this, the pick-up wires were placed with their axes perpendicular to the pulsed wire axis. The pulsed wire was 0.0002 inch diameter platinum and about 0.2 inch long. The two resistance wires were also 0.0002 inch diameter of similar length and about 0.06 inch apart. The use of two pick-up wires ensured that even in a reverse flow region, the heat pulse would be sensed by one or the other of the two pick-up wires. The voltage

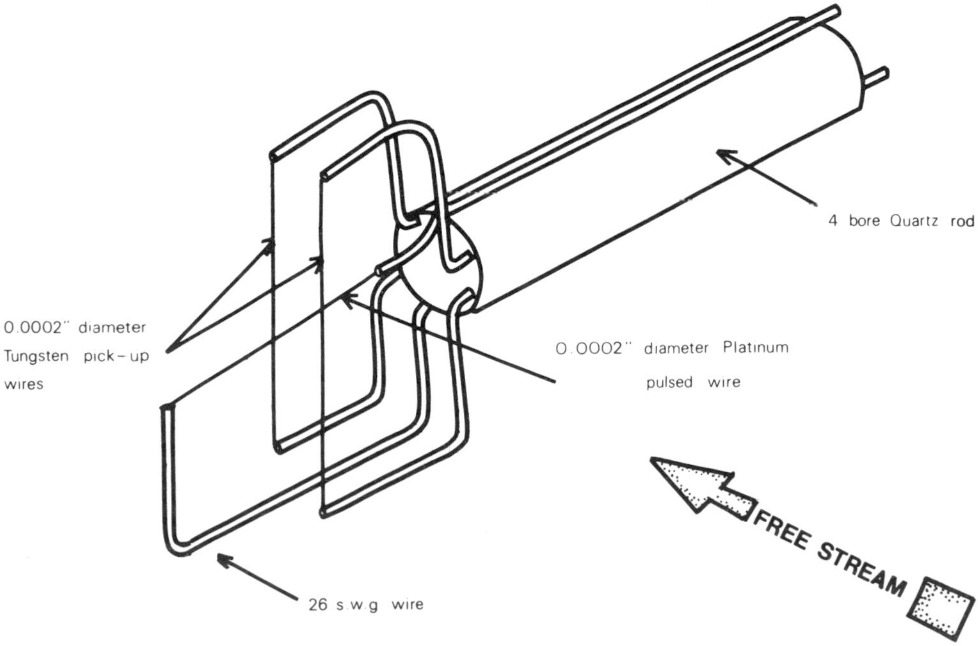

Figure 4.6 A Sketch of the pulsed wire probe

applied to the pulsed wire was typically about 30 volts for a duration of about 5 μsec. A simple pulse generator was used to provide pulses either on a single shot basis or repetitive with a variable frequency between 30 Hz to 100 Hz. The two pick-up wires were operated as simple resistance thermometers in a constant current mode with a current of about 1 mA and the voltage across them was fed into a low noise differential amplifier. An oscilloscope was used to observe the time taken for the signal to reach the pick-up wires.

Two practical difficulties with this technique should be mentioned. Even at low current passing through the pick-up wires, some direct anemometer sensitivity to velocity fluctuations seemed to remain. The size of this signal is proportional to the length of the pick-up wire, whereas in the crossed-wire probe, the signal from the heat pulse is independent of the wire length. It would seem therefore that there is an advantage in keeping the pick-up wires as short as possible. But, in order to maintain an adequate yaw response, this would require the wire spacing to be reduced proportionally. Two limitations seem to arise in doing this. First, if the tracer is to be convected with effectively the same velocity as that of the stream, it is necessary that the pick-up wire should be located not less than about a hundred diameters downstream from the pulsed wire. Secondly, electrical coupling occurs between the pulsed wire and resistance wire circuits, probably due to stray capacitance.

Although the pulsed wire technique has the advantage of somewhat less sophistication and directional sensitivity, it still suffers from poor spatial resolution, poor frequency response and inability to extract spectra and correlation coefficients. These are overcome with the recent developments in laser-based diagnostic techniques; for example, laser doppler anemometry, laser dual focus.

Laser Velocimetry

The recent availability of laser as a highly monochromatic, coherent light source has created a new era in high resolution optical spectroscopy. The usefulness of laser doppler technique for fluid flow measurement, first demonstrated by Yeh and Cummins[45], has been widely reported in the literature[46-53]. The potential benefits of laser velocimetry, LV, include good optical resolution, a linear relationship between instantaneous velocity and the measured signal, sensitivity to one velocity vector at a time, lack of dependence of the measured signal on thermodynamic properties, and no need for calibration. In this section a brief review is given of LV principles with particular reference in their application to swirl flows, both without and with combustion. Nevertheless, it is not our intention to cover here the entire field of laser velocimetry; readers are recommended to consult references[46-53] for further information and experience.

The LV has now become a practical laboratory and field test instrument for the measurement of local velocity. These velocity measurements can rival the hot film probe in spatial resolution, and the data obtained can now provide mean and turbulence velocity as well as turbulence length scales and spectra. The LV is now a widely used successful diagnostic tool for measurements in both isothermal and combustion systems.

In this section some basic principles, and optical arrangements of LV with specific application to swirl flows, both without and with combustion, are described. Various components of the optical systems, methods of particle generation and seeding the fluid flow, and the successful techniques used for processing the doppler signal are discussed in some detail.

Doppler Effect: Basic Theory

The Laser velocimeter is based on the principle of the doppler effect; the frequency of the radiation scattered by an object moving relative to a radiating source is changed by an amount that depends on the velocity and the scattering geometry. If V is the velocity of the scatterer, the doppler shift is given by (*see* fig. 4.7(a))

$$\Delta\nu = (K_s - K_o) \cdot V \tag{4.18}$$

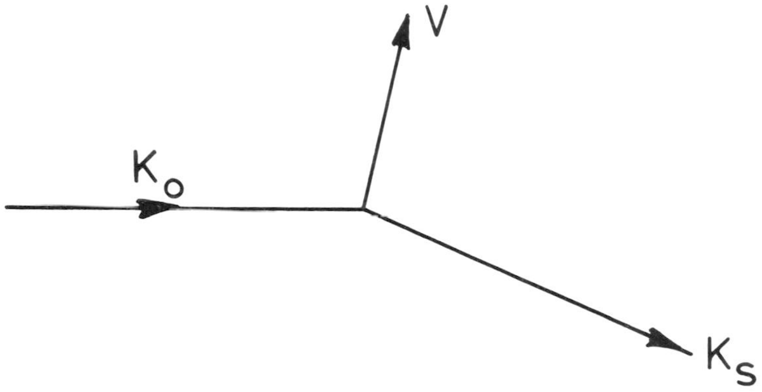

Figure 4.7(a) Scattering geometry – basic doppler effect

where K_o is the incident wave vector $= \dfrac{2\pi}{\lambda_o}$, and K_s is the scattered wave vector.

The above relation implies that an observer of a particle moving away from a fixed source of light would see the light at a lower frequency than the source frequency, and to a stationary observer, the light scattered from the particle would also appear to have a different frequency. The disadvantages such as frequency broadening, difficult optical geometry, alignment sensitivity in hostile environments and restricted accuracy of frequency measurement in the above can be overcome by using a doppler differential arrangement as shown in Fig. 4.7(b).

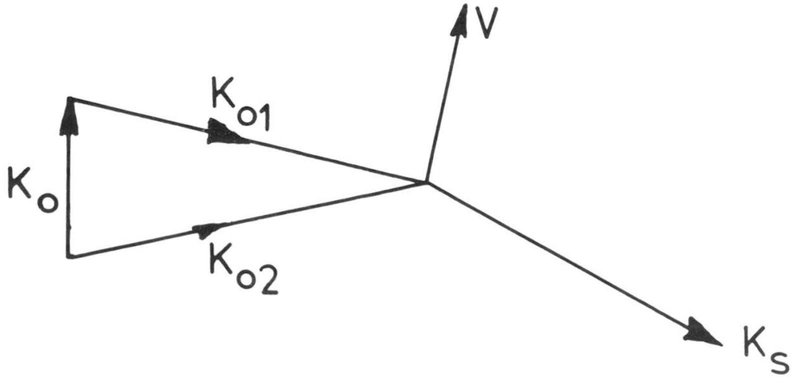

Figure 4.7(b) Scattering geometry – doppler difference effect

Here, two incident radiation is convergent on the particle from the two directions with wave vectors K_{01} and K_{02}. Thus,

$$\Delta\nu_1 = (K_s - K_{01}) \cdot V$$

$$\Delta\nu_2 = (K_s - K_{02}) \cdot V$$

so that $\Delta\nu_1 - \Delta\nu_2 = (K_{02} - K_{01}) \cdot V = K_O \cdot V$ (4.19)

$$\text{Now } |K_{01}| = |K_{02}| = \frac{2\pi}{\lambda_o}$$

$$\text{So that } |K_O| = |(K_{02} - K_{01})| = 2 \sin(\phi/_2)\, \frac{2\pi}{\lambda_o}$$

$$\text{and } \Delta\nu_1 - \Delta\nu_2 = \frac{4\pi u}{\lambda_o} \sin \phi/_2$$

where u is the component of V in the direction of K_0, or

$$f = \frac{2\, u \sin(\phi/_2)}{\lambda_o}\ Hz \tag{4.20}$$

which is independent of the scattering direction. The collection efficiency therefore, can be enhanced by using a large light-collecting lens.

The scattering direction K_s in some arrangements is taken to be either 0° or 180° with respect to the axis of symmetry of the incident beams. In other cases an intermediate angle is used to give a useful degree of control over the scattering volume and to avoid unwanted reflections.

Modes of Operation

Doppler-difference System

The basic arrangement of a practical doppler-difference system is shown in Fig. 4.8(a). The laser light is split into two equal parts by a beamsplitter and a mirror. The point in space at which these two beams cross, together with the field stop on the face of the detector, define the scattering volume from which velocity information is being obtained.

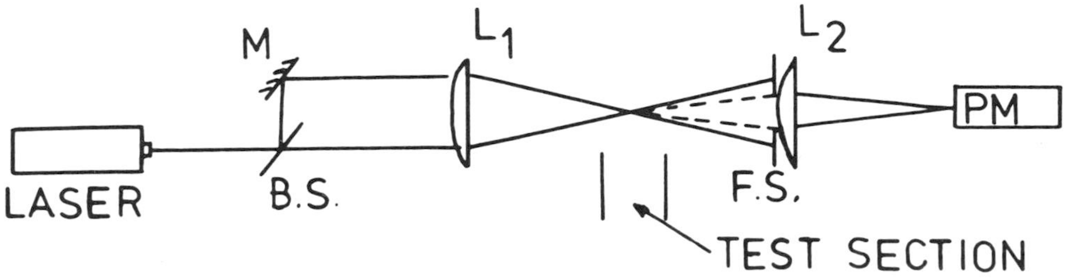

Figure 4.8(a) Doppler difference system

The doppler-difference mode—also known as "Fringe-mode" because the beams form a fringe system in the volume of intersection—is used where the intensity of scattered light is low.

Ideally, at any instant, there should not be more than one particle present in the scattering volume. If two or more particles are present in the scattering region at the same time the radiated fields are, in general, out of phase and the detected signal will have a lower depth of modulation due to partial cancellation.

The velocity component measured in the doppler difference mode on forward scatter is parallel to K_{01} and K_{02}. In the back-scatter mode, the flow is attacked from only one side. This may be useful in some measurements, but, even at high concentrations of scattering particles in the flow, these measurements require a powerful laser. Since the doppler difference mode is independent of the direction of the scattered light, the expression above, eqn. 4.20, is valid for both forward and backward scatter mode.

Reference-Beam System

If the average number of scatterers present at any instant in the scattering volume is significantly greater than one, the reference beam mode is preferable. In this arrangement, Fig. 4.8(b), the detector aperture is small enough for rays from any point of the scattering volume to arrive in approximately the same relative phase, and the cancellation referred to above does not take place.

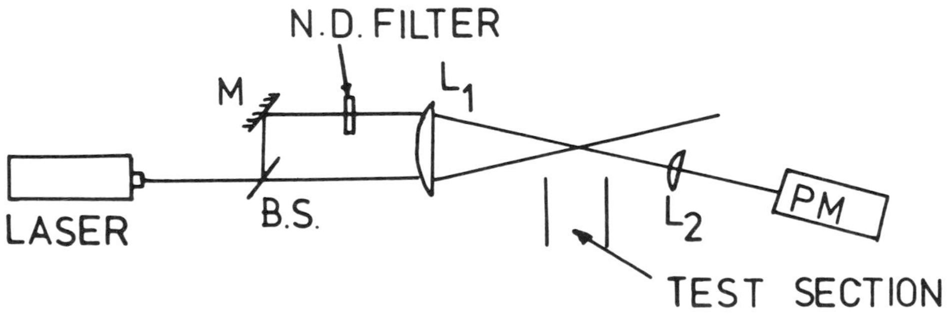

Figure 4.8(b) Reference beam arrangement

In the reference-beam mode the laser light is split up into two beams; one of the beams is further attenuated by approximately a factor of 100 or more with a neutral density, ND, filter. The intensity of the reference beam is reduced by the ND filter in order to optimise the quality of the doppler shifted light signal which is picked up by the photomultiplier, PM. The two beams, after passing through the lens, cross at a point within the flow in the test section.

On the receiving side, the weaker beam passes through an aperture (approx. 1 mm diameter or less) and enters a PM tube. Here the light from the weak reference beam is mixed with light from the brighter beam which has been scattered from the volume in which the two beams intersect. The scattered light is doppler shifted by the motion of the scattering particles which are assumed to move with the local fluid velocity. Thus, the scattered light has a slightly different frequency from the reference light and the combination of the two produces a beat frequency in the PM tube. The beat frequency is directly proportional to one component of the fluid velocity.

Several other optical geometries can be devised for LV; for instance a single incident beam and two scattering directions[49, 51, 54].

In the above discussions the fringe velocimeter and doppler shift velocimeter were broadly classed in one group, but it is important to distinguish between them.

Fringe and Doppler Shift Velocimeters

In fringe velocimeters, the frequency signal corresponds to the rate at which fringes are crossed by scattering particles. Thus, such instruments require a discontinuous light intensity distribution, that is, a fringe pattern at the measuring point. The scattered light also shows an apparent change in frequency due to the doppler effect; this frequency shift is not detected provided a light combining system is not used. Various optical arrangements for fringe velocimeters are shown in Fig. 4.9.

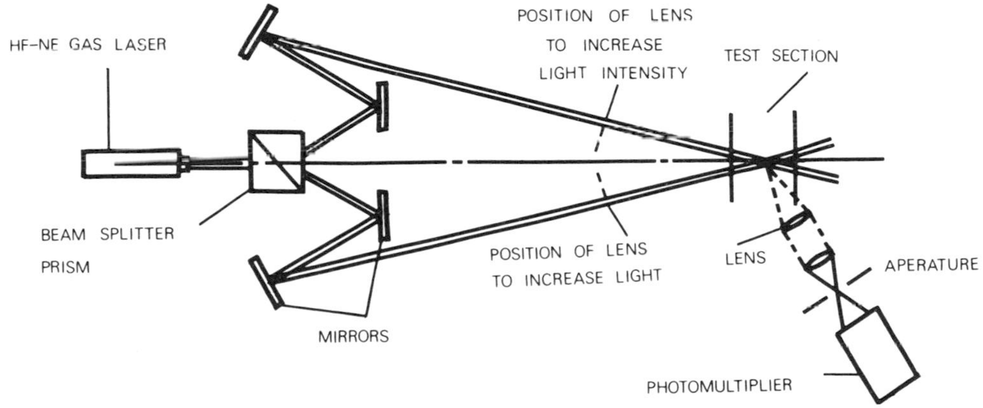

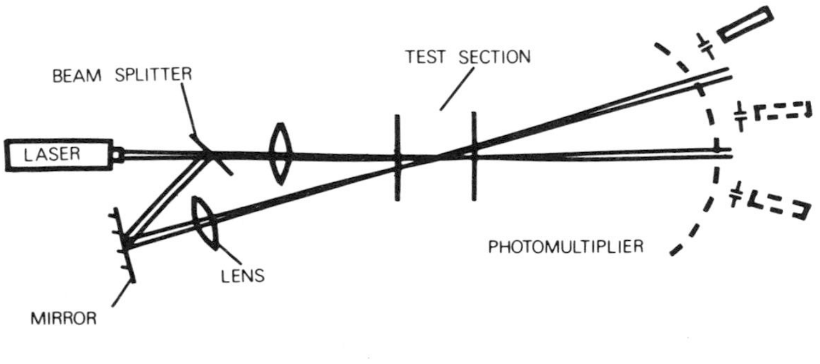

Figure 4.9 Optical arrangements for fringe anemometers[54]

In doppler shift velocimeters, the relation between doppler frequency shift and mean and fluctuating flow properties is based indirectly on the assumption that the light distribution in the measuring control volume, MCV, from which light is collected is continuous over a distance x, the dimension of light beam at the MCV in the direction of sensitivity of optical velocity meter. Thus, continuous light rays are emitted by particles over a time 'δt' given by

$$\delta t = \frac{x|n_i|}{u_i' (n_i)}$$

where n_i = vector, direction of sensitivity of optical meter.

u_i' = fluctuating component of velocity.

The time δt must be larger than the reciprocal of the beat frequency $\Delta\nu$ for the signal to be observed over a long enough time. Various optical arrangements for doppler shift velocimeters are shown in Fig. 4.10.

It was pointed out in the section on fringe (or dual beam) velocimeters that the light scattered by particles passing through a set of fringes also shows a frequency shift due to the doppler effect. The light scattered from the MCV can be processed not only in the manner of fringe velocimeters but also by combining the two beams to obtain the doppler frequency shift—which can be utilized to determine the velocity component in the direction n_i given by the light-collection system. In the fringe velocimeter the fringe pattern is utilized to obtain the velocity component perpendicular to the fringe pattern.

It is clear from the brief description given above that two different phenomena can be used to measure fluid flow velocity, Fig. 4.11. The frequency shift due to the doppler effect can be measured only if the two light beams are superimposed to produce a frequency difference; that is, the doppler frequency shift. For such measurements, optical arrangements are required to combine the two beams. In the case of distinct fringe pattern, no combining system is required to isolate the frequency of interest.

After the initial work on fringe velocimeters, several convenient ways of splitting the light beams were tried by several research workers in an attempt to develop a simple system adaptable to the laser doppler velocimeter. Among the different beam-splitting devices were Wollaston prisms, Savart plates, diffraction grating and other birefringe beam splitters. These devices had great advantages in comparison with the other systems since the two light beams of a velocimeter could be created without the use of mirrors; the latter yield geometrical arrangements which are very sensitive to tilt. A small tilt of the mirror causes a deviation in the reflected beam by twice that amount, whereas a good transmitting system is, at least to a first order, immune to misalignments. This greatly facilitates the alignment of optical systems in two or three channel systems and also for their use in successive measurements of several velocity components by means of a single-channel velocimeter.

Figure 4.12 shows the laser doppler system in which a Wollaston prism and a Savart plate are used to split the incident beam into two beams of equal intensity. The two outgoing beams from these have two orthogonal directions of polarization, and a polarization rotator has to be used in one of the beams to yield an interference fringe pattern inside the measuring control volume.

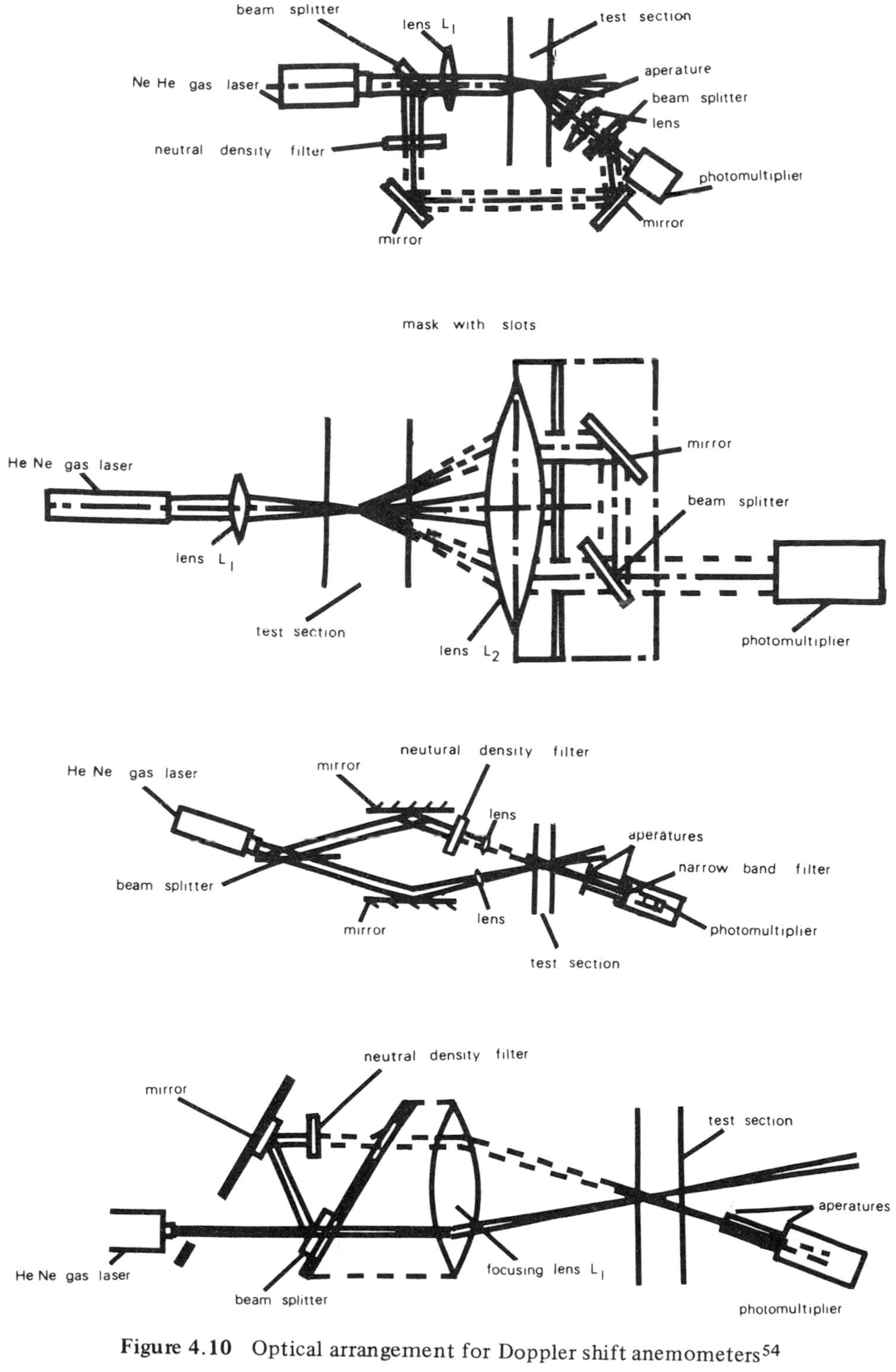

Figure 4.10 Optical arrangement for Doppler shift anemometers[54]

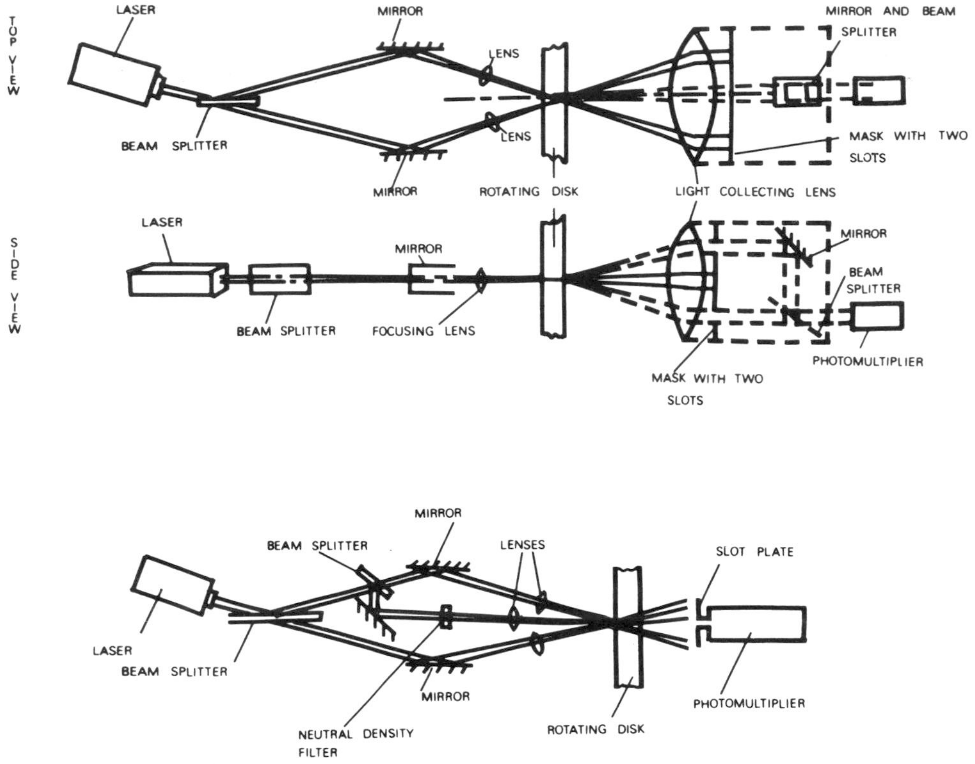

Figure 4.11 Combined anemometers[54]

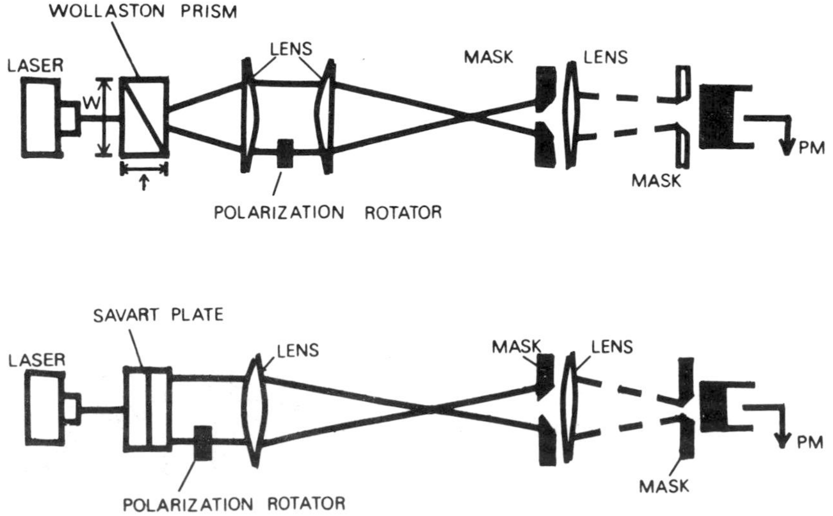

Figure 4.12 Configuration for laser Doppler, anemometers[49]

In the above systems it is important that the prisms used as beam splitters are made to the correct dimensions. In the case of a Wollaston prism this can be done by considering the angular deviation between the two emerging beams of the Wollaston prism according to the following relationship:

$$\Theta = \frac{2x}{W}(n_o - n_e)$$

where x = thickness of the prism
W = width of the prism
n_o and n_e = refractive index for ordinary and extraordinary beams respectively.

Polarization properties have been used by several research workers to measure velocity direction[55, 56].

Diffraction Gratings

Diffraction gratings have also been successfully used to create the two light beams needed for laser velocimetry measurements. Diffraction gratings can be arranged to yield two beams of equal intensity that can be utilized for dual beam systems or two beams with a large light intensity difference to permit operation in the reference beam mode. The latter has been used by Stevenson[57] who employed a radial rotating grating to measure the velocity field in a pulsating flow where both the magnitude and direction of the flow were needed simultaneously. Oldengarm *et al.*[58] also used rotating gratings in several flows for dual-beam laser doppler measurements. Ballantyne[59] obtained the frequency shift by scattering achieved by a rotating disc. Gupta and Beér[51] used a bleached rotating grating for measurements in swirl flows with recirculation, Fig. 4.13.

Like optical arrangements based on transmitting beam splitter prisms, the laser doppler systems employing diffraction grating are insensitive to tilt, at least for first order error calculations. This is of great help when setting up laser doppler systems and eliminates realignment problems when multicomponent velocity measurements are made by successive measurements in several directions.

Practical Considerations for Diffraction Grating

The velocity component measured with a LV system, without the use of frequency shifting, has a directional ambiguity of 180°. This limits the measurements to flows with low turbulence intensities, a problem that can be overcome by applying a fixed frequency shift on one or both of the laser beams to bias the beat frequency. With such an arrangement, measurements are made relative to a moving coordinate system (or moving set of fringes) and it becomes possible to measure zero velocity of a particle in the MCV, which becomes represented by the bias frequency. Positive and negative velocities are represented by frequencies above or below the frequency offset. There are at least three following reasons that one needs to introduce a frequency shift:

(i) allows one to discriminate between positive and negative velocities, for example, in swirl flows, oscillatory flows.

(ii) simplifies measurement problems encountered at very low velocities due to low

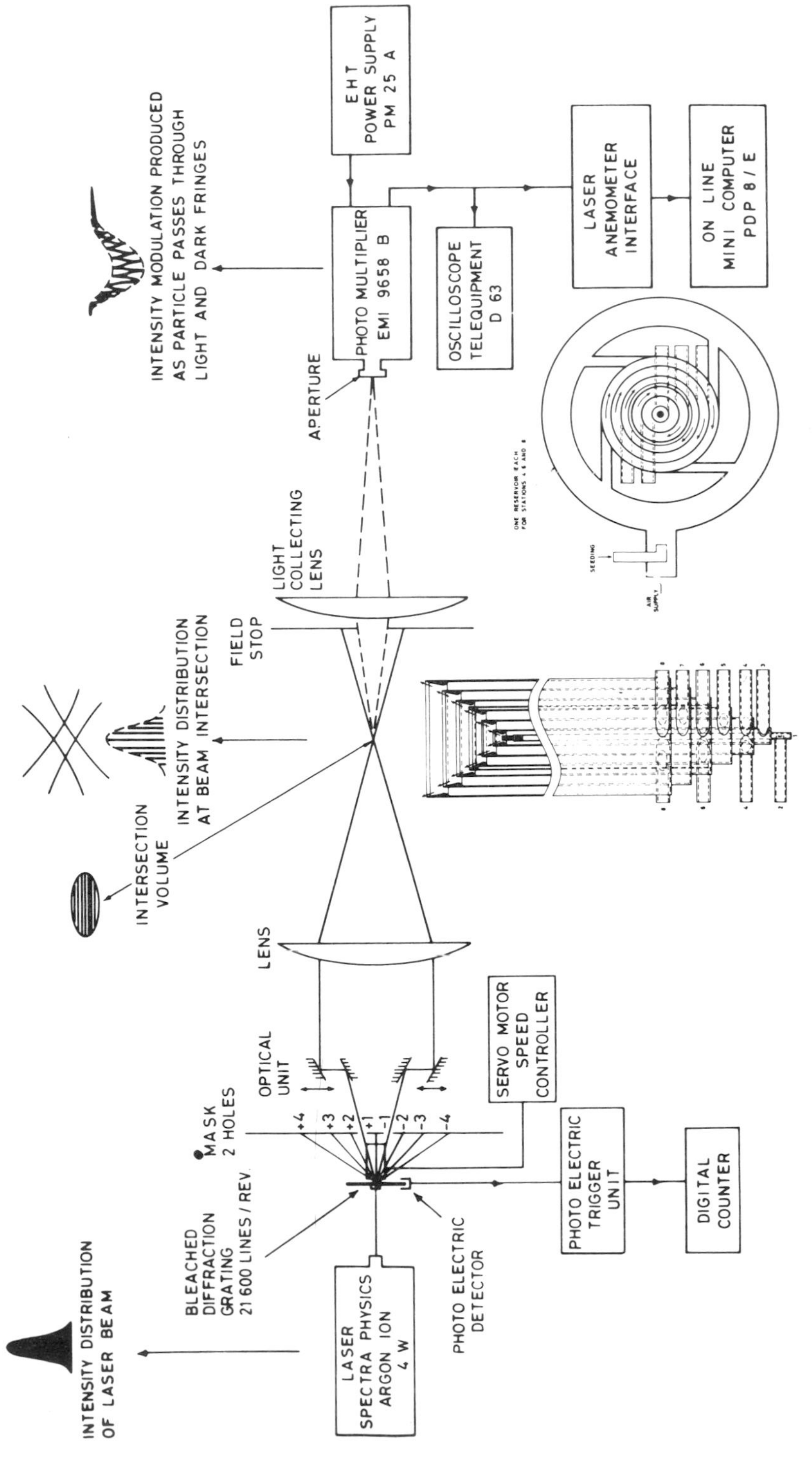

Figure 4.13 Schematic diagram of laser velocimeter using diffraction grating[51]

frequency noise from the electronics, laser, 50 or 60 Hz power supply source and mechanical vibrations.

(iii) allows one to match the heterodyne frequency to the characteristics of the signal processing equipment over a wide velocity range.

The principal means of obtaining frequency shifting are by the use of rotating grating, acousto-optic and electro-optic techniques,[60,66]. Although they offer high frequency shift, stability and high light efficiency, they have inherent disadvantages when compared with the moving grating method[57,62] in the frequency range where the latter method is usable. Both the electro-optic and acousto-optic require expensive modulating devices, and high-frequency power supplies. The power supplies for electro-optic modulators must operate at high voltages also. Alignment of these devices is very critical. Frequency shifts below 10 MHz are not practicable when using an ultrasonic cell; this introduces some problems in signal processing.

The cheapest and most convenient method of frequency shifting is to use a rotating diffraction grating, mounted perpendicular to the direction of the incident light. The laser beam passing through the grating is split into a number of diffraction orders (up to 32) from which the first order (+1 and −1) are selected. The disadvantage of the grating is that the efficiency of transmission of light is poor, but, if a bleached grating is used, efficiencies of the order of 57 per cent in the first order can be achieved[62,63].

General Description of Diffraction Grating

Diffraction pattern is the result of light coming from different parts of the same wave front[64,65]. The diffraction fringes formed are not of the same width. Hence, many of the important properties of diffraction grating (dispersion, resolving power, etc.) are associated with interference effects between disturbances from corresponding parts of the separate elements.

The radial grating shown in Fig. 4.14 differs from infinite linear grating in two respects; the velocity and the grating spacing both vary with the radius. At a particular radius r, the frequency in the +1 order (*see* Fig. 4.14) will be–

$$\nu(r) = \nu_o + \left(\frac{v}{a}\right)$$

but $v = r\omega$ and $a = Kr$

where $\omega =$ angular velocity and K is a positive constant

Thus, $f = f_o + \left(\dfrac{\omega}{K}\right)$

One characteristic of the radial grating that may pose problems in some applications is the broadened angular spectrum in the diffracted orders due to the varying grating spacing.

If precise focusing of the diffracted beam is not required, the broadened angular spectrum can actually be advantageous, since it makes alignment of the two beams at

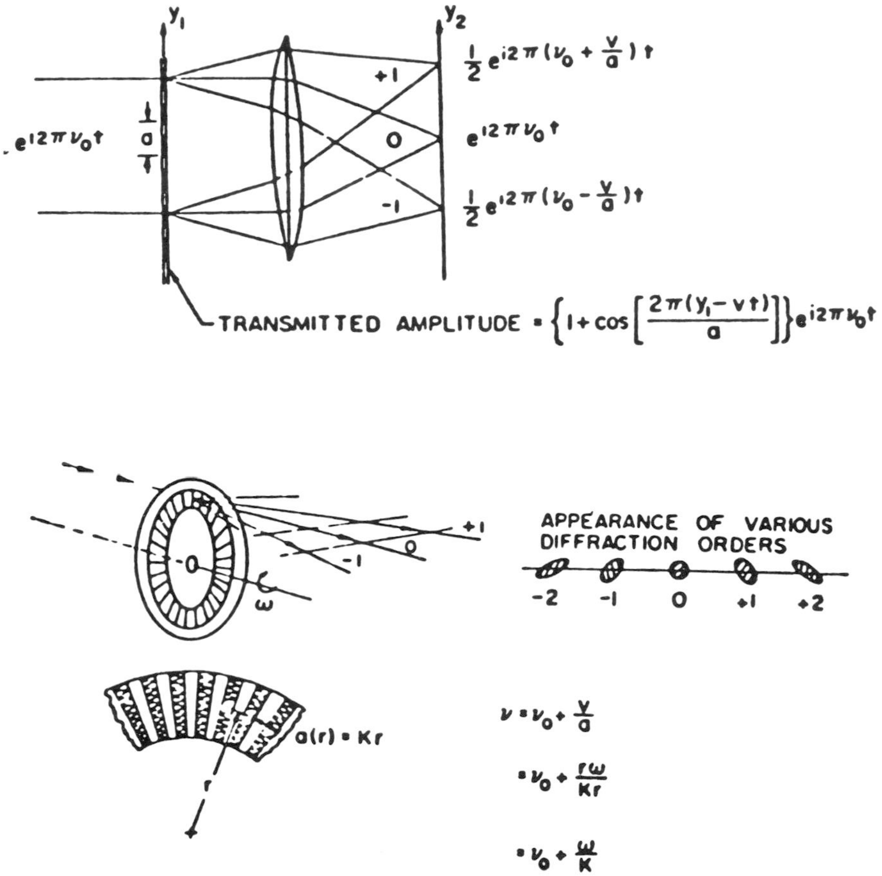

Figure 4.14 Radial diffraction grating[62]

the photo-surface much easier. On the other hand, heterodyning efficiency will be reduced if the angular spectrum is too broad.

Other effects that can limit the performance of a grating modulator include errors in the ruling, variation in the angular velocity, and vibrating motion caused by poor motor bearings or by the grating not being perfectly flat. All these defects in the grating or its driving mechanism increase the frequency spread in the shifted signal. The broadened angular spectrum in a given diffraction order, the low optical frequency, and the various mechanical effects may limit its applicability in certain situations.

General Theory of Diffraction Grating

Diffraction grating is made up of clear lines of width a and opaque lines of width b, Fig. 4.15.

The intensity distribution of the diffracted light is usually given for incident plane

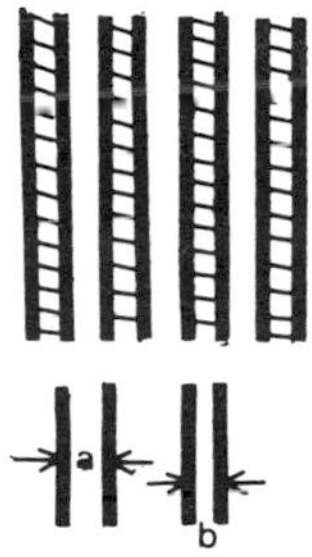

Figure 4.15 Representation of diffraction grating

waves of equal intensity. The intensity distribution resulting from using a laser light source is assumed to be given by similar relationships together with a gaussian profile.

For the light beam on a diffraction grating at an angle i (to the normal) the condition for a principal maximum in the diffracted light at angle 'θ' (Fig. 4.16) is —

$$\sin\theta_p - \sin\theta_i = \frac{P\lambda_o}{a+b} = \frac{P\lambda_o}{d} \tag{4.21}$$

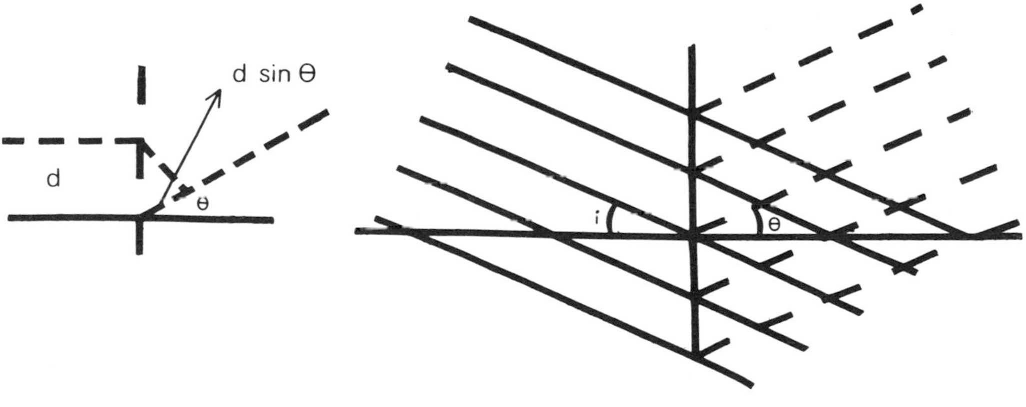

Figure 4.16 Oblique incidence of light on to the diffraction grating

Where P is an integer (positive or negative) defining the diffraction order about the zero order beam, and λ_o is the wavelength of the incident beam. The angular width of the principal maxima, measured between the minima on either side is '$d\theta$' where

$$d\theta = \frac{2\lambda_o}{N\,d\cos\theta} \tag{4.22}$$

Secondly, periodic maxima occur between the principal maxima. They are (N–2) in number but for $N \geqslant 20$ are seldom seen except very close to the principal maxima. The contribution of each line pair to the intensity of the total diffraction pattern varies with the diffraction angle. The resultant intensity, I, is according to:

$$I = \left(\frac{\sin \alpha}{\alpha}\right)^2 \left(\frac{\sin N\beta}{\sin \beta}\right)^2 \tag{4.23}$$

where $\alpha = \dfrac{\pi a (\sin \theta - \sin i)}{\lambda_o}$

and $\beta = \dfrac{\pi d (\sin \theta - \sin i)}{\lambda_o}$

The first term in eqn. (4.23) gives the amount of light from each line pair reaching any point in the diffraction pattern, whereas the second term gives the result of the interference between disturbance from 'N' line pairs.

If the principal maximum given by eqn. (4.21) coincides with the minimum of the first term in eqn. (4.23), then the principal maximum of that order, and its multiples, will be absent. If P defines the order of the diffraction maximum and q the minimum order, then

$$\frac{P}{a + b} = \frac{q}{a}$$

that is, the principal order P will be absent; for example, if $a = b$, then $P = 2q$.

To concentrate as much light as possible in the first and second diffracted orders the first maximum of the first term in eqn. (4.23) must be made to vary slowly; that is, for a fixed grating spacing d then $a > b$.

It is possible to construct gratings in which most of the incidence light is concentrated into one or two orders. Consider the production of a grating with wedge-shaped elements, then most of the light would be concentrated into the regions corresponding to specular reflection/refraction from the wedge; these are called blazed gratings. Alternatively, if the opaque lines were constructed so that they transmitted light and their thickness gave the transmitted light a phase shift of $\lambda_o/2$ compared to that transmitted through an adjacent clear line, then the zero order maximum would be suppressed entirely and the light thrown into the higher diffracted orders. This type of grating can readily be made by using an ordinary replica diffraction grating and etching or photographically bleaching the grating line to the correct $\lambda_o/2$ thickness for the intended light source.

Radial Diffraction Grating

The frequency of the diffracted beams of order P is ν_p given by

$$\nu_P = \nu_o + \frac{u \sin \theta_P}{\lambda_o} \tag{4.24}$$

where u is the magnitude of the linear velocity of the grating through the incident beam.

Combining eqns. (4.24) and (4.21) gives the frequency shift

$$\nu_P = \nu_o + \frac{u}{\lambda_o}\frac{P\lambda_o}{d} + \sin i = PN_r\omega \qquad (4.25)$$

Where N_r is the number of line pairs per revolution and ω is the frequency of rotation.

The frequency difference in the two beams causes a moving fringe pattern in the control volume, the direction depending upon the rotation of the grating. The clockwise rotation produces an upward shift in frequency of the light scattered from the control volume. The combined frequency shift therefore from the diffracted + 1 and −1 orders is

$$\nu_S = 2|\nu_P|$$

In an attempt to reduce the elliptical nature of the diffracted beams several workers have focused the laser beam on to the grating. This, however, causes a broadening of the diffraction maxima, $d\theta$, as well as a divergence of the diffracted beam due to the focusing action of the lens, $f\theta$. The resultant frequency shift of each diffracted beam can then be written as

$$\nu_P = \nu_o + \frac{u}{\lambda_o} \sin(\theta_P + d\theta + f\theta$$

If the laser is focused after the radial grating then $f\theta$ may very well be negative.

Effect of Irregularities in Diffracting Grating

(i) Non-uniformity in line spacing

(a) error random and restricted to a very small percentage of lines seen by the incident beam—the result is a background illumination across the diffracted beams and is unimportant if apertures are used after the grating.

(b) if random, that is, if the line spacing increases or decreases progressively across an area of the grating that is comparable to the incident beam diameter, then the diffracted beam will be non-circular in cross-section.

(ii) If the progressive error occurs over a much larger area, then the diffraction angles will depend on the positioning of the grating. With the rotating grating these progressive errors will produce a periodic "wonder" in the direction and shape of the diffracted beams—therefore an uncertainty in size and location of the control volume. Also this has the effect of broadening the bandwidth of the frequency shift which is directly proportional to the rotational speed.

(iii) For bleached grating a variation in the thickness of the grating will cause a variation in the amount of light in the diffracted orders. The signal scattered from a stationary particle in the control volume will be of frequency $PN_r\omega$. This signal will be amplitude modulated resulting in a lower signal to noise ratio in the scattered signals.

Frequency Shifting by Electro-Optic and Acousto-Optic Devices

Laser light frequency shifting by electro-optic means is obtained by generating a rotating electric field in one or several electro-optic cells. The incident circularly polarized light is either accelerated or decelerated, depending on the relative direction of rotation of the two fields. The frequency of the outgoing light is therefore either upshifted or downshifted. The electro-optic cell method has the advantages of having no moving parts, accurate control of the frequency and the possibility of obtaining rapid frequency shifts. Nevertheless, in order to obtain low values of frequency shift with high conversion efficiencies, high voltage supplies of several kV are required.

Acousto-optic frequency shifting is based on the principle that ultrasonic energy, propagating through a liquid medium, forms a moving time dependent three dimensional diffraction grating as a result of the variations in the index of refraction of the liquid. In practice, acousto-optic cells are excited with ultrasonic waves of frequencies greater than 30 MHz.

In general, the frequency shifts achieved by acousto-optic cells are much higher than those with the rotating grating. Typical frequency shifts provided by commercially available arrangements are around 40 MHz. Small frequency shifts can be achieved at high efficiency by using two cells of slightly different frequency either in parallel (shifting in the same direction) or in series (shifting in opposite directions).

The other possible methods for obtaining frequency shift involve the use of polarized light and multi-mode laser beams. Durst[66] has drawn up a table comparing the different methods of direction sensing in LV which can be used as a basis for selecting the most suitable method for any given application. The literature, however, does suggest that for measurements in combustion systems, the rotating diffraction grating has been preferred, because of its low cost, availability of variable frequency shifts, and relative ease of operation.

Response of Particles Used for Seeding the Flow in LV

The operation of laser velocimeter depends on the presence of particles to scatter the incidence light wave into the photomultiplier and, hence, to provide a measurable current modulated signal at the photomultiplier at a frequency proportional to a component of the particle's instantaneous velocity. In gaseous flows it is important to consider the acceptable limits on the physical properties of scatterers (suspended particles) for their ability to follow turbulent fluctuations in the flow to a prescribed upper frequency limit within a set accuracy. The lower limit on acceptable particle size is, somewhat, of less importance. It is questionable whether any lower limit is necessary at all since the amplitude of Brownian motion do not normally exceed the optical fringe spacing. The RMS displacement (Δx^2) of a particle by Brownian motion in time t using Einstein's formula is given by:

$$(\overline{\Delta x^2}) = \frac{ktT}{3\pi rn} \tag{4.26}$$

where k is Boltzmann's constant and T the absolute temperature. Assuming that eqn. (4.26) has meaning over very small time intervals, a 0.4μm diameter particle crossing 1μm wide fringes at 10 m/sec would suffer an additional displacement of only 0.03μm through Brownian motion.

The upper size limit has been approached analytically, which requires the following assumptions:

(i) turbulence intensities should be homogeneous and time invariant

(ii) particles should be much smaller than the microscale of turbulence but large enough so that the Brownian motion is negligible
(iii) no interaction between the particles
(iv) Reynolds number based on the relative velocity be of the order of one or less so that Stokes drag law apply.

Bassett[68] derived the following expression for the motion of single particles in a moving fluid based on the relative velocity for the balance between acceleration forces on a particle and a stationary displaced fluid:

$$\frac{\pi d^3}{6}\rho_p\frac{du_p}{dt} = \frac{\pi d^3}{6}\rho_f\frac{du_f}{dt} - \frac{1}{2}\frac{\pi d^3}{6}\rho_f\frac{d(u_p - u_f)}{dt} - 3\pi\nu\rho_f d(u_p - u_f)$$
$$- \frac{3}{2}d^2\rho_f\sqrt{\pi\nu}\int_{t_o}^{t}\frac{d(u_p - u_f)}{d\xi}\frac{d\xi}{\sqrt{t-\xi}} \tag{4.27}$$

where d is the particle diameter, ρ_p and ρ_f are the densities of the particle and fluid respectively, and ν is the kinematic viscosity of the fluid. The four terms on the right-hand side of eqn. (4.27) represent, respectively, the acceleration of the fluid, the resistance of an inviscid fluid to the accelerating sphere, the Stokes drag force and a drag force (history integral) which takes into account the unsteady motion of the particle. A solution to the above equation provides an indication of the upper size and density limits for spherical particles. For particles suspended in gases the density ratio, ρ_p/ρ_f, is normally of the order of 10^3 and, provided the Stokes number $N_s = \nu/\omega d^2$ with ω the angular frequency of turbulence fluctuations is greater than about 8, eqn. (4.27) reduces to:

$$\frac{du_p}{dt} + \frac{18\nu}{d^2}\frac{(u_p - u_f)}{(\rho_p/\rho_f)} = 0 \tag{4.28}$$

The solution of eqn. (4.28) is

$$\eta = \frac{x}{x^2 + 1}, \quad \beta = \tan^{-1}\left(\frac{1}{x}\right)$$

where $x = \dfrac{18\, N_s^{\,2}}{\rho_p/\rho_f}$

η and β are the amplitude and phase response respectively.

Table 4.2 shows typical results obtained by solving eqn. 4.28 (by requiring that particles follow the fluid motion within 1%).

In high velocity flows (transonic and supersonic), compressibility effects of the fluid introduces further problems. Under these conditions one dimensional flow of a gas-solid mixture is usually analyzed by assuming equilibrium flow and that a particle lags behind

TABLE 4.2

Particle Properties and Their Response to Turbulent Fluctuations[67]

Particle	Fluid	Density Ratio	Viscosity kg/msec	Particle Diameter (μm) f=1 Hz	f=10 KHz
Silicone Oil	Atmospheric Air	900	1.8×10^{-5}	2.6	0.8
MgO	Methane-Air Flame (1800 K)	1.8×10^4	5.9×10^{-5}	2.6	0.8
TiO_2	Oxygen Plasma (2800 K)	3.0×10^4	1.1×10^{-4}	3.2	0.8
TiO_2	Atmospheric Air	3.5×10^3	1.8×10^{-5}	1.3	0.4
PVC	Water	1.54	1.0×10^{-3}	16.0	5.0
Aerosil 200 (SiO_2)	Methane-Air Flame (1800 K)	306.0			

the fluid in velocity and temperature by a constant fraction. Calculations based on the constant fractional lag concept have shown that the smaller particles with lesser lag are distributed fairly uniformally in the flow field while larger particles are projected along paths closer to the jet axis.

Particles used for measurements in laser velocimetry may also be subjected to forces arising from photophoresis, diffusiophoresis, and thermophoresis. Photophoresis is the movement of an aerosol particle as a result of temperature differences within its surface induced by irradiation with light. The movement of aerosol particles with concentration gradients, called diffusiophoresis, can be relevant for measurements in laminar jets or mixing flows, but in turbulent swirl flows it is likely to be eclipsed by thermophoresis, the diffusion of particles due to a temperature gradient.

Aerosol Generation and Seeding of Gas Flows

Table 4.3 gives the various techniques used for generating and seeding the gas flows in laser velocimetry. The methods are given in order of decreasing preference with regard to size and concentration control and the convenience in its operation. Aerosol generation by chemical reaction is not recommended as it is inferior to all the other methods. Pressure jet or rotating disc atomizers are less suitable for LV because they produce larger droplets of larger diameter than required. The former method achieves liquid break-up by forcing the liquid through an orifice from which it emerges as a sheath in the form of a cone. This conical liquid film subsequently disintegrates into droplets of a relatively large size. In the latter rotating type atomizer, a thin liquid film sheet flows in the radial-tangential plane of the disc and disintegrates at the edge to produce droplets of diameter d_p given by

$$d_p = K \frac{1}{\omega} \left(\frac{\sigma}{\rho d}\right)^{1/2}$$

TABLE 4.3

Aerosol Generation and Seeding of Gas Flows in LV[67]

Material	Aerosol Generation Technique	Size d, μm	Size Control	Concentration Control	Operational Convenience	$\rho, \frac{Kg}{m^3}$	Refractive Index m	Application
Silicone Oil	Atomization	<5	Fair	Good	Good	970	1.47	Cold Flows
Water	Atomization	$1 \sim 2$	Fair	Good	Good	1000	1.33	Cold Flows
DOP	Atomization	$0.35 \sim 1$	Fair	Good	Good	984	1.48	Cold Flows
MgO	Fluidization	1-10	Poor	Fair	Good	3580	1.74	Hot Flows
TiO_2	Fluidization	0.5-2	Poor	Fair	Good	4200	2.6	Hot Flows
Aerosil 200 (SiO_2)	Fluidization	<1	Poor	Fair	Good	60	1.45	Hot Flows
Al_2O_3	Fluidization	<8	Poor	Fair	Good	3970	1.76	Hot Flows
Bakelite Phenolic Microballons	Fluidization	40	Poor	Fair	Good	104		Cold Flows
Polystyrene	Fluidization	3	Poor	Fair	Good	1050	1.59	Cold Flows
Tobacco (or MgO)	Combustion	0.1-1.0	Bad	Bad	Poor			Not Recommended
Ice	Sublimation	0.5	Fair	Poor	Fair	920	1.31	Not Useful
Ammonium Chloride (or Stannic Chloride)	Chemical Reaction	1.2	Good	Poor	Poor			Hot Flows (particles are toxic and corrosive)

where ρ, d, σ, and ω are density, disc diameter, surface tension and rotational speed of the disc respectively. Both the above devices permit the dispersal of large mass flows of liquids and produce polysize droplet distribution. Separation between large and small size droplets, although possible, is not very convenient to apply and the whole process is rather inefficient. Under isothermal conditions, the use of air-blast (or twin-fluid) atomizers are most suited to LV measurements since they can produce much smaller droplets than other types of generators and, at low flow rates, diameters down to about 1 μm can be obtained. They use a jet of air to break up a liquid film, Fig. 4.17, and has been used successfully by the authors with silicone oil under nonburning conditions. Atomized silicone oil droplets have also been used successfully in low temperature zones of flames. In the glass atomizer design shown in Fig. 4.17, liquid from the reservoir is drawn up the tube *A* by the injector effect of the air jet from tube *B*. As the liquid emerges from tube *A*, the shearing effect of the air jet breaks the liquid film into a fine spray. Droplets of large size tend to strike the size of the atomizer walls and drain back into the reservoir, while the smaller drops follow the flow of air. With the above air blast atomizer it is possible to obtain approximately 10^{10} particles per m^3 at a flow rate and pressure of 10 ℓ/min. and 1.4 x 10^5 N/m^2 respectively, using silicone oil of 500 centistroke kinematic viscosity. The performance of these atomizers depends critically on the relative positions of the tips of the two tubes and also on the orifice diameter of tube *A*. The mean diameter of aerosols generated by the design shown in Fig. 4.17 is of the order of 1 to 5 μm.

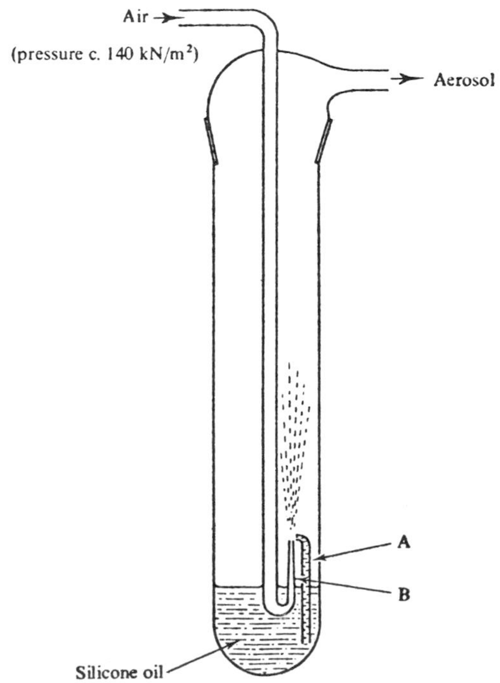

Figure 4.17 Silicone oil atomizer[67]

Seeding by solid particles has certain advantages for velocity measurements in swirl flames or high temperature flows where liquid droplets will evaporate or burn. The fluidised bed, shown in Fig. 4.18, can be used to fluidise a powder of submicron particles and the aerosol drawn off from the top of the bed. Although particles of suitable size can be obtained as powders (for example, MgO, TiO_2, Aerosil 200 (mainly SiO_2), micro-ballons), the suspended particles are usually several times larger because of particle agglomeration. At low flow rates the particle agglomeration is not too severe a problem, but as the flow rate through the bed is increased, the agglomeration tends to increase; the bed density also becomes non-uniform due to the bursting of the continuously growing bubbles. Design of fluidised beds is not considered here since it is largely a matter of experience. The fluidised bed shown in Fig. 4.18 has been used to fluidise 0.25 μm, TiO_2 and 0.12 μm Aerosil 200 (mainly SiO_2) particles for seeding swirl flames. The mean diameter of the particles obtained from the fluidised bed were 2 μm and 1 μm respectively; wide range of flow rates could be obtained depending on the input air flow rate to the bed.

Controlled concentration and size of solid particles can also be produced by atomizing solutions or suspensions and allowing the solvent to evaporate prior to the introduction of solid particles into the measurement control volume (as is done, for example, with Teflon-Freon suspension). The direct oxidation of titanium tetrachloride to titanium dioxide has also been used for some measurements in flames. Magnesium oxide produced by burning magnesium powder has also been used.

In the reference beam mode optical systems, the signal to noise ratio is improved by increasing the concentration of scatterers in the flow under study. However, the practical difficulty or high seed concentration is that particle coagulation occurs in the equipment used to generate the seeding particles. The coagulation between small, near monosize particles occurs more readily and the probability of coagulation between particles of unequal sizes increases as the difference between their diameters increases. Thus, even though the particles can be generated with a high number concentration, its size will rapidly change by coagulation to yield a much smaller concentration of larger particles. Similarly, when a liquid monosize aerosol is generated at high concentration it will tend to become polysize by coagulation. The coagulation of aerosols is also enhanced by the electrostatic charge present on almost all particles. These may arise during the actual process of aerosol generation, for example, in atomizing a liquid or fluidising a powder, or by the capture of gaseous ions which is the main source of charge on aerosols manufactured by condensation. In some applications it may also be necessary to consider the external electric fields or electrostatic charges on the walls of confined flows.

It is recommended that prior to choosing the type of particles for seeding the gaseous flow, either with or without combustion, pollution and associated health effects due to submicron particles be considered. Particles near 1 μm in size or less deposited on the inner surface of the respiratory system can have harmful effects, and great care should be taken to avoid the possible inhalation of small particles; the LV should therefore be operated in a large space with adequate ventilation.

Photodetectors

In order to measure the flow velocity of moving scattering particles the doppler signal is measured. This shows intensity variations of light signals and has frequencies that contain

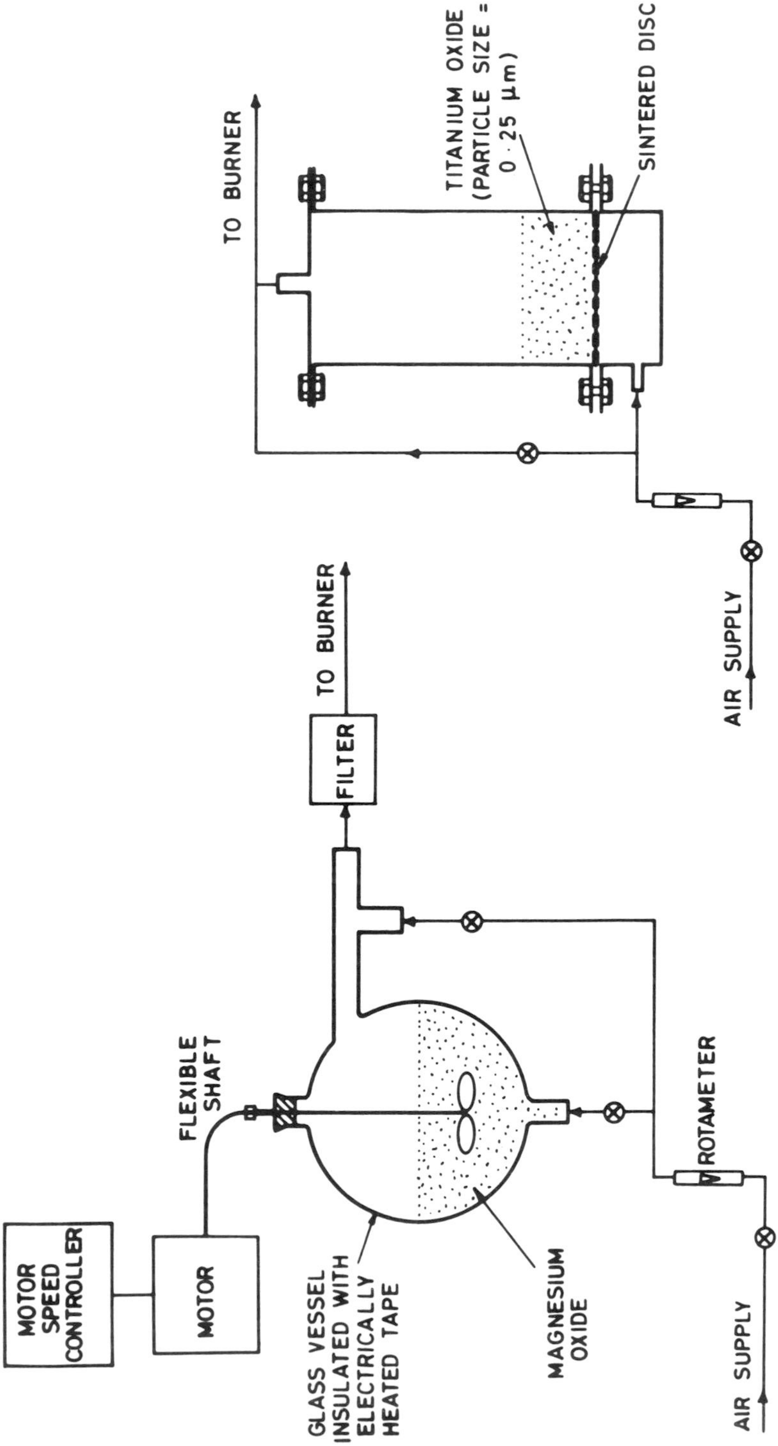

Figure 4.18 Schematic diagram of particle generator.[51] Left diagram: fluidised bed type with stirrer to break the coagulated particles. Right diagram: fluidized bed.

the required velocity information. Signals of this kind are usually processed by using opto-electronic devices which convert the optical signals into the electrical signals and are often referred to as photo detectors or quantum detectors. The arriving photons at the detector (for example, photoelectric cell, photomultiplier) cause electrons to change its energy state with the result that the photon flux of the optical signal causes an electron flux. The cathode of a photoelectric cell is made up of a light sensitive film (the emission layer) and a supporting layer on which the emission layer is deposited. The emission layer is made of different materials and must be chosen according to the application. The photocathode has similar features to those of photoelectric cells and opaque or semi-transparent photocathodes are used in different designs. The photomultiplier consists of a photocathode, electron-optical input system, dynode chain (secondary emission), and the anode. The electron-optical system focuses the electrons onto the first dynode. This mainly determines the spread of the electron transit times and thus the quality of the photomultiplier (in conjunction with the collection efficiency). The secondary emission multiplier consists of several stages usually referred to as dynode chain. The anode (end of the chain) collects the electrons originated from the cathode and multiplied by each dynode stage to yield a gain of $G = e^n$, where e is the ratio of secondary electrons leaving a dynode to the number of electrons falling on it and n is the number of stages in the dynode chain. The signal-to-noise ratio obtained in the photodiodes and photomultipliers are not considered here. The reader is referred to the handbook on photomultipliers and photodiodes (for example, EMI, RCA, Centronic, Harshaw, Rofin, Space Technology Products, Infrared Industries, etc.).

Control Volume Dimensions and Fringe Spacing

The calculation of the control volume dimensions is based on the assumption that a laser beam has a Gaussian distribution and that beyond $1/e^2$ point the light intensity is too weak for measurements by LV. The light intensity distribution of a laser light beam is given by

$$I = I_o \exp\left[\frac{1}{2}\,\frac{x^2}{\sigma}\right] \tag{4.29}$$

The $1/e^2$ intensity corresponds to a beam diameter D_o of 4σ (4 standard deviations) and contains 86.5 per cent of the emitted light. The waist diameter of the laser beam, length and height of the control volume, fringe spacing and number of fringes in the volume can be calculated from the following relations:

$$\text{Waist diameter, } D = \frac{4\lambda_o F}{\pi D_o} \tag{4.30}$$

$$\text{Length of control volume} = \ell_m = \frac{4\lambda_o F}{\pi D_o \sin\frac{\theta}{2}} = \frac{D}{\sin\frac{\theta}{2}} \tag{4.31}$$

$$\text{Height of control volume} = d = \frac{4\lambda_o F}{\pi D_o \cos\frac{\theta}{2}} = \frac{D}{\cos\frac{\theta}{2}} \tag{4.32}$$

$$\text{Fringe spacing, } \Delta x = \frac{\lambda_o}{2 \sin \frac{\theta}{2}} \tag{4.33}$$

Number of fringes in the volume

$$N = \frac{8F\tan\frac{\theta}{2}}{\pi D_o} = \frac{2D\tan\frac{\theta}{2}}{\lambda_o} = \frac{4S}{\pi D_o} \tag{4.34}$$

$$\text{Actual height observed, } d_{act} = \frac{d}{M}$$

where λ_o is the wavelength of laser light, F is the focal length of the lens, d_{act} is the aperture in front of the photomultiplier, M is the magnification of the receiving optics, θ is the angle subtended between the two beams, and S is the distance between the beams before the lens.

The size of the control volume and the number of fringes in the control volume are selected by the diagnosticist, depending on the flow under investigation and also on the resolution required.

Doppler Signal Processing Techniques

Spectrum Analyzers

This is the simplest approach to the signal processing problem and was the technique used for all early work on laser velocimetry[46,48,49].

To obtain information on mean velocity and turbulence, one needs to know the probability density function, P (f), of doppler frequency and, hence, the probability density function of velocity. Nevertheless, the instrumentation to measure the frequency probability density function is not readily available, but it is possible to measure how the energy of a signal is distributed in the frequency domain, in which case the frequency domain is divided into small frequency bandwidths of equal widths, Δf, Δf_2, ... Δf_n.

For any signal $\phi(t)$ the energy contained in the band Δf_i is given as

$$\frac{1}{N}\int_O^N \Phi^2_{\Delta f_i}\, t\, dt$$

$$\text{Lim } N \to \infty$$

where $\Phi_{\Delta f_i}(t)$ is the signal obtained by an ideal filter.

The frequency density distribution is given by

$$P(f) = \frac{1}{\Delta f N} \int_O^N \Phi^2_{\Delta f_i}(t)\, dt. \tag{4.35}$$

$\lim \Delta f \to 0$

$\lim N \to \infty$

– an expression often called Power Spectral Density Function.

The device which enables P (f) to be plotted against f is called "Spectrum analyzer" and the type commonly used in LV is Heterodyne analyser.

The plot of $P(f) \sim f$ will only be an approximation to the true spectrum owing to the finite bandwidth. The effect of this finite bandwidth is to produce a broadening effect in the peak on the spectrum. Moreover, the filter will not have the absolutely sharp cut-off points of an ideal filter, which will produce further broadening.

Further broadening of the peak results from the presence of velocity gradients across the measurement volume.

The effect of turbulence in the flow is to produce rapid fluctuations in the doppler frequency and since these fluctuations are much faster than the sweep rate of the filter they produce a broader peak on the spectrum than would be obtained from a laminar flow.

Information about the turbulence intensity can be obtained from the width of the doppler spectrum, after allowance has been made for transit time broadening, velocity gradient broadening, filter bandwidth, and non-uniform seed concentration because of density changes. If the spectrum is symmetrical, the mean doppler frequency, $\bar{f}$, will be equal to the most probable frequency, corresponding to the peak of the distribution. In addition, the spectrum is assumed to be Gaussian, the standard deviation, σ, of the doppler frequency can be evaluated from:

$$\frac{\text{Width of doppler spectrum at half height}}{2.36} = \frac{\sigma}{2\pi}$$

It is clear that the error introduced in evaluating the RMS level is likely to be substantial, because it depends strongly on the smoothness and accuracy of the plotted spectrum in the region of the half height. The major problem in highly turbulent swirl flows is that there is a directional uncertainty of 180 degrees in the velocity component determined by LV, and the tail of the spectrum, which corresponds to negative velocities, is superimposed on that part of the spectrum corresponding to positive velocities. A further complication arises from the zero spectrum which becomes broader as the turbulence intensity increases. Both the above problems can be overcome by shifting the frequency of one of the beams relative to the other, thus creating a moving set of fringes in the differential mode.

The doppler spectrum must be based on a large enough number of doppler signals to define the mean frequency, standard deviation (rms frequency) within narrow confidence limits. If the doppler signals are infrequent enough for counting spectrum analysis to be employed, the number of particles contributing to the spectrum can be counted. Statistical criteria for the confidence limits on mean and RMS can be employed, although the standard criteria is applicable only to Gaussian distributed variables. A disadvantage of the spectrum analyser is that the real time information is lost and the interpretation of data is not straightforward. No information can be obtained on the energy spectrum of turbulence or the scale of turbulence.

Frequency Trackers

This is a device that follows the doppler signal giving an output voltage proportional to the instantaneous input frequency.

In a frequency tracker, the doppler signal is combined with the output from a voltage-controlled oscillator in a mixer. The output signal at the different frequency is narrow band filtered (I.F.) to remove noise, and then through a limiter to remove amplitude fluctuations inherent in the doppler signal and thence to a sensitive frequency discriminator. This provides a d.c. output proportional to I.F. frequency deviation from a fixed centre value f_o; after suitable smoothing and d.c. amplification the resulting voltage is fed back to the control input of the voltage control oscillator. The result of the feedback is that, provided a suitable value of loop gain is chosen, the oscillator frequency tracks that of the doppler signal.

Nevertheless, the doppler signal is such that from time to time it vanishes, even with high light flux, and thus the tracker will 'drop out'; requisition of the signal is then necessary, and although this can be done automatically, it can present problems. Even when locked, the performance will still be subject to distortions arising from the presence of finite fringe numbers, pedestal effects, non-uniform particle concentration in flows with density changes in the fluid, and noise in a similar way to the Counters (later section) but compounded by the finite response time of the tracking loop.

Some commercially available trackers together with their important specifications are listed in Table 4.4.

Filter Banks

Banks of filters designed and described by Baker[69] to process doppler signals have been used successfully for velocity measurements both in isothermal and combustive conditions. The instrument is more useful where the doppler signal occurs over a comparatively wide frequency bandwidth. Here the amplified photomultiplier signal within an adjustable range is delivered to the parallel inputs of a number of tuned filters. The instrument has been operated with 50 filters covering the range from 631 KHz to 6.02 MHz; the adjacent filters were arranged to overlap at the –3 dB level. The probability density distribution of signal frequencies is measured by recording the outputs from the filters after a preset measuring time. Alternatively each filter can be continuously monitored to provide a real time (at low frequency of operation) record of voltages proportional to the center frequency of the resonant filters and hence the instantaneous velocity. The filter banks are claimed to be more efficient than frequency analysers[69]. The filter bank is considerably less susceptible to the signal to noise limitations and is intended to work with values of duty cycle considerably less than those at which tracking would normally be employed.

Autocorrelation Function of the Laser Anemometer Signal (Photon Correlation Spectroscopy)

Laser velocimeters rely on some kind of artificial seeding to the flow. The size and distribution of particles are usually the limiting factors by which these particles can follow the turbulence fluctuations. Photon correlation spectroscopy offers particular ad-

TABLE 4.4

Some Available Frequency Trackers

Tracker Model and Country of Manufacture	Frequency Range	No. of Ranges	Tracking Range	Slew Rate	I.F. Bandwidth (% fsd)
DISA 55 L20 or 55 L22 (Denmark)	2 KHz–15 MHz	7	60:1	9×10^{-4}	0.5–8.0
Cambridge Consultants (England)	100 Hz–10 MHz	5	20:1	3×10^{-3}	Autodyne Loop
Southampton University (England)	20 KHz–10 MHz	8	45:1	Variable	Autodyne Loop
TSI 1090–1A (U.S.A.)	2 KHz–50 MHz	3	over 200:1	4×10^{-4}	10
Nikon Kagaku Kogyo (Japan)	2.5 KHz–20 MHz	7	8:1 (minimum)		
TNO 1057 (Netherlands)	10 KHz–5 MHz	2 (low & high)	40:1 and 500:1	1.8×10^{-4} 1.2×10^{-5}	5 0.4 or 3.0
BBC Goerz LSEI (Austria)	5 KHz–16 MHz	3	32:1	4×10^{-5}	1.25

vantages in situations where the intensity of scattered light and/or the signal to noise ratio is low. These circumstances arise when the particles are of very small diameter, when there is low laser light intensity or an inefficient light collection arrangement. The single electron pulse arriving at the anode of the photomultiplier contains information on the intensity variation of the scattered light and, therefore, also on the velocity with which scattering particles enter the interference fringe pattern in the measurement control volume. In this method an autocorrelation process is used to determine the frequencies present by correlating the digital signal with itself after fixed delays, generated by shift registers, Fig. 4.19. The autocorrelation $\Phi(T)$ of the input $f(t)$ is defined as

$$\Phi(T) = \int f(t)\, f(t-\tau)\, dt$$

If delay exactly equals the period of a component of the signal then the groupings will match up and the product of the delayed and direct signals will provide a constructive interference maxima. If, however, the delay does not exactly equal then a phase mismatch will occur providing a complete destructive interference at a half period delay.

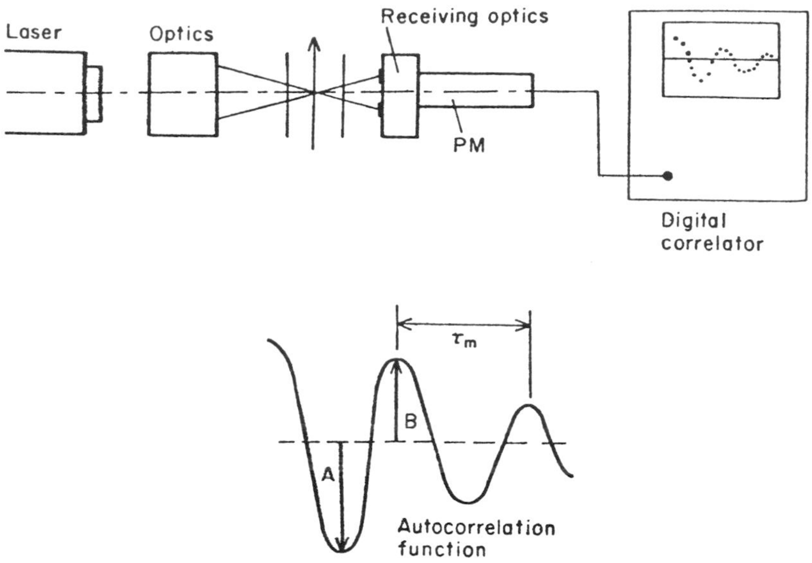

Figure 4.19 Photon correlation technique for velocity measurement via determination of autocorrelation function.[49]

In general, all the correlations present show themselves in the output, each frequency component appears as a cosine wave of the same period.

The autocorrelation of the signal from a single particle can be formed if a sufficient number of photons is received at the detector. The autocorrelation will then be formed in a time that is short compared with the integral and microscales of the turbulence and will indicate no damping, other than that due to the finite transit time; thus a single velocity will be deputised by the correlogram. From the computed optimum correlation curve the frequency distribution of the desired input signal is derived. The shortest measuring period in the photon correlator is 10 nsec. and the maximum observable doppler frequency with the instruments available at present is of the order of 50 MHz.

Mean flow velocity is calculated via the time t_m between the two maxima from the record of the autocorrelation curve using the relationship $u = \dfrac{\lambda_o}{2t_m \ \mathrm{Sin}\ \phi/2}$.
The turbulence intensity is calculated, for the particular case of Gaussian turbulence, from the amplitude decay of the sinusoidal part of the correlogram using the relationship (*see* Fig. 4.19)

$$\frac{u'}{u} = \frac{1}{\pi}\sqrt{0.667 \ln\left(\frac{A}{B}\right)} \tag{4.36}$$

Photon correlation spectroscopy has been widely described in the literature and readers are recommended to[70-73] for further information.

The above assumption of Gaussian velocity probability distribution is only true in small fractions of flow locations in limited flow cases. It is therefore necessary to determine the deviation in values of velocity for non-Gaussian velocity distribution and different values of skewness factors (a measure of symmetry)

$$\text{skewness factor} = \frac{\overline{u'^3}}{\left(\overline{u'^2}\right)^{3/2}} = \frac{\overline{u'^3}}{\sigma^3} \quad (\sigma = \text{standard deviation})$$

and flatness factor (a measure of the length of the tail in the probability density distribution). The flatness factor is given by:

$$\text{flatness factor} = \frac{\overline{u'^4}}{\overline{u'^2}} = \frac{\overline{u'^4}}{\sigma^4}$$

Birch *et al.*[74] provides some information in order to meet the case of non-Gaussian velocity distribution. A general relationship between the auto-correlogram and the velocity probability density was derived given as:

$$G(\tau) = I\,\frac{\pi d_2}{4} \int_{-\infty}^{+\infty} \int_{-\infty}^{+\infty} \exp\left\{-(\hat{u}^2+\hat{v}^2)\frac{4\tau^2}{d_2^2}\right\}\left\{1 + 0.5\cos 2\pi\tau\frac{\hat{u}}{\Delta x}\right\} P(\hat{u}\hat{v})\, d\hat{u}\, d\hat{v} \qquad (4.37)$$

The inversion of this integral is difficult in an exactly analytic manner. The technique suggested by Lumley[75] and used by Ribeiro and Whitelaw[76] was employed to obtain an explicit equation. The difference between the Gaussian and non-Gaussian velocity distribution models indicated differences in mean velocity and turbulence intensity of 4 per cent and 2 per cent respectively at a skewness factor of 0.5 and turbulence intensity of 50 percent. Nevertheless, for smaller values of skewness factor and turbulence intensity the differences were small and negligible.

A Computer in Connection with a Fast A/D Converter

In this method, the photomultiplier signal is digitized using an ultrafast A/D converter, and the subsequent signal is stored in a computer. Data reduction is performed using a mini computer, by means of specially developed programs[77]. Three different methods of processing the data will be described here. Readers are recommended to [48, 77, 78] for further advancement on the above method of data analysis. This method of signal processing is recommended where doppler signals are of low frequencies.

Off-line Data Processing

This method utilizes a prechosen number of J signals, each consisting of a given number of digital words which can be stored into a computer with a good resolution in amplitude (say 7 bits). The signals are then rewritten on magnetic tape after recording the desired number of signals for velocity information. The magnetic tape is used for later analysis after the completion of selected number of measuring points. Zero crossings in signal processing are determined by setting a condition for positive slope in the computer program. Mean frequency (and hence velocity) and standard deviation are calculated from the known time spacing of the digital words (this is given by the sample rate of the A/D converter), and the number of words between each pair of positive axis crossings. With this method, a fairly reasonable data acquisition rate (about 400 signals/sec) has been reported[78]. Nevertheless, a disadvantage of the method is that the data transfer from computer to the magnetic tape takes too long (about 35 sec) so that the total cycle time for one measuring position is about 40 sec.

On-line Data Processing

In this method there is a prechosen number of J signals, consisting of a selectable number of B words. It is digitally stored into the computer as before, but instead of transferring them to the magnetic tape or disc the signals are analysed immediately in the same way as in off-line data processing. For a greater number of signals, however, it is necessary to record and process the signal analysis more than once. With this method data processing reduction time, including analysis and storing, is about 100 msec. per signal.

On-line Data Processing Directly After Storage

Both the above methods have the disadvantage that one has to find a varying number of signals for each measuring position, because different signals have to fulfil different imposed conditions. As a result of this, the efficiency for data analysis varies between 60 to 80 per cent. In order to overcome these disadvantages, the signal is analysed directly after storage, and only the results are stored into the computer for further calculations. Those signals that do not satisfy the validation conditions are eliminated. In comparison with the on-line processing, the time required by this method can vary and depends on the particle density in the flow and the local mean velocity.

In the system used by Gupta[77] an A/D converter of very high maximum throughput (up to 500 MHz into 6 bits) together with a fast back-up memory of 1024 words and a mini computer was used for signal processing. A/D converters faster than 1 GHz are also available nowadays. This system could essentially be used where the captured data appears on an intermittent basis (for example, in LV). The A/D converter digitises the input wave or pulse until the back-up memory (which is conveniently varied as a shift register) is filled. The completion of this fill initiates the transfer of data from the last memory to the microcomputer memory at a somewhat slower rate (i.e. 100 KHz) where it forms the raw data for any further data processing to be carried out. Additional words, for example, those indicating real time may also be transferred. The real time capability is useful for studying oscillatory flows or time dependent flows, for example, swirl flows with precessing vortex cores. Results from the latter process may be stored in other memory locations in the minicomputer (for example, a series of slots for LV measurement) for later display via the controlling teletypewriter.

It is also desirable that the controlling computer may be able, by means of its digital output bus, to control all the relevant operations of the primary A/D converter such as triggering, gain level control, and capture rate, so that optimization of the performance or response of the entire system can be derived from the control loops emanating from the minicomputer program[77].

Two-Spot Method

In this method two laser beams are focused at a fixed distance apart in the measuring control volume and the flow velocity is measured by measuring the time a particle takes to cross the two beams (time of flight)[79].

When a particle passes through both the focal points in succession it causes two scattered light pulses which are registered at the photomultiplier. The time interval between the two pulses gives a measure of instantaneous flow velocity. By measuring the time of flight of many scattering particles a frequency distribution is obtained from which the flow velocity distribution can be calculated. The measuring control volume is defined by two laser beams. Thc ratio between the beam spacing and beam diameter determines the accuracy of the measuring volume and for an accuracy of better than 1 per cent an optimum value of 40:1 is recommended. Velocity components in various directions (for example, u, v, w) can be measured by rotating the two beams around the optical axis. Thus, it is possible to determine the two-dimensional frequency distribution of the flow vectors regarding magnitude and direction at a certain point in the flow field. From this frequency distribution, information about absolute value and direction of the mean velocity, turbulence level and intensity, skewness factor, and Reynolds stress can be derived.

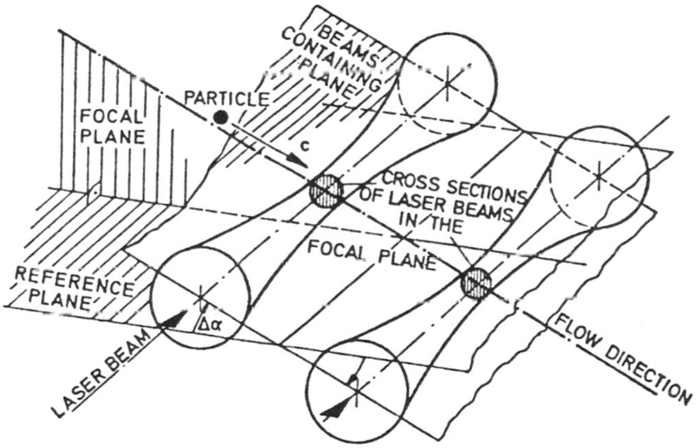

Figure 4.20 Light intensity distribution in the probe volume with a two spot method.[79]

Since not all the particles are moving in the defined measuring direction, certain particles will cross only one of the focal points. Therefore, in addition to the time of flight values (correlated signals) some meaningless time intervals (uncorrelated signals) are measured due to the fact that two light pulses are generated by two different particles independent of each other in the measuring control volume. Because the particles are randomly distributed in the fluid there is no preferred value for these uncorrelated signals; they appear as homogeneously distributed statistical noise in the frequency distribution of the measured time intervals. It is, therefore, necessary to take as many samples as will allow the frequency distribution to be evaluated statistically.

The advantages of the two-spot method are: very high velocity measurement capability, and that the flow velocity measurements can be made close to the walls, for example boundary layer, turbine blade, etc. Relatively large size of the measuring volume means that the maximum resolution or the minimum eddy size that can be investigated is equal to the distance between the two beams at focus. In highly turbulent swirl flows significant error can be introduced under conditions when many flow velocities are present or the flow recirculates within the two focused beams. Under conditions of high seed concentration the two signals can be generated by two different particles independent of each other to give erroneous results.

Period Counting Method

Here the signal from the photomultiplier is passed through a high pass filter to remove the low frequency pedestal that occurs due to the finite particle transit time; the resultant doppler frequency may be measured by counting zero crossings. The symmetrical doppler burst is processed by the amplitude and zero crossing detector (Schmitt trigger) to provide sets of pulses that can be used to operate the zero crossing counter and the different logics incorporated for testing the validity of frequency information.

The counter system must be gated to count only those zero crossings close to the center of the doppler burst, since phase changes occur between bursts and produce errors in the count. The signal levels can be used to initiate the count and the counter can be gated for either a fixed time (fixed gate counting) or a variable time (variable gate counting). The gate time 't_g' must be matched to the duration of the signal burst. Fixed gate counting can only be used in laminar or low turbulence flows where the transit time of a particle across the measurement volume remains nearly constant.

In highly turbulent flows the signal level is used to end the count and the gate time 't_g' measured with a separate electronic clock counter, gated by the same control pulses and driven by a fast electronic clock, Fig. 4.21. Since the gate time may or may not be in phase with the clock pulses, the measured time is, therefore, subjected to ±1 count ambiguity error. The clock frequency should be selected to keep this error smaller than the predetermined percentage. The accuracy of gate time measurements can be defined as

$$a = \frac{2}{N_{clock}} \qquad \text{where } N_{clock} = \text{No. of clock pulses}$$

which has to be better than a predetermined value

$$\text{that is, } a \leqslant \frac{2}{(N_{clock})_{min}} \tag{4.38}$$

Also the number of pulses, $(N_{clock})_{min}$, from the electronic clock of frequency f_{clock} is given by

$$(N_{clock})_{min} = \frac{N_{min}}{f_{max}} f_{clock} \tag{4.39}$$

where N_{min} = minimum number of zero crossings and f_{max} = maximum doppler fre-

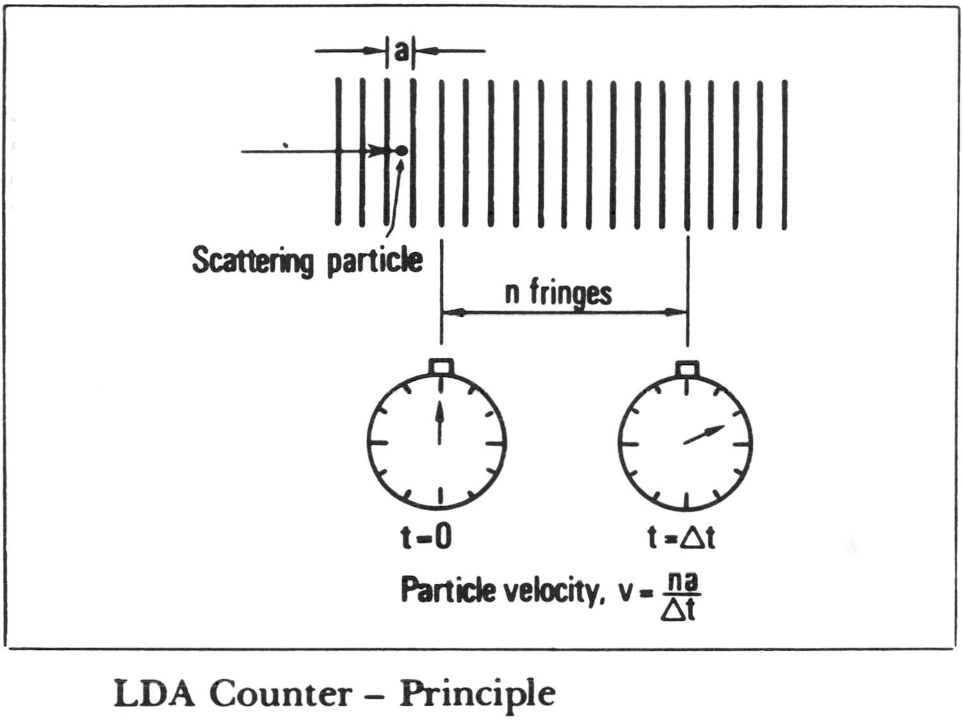

Figure 4.21 Principle of the laser velocimeter counter system.

quency. Combining eqns. 4.38 and 4.39 yields the final relationship for the clock frequency

$$f_{clock} \geqslant \frac{2}{a} \frac{f_{max}}{N_{min}} \tag{4.40}$$

for an accuracy of 0.1 per cent and 50 zero crossings, the clock frequency should be

$$f_{clock} \geqslant 40 f_{max}$$

With the counter system new data is available at the output at the end of each count. In counters, errors can arise in the count from spurious zero crossings due to noise in the signal and phase changes that occur as particles enter and leave the measuring volume. Errors also occur due to velocity and fringe bias. Various particle bias errors in counters, trackers and spectrum analysers are described[81].

With a suitable selection of data handling system linked to the output of a counter, mean and RMS velocity, higher order moments of the velocity fluctuations, scale of turbulence, and energy spectra can be evaluated.

The data processing and handling system used by Gupta *et al.*[82] consisted of a real time electronic counter interfaced to a PDP 8/E for processing the doppler signal and subsequent evaluation of the statistical properties of the flow. The data acquisition system of Gupta *et al.*[82] incorporating a digitiser and a computer based transmission path is described in the following two sections:

Data Acquisition System

The above system can be divided for convenience into two separate sections—the Digitiser and the Computer-based Data Transmission Path. They are described in that order below:

The Digitiser

The output of the photomultiplier which monitors the interference grid set up by two laser beams gives rise to low-level bursts of negative-going signals modulated at frequency dependent on the particle velocity and other physical characteristics of the optical system. The digitiser is based on the 'pulse-counting' technique where a specific number of oscillations taking place in the input pulse signal are timed against the oscillations of a fixed 'clock' oscillator which runs at as high a frequency as possible to improve the resolution of the measurement.

The most difficult decisions that have to be made by the circuitry lie in defining those instants where timing of the oscillation cycles may begin because an acceptable signal is present, and where the timing must cease because the signal is in the process of deterioration. The acceptable timing zone starts and ends on a positive oscillation transition and the acceptability of the signal is monitored by observing simultaneously two other functions which are derived electronically from the incoming signal. These monitor functions are derived from the photomultiplier signal by passage through two amplifiers of very different characteristics – one a high-pass configuration which eliminates the unidirectional nature of the input wave and a second of low-pass configuration which in effect produces the envelope caused by the asymmetry of the input signal. The high-pass amplifier output is fed to a Schmitt trigger at T.T.L. levels and also to a half-wave rectifier which after a little smoothing yields a profile proportional to the signal amplitude. The two raw analog signals are then each fed to an identical Butterworth filter configuration which combines smoothing with an optimised response to an input signal 'step'. The filter outputs are then translated to T.T.L. levels by a pair of variable level comparators which can be adjusted to determine the signal levels accepted as satisfactory.

At this point in the circuitry all relevant signals are expressed as T.T.L. levels and they are combined into a logic system based on T.T.L. devices. The digitiser has three output lines – an 'events' line which goes 'High' when an acceptable signal is present, a 'cycles' line which is derived from the output of the Schmitt trigger by "AND" logic with the events line, and a 'clock' line which is similarly derived from the clock oscillator line. The logic is arranged so that an 'event' begins when both comparators described above give a 'High' indication; the event terminates when either one of those comparators drops to the 'low' state, and a new event cannot be cleared until both comparators have dropped back to the 'low' state after the passage of the signal pulse. The leading edge of the pulse train to excite can also be used to provide pulse which updates a latch linked to a 1.3 MHz real time clock for real time LV work. This interlock helps to minimize transmission of any signal information of inferior quality that may give rise later to inaccurate results.

Computer-based Data Acquisition System

It is necessary to convert the pulse trains appearing randomly on the three signal line described previously into a form in which they can be transmitted to and be stored by a PDP 8/E Computer, and the procedure is described here by following the signals through the system. The two pulse trains, corresponding to the cycle and 'clock' oscillations are first passed to a pair of 12-bit counting registers, whose counting or resetting status is controlled by separate logic which, in turn, is influenced by the event signal and by the computer. The termination of an event (appearing as a resumption to the 'low' level of the event line) initiates the next stage of the sequence. Physical contact with the computer is via a 12-bit digital interface which is capable of transferring 12-bit parallel information both into and out of the machine. On the input mode, one bit is used as a flag from the signal processor (bit zero) and the remaining eleven bits carry a binary number expressed as eleven bits into the computer. On the output mode, one bit (bit zero) is used to feed back the computer status to the signal processor, and of the remaining bits two are used to select a local multiplexer/demultiplexer system so that access from up to four experiments can be made to the machine with identical programs apart from the bit combination or 'mask' which sets out the interface output lines.

When an 'event' has been accepted and terminated, the counts resting on the two twelve bit registers (conditions never require the use of the most significant bit, so it is always zero and never transmitted) are locked into two twelve bit latches, and the counting circuits are reset and able to start the processing of a further pulse train from the experiment as soon as one arrives. The control logic immediately signals to the computer by setting input bit zero to a 'High'. The two 12-bit latches are linked to a local multiplexer whose control is derived from the bit zero on the computer output side. The computer immediately reads the state of the eleven input logic lines and stores the result as an eleven bit word in one indexed location in memory. The computer program then switches the output bit zero from 'Low' to 'High', thus changing the status of the local multiplexer and exposing the second input word to the transmission line. This is also read and stored in memory. Finally, the computer program reads the value of an indexing register which is set in a program delay loop and also stores it similarly. This computer register is indexed every time the transmission flag is interrogated and found to be 'Low' (unset), and since that in effect measures the time interval between the arrival of successive signals at the computer, it can be interpreted as a real time equivalent to supply the real time status of every event input to the computer.

Once the entire read process has taken place, the computer output line reverts to 'Low', resetting the local multiplexer and providing a clear pulse which allows the whole process to begin again once the input flag is set to a 'High'.

The program that leads the information into the Computer memory is supplied with a comand-word decoder which allows up to ten separate operations to be carried out as required. These allow the information acquired to be examined, punched on paper tape, or loaded on to a magnetic tape file which can then be later readdressed by a program written in one of several high level languages.

Two-dimensional Laser Velocimetry System

Although information on axial, radial and swirl velocity and one point correlations of velocity fluctuations can, in principle, be obtained with a one-channel optical system by velocity measurements in different directions, experimental errors may prevent the precise measurement of higher order correlations. In swirl flows, it is apparent that the simultaneous measurements of two or three velocity components by a two or three channel LV respectively would reduce the total experiment time and measuring errors and that the two output signals can be processed to yield higher order correlations of one point velocity fluctuations, $\overline{u_i'^n u_j'^m}$. The need for a two-dimensional system becomes particularly important if correlations between different fluctuating velocity components have to be studied. A considerable number of two-dimensional laser velocimeter systems have been reported in the literature[49, 91]. Most of these operate in the 'fringe mode' in which provisions have to be made to separate the Doppler signals into two non-interfering channels. Channel separation can be accomplished by different methods namely two color optics[86], cross polarization[84,90], or a system in which two beams are frequency shifted by different amounts. Two-dimensional optical systems operating in the reference beam mode are described in Oldengarm[91].

The two-dimensional system described by Durst and Zare[90] is shown in Fig. 4.22. The system is based on two very similar beam splitter-prisms that produce two sets of parallel light beams with mutually perpendicular plane of polarization. In this way two sets of parallel light fringes can be obtained by focusing the light beams inside the measuring control volume. Scattering particles passing through the measuring region will cross both fringe systems and yield information on the two velocity components perpendicular to the two sets of fringes. The two velocity components are separated by using a light collecting lens and a polarizing beam splitter; the two signals are detected by two separate photodetectors, Fig. 4.22. The signals from the two detectors are processed by two electronic signal processing units.

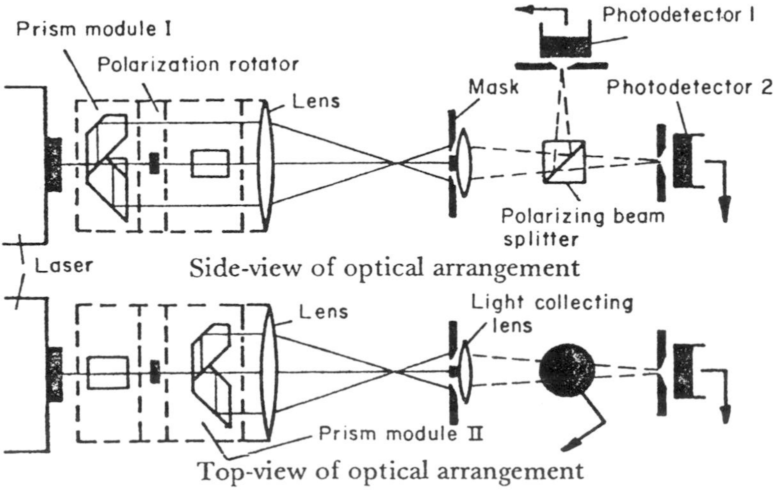

Figure 4.22 Dual beam arrangement for simultaneous measurement of two velocity components.

In general, several different optical arrangements can be realized for two-dimensional LV. Some representative beam configurations in either reference beams or fringe mode are shown in Fig. 4.23. Beam configuration A uses four illuminating beams and it operates in the 'fringe mode'. It gives two orthogonal velocity components in a plane normal to the optical axis of the focusing lens. Channel separation is obtained by using two colors or two states of polarization for each pair of beams. Configuration B utilises one illuminating beam and two weak reference beams and also gives two orthogonal velocity components. Configuration C also uses one illuminating beam and two reference beams. It gives two velocity components, each of which makes a small angle with the main velocity component. In configuration D two additional reference beams are used. It gives four velocity components from which all three orthogonal velocity components can be derived, Fig. 4.24. This system has been successfully used for velocity measurements in the wake field of a moving ship model. A similar beam configuration has also been proposed by Durst and Whitelaw, where four scattering beams, rather than reference beams, are used. These scattering beams are mixed in pairs in order to give two ortho-

TYPE	BEAM CONFIGURATION	CHARACTERISTICS
A	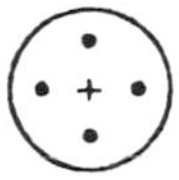	– 4 ILLUMINATING BEAMS – FRINGE MODE
B	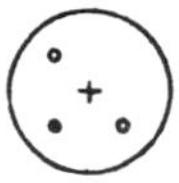	– 1 ILLUMINATING BEAM – 2 REFERENCE BEAMS
C	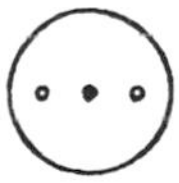	– 1 ILLUMINATING BEAM – 2 REFERENCE BEAMS – GIVES THIRD ON-AXIS COMPONENT INDIRECTLY
D	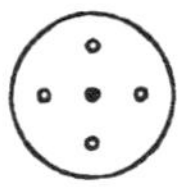	– 1 ILLUMINATING BEAM – 4 REFERENCE BEAMS – SUITED FOR THREE-DIMENSIONAL WORK – (ALTERNATIVE ARRANGEMENTS HAS 4 SCATTERING BEAMS)
E	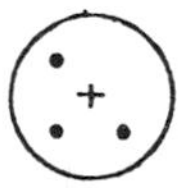	– 3 ILLUMINATING BEAMS – FRINGE MODE – ONE PHOTODETECTOR
F	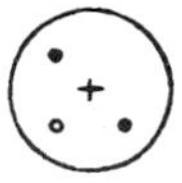	– 2 ILLUMINATING BEAMS – 1 REFERENCE BEAM – ONE PHOTODETECTOR

Figure 4.23 Basic beam configurations.[91]

gonal velocity components directly. For configurations B, C, and D no special provisions are required to obtain channel separation. The only strict requirement is that the reference beams are sufficiently weak to avoid disturbing cross interference.

Configurations E and F are convenient if channel separation could be achieved by introducing two different frequency shifts. Configuration E operates in the fringe mode and is possibly best suited for acousto-optic frequency shifting. If one operates at two different frequency shifts the two doppler signals could be received by one photodetector and subsequently these signals could be separated electronically and processed independently. In the same way this can be done for the reference beam configuration *F* shown in Fig. 4.24.

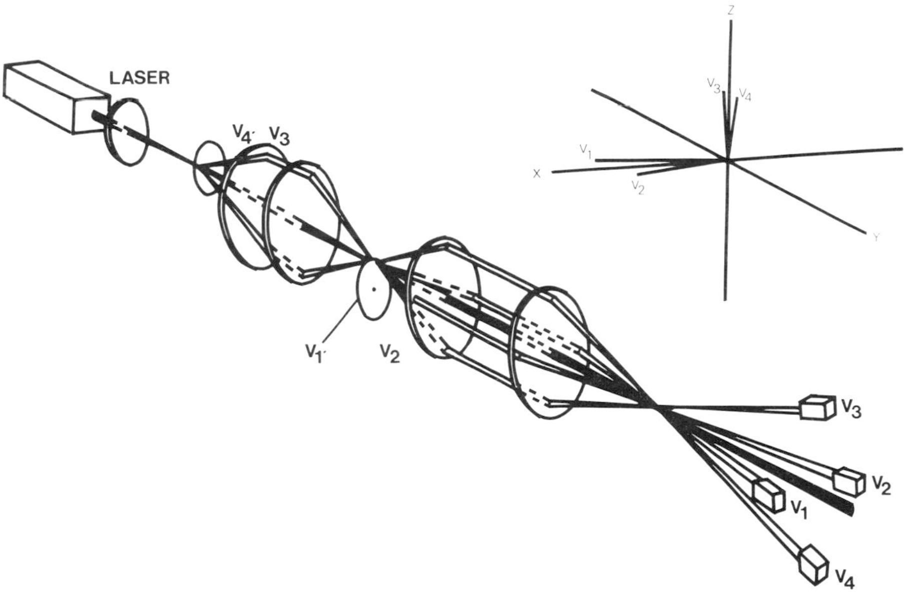

Figure 4.24 Arrangement for simultaneous measurement of three velocity components using two rotating diffraction grating

Evaluation of Doppler Signals in Two-Dimensional LV

In two scattered beam LV, the two 'sensitivity vectors' $(K_1)_i$ and $(K_2)_i$ are normal to each other and normal to the scattering beam, Fig. 4.25. If the latter is normal to the plane in which the velocity measurements are to be made, for example, the $x_1 - x_2$ plane, then the following equations hold:

$$(K_1)_i = \frac{2 \sin\phi_1}{\lambda_o} \left\{ \sin\alpha, \cos\alpha, 0 \right\}$$

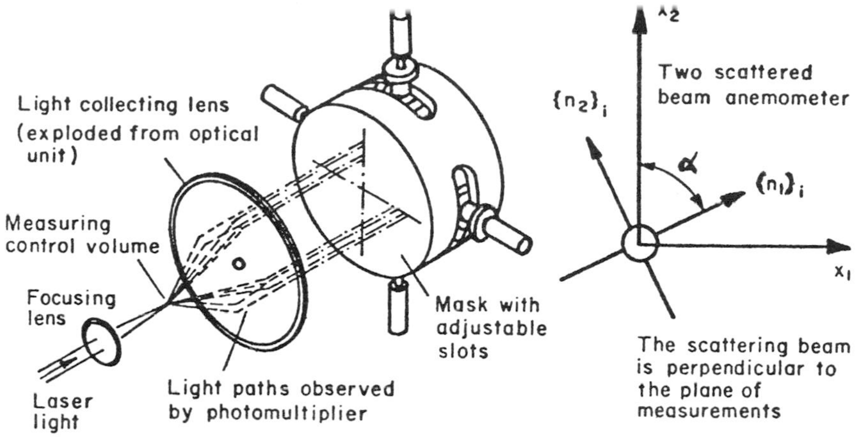

Figure 4.25 Two scattered beam anemometer systems for simultaneous measurement of two velocity components.[49]

$$(K_2)_i = \frac{2\sin\phi_2}{\lambda_o}\left\{-\cos\alpha, \sin\alpha, 0\right\}$$

$$(\hat{u})_i = \hat{u}_1, \hat{u}_2, 0$$

where α is the angle between the vector $(K_1)_i$ and the x_2-axis. Thus,

$$\hat{f}_{D_1} = \frac{2\sin\phi_1}{\lambda_o}(\hat{u}_1 \sin\alpha + \hat{u}_2 \cos\alpha)$$

$$\text{and } \hat{f}_{D_2} = \frac{2\sin\phi_2}{\lambda_o}(-\hat{u}_1 \cos\alpha + \hat{u}_2 \sin\alpha).$$

Introducing $\phi_1 = \phi_2 = \phi$ the instantaneous velocity components read as:

$$\hat{u}_1 = \frac{\lambda_o}{2\sin\phi}(\bar{f}_{D_1} \sin\alpha - \bar{f}_{D_2} \cos\alpha) \tag{4.41}$$

$$\hat{u}_2 = \frac{\lambda_o}{2\sin\phi}(\bar{f}_{D_1} \cos\alpha + \bar{f}_{D_2} \sin\alpha). \tag{4.42}$$

The mean velocity components are obtained by time averaging the above two equations 4.41 and 4.42.

Introducing $\hat{u}_i = u_i + u_i'$ and $\hat{f}_{D_i} = f_{D_i} + f_{D_i}'$, for $i = 1, 2$

into the equations 4.41 and 4.42 and subtracting the expressions for the mean velocity components yields:

$$u_1' = \frac{\lambda_o}{2\sin\phi}\left[\Delta f_{D_1}\sin\alpha - \Delta f_{D_2}\cos\alpha\right]$$

$$u_2' = \frac{\lambda_o}{2\sin\phi}\left[\Delta f_{D_1}\cos\alpha + \Delta f_{D_2}\sin\alpha\right].$$

For $\alpha = \pi/4$ the above equations reduce to

$$u_1' = \frac{\lambda_o}{(2)^{3/2}\sin\phi}\left[\Delta f_{D_1} - \Delta f_{D_2}\right]$$

$$u_2' = \frac{\lambda_o}{(2)^{3/2}\sin\phi}\left[\Delta f_{D_1} + \Delta f_{D_2}\right].$$

Simultaneous records of the sum and the difference of the frequency fluctuations allows $\overline{u_1'^2}$, $\overline{u_2'^2}$ and $\overline{u_1' u_2'}$ to be computed

$$\overline{u_1'^2} = \frac{\lambda_o^2}{8\sin^2\phi}\overline{\left[\Delta f_{D_1} - \Delta f_{D_2}\right]^2} \tag{4.43}$$

$$\overline{u_2'^2} = \frac{\lambda_o^2}{8\sin^2\phi}\overline{\left[\Delta f_{D_1} + \Delta f_{D_2}\right]^2} \tag{4.44}$$

$$\overline{u_1' u_2'} = \frac{\lambda_o^2}{8\sin^2\phi}\overline{\left[\Delta f_{D_1} - \Delta f_{D_2}\right]\left[\Delta f_{D_1} + \Delta f_{D_2}\right]}. \tag{4.45}$$

Similar derivations can be derived for the other velocity correlations, for example, $\overline{u_3'^2}$, $\overline{u_1' u_3'}$ and $\overline{u_2' u_3'}$.

Similar relationships can easily be derived for two-dimensional reference beam velocimeters.

4.2 TEMPERATURE

There is a growing need for accurate methods of temperature measurements in high temperature gases in the presence or absence of solid or liquid particles. The definition of the temperature of flame gases is hampered by the thermodynamic equilibrium, the Boltzmann distribution of the molecules between various energy states may not be fully established in the gas at the point being considered. This leads to the concept of differing temperatures corresponding to the various modes of excitation (vibrational, rotational, translational, electronic), and the possibility even of a different value for each mode in each molecular species present. There is also the possibility of chemical non-equilibrium, and in practical systems (not involving "black bodies") a very high probability of departure from radiation equilibrium (that is, a net loss of energy by radiation) which may itself affect the internal equilibrium of the various molecular states.

These departures from equilibrium (with the occasional exception of the chemical and radiative types) are comparatively small for the burnt gases of many flames, and for these the temperature is a valid and valuable property. Nevertheless, in the reaction zone or flame front (for example swirling flame where the hot and active species are transported from downstream of the flame to upstream of the flame near the nozzle exit) major departures from equilibrium are to be expected, and the determination of the effective temperatures of the various modes, giving a measure of the extent of such divergences, may be of much value in mechanistic studies of flame propagation and ionization.

The various methods that have been developed for the measurement of temperature in flame gases under differing conditions refer, strictly speaking, to different modes of excitation. Thus, the much used line-reversal method gives the effective electronic excitation temperature for the element used (or, more precisely, the particular excited state of the element used). Methods depending on brightness and emissivity similarly yield information which is strictly relevant only to the particular transition employed. Rotational and vibrational temperatures may be determined by measuring the intensity distribution of the appropriate spectra[92]. Doppler broadening of spectral lines have also been employed to investigate the translational temperature of a single species in the reaction zones of flames.

For many practical applications and research, however, the essential requirement is for a measure of the mean and possibly fluctuating translational temperature of the gas molecules. This may be achieved, for example, by refractive index (interferometric or schlieren) methods, by methods depending essentially on the density, or (for flames at comparatively low temperatures) by hot wire methods. These latter, in turn, include resistance thermometry, optical pyrometry and the use of thermocouples.

Nonintrusive optical methods (including spectroscopic) are more advantageous than the resistance thermometers because of their not disturbing the flow, there is no melting point limitation and very high range of maximum temperature measurement, Table 4.5. Nevertheless, solid thermoelements are usually more convenient and give better spatial resolution. Such probes give an electrical signal, which can be translated into probe temperature with the aid of reliable calibration. Fine wire thermocouples have more stable calibration than resistance wires at high temperature. The gas temperature may be found from the temperature by using the energy equation.

In general, the probe does not attain the same temperature as the hot gas. The gas is contained by solid walls and there is a radiative energy exchange between these and the probe. The probe usually radiates energy to cooler walls and in the steady state this is balanced by convective energy transfer from the gas to the probe. In the absence of any heat release by chemical reaction this means that the wire is at a lower temperature than the gas. The value of the temperature difference is called the radiation correction. Because the radiation from the probe increases as the fourth power of the probe temperature; this correction increases very sharply with temperature. Consideration of the energy balance for the probe also shows that the magnitude of the correction decreases with the size of the probe. For example, at a gas temperature of 1300 K, a 0.0005 in. diameter platinum wire probe may have a radiation correction of 5 degrees rising to 60 degrees for a gas temperature of 2100 K. The corresponding values of the correction for a 0.002 in. diameter probe would be 35° and 200°. The radiation correction may be

TABLE 4.5

Some Methods of Temperature Measurement

Instrument	Measurement Range, K Normal	Maximum	Accuracy	Comments
Thermocouples				
(a) Bare Metal	1400	2000	± 0.75%	
(b) Rare Metal	2000	2800	± 1° at 1300 K ± 5° at 2000 K ± 1% above 2000 K	Moderate cost, radiation correction required.
Resistance Thermometer	900	2000	± 0.01° at 800 K ± 0.5%	Used in laboratory and industrial applications, moderate cost, radiation correction required.
Suction Pyrometer	1800	2100	1–2%	Moderate cost.
Venturi Pneumatic Pyrometer	2100	2800	2% at 1900 K	Moderate cost.
Radiation Pyrometer				
(a) Total	2100	2800	± 0.75%	
(b) Disappearing Filament	2600	None	± 5° at 1600 K	Can give large variations in accuracies between different instruments, moderate cost.
(c) Partial	2800	None	± 0.75%	
(d) Ratio (or two color)	2000	None	± 2%	
Schmidt Method	2300	2800		See text.
Line Reversal	2800	5000	± 1–2% at 2800 K ± 5–10% at 800 K	See text.
Line Intensity		10,000	± 10%	See text.
Laser Schlieren Interferometry	2000	2800	± 10%, depends upon a knowledge of the concentration distribution	See text, moderate to high cost.

advantageous, in that gas temperature higher than the fine wire melting point may be measured, provided the value of the radiation correction can be calculated.

The disadvantage of fine wires lies in their fragility. Because of the limited strength of fine wire thermocouples and of the need for accurate location of the hot junction, the wires must be supported by thicker wires of the same material. The support leads will have a larger radiation correction than the fine wire and with the containing walls cooler than the gas, energy is conducted along the fine wire to the support. This conduction can cool the hot junction, and the amount by which it does so depends upon the length of wire between the junction and the support. The decrease in hot junction temperature as a result of this effect is called the conduction correction.

In conditions where it is impossible to use fine wires because of strength limitations, the radiation correction may be reduced by a local increase in velocity over the sensing element, as in the suction pyrometer.

Thermocouples

Bare Metal

There has been no major change in materials used in this field for many years. Iron vs constantan can be used under reducing condition up to 700/800°C. Nickel/chrome/aluminium alloys such as Chromel vs Alumel, etc. (all made to the same output standard BS1827) give good service under oxidising conditions up to about 1200°C for thick wire. The most common causes of failure of the Ni/Cr/Al alloy thermocouples are, attack by sulphur-bearing compounds (or gases) and, alternate oxidising – reducing conditions which can result in the formation of a nickel layer that partially shorts the normal thermocouple, giving low readings.

A most significant recent development has taken place, however, in the method of constructing the thermocouples. Both iron vs constantan and Ni/Cr thermocouples are available, with a variety of protective sheaths, in the mineral packed construction developed for heavy duty electrical wiring. This mode of construction, used unprotected, gives a small diameter flexible thermocouple ($\frac{1}{16}$, $\frac{1}{8}$ and $\frac{1}{4}$ in. diameter thermocouples are available as standards, and smaller sizes are made in certain materials). Used in place of a conventional thermocouple, with an external protection sheath, the assembly has double protection against contamination. The resulting longer life may frequently offset the extra cost.

Rare Metal

In the rare metal thermocouples, platinum vs platinum 13 per cent rhodium is still the most common and accurate thermocouple combination for applications up to about 1800°C. Nevertheless, in recent years some new combinations have been developed; some of these are listed in Table 4.6.

The first two combinations were developed in different countries for the same purpose, namely to minimise errors caused by the migration of rhodium to platinum in the thermocouple.

The 6/30 combination has the considerable advantage of not requiring compensating leads up to a cold junction temperature 70/100°C. It appears sensible to standardise on

TABLE 4.6

Thermocouple Properties

Combination	Maximum Temperature, K	Suitable Environment	Comments
Platinum–5% Rhodium vs. Platinum–20% Rhodium	1600–2100	No Special Atmosphere Required	Relatively strong, stable calibration.
Platinum–6% Rhodium vs. Platinum–30% Rhodium	1600–2100	No Special Atmosphere Required	Relatively strong, stable calibration.
Platinum–20% Rhodium vs. Platinum–40% Rhodium	2150	Oxidizing or Reducing	Relatively strong, stable calibration.
Iridium vs. 40% Rhodium Iridium	2300	Inert, Oxidizing for Short Periods	Embrittles in reducing atmosphere. Difficult to draw to small diameter.
Iridium vs. Tungsten	2600	Neutral	Embrittles in reducing atmosphere. Tungsten embrittles after recrystallization.
Tungsten vs. 26% Rhenium Tungsten	3000	Neutral or Reducing	Cannot be used in oxidizing atmosphere.
5% Rhenium Tungsten vs. 26% Rhenium Tungsten	3000	Clean Neutral or Reducing	Cannot be used in oxidizing atmosphere, or with hydrocarbons.

this combination in applications requiring continuous operation in the range 1300-1600/1800°C.

The remaining very high temperature combinations are less well tried and are still undergoing application evaluation. Better protective sheaths and insulators are required for these thermocouples and this field still warrants some attention from the manufacturers.

Noncatalytic Coating for Platinum-Rhodium Thermocouples

There are two basic reasons for coating platinum-rhodium thermocouples when their application is to measure flame temperatures. Platinum placed in certain flames acts as a catalyst; the reaction taking place on the surface of the junction brings about a rise in temperature which deviates from the true flame temperature. It is therefore necessary to insulate the catalytically active thermocouple from the flame with an inert coating. Another reason for coating the platinum-rhodium thermocouples is that these alloys are subjected to contamination at high temperatures with a variety of elements, for example, carbon and hydrogen, which occur naturally in the flame. Contamination frequently leads to embrittlement of the thermocouple and alters its calibration. Any coating applied to the thermocouple suitable for flame temperature measurement should have the following general properties:

(a) noncatalytic to flame
(b) inert to the thermocouple material at all temperatures
(c) impermeable to gases so as to afford protection from the environment
(d) poor conductor of electricity, especially at high temperatures; otherwise the thermocouple will be short-circuited.
(e) stable at high temperatures. Forms of instability include oxidation, reduction, hydration, volatization, and crystalline change.
(f) capable of being applied evenly and smoothly to the thermocouple surface and must cover it completely.
(g) minimum thickness of the coating so as to avoid appreciable losses through conduction.

For flame temperature measurements up to about 1100°C with platinum-rhodium thermocouples, a coating containing a small proportion of silica can be used. A silica coating can be applied to the thermocouple either by drawing it into a fine silica tube of appropriate diameter or by holding it in a flame in which a volatile silicon-containing compound (for example, methylated spirit and 10 per cent hexamethyldisiloxane) is being burnt. Trimethylethoxysilane has also been found best to deposit silica in solid granules from a fuel-rich coal gas/air flame with an outer sheath of nitrogen to restrict secondary combustion. The temperature is then raised to fuse the silica so as to form a clear uniform coating around the wire.

Nevertheless, at higher temperatures, the silica is reduced by hydrogen in the flame, and the diffusion of free silicon into platinum produces platinum silicide. It has been reported that even 0.2 per cent silica present in the thermocouple sheath is enough to bring about the formation of embrittling silicide[93]. It is therefore necessary to remove silica completely for measurements in high temperature flames. Consequently all the common porcelains and clays must be excluded from consideration when choosing a coating material. Contact at high temperatures with carbon, sulfur, phosphorous, arsenic, and their oxidizable compounds and with metallic vapors, especially lead and zinc, should be avoided[93].

Kent[94] has reported that a combination of yttrium oxide or yttrium chloride and beryllium oxide is best suited when tested for properties outlined above. The actual proportion of beryllium oxide depends on the required fusing temperature of the coating and must always be kept below the melting point of platinum (1769°C) and above the working temperature of the thermocouple (1600°C). A composition of approximately 10-15 per cent beryllium oxide in yttrium oxide fulfils these conditions. An increase in beryllium oxide content lowers the fusing temperature. The coating is prepared by dissolving both ingredients (yttrium chloride and beryllium oxide) in hydrochloric acid. Yttrium oxide forms an insoluble intermediate compound in the acid, which then had to be broken down. The chloride is quite soluble and converts to oxide when the coating is fired.

Fluctuating Temperature Measurement with Thermocouples

Thermocouples with an element of usable size have large time constants compared to the level required for signals of acoustic frequency to be followed. This time constant depends on the physical properties of the thermocouple wire and on the aerodynamic conditions where it is used and can be effectively reduced by using an electrical circuit applied to the thermocouple output. Some of the earliest papers on fluctuating temperatures were by Shepard and Warshwasky[95] and Kunugi and Jinno[96]. The former was the first survey on the measurements of fluctuating temperatures in flames. The importance of fluctuating temperatures was not recognized for a long time and only recently have efforts been made to improve this[97, 98].

The time response of a bare-wire thermocouple can be described by the following differential equation

$$\tau \frac{dT_w}{dt} + T_w = T_g \qquad (4.36)$$

where T_g and T_w are the temperature of the gas and temperature of the wire respectively, and τ 'the time constant' defines the ability of the thermocouple to follow gas temperature variations. In terms of step response, τ is the time required for the thermocouple output to cover 63 per cent of the total change as shown in Fig. 4.26(a). An electrical lag compensation could be produced if an electrical network was found that could perform upon the primary element output signal 'T_w', the operations described by the left side of equation 4.36. The result obtained would be a voltage representation of the true gas temperature.

Principles of Compensation

It is evident from Fig. 4.26(b) that the response drops at frequencies greater than $\frac{1}{2\pi\tau}$, the cut-off frequency of the thermocouple. The compensating network used has a response inverse to that of the thermocouple, so that over the frequency range of interest, the combined response is flat. The method used is to reduce the impedance of a network with rising frequency at the same rate so that the response of the thermocouple falls off[95-97], that is, the frequency response is extended by a certain factor F (so that the cut-off frequency of the thermocouple-compensator combination is $\frac{F}{2\pi\tau}$). The time required to complete 63 per cent of the change will be reduced by F, and the combined system will act as though it had an effective time constant τ/F. Scadron and Warshwasky[99] have shown that the time constant of a thermocouple can be given by the following

$$\tau \propto \left[\frac{(\rho c)_w}{(\rho c)_{pt,0}}\right]\left(\frac{289}{T_g}\right)^{0.18} \left[\frac{(D_w{}^3)^{\frac{1}{2}}}{(MP_s)^{\frac{1}{2}}}\right] \qquad (4.37)$$

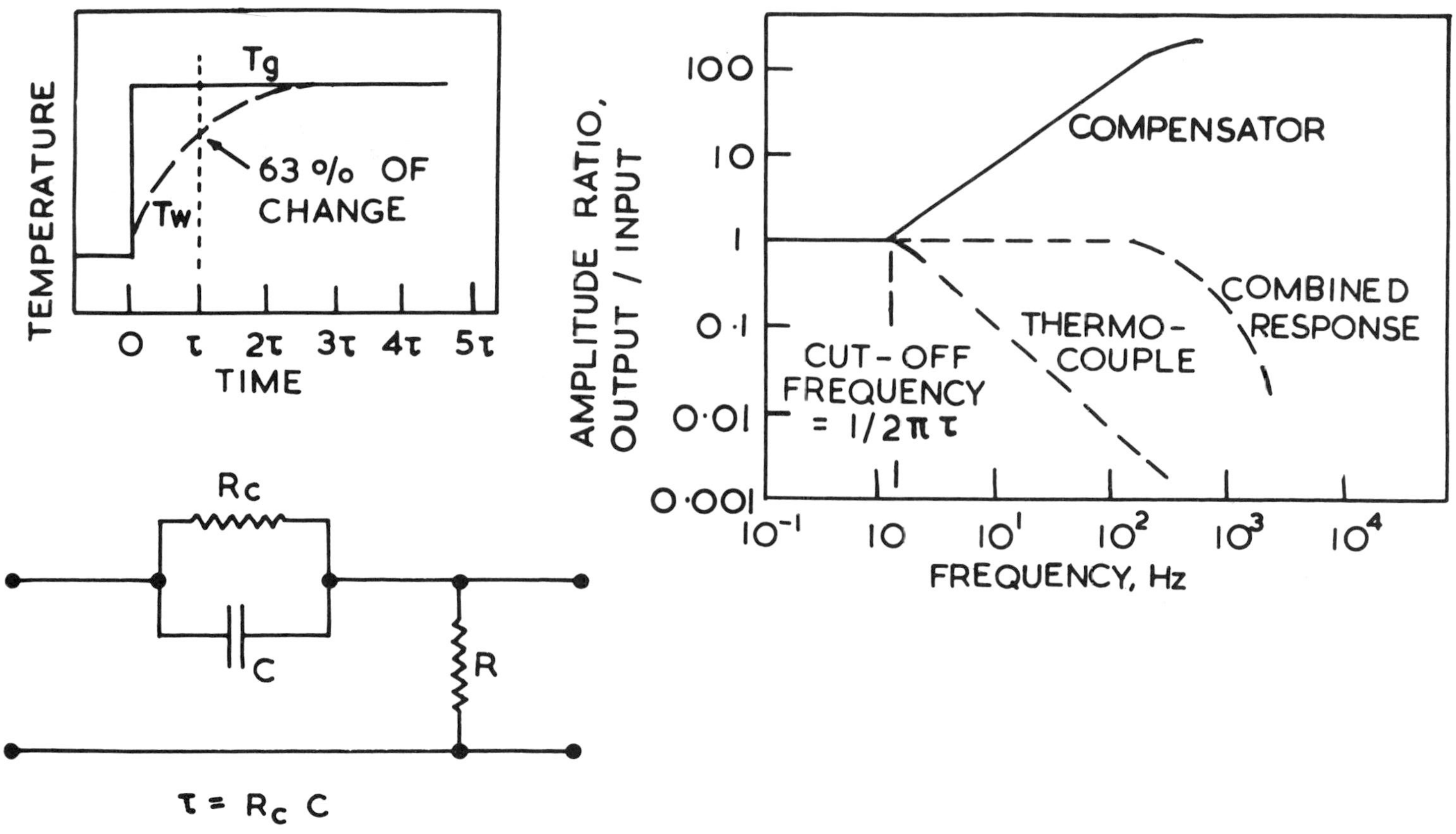

Figure 4.26 Top left: Response of the thermocouple to step gas temperature changes; bottom left: the R-C compensator network; right; frequency response characteristics[63]

where pt, 0 refers to condition of the cold junction of the thermocouple and M and P_s are the Mach no. and static pressure, respectively.

A detailed description of the various electrical techniques for the time lag compensation of the thermocouples and the basic principles applied are given in Bennett[93].

The Compensating Circuit

An R-C compensator network is shown in Fig. 4.26 (c). In this, the summation is obtained by choosing R and C so that a current flows through R proportional to the time rate of change of the thermocouple temperature and by choosing R_c so that an additional current is produced through R proportional to the thermocouple temperature. The voltage drop produced by the sum of the two currents flowing through R is then approximately proportional to the gas temperature. The criterion for correct compensation is then

$$R_c \quad C = \tau \tag{4.38}$$

and the cut-off frequency of the thermocouple (of low resistance) is effectively improved by factor F given by

$$F = 1 + \left(\frac{R_c}{R}\right) \tag{4.39}$$

Equations 4.38 and 4.39 are the basic equations of an idealized R-C compensator and serve to establish the relationships between R, R_c and C in terms of τ and the frequency response improvement factor F. Nevertheless, in actual practice the frequency response improvement factor obtained is smaller than F because of the simplified assumptions made in arriving at equation 4.39.

As pointed out earlier, the time constants of thermocouples of usable element size are large and depend on the physical properties of the thermocouple wire and on the aerodynamic conditions where it is used (*see* eqn. 4.37). The instrumentation used by various workers to determine the thermocouple time constant is shown in Fig. 4.27(a) and Fig. 4.27(b). With the technique used by Gupta *et al*[97], linear response of several kilo hertz (typically 4-5 KHz) can easily be obtained. Nevertheless, the level of compensation involves a penalty in detectable signal amplitude in which, for correct compensation, all signals are attenuated from the true response amplitude given by the thermocouple. A typical radial distribution of mean and RMS temperatures and the thermocouple time constant in a turbulent diffusion methane flame is shown in Fig. 4.28.

Radiation Correction to Thermocouples

Figure 4.29 shows a generalized temperature profile associated with a simply supported fine wire thermocouple. The support at A, because of radiative and conductive energy losses, will be at a temperature below that of the gas and the fine thermocouple wire. The profile ABC shows the cooling effect of the support by the conduction of heat along the wire, which becomes negligible at C. The profile CD shows the wire at a steady temperature somewhat below gas temperature, such that radiative energy loss to the cool surrounding walls is balanced by convective energy gain from the gas. The hot junction

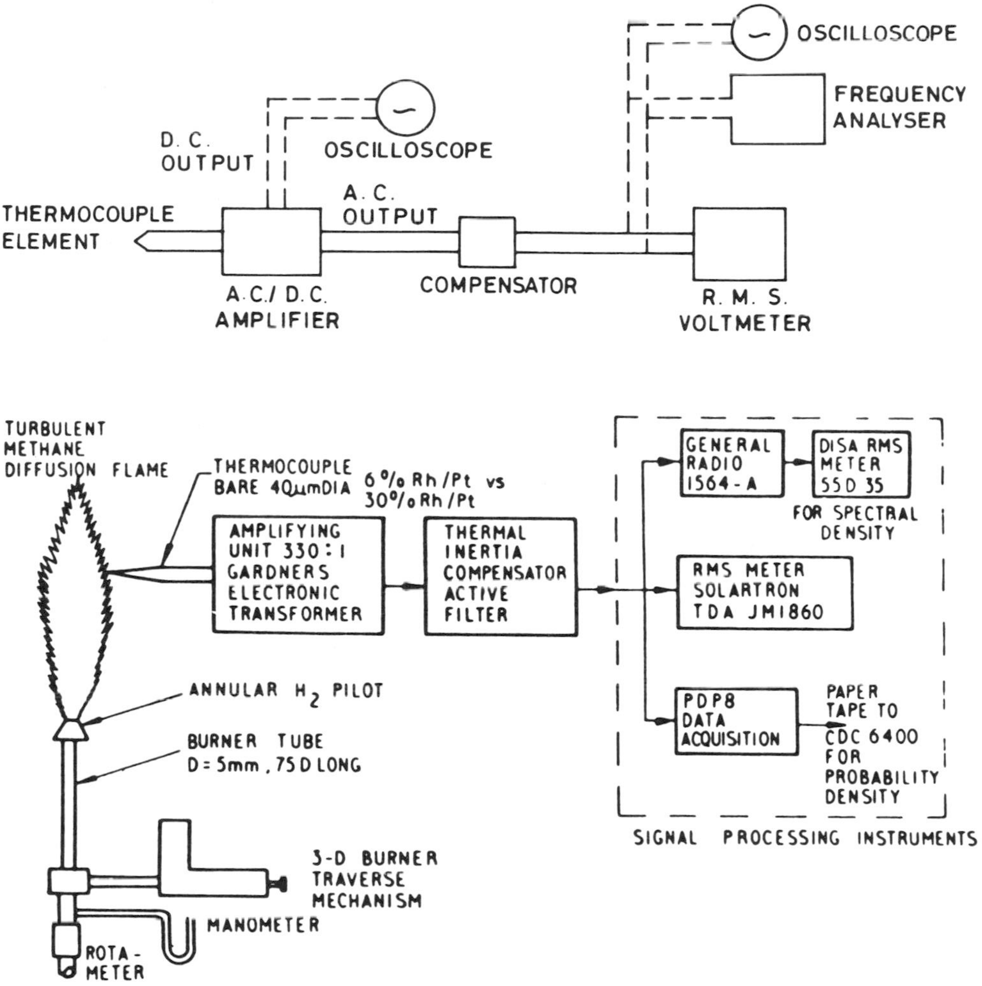

Figure 4.27 Instrumentation for the measurement of fluctuating temperatures. Top diagram: as used by Gupta et al[97]; bottom diagram: as used by Lockwood et al[98]

of the thermocouple, formed by fusing the two component wires together, is essentially of somewhat larger diameter than either of them. The increase in diameter creates a relatively larger energy loss by radiation than energy gain by convection and the junction temperature is lower than that of the adjoining component wires. This is shown by point *E* in Fig. 4.29 and the curve *DEF* represents this cooling effect of the junction globule on the component wires. The curve *FGHJ* represents the temperature profile for the other component wire. Both the right-hand side wire and its support will, in general, have different temperatures, at corresponding positions, from those of the left-hand side, mainly because of differences in emissivities, thermal conductivities and possibly the diameters of the two materials.

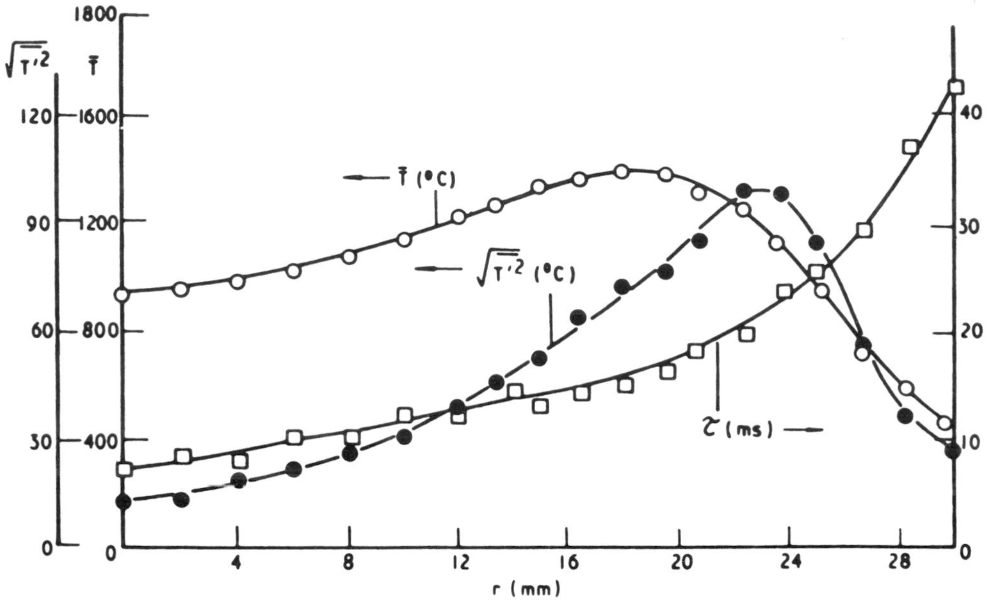

Figure 4.28 Radial distribution of mean and r.m.s. temperatures and thermocouple time constant in a turbulent diffusion methane flame.[98]

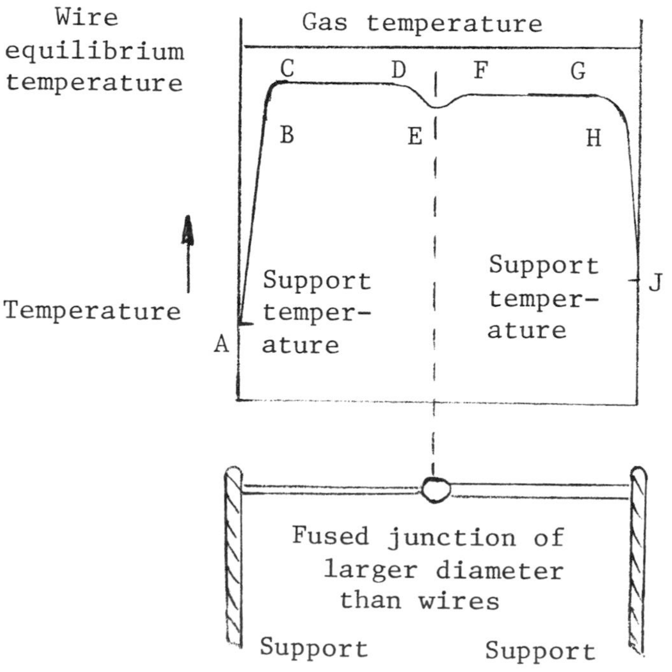

Figure 4.29 Wire temperature distribution.[105]

Assuming that the surrounding walls are black to radiation from the wire and that radiant energy exchange between the wire and the gases is negligible, the steady state energy equation for an uncoated wire can be written as follows:

$$\frac{d}{dx}\left(k\frac{dT}{dx}\right) + \frac{4h}{D}(T_g - T) - \frac{4\sigma}{D}(\epsilon T^4 - \alpha T_b{}^4) = 0 \tag{4.40}$$

where ϵ and α are the wire emissivity and absorptivity of wire respectively.

It is worthwhile to consider briefly the general validity of this equation. For a clean gas the assumption of negligible radiant energy exchange between gas and wire is valid. For a gas containing suspended particles this would not be so and an extra term would be necessary in the equation to allow for the emissivity of the particles.

With regard to radiative energy exchange with the container walls, it is assumed that the wall is an isothermal, radiatively black surround at constant temperature. If this is not so, then the actual geometry and wall temperature distribution must be taken into account.

The present assumptions, however, of a clean gas and black surround give a treatment of sufficient generality.

When there is no thermal conduction along the wire it may be said to be at its 'semi-infinite equilibrium temperature', T_∞. The difference between this temperature and the gas temperature is the radiation correction. In this case the first term in eqn. 4.40 is zero and therefore

$$\frac{4h}{D}(T_g - T_\infty) - \frac{4\sigma}{D}(\epsilon T_\infty{}^4 - \alpha T_b{}^4) = 0$$

In practice, for wire temperatures above 1000°C and low wall temperature the absorption term $\alpha T_b{}^4$ is usually negligible and we can write

$$T_g = T_\infty + \frac{\sigma\epsilon T_\infty{}^4}{h} \tag{4.41}$$

where $\sigma = 1.355 \times 10^{-12}$ cal/s cm K^4 [Stefan Boltzmann constant]

The importance of reliable values of emissivity now becomes apparent. Unfortunately, there is a dearth of experimental data for thermocouple materials at high temperatures, although some values for platinum and platinum-10 per cent rhodium have been obtained[100, 101]. Another approach is to derive values of emissivity from electrical resistivity on the basis of electromagnetic theory. Davisson and Weeks[101] give a theoretical expression for the hemispherical emissivity ϵ integrated over all wavelengths. This expression is

$$\epsilon = 0.751\,(\mathrm{Tr_e})^{1/2} - 0.632\,(\mathrm{Tr_e}) + 0.670\,(\mathrm{Tr_e})^{3/2} - 0.607\,(\mathrm{Tr_e})^2 \tag{4.42}$$

and its validity is discussed by Davisson and Weeks[101]. Resistivities, r_e, for the platinum-rhodium alloys can be estimated from the data presented by Wise and Vines[102].

For coated wires the emittance depends on the diameter of the wire and the thickness of the coating. Bradley and Entwistle[100] give theoretical and experimental values of total hemispherical emittance for silica coated platinum-10 per cent rhodium wires. The emittance is close to the uncoated wire emissivity at high temperatures. This is because the coating is almost transparent to the energy radiated in the shorter wavelengths, where most of the energy is transferred at the higher temperatures. On the other hand, at lower temperatures, the emittance is increased as a consequence of the high absorption at the longer wavelengths. There is a need for much more data on emissivity at high temperatures as this is essential for the accurate derivation of gas temperature from thermocouple temperature.

The heat transfer coefficient, h, in equation 4.41 is determined from the expression of Kramer, quoted by Hinze[103]. This expression, which holds for $0.01 < \mathrm{Re} < 10{,}000$, is

$$\mathrm{Nu} = 0.42\mathrm{Pr}^{0.2} + 0.57\mathrm{Pr}^{0.33}\mathrm{Re}^{0.5} \tag{4.43}$$

It is frequently used in anemometry, for cross flow to a wire.

Gas properties in eqn. 4.43 are evaluated at the mean value of T_g and T_∞. Data on the properties of gas mixtures at high temperatures are somewhat uncertain.

Conduction Correction to Thermocouples

In a well-designed thermocouple the junction will be cooled only a few degrees by conduction along the fine wires. Nevertheless, if the fine wires are too short serious cooling of the junction can result. A short thermocouple may be necessary in order to keep the probe robust, for instance, when high velocities are encountered. To ascertain the minimum length of fine wire required to avoid excessive cooling of the hot junction it is necessary to calculate the wire temperature profile by solving the energy eqn. 4.40. To do this, the equation is first put into finite difference form for any three adjacent points $-1, 0, +1$ distance δ apart and becomes

$$\frac{T_{+1} - 2T_0 + T_{-1}}{\delta^2} + W_x = 0 \tag{4.44}$$

where

$$W_x = \frac{4h}{Dk}(\mathrm{T}_g - T) - \frac{4\sigma}{\mathrm{Dk}}(\epsilon T^4 - \alpha T_b{}^4) \tag{4.45}$$

For a given wire in a constant gas temperature field, W_x is a function of the wire temperature only, and the normal relaxation techniques can be modified to determine the wire temperature profile. To allow for the variation of W_x with T, the relaxation pattern is modified to

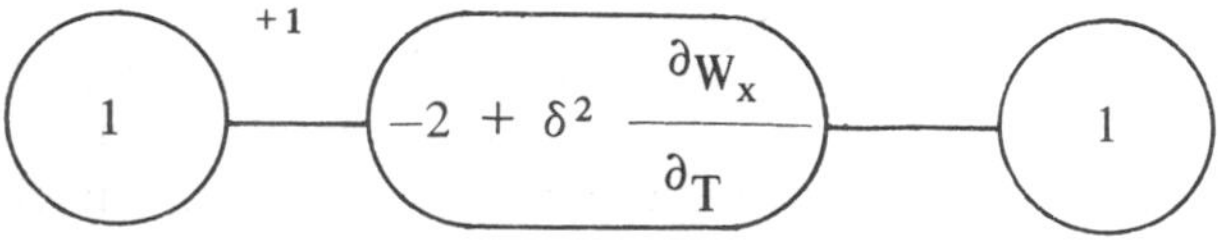

It should be noted that when $\partial W_x/\partial T = 0$ and also when δ is very small the relaxation pattern reduces to the normal simple form

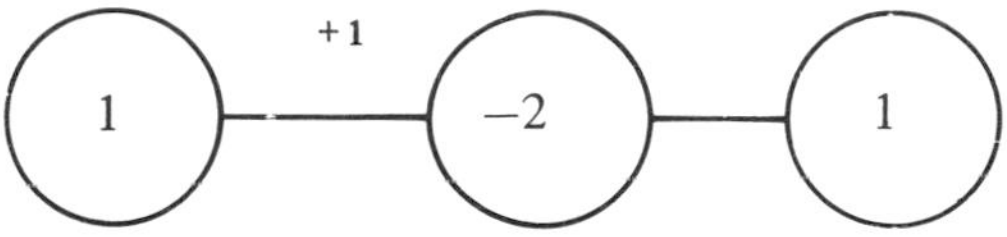

Once again the calculation is made more difficult by the lack of reliable high temperature data. In addition to the lack of wire emissivity and gas property data discussed above, there is also considerable doubt concerning the value of wire thermal conductivity data. The thermal conductivity, k, can be calculated from wire electrical resistivity, r_e, using the Wiedemann-Franz relationship

$$k = \frac{4T}{r_e} \times 10^{-10} \qquad \text{chu/ft s deg K}$$

In practical terms, the calculations for conduction cooling show that with a thermocouple wire length of about 0.125 in. the conduction cooling is unimportant with a wire diameter of 0.0005 in. As the wire length is decreased the junction will be cooled by conduction of heat energy along the wires to the supports. With larger diameter wires the conduction cooling effect will be considerably greater and consequently longer wires will be required in order to minimize error in the measured temperature. In order to reduce the error due to conduction it is necessary to immerse the thermocouple wires in the flow with as great a length as possible of small diameter and low thermal conductivity k.

For further discussions on conduction correction and to design a thermocouple with known implicit (minimum) conduction cooling error, see Bradley and Matthew[104].

Resistance Thermometers

In resistance thermometers the change in resistance of the wire at the unknown temperature is measured; the unknown temperature is calculated using the relationship[105]

$$R_t = R_o \, [1 + AT + BT^2 + \ldots\ldots]$$

Although platinum resistance thermometers have been accepted for many years as the most accurate method of measuring temperatures up to 600°C it is only recently that they have become available for use up to 1000°C and sometimes even up to 1400°C. This development will almost certainly continue and we may see resistance thermometers used in many applications, at present the exclusive domain of the thermocouple. Certainly the resistance thermometer may replace the thermocouples as the interpolating standard for the International Practical Temperature Scale up to 1063°C.

It is possible to apply the above method for measuring fluctuating temperatures. Nevertheless, the limitation is that the heat balance equation depends upon the temperature difference between the hot wire and its surrounding environment. In addition to this, the wire probe is also sensitive to concentration fluctuations.

Suction Pyrometers

In order to eliminate the various sources of error enumerated in the previous section, the use of a suction pyrometer is recommended. In this method the true temperature of the gas is made by minimising the heat transfer from the surroundings by shielding the thermocouple with a number of concentric shields and by maximising the heat transfer from the gas by aspirating a sample at high speed, past the thermocouple. The performance of the pyrometer as a function of the pyrometer and operational variables can be made by considering the convective heat transfer in a tube, or between two concentric tubes under turbulent conditions ($R_e > 2500$)

$$\mathrm{Nu} = \frac{h_c d}{k} = 0.2 \left(\frac{\rho u d}{\mu}\right)^{0.8} \tag{4.46}$$

where d is the internal diameter of the tube or an equivalent distance (diameter) separating two concentric tubes. The coefficient h_c varies only slightly with d so that in order to reduce the size of the pyrometer with large number of shields, d should be chosen as close as possible to the minimum diameter that would allow turbulent flow to be conserved. In practice, however, the turbulent flow is conserved over a certain distance from the entrance to the tube so that if the thermocouple is placed near enough to the entrance of the tube the efficiency is not reduced for Reynolds numbers considerably lower than 2000. Since h_c increases with turbulence it is best to augment the turbulence by creating an irregular flow at the tube entry and placing the thermocouple close enough to the gas entry without creating any additional losses and errors. Convection is further increased by increasing u, that is, sucking the gas at as high a suction rate as possible. It must be remembered, however, that an increase in velocity also causes an error which should be kept to a minimum. The error caused due to velocity is small, typically it is about 3°C for a suction velocity of 80 m/s and 7°C for 300 m/s.

The change in temperature created by increasing the velocity of the gas is resolved by 'choking' the flow at the thermocouple by means of a venturi restriction in a sonic suction pyrometer. In the sonic suction pyrometer the hot junction of the thermocouple is placed in the throat at the head of the suction tube where the gases are flowing at the speed of sound, Fig. 4.30. The measured temperature T_m is related to the total temperature of the gas T_o by the following relationship

$$T_m = AT_0$$

where $A = \dfrac{2 + r(\gamma - 1)}{(\gamma + 1)}$; r = recovery factor.

The value of A, measured at ambient temperature, is corrected for high temperatures by using the law of the variation of γ as a function of this variable.

The response of the sonic pyrometer is very fast and the error due to radiation at high suction velocities, even with only one shield, is negligible.

The sonic pyrometer is, in general, constructed of 'inconel' and can be used at temperatures up to about 1200°C. It can also be manufactured in alumina or calcium oxide stabilized zirconia for use at high temperatures.

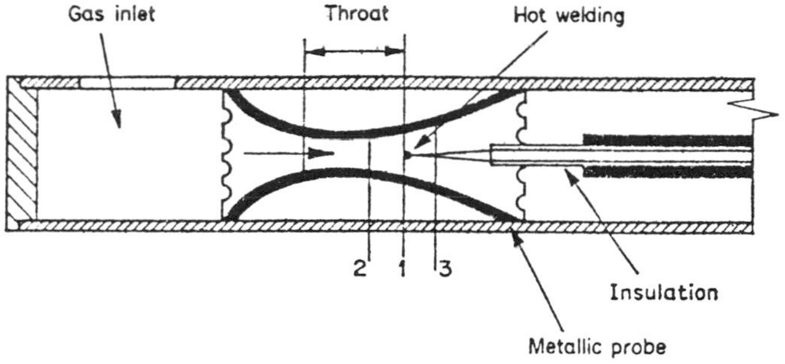

(a) Scheme of apparatus

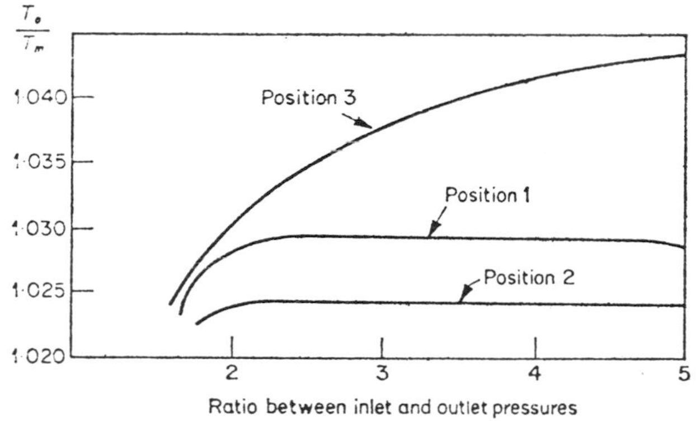

(b) Influence of the position of hot welding in the throat

Figure 4.30 Sonic suction pyrometer.[5]

Venturi Pneumatic Pyrometer

The standard suction pyrometer is not very suitable for making temperature measurements that are very high or to make measurements in gases heavily laden in dust.

The venturi pneumatic pyrometer is somewhat similar in principle to the constant pressure gas thermometer in that the temperature is calculated from a knowledge of the density of the gas at the unknown temperature and at a known lower temperature. In the venturi pneumatic pyrometer method the ratio of the densities is measured by aspirating a sample of the gas down a water-cooled probe with a venturi restriction further down the probe. The temperature of the gas is measured by a platinum resistance thermometer at the 'cold' venturi. The ratio of densities is determined by measuring the ratio of the differential pressures generated at the venturi restrictions. The pyrometer is calibrated by initially aspirating cold gas at a known temperature. A useful feature of this venturi pyrometer is that no part need be very hot.

Radiation Instruments

In the last couple of decades, a large number of developments have taken place in the area of radiation instruments for temperature measurement, for example, total radiation pyrometer, disappearing filament pyrometer, partial radiation pyrometer, ratio (or two color optical) pyrometer. Radiation pyrometers are instruments that measure the rate of energy emission per unit area over a relatively broad range of wavelengths.

In the disappearing filament method, temperature is measured by comparison of the flame emission with a light source at known temperature. In commercial pyrometers, the filament of an incandescent lamp is superimposed optically on the image of the flame region under study. Filament temperature is adjusted by changing the applied voltage, and when the two images are at the same temperature, they will tend to merge. The equivalence point can be determined visually or by the use of a photocell to within a precision of a few degrees. Carbon, tungsten, or xenon lamps can also be used and can be calibrated against a black body whose temperature is measured by some auxiliary method. This method together with the total and partial radiation pyrometers and their method of calibration are covered in some detail in Fristrom and Westenberg[1] and Forsythe[106].

Two-Color Optical Pyrometer

A radiation pyrometer compares the intensity of light at a particular wavelength, λ, emitted by an object whose temperature T is being measured to the intensity of light at the same wavelength emitted by a black body source whose temperature T_B is known. If the object being measured is a black body, then matching the radiation intensities of the objects is equivalent to matching their temperatures. This is because, by Planck's radiation law, emitted intensity is a function of temperature, emissivity, and wavelength. If the object being measured is not a black body, then its emissivity ϵ_λ must be known in order to determine its temperature. The temperature of a non black body can be found by knowing its emissivity and by determining its "brightness temperature", that is, the temperature of the black body whose radiation intensity at a specified wavelength equals that of the non-black body.

It is often required to know the temperature of an object whose emissivity is unknown. A method to overcome this difficulty is to use a two-color pyrometer. In two-color pyrometry the ratio of the two light signals at two discrete narrow bands of emitted radiation from the object say, for example, burning particles gives an output that is a function of the particle temperature[107-109]. An advantage of the two-color approach is that the emissivity terms drop out if the object is a grey or black body ($\epsilon_\lambda \equiv \epsilon(\lambda) = \text{const.}$). The constant C, built into the two-color detection system, is determined by calibration[109]. A background to the radiation theory together with principles of two-color pyrometer operation are given below.

Planck's radiation law gives an expression for radiative energy emitted per unit area from a surface at temperature T:

$$\Delta\lambda \cdot \epsilon(\lambda, T) = \epsilon_\lambda \frac{C_1}{\lambda^5} \left(\exp\left\{\frac{C_2}{\lambda T}\right\} - 1 \right) \Delta\lambda \tag{4.47}$$

where $\Delta\lambda \cdot \epsilon(\lambda, T)$ = energy emitted per unit area over a fraction of the spectrum defined by λ and $d\lambda$, Watt/cm^2

λ = wavelength of band center, cm

$\Delta\lambda$ = bandwidth, cm

C_1 = Planck's first radiation constant
= 3.74 10^{-12}, watt/cm^2

C_2 = Planck's second radiation constant
= 1.44 cm°K

T = source temperature, K

ϵ_λ = spectral emissivity of the source for wavelength λ.

From the above equation the relationship between the ratio of two narrow bands of emitted radiation and the temperature of the emitter can be easily derived:

$$\frac{I_A}{I_B} = \frac{E_{\lambda A} \quad \Delta\lambda_A}{E_{\lambda B} \quad \Delta\lambda_B} = \frac{\epsilon_A}{\epsilon_B} \frac{\Delta\lambda_A}{\Delta\lambda_B} \frac{\lambda_B{}^5}{\lambda_A{}^5} \frac{\exp \frac{C_2}{\lambda_B T} - 1}{\exp \frac{C_2}{\lambda_A T} - 1} \tag{4.48}$$

For $\frac{C_2}{\lambda T} > 4$, the following mathematical approximation is valid to within 1 per cent:

$$\exp\left(\frac{C_2}{\lambda T}\right) - 1 \simeq \exp\left(\frac{C_2}{\lambda T}\right) \tag{4.49}$$

Substituting into eqn. 4.48 gives

$$\frac{I_A}{I_B} = \frac{\epsilon_A}{\epsilon_B} \frac{\Delta\lambda_A}{\Delta\lambda_B} \frac{\lambda_B{}^5}{\lambda_A{}^5} \exp\left\{\frac{-C_2}{T}\left(\frac{1}{\lambda_A} - \frac{1}{\lambda_B}\right)\right\}$$

defining $C \equiv \frac{\Delta\lambda_A}{\Delta\lambda_B} \frac{\lambda_B{}^5}{\cdot\lambda_A{}^5}$ (detector response and optical correction factors in the detection system)

and R ≡ the ratio of the measured signals:

$$R \equiv C \frac{\epsilon_A}{\epsilon_B} \exp\left\{\frac{C_2}{T}\left(\frac{1}{\lambda_B} - \frac{1}{\lambda_A}\right)\right\}$$

$$\text{or } T = \frac{C_2 \left(\dfrac{1}{\lambda_B} - \dfrac{1}{\lambda_A} \right)}{\ln R - \ln \dfrac{\epsilon_A}{\epsilon_B} - \ln C} \tag{4.50}$$

A two-color pyrometer simply measures *R* and then the above relationship is used to determine the object source temperature.

For selecting the wavebands the choice is inherent in the grey body assumption for determining the temperature from the signal ratios for unknown $\epsilon_{\lambda A}$ and $\epsilon_{\lambda B}$. The assumption that $\epsilon_{\lambda A} = \epsilon_{\lambda B}$ is best for λ_A close to λ_B. Another consideration for obtaining a good correlation between *R* and *T* is that

$$\frac{d\,(E_{\lambda A}(E_{\lambda B})}{dT}$$

should be large and that the selected bands do not overlap the absorption bands of species which might be present in the gases surrounding the burning particles. A final requirement is that $\Delta\lambda$ be small so that eqn. 4.47, on which the correlation between *R* and *T* is based, is valid.

A schematic diagram of the two-color optical pyrometer is shown in Fig. 4.31 in which a fiber optic is used to transmit the light signals from the particles to a filter detector assembly[109]. The interference filters used were centered at $\lambda_A = 0.94\mu m$, $\lambda_B = 0.74\mu m$ bands with $\Delta\lambda_A = \lambda_{\lambda B} \simeq 13.2$ nm. A fast response current amplifier with a high gain (approx. 2×10^8 V/A) was also used to amplify the detector signals. The signal strength from the detectors can be increased by increasing the bandwidth of the two filters. In this case the integrated bands beneath the radiation curve must be used rather than using a point-to-point ratio.

The calibration of the pyrometer is carried out by using a tungsten strip lamp over a range of temperatures. The temperature of the tungsten strip lamp can be determined by using a disappearing filament optical pyrometer in conjunction with the following emissivity correction equation:

$$T_c = \frac{1}{\dfrac{1}{T_m} + \dfrac{\lambda}{C_2} \ln \epsilon_\lambda}$$

where T_m = measured temperature, K

T_C = emissivity corrected temperature, K

λ = wavelength passed by the optical pyrometer filter

ϵ_λ = spectral emissivity of tungsten

Applying the equations below, a value for ln C is determined from calibration measurements.

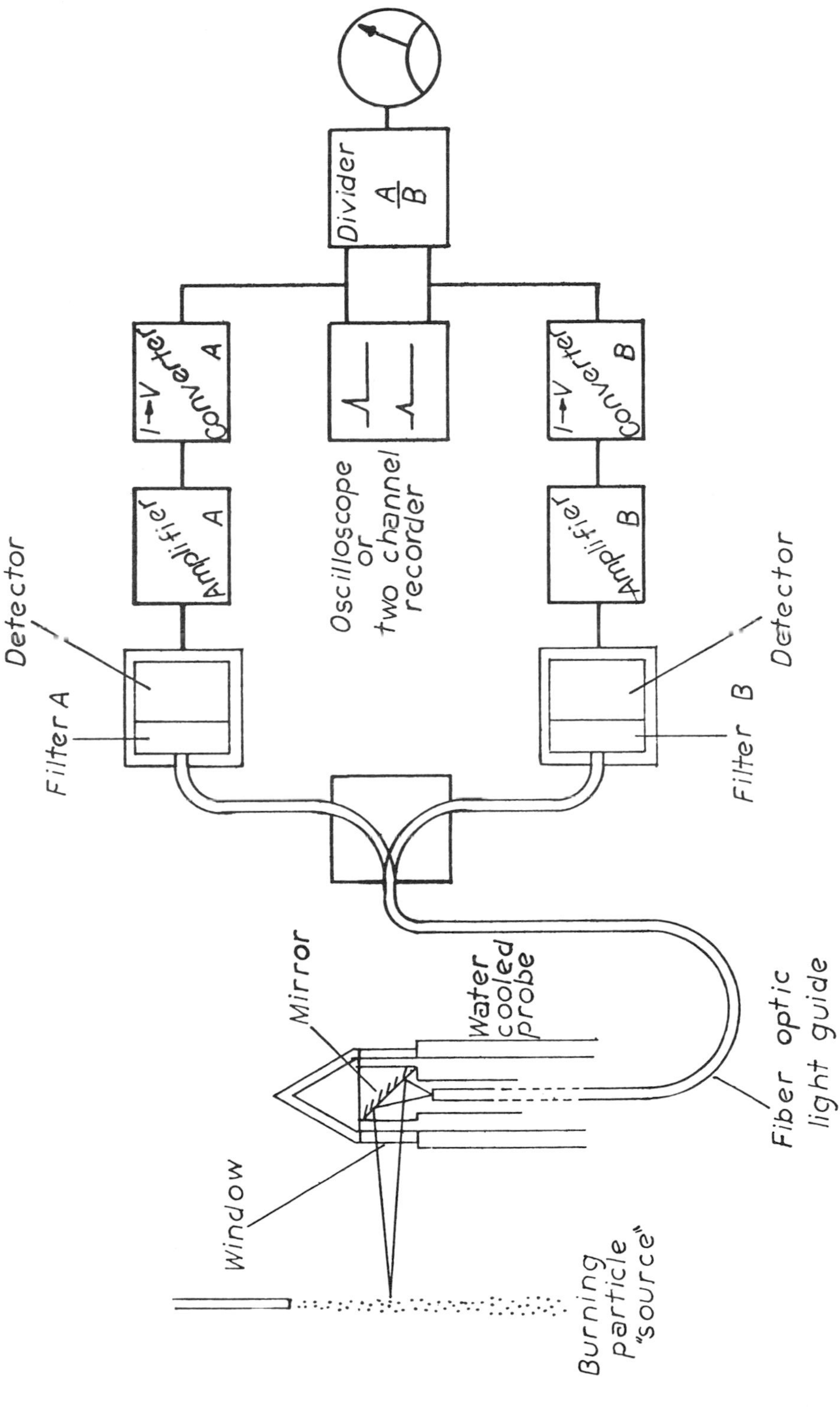

Figure 4.31 Schematic diagram of the two-color optical pyrometer for the burning particle temperature measurement.

$$\left(\ln C + \ln \frac{A}{B}\right) = \frac{-C_2\left(\frac{1}{\lambda_B} - \frac{1}{\lambda_A}\right)}{T_C} + \ln R \qquad (4.51)$$

(from eqn. 4.50)

$$\ln C = \left(\ln C + \ln \frac{\epsilon_A}{\epsilon_B}\right) - \ln \frac{\epsilon_A}{\epsilon_B}$$

where T_C = temperature of the tungsten strip determined from disappearing filament pyrometer measurements, K

$\frac{\epsilon_A}{\epsilon_B}$ = ratio of spectral emissivities for tungsten ($\simeq -0.08$ for temperatures below 1600K)

R = the ratio of the voltage outputs from the two-color pyrometer

The two-color pyrometer described above has been used successfully for measuring burning coal particle temperatures in a laminar flow furnace[109].

Schmidt Method

Gas temperature measurement by optical methods are usually handicapped by the translucent nature of the gas. This problem can be overcome by sighting a radiation pyrometer, for example, a total radiation pyrometer, through the flame of temperature T_f K. Two readings are taken, one with a cold background and the other with a hot background at a known radiating temperature T_B K. If the outputs V_1 and V_2 are proportional to the energy received, then:

$$V_1 = K\epsilon\sigma T_f^4 \qquad (4.52)$$

$$V_2 = K\left[\epsilon\sigma T_f^4 + (1-\epsilon)\sigma T_B^4\right] \qquad (4.53)$$

$$(1-\epsilon) = \frac{1}{K}\,\frac{(V_2 - V_1)}{\sigma T_B^4} \qquad (4.54)$$

(N. B. absorptivity = emissivity)

where K is the calibration constant of the pyrometer.

The flame temperature, T_f, can then be calculated from Eqn. 4.52 by using equation 4.54.

These measurements can be made with a single pyrometer viewing alternately a cold background and a hot furnace (usually a black body furnace) through the flame. In furnaces with brick linings, temperature measurements can be made with a special twin-beam pyrometer with one beam sighted on a hole in the furnace and the second on a hot brick containing a thermocouple. It must be remembered, however, that with this method the temperature value obtained will depend on the absorptivity of the flame when a gradient exists along the line of sight.

The measurement of temperature with Schmidt method is closely allied to effective gas emissivity and can therefore be used for emissivity measurement.

Sodium-Line Reversal Method

The spectrum-line reversal method is often carried out in practice using sodium salt and is very similar in principle to the disappearing filament optical pyrometer. It is well known that when sodium salt is introduced into a flame it emits the two yellow D lines at 5890 and 5896 Å. In addition to this, when light from a bright background source is passed through sodium vapor, these same two lines appear dark, in absorption, against the continuous spectrum from the background. It can be easily shown using Kirchhoff's law that when light from a bright background source giving a continuous spectrum is passed through a flame containing sodium vapor, the sodium lines will appear either in absorption, as dark lines against the continuum, depending upon whether the brightness temperature of the background source is higher or lower than the flame temperature. When the brightness temperature of the background exactly equals the flame temperature then the lines become invisible and have the same brightness as the background. The flame temperature can be determined by varying the background lamp temperature until the sodium D line becomes indistinguishable from the background. Background lamp temperature can be measured with an optical pyrometer. Tungsten lamps can be used as a background source up to 2800°K and special xenon lamps are used up to a brightness temperature of 5000°K. Unfortunately, the signal is non-linearly integrated along the line of sight, however, the result is close to the maximum temperature in the beam path. This method has been described and used, with small modifications, by a number of authors[92, 110-112].

In operation, the light from either a tungsten lamp or a xenon lamp, is focused with a lens L_1 to give an image of the lamp in the flame F. A second lens L_2 placed at some distance from the flame forms an image of both the flame and lamp at S, Fig. 4.32. A field stop aperture A is placed between L_2 and S to restrict the aperture so that the solid angle of light taken from the flame is the same as that from the image of the lamp; the correct position for this aperture stop is at the position of the image of the lens L_1 formed by L_2. In practice, however, the aperture is placed close to the lens L_2.

Both the lenses used should be of good quality so as to give a good image of the background source on S. Poor quality lens or poor focusing will tend to weaken the image of the small background source more than that of the larger flame, and thus will require a higher intensity background source for the reversal. It is also important that the system is completely lined up. The lens L_1 should be a single biconvex or plano-convex lens; complex lenses; for example achromats, triple aplanat are not recommended.

Line Intensity and Profile Methods

Further spectrographic methods which do not require other sources are often used in the general area of high temperature devices, for example, MHD combustors, plasma arcs, etc. Both the intensity of individual emission lines and the width (or shape) of these lines can be used for measuring the temperature. This is a rather specialized field of temperature measurement and is described at length in a recent text[113].

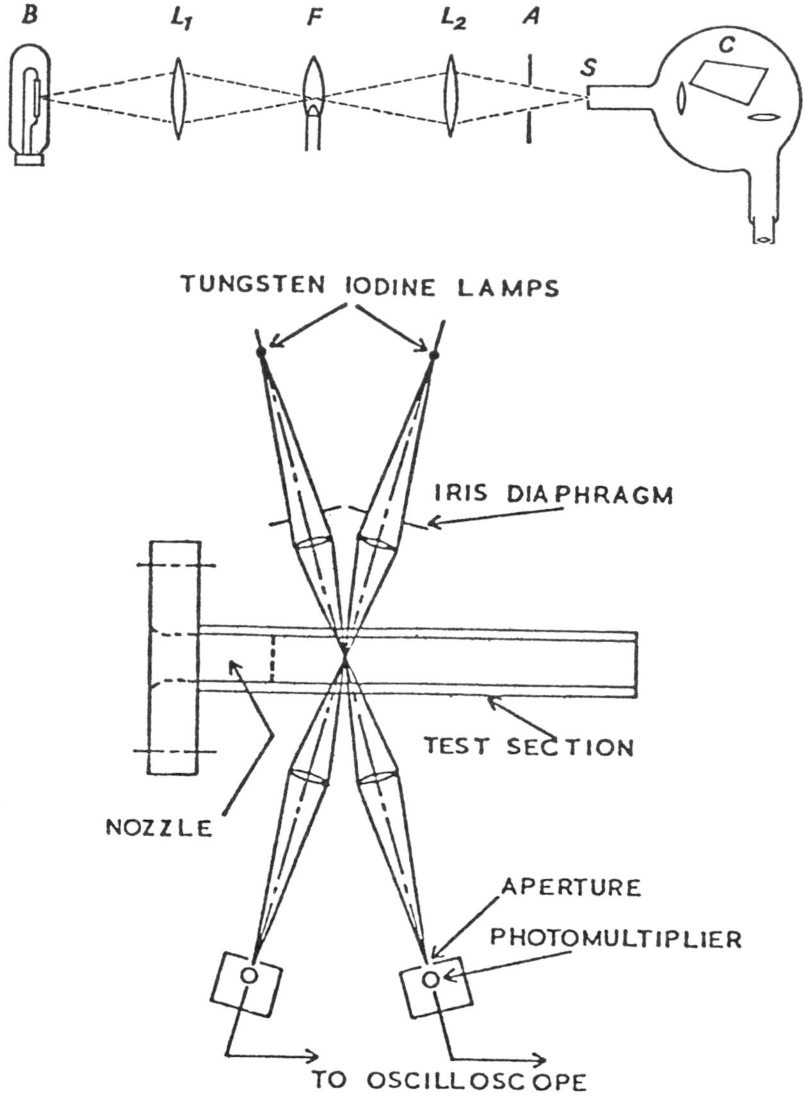

Figure 4.32 Top diagram: Sodium line reversal method for temperature measurement. Bottom diagram: double sodium line reversal apparatus.

A useful survey of the subject is contained in a Review No. 243 published as a monthly bulletin by the British Coal Utilization Research Association (BCURA).

Temperatures Derived From Gas Density Gradient Measurements

In this method, mean temperatures within a hot gas are determined by optical methods; for example, first derivative by schlieren and the second derivative by shadowgraph.

Strictly speaking the schlieren system measures $d\rho/dz$, shadowgraph measures $d^2\rho/dz^2$, and the Mach-Zehnder interferometer measures absolute changes in gas density. Most optical studies of flame structure have used some variant of schlieren system[114-126].

During the past decade, a range of interferometers based on schlieren system has come into use[114-127]. There are at least three important advantages in basing an interferometer on a schlieren system. The first is the availability of a large test section as compared with most existing interferometers. Secondly, the adjustment of these interferometers is in general fairly simple. This is because they operate by splitting the beam at or near the focus of a schlieren mirror with the focal length of the order of several meters. Lastly, these tend to be inexpensive because the laboratories in which they are most useful are normally equipped with the required schlieren mirrors and also because the beam splitters are used over such a small area that their optical quality is not very important. An additional advantage of using a laser in the interferometric system is that one can have a relatively large angle between the beams at the splitter; the resultant fine-fringe interferogram can be used subtractively by a double exposure method. This yields an infinite fringe interferogram which automatically subtracts the aberrations of the optical system and imperfections in any windows surrounding the test section. This property of subtraction has been utilized in the elimination of end effects where the extremities of hot medium interface with cold air. This method has many advantages and applications in particular when applied to combustion and heat transfer studies.

Interferometry of phase object requires at least one of the two interfering beams to have passed through the phase object. The resultant intensity distribution, $I\ (x, y, z)$, of two interfering beams I_1 and I_2 focused at a recording plane (that is, fixed value of x) is given by[114].

$$I(y,z) = I_1 + I_2 + 2\,(I_1 I_2)^{1/2} \cos\phi\,(y,z) \tag{4.55}$$

The significance of focusing the test object on to the recording plane is that I_1 and I_2 become independent of $(y,\ z)$ and the resultant intensity distribution is a function of the phase difference, ϕ, only. Here x, y, z represent rectangular coordinates. $\phi(y,z)$ can be expressed as follows:

$\phi\,(y, z)$ = (phase difference between the beams due to their passage through regions of unknown, varying refractive index) + (phase difference arising from geometrical path difference) + (phase difference created by abberations in the optical systems).

or
$$\phi\,(y,z) = \phi_{p_1}(y, z) - \phi_{p_2}(y, z) + \phi_{g_1}(y,z) - \phi_{g_2}(y,z) + \phi_{a_2}(y, z) - \phi_{a_2}(y,z) \tag{4.56}$$

ϕ is obtained by the line integral along the path of the ray, that is,

$$\phi_p\,(y,z) = k \int_{\text{ray}} n\ (x, y, z)\,dl$$

where $k = 2\pi/\lambda_o$, $n(x, y, z)$ is the refractive index distribution within the region of interest, dl is a distance along the ray and λ_o is the wavelength of the transluminating (laser) beam. For small deflections $d\ell \simeq dx$ so that

$$\phi_p(y,z) = k\int_0^X n(x,y,z)\,dx$$

where X is the geometric path length through the test space. The absolute phase distribution in the test space relative to some reference medium is given by

$$\phi_{p_1}(y,z) - \phi_{p_2}(y,z) = k\left[\int_0^x n_{p_1}(x,y,z)\,dx - n_o X\right] \qquad (4.57)$$

where $n_{p_1}(x, y, z)$ is the refractive index distribution within the test region, and n_o is the refractive index of the reference space. The two interfering beams may be inclined to each other and to the recording plane as shown in Fig. 4.33. Nevertheless, it is convenient to make the angles of incidence, i_1 and i_2, equal so that the scales of the two projected images are the same. For sufficiently small angles of incidence both the images are in reasonably good focus over the whole of the recording plane. As a consequence of this the phase distributions in the recording plane can then be related directly to the refractive index distributions in the test object space. The overlap between the two images is referred to as 'shear' and its amount determines whether the interferometer is utilized in a differential or absolute capacity. A small shear results in a differential interferogram. The theory concerning this will not be described here and may be found in Gupta and Rossi[127], and Jones *et al*[116]. In absolute interferometry, a ray passing through a phase object interferes with one that by-passes it. For this case, the phase difference is given by

$$\phi(y,z) = kX\left[n_p(y,z) - n_o\right] + k\,2n_o Y_i + \phi_{a_1}(y,z) - \phi_{a_2}(y,z) \qquad (4.57)$$

where $n_p(y, z) = \frac{1}{X}\int^X n_{p_1}(x,y,z)\,dx$, and Y_i is the lateral displacement between the two images. In terms of fringe order number distribution, $P(y,z)$, above eqn. 4.57 becomes

$$P(y,z)\lambda_o = X\left[\bar{n}_p(y,z) - n_o\right] + 2n_o Y_i + P_{a_1}(y,z) - P_{a_2}(y,z) \qquad (4.58)$$

It is clear from the above equation for the order number distributions that the position of the resulting fringes depends on the aberrations of the system as well as on its geometry and the nature of the phase object being studied. The effect of residual fringes can be eliminated by using double exposure technique. The principle is to record on the same photographic plate two interferograms (with and without the phase object). If $P(y, z)$ and $P_o(y,z)$ are the recorded fringe order number distributions for these two exposures respectively, the order number distribution, $P(y,z)$ of the resulting Moire pattern is given by

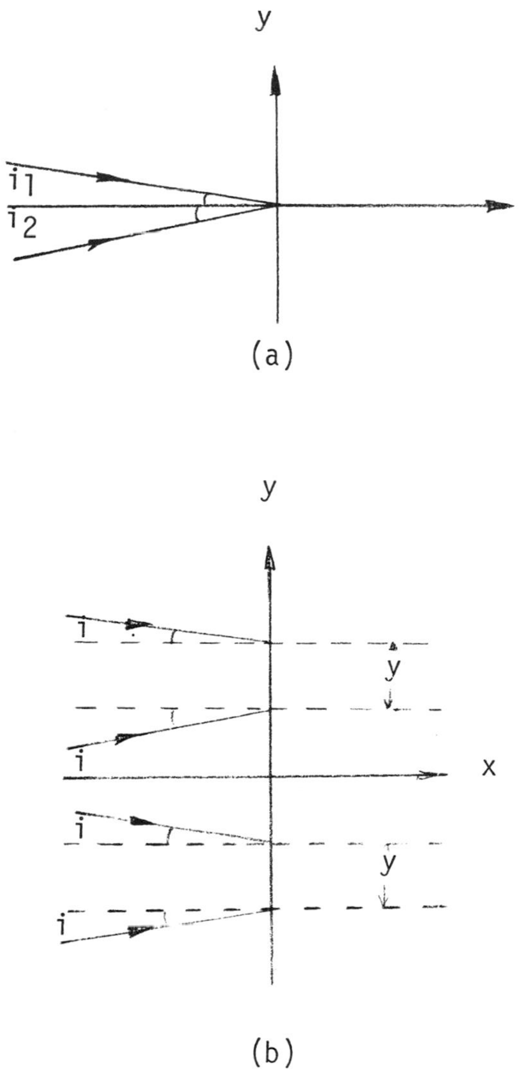

Figure: 4.33 A schematic representation of the two interfering beams inclined to each other (upper) and to the recording plane (lower).[125]

$$P(y, z) = P(y, z) - P_o(y, z) \ .$$

When this equation is applied to the case described by eqn. 4.58, the resultant distribution represents the so-called 'infinite fringe' absolute interferogram, that is,

$$P(y, z)\,\lambda_o = X\left[\bar{n}_p(y, z) - n_o\right] \qquad (4.59)$$

Two optical systems successfully used by employing either a holographic grating[127] or a small angled prism[124] are shown in Figures 4.34(a) and 4.34(b) respectively.

One half of the collimated beam from the first mirror M_1 acts as the 'object beam' and the other half as the 'reference beam'. On subsequent reduction of the cross-section the beam is split by employing either a holographic grating (Fig. 4.34(a)) or a small angled (less than about 2°) prism (Fig. 4.34 (b)). The two beams (±1 orders for grating or front and first rear surface reflected beam for the case of prism) are made to interfere at the position of the recording plane. Two exposures, with and without the test object (for example, flame, burning droplet, hot surface, etc.), are recorded on the photographic plate; each exposure producing an interference pattern. Many different types of photographic plates are available, depending upon the application for which it is to be used (for example, Kodak 649-F, SO-173, SO-253, SO-115, 2479, 2475 or 2485). For many applications SO-115 is found to be quite suitable which has a resolving power of 320 lines/mm and an energy exposure requirement of 0.3 ergs/cm^2 for He-Ne laser light source with λ_o = 632.8nm. Details of the various types of plates and films for use with different laser light sources are given in Table 4.7. A fine fringe interferogram is obtained after processing the photographic plate. The processed plate is placed in the laser beam to obtain the resultant interference pattern due to the phase object only. The optical system shown in Fig. 4.35 can be used to reconstruct the interferogram. The plate is illuminated with the laser light having the same wave length as that used during the original recording. One of the ±1 orders is allowed to pass through the stop and the interferogram is recorded on a photographic plate, Fig. 4.35. The resultant interferogram can be translated into the corresponding refractive index (or mean temperature) distribution.

The holographic grating used in Fig. 4.34(a) acts as a beam splitter by the use of the principle of diffraction. The grating, which is most conveniently made as a hologram of a plane wavefront by using a second inclined plane wavefront as a reference beam, produces overlapping focused images on the receptor (a photographic plate). The irregularities present in mechanically ruled gratings make them unsatisfactory for use with laser light as they introduce an unacceptable amount of speckle in the image plane[118]. The ± orders produced by the holographic grating are of equal intensity which is a requirement to maximize fringe legibility in the interference pattern obtained by two beams. The small angled prism, which is partially reflecting on the front and fully on the rear surface, provides one beam reflected from the front surface and one (or more than one) beam from the rear surface. The transmitted part of the beam incident on the front surface of the prism undergoes reflection and partial transmission alternately on the back and front surface, resulting in first rear surface reflected beam. In the same way the second reflected beam is produced. The intensity of the successive reflections decreases. Nevertheless, it is found that only the first two of the reflected beams are visible[124]. The intensity of one beam is comparable to that reflected from the front surface; these two are used as interfering beams.

Figure 4.34(a) shows that the separation of the adjacent images is equal to $Ma\Psi$, where M is the magnification produced by the final imaging lens and Ψ is the angular separation of the diffraction orders. By blocking off all the diffraction orders except ±1, by using slit S, the shear or lateral displacement, Y_i (=$2Ma\Psi$), of the two remaining images can be controlled. $2Ma\Psi$ represents the shear of the two interfering beams in the recording plane. Y_i is also equal to mY_o, where m is the overall magnification of the

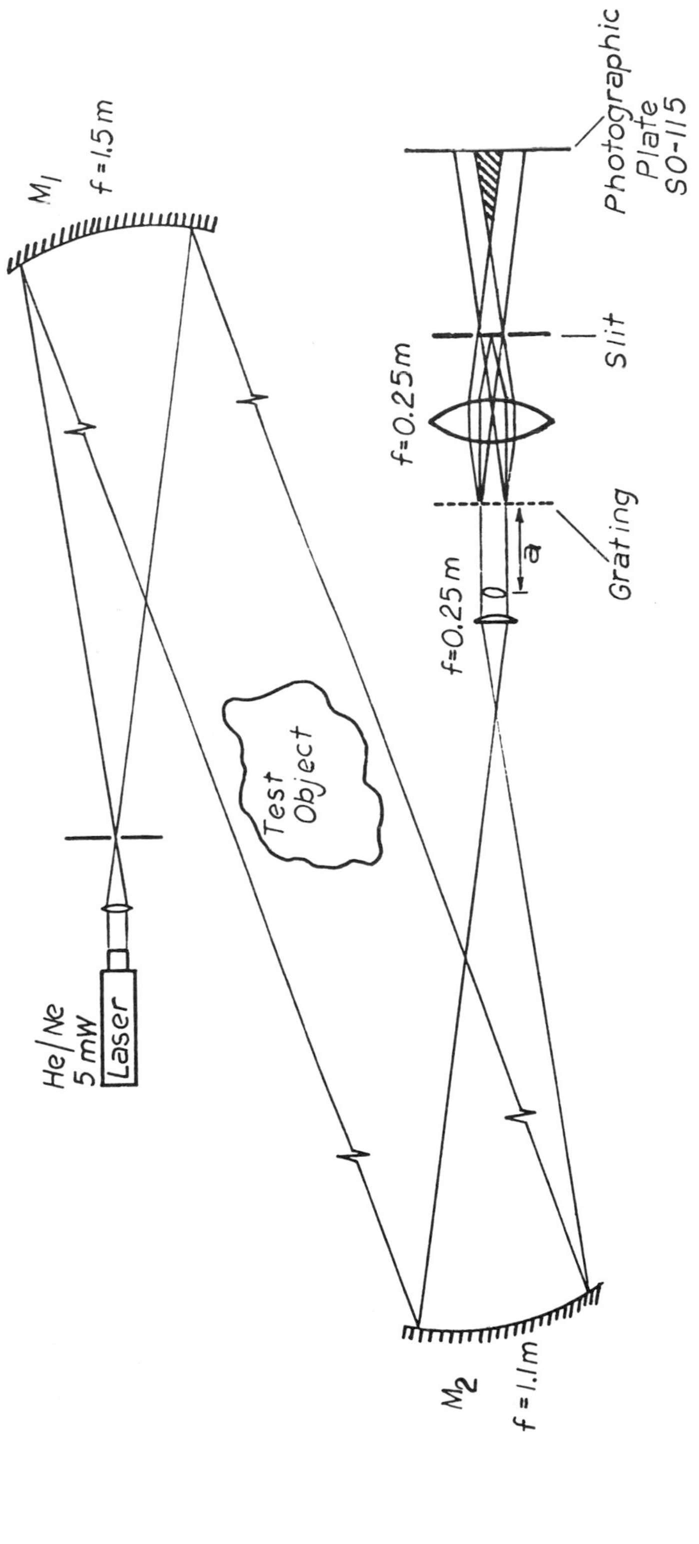

Figure 4.34(a) A schematic diagram of the laser Schlieren interferometric system using a holographic grating as the beam splitter[127]

TABLE 4.7

Holographic and Photographic Films and Plates

Kodak	Exposure to Achieve D = 1.0 (ergs/cm^2) HeCd 325	HeCd 442	Ar 448	Ar 515	Nd:YAG 532	HeNe 633	Kr 647	Ruby 694	Resolving Power 1000:1	@ TOC 1.6:1	Granularity @ D = 1.0 48 μm	6 μm	Contrast γ	Emulsion Thickness (μm)		Standard Base	Development
High Resolution Plate, Type 1A	(400)	1000	1500	1000	800	–	–	–	2000+		<5	<10	8	6	No	.060 BKD	6-8′ HRP/D-19
High Resolution Film, SO-343									2000+		<5	<10		7	No	E7B	6-8′ D-19
Spectroscopic Film, Type 649-GH									2000+		<5	<10		7	No	E4AH	6-8′ D-19
High Resolution Plate, Type 2A	(1000)	3000	2500	2000	2000	–	–		2000+		<5	<10	5	6	No	.060 UNB	6-8′ FRP/D-19
									2000+		<5	<10	5	17	No	.040 UNB	6-8′ D-19
Spectroscopic Plate, Type 649-F		500	800	800	1000	900			2000+		<5	<10	4	6	No	E4AH	6-8′ D-19
Spectroscopic Film, Type 649-F									2000+		<5	<10	5	5	No	.040 UNB	6-8′ D-19
Holographic Plate, Type 120-02							400	400	2000+		<5	<10	4	6	No	E4B	6-8′ D-19
Holographic Film, SO-173														7	No	.040 UNB	6-8′ D-19
Special Plate, Type 125-02							–	–	1250	630	<5	13	4	<3	Yes	A5CB	6-8′ D-19
MINICARD II Film, SO-424														9	No	.040 UNB	6-8′ D-19
H. S. Holographic Plate, Type 131-02		20/35	40/65	25/35	20/30	5/8	3.5/6	1000+	1250	800	<5	14	7	9	No	E4B	6-8′ D-19
High Speed Holographic Film, SO-253																	
Direct Positive Laser	–	35	35	55	75	30	50	–	1250	630	<5	14	−2	<4	Yes	A5C	5′ D-19
Recording Film, SO-285																	
RECORDAK Direct Duplicating	5	100	100	50	40	–	–	–	1000	400	5	17	-1.9	3	No	A5C, A7C	5′ D-19
Print Film, 5468, 8478																	
High Definition Aerial Film, 3414	0.4	0.6	3	2	2–	2	2–	5	630	250	9	33	0.8-2.4	<4	No	E2.5 B	D-19, D-76
High Contrast Copy Film, 5069	0.4	1	4	2	1	6	–	–	630	200	9	43	1.0-2.8	<4	Yes	A5C	D-19, D-76
Technical Pan Film, SO-115	0.25	0.35	0.6	0.6	0.55	0.3	0.3	1.6	–	–	–	–	4			E4AH	4′ D-19
	0.4	0.45	0.8	0.8	0.7	0.35	0.3	2	320	125	8	–	1-3	7.5	No		8′ HC-110 (D)
LINAGRAPH SHELLBURST Film, 2474	0.15	0.09	0.3	0.3	0.2	0.15	0.15	2	125	50	24	–	0.5-2	–		E4B	D-19, D-76
LINAGRAPH SHELLBURST Film, 2476	0.15	0.09	0.3	0.3	0.2	0.15	0.15	5	160	63	22		0.5-2	–	Yes	E4AH	D-19, D-76
2479 RAR Film	0.1	0.05	0.2	0.3	0.2	0.08	0.08	0.5	100	40	24	–	0.6-1.8	–	Yes	E4AH	D-19, D-76
2475 Recording Film	0.07	0.03	0.06	0.07	0.06	0.05	0.05	0.05	63	22	32	–	0.4-2	–	No	E4AH	D-19, DK-50
2485 High Speed Recording Film	0.03	0.007	0.04	0.05	0.04	0.03	0.03	0.04	50	20	47	–	0.9-1.8	–	No	E4AH	857, D-19
Agfa-Gevaert																	
10 E56 Plate/Film		60	30	20	20				1500+				7	7/5	No	0.050/A5	5′, D-19
8 E75 Plates		150	1500	250	250	75	75	50	2000+				3	7	No	0.050	5′, D-19
10 E75 Plates/Film		60	300	120	60	20	20	20	1500+				4	7/5	No	0.050/A5	5′, D-19

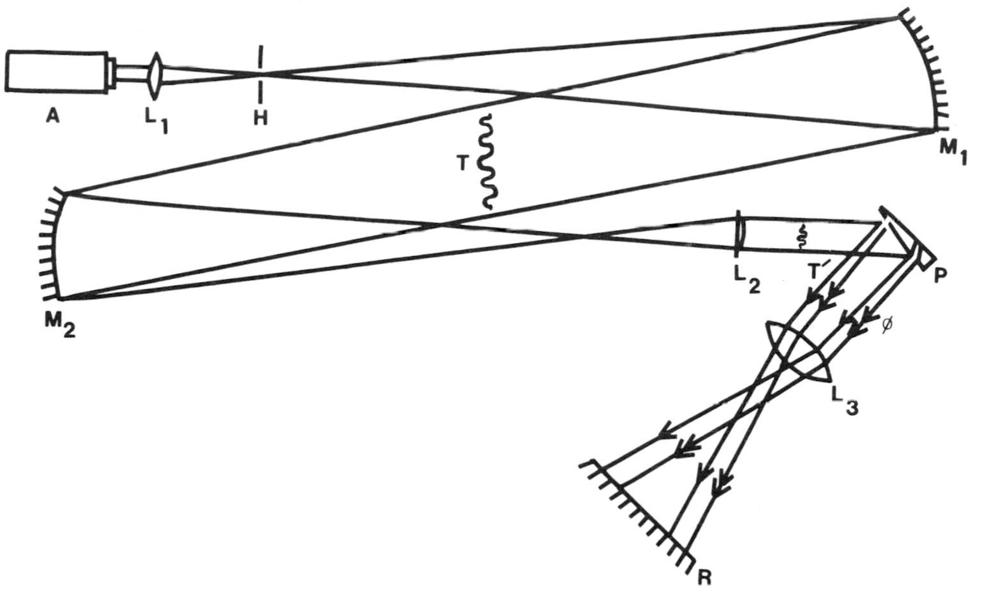

Figure 4.34(b) A schematic diagram of the laser Schlieren interferometric system using a small angled prism as the beam splitter.[124]

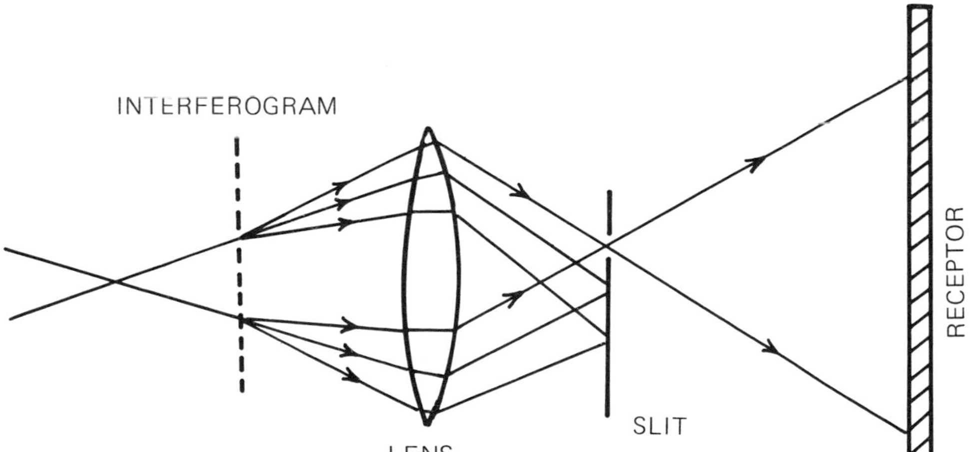

Figure 4.35 Reconstruction system for the interferogram[124, 127]

optical system. Y_o can be varied by altering *M, a* or Ψ. In practice, the simplest variable is *a*.

Fringe spacing between the two interfering beams in the absence of a test object is equal to $\frac{\lambda_0 M}{2\psi}$. This should be smaller than the smallest distance in the image that is to be resolved. Another requirement that must be satisfied is that ψ must be greater than $2\Theta_{max}$[118], where Θ_{max} is the maximum ray deflection by the phase object in the *y* direction. By arranging for the width of the test object to be less than half of the available mirror aperture and if w_i is the width of each of the beams at the receptor, absolute interferometry requires that $Y_i \simeq \frac{1}{2} w_i$. When the shear, Y_i, is made so large that $Y_i > w_i$ the two beams are completely separated. When differential interferometry is desired, Y_i should be made smaller than w_i. If the resulting interferogram is to be interpreted in terms of ray deflections then the shear should be infinitesimally small.

In the laser schlieren interferometry it is important that the collimated light from the second mirror should be brought to a point focus. Failure to do this results in optical obscuration. Distortion in the image occurs by the adaptation of large angles between the collimated light and the incident light and/or reflected light, or also by the use of small focal length mirrors. This effect is often referred to as 'vignette' and it is vital that it should be considered prior to any experimental set-up.

Figure 4.36 shows some magnified reconstructed interferograms obtained by using the optical arrangements shown in Figs. 4.34(a) and 4.35. The corresponding temperature distribution of an interferogram in Fig. 4.36 is shown in Fig. 4.37.

The apparatus in Figs. 4.34(a) and 4.34(b) can briefly be compared as follows:

(a) In Fig. 4.34(a) the test space remains conjugate with the receptor irrespective of '*a*' whereas it goes out of focus with a change in '*a*' in Fig. 4.34(b).

(b) Shear from complete overlapping to complete separation could be achieved by using a grating whereas in the case of a prism there would be a limit set to the minimum shear by the finite thickness of the prism. For this reason truly infinitesimal differential interferograms cannot be obtained in this system.

(c) The illumination obtained with the prism interferometer is about fifteen times that of the grating interferometer by comparison of the two exposure times.

Other Potential Methods of Temperature Measurement

Other gas temperature measuring devices, such as laser Raman, can indicate either mean gas temperature or local temperatures in regions of the order of 100μm dimensions. Unfortunately, the associated optical components are very expensive and they are not yet widely available for practical purposes. This technique has, as yet, not been developed to the extent that it can be applied to complex and swirling flames of large size. The attraction of this method is due to its high frequency capability and high spatial resolution which can help to resolve many fundamental problems.

The Raman effect results in a scattered spectrum on both the low frequency side (Stokes lines) and the high frequency side (anti-Stokes lines of the incident laser frequency). Both pure rotational spectra and vibration-rotation spectra occur shifted by frequencies corresponding to characteristic molecular energy level differences. The former lie very close to the laser line and overlap the Rayleigh scattered spectrum, but

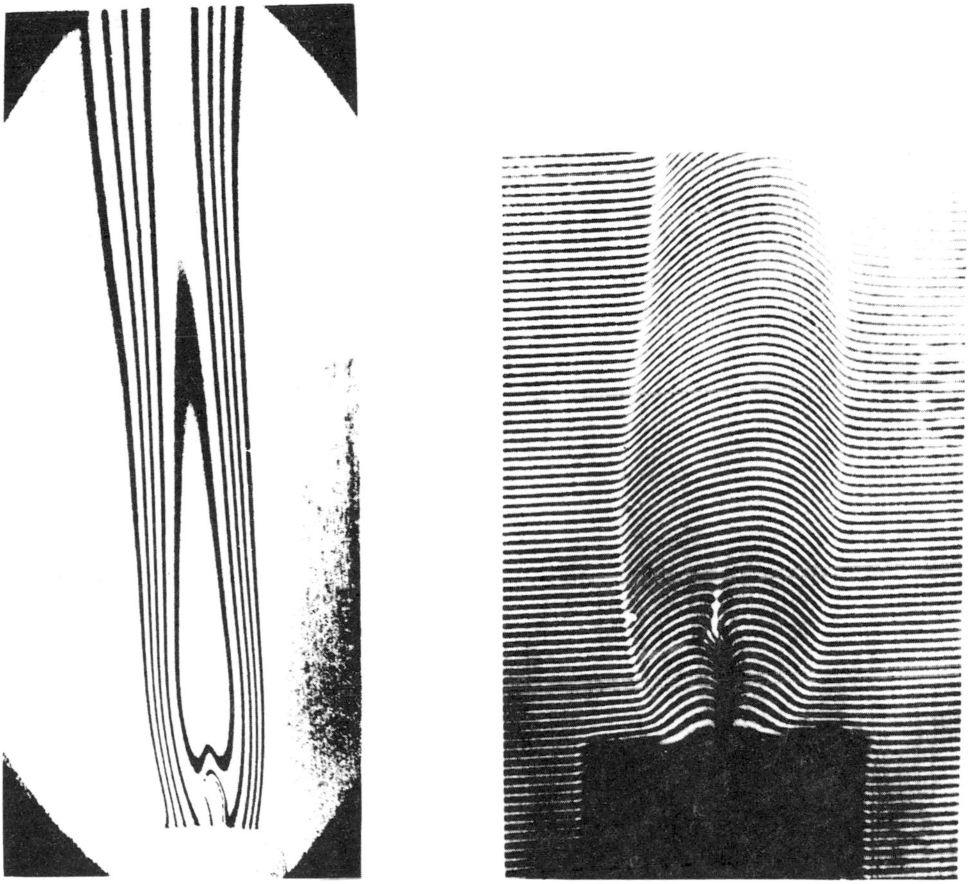

Figure 4.36 (a) Reconstructed interferograms of a candle flame in the infinite fringe absolute mode (left diagram) and finite fringe absolute mode (right diagram[127].

the latter exhibit large shifts (up to $\simeq$ 1000Å in the visible) and are particularly suitable for temperature measurements in hot gases and flames. In the past several years considerable effort has been applied by several groups[128,131] to develop laser Raman scattering as a technique for point measurements of temperature (and species concentrations) in gases, including flames. Temperature measurement is less difficult than species concentration, especially for minority species, since it is a relative measurement and can be made on a suitable majority species; for example, N_2 in combustion with air. The temperature can be determined from the distribution of populations in the vibrational levels of either the Stokes or anti-Stokes spectra or from the ratio of corresponding lines in the two. While the anti-Stokes lines are weaker, they have the advantage of being free from interference due to fluorescence.

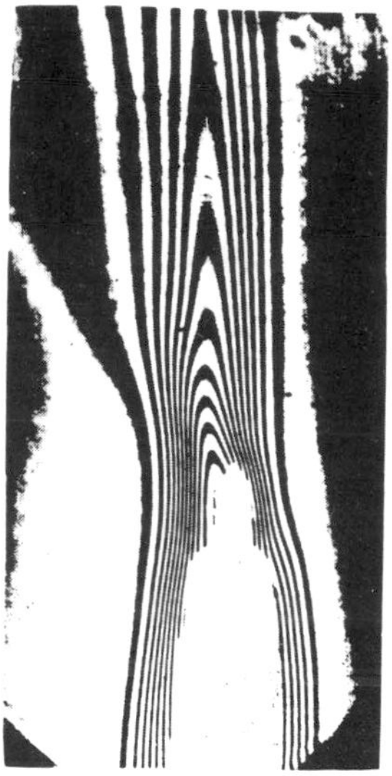

Figure 4.36 (b) Reconstructed interferogram of a soldering iron in the infinite fringe absolute mode[127]

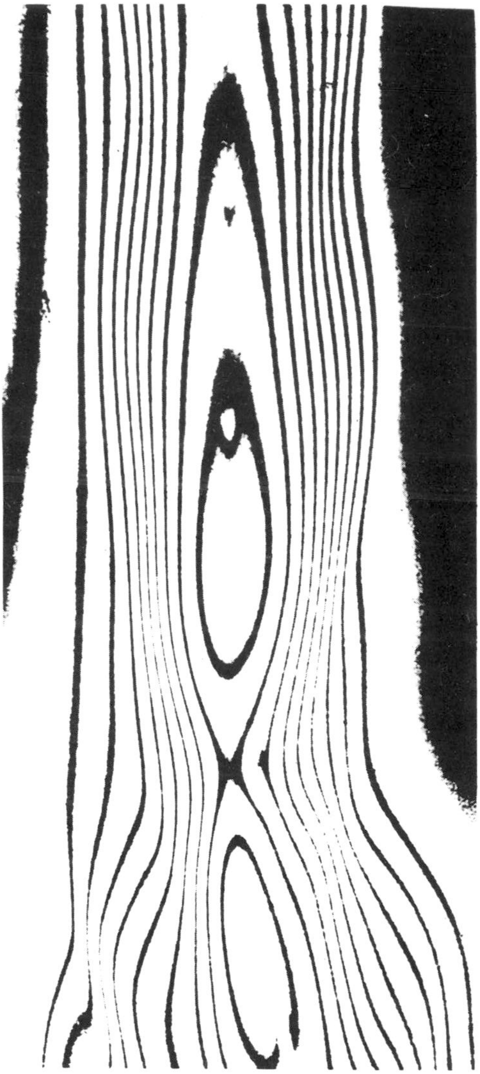

Figure 4.36 (c) Reconstructed interferogram of a burning droplet train in the infinite fringe absolute mode.[127]

Two basic types of laser Raman systems have been employed, using continuous and pulsed lasers respectively. In the first, a CW laser, usually an Argon laser at the level of several watts, is used and the effective power is commonly enhanced a factor of 10-100 by multiple-passing using a mirror cavity. With this method, the integration time necessary to obtain good data effectively limits the measurements to mean temperature values.

In the pulsed method, a high-power pulsed laser, for example, ruby- or flash lamp-pumped dye laser is used. The pulse length is short compared with typical temperature fluctuation times and the power high enough to determine the temperature on a single pulse by using a polychromator. Such high power lasers, however, have low repetition

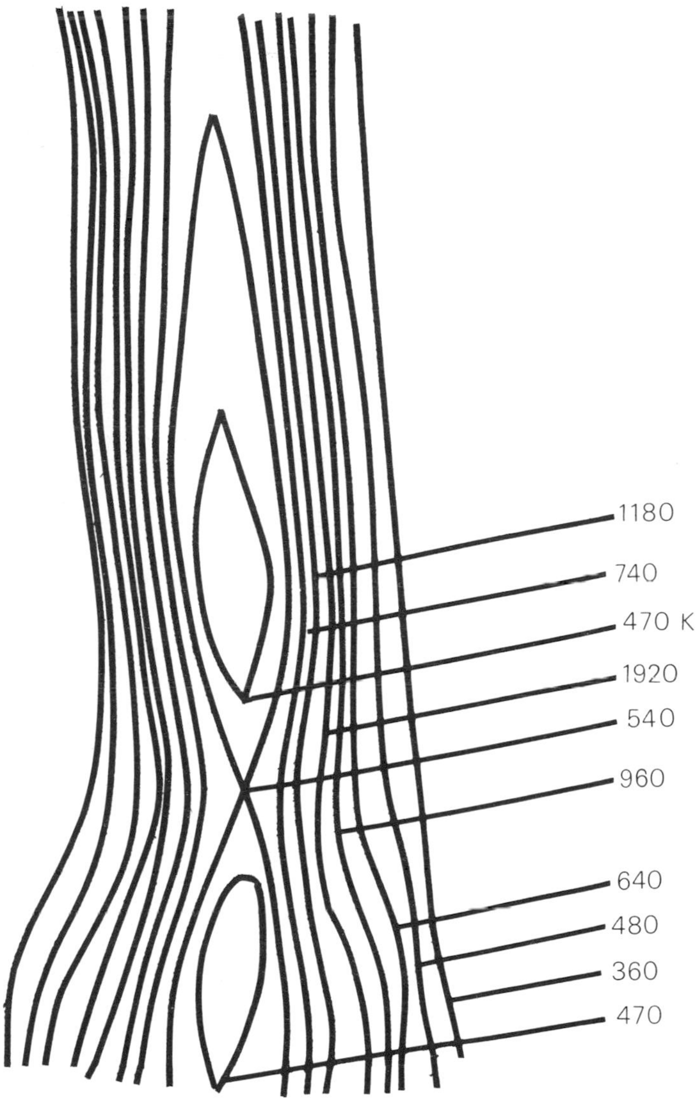

Figure 4.37 Temperature distribution derived from the burning kerosene droplet train interferogram in Fig. 4.36 (c).[127]

rates, usually no more than a few per second, so that many pulses are required to determine the mean temperature and RMS fluctuation. Without some further significant advance it seems unlikely that time resolution on the scale of the turbulent fluctuations is possible.

Laser fluorescence also offers the possibilities of determining temperature (and species concentrations). This method is a resonant process and has very much larger cross-sections[132, 133]. The basic idea is to pump a suitable absorption line with a tunable laser, and detect the side-scattered radiation either at the same wavelength or, preferably, to facilitate spectral filtering of elastically scattered light, at a different wavelength corresponding to some other allowed decay transition from the upper level of the pumped transition. If the lower level of the absorption line is itself an excited level, for example, potassium 4P, the fluorescence signal will be exponentially dependent on temperature through the Boltzman relation. Since the induced fluorescence signal must be detected against the background, spontaneous emission from the same line, a modulated CW laser or pulsed laser is used with suitable electronics to subtract the background. In practice, since there are strong collisional quenching processes competing with the radiative decay to maintain the original Boltzman distribution of levels, it appears that to obtain sufficient signals the pumped transition must be strongly pumped—even saturated. For relative temperature measurements, the relative intensity should be approximately independent of the quenching cross-section, as long as its temperature dependence is weak in comparison with that of the Boltzman factor of the lower level for absorption. Alternatively, it may be possible to pump two transitions having the same upper level and compare the fluorescence on the same wavelength.

The coherent anti-Stokes Raman scattering (CARS) is a coherent, resonant, four-wave parametric interaction, or four-wave mixing process[134]. The CARS may be qualitatively described as a process by which a photon interacts with a tunable photon (Stokes photon of the given specie of interest) through the third order nonlinear susceptibility to generate a polarization component of the anti-Stokes frequency. In this method the gas is illuminated with a high power pulsed laser beam (the pump) at frequency ν_1 and simultaneously and colinearly with a lower power tunable laser at frequency ν_2. When the latter is tuned to a Stokes line, so that $\nu_1 - \nu_2 = \nu_R$, the vibrational frequency of a Raman mode, the Stokes radiation is parametrically amplified and simultaneously, anti-Stokes radiation at $\nu_3 = \nu_1 + \nu_R$ is generated coherently. Compared with ordinary incoherent Raman scattering there are two principal advantages. First, the anti-Stokes signal is emitted as a diffraction-limited coherent beam all of which can be collected, rather than being distributed over 4π steradians, and allows much greater rejection of background radiation by spatial filtering. Second, the total signal is proportional to the square of the population density and on majority species is therefore much larger than for incoherent Raman. For temperature the relative strengths of two or more anti-Stokes lines on a suitable majority species (for example, N_2) measures the relative populations in the associated vibrational levels, and hence the temperature. Signal enhancements of 10^6 or more relative to incoherent Raman scattering are possible, allowing temperature measurements to be made in a single pulse if the bandwidth of the tunable laser (ν_2) is broad enough to encompass at least two Raman modes. Nevertheless, as in incoherent Raman scattering using pulsed lasers, the repetition rate is low compared with the fluctuation frequencies of interest, only the time-average temperature and fluctuation amplitude can be obtained. The anti-Stokes signal beam appears in the forward direction, in the same solid angle as the pump and tunable laser beams from which it must be separated by heavy spectral filtering. Furthermore, unlike the incoherent Raman method, where three-dimensional resolution is obtained by the use of side scatter, such resolution must be obtained by focusing the incident beams to form an elongated control volume.

In summary, CARS shows promise as offering a more sensitive method for temperature measurement in hot gases, which may be less susceptible to interference due to fluorescence and particulates. This is a currently active research area, and further results in combustion flows reveals that it is indeed a viable technique for its application in high intensity combustors.[130]

4.3 PRESSURE

Pressure, defined as force per unit area, is normally expressed in terms of familiar units of weight-force and area or the height of a column of liquid. Pressure measuring devices may be classified into three groups: (1) those based on measurement of the height of a liquid column, (2) those based on measurement of the distortion of an elastic pressure chamber, and (3) electrical sensing devices.

Liquid-column pressure-measuring devices are those in which the pressure being measured is balanced against the pressure exerted by a column of liquid. If the density of the liquid is known, the height of the liquid column yields the pressure. Most forms of liquid column pressure-measuring devices are often called manometers.

Elastic-element pressure-measuring devices are those in which the measured pressure deforms some elastic (metallic) material within its elastic limit; the magnitude of the deformation is approximately proportional to the applied pressure.

When a wire or other electrical conductor is stretched elastically, its length is increased and its diameter is decreased. Both of these dimensional changes result in an increase in the electrical resistance of the conductor. Devices utilizing resistance-wire grids for measuring small distortions in elastically stressed materials are called strain gauges. Strain gauges are available in two basic forms: bonded and unbonded.

Pressure transducers are usually based on a thin cylinder or diaphragm which is fitted with bonded or unbonded strain gauges. The resonant frequency of such systems is typically a few kilohertz. Nevertheless, due to the temperature sensitivity of the strain gauges, the transducer must be thermally isolated from a combustion environment, and the overall frequency response is generally governed by the coupling technique.

The simplest technique is to mount the transducer on a short swan neck coupling pipe (to isolate it from vibration) then fill the transducer and pipe with oil, sealed in by a short plug of petroleum jelly. This method is frequently used on rocket motors where a response up to 100 Hz is necessary to monitor mean chamber pressure for test duration of several seconds.

When gas coupling is used, the transducer may be mounted at the end of a long tube to isolate it from the heat. At first sight the long neck and chamber volume may be thought to form a Helmholtz resonator whose frequency is given by:

$$f_h = \frac{c_t}{2\pi}\left(\frac{A_t}{V_c\,\ell_{eff}}\right)^{1/2} \tag{4.60}$$

where c_t = sound speed in the tube (i.e. at tube temp.)

A_t = tube area

ℓ_{eff} = effective tube length

V_c = transducer chamber volume

In practice, the viscous damping is usually so large that the model must be modified; however, the important factor is to reduce the chamber volume as far as possible. This may often be accomplished by temporarily fitting a thin piece of cellulose tape to the diaphragm surface, then adjusting the transducer mounting shims until the transducer just bottoms, and finally removing the tape. In this way a transducer volume of the order of a few mm^3 can be achieved. For tubing of 1m length, a frequency response of up to about 100Hz may be obtained (i.e. close to the 1/4 wave frequency $f = c/4\ell$). This response is often sufficient for high speed pitot traverses, scanning valves, etc. but is inadequate for studying phenomena such as combustion instability which occur throughout the audio range and beyond. The common answer is to increase the sound speed in the pipe by using a small helium bleed, and shorten the pipe to the limit of a few mm. Frequency response extending beyond 20kHz can then be achieved by using a very high frequency transducer such as a quartz (or other piezo-electric crystal).

One alternative solution that is often used satisfactorily in combustion systems is the water-cooled diaphragm transducer. A thin water-cooled diaphragm is exposed to the hot gas and the pressure is transmitted mechanically to a protected cool diaphragm within the body of the instrument. Clean filtered water must be used, and in common with all other close coupled systems, care must be taken to check for vibration sensitivity of the transducer. Resilient mountings may often be made from 0-rings or by potting an air-curing rubber.

In many cases the phase of the signal is important in the interpretation of oscillatory combustion phenomena, and determination of the overall instrument transfer function can be achieved with a simple shock tube test which imposes a square wave forcing function.

Studies in very rapidly varying combustion systems such as detonations require extremely high response, and flush mounted piezoceramic gauges may be used. In this case, the transit time of the wave over the sensitive surface must be minimized, and a gauge with a sensitive diameter of 1mm can give a response of a fraction of a microsecond.

Noise measurements are closely related to pressure measurements except that the fluctuating pressures to be measured are extremely small. The most satisfactory technique is the capacitative (condenser) microphone in which a small bleed flow is used to balance the d.c. pressure difference across the diaphragm. When using such instruments in a pressurized combustor, care must be used to ensure that the bleed flow is taken from the combustor, rather than from atmosphere. Similarly, care must be taken in expressing the results in dB or relative amplitude since the instrument calibration usually assumes ambient pressure. Matching impedences in probe microphones when there are large temperature gradients can present problems if absolute measurements are required. However, relative measurements are usually sufficient to define the modes of oscillation in an oscillatory combustion system. In cylindrical chambers the tangential modes of oscillation follow Bessel functions and the amplitudes of the wave depend on which antinode measurements are made. Further details on noise measurements are given in Gupta[135] and Peterson and Gross[136]. Noise and vibration measuring instruments are manufactured by a number of companies such as, Brüel & Kjaer, Copenhagen, Denmark and BBN, Cambridge, Mass.

Static Pressure-Disc Probe

An exact measure of the static pressure in swirl flows is difficult due to the influence of the velocity and pressure fluctuations on the pressure measuring device which is introduced into the flow. For swirl flows and flows in the wake of stabilizer discs where there are significant radial and axial pressure gradients, the measurement of the static pressure distributions is required in order to determine the flow pattern. A review of the methods for measuring static pressure has been made in Fechheimer[12], Miller *et al.*[137], Bryer *et al*[138]. In strongly swirling flows there may be a significant change in the static pressure between the total head and static holes of a normal pitot. Under these conditions it is often found necessary to measure the total head with an impact probe (section 4.1) and subsequently the static pressure with a disc probe at the same position. In order to measure the static pressure it is necessary to align the disc so that the resultant velocity is in the plane of the disc at each measuring point of interest. For flows in which there are only axial and radial components of velocity it is unnecessary to rotate the probe.

Nevertheless, when a tangential component of velocity is present, it is necessary to rotate the probe until the measured differential pressure on the two side tubes is zero. The pressure registered on the central hole gives a direct measure of the static pressure. It must be remembered, however, that the static pressure measured with the above disc probe can yield erroneous results at certain points in strongly swirling jet flows.

4.4 DENSITY

The determination of rapidly varying gas density is most often carried out by non-intrusive optical methods. Since the gas density, ρ, is related to the refractive index, n, by the Gladstone and Dale law

$$M(n-1) = \text{Const.}\,\rho \tag{4.61}$$

where M is the molecular weight, the density ρ and the constant can be computed for any given gas[114].

From the above relationship it can be seen that $(n-1)$ varies hyperbolically with temperature, thus at high temperatures the refractive index variations [actually $(n-1)$] are very insensitive to temperature, whereas at low temperatures the converse is true. Care must therefore be taken with the use of direct refractive index measuring techniques, and beam deflection techniques may be advantageous provided the reference level (preferably at high temperatures, that is, low density) can be accurately established.

The laser schlieren interferometric technique (discussed in section 4.2) for refractive index measurement can be used to evaluate density through eqn. 4.61. It is a very powerful technique which can be used in either differential or absolute fringe mode (finite or infinite) and the abberations in the optical components may be subtracted out by the double exposure technique, Fig. 4.34.

Schlieren System

The word schlieren originates from German and designates streaks or striae (an irregular light deflection in a transparent medium having local inhomogeneity). The basic idea of the schlieren system is that part of the deflected light is intercepted before it reaches the receptor, so that the parts of the field it has traversed appear darker. The illumination of the image can be reversed by adapting an optical arrangement in which the undeflected light is intercepted and the deflected light passes through. The principle of the schlieren method was developed more than a century ago[139] and was utilized for visualizing compressible flows by the schlieren knife-edge method (also called Toepler schlieren method).

In the knife-edge method, Fig. 4.38(a), an image of the light source *LS* is formed in the plane of the knife-edge, which is placed in the focal plane of the second spherical lens or mirror M_2, sometimes called as 'schlieren head'. The knife-edge is perpendicular to the plane of the figure, and the light source is either a point source or a narrow slit parallel to the knife edge. If part of the light in the image plane is intercepted by the knife edge, then the illumination at the receptor will be decreased. If part of the light is deflected by an angle α, due to inhomogeneity in the test section, however, then it would not overlap with the other light at the focal plane. Its image point at the receptor would be darkened by a different amount, and the point would appear darker or brighter than the rest of the field, depending on how the light is intercepted. The displacement of the light at the source image due to an angular displacement α at M_2 (for small apertures) is

$$h = \Delta f_2 \alpha$$

where f_2 is the focal length of M_2. There may also be a displacement $\Delta \ell$ due to the deflection in the other direction. A ray of light that is deflected arrives at the same point

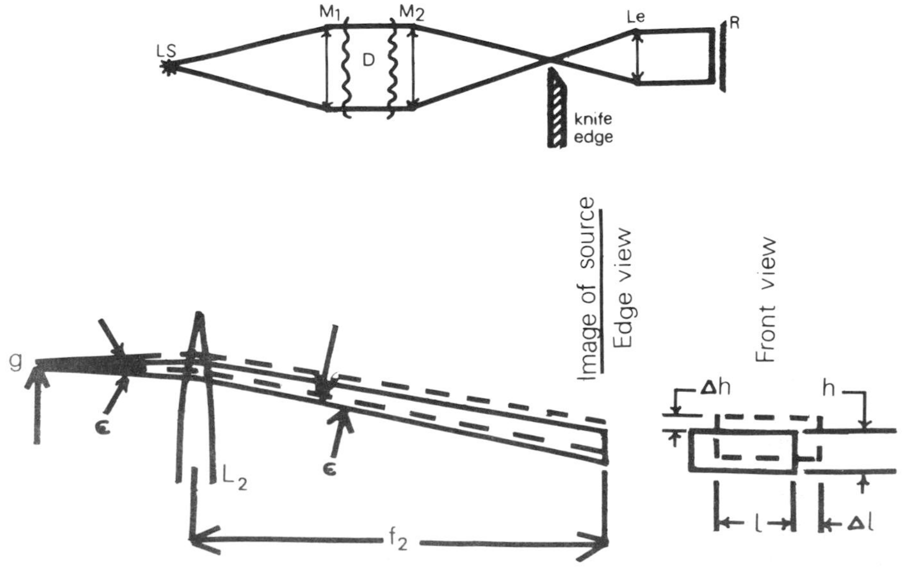

Figure 4.38 (a) Schematic arrangement of a Schlieren knife-edge method
(b) Displacement of the light source image in the plane of the knife-edge

on the receptor as the undeflected light, and thus the image on the receptor remains sharp. Only the illumination is affected.

The component of density gradient that is displayed depends on the orientation of the source (and the knife-edge). Fig. 4.38(b) reveals that only the displacement Δh affects the illumination; the light corresponding to displacement $\Delta \ell$ is not intercepted. Thus, the schlieren method gives the density gradient normal to the knife-edge. The density gradient in any direction in the flow may be obtained by setting the knife-edge (and source) perpendicular to it; the settings often used are parallel and perpendicular to the general flow direction. The sensitivity of the system is defined as the fractional deflection obtained at the knife-edge for unit angular deflection of the ray at the test section

$$s = \frac{\Delta h}{h_1 \alpha} = \frac{f_2}{h_1} = \frac{c}{\alpha}$$

where c is the contrast and is defined as

$$c = \frac{\Delta h}{h_1} = \frac{f_2 \alpha}{h_1} = \frac{f_2 L \beta}{h_1 \rho_o} \left(\frac{d\rho}{dy} \right) \tag{4.62}$$

where L is the width of the test section, ρ_o is the reference density and the value of dimensionless parameter, β, varies with the gas. Typical values of β for air, carbon dioxide, and Helium for $\lambda_o = 5893$ (D-line) are 0.000292, 0.000451, and 0.000036 respectively. The contrast is therefore determined by focal length of the second lens M_2, width of the test section, density gradient, refractivity of the fluid, and the uncovered width of the basic image.

In practice, it is usually desirable to have high sensitivity but unfortunately there is an upper limit that is determined by the fact that spurious density gradients are normally encountered by the light. The system, therefore, should not be made so sensitive as to make these visible. Another sensitivity limit is that Δh must not be so large that the secondary image is deflected completely off (or completely onto) the knife-edge, for then any additional deflection would not produce corresponding changes of illumination at the screen.

In practice, it is usual to employ schlieren mirrors, rather than the lenses, because large aperture mirrors are less expensive and lose less light by reflection. A typical arrangement is shown in Fig. 4.39 which appears to be a simple version of the powerful laser Schlieren interferometer shown in Fig. 4.34.

Color Schlieren System

In this system the knife edge in the conventional system is replaced by commercially available gelantine filters[140] which are in the form of several parallel, transparent colored strips. This method can be interpreted as an analogy to the system using a grid, when the opaque fringes would be reduced to a thickness of zero and the transparent fringes could be discriminated by different colors. It is usual to use no more than three colored sheets

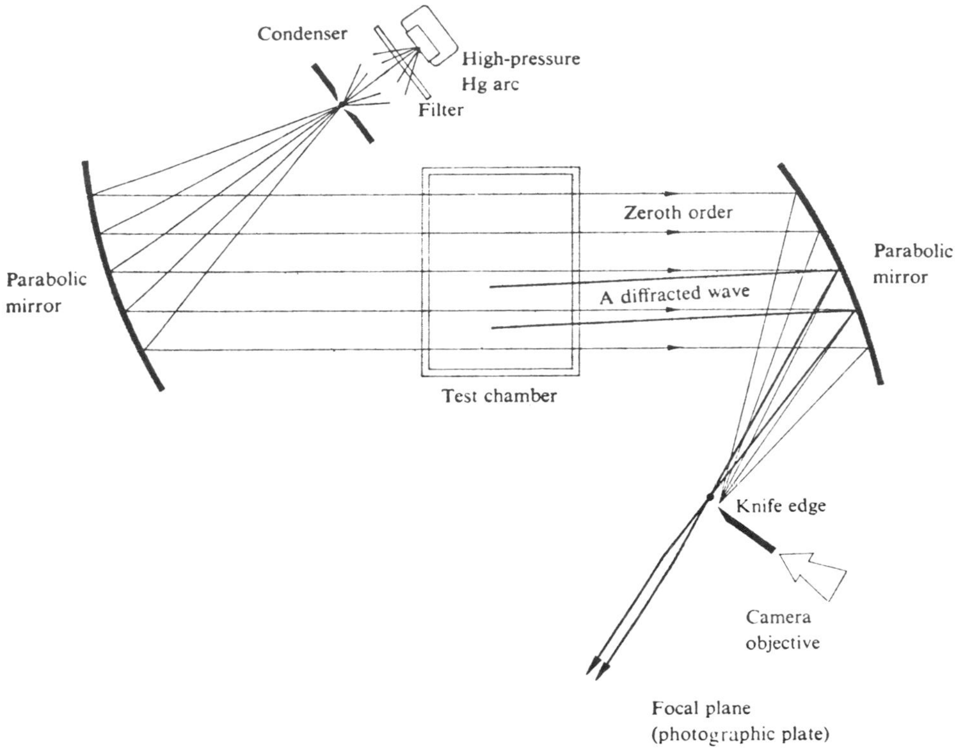

Figure 4.39 A Schlieren system set-up with two mirrors.

and this tricolor filter is placed parallel to the light source slit; the width of the central filter section being approximately equal to that of the slit image. The choice of the colors depends on the appearance and discrimination by the eye in addition to the color sensitivity of the film. The colors should have approximately the same transmission and a combination of blue, yellow and red gives the best contrast.

Mach-Zehnder Interferometer

The Mach-Zehnder interferometer, MZI, is sensitive to absolute changes in gas density while the schlieren method is sensitive to changes of the density gradient.

In the classical Mach-Zehnder interferometry (named after L. Mach and Zehnder) the phase of the disturbed light ray is compared with the phase of the undisturbed ray by making them interfere with each other[141-143].

In the basic arrangement of an MZI two plane and two partially reflecting mirrors are arranged so as to form a rectangle, Fig. 4.40. The coherence between the test beam and reference beam paths is obtained by placing two glass windows in the reference beam path identical to those used in the test beam path. The corresponding two light beams interfere behind the partially reflecting mirror M_2' to produce interference fringes on the

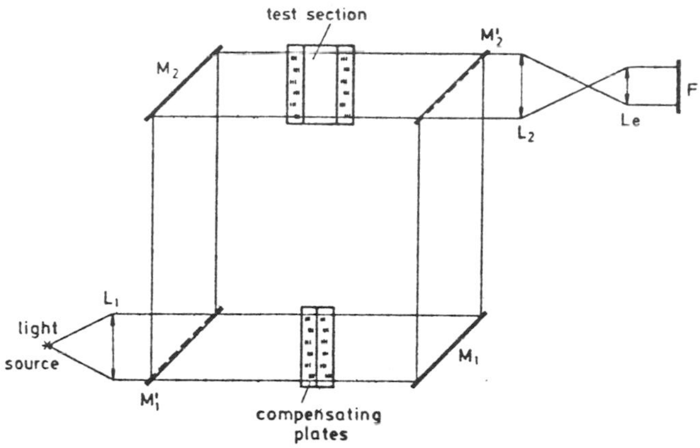

Figure 4.40 Mach-Zehnder interferometric system[141]

receptor (a photographic plate) which is focused on to a plane in the test section by means of a camera. An inhomogeneity in the test section produces an interference fringe pattern which can be quantitatively related to the density distribution of the flow field. Readers are referred to Merzkirch[163] for further details on Mach-Zehnder interferometers.

4.5 SPECIES CONCENTRATION

The composition of gas and liquid or solid particles within a flame zone is of great interest to combustion engineers and provides an insight into the chemical kinetic processes taking place within the flame. In most industrial and laboratory flames, concentration measurement by direct probe sampling has proved to be the most successful technique. The principle of this technique is fairly simple; a suitable probe is inserted in the desired test section of the flame and a sample is withdrawn, quenched and analyzed for gas (stable species) and liquid or solid particles[1,4,144-147].

In gas sampling the fundamental problem is to obtain a sample, representative of the composition of the fluid at the sampling point, and then to quench it with a suitable cooling system. The presence of the probe in the flame and the disturbances caused by the gas flow into the probe distorts the flow pattern. This may have two effects. First, it may directly affect the combustion process if it interferes with a combustion wave; and secondly, it may have a mechanical influence on the sample composition. In two-phase flows the pressure and velocity gradient produced by the probe can cause particles or gas pockets of unequal size and density to behave differently. Gas and solid (or liquid) particles can be separated by using a cyclone, cascade impactor or a sintered disc filter. A sampling probe introduced into a flame acts as a heat sink and causes thermal gradients around it.

Ideally, quenching should freeze chemical reaction, thus preserving the initial composition of the sample. In general, the slower the cooling the greater the alteration, provided the gas is capable of chemical reaction. Moreover, even after quenching, the sample can change during its passage through the sampling probe due to the condensation of the vapor phases.

Summing up, possible sampling errors may be grouped into two groups, depending upon whether they originate outside or inside the probe. Factors contributing to the first kind are:

(a) physical and chemical properties of the flow being sampled. This refers to the nature of the chemical species and to their distribution as well as to the physical conditions in the vicinity of the sampling point
(b) size and shape of the sampling probe and its disposition relative to the gas stream
(c) sampling flow rate
(d) temperature of the outer walls of the probe

The factors contributing to the second kind are:

(a) quenching system
(b) dynamic properties of the gas flow inside the probe
(c) catalytic properties of the inner probe walls
(d) length and geometry of the sampling line
(e) physical and chemical properties of the sample entering the probe

In gaseous flows, water-cooled probes sampling at stream velocity (iso-kinetic sampling) are often used, although they are known to be unsatisfactory in many respects. Fristrom and Westenberg[1] have shown that chemical reactions can be quenched at the entrance to the probe by the use of a sonic orifice. The pressure drop across the sonic orifice is sufficient to quench the reactions, hence, no water cooling of the probe is necessary. The probes are constructed from fine quartz tubing with one end tapered down to a fine orifice (about 30° taper). It has been shown that the results obtained using such a probe are independent of the size of sampling orifice, probe orientation, sampling pressure, precise construction of the probe and whether it is cooled or not. The sample can also be quenched using inert gas by dilution.

In two phase flows, the problem is to separate the liquid or solid from the gas. A sampling probe similar to that described in Beér & Chigier[4] and Chedaille & Braud[5] fitted with a sintered bronze or stainless steel filter may be used. The transpiring wall sintered tube sampling probe has also been used successfully to quench the reaction in multiphase flows, where solid, liquid, fog, soot, and gases are all present simultaneously. In this method inert gas is forced through the porous sintered tube radially inwards and the sample (with the inert gas) is withdrawn through the center of the tube. The transpiring wall prevents deposition of soot by thermophoresis and condenses the condensable hydrocarbons into a submicron fog. The soot, fog, droplet residue and condensable can be filtered using a sampling train (cascade impactor, filter) leaving dry gas which can be analyzed using a gas chromatograph-mass spectrometer combination. The above sampling method has been successfully used to sample gas and heavy fuel oil droplets in a laminar flow furnace[149]. Sampling probes for high temperature and high pressure flows have recently been reviewed by Blann[147]. They are designed to sample iso-kinetically to ensure a representative sample and may either catch the particles on a filter for subsequent weighing and microscopic examination or be plumbed to provide an input to a particle sizing device such as a cascade impactor[148].

Gas chromatography or mass spectrometry is often used for analyzing the sampled gas. Gas chromatography is a physical method for separating the constituents of a mixture of volatile compounds. A small discrete sample of the mixture is introduced into the stream of carrier gas which passes continuously through a tubular 'column'. The column is packed with adsorbent granuals (adsorption partition effects) for gas/solid chromatography. The progress of individual constituents through the column is retarded, the magnitude of the effect being dependent on the appropriate partition coefficient. If suitable conditions are chosen the total amount of each constituent leaves the remote end of the column separately from the others at a characteristic time after sample injection.

The mass spectrometer is a very sensitive and accurate instrument and is suitable for highly complex analysis. It is, however, very costly and requires skilled personnel for operation.

Most conventional methods of concentration measurement involve gas sampling and are generally slow, i.e. they respond to the 90 per cent level of the input signal in about 15 sec. If care is taken to maintain a high velocity through the sampling line and use 'fast' instruments, this time can be reduced to about 0.5 seconds. It is usually recommended that the line connecting the probe to the instruments be heated to 150°C with a flow rate of 5 ℓ/m. Filters, pumps, and sometimes drying tubes are incorporated into the line and a typical instrumentation system comprises a flame ionization detector (for total hydrocarbons), non-dispersive infra-red gas analysers for CO and CO_2, a paramagnetic oxygen analyser and a chemi-luminescent NO analyser. This system may be conveniently backed up by a gas chromatograph operating at about 105°C which can detect all these gases except NO_x (by a catharometer) plus others such as H_2 and CH_4, with two columns containing molecular sieve and silica gel respectively. A higher series of hydrocarbons can be detected with a flame ionization detector and a column containing alumina or OV-17 by temperature programming the oven (i.e. the column). When there are large fluctuations in density, as in unmixed hydrogen/air or two phase flow situations, the lighter constituent is preferentially introduced when the sample tube entry velocity is above the local velocity. Conversely, the heavier component is preferentially drawn in when the probe entry velocity is below the local stream velocity. The optimum would be isokinetic sampling for an infinitely thin probe tip. In practice, the probe tip is thick and, in general, a velocity higher than the isokinetic velocity is optimum, Fig. 4.41.

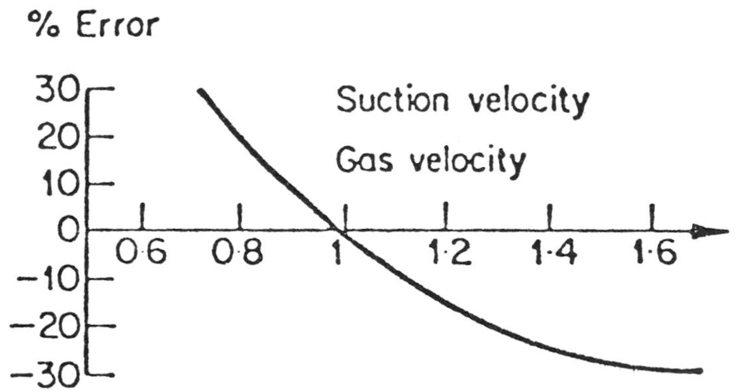

Figure 4.41 Correction curves for non-isokinetic sampling (Error in concentrations of pulverised coal measured at IFRF, Ijmuiden; 80% of weight < 75 μm).[5]

The ideal concentration measuring system avoids sampling the flow since it is prone to sampling errors and a brief discussion of optical concentration measuring methods is appropriate. Several physical/optical phenomena can be used; the most obvious being the refractive index variation. Unfortunately, the refractive index depends on temperature and concentration in addition to pressure and this often invalidates its use in combustion and other reacting systems. Similar criticisms apply to the Rayleigh scattering technique. This technique consists of a laser beam focused on some point in the flow. The light scattered from this point at some angle (for example, 90°) depends on the Rayleigh scattering coefficient, which, in turn, depends on species. If a lens is used to focus this light on to a photomultiplier tube, the fluctuations in local concentration can be monitored at frequencies up to the MHz region. The system is, of course, only applicable to isothermal binary mixing systems. The only light scattering process that is directly sensitive to species is the Raman scattering which is at a wavelength that varies with the species. However, under certain conditions the spontaneous Raman technique can fail due to excessive noise, unwanted fluorescence, and other sources of interference. CARS diagnostic technique can be used to alleviate somc of the above problems.

The main difficulty with the laser Raman technique lies in the fact that the ratio of the Raman scattered intensity to the input intensity is so low. Fortunately, high power pulsed ruby lasers permit high input intensities to be achieved, and using narrow band filters together with photomultipliers to measure the intensity at selected wavelengths, instantaneous concentration measurements can be obtained. Temperature measurements require a rejection ratio of about 10^{-11} at 10 Å from the preset line, hence narrow band filters are ruled out, and expensive double monochromators must be used.

The applicability of the Raman scattering technique to combustion systems is still in a primitive but very active stage of development and we are optimistic about its prospects.

4.6 PARTICLE AND DROPLET SIZE DISTRIBUTION

The size* of a particle is that dimension that best characterizes its subdivision. For a spherical, uniform particle, the diameter is that dimension. Particles of irregular shape can be characterized in various ways. The actual scientific measurement of this simple descriptive term is extremely difficult in all but the most simple instances of perfectly symmetrical spheres, cylinders, cubes or blocks. If the particle is of an irregular form, complex equations must be used to define the shape relationship. A term used to assist in the description of the shape is called sphericity, defined as:

$$\text{Sphericity}, \Psi = \pi d_v^2 / \pi d_s^2 = \left(\frac{d_v}{d_s}^2\right)$$

where d_v and d_s are the diameters of a sphere of equivalent volume and surface respectively. Typical values of Ψ vary from 0.216 (for very thin flakes of mica, graphite, aluminum, etc.) to 0.817 for rounded particles of water worn sands, atomized metals. Sphericity for pulverised coal particles lie in the range of 0.6 to 0.7.

*Size is referred to both the liquid droplets and solid particles

Another parameter used to define the shape is the surface coefficient defined as.

$$f = 1.57 + \frac{4C}{3}\frac{k}{m}\frac{(n+1)}{n}$$

where f = surface coefficient ($fd_a{}^2 = \pi d_s{}^2$)

k = volume coefficient ($kd_a{}^3 = \pi d_v{}^3$)

n = elongation ratio ($= \frac{\text{length}}{\text{breadth}}$)

m = flatness ratio ($= \frac{\text{breadth}}{\text{thickness}}$)

C = coefficient depending on geometric form

Because of the difficulties of describing the shape of a particle, it is usual to define the size of a particle by a single dimension, a diameter. This can be accomplished by expressing the size of the particle in terms of the diameter of a sphere that is equivalent to the particle with respect to some property. Various equivalent diameters can be extracted from techniques that measure different size dependent properties, for example, surface, volume, resistance to motion in a gas, scattered light from the particles.

Log-normal particle size distribution can be described completely by two values, the geometric median diameter, d_g, and the geometric standard deviation, σ_g. In log-normal distribution the mean, median and mode coincide and have identical values. These values, while completely describing the distribution, have no physical significance to aid in the interpretation of experimental results. An average diameter is the diameter of a hypothetical particle which in some way represents the total number of particles in the sample. Diameters representing length, surface area, volume, and specific surface may be determined. The size of an irregularly shaped particle may be defined as the diameter of a sphere that is equivalent to the particle with respect to some conveniently measurable property. The aerodynamic diameter, which is actually a measure of the particle's terminal settling velocity, is an equivalent diameter of this type. Consequently, the aerodynamic diameter is a common deposition parameter and is defined as the diameter of a sphere of unit density having the given value of the settling velocity. The terminal settling velocity is given by

$$V_t = \frac{\rho_p C d_p^2 g}{18\mu}$$

where g is the acceleration due to gravity and C is the Cunningham slip correction factor. The settling velocity is also used to define another equivalent diameter called Stokes diameter. The Stokes diameter, d_s, is the diameter of a sphere having the same bulk density and terminal settling velocity as the particle.

A particle's aerodynamic diameter can be determined by knowing the information concerning the material density of the particle and the measured diameter, d. This is achieved by application of a volume shape factor, α, and a resistance shape factor, both related to the measured diameter. Therefore the aerodynamic diameter is

$$d_a = \left(\frac{6}{\pi} \frac{\rho_p}{\rho_{p_o}} \frac{\alpha}{\beta}\right)^{1/2} d$$

where ρ_{p_o} represents unit density. After the ratio, α/β is determined experimentally for a specific measured diameter and for particles of a given material, it can be applied to similar measurements of diameter, made on particles of the same type, to estimate their aerodynamic diameters. Some of the other used average diameters are given in Table 4.8.

There is an increasing area of research concerned with the physical and chemical transformations of solid and liquid aerosols and particulate clouds where accurate particle size analysis is required. Droplet and particle size distribution plays a key role in the ignition and subsequent combustion in stationary combustion systems, for example, industrial combustors, gas turbine combustors, diesel engines, etc. During the last two decades considerable efforts have been made towards the development of non-intrusive optical instruments for the measurement of size distribution. The mechanical methods such as the coated-slide system, cascade impaction, frozen drop and wax method, pulse counting technique, have many disadvantages in which the sampling process always disturbs the flow field, and in highly turbulent combustion systems, it is particularly difficult to extract a representative sample with any degree of confidence. Also, particle agglomeration and deposition in the sampling system can alter the size distribution prior to measurement. The mechanical methods do not provide real time measurements and

TABLE 4.8

Mathematical Definition of Average Diameters

Average Diameter	Symbol	Mathematical Definition	Description
Arithmetic Mean	d_{av}	$\Sigma Nd/\Sigma N$	The sum of all diameters divided by the total number of particles.
Surface Mean	d_s	$(\Sigma Nd^2/\Sigma N)^{1/2}$	The diameter of a hypothetical particle having average surface area.
Volume Mean	d_v	$(\Sigma Nd^3/\Sigma N)^{1/3}$	The diameter of a hypothetical particle having average volume. The median value of this frequency distribution is often called the mass median diameter.
Volume-Surface Mean (also Sauter Mean)	d_{vs}	$\Sigma Nd^3/\Sigma Nd^2$	The average size based on the specific surface per unit volume.
Weight Mean Diameter (also DeBroucker mean)	d_w	$\Sigma Nd^4/\Sigma Nd^3$	The average size based on the unit weight of the particles.

in some cases sample preparation and analysis may actually occupy many hours. A brief review of the mechanical methods for particle sizing is given in McCreath and Beer[150] and Giffen & Muraszew[152]. The optical methods, however, are somewhat less tedious and cause no disturbance to the flow. Several different optical phenomena have been utilized as the basis for specific instruments. Optical methods have their own limitations, the major one being the need for high quality optical access to the region of interest. As yet no single device has proved completely satisfactory over a wide size range (0.05 to 1000 μm); the recent advances indicate that this goal can eventually be realized.

In this section some of the recently developed optical diagnostic techniques used for the measurement of drop or particle size distribution, with special reference to their application in combustion systems, are described. Some of the optical fundamentals relevant to optical particle-sizing instruments are also discussed. The optical techniques considered here are: photography, laser holography, laser diffraction, laser anemometry and various other techniques based on light scattering.

Photographic Techniques

Single-flash Photography

This technique can provide information on the drop size frequency distribution[153-155]. In the system used by Nuruzzaman[154], a camera was focused on the droplet stream by using a tungsten filament lamp and a 203 mm diameter brass spinning disc (having eight holes) as the source of intermittent light. The source of light, although it can be replaced by a pulsed laser for shorter exposure times can introduce difficulties due to the coherent nature of the laser light. The continuous light source and the spinning disc were then replaced by a flash tube, since the photographs obtained using the spinning disc were found not of a sufficiently sharp quality for accurate drop size measurement. The photograph of the droplet stream was taken quite successfully, using a flash duration of 1-2 μsec. It was, however, found necessary to keep the camera shutter open for 1/25 second for the recording time[154]. The particle size distribution and the mean diameters were then determined from the photographic film by projecting the film on to a screen with some magnification (of the order of 100). Alternatively, the photographs can be analyzed, using a particle analyzer similar to that described by Sato *et al.*[156]. In their automatic particle size analyzer the photograph is placed on a drum revolving at constant speed and is scanned with a focused light beam. The signals, corresponding to the brightness of the photograph, are detected and converted directly into digital signals which are then punched out on a paper tape. The data on the paper tape can then be analyzed using a mini-computer. The advantages and limitations of single spark photography are given in Table 4.9.

Double Flash Photography

This technique is very similar to the above single flash photography and essentially consists of superimposing two photographs separated by a variable time interval so as to provide additional information on velocity and direction of flight of particles. A careful choice of film and the use of various filters can enable one to make measurements in highly luminous flames.

TABLE 4.9
Comparison of Various Sizing Methods

Method	Size of Measurement Control	Particle Size Range	Particle Size Distribution	Particle Velocity	Particle Trajectory	Remarks
SINGLE SPARK PHOTOGRAPHY	small (width < 1mm) –plane measurement	$5<d<2000\ \mu m$ (0-75 m/sec velocity)	possible by future analysis	No	No	Simple to use, fairly laborious. Can be used both in nonburning and burning sprays; require fairly high light intensity source. Depth of field must be small.
DOUBLE SPARK PHOTOGRAPHY	small (small size as in single spark photography)	$5<d<2000\ \mu m$ (0-75 m/sec velocity)	possible by further analysis	Yes	Yes	Simple to use. Depth of field $D_f = u \left[\dfrac{2\left(\dfrac{u}{f}\right)\left(\dfrac{R_r}{1720}\right)}{1-\left\{\left(\dfrac{u}{f}\right)\left(\dfrac{R_r}{1720}\right)\right\}^2} \right]$ must be small. Useful for both nonburning and burning sprays.
LASER DIFFRACTION	Usually large (a cylinder ∿ 1 cm diam. and few cms. long)	$5<d<1800+\mu m$ (stationary or moving at any velocity)	on-line analysis hard copy printout	No	No	Simple, fast, and fairly straight forward to use; particle may be stationary or moving at any speed. Requires only small laser power; Can be developed for use in burning sprays. Expensive.
LASER HOLOGRAPHY	Usually large (∿ few cms)	$5<d<1500+\mu m$ (0-100 m/sec)	possible by further analysis	possible	possible	Require high power laser specially for use in burning sprays; permissible movement of object = 10% of particle diameter; no depth of field restriction $(100d^2/\lambda_o)$. Reconstructed hologram may be projected with uniform magnification.
LIGHT SCATTERING (LDA and others)	Usually small (∿1-2mm x 1-2mm)	$0.5<d<1000+\mu m$	possible by further analysis	Yes. Can be linked to an on-line mini-computer for size and velocity	Possible, but rather difficult.	Require fairly high laser power in burning sprays; signal processing in L.D.A. for size difficult. Particles may be stationary or moving; MCV size small.

Photographic technique can be applied to isothermal or burning sprays within the size range of 5 μm to 2000 μm having velocities in the range of 0 to 75 m/sec and flight angles between 0 deg. and 360 deg. (*see* Table 4.9).

The double flash photographic system, shown in Fig. 4.42, has been used successfully to photograph high luminosity burning kerosene spray droplets[155] and synthetic fuel droplet streams. The apparatus consists essentially of two spark sources, fired at variable time intervals controlled electronically, an optical system and a camera to record the droplet/particle images produced.

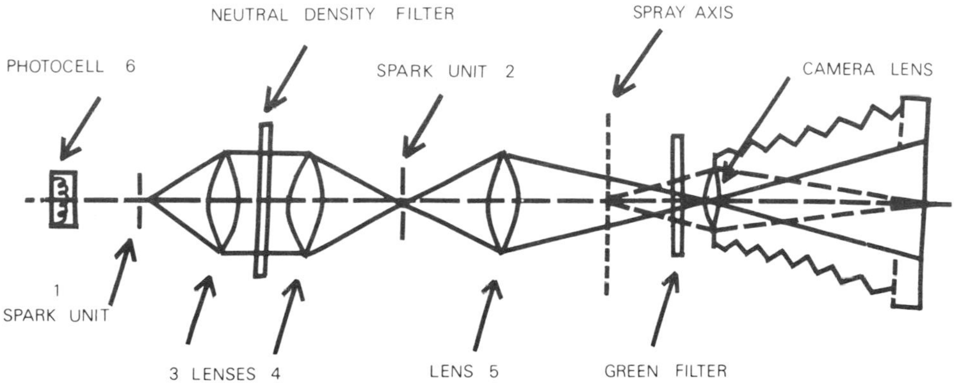

Figure 4.42 An optical arrangement for the double flash photographic system.[155]

The sequence of events consist of the spark labelled 1 discharging and the resultant light being focused onto the point of origin of the second spark 2 by the lenses 3 and 4, each of 75 mm focal length. The light is then focused by lens 5, focal length 140 mm, on to the camera shutter, thus illuminating a small area of spray or particles. The camera, which is focused onto a particular diameter plane in the spray, then records the image produced. After an electronically-controlled variable time interval the second spark is discharged. To the camera, the illumination emanates from the same point as that from the first spark. The second image produced is superimposed on to the same photographic negative. After development, the resultant negative can be projected at greatly increased magnification to obtain directly the droplet size, angle of flight and also, velocity (provided the time interval between the spark is known). The time interval between the two sparks is obtained by using a photoelectric cell, which basically monitors the light output from the sparks and displays it on an oscilloscope. The trace is recorded by means of a storage oscilloscope or a Polaroid camera. The accumulation of data from the photographic plate is carried out by a data logging system, which can then be analyzed using a computer.

Because the illumination time is short, the use of a relatively fast film is a necessary prerequisite for good particle image formation. The small objects being photographed and the large magnifications necessary dictate the use of a film having good contrast and high acutance, together with small wavelength sensitivity, in order to provide less image obscuration by flame light.

Kodak or Ilford commercial orthochromatic film gives the best results but the films are still affected by some flame radiation. Freshly prepared Paterson's Acutol-S developer gives high acutance characteristics using a development time of 600 sec at 20°C. Some commercially available photographic films together with their properties are given in Table 4.7.

Image obscuration by flame radiation is overcome by using a filter to obviate as much flame light as possible from the negative, matching the spark light with the most sensitive wavelength range of the photographic plate and using a high shutter speed (1/200 sec or less).

The commercial orthochromatic plates are known to respond only to wavelengths between 360 nm and 590 nm, the most effective region being around 560 nm. Polaroid T55 film, although expensive, gives better results than commercial ortho film. Kodak commercial film 4127 also gives good results. McCreath *et al*[155] used a wratten 61 filter which allowed all wavelengths between 480 nm and 600 nm to pass and had a maximum transmittance at 540 nm. In these days, filters are available and can be used to transmit precisely the desired wavelengths. The efficiency of this filter[155] in avoiding blackening of the photographic emulsion due to the flame light was checked by photographing the flame at f/2.8 and 1/200 sec exposure time both with and without filter in position for a range of spark energies. The spark energy was controlled via the mains voltage supply to the EHT unit. A 180V supply was found to give the best results. The 0.1 μF capacitors charged to a voltage corresponding to a 180V input supply gave no indication of image blur.

Apart from precautionary measures to exclude flame light from the photographic emulsion, it is necessary to avoid exposing the photographic plate excessively to illumination from the first spark. If this precaution is not observed, insufficient "reactivity" of the emulsion remains to record clearly the second superimposed droplet/particle image. This problem is overcome by inserting a xl-1/4 neutral density filter between the two spark units, Fig. 4.42. A better quality photograph also results by using electrodes having round ends, which enabled higher voltages to be used prior to self-discharge, and obviated corona effects.

The depth of field of a lens is given by

$$D_f = u\left[\frac{2\left(\frac{u}{F}\right)\left(\frac{R_r}{1720}\right)}{1-\left\{\left(\frac{u}{F}\right)\left(\frac{R_r}{1720}\right)\right\}^2}\right]$$

where u = distance between the lens and the object, R_r the relative aperture, and F the focal length.

The depth of field must be small to obviate errors in velocity calculations due to foreshortening of inter-image distances. In addition, the relative aperture has to be physically small to reduce fogging of the photographic plate by flame radiation. A compromise is often made between the above two incompatible factors. This compromise is biased towards obtaining the smallest possible depth of field while maintaining a sufficient number of 'in focus' drops to obviate taking an excessive number of photographs for the same information. The incompatibility problem is offset by selecting a magnification large enough to effect a reduction in the depth of field. This means that the objective distance of the camera lens must be small, which results in an increase of heat incident upon the lens; a high pressure curtain of compressed air is therefore introduced in front of the lens, the curtain also serving to prevent wetting by spray droplets. In addition, heat insulated asbestos shields, fitted with pneumatically-controlled sliding doors, can be used. These are opened only during the period of photography.

The photographic negatives of the droplets/particles are processed in large batches to give time mean results of sizes, velocities and angle of flight. The positions of droplet/particle images on the photographic negative are recorded semi-automatically on punched tape in terms of three pairs of coordinates. Flight angles and the velocities of drops are calculated from the relative position of each drop and its image. The photographic negatives are projected onto a 1m square translucent screen by a projector to an overall magnification of 100. The screen is mounted in a frame with adjustable jack to hold it perpendicular to the projected light.

The advantages of flash photographic technique are: simplicity and relative lack of expense of photographic apparatus, flexibility, capability of detecting and analyzing non-spherical particles, and the relative insensitivity to optical properties of particles and multiple scattering (*see also* Table 4.9). The disadvantages are that the technique is very laborious (or expensive post-processing is needed to extract the data).

The data processing problem has been alleviated to a great extent with the TV analyzer developed at Parker-Hannifin Corporation[157], or a Quantimet Image Analyzer[158]. In the TV analyzer a strobe light is used to "burn" temporarily an image on to the TV camera Vidicon tube. The image is scanned to obtain drop size information and then erased at a frequency of 15 Hz. Output is recorded on videotape for subsequent processing using appropriate computer programs. Sauter mean diameter, complete size distribution, and other information can be obtained at each point within the spray. Suitable instrument correction factors can easily be incorporated into the data analysis. One correction factor required is the effective depth of field vs. droplet size (larger particles are visible over a larger axial distance from the object plane than small particles). Another correction factor needed to obtain correct data for total spray parameters is the radium weighting. This accounts for the fact that the viewing area (relative to the total cross-sectional area of the spray at a given radius) decreases with increasing radius.

The TV image analyzer is a very convenient method of droplet/particle sizing under cold flow conditions. It is straight forward to use and appears to give reasonably accurate results. One limitation is the resolution limit of four microns imposed by the TV scan raster. Nevertheless, in practice, the other imaging methods have a similar lower limit of resolution in cold flows. In hot flows one would expect poorer results due to distortion by density and refractive index fluctuations in the flow. Resolution would also suffer in high pressure tests or any other situation where windows must be placed between the spray and the TV camera, particularly when the optical aperture is limited. This problem is, of course, common to all imaging methods. In a recent study of optical methods for Diesel engine research, for example, the threshold of size detection was 35 μm for high-speed photography and 8 μm for holography[159].

Recently, Yule *et al.*[160] used an image analysis computer (IAC) to reduce the time of analysis and to improve the accuracy of spray photographs. Here, essentially, the photographs are scanned by an epidiascope or a microscope and the signal is digitized to give a measurement of light intensity in a matrix of 700 x 1000 picture points. The IAC counts the number of picture points bounded by contours at the measurement light level for each droplet/particle image. The data is acquired by an HP9830 calculator which converts the data into projected areas and thus measured image diameters. The computer program then prints out plots of particle number and volume size distribution, calculated numerical, mass and Sauter mean diameters and also any additional data such as particle shape information. The lowest measurable particle size limit with this technique is about 5 μm. Although the IAC reduces the spray photograph analysis time, the method is fairly expensive and is only worthwhile for those already having a Quantimet System.

Another inexpensive method of obtaining the drop size and velocity information is a fast image digitizer. Essentially, this consists of an array of multi-element detectors positioned in place of the photographic plate which gives a signal output when a droplet image is present. The digitized signal can be calibrated to provide information upon size distribution, velocity, number density and particle shape factor using a mini-computer. This method of data processing is very fast and avoids the laborious technique of film development and its subsequent processing.

Laser Holography

In conventional photography, light from an object is focused by a camera on to the photographic plate to produce a negative picture of the original object. A hologram, on the other hand, is produced without a lens between the object and the recorded medium, and its appearance usually gives no indication of the scene that it represents. The photographic emulsion is used to record phase and amplitude information from superimposed light waves (fringe pattern) arriving simultaneously from the object and from a reference beam.

The holographic or photographic technique by wavefront reconstruction is about 30 years old. It was invented in 1948 by Dennis Gabor[161] as a possible means of improving the resolving power of the electron microscope. It was not until the early 1960's that the holographic technique began to attract widespread attention, for example, by using the off-axis reference-beam method one was able to make holographic images of far better quality than had previously been achieved. By exploiting the intense coherent laser light, it was found possible for the first time to make startlingly realistic holographic images of various types of three-dimensional reflecting objects[162-167].

The unique feature of a hologram is that it stores all information carried by a wavefront, independently of whether it is electromagnetic or mechanical in origin and that this wavefront is available at any time for interrogation. By using interferometric techniques, information can be recovered from several wavefronts carrying slightly different information, of which at least one has been recorded on a hologram before the actual measurement is performed. The holographic interferometry basically differs from conventional interferometry in that the wave fronts to be compared exist at different times. Conventional photography, however, makes use of only the intensity and wavelength. The holographic technique, because of its ability to store amplitude and phase information, has been used successfully in reacting liquid sprays[168-172] and also in Biology and Medicine for three-dimensional imaging of biological structures[173].

Holography is a comparatively straightforward process and is a mere technique of recording images of an object using the intensity, the wavelength, and the phase of the light reflected or transmitted by that object. A schematic representation of the formation of a hologram is shown in Fig. 4.43. Coherent light from a laser light source is split into two beams, and the portion of the beam that is reflected from the object falls on a photographic plate. The other is aimed directly at the plate by means of a mirror. The light from the mirror, called the reference beam, combines at the plate with the light reflected from the object to form a complex interference pattern. The developed plate, which records that interference pattern, is a hologram.

When a hologram of this type is illuminated with the reference beam alone, the light rays passing through the plate are selectively transmitted or absorbed in such a way as to create in the emerging beam a component that exactly duplicates the original light waves that were reflected from the object to the plate when the hologram was formed. An observer receiving these waves will perceive them as emanating from the original object; in effect one will "see" the object as if it were actually there.

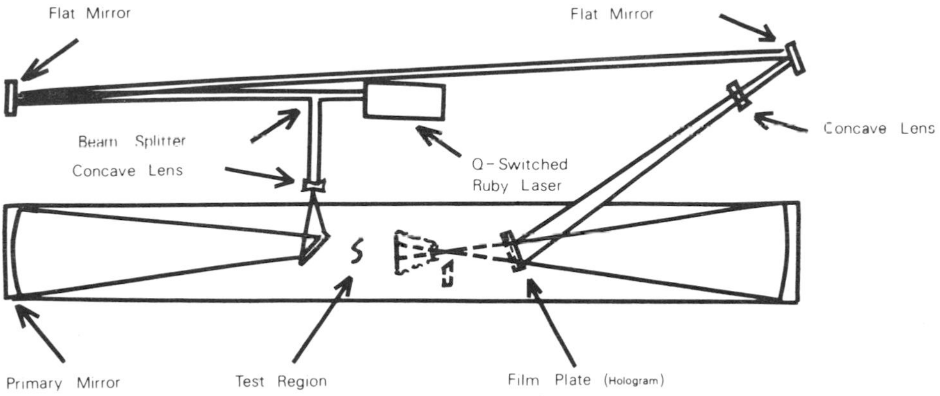

Figure 4.43 (a) A schematic representation of the formation of a hologram

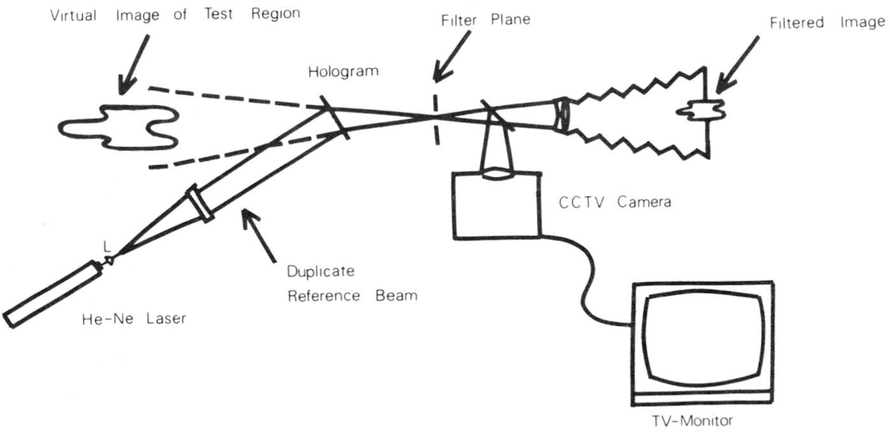

Figure 4.43 (b) The reconstruction system

The coherence requirement arises because the hologram is a record of the interference of two waves, and in general (but not always) coherent light produces interference patterns and incoherent light does not. This requirement has definitely inhibited the development of holography, particularly for display purposes, since coherent light sources are not only more expensive but also less convenient.

There are two types of coherence: temporal coherence and spatial coherence, and light is said to be coherent when it possesses both types. Temporally coherent light is light that is monochromatic, that is, it has only one wavelength. Spatially coherent light is light that is derived from a point source or is capable of being focused to a point. Laser light is the usual source of coherent light. Coherent light can also be obtained from incoherent sources. Spatial coherence can be achieved, for example, by placing a pinhole in front of the source, so that the light emanates from a point. Temporal coherence can be achieved by placing an interference filter in front of the source, so that only light in a narrow spectral band is transmitted. Each process involves throwing away by far the greater part of the light; hence, to obtain a small amount of coherent light a very powerful incoherent source is necessary.

There are two distinct advantages of holograpy for recording the images of droplets/ particles in two phase flows. The first is that there is little depth of field restriction and the second is that a reconstructed hologram when projected will always have a uniform magnification of particles operated longitudinally.

The scale of the diffraction pattern formed by a point object, for example, a droplet, is proportional to the wavelength of the incident light. Because the patterns for the different wavelengths differ in size, a beam with a wide band of wavelenghts will blur the resulting pattern, the finest lines being blurred the most. The acceptable spectral bandwidth becomes narrower as the distance between the object and hologram is increased or as the size of the resolution element is decreased. The ratio of the size of the diffraction pattern to the size of the resolution element is called the expansion ratio. In order to minimize the blurring, caused mainly due to the use of polychromatic light source, the spectral bandwidth should be less than four times the average wavelength divided by the expansion ratio.

Webster[174] used holographic technique to measure drop size distribution in the range of 20 to 500 μm moving at velocities up to 70 m/sec using a chemically switched double pulse ruby laser as the light source. A specially constructed spatial filter was used to reduce noise interference. Webster points out that permissible subject movement is 10 percent of the subject diameter that is, for a pulse width of 2×10^{-8} sec the maximum permissible velocity of a 20 μm diameter droplet is 100 m/sec (*see also* Table 4.8). This droplet velocity is somewhat greater than that covered by the conventional type of double spark photographic technique[155].

Thompson[169, 170] also used far field holographic technique to measure particle size distribution within the range 5-300 μm using a pulsed ruby laser. He has also given an excellent bibliography on the application of holography to drop size measurement.

Holographic technique applied to reacting liquid sprays by Belz and Dougherty[168] used in-line holography. In-line holography is simple to set up and align and also gives maximum resolution with respect to the cut-off frequency of the film[167]. The set-up essentially consists of a coherent light source from a passively Q-switched ruby laser illuminating the spray. A 15-nanosecond duration pulse width, spatially filtered by a

100 μm pinhole and collimated to three-inch diameter, was used and effectively freezes the droplet motion during film exposure. Holograms were reconstructed using a collimated He-Ne laser light. A resolution of 15μm in combustion environments with holography has been obtained although thermal density effects have been reported to degrade the reconstructed image in certain cases[168, 172].

The depth of field in laser holography is related to the particle size, laser power and the optical resolution of the system. This has been empirically assessed to be of the order of 100 d^2/λ_o where d is the droplet/particle diameter and λ_o is the wavelength of incident light.

This empirical assessment shows that the depth of field criterion, important in the photographic assessment of velocity in sprays, does not apply to holography. In addition, the magnification of the system is not a function of objective distance, as in conventional photography, but can be varied by using a divergent reconstruction beam. Reconstruction beam requirements for the hologram are not stringent; any He-Ne laser light or mercury arc lamp is adequate.

A number of photographic materials exist to record holographic images capable of the resolution requirements. Nevertheless, for work in far red wavelengths (He-Ne laser light) a material with extended red sensitivity is more practicable. Materials conforming to these specifications are given in Table 4.7. The choice of the film depends upon many factors, for example, light source, resolving power, granularity, contrast, and the object whose hologram is to be taken. The light energy requirements for recording the hologram vary from 900 erg/cm^2 (for 649-F) to 0.3 erg/cm^2 (for SO-115), Table 4.7.

Holographic technique has been used successfully in a variety of dilute spray systems[175-177]. Nevertheless, its application to more dense sprays has until recently been uncertain. The main problem in dense sprays is to obtain a high quality hologram so that analysis could be carried out using a Quantimet Image Analyzer in a similar manner to that previously described for photography[158]. For drops or particles to be reconstructed clearly, the coherent light diffracted by each drop at the imaging stage must pass largely unobstructed to the film plane. In dense sprays, however, the high concentration of droplets between the light source and the recording plane gives rise to further scattering of the light originally diffracted by one droplet. This results in the reconstructed droplets being ill-defined against a background of variable intensity. The only remedy for obtaining good quality holograms in dense sprays is to reduce the number of droplets through which the laser light must pass[178].

It is therefore apparent that holographic technique is difficult to apply to large, dense atomizer sprays. The method could, however, be of some use in its present form for determining the upper limit of drop size in dense sprays.

Double exposure holography is also a well-established technique and can provide information on velocity, direction and temporal variation of particle size. Holographic technique can also be applied to monitor the bubble size growth in a fluidized bed combustor.

Laser Diffraction

Hodkinson and Greenleaves[179] showed that for large particles ($d \geqslant 2$ μm) with size parameter $\alpha \gtrsim 3/(n-1)$ the scattering may be treated with reasonable accuracy as a linear combination of diffraction, refraction and reflection, Table 4.10 (see also Self

TABLE 4.10

Scattering Theories

Size Range	Appropriate Theory	Size Parameter $\alpha = \frac{\pi d}{\lambda_o}$	Diameter for $\lambda_o = 0.5\ \mu m$
Small	Rayleigh approximation	$\alpha \lesssim 0.3$	$d \lesssim 0.5\ \mu m$
Medium	Full Mie theory necessary	$0.3 \lesssim \alpha \lesssim \frac{3}{(n-1)}$	$0.05 \lesssim d \lesssim 2\ \mu m$
Large	Approximation by Diffraction and geometrical optics	$\alpha \gtrsim \frac{3}{(n-1)}$	$d \gtrsim 2\ \mu m$

and Kruger[180]). Geometrical optics can be used to compute the refraction and reflection contributions and the Fraunhofer diffraction pattern of a circular aperture gives the diffraction component. It is important to note that the diffraction contribution is independent of refractive index and is the dominant far field effect in the forward direction.

The Fraunhofer diffraction by a particle is the same as that from an opaque disk or aperture of the same shape and size. For the sphere the scattering efficiency is given as:

$$I_{diff} = \frac{\alpha^2}{4\pi} \left[\frac{2J_1 (\alpha \sin \theta)}{\alpha \sin \theta} \right]^2$$

where J_i is the first order Bessel function, θ the scattering angle, and the size parameter $\alpha = \pi d/\lambda_o$.

Figure 4.44 shows the normalized angular intensity distribution in the diffraction pattern of a circular disc or aperture as determined by the relation

$$\frac{I(\theta)}{I(0)} = \left[\frac{2J_1 (\alpha \sin \theta)}{\alpha \sin \theta} \right]$$

where $I(0)$ is the scattered intensity at $\theta = 0$, that is, in the forward direction. This approximation to the normalized intensity distribution in the forward direction is valuable because it permits a closed form analytical treatment of the scattering problem applicable to a number of instruments. It should be emphasized, however, that it predicts only the relative intensity. The actual intensity may differ by few orders of magnitude.

A general arrangement of particle size measurement by laser diffraction technique is shown in Fig. 4.45. A collimated laser light beam illuminates the particles which may be stationary or moving at any speed. The Fourier transform lens collects the light scattered by the particles. If all particles are identical, each will produce the same Fraunhofer pattern, that is, a series of alternate light and dark concentric rings, at the back focal

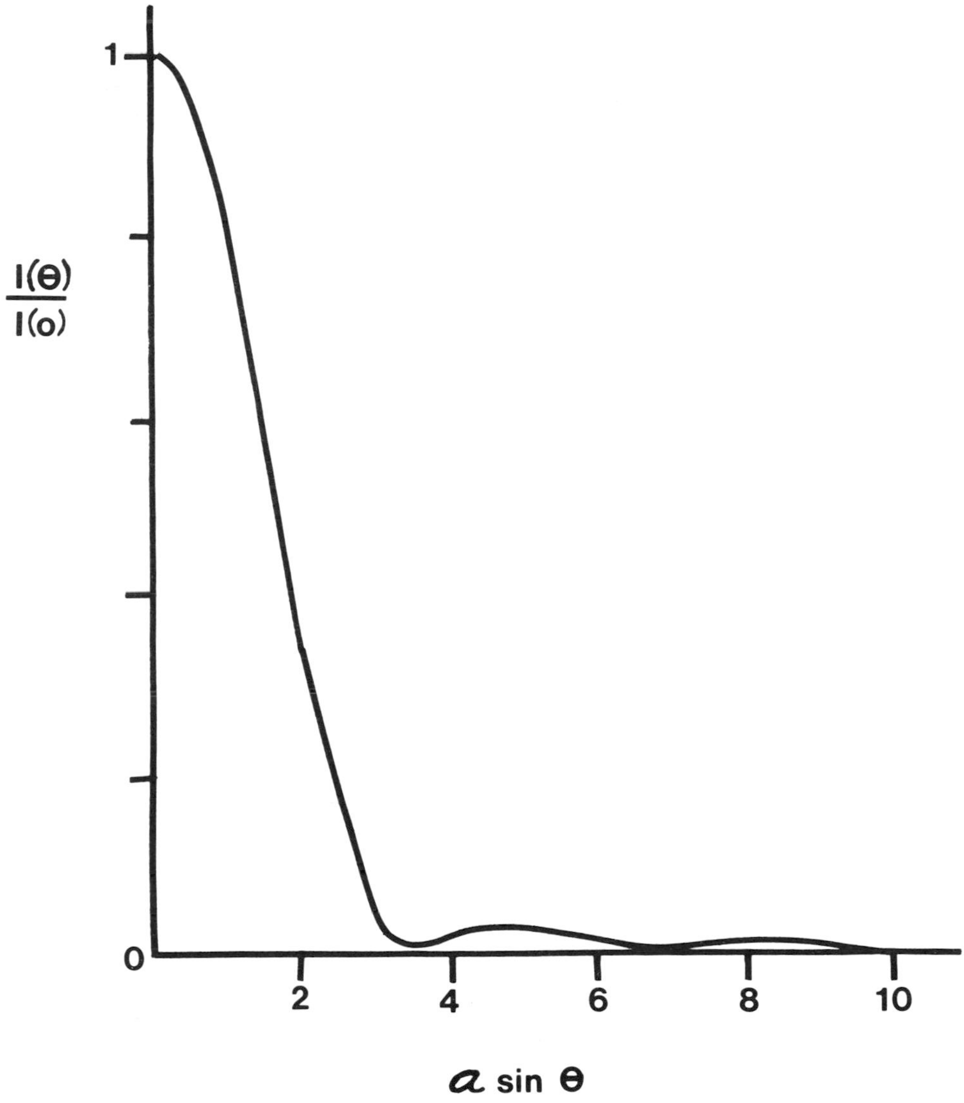

Figure 4.44 Fraunhofer diffraction pattern for a circular disk.[186]

plane of the lens. All of these patterns will be centered on the optical axis and will overlap exactly regardless of the particle position. This is because all light scattered through a given angle at any point in front of the lens is brought together at the same point in the back focal plane. A strong central intensity peak will also exist due to unscattered light from the incident beam. If the particle field is dense then a substantial portion of the light will be scattered and the resultant intensity distribution will be a sum of the individual patterns. Interference effects will influence the pattern if too many

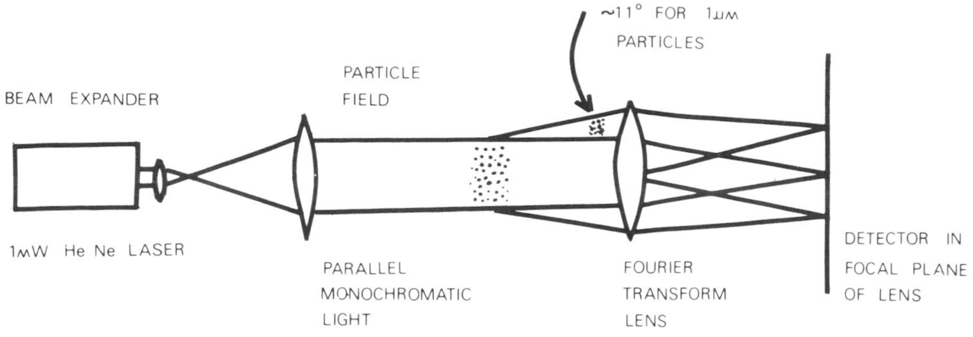

Figure 4.45 A schematic diagram of the laser diffraction particle size analyzer[186] [NB All light scattered by a particle at angle θ is focused at a position $L_{FP}\,\theta$ in the focal plane of the fourier transform (collecting) lens, where L_{FP} = focal length of the fourier transform lens]

particles are present. In most cases of practical interest a polydisperse particle field exists and the integration over all sizes smooths out the secondary maxima.

The simplest diffraction method is based on a direct measurement of the scattered intensity profile using a collecting lens[181]. It is found that for particle distributions defined by an upper limit distribution Function (no particles larger than some d_∞) the scattered intensity vs the parameter $\pi d_{vs}\theta/\lambda_o$ is independent of the most probable diameter d, Fig. 4.46, where d_{vs} is the Sauter Mean Diameter (SMD). From the measurement of intensity vs radius in the focal plane of the receiving lens SMD can be obtained directly. In practice, this is accomplished by measuring the radial distance at which the scattered intensity falls to 10 per cent of its on-axis value I (0). Some ambiguity exists due to the strong on-axis peak from the direct unscattered beam. Thus, I (0) must be determined from extrapolation as shown by the dashed line in Fig. 4.46 (bottom graph). The resulting error proves to be rather small. It is, therefore, appropriate to calibrate the instrument which correlates the SMD with the radial distance at which the measured intensity falls to 10 percent of I (0).

The sensitivity of the above Dobbins method[181] to the form of the size distribution was found to be applicable to essentially any unimodal bidisperse distribution. A monodisperse will, as was pointed out, produce definite maxima and minima in the intensity distribution, which can be used to compute the particle diameter directly.

Droplet size measurements using Dobbin's method have been made in liquid fuel sprays and the results showed good agreement with other independent measurements[182-184]. One obvious limitation is the fact that SMD rather than the complete distribution is measured. This may not be of great concern since it has been found that there is a direct relation between SMD and the width of the size distribution for fuel nozzles tested by the TV imaging method[185]. This technique gives *in-situ* measurements rather than point measurement. The approximate size range of the instrument is 10-200 μm and provides no information on the particle velocity. The main disadvantage of this technique is the limited range of spray density over which the instrument is operable. In

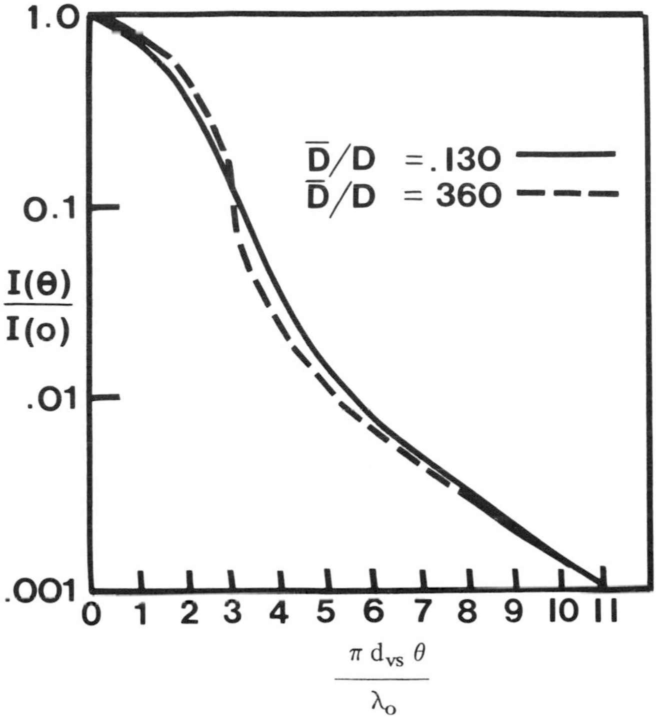

ILLUMINATION PROFILE FOR DIFFERENT SIZE DISTRIBUTIONS OF THE ULDF TYPE

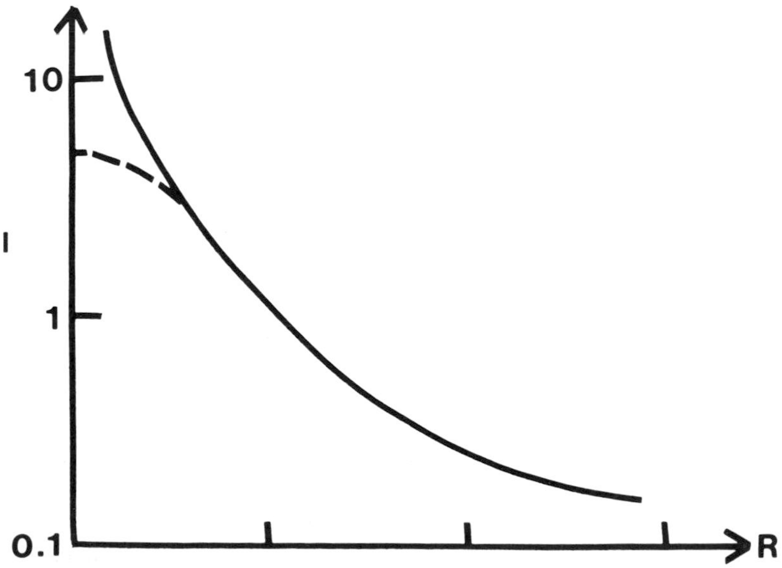

Figure 4.46 Typical intensity profile observed with polydisperse sprays[181]

dense sprays multiple scattering becomes significant and, therefore, a reliable interpretation of diffraction pattern becomes difficult.

Another method of particle size measurement based on diffraction utilizes special masks in the focal plane which pass scattered flux proportional to the second, third, and fourth power of the particle radius. The resulting signals can be used to obtain various statistical parameters for the distribution. There appears to be no particular advantage over Dobbin's method for most applications.

Recently, Swithenbank *et al.*[186] proposed a modified version of Dobbin's method wherein measurement is made of the scattered "energy distribution" rather than intensity distribution. The experimental set-up is similar to that shown in Fig. 4.45. Light energy information is extracted from the diffraction pattern by a photoelectric detector consisting of thirty-one semicircular photosensitive rings surrounding a central circle. The innermost central circle is divided into four quadrants for alignment of the optics. Each semicircular ring is sensitive to a particular size range of drops. Measured light energy distribution is converted to particle size distribution using a mini-computer (PDP8/A). One particular advantage of laser diffraction technique is that diffraction pattern generated by particles is independent of the position of particles in the laser light beam. Hence, measurements can be made with the particles stationary or moving at any speed. Also, for a group of particles, the combined diffraction pattern is directly related to their size distribution. As for the photographic method, this analyzes *in-situ* particles and hence produces spatial particle size distributions. Size distribution in the range of 2-1800 μm has been obtained with this technique; a lower limit of resolution is claimed to be about 1 μm.

Rosin-Rammler distribution is used for the characterization of the particles. The Rosin-Rammler distribution, which is really a simplified form of the Nukiyama-Tanasawa expression, is defined as that weight or volume fraction of particles or droplets larger than size d is given by R where

$$R = e^{-\left(\frac{d}{\bar{d}}\right)^n}$$

conversely, the cumulative weight fraction is given by

$$1 - R = 1 - e^{-\left(\frac{d}{\bar{d}}\right)^n}$$

where $\bar{d}$ is a characteristic size and that a weight fraction $\frac{1}{e}$ (= 0.368) is larger than $\bar{d}$, and 63.2 per cent of particles or droplets are less than $\bar{d}$. n is a measure of the spread of the size distribution such that it is equal to infinity for mono-disperse size distribution and $3 < n < 1.5$ for most fuel spray nozzles. The above equation for R may also be written as

$$\log \log \frac{1}{R} = n \log d - k$$

where k is a constant.

Thus, when $\log \log \frac{1}{R}$ is plotted against $\log d$ the experimental results should lie on a straight line, the slope of which gives the value of n, the spread of the size distribution.

The laser light power requirement is low, typically 0.5–1 m watt. This technique is extremely rapid to apply; a liquid spray nozzle can be completely calibrated in a few minutes, unlike the photographic or holographic techniques. The size distribution display with Swithenbank's method is grouped into fifteen size ranges.

Measurements in non-burning sprays or aerosols have been made successfully using Swithenbank's laser diffraction method. However, for measurements in burning sprays with high ambient lighting, parasitic effects become significant and the photodetector needs to be protected by an appropriate filter for the particular laser light wavelength. Interference filters can be used but, unfortunately, their pass band (hence, the light energy) depends upon the angle of incidence of the light beam. The use of high-power lasers, followed by attenuators before the detector or the application of a chopper to modulate the laser beam before it is passed through the flame, used in conjunction with a synchronous detector, have been proposed. However, no measurements have been reported to date in burning spray flames.

Light Scattering Fundamentals

Light scattering by particles is often used for *in-situ* particle size measurement and it is, therefore, appropriate to outline brief fundamentals of light scattering phenomena.

The general theory of light scattering from small uniform spherical particles was developed by Mie in 1908[187]. Exhaustive treatment of the light scattering from particles are given in Kerker[188], Crosignani *et al.*[190] scattered radiant flux F in the direction (θ, ϕ) is given by the relation (*see* Fig. 4.47)

$$F = \frac{I_o \lambda_o^2}{4\pi^2} \int_{\theta_1}^{\theta_2} \int_{\phi_2}^{\phi_2} [i_1(\theta, \alpha, \hat{n}) \sin^2 \phi + i_2(\theta, \alpha, \tilde{n}) \cos^2 \phi] \sin\theta \, d\theta \, d\phi$$

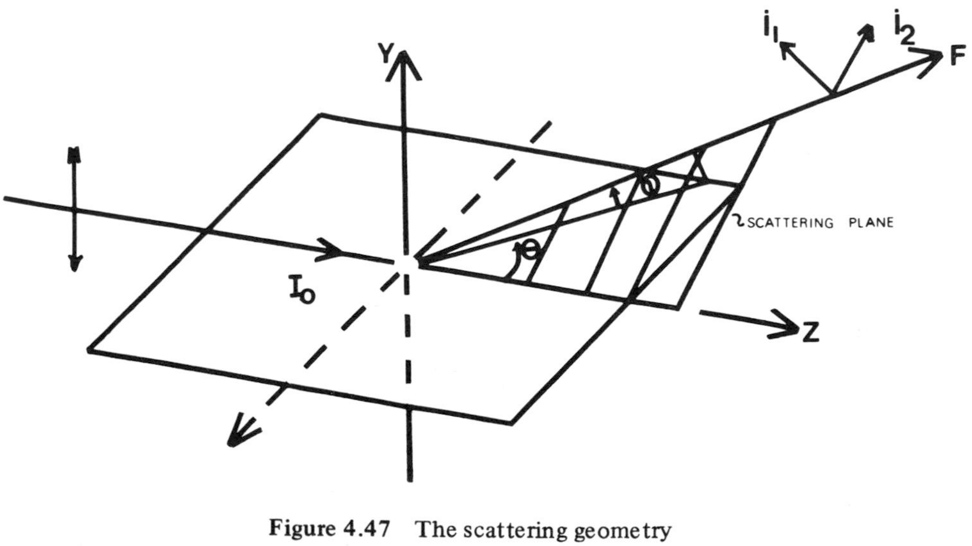

Figure 4.47 The scattering geometry

where θ and ϕ are the space angles as described in Fig. 4.47. The above equation assumes that the incident light is linearly polarized with wavelength λ_o and intensity I_o. i_1 and i_2 are the Mie coefficients for components perpendicular and parallel to the scatter plane containing the incident direction and the direction (θ, ϕ). They are seen to depend on the scattering angle θ and the particle parameter α and $\tilde{n}$ where $\alpha = \pi d/\lambda_o$ (a non-dimensional size parameter), d = particle diameter, $\tilde{n}$ = complex refractive index and is equal to $(n - ik)$, where n = real refractive index, and k = adsorption index.

The above equation indicates that, for monochromatic illumination, if all particles are of the same material the angular distribution of scattered light will depend only on particle diameter. Typical Mie scattering diagrams for soot-like particles are shown in Fig. 4.48. The polar plots of intensity vs. angle θ use a logarithmic scale with each ring

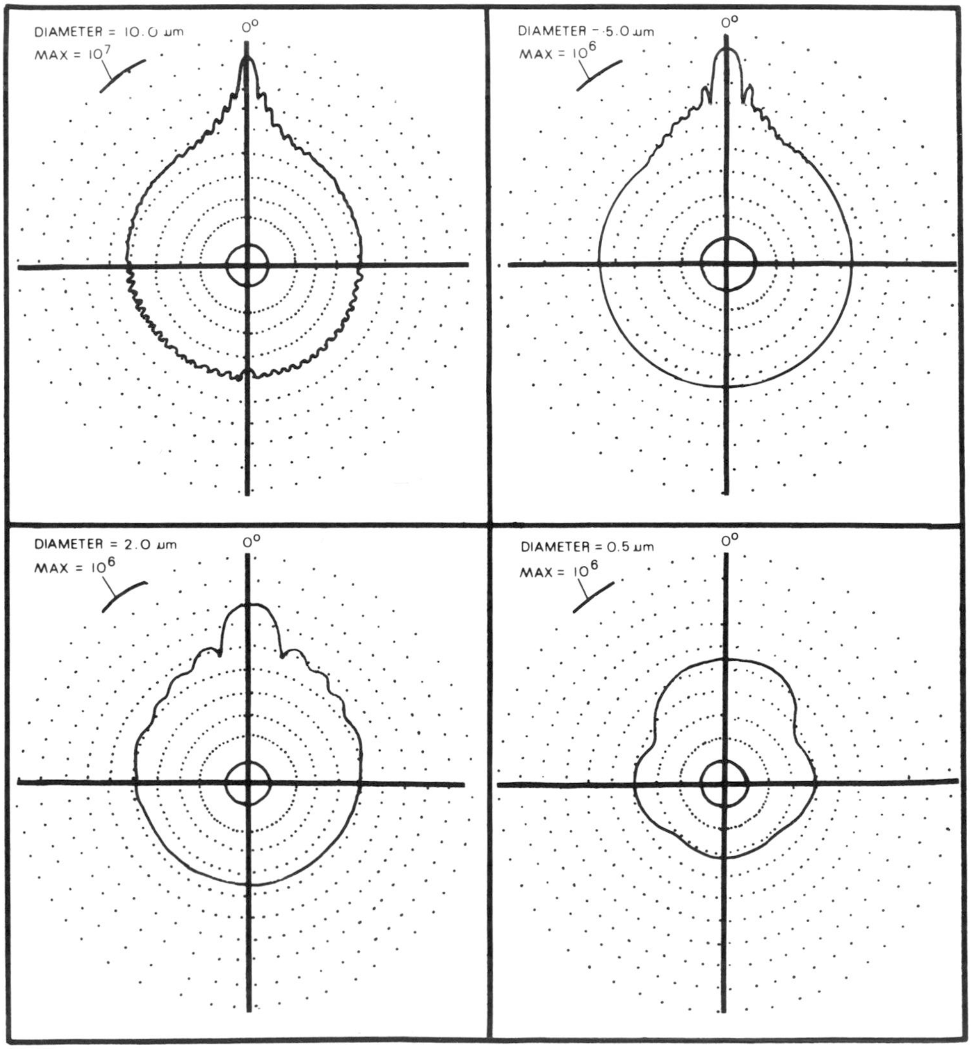

Figure 4.48 Polar plots showing the magnitude of the Mie scattering functions for typical soot like particals (u = 1.57 – 0.56i and λ_o – 05145 μm)

representing a factor of 10 and the dots representing 5 degree angular increment. Incident light propagates toward the top of the figures. Differences in the scattered light distribution over the 0.5 to 10 μm size range shown are apparent. There are also significant differences in the scattered light distribution due to refractive index variation.

It is, therefore, apparent that no simple functional relationship can describe the scattering light distribution for all particle sizes. The dependence on size parameter can be broadly classified into three ranges; namely: small, medium and large particles as shown in Table 4.10[180, 191]. The values in Table 4.10 are for transparent particles and will be altered slightly for absorbing particles. The effect of absorption on scattering is clearly illustrated in Fig. 4.49.

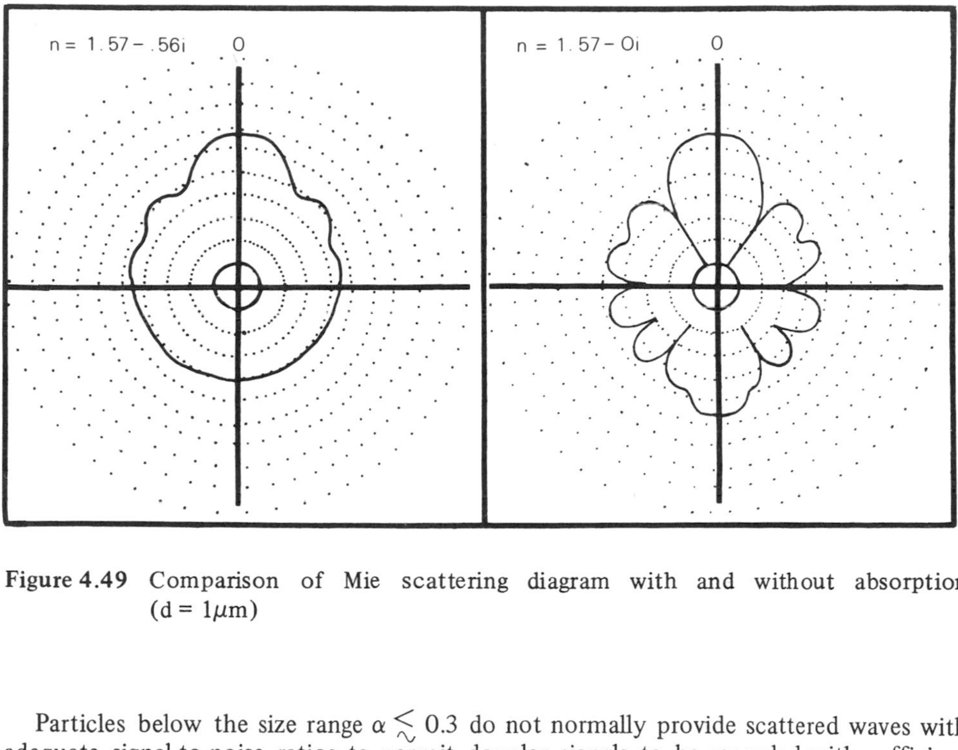

Figure 4.49 Comparison of Mie scattering diagram with and without absorption (d = 1μm)

Particles below the size range $\alpha \lesssim 0.3$ do not normally provide scattered waves with adequate signal-to-noise ratios to permit doppler signals to be recorded with sufficient accuracy. Only a few photons are scattered in this size range. Mie theory of light scattering is also valid for $0.3 \gtrsim \alpha \gtrsim 3/(n-1)$. Nevertheless, for $\alpha \lesssim 0.3$ the simple Rayleigh formula can be used, and for particles $\alpha \gtrsim 3/(n-1)$, the numerical calculations become very tedious. Calculations using laws of geometrical optics can then be applied to provide the necessary information on the reflected and refracted light waves emerging from these large particles. Dave[192] has developed a computer program for this purpose. Since a direct comparison between the measured angular distribution of scattered light and the Mie theory is nearly impossible in practice, most instruments rely on the measurement of intensity ratios, integrated intensity over a fixed solid angle, or some other characteristic which is reasonably well behaved in a given size range. These various approaches are examined later in connection with their application to specific measurement devices.

Mie theory applies only to single particles. When the optical system receives light from more than one particle, it becomes necessary to consider multiple scattering from particles. Generally one can assume that the Mie scattering distribution is applicable if all particles are of the same size ($0.05 < d < 2\ \mu m$) and are separated far enough for the light scattered by one particle not to be strongly influenced by the surrounding particles. This, of course, depends not only on the particle number density but also on the length over which the particles scatter light. If the particles are poly-disperse (not all of the same size) then some average spatial distribution of the scattered light will exist. Useful information can still be obtained in this case. However, if the number density measurement volume length is so high that single scattering cannot be assumed it will be very difficult to make measurements with any degree of confidence. Fortunately, it is to our advantage that in most practical combustion system single scattering assumption can be made.

In considering light scattering from various types of particles, it is important to consider non-spherical particle effects. It is reasonable to assume that liquid droplets are spherical, but soot, ash, and other solid particulates are usually not. Various extensions of the Mie theory to ellipsoids, cylinders, and other non-spherical particles have been made but these have only limited usefulness in practice. Soot tends to form chain-like agglomerates of varying lengths, for example, and the orientation may or may not be random depending upon the flow situation. In the Rayleigh limit ($d < \lambda_o$) particle shape is less important and some reasonable approximation may be made. In most cases, the particles are treated as spheres of some equivalent diameter. The study by Holland and Gagne[193] shows that this approximation is valid for polydisperse systems of irregular particles, at least in the forward scatter.

Light Scattering – Based on Laser Velocimeter

When a particle passes through a control volume at the intersection of two laser beams, it will scatter light in proportion to the integrated light intensity it sees. This results in a sinusoidal variation in scattered light due to the formation of interference fringe pattern in the control volume. The frequency of this signal is proportional to the particle velocity and the signal modulation is a function of particle size[194-198]. A particle with a diameter very small relative to the fringe spacing will produce a signal with full modulation, whereas a particle nearly equal in diameter to the fringe spacing will see the same integrated light intensity at any position and the resulting signal modulation will be nearly zero. Farmer[194-197] has proposed that this effect can be used for particle sizing. Unfortunately, it is found in practice that other factors, for example, the refractive index of the particle, laser power, size and position of the receiving aperture, also influence signal modulation.

These effects have been analyzed by several investigators and the general conclusions are that for small beam angles, fairly accurate measurements can be made using a forward scatter collection geometry. Lennert *et al.*[159] used this system to study fuel spray in Diesel engines but, unfortunately, without success.

The data analysis system described by Gupta[77] has many advantages and can be applied for simultaneous measurement of particle velocity and size.

Recently Yule *et al.*[199] proposed another technique for sizing large particles based on the use of a laser velocimeter (LV). Rather than measure signal modulation they measure the peak mean value of the Doppler signal for particles larger than the fringe spacing. An analysis predicts that the peak mean signal should increase monotonically with particle size for particles above a certain diameter. As in the case of Farmer's method such a system does allow simultaneous measurement of particle size and velocity. The authors do not present information on the useful particle size range for this method and, in fact, it appears that this would be severely limited, particularly at the lower end. Another problem is that this is an absolute intensity method and therefore suffers from all of the defects common to such techniques, including a direct dependence on particle trajectory through the probe volume. This limitation will be difficult to overcome.

Fristrom[200] proposed a variety of optical systems for measuring sizes of droplets, particles, fibres, etc., under different conditions. These optical methods were for particle sizes larger than a few wavelengths of laser light source. In these methods of particle sizing, the fringe spacing was varied and the zeros in the AC amplitude were observed. The fringe spacings at which these zeros occur were directly related to the size of the particle.

Waterston and Chou[201] used two photomultipliers and two tracking filters to measure the ratio between the forward and back scattered light and found that this ratio is a monotonic function of particle size over the nominal range of 0.015-0.5 μm. This technique is capable of measuring both the size and velocity and gives a point measurement.

Durst[202] also used two photomultipliers on either side of the optical axis of a forward scattering LV arrangement. Under certain conditions it was found that the phase difference between the signals could be related to the particle size.

Droplet Sizing by Means of Fluorescence

All of the sizing methods described in previous sections are based on the collection and detection of light elastically scattered by the droplets. With the exception of the imaging methods they therefore suffer from inherent limitations imposed by the nature of the scattering process. Stevenson[303, 304] proposed a derivative of Farmer's method based on fluorescence rather than scattering. Unless the particles are naturally fluorescent this requires the addition of a suitable fluorescent dye to the liquid being atomized. However, the method is free of many difficulties found in Farmer's method. A major experimental advantage is the fact that a "backscatter" configuration can be employed. This is not possible with any of the non-imaging scattered light techniques due to the complicated lobe structure observed in backscatter. Fluorescence emission is, by contrast, essentially isotropic and location of the receiving optics is unimportant.

The principle of the fluorescence particle sizing method is that in a crossed beam arrangement liquid droplets passing through the probe volume both scatter light and fluoresce. The scattered light is at the laser wavelength, but the fluorescence is in a band at longer wavelengths. This is illustrated in Fig. 4.50, which shows the excitation (absorption) and emission spectra for the fluorescent dye Rhodamine 6G in ethylene glycol solution. Light at any wavelength in the excitation band will be absorbed and result in nearly instantaneous ($\sim 5 \times 10^{-9}$ sec) emission of fluorescence over the entire emission band. The two strongest lines of the argon laser are indicated in Fig. 4.50 and are seen to be well suited for exciting this particular material. With an appropriate optical filter the scattered light at these wavelengths can be blocked while allowing the fluorescent emission to be transmitted to a photodetector without interference from reflections and scattering at windows and other surfaces.

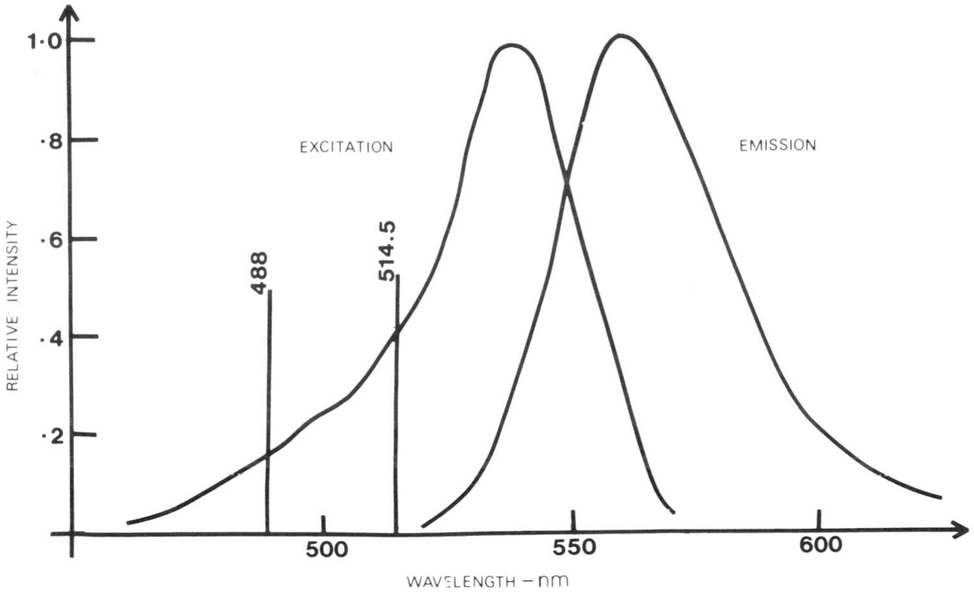

Figure 4.50 Fluorescence spectrum for Rhodamine 6G in ethylene glycol solution[204]

Analysis shows that signal modulation (fringe visibility), V, should vary with cylinder diameter, d, as a sine function, that is,

$$V = \frac{I_{max} - I_{min}}{I_{max} + I_{min}} = \frac{\sin(\pi d/a)}{(\pi d/a)}$$

where a is the fringe spacing in the probe volume. I_{max} and I_{min} are the maximum and minimum photodetector outputs observed as the micropipette passes through the probe volume. Good agreement was obtained between the experimental and theoretical signal visibility by the fluorescence method for particle size around 10 μm.

Practical problems that must be overcome in order to develop a reliable instrument for fuel spray analysis include (a) means of correcting for errors that may result when droplets pass through the edges of the probe volume and (b) ways of accounting for the finite size range that can be covered at one instrument setting. Both of these problems are also present when using Farmer's method, and he has considered the first in some detail[197]. The second problem is caused by the multiple lobes characteristic of the visibility function. Obviously it is desirable to work in the linear region of the lobe at V values above that corresponding to the second maximum. This limits the particles that can be sized to those ranging from about $d = 0.2\delta$ to $d = 0.8\delta$. Thus, for example, with a fringe spacing of 10 μm one could measure droplets with diameters ranging from 2 to 8 μm. A fringe spacing of 40 μm would permit sizing of droplets from 8 to 32 μm and so on. The fringe spacing is easily changed by altering the separation of the two input beams or changing the focal length of the receiving lens. Nevertheless, there are practical limits on the variation of fringe spacing that can be achieved. In any case particles outside the chosen range must be detected by peak intensity or some other means to eliminate ambiguity due to the multiple lobes. One significant advantage of the fluorescence method is that it affords a means of accurately calibrating other single particle instruments.

Extinction Methods

None of the optical methods previously described has been proved useful for sizing particles below about 0.5 μm except under ideal conditions, particularly when the particles are highly absorbing. Therefore, research on topics such as soot formation and growth requires a different approach. One technique has been to measure the extinction of light passed through a relatively dense collection of particles. This is often referred to as a turbidity measurement.

Dobbins and Jizmagian[205] showed that, if the refractive index and volume concentration of the particles are known, the Sauter Mean Diameter (SMD) can be determined by a single light transmission measurement. When concentration is unknown a measurement at two discrete wavelengths is required. Lester and Wittig[206] employed a similar "dispersion quotient method" for soot growth studies in a shock tube. Nevertheless, more recent work at Purdue has shown that interpretation of the data is more complex than originally believed. Preliminary measurements by Holve and Self[207] in an ash-laden coal fired MHD channel with an extinction method indicated some potential for average size determination in the case of relatively dense flows with large particles.

Extinction methods require a significant fraction of the incident light to be attenuated if accurate measurements are to be made, but if the light transmission is less than 75 per cent multiple scattering exists and the results are invalid. In addition, the number density of the particles must be known or assumed to uncouple the particle size. Such methods therefore are usable only under special conditions and are of limited utility for most combustion studies.

Other Methods

A number of optical sizing methods that do not fall directly within previously mentioned categories appear to offer some promise for combustion studies. Several of these, including two that are actually a combination of other methods, are discussed here to illustrate different approaches that are being taken.

Bachalo[208-209] described a system for application in fluidized bed combustion studies which utilizes the multiple ratio method of Hirleman and Wittig in combination with the fringe visibility method of Farmer. A single low power argon laser serves as the common source. The multiple ratio system has a predicted range of 0.5–10 μm while the visibility system range is 2–100 μm. The 0.5145 μm wavelength of the argon laser is focused to a spot of approximately 50 μm diameter to obtain a high probe volume intensity for the smaller particles sensed by the ratio detection electronics, while the 0.488 μm wavelength is focused to 500 μm diameter at the intersection of the crossed beams in the fringe visibility system. The visibility system electronics allow measurement of size and velocity simultaneously for the larger particles. Rather sophisticated electronics are obviously required to produce the desired output information. There are no breakthroughs here, but rather a straightforward utilization of recent developments resulting in a versatile (albeit expensive) instrument.

Bernard and Penner[210] used the photocurrent power spectrum resulting from Brownian motion of soot particles (50–1000 Å) in hydrocarbon flames as a measure of particle size. Good accuracy and spatial resolution were obtained in a flat flame burner study, but the technique would not be applicable to more complex situations.

Powell, *et al.*[211] employed a combination of the forward lobe ratio method and a spectral turbidity measurement to obtain mean particle diameter, refractive index, and volume concentration in smoke. Good results were obtained for the small ($\sim$1 μm) nearly transparent particles of smoke. The method is not useful for particles exhibiting absorption, however.

Another *in-situ* measurement device only recently developed is the "optical particle-sizing counter" of Holve and Self[212]. This utilizes a single focused He-Ne laser beam with slightly off-axis forward scatter collection to obtain a small probe volume. The demonstrated range in cold flows is 2–25 μm at present. Particle size is determined from peak scattered intensity which implies that a stable laser is necessary. Since particle path through the probe volume also affects peak intensity, a rather complex numerical inversion scheme is used to unfold the true size distribution. Apart from this numerical inversion which can be implemented on a mini-computer, the system is simple and low cost.

Driscoll *et al.*[213, 214] used spectral broadening of scattered light due to the particles to measure *in-situ* measurements of submicron particles (range 0.04 to 0.25 μm) in an acetylene-oxygen flame.

A final and unique sizing device is the single particle extinction measurement system of Faxvog[215]. This has not been designed as an *in-situ* instrument, but it may be possible to extend the concept involved to such measurements. Fig. 4.51 illustrates the system. A stable He-Ne laser is forced to operate in the so-called doughnut mode (TEM_{01}*) by precisely placing an ink spot on a Brewester angle window in the laser cavity. The output is then a ring of light with an intensity minimum on axis as shown in Fig. 4.51. A $\lambda/4$ plate and polarizing prism are used to produce parallel and perpendicularly polarized output beams which are brought to a common focus by a lens. No fringes are formed since the beams are cross-polarized. This arrangement permits electronic discrimination so that only particles passing through the exact center of the beam-crossing region are sampled. In this case simultaneous double pulses will be detected on both channels. The photodiodes measure single particle extinction which was previously shown to be directly related to scattering cross-section for small particles[215]. The instrument has been successfully used for measuring the size distribution of opaque particulates in the 0.05-5 μm size range in a diesel exhaust[216].

Soot Size and Concentration Measurement by Laser Light Scattering (LLS)

The studies on the structure and properties of spray combustion of liquid hydrocarbon fuels have always been a subject of great interest in connection with technologies of industrial burners, gas turbine combustors, and diesel engines, etc. In recent years particular attention has been focused upon the formation and evolution of carbonaceous particulates in the above systems which occurs due to the local variation in the rates of mixing and the degree of completeness of combustion. A major reason for the research

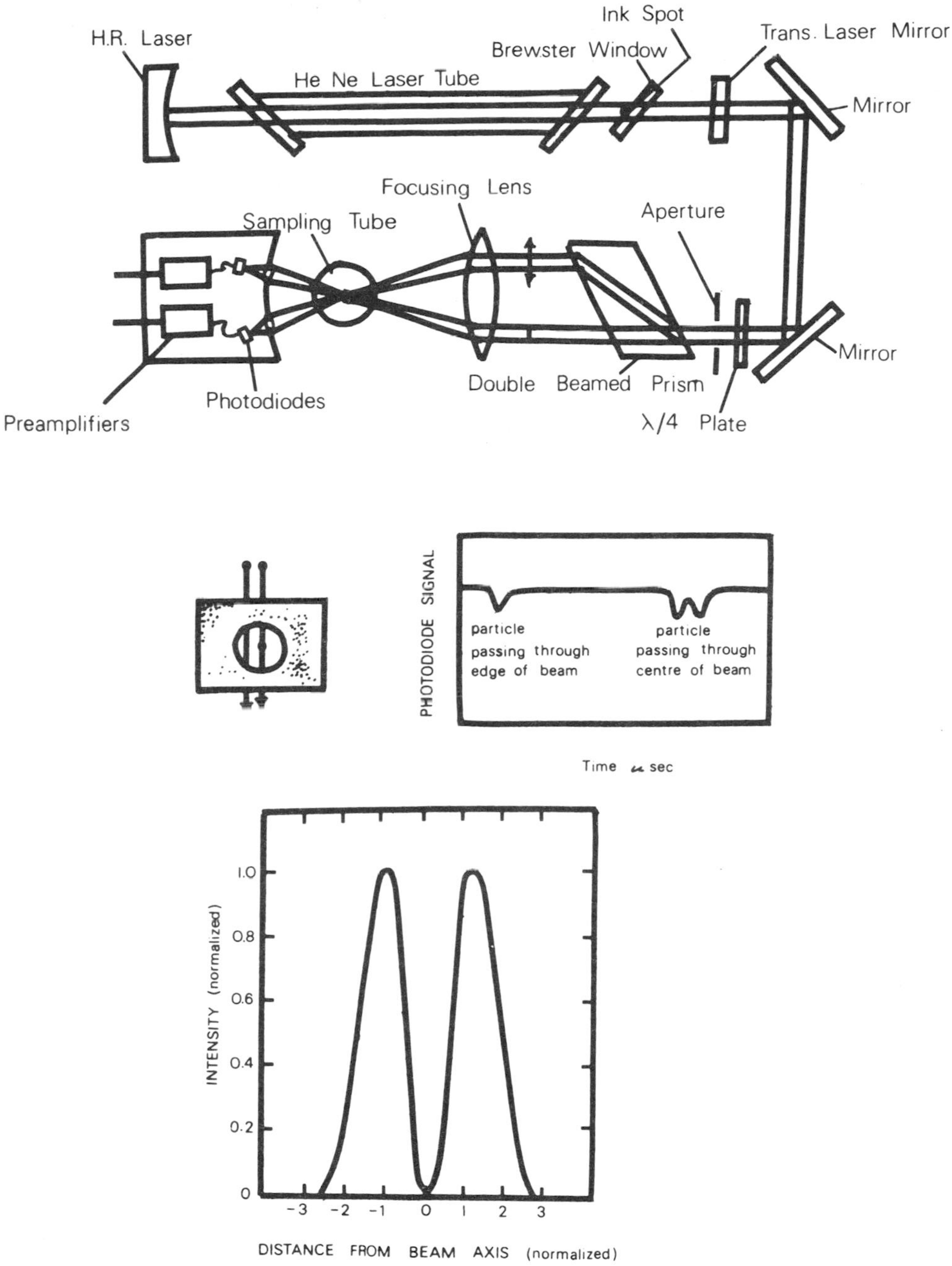

Figure 4.51 Single particle extinstion method of Faxvog[216]

effort in this direction is the growing concern with the health effects of fossil fuels utilization and also with the increased need of using heavy fuel oils with high carbon-to-hydrogen ratio, high aromatic content and coal slurries in the existing combustion systems. The formation of soot in turbulent diffusion flames is highly complex and involves many chemical and physical processes, several of which are still unknown. There is therefore an urgent need for a more powerful diagnostic technique which can provide information on soot formation and evolution in practical combustion systems.

The laser light scattering (LLS) techniques have the unique potential of space and time-resolved measurements without any physical disturbance to the flow.

Theoretical Background for Laser Light Scattering and Extinction

The monochromatic energy flux scattered $F(\theta)$, in the experimental condition, by a scattering volume ΔV under a solid angle of the collecting optics $\Delta\Omega$, at a scattering angle θ, is given by the expression[217, 218].

$$F(\theta) = \dot{Q}(\theta)\, \Delta V\, \Delta\Omega\, I_o$$

where I_o is the intensity of the laser light beam incident on the scattering volume.

The quantity $\dot{Q}(\theta)$ [cm^{-1}, str^{-2}], which is the energy flux scattered at an angle θ per unit solid angle from a unit volume and unit incident energy flux density, depends both on the number density of the scatterers N[cm^{-3}] and on the physical nature of the scattering interaction, through a differential cross-section C[cm^2, str^{-1}]. $\dot{Q}(\theta)$ is given by the following expression:

$$\dot{Q}(\theta) = N\ C(\theta)$$

The scattering cross-sections are functions of the physical and chemical properties of the scatterers, wavelength of the incident beam λ_o, polarization properties of the incident and scattered beams, and the scattering angle θ, which is defined by the direction of the incident and scattered beams. When different non-interfering i scatterers are present in the probe volume, $\dot{Q}$ is given by the expression

$$\dot{Q}^{\lambda_o}_{\ell,\kappa}(\theta) = \sum_i N_i C^{\lambda_o}_{\ell,\kappa}(\theta)$$

where the subscripts ℓ and κ refer to the polarization state of the scattered and incident beams.

More precisely $C_{V,V}$ and $C_{H,V}$ are the cross-sections relative to a vertically polarized incident beam when the scattered light is analyzed in the vertical and horizontal planes respectively.

$C_{H,H}$ and $C_{V,H}$ are the cross-sections when the incident light is horizontally polarized and the scattered light is analyzed in the horizontal and vertical planes respectively.

The transmissivity I/I_o of a collimated beam through a scattering/absorbing medium of thickness L is given by the expression

$$I/I_o = \exp\left[-\int_o^L C_{ext}(\ell)\, N(\ell)\, d\ell\right]$$

where C_{ext} is the extinction cross-section.

The quantitative definition of the relevant cross-sections is presented in many text-books[217-219] and an analysis applied to sooting flames was carried out by D'Alessio *et al.*[220-221].

Rayleigh Scattering

The Rayleigh scattering occurs when the scatterers have characteristic dimensions much smaller than the wavelength of the incident light beam. In the Rayleigh approximation the scattering angular cross-sections $C_{V,V}$, $C_{H,V}$ and $C_{V,H}$ are independent of the scattering angle θ, whereas the $C_{H,H}$ cross-section varies with θ given by the expression

$$C_{H,H} = C_{V,V} \cos^2\theta + C_{H,V} \sin^2\theta$$

Moreover from the reciprocity law $C_{H,V}$ is equal to $C_{V,H}$. The ratio $\rho_V = C_{H,V}/C_{V,V}$ is defined as depolarization ratio. When the scatterer does not present any optical or geometrical anisotropy its polarizability is a scalar quantity and the depolarized cross-sections $C_{H,V}$ and $C_{V,H}$ are equal to zero. For a spherical absorbing particle the angular scattering cross-section by a vertically polarized light is given as

$$C^{\lambda_o}_{V,V} = \frac{\lambda_o^2}{4\pi^2}\left[\frac{m^2-1}{m^2+2}\right]^2 \alpha^6$$

and the absorption cross-section is equal to

$$C^{\lambda_o}_{abs} = -\frac{\lambda_o^2}{4\pi^2}\, I_o\left[\frac{m^2-1}{m^2+2}\right]\alpha^3$$

where $\alpha = \pi D/\lambda_o$ is the ratio of the peripheral length of the particle to the wavelength of the initial light and $m = n{-}ik$ is the complex refractive index of the substance (particle). It is customary to refer to non-dimensional parameters in the theory of scattering and absorbing spherical particles. The efficiencies for scattering and absorption (Q_{scatt} and Q_{abs}) are defined as the ratio between the physical cross-section and the geometrical cross-section of the particle, and the angular cross-sections, $i(\theta)$, can be given by the following expressions:

$$C^{\lambda_o}_{V,V} = \frac{\lambda_o^2}{4\pi^2}\, i_\perp(\theta)$$

$$C^{\lambda_o}_{H,H} = \frac{\lambda_o^2}{4\pi^2}\, i_\parallel(\theta)$$

where the subscripts ⊥ and || mean perpendicular (vertical) and parallel (horizontal) components of the scattered light respectively.

Finally, the Rayleigh Theory can be summarized by the following equations:

$$Q_{abs} = A\alpha$$

$$Q_{scatt} = B\alpha^4$$

$$i_{\perp}(\theta) = \frac{3}{2} B\alpha^6$$

$$i_{||}(\theta) = \frac{3}{2} B\alpha^6 \cos^2\theta$$

where A and B are algebraic functions of the complex refractive index of the particles.

Lorenz-Mie Scattering

Lorenz-Mie is applicable in the range when the scatteres have characteristic dimensions comparable with the wavelength of the incident light beam and the Rayleigh Theory is not adequate. The Lorenz-Mie equations provide a complete characterization of the absorption and scatter of a spherical particle as a function of the perimeter/wavelength ratio ($\alpha = \pi D/\lambda_o$) and the complex refractive index $m = n - ik$.

They can be used to calculate the efficiency of extinction (Q_{ext}), radiation from the particles, scattering efficiency (Q_{scatt}), angular distribution and state of polarization of the scattered radiation through the parameters $i_{\perp}(\theta)$ and $i_{||}(\theta)$.

$$Q_{ext} = Q_{ext}(\alpha, m)$$

$$Q_{scatt} = Q_{scatt}(\alpha, m)$$

$$Q_{abs} = Q_{ext} - Q_{scatt}$$

$$i_{\perp}(\theta) = i_{\perp}(\theta, \alpha, m)$$

$$i_{||}(\theta) = {}_{||}(\theta, \alpha, m)$$

These functions have been calculated by D'Alessio *et al.*[220,222] for soot particles assuming a complex refractive index m = 1.57 – 0.56 i[222] and are depicted in Figs. 4.52 and 4.53. For values of $\alpha \leqslant 0.5$, the extinction is almost exclusively due to true absorption and increases linearly with α; for $0.5 < \alpha < 0.7$, it increases more than linearly. For $\alpha > 0.7$ the extinction efficiency passes through a maxima at $\alpha \simeq 3$ and finally levels off to an asymptotic value near two. The scattering efficiency increases initially with the fourth power of α, as expected from the Rayleigh theory, and has a minor increase for larger α. Nevertheless, for $\alpha \geqslant 1$ the contribution of scattered light to the total extinction is comparable with that due to true absorption. In Fig. 4.53 the angular patterns of $i_{\perp}(\theta)$ and $i_{||}(\theta)$ are illustrated for different values of α. For values of α up to 0.3 (particles diameter less than 500 Å with λ_o = 514.5 mm) the patterns are similar to those predicted by the Rayleigh theory. The vertical component is independent from the

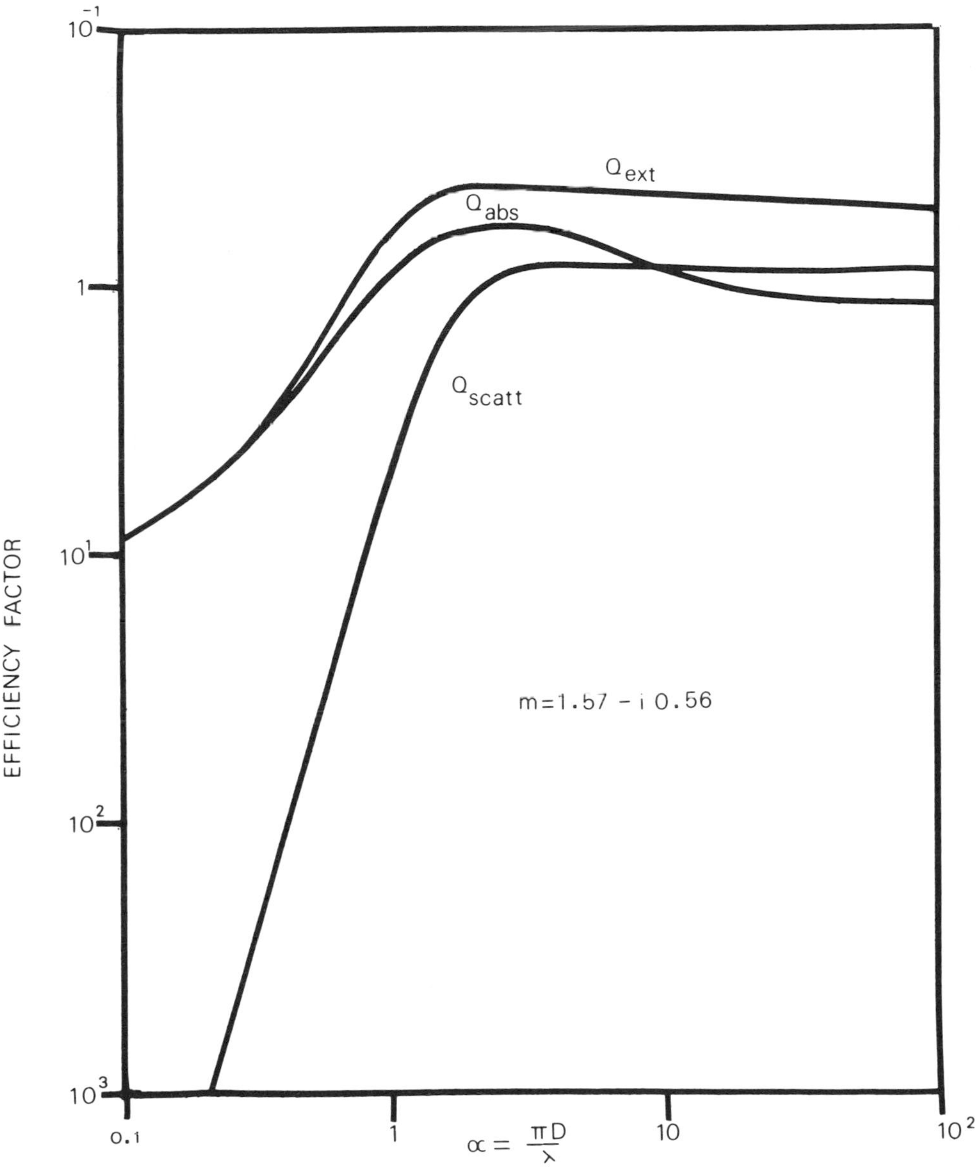

Figure 4.52 Efficiency factors of soot particles for extinction (Q_{ext}), absorbtion (Q_{abs}) and scattering (Q_{scatt}) as function of the parameter.[224]

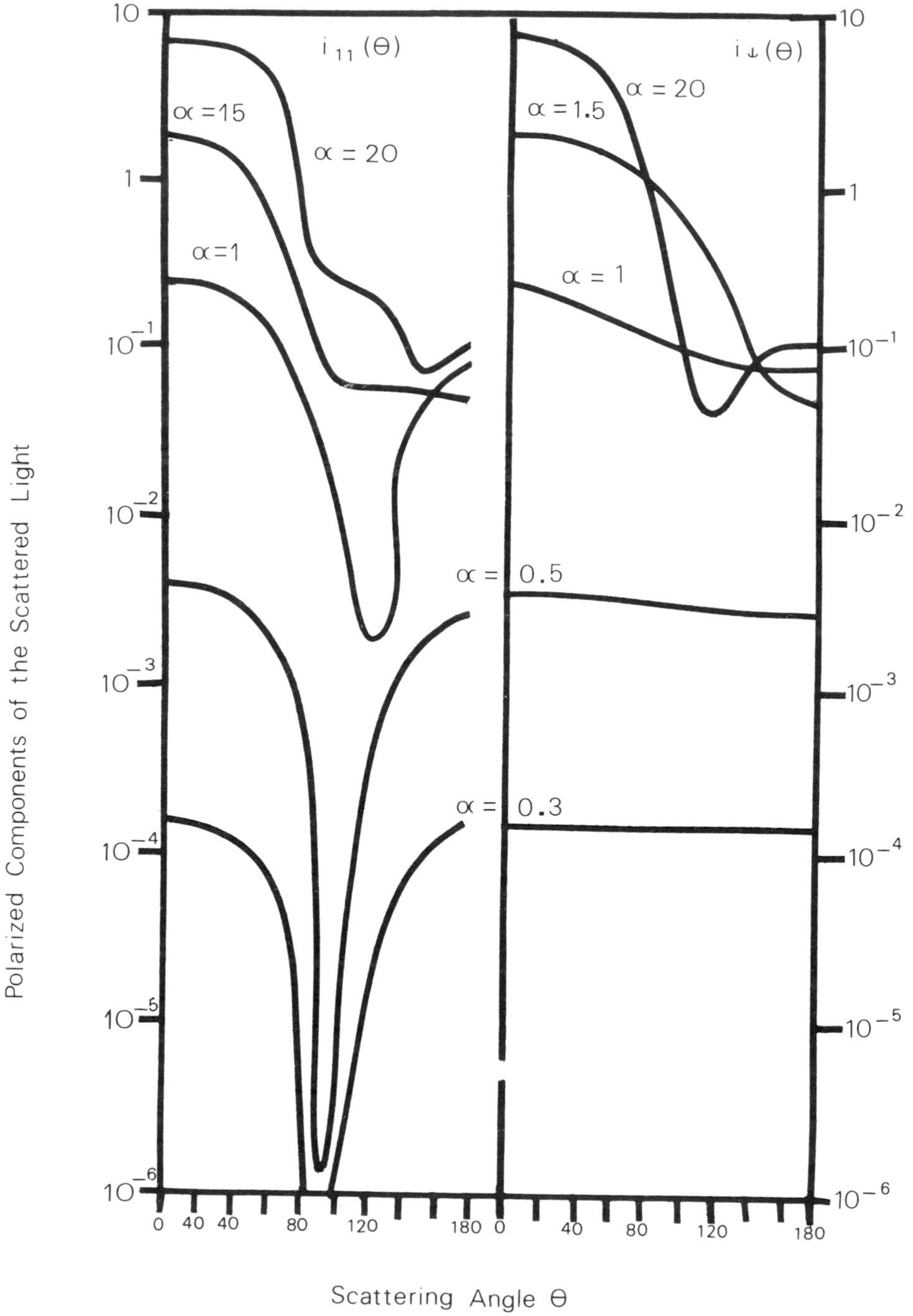

Figure 4.53 Angular pattern of the scattering components polarized in the vertical and horizontal plane for different values of α.[224]

scattering angle while the horizontal component follows a $\cos^2$ dependence. Both cross-sections increase with increase in particle size when the scattered radiation is more in the forward lobe than the backward lobe. For particles with α larger than one ($D >$ 1500 Å) the scattering patterns in the backward directions begin to exhibit oscillations with α.

The scattering parameter for soot, α, is less than unity and therefore it is possible to utilize either forward or backward scattering. Fig. 4.54 shows a sketch of the experimental apparatus. Measurements are carried out of the scattered light signal (light signal collected at small angle relative to the laser light beam, typically 5–10°) and extinction signal due to the presence of the soot particles. The electronic signal of the scattered light is processed using a lock-in amplifier. In this an analog phase sensitive detection system is used wherein only those signal components which are synchronous with the reference yield a net output.

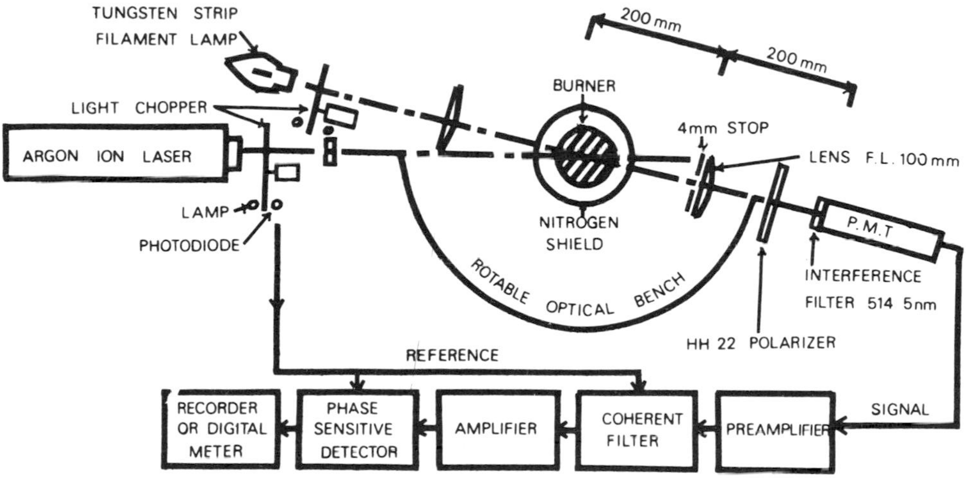

Figure 4.54 Schematic of the optical and electronic apparatus for the laser light scattering and extinction experiments.[224]

Application to Combustion Systems

In a combustion system the hot fluid can be assumed to consist of Rayleigh scatterers (gas phase) and Rayleigh and Mie scatterers (soot particles). The soot cross-sections are several orders of magnitude larger than the gas cross-sections and therefore the contribution of gases to the scattering is not significant. The soot concentration can be obtained with the measured value of the absolute value of the scattered light and the soot particle size. The measurement of soot particle size is not very easy. The size of soot particles lies in the range of 10 Å to 1500 Å[223-225] and spread in both the Rayleigh and Mie regimes. In the Rayleigh regime the angular patterns of the $C_{V,V}(\theta)$ and $C_{H,H}(\theta)$ cross-sections do not depend upon the size of the particles. Nevertheless, it is possible to exploit the different dependence law from the size of the scattering cross-section and the absorption cross-section. For spherical particles, the ratio between the scattering and absorption cross-section is proportional to α^3. The ratio therefore depends upon the volume of the particle. The quantities $\dot{Q}^{\lambda_o}_{V,V}(\theta)$ and $k^{\lambda_o}_{ext}$ are determined through scattering and extinction measurements and are given by

$$\dot{Q}_{V,V}(\theta) = NC_{V,V}(\theta)$$

$$k^{\lambda_o}_{ext} = \frac{1}{L} \ln \frac{I_o}{I} = NC^{\lambda_o}_{ext}\, NC^{\lambda_o}_{abs}$$

Since the system is not spatially homogeneous, local values of the extinction coefficient must be obtained.

In the Mie regime, both the $C_{V,V}$ and $C_{H,H}$ angular behavior are a function of the size of the particles through the α parameter. Furthermore, the ratio of $C_{H,H}/C_{V,V}$ is a function of α for a fixed scattering angle. Therefore the quantities $\dot{Q}_{V,V}(\theta)/\dot{Q}_{V,V}(\pi-\theta)$, $\dot{Q}_{H,H}(\theta)/Q_{H,H}(\pi-\theta)$ and $\dot{Q}_{H,H}(\theta)/\dot{Q}_{V,V}(\theta)$ are suitable for determining the size of the particles. The ratio between scatter and extinction $\dot{Q}_{V,V}(\theta)/k_{ext}$ is still usable.

The choice between the above two approaches requires an analysis of the sensitivity of the above quantities with the variation in particle size and other experimental conditions.

References

1. Fristrom, R. M., and Westenberg, A. A.: *Flame Structure,* McGraw Hill, New York, 1965.
2. Folson, R. G.: *Trans. A.S.M.E.* **78,** October, 1956, p. 1447.
3. Hubbard, C. V.: *Trans. A.S.M.E.*, **61,** August, 1939, p. 447.
4. Beér, J. M., and Chigier, N. A.: *Combustion Aerodynamics*, Applied Science Publishers, London, 1972.
5. Chedaille, J., and Braud, Y.: *Industrial Flames,* **I:** Measurements in Flames, Edward Arnold, 1972.
6. Liepmann, H. W., and Roshko, A.: *Elements of Gas Dynamics,* Wiley, 1957.
7. Becker, H. A., and Brown, A. P. G.: Response Functions for Pitot Probes in Turbulent Streams, *Report 2-72, Department of Chemical Engineering, Queen's University, Ontario,* May 1972.
8. Becher, H. A., and Brown, A. P. G.: Response Characteristics of Pitot and Static Pressure Probes, with Application to Measuring Turbulence Intensity, *Report 1-71, Department of Chemical Engineering, Queen's University, Ontario,* Sept. 1971.
9. Ebrahimi, I.: *Combustion and Flame,* **11,** 1967, p. 255.
10. Lenze, B.: Doktor-Ingenieurs Dissertation, Universität Karlsruhe, 1971.
11. Eickhoff, H.: *Chem. Ing. Techn.* **40,** 22, 1968, p. 995.
12. Fechheimer, C. J.: *Trans. A.S.M.E.,* **48,** 1926, p. 965.
13. Hiett, G. F., and Powell, G. E.: *The Engineer,* Jan. 1962, p. 165.
14. Lee, J. C., and Ash, J. E.: *Trans. A.S.M.E.,* **48,** 1926, p. 965.
15. MacPharlane, J.: NGTE Pyestock, Farnborough, England. Also see Gupta, A. K., Syred, N., and Beér, J. M.: *Gas Wärme International,* **23,** 2, 1974, p. 39.
16. Beér, J. M., Chigier, N. A., Koopmans, G., and Lee, K. B.: Intl. Flame Research Foundation, Ijmuiden, Holland, *F72/2/9*, 1965.
17. Poulston, B. V., and Winter, E. F.: Techniques for the Study of Air Flow and Fuel Droplet Distribution in Combustion Systems, *6th Symp. (Int.) on Comb.,* 1956, p. 833.
18. Chesters, A. K.: The Influence of Velocity Gradients on Five-hole Pitot Measurements, I.F.R.F., Ijmuiden, *Doc. nr. G 02/9/10,* Nov. 1965.
19. Bradshaw, P.: *An Introduction to Turbulence and its Measurement*, Pergamon Press, 1971.

20. Gupta, A. K.: M.Sc. Dissertation, The University of Southampton, Department of Aeronautics and Astronautics, 1970
21. King, R. O.: *Engineering* **117**, 1924, 249.
22. Tyler, E.: *J. Scientific Instruments,* **6**, 1929, p. 310.
23. Ziegler, M.: The Construction of a Hot Wire Anemometer With Linear Scale and Negligible Lag, Verk Konikl, *Akad. van Wetenshap,* **15**, 1934, p. 3.
24. A Bibliography of Thermal Anemometry, *TSI Quarterly*: Nov./Dec. 1978.
25. Weske, J. R.: Methods of Measurement in High Air Velocities by the Hot Wire Method, *NACA TN. No. 880*, 1943. See also *NACA TN No. 881.*
26. Kovasznay, L. S. G.: Development of Turbulence Measuring Equipment, *NACA Report 1209*, 1951.
27. Shepard, C. E.: A Self-Excited, Alternating Current, Constant Temperature Hot Wire Anemometer, *NACA TN No. 3406*, 1955.
28. Hassan, K. E.: A New Type of Hot-Element Directional Anemometer, *ASME Paper No. 57-A-197*, 1957.
29. Wise, B., and Schultz, D. L.: The Hot Wire Anemometer for Turbulence Measurements, part I-IV, Aero Res. Council, London, *Paper No. 273-276*, 1956.
30. Cowdery, C. F.: *J. App. Phy.* (British), **9**, 1958, p. 112.
31. Davies, P. O. A. L., and Davis, M. R.: The Hot Wire Anemometer, University of Southampton, *ISVR Reports No. 155 and 159*, 1966.
32. Davies, P.O.A.L., and Bruun, H. H.: Evaluation of Hot Wire Anemometer Measurements in Turbulent Flows, University of Southampton, *ISVR Memorandum No. 284*, 1969. See also *Report No. 16 and 189.*
33. Siddal, R. G., and Davies, T. W.: The Interpretation of Anemometer Response in Highly Turbulent Flows, *Int. Seminar Heat Mass Transf. in Flows, Herceg Novi, Yugoslavia*, 1969.
34. Bruun, H. H.: *J. Phy. E.*, **4**, 1971, p. 815. See also **4**, 1971, p. 225 and **5**, 1972, p. 812.
35. Durst, F.: Evaluation of Hot Wire Anemometer Measurements in Turbulent Flows, Imperial College, Dept. of Mechanical Engineering *Report ET/TN/A/9*, 1971.
36. Durst, F., and Rodi, W.: Evaluation of Hot Wire Signals in Highly Turbulent Flows, *Proc. DISA Conference, Univ. of Leicester*, 1972.
37. Dvorak, K., and Syred, N.: The Statistical Analysis of Hot Wire Anemometer Signals in Complex Flow Fields. *Proc. DISA Conference, Univ. of Leicester,* 1972.
38. DISA Information – Several papers in various issues from No. 1 to No. 24.
39. Favier, D., and Pallerin, N.: *Rev. Sci. Instrum.*, **47**, 1976, p. 368.
40. Bradbury, L. J. S.: A Pulsed Wire Technique for Velocity Measurements in Highly Turbulent Flows, *Not. Phy. Lab. Report 1284, A.R.C. 30 851, A.C. 1403,* Jan. 1969.
41. Acrivlellis, M.: *DISA Information 23,* 1978, p. 11. See also **23**, p. 17 and **22** p. 15.
42. Collis, D. C., and Williams, M. J.: *J. Fluid Mech.*, **6**, 1959, p. 357.
43. Rodi, W.: Imperial College of Science and Technology, Dept. of Mechanical Eng., *Report No. ET/TN/B/10*, 1971.
44. Bauer, A. B.: *AIAA Journal,* **3**, No. 6, 1965, p. 1189.
45. Yeh, Y., and Cummins, H. Z.: *App. Phys. Letts.,* **4**, 1964, p. 176.
46. Laser Velocimetry, *Proc. of the 2nd Intl. Workshop, Purdue University,* March, 1974.
47. The Accuracy of Flow Measurements by Laser Doppler Methods, *Proceedings of the LDA Symposium,* Copenhagen, 1975.
48. Thompson, H. D. and Stevenson, W. H. (Eds.): *Laser Velocimetry, First International Workshop,* Purdue University, March, 1972.
49. Durst, F., Melling, A., and Whitelaw, J. H.: *Principles and Practice of Laser Doppler Anemometry*, Academic Press, 1976.
50. Thompson, H. D. and Stevenson, W. H. (Eds.):, *Laser Velocimetry and Particle Sizing, Third International Workshop,* Purdue University, July, 1978.
51. Gupta, A. K., and Beér, J. M.: Laser Doppler Anemometry, *Report No. CEFT/102,* Department of Chemical Engineering and Fuel Technology, Sheffield University, 1975.
52. Durst, F., and Zare, M.: Bibliography of Laser Doppler Anemometry, Sonderforschungsbereich 80, Universität Karlsruhe, DBR, 1974.
53. Abbis, J. B., Chubb, T. W., and Pike, E. R.: *Optics and Laser Tech.,* December, 1974, p. 249.
54. Durst, F., and Whitelaw, J. H.: *Proc. Roy. Soc., London, A324,* 1971, p. 157.
55. Goethert, W. H.: Balanced Detection for the Dual Scatter Laser Doppler Velocimeter, Arnold Engineering Development Center, *AEDR-TR-71-70,* 1971.
56. Dändliker, R., and Iten, P. D.: *App. Optics,* **13**, 1974, p. 286.
57. Stevenson, W. H.: *App. Optics,* **9**, 3, March, 1970, p. 649.
58. Oldengarm, J., van Krieken, A. H., and Raterink, H.: *Optics and Laser Tech. 5*, 1973, p. 249.

59. Ballantyne, A.: Ph.D. Thesis, University of Southampton, 1975.
60. Drain, L. E., and Moss, B. C.: *Opto-Electronics,* **4,** April, 1972, p. 429.
61. Cummins, H. Z., Knable, N., and Yeh, Y.: *Physical Rev. Lett.,* **12,** 6, 1964, p. 150.
62. Wigley, G.: The Application of Radial Diffraction Grating to Laser Anemometry, *AERE Report No. R.7886,* Harwell, 1974.
63. Gupta, A. K., Swithenbank, J., and Beér, J. M.: *J. Inst. Fuel,* Dec. 1977, p. 163.
64. Longhurst, R. S.: *Geometrical and Physical Optics,* Longmans, 1963.
65. Hecht, E., and Zajac, A.: *Optics,* Addison-Wesley, Reading, Mass., 1976.
66. Durst, F., and Zare, M.: Removal of Pedestals and Directional Ambiguity of Optical Anemometer Signals, *Sonderforschungsbereich* 80, University of Karlsruhe, May, 1973.
67. Melling, A.: Scattering Particles for Laser Anemometry in Air; Selection Criteria and their Realization, *Imperial College Report No. ET/TN/B/7,* 1971.
68. Bassett, A. B.: *Treatise on Hydrodynamics,* **II,** Deighton Bell and Co., London, 1888.
69. Baker, R. J.: A Filter Bank Signal Processor for Laser Anemometry, *AERE Report No. 7652,* 1973.
70. Cummins, H. A., and Pike, E. R.: Photon Correlation Spectroscopy and Velocimetry, NATO Advanced Study Institutes Series, Series B: *Physics,* **23,** Plenum Press, 1977.
71. Abbis, J. B., Chubb, T. W., and Pike, E. R.: Supersonic Flow Investigations with a Photon Correlator, *Proc. 2nd Int. Workshop on Laser Velocimetry, Purdue University,* March, 1974.
72. Durrani, T. S., and Greated, C.: *Trans. IEEE AES* **10,** 17, 1974.
73. Fog, C.: A Photon-Statistical Correlator for LDA Application, *Proc. of the LDA-Symposium, Copenhagen,* 1975.
74. Birch, A. D., Brown, D. R., and Thomas, J. R.: *J. Phys. D.: App. Phy.* **8,** 1975, p. 438.
75. Lumley, J. L.: *Stochastic Tools in Turbulence,* Academic Press, 1971.
76. Ribeiro, M. M., and Whitelaw, J. H.: *J. Fluid Mech.,* **70,** 1, 1975.
77. Gupta, A. K.: Improvements in or Relating to the Methods of Data Acquisition and Processing for Laser Diagnostic Analysis, Dept. of Chemical Engineering, M.I.T., Cambridge, Mass., Sept. 1977.
78. Petersen, J., and Maurer, F.: *Proc. LDA Symposium, Copenhagen,* Denmark, 1975.
79. Schodl, R.: A Laser Dual Beam Method for Flow Measurements in Turbomachines, *ASME Paper No. 75-GT-157,* 1975. See also *LDA Symposium,* Copenhagen, 1975, p. 481.
80. Smart, A. E.: *Proc. 3rd Int. Workshop on Laser Velocimetry*, Purdue University, July, 1978, p. 273.
81. Edwards, R. V.: *Proc. 3rd Intl. Workshop on Laser Velocimetry, Purdue University,* July, 1978, p. 79.
82. Gupta, A. K., Beér, J. M., and Swithenbank, J.: *Comb. Sci. and Tech.,* **17,** 1978, p. 197.
83. Bourke, P. J. *et al.:* Measurements of Reynolds Shear Stress in Water by Laser Anemometry, *Disa Information No. 12,* 1971.
84. Blake, K. A.: *J. Phy. E.* **5,** 1972, p. 623.
85. Farmer, W. M.: *App. Opt.,* **11,** 1972, p. 770.
86. Grant, C. R., and Orloff, K. L.: *App. Opt.,* **12,** 1973, p. 2913.
87. Farmer, W. M., and Hornkohl, J. O.: *App. Opt.,* **12,** 1973, p. 2636.
88. Brayton *et al.: App. Opt.,* **12,** 1973, p. 1145.
89. Sullivan, J. P., and Ezekiel, S.: *J. Phys. E.* **7,** 1974, p. 272.
90. Durst, F., and Zare, M.: Optical Developments in Laser Doppler Anemometry, University of Karlsruhe, *Sonderforschungsbereich 80, Report No. SFB 80/E/65.*
91. Oldengarm, J.: *Proc. of the LDA Symposium, Copenhagen,* 1975, p. 553. See also A Three-Dimensional LDV System, Proc. Fotonica Symp., Eindhoren, April, 1975.
92. Gaydon, A. G., and Wolfhard, H. G.: *Flames, Their Structure, Radiation and Temperature,* Chapman and Hall, London, 1970.
93. Bennett, H.: *Platinum Metals Rev.,* **5,** No. 4, 1961, p. 132.
94. Kent, J. H.: *Comb. and Flame,* **14,** 1970, p. 297.
95. Shepard, C. E., and Warshwasky, I.: (a) Electrical Techniques for Compensation of Thermal Time Lag of Thermocouples and Resistance Thermometers, *NACA Tech. Note 2703 (18),* May, 1952. (b) Electrical Techniques for Time Lag Compensation for Thermocouples Used in Jet Engine Gas Temperature Measurements, *ISA Journal,* 9, 1953.
96. Kunugi, M., and Jinno, H.: *7th Symp. on Comb.,* 1974, p. 1367.
97. Gupta, A. K., Syred, N., and Beér, J. M.: *15th Symp. (Intl.) on Comb.,* 1974, p. 1367.
98. Lockwood, F., and Odidi, A. O.: *15th Symp. (Intl.) on Comb.,* 1974, p. 561.
99. Scadron, M. D., and Warshwasky, I.: *NACA Tech. Note No. 2599,* 1952.
100. Bradley, D., and Entwistle, A. G.: *Brit. J. App. Phys.,* **12,** 1961, p. 708. See also **17,** 1966, p. 1155.

101. Davisson, C., and Weeks, J. R.: *J. Opt: Soc. Amer.*, **8**, 1924, p. 581.
102. Wise, E. M., and Vines, R. F.: *The Platinum Metals and Their Alloys*, International Nickel Co., New York, 1941.
103. Hinze, J. O.: *Turbulence*, McGraw Hill, New York, 1975.
104. Bradley, D., and Matthews, K. J.: *J. Mech. Eng. Sci.*, **10**, 4, 1968, p. 299.
105. Barber, R.: *The Chemical Engineer*, April, 1967, p. 81.
106. Forsythe, W. E.: *Optical Pyrometry, Temperature: Its Measurement and Control in Science and Industry*, 1, Reinhold Publishing Corporation, New York, 1941.
107. Ayling, A. B., and Smith, I. W.: *Comb. and Flame*, **18**, 1972, p. 173.
108. Bach, J. H., Street, P. J., and Twamley, C. S.: *J. Phy. E.: Sci. Inst.*, **3**, 1970, p. 281.
109. House, K.: B.S. Dissertation, M.I.T., Dept. of Chemical Engineering, May, 1978.
110. Kurlbaum, F.: *Phys. Z.*, **3**, 1902, p. 187.
111. Penner, S. S.: *Amer. J. Phys.*, **17**, 1949, p. 422.
112. Thomas, D. L.: *Comb. and Flame*, **12**, 1968, p. 569.
113. Quinn, T. J.: *Temperature*, Academic Press, 1983.
114. Weinberg, F. J.: *The Optics of Flames and Methods for the Study of Refractive Index Fields in Gases*, Butterworths, London, 1963.
115. Pandya, T. P., and Weinberg, F. J.: *Proc. Roy. Soc.*, A 297, 1964, p. 544.
116. Sterrett, J. R., and Erwin, J. R.: *NACA Tech. Note No. 2827*, 1952.
117. Schwar, M. J. R., and Weinberg, F. J.: *Comb & Flame*, **13**, 1969, p. 335.
118. Jones, A. R., Schwar, M. J. R., and Weinberg, F. J.: *Proc. Roy. Soc.*, A 322, 1971, p. 119.
119. Oppenheim, A. K., Urtiew, P. A., and Weinberg, F. J.: *Proc. Roy. Soc.*, A 291, 1966, p. 279.
120. Kraushaar, R. J.: *J. Opt. Soc. Amer.*, **40**, 1950, p. 480.
121. Hariharan, P., and Sen, D. J.: *J. Opt. Soc. Amer.*, **49**, 1959, p. 1105.
122. Goldstein, R. J.: *Rev. Sci. Instrum.*, **36**, 1965, p. 1408.
123. Weinberg, F. J., and Wilson, J. R.: *Proc. Roy. Soc.*, A 314, 1970, p. 175.
124. Sandhu, S. S., and Weinberg, F. J.: *J. Phy. E.: Sci. Inst.*, **5**, 1972, p. 1018.
125. Sandhu, S. S., and Weinberg, F. J.: *Comb. & Flame*, **25**, 1975, p. 321.
126. Meyer, J. W., Cohen, L. M., and Oppenheim, A. K.: *Comb. Sci. and Tech.*, **8**, 1973, p. 185.
127. Gupta, A. K., and Rossi, I.: Application of Laser Schlieren Interferometry to Burning Droplets, AIAA Aerospace Sciences Meeting, Pasadena, Cal., January, 1980. *Paper No. 80-0349*.
128. Lapp, M., and Penney, C. M. (Ed.), *Laser Raman Gas Diagnostics*, Plenum Press, New York, 1974.
129. Lederman, S.: *AIAA*, **53**, [B. T. Zinn (Ed.)], 1977, p. 479.
130. Eckbreth, A. C.: *AIAA*, **53**, 1977, p. 517.
131. Setchell, R. E.: *AIAA*, **53**, [B.T. Zinn, (Ed.)] 1977, p. 499.
132. Kowalik, R. M., and Kruger, C. H.: Laser Fluorescence Temperature Measurements, *WSS/CI Paper No. 78-17*, Spring, 1978.
133. Cattolica, R. J.: OH Rotational Temperature from Laser Induced Fluorescence, *WSS/CE Paper No. 78-18*, Spring, 1978. Also available as Sandia Laboratories Report No. 78-8614, California.
134. Moya, F., Druet, S., Pealat, M., and Taran, J. P.: *AIAA*, **53**, 1977, p. 549.
135. Gupta, A. K.: Ph.D. Thesis, Sheffield University, Department of Chemical Engineering and Fuel Technology, England, 1973.
136. Peterson, A. P. G., and Gross, E. E.: *Handbook of Noise Measurement*, GenRad, Concord, Massachusetts, 1974.
137. Miller, R. D., and Commings, E. W.: *J. Fluid Mech.*, **7**, 2, 1960, p. 237.
138. Bryer, D. W., Walshe, D. E., and Garner, H. C.: *Aero Res. Council R & M No. 3037*, 1958.
139. Toepler, A.: *Beobachtungen Nach Einer Neuen Optischen Methode*, Max Cohen, U. Sohn, Bonn, 1864.
140. Smith, L. L., and Waddell, J. H.: Techniques of Color Schlieren, *Proc. 9th Int. Congress on High Speed Photography*, 1970, p. 368.
141. Zehnder, L.: *Z. Instrumentenkunde*, **11**, 1891, p. 275.
142. Grönig, H.: *AIAA J.*, **5**, 1967, p. 1046.
143. Winckler, J.: *Rev. Sci. Instrum.*, **19**, 1948, p. 307.
144. Tiné, G.: *Gas Sampling and Chemical Analysis in Combustion Processes*, Pergamon Press, 1961.
145. Lengelle, G., and Verdier, C. V.: Gas Sampling and Analysis in Combustion Phenomena, *AGARDograph No. 168*, July, 1973.
146. Holderness, F. H., and Witcher, F. S. E.: A Gas Chromatographic Technique for the Determination of All Major Components in Combustion Products, *N.G.T.E., Report No. R 299*, Dec. 1977.

147. Blann, D. R.: Measurement Methods at High Temperature and Pressure, *Symp. on Particulate Control in Energy Processes,* San Francisco, May 11-13, 1976.
148. Pilat, Mark III Source Test Cascade Impactor, *Operations Manual, Pollution Control Systems Corporation,* Washington, May, 1976.
149. Hanson, S. P.: Private Communications, M.I.T. Dept. of Chemical Eng., 1980.
150. McCreath, C. G., and Beér, J. M.: *Applied Energy,* **2,** 1976, p. 3.
151. Jones, A. R.: *Prog. Energy & Comb. Sc.,* **3,** 1977, p. 225.
152. Giffen, E., and Muraszew, A.: *The Atomization of Liquid Fuels,* Wiley, New York, 1953.
153. York, L. L., and Stubs, H. E.: *Trans. Am. Soc. Mech. Eng.,* **74,** 1952, p. 1157.
154. Nuruzzaman, A. S. M., Hedley, A. B., and Beér, J. M.: *J. Inst. F.,* Aug. 1970.
155. McCreath, C. G., Roett, M. F., and Chigier, N. A.: *J. Phy. E.: Scientific Instruments,* **5,** 1972, p. 601.
156. Sato, M., Shimizu, K., and Sakai, T.: *J. Inst. F.,* March, 1977, p. 19.
157. Simmons, H. C., and Lapera, D. L.: A High Speed Spray Analyzer for Gas Turbine Spray Nozzles, *ASME Gas Turbine Conference,* Cleveland, Ohio, March 12, 1969.
158. Bexon, R., Bishop, G. D., and Gibbs, J.: *News of Imanco Equip. and Applications,* **3,** 1975.
159. Lennert, A. E., Sowls, R. E., Belz, R. A., Goethert, W. H., and Bentley, H. T.: *Prog. in Astro. and Aero.,* **53,** 1977, p. 629 [Zinn, B. T. (Ed.)]
160. Yule, A. J., Chigier, H. A., and Cox, N. W.: Measurement of Particle Sizes in Sprays by the Automated Analysis of Spark Photographs, Particle Size Analysis, *Paper 22,* Heydon, London, 1978.
161. Gabor, D.: *Nature,* **161,** 1948, p. 777.
162. Collier, R. J., Burckhardt, C. B., and Lin, L. H.: *Optical Holography,* Academic Press, New York, 1971.
163. Merzkirch, W.: *Flow Visualization*, Academic Press, New York, 1974.
164. Hecht, E., and Zajac, A.: *Optics,* Addison-Wesley Publishing Co., Reading, Mass., 1976.
165. Leith, E. N., and Upatnieks, J.: *J. Opt. Soc. Am.*, **54,** 1964, p. 1295.
166. Leith, E. N., and Upatnieks, J.: *Sci. Inst.*, June, 1965.
167. Develis, J. B., and Reynolds, G. O.: *Theory and Applications of Holography*, Addison-Wesley Publishing Co., Reading Mass., 1967.
168. Belz, R. A., and Dougherty, N. S.: In-Line Holography of Reacting Liquid Sprays, SPIE *Proc. Symp. on Engineering Applications of Holography*, Los Angeles, 1972, p. 209.
169. Thompson, B. J.: IEEE *Ninth Annual Symposium on Electron Ion and Laser Beam Technology*, San Francisco Press, Inc., 1967.
170. Thompson, B. J.: *Diffraction and Holographic Techniques for Particle Size Analysis*, A Review, ASME Fluids Engineering Conference, Pittsburgh, Penn., 1971.
171. Hickling, R.: *J. Opt. Soc. Am.,* **59,** October, 1969, p. 1334.
172. Clayton, R. M., and Wuerker, R. F.: Applying Holography to Reacting Spray Studies, Holographic Instrumentation Applications, *NASA SP-248*, January, 1970.
173. Greguss, P.: *Optics and Laser Tech.*, December, 1975, p. 253.
174. Webster, J. M.: CEGB Marchwood Engineering Labs, *Internal Report No. RD/M/R132*, 1971.
175. Fourney, M. E. Matkin, J. H., and Waggoner, A. P.: *Rev. Sci. Inst.,* **40,** 1969, p. 205.
176. Bexon, R.: *J. Phy. E. Sci. Inst.*, 6, 1973, p. 245.
177. Thompson, B. J.: *J. Phy. E. Sci. Inst.,* **7,** 1974, p. 781.
178. Royer, R.: Nouv. *Rev. Optique,* **5,** 1974, p. 87.
179. Hodkinson, J. R., and Greenleaves, I.: *J. Opt. Soc. Am.,* **53,** 1963, p. 577.
180. Self, S. A., and Kruger, C. H.: *J. Energy,* **1,** 1977, p. 25.
181. Dobbins, R., Crocco, L., and Glassman, I.: *AIAA Journal*, **1,** 8, August, 1963, p. 1882.
182. Rao, K. V. L., and Lefebvre, A. H.: *J. Fluids Eng.,* **97,** 1975, p. 316.
184. Lorenzetto, J., and Lefebvre, A. H.: *AIAA Journal,* **15,** 1977, p. 1006.
185. Simmons, H. C.: The Correlation of Drop Size/Volume Fraction Distribution, *ASME Paper 76-WA/GT-9*; Part II: The Drop Size/Number Distribution, *ASME Paper 76-WA/GT-10*, 1976.
186. Swithenbank, J., Beér, J. M., Taylor, D. S., Abbot, D., and McCreath, C. G.: *Prog. in Astro. and Aero.,* **53,** 1977, p. 421.
187. Mie, G.: *Annalen der Physik,* **25,** 1908, p. 373.
188. Kerker, M.: *The Scattering of Light and Other Electromagnetic Radiation,* Academic Press, New York, 1969.
189. Chu, B.: *Laser Light Scattering,* Academic Press, New York, 1974.
190. Crosignani, B., Diporto, P., and Bertolotti, M.: *Statistical Properties of Scattered Light,* Academic Press, New York, 1975.
191. Durst, F., and Eliasson, B.: Properties of Laser Doppler Signals and Their Exploitation for Particle Size Measurement, *Proc. LDA Symposium Copenhagen*, 1975, p. 1975.

192. Dave, J. V.: Subroutines for Computing the Parameters of the Electromagnetic Radiation Scattered by a Sphere, IBM Palo Alto Scientific Center, CA, *Report No. 320-3237*, 1978.
193. Holland, A. C., and Gagne, G.: *App. Optics*, **9**, 1970, p. 1113.
194. Farmer, W. M.: *App. Optics,* **11**, No. 11, 1972, P. 2603.
195. Farmer, M. W.: Ph.D. Thesis, University of Tennessee, 1973.
196. Farmer, M. W.: *App. Optics,* **13**, 1974, p. 610.
197. Farmer, W. M., Hornkohl, J. O., Tidewell, E. D., Enis, C. P., and Blanks, J. R.: Particle Sizing Interferometer, Measurements of Simulated Clouds, *SDL-75-6805,* 1975.
198. Ogden, D. Dm. and Stock, D.E.: *Proc. Third International Workshop on Laser Velocimetry, Purdue University, 1978.*
199. Yule, A., Chigier, N. A., Atakan, S., and Ungut, A.: Particle Size and Velocity Measurement by Laser Anemometry, *AIAA 15th Aerospace Sciences Meeting,* Los Angeles, Cal., January, 1977, Paper No. 77-214.
200. Fristrom, R. M., Jones, A. R., Schwar, M. J. R., and Weinberg, F. J.: *Faraday Symposium of the Chemical Society,* **7**, 1973, p. 183.
201. Waterston, R. M., and Chou, H. P.: A New Crossed Laser Beam Technique for Particle Sizing and Application to Measurements Behind Shock Waves, *AASU Departmental Report,* Southampton University, England, 1976.
202. Durst, F., and Umhauer, H.: *Proc. LDA Symposium, Copenhagen,* Denmark, 1975.
203. Stevenson, W. H.: Spray and Particulate Diagnostics in Combustion Systems: *A Review of Optical Methods,* Central States Section Meeting, Combustion Institute, West Lafayette, Indiana, April, 1978.
204. Santos, R., and Stevenson, W.: *App. Physics Letters,* **30**, 1977, p. 236.
205. Dobbins, R. A., and Jizmagian, F. S.: *J. Opt. Soc. Amer.*, **56**, 1966, P. 1351.
206. Lester, T. W., and Witting, S. L. K.: *Proc. Tenth (Intl.) Shock Tube Symposium*, Kyoto, Japan, 1975.
207. Holve, D., and Self, S. A.: Optical Measurements of Mean Particle Size in the Exhaust of a Coal-Fired MHD Generator, *Paper No. 76-53,* Western States Section Meeting, Combustion Institute, La Jolla, Cal., 1976.
208. Bachalo, W. D.: *Paper No. THIII15,* Conference on Laser and Electro Optical Systems, San Diego, February 7-9, 1978.
209. Bachalo, W. D.: *Proc. Third Intl. Workshop on Laser Velocimetry,* Purdue University, 1978.
210. Bertrand, J. M., and Penner, S. S.: *Prog. in Astro. and Aero.*, **53**, 1977, p. 411.
211. Powell, E. A., Cassonova, R. A., Bankston, C. F., and Zinn, B. T.: *Prog. in Astro. and Aero.*, **53**, 1977, p. 449.
212. Holve, D., and Self, S.A.: Particle Sizing Counter for In-Situ Measurements, *Western States Section Meeting, Combustion Institute,* Spring, 1978.
213. Driscoll, J. H., Mann, D. M., and McGregor, W. K.: *Comb. Sci. and Tech.*, **20**, 1979, p. 41.
214. Driscoll, J. F.: Submicron Particle Size Measurements Using Diffusion Broadening Spectroscopy, AIAA Aerospace Sciences Meeting, Pasadena, January, 1980.
215. Faxvog, F. R.: *App. Optics,* **13**, 1974, p. 1913.
216. Faxvog, F. R. (1978) "Instrument for Sizing Submicron Airborne Particles", Presented as Paper THHH, *Conference on Laser and Electro-optical Systems, San Diego,* Feb. 7-9, 1978 (Related paper available as SAE, Paper No. 770140).
217. Born, M., and Wolf, B.: *Principles of Optics,* Pergamon Press, New York, 1970.
218. Van der Hulst, H. C.: *Light Scattering by Small Particles,* Chapman and Hall Company, London, 1957.
219. Kerker, M.: *The Scattering of Light,* Academic Press, New York, 1969.
220. D'Alessio, A., Ambrosio, M.: *La Termotecnica,* **30**, 1976, p. 460.
221. Beretta, F., Borghese, A., D'Alessio, A., Venitozzi, C.: Laser Light Scattering Investigations on Rich Methane-Oxygen Flames, presented at the *Workshop on "Laser Measurement Methods in Combustion,"* Urbino, Italy, 7-9 September, 1977. See also *18th Symp. (Intl.) on Comb., The Comb. Inst.*, 1981.
222. Dalzell, W. H., Sarofim, A. F.: *J. Heat Transfer, Trans. ASME Ser. C,* **91**, 1969, p. 100.
223. D'Alessio, A., Di Lorenzo, A., Beretta, F., Venitozzi, C.: *14th Symp. (Intl.) on Comb., The Comb. Inst.*, 1974, p. 941.
224. D'Alessio, A., Di Lorenzo, A., Sarofim, A. F., Beretta, F., Masi, S., Venitozzi, C.: *15th Symp. (Intl.) on Comb., The Comb. Inst.*, 1976, p. 1427.
225. D'Alessio, A., Di Lorenzo, A., Borghese, A., Beretta, F., Masi, S.: *16th Symp. (Intl.) on Comb., The Comb. Inst.*, 1978, P. 1439.

CHAPTER 5

PROBLEMS AND PROGRESS

5.1 POLLUTANT EMISSION

The combustion design engineer always desires to be able to select operating conditions that yield minimum emission of pollutants and maximum combustion efficiency[1-6]. In doing this, he can be guided by the past experience, general 'rule-of-thumb', and qualitative or semi-quantitative understanding of the basic processes involved. Large combustors and furnaces used in the utility and process industries often make use of swirl for the stabilization of flame. Such furnaces/boilers represent major capital investments, hence their design and operating characteristics are necessarily based on requirements of reliability, operating flexibility, cost, and emission of pollutants. It is important, therefore, that the combustion engineer, in addition to understanding the phenomena, appreciates these considerations because they influence controllability, safety, material limitations and compatibility.

A real combustion process will involve some or all of the physiochemical phenomena, for example, fluid mechanics, heat transfer, chemical kinetics, turbulence, radiation, two-phase flow. A complete quantitative treatment of any individual process can be quite complex. The emphasis on emissions control, in particular, the desire for simultaneous elimination of reducing species (hydrocarbons, carbon monoxide) and oxidizing species (nitrogen oxides), calls for new concepts in combustion design. The other pollutants of interest are smoke, particulates, SO_x, noise, CO_2 and thermal pollution. The goals to be considered now are high efficiency, reasonable size, and low emissions. In order to achieve all these goals in new designs a better understanding of the combustion process is required. Reduction in the emission of pollutants, and improvements in combustion efficiency from swirl combustors are limited by numerous practical considerations; for example, heat transfer requirements are as important as combustion considerations in the determination of furnace volume. Combustion air, being four-fifths inert nitrogen, is often considered more of a heat transfer working fluid than a primary combustion variable.

Pollutant emissions from combustors and furnaces originate from three sources: (1) fuel contaminants; (2) species resulting from incomplete combustion; and (3) species formed as part of complete combustion. In each case, emissions can be controlled to a greater or lesser extent by pre-combustion fuel treatment, combustion control techniques, and/or, finally, stack gas clean up. In alternative fuels, the impacts of reduced hydrogen content are associated with increased rates of carbon particle formation and higher smoke emissions. A reduction in volatility reduces the time available for chemical reaction within the combustion system and results in reduced combustor stability, increased emissions of CO and hydrocarbons and associated loss in combustion efficiency. With any pollution-controlling technique, consideration must be given to energy usage and the possible pollution of water or the production of concentrated solid waste for disposal.

The oxidation of compounds that contain metallic elements in the fuel can have far-reaching implications: mercury, arsenic, lead and boron, which remained inert as ground minerals for millions of years, are converted to oxidized, water-soluble forms during the combustion process. Although these oxidized, water-soluble compounds may be removed from the stack gases by a precipitator, scrubber or a baghouse, along with other particulates and sulfur compounds, they may eventually enter groundwater in toxic form rather than in the original stable forms. In addition, there is the better-known problem of particulates, oxidants, and organic molecules that contribute to the widely recognized problem of air pollution. Control of these pollutants may involve complex interactions between boiler design and operating constraints such as efficiency, slagging and safety. The control techniques used for the emission of pollutants from combustors can be conveniently grouped into three categories, depending upon their application; (that is; before, during, or after combustion).

Fuel cleaning processes such as coal washing can not only be helpful in reducing emissions of ash, water-soluble metallic oxides, and of SO_x, but can also help to alleviate boiler corrosion, slagging, plugging, and erosion problems. The major disadvantage of fuel cleaning processes is that some of the fuel value is lost in the cleaning.

Removal of organically bound sulfur and nitrogen is also a useful concept, although the present commercial process, hydrogenation, demands a very large capital investment and is at present suitable only for oils. Since hydrogen has more value for other uses, methods that employ selective oxidizers are being developed for sulfur and nitrogen removal.

Another clean-fuel alternative for some US boiler users, mainly in the midwest region, is to use the low sulfur content coals located in some of the western states.

Stack gas clean-up devices of very high efficiencies are now in demand. Efficiencies of more than 99.8 per cent for particulate control are needed in some cases, for which purpose, fabric filters (baghouses) are competitive with high efficiency electrostatic precipitators, even for large combustors. SO_x scrubbers of 90 per cent efficiency are now available and beginning to gain acceptance. In the Los Angeles area, 90 per cent clean up of NO_x from existing power plants is required to be in operation by 1987, even though the technology has not yet proved itself on units fueled with heavy oils.

Stack gas clean up is the last resort for reducing emissions because normally, the quantity of materials that requires processing is about twenty times the mass, and twenty thousand times the volume of the fuel. Other problems are that if wet scrubbing is necessary, as it is in many SO_2 scrubbers that employ water slurries of lime or limestone, additional heat or fuel must be used downstream to restore the buoyancy of the emitted plume, and that solid or liquid wastes, which often contain water-soluble metallic oxides, are accumulated.

With regard to mathematical modeling of pollution formation in combustion processes, many models have appeared over the years. Most of these have been established for specific devices for the prediction of trends, and many of them have some common features. One found in most models is their treatment of the basic chemical mechanisms. Although some reactions that may be important at temperatures and pressures in one device may not be significant in another. Nevertheless, many chemical kinetic schemes can be used in a wide variety of practical systems.

A basic practice in the formation of the model is identification of the critical, rate-limiting steps. It is important that these steps should be modeled most carefully. The effects of processes that are very fast in comparison with this rate-limiting step can be estimated from some equilibrium considerations (mechanical, thermal or chemical equilibrium). Processes that are too slow to exert a significant effect can be ignored in the model. A careful selection of the processes to be modeled accurately is necessary to achieve a useful model.

Some simplifications to chemical kinetics are often used for the modeling of pollutants from practical combustion systems. The review of pollutant kinetics by Bowman[7] has described the basic kinetic mechanisms for major pollutant species. It was noted that mechanisms for reactions of carbon monoxide and the nitrogen oxides formed from atmospheric nitrogen are fairly well understood. A detailed kinetic mechanism can be used to describe the oxidation of methane, but such detailed mechanisms are not known for the higher hydrocarbons, (for example, kerosene, petroleum or derived and heavy fuel oils). If such mechanisms were known, it is likely they would include a large number of intermediate species, which would place a heavy burden on the modeler who would seek to couple such mechanisms with a description of the physical operation of a given combustor.

A description of the fuel kinetics is important, not only for prediction of the amount of unburned fuel, but also for the prediction of concentrations of species that participate in both the combustion and the pollutant species reactions. Although carbon monoxide and nitric oxide kinetics are fairly well understood, the use of these kinetic mechanisms in quantitative predictions depends on an accurate knowledge of the amounts of species such as O, OH, H, H_2, H_2O, and O_2. When a detailed picture of fuel combustion kinetics is not available, some approximations are required to obtain estimates of these concentrations for calculations of carbon monoxide and nitrogen oxide emissions. In addition, some authors have used approximations to the known CO and NO kinetics to make the final model of the actual combustion device more tractable.

Carbon Monoxide

Carbon monoxide is inevitably formed as an intermediate product of hydrocarbon oxidation. When it is found in the exhaust or flue gases of a combustion system the cause is usually localized fuel-rich areas followed by rapid quenching. Fig. 5.1 shows the variation of CO, HC, and NO_x concentrations with mixture ratio for a commercial swirl burner. Minimum levels always occur at fuel-lean combustion conditions in the primary zone. Excess CO levels can also be caused by inadequate burning rates in the primary combustion zones combined with quenching of post-flame products downstream of the flame.

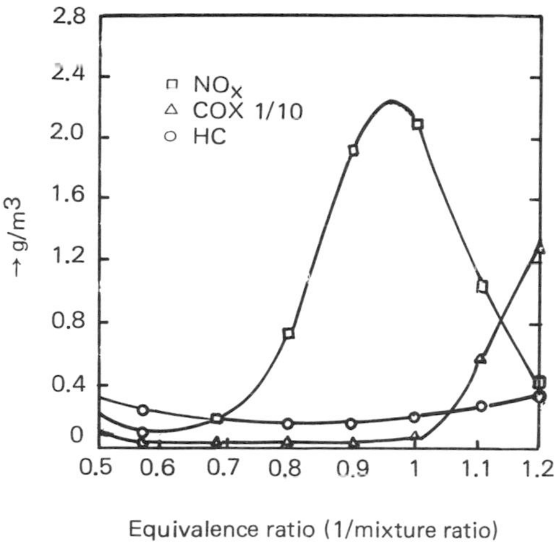

Figure 5.1 Variation of CO, H.C. and NO_X Concentrations with Mixture Ratio

The relationship between CO, HC and NO_x emissions can be clearly seen from Fig. 5.1 in that NO_x emissions peak at mixture ratios where CO and HC levels are minimal, thus giving rise to problems in minimizing emissions of all three pollutants. Gas concentrations measured in the two exit planes of a natural gas-fired swirl burner of similar configuration but scaled down by a factor of five, showed that close to the burner exit ($X/D_e = 0$) high levels of CO are formed near to the boundary of the recirculation zone and flame front (up to between 5 and 6 per cent). By two exit diameters downstream of the flame, near the end of the visible flame, almost complete burnout of the CO had taken place; this was particularly apparent with two-stage combustion in which there had been axial/radial fuel injection into the swirl burner.

Similar effects are seen in cyclone combustors, some designs create a 'two-stage' combustion system with two combustion zones, for example, the Enin cyclone shown in Fig. 5.23[1] has a fuel-rich zone in the main body and a secondary afterburning zone in the exhaust region which is quite common in such cyclones. Gasification of fuel occurs in the fuel-rich zone and CO and H_2 concentrations reach 10 to 13 per cent, complete CO and H_2 burnout taking place in the exhaust region.

Gas turbine combustors also suffer from problems of CO emission, similar to high intensity combustors. Basically, any combustor modification that improves combustion efficiency, automatically reduces CO levels. Approaches that have yielded worthwhile CO emission level reduction include[8]:

1. Improved fuel atomization. Normally, this implies the use of an airblast atomizer, but, if a separate supply of compressed air is available, an alternative approach is to employ air assistance to improve atomization at low fuel flows.
2. Redistribution of the air flow to bring the primary-zone equivalence ratio closer to an optimum value of around 0.85.
3. Increase in primary-zone volume or residence time.

4. Reduction of film-cooling air. This air, which issues from the primary zone, normally contains high concentrations of CO and HC. Unless these species are subsequently entrained into the hot central core in sufficient time to react for the completion of combustion they will appear in the exhaust gas. Thus, reduction in film-cooling air, especially in the primary zone, is often effective in reducing CO.
5. Compressor air bleed. This consists of bleeding air from the compressor during low power operation. It reduces CO emissions by virtue of an increase in primary zone fuel/air ratio, which, in turn, improves combustion efficiency.
6. Fuel staging. This technique is based on cutting off the supply of fuel to some nozzles and diverting it to the remainder. It reduces emissions at low power conditions by improving atomization quality and raising the local fuel/air ratio in the burning zones.

Conversion of CO to CO_2

The reaction of CO to CO_2 is almost exclusively due to the elementary step[9]

$$CO + OH \leftrightharpoons CO_2 + H \qquad R1$$

This reaction is very fast under normal combustion conditions in both the flame region and the post-flame gases. In many cases reaction (R7) can be assumed to be in a state of partial equilibrium[3] so that the CO/CO_2 ratio is given by

$$\frac{[CO]}{[CO_2]} = \frac{1}{K_1} \frac{[H]}{[OH]} \qquad (5.1)$$

Thus, the conversion of CO to CO_2 is governed by the reactions of hydrogen atoms and hydroxyl radicals. These species react via the fast bimolecular reactions:

$$H + O_2 \leftrightharpoons OH + O \qquad R2$$

$$O + H_2 \leftrightharpoons OH + H \qquad R3$$

$$H + H_2O \leftrightharpoons OH + H_2 \qquad R4$$

$$OH + OH \leftrightharpoons H_2O + O \qquad R5$$

and the slower termolecular recombination reactions:

$$O + O + M \leftrightharpoons O_2 + M \qquad R6$$

$$O + H + M \leftrightharpoons OH + M \qquad R7$$

$$H + H + M \leftrightharpoons H_2 + M \qquad R8$$

$$H + OH + M \leftrightharpoons H_2O + M \qquad R9$$

Kaskan[10] showed that the oxidation of CO in post flame gases could be explained by assuming that reactions R2-R7 (in addition to reaction R1) are in a state of partial equilibrium, because of which, any change in the H and OH concentrations will come about only through the thermolecular recombination reactions. Bowman[7] has shown experimentally that partial equilibrium is not a good assumption for predicting peak O-atom concentrations that follow the induction period for methane oxidation in a shock tube. This partial equilibrium model for CO oxidation has been shown to be a good model for CO oxidation kinetics in post flame gases[7] and in spark-ignition internal combustion engines[3,11].

The reaction steps given here describe the conversion of CO to CO_2. A complete model of CO kinetics must include the initial fuel kinetics that form CO. Because such kinetics are not known, some approximations are required in modeling CO emissions from practical systems even if the full mechanism (reactions R1-R7) is used. A commonly used assumption is that the initial combustion reactions produce high temperature equilibrium products at some specified point in the process[3,6,11]. Another approximation is the quasi-global model for hydrocarbon kinetics[5].

Unburnt Hydrocarbons (HC)

Unburnt hydrocarbons are primarily a problem found in high intensity combustors of the gas-turbine type fired with liquid or solid fuels; they are caused by poor fuel atomization, inadequate burning rates, the chilling effects of film cooling air, or any combination of these. The same factors also govern the levels of CO, and it has been shown by Verkamp[12] that HC emissions parallel CO emissions, but at a much lower level.

To reduce HC emissions, similar treatment to that used for CO emissions but with slightly more emphasis on reductions in film cooling air. Improvements in fuel atomization, airblast and air-assist nozzles have also proved very beneficial.

In conventional, lower intensity combustion systems, HC emission has not proved to be a problem because the reduction of CO emission (that is, 20-40 ppm) and smoke emissions to low levels ensure that HC emissions are negligible.

For the modeling of HC pollutant formation and emission, detailed kinetic schemes for hydrocarbon oxidation are required. These are unknown for the real fuels (fossil or derived) which have complex fuel mixture composition. Computations of product distributions resulting from methane/air flame have been carried out for simple, static flow systems. These computations are useful because they form a basis for comparing approximate kinetic schemes with detailed mechanisms from real fuels.

Several global rate expressions for hydrocarbon/air reactions have been proposed. The application of such expressions is usually limited to the narrow region of temperature, pressure and fuel/air ratio in which the original data, used to determine the empirical constants, were obtained. These expressions are also limited in that they do not give any predictions of radical concentrations required to link hydrocarbon kinetics to CO and NO kinetics.

This latter difficulty was resolved by the quasi-global scheme of Edelman and Fortune[13], in which scheme the initial hydrocarbon fuel is assumed to undergo an overall reaction of the following form:

$$C_nH_m + (n/2 + a/2)O_2 \rightarrow nCO + aH_2O + (m/2 - a)H_2$$

The rate parameters and the stoichiometric coefficient, a, in this reaction are determined empirically. This overall first step can then be coupled with a detailed kinetic scheme for CO oxidation, (for example, reactions R1-R9) to predict the concentration-time histories of radical species. The reaction rate for the hydrocarbon can be given by an empirical equation, or it can be assumed to be infinite, in which case, the 'initial composition' of a given fuel/air mixture will consist of CO, H_2O, and H_2 (instead of fuel) and N_2 and excess O_2.

The quasi-global model of hydrocarbon combustion was initially developed for application to gas-turbine combustors. Bowman has compared the results of the quasi-global mechanism (with both finite-rate and infinite-rate first steps) to the results of a detailed mechanism for constant-volume methane/air combustion[14]. The quasi-global mechanism gives a smooth and gradual temperature rise compared with the sharp, nearly-instantaneous temperature rise (ignition) predicted by the detailed mechanism. The nitric oxide formation rates predicted by the finite-rate quasi-global mechanism agreed closely with those predicted under conditions of high temperature and pressure and lean mixtures. Agreement, however, was poor at other conditions.

In terms of pollutant modeling, the hydrocarbon kinetics are usually important in providing information on species that participate in both pollutant and fuel-combustion mechanisms. Emissions of unburned hydrocarbons as a pollutant are usually due to a quenching of the combustion reactions by cold surfaces rather than by any limitations due to slowness of gas-phase kinetics. Four models of fuel kinetics are possible: 1. detailed kinetics; 2. quasi-global, finite-rate; 3. quasi-global, infinite rate; 4. CHO equilibrium. Each of these provides a prediction of species such as H, O, and OH which enter into the mechanisms for carbon monoxide and nitric oxide. (The CHO equilibrium model is not useful for describing kinetically-limited CO formation as it always predicts equilibrium CO.) In most cases detailed kinetic models are not available and some approximation is required. All the approximate models give better agreement with detailed kinetics as pressure, temperature or air/fuel ratio increase. In many cases, the observed agreement, even to within a factor of ten, is fortuitous. As an example, the CHO equilibrium model applied to NO kinetics underpredicts the rate of NO formation but overpredicts the time available for the reactions to occur. Consequently, the use of approximate models of hydrocarbon kinetics should be regarded as a necessity (except for methane) albeit an undesirable one. The application of such kinetic models is reasonable when the object is the prediction of trends. Good agreement between a model and experiment cannot be considered a verification of the validity of the approximate model. Instead, such good agreement between model and experiment should be regarded as a verification of the application of the model for prediction under the same conditions as that used during the experiment.

5.2 OXIDES OF NITROGEN EMISSION

Nitrogen oxides are formed in all combustion processes (swirl combustors, gas turbine combustors, I.C. engines, process heaters and many other types of furnaces, combustors and power systems) either by the high temperature oxidation of atmospheric nitrogen (thermal NO_x), fixation and subsequent oxidation of atmospheric nitrogen via fuel species (prompt NO_x), or by the oxidation of the fuel-bound nitrogen compounds. The principal reactions for the fixation of atmospheric nitrogen in combustion systems are generally recognized to be those proposed by the following three extended Zeldovich mechanisms[15].

$$N_2 + O = NO + N \quad \ldots\ldots \quad R10$$

$$N + O_2 = NO + O \quad \ldots\ldots \quad R11$$

$$OH + N = NO + H \quad \ldots\ldots \quad R12$$

For stoichiometric and fuel lean flames, with proper evaluation of oxygen atom concentrations, which often greatly exceed equilibrium values, the Zeldovich mechanism has been found to predict nitrogen oxide levels adequately from atmospheric nitrogen. The fixation of molecular nitrogen forming thermal NO is a temperature-dependent process, and it has been shown that the emission of thermal NO can be controlled adequately by the use of flue gas recirculation. The mechanism of thermal NO_x formation is now well known, and numerous papers and surveys are available for discussing it[16-18]. Nevertheless, in fuel-rich hydrocarbon flames, another mechanism for the formation of NO_x has been postulated, (additional to the Zeldovich mechanism) which leads to rapid formation of large quantities of NO_x (prompt NO_x) and is believed to operate in or very close to the reaction zone of a flame; it involves some hydrocarbon fragment attacking molecular nitrogen, one example of such a scheme being $CH + N_2 = HCN + N$. Nitric oxide is then produced by R11, as well as the oxidation of HCN[19,20].

$$HCN + \text{Oxidant} \rightarrow \ldots\ldots \rightarrow NO$$

It should be noted that hydrocarbon radicals such as CH are generally found only in or close to the reaction zone of a flame, since they disappear in the burnt gases downstream by rapid bimolecular processes, such as $CH + O_2 = CO + OH$.

It can be expected that high nitrogen content coal-derived fuels, shale oil, tar sands, and low-grade petroleum will play an important role as fuels during the 1980s. The combustion of these fuels in combustors is complicated due to high nitrogen content (*see* Table 5.1), high aromatic content and low H/C atomic ratio. Typical H/C ratio of petroleum fuels is about 2.0, 1.75 for tar sands, 1.25 for synthetic coal liquid and only 0.75 for coal[21]. The combustion problem is to reduce the oxidation of fuel-nitrogen to NO_x without the emission of any carbonaceous particulates. The pollutant emission

TABLE 5.1

Nitrogen Content of Some Petroleum and Alternative Fuels

Fuel	Nitrogen Content, % wt
Coal-Derived Low-Btu Gas	0.04 (as ammonia)
Californian Distillate	0.53
East Coast	0.16
Middle East	0.18
Indonesian/Malaysian	0.24
Venezuelan Desulfurized	0.24
Gulf Coast	0.4
Venezuelan	0.40
Alaskan	0.51
Coal-Oil Slurry	0.65 (Oil 0.42, Coal 0.78)
Wilimington California	0.77
California	0.79
SRC-II Middle	0.9
SRC-II Heavy	1.15
H-Coal	0.5-1.1
Shale (Raw Paraho)	2.1

(NO_x, particulate matter, SO_x) potential of alternative fuels is linked very strongly to their chemical properties. This section concentrates upon the production of NO_x from these fuels, in addition to the petroleum fuels.

Conversion of Fuel Nitrogen to NO_x

In contrast to thermal NO_x, the rate of formation of which is a strong function of temperature, the formation rate of nitric oxide from fuel-bound nitrogen is only slightly dependent upon temperature but increases markedly with increased oxygen concentrations. This is because the conversion efficiency of fuel nitrogen to NO is thought to depend on the rate of competing reactions that cause nitrogen fragments to produce NO or N_2. The conversion of fuel nitrogen to NO in flames is dependent upon a number of chemical and physical factors, for example, rate of evolution of fuel nitrogen in residual heavy fuel oils, chemical composition of fuel and its surrounding chemical and thermal environment, and kinetics of the reduction of NO by char. The exact mechanism of fuel nitrogen conversion is still unknown and several studies carried out using fuels doped with various nitrogeneous compounds of relatively low boiling fraction ranges have shown that the form of nitrogen compound does not significantly influence conversion to NO[22,23]. It is, indeed, doubtful whether the same conclusions may be drawn from residual heavy fuel oils which have a wide range distribution of nitrogeneous compounds. Recently, measurements were reported of nitrogen evolution from a stream of 150 μm droplets injected into a heated helium gas in a laminar drop-tube furnace at temperatures up to 1400 K, using Raw Paraho Shale oil (fuel N in oil = 1.9%) and Indo-Malaysian (fuel N in oil = 0.24%) residual fuel oil[24]. The nitrogen evolution during vaporization of the dispersed oil droplets was found to depart significantly from that obtained under equilibrium distillation conditions. For the Raw Paraho Shale oil the rate of nitrogen evolution under the rapid heating experienced in the drop-tube furnace by the droplets was retarded relative to that observed under equilibrium conditions. By contrast, preferential vaporization of the nitrogen was observed for the Indo-Malaysian residual fuel oil.

In fuel-lean flames, fuel nitrogen is converted with high efficiency to NO_x. The conversion is reduced as the equivalence ratio and fuel nitrogen content is increased[20,25,26] but the important question is whether the fuel nitrogen can be converted in fuel rich regions of the flame to the more stable molecular nitrogen, otherwise their conversion to NO_x will proceed in the fuel lean combustion stage. According to current thought, fuel nitrogen is rapidly converted in fuel-rich flame regions to HCN, an intermediate that is then oxidized to NO_x. The mechanisms by which HCN is converted to NO_x are not, as yet, fully understood. Nevertheless, there is evidence to show that it occurs by reactions that are mixed first and second order kinetics in OH concentrations according to[20,26]

$$-\frac{d}{dt}\ln\,[HCN] = k_I[OH] + \frac{k_{II}[OH]^2}{k_{eq.}[H_2O]}$$

where k_{eq}. is the equilibrium constant for the HCN/CN equilibrium.

$$CN + H_2O = HCN + OH$$

which is considered to be balanced.

The production of an HCN intermediate and its decay coupled with NO_x formation has been well documented[20,25,27], though postulated intermediates have not been observed. Efforts to postulate a decay mechanism[20,27] for HCN currently favor reactions that convert the stable CN species to a composite oxycyanogen species (NCO, HNCO) whose C-N bond is more amenable to rupture[20,26,27]. Specifically

$$HCN + OH \rightarrow HNCO + H$$

$$CN + OH \rightarrow NCO + H$$

followed by rapid destruction of the intermediate oxycyanogens according to

$$NCO + H \rightarrow NH + CO$$

$$NCO + H_2 \rightarrow NH_2 + CO$$

$$HNCO + H \rightarrow NH_2 + CO$$

The amines then undergo further oxidation to form nitric oxide. It is noteworthy that neither NCO nor HNCO has been observed in any of the flames studied.

Oxidation of NH_i and Formation of NO_x

Following the suggestion of Fenimore[28], NH_i species resulting from the decay of HCN can undergo two types of reactions which either form or destroy NO according to

$$NI + \text{Oxidant} \rightarrow \ldots\ldots \rightarrow NO + \ldots\ldots$$

$$NI + NO \rightarrow \ldots\ldots \rightarrow N_2 + \ldots\ldots$$

where NI is a nitrogen-containing intermediate generally thought to be a composite NH_i species, and the oxidant is generally accepted to be OH[20,25,27]. The exact identity of NI is currently in dispute, though it is most likely, primarily, either NH_3, NH_2, NH, or N atoms. The problem is that due to rapid hydrogen abstraction, reactions by H, O, or OH, the various NH_i species are rapidly interconnected. Despite attempts to resolve this issue, the degree of partial equilibrium among the NH_i species remains uncertain. A recent study of $NH_3/O_2/N_2$ flames has, however, confirmed the equilibrium of NH, NH_2 with NH_3 through reactions with OH and H[29].

It appears, therefore, that a possible path for the mechanism of the fuel nitrogen conversion proceeds through a fast conversion to the HCN intermediate, followed by reactions with OH in which oxycyanogens are formed and then react with molecular and/or atomic hydrogen to form amines. In strongly oxidizing atmospheres the amines react with OH or O_2 to produce NO; but at low concentrations of oxidizing species the NO can react with NH_i species to form molecular nitrogen. Schematic pathways of fuel nitrogen transformation during combustion processes are illustrated in Fig. 5.2. A listing of the fuel nitrogen reaction mechanism set is presented in Table 5.2[18]. It is clear, from consideration of the reaction set, that the common flame radicals H, OH, and O are the most active species in interconverting the fuel nitrogen. Clearly, the kinetics of NO formation will depend upon the concentrations of these species which, in turn, are closely coupled to the detailed reaction kinetics of the hydrocarbon fuel, which, in most cases, is unknown.

Control Strategies for NO_x Emission

Several approaches are used to reduce NO_x from a combustion system; they may be grouped as:

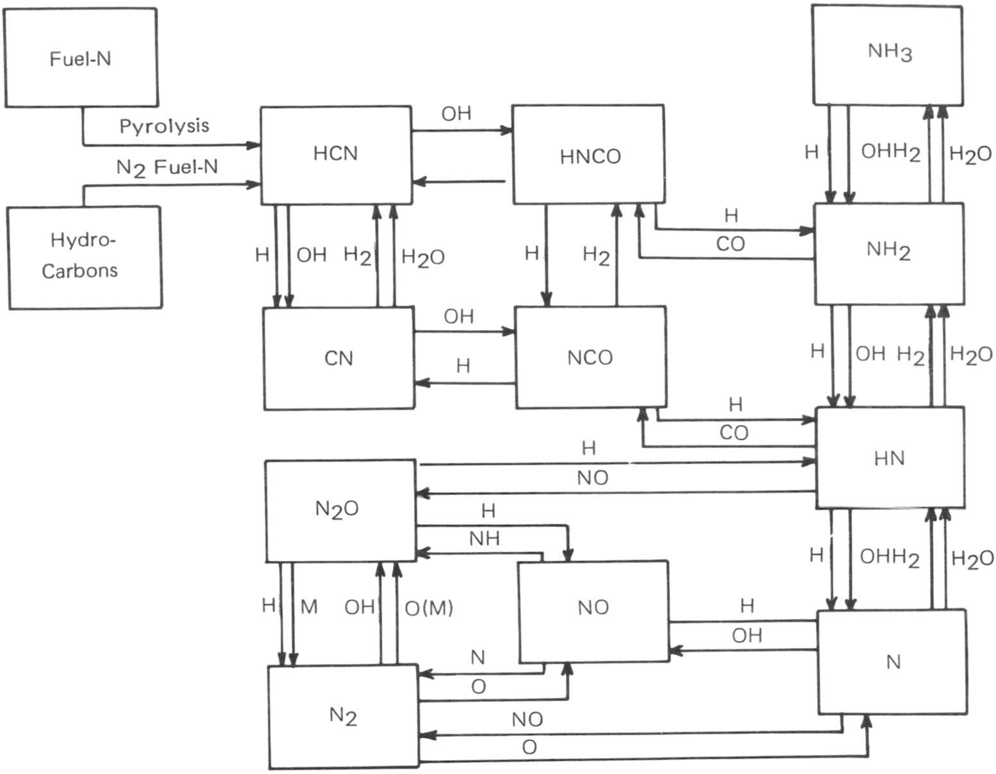

Figure 5.2 The basic fuel-nitrogen mechanism[18]

TABLE 5.2

Fuel-Nitrogen Mechanism

Reaction	$k_f = AT^N \exp(-E/RT)$		
	$A(\frac{cm^3}{mole\ sec})$	N	E(cal/mole)
1. $NO + OH = N + HO_2$	2.1×10^{11}	0.5	76,800
2. $N + N + M = N_2 + M$	3.02×10^{14}	0	-990
3. $NH + NH = N + NH_2$	3.6×10^{11}	0.55	1,900
4. $N + NH_3 = NH + NH_2$	2.1×10^{11}	0.5	23,160
5. $N + NO_2 = NO + NO$	3.6×10^{12}	0	0
6. $N + N_2O = N_2 + NO$	5.0×10^{8}	0	10,000
7. $N + H + M = NH + M$	2.5×10^{17}	-0.5	0
8. $NH + H = N + H_2$	6.3×10^{11}	0.5	8,000
	1.0×10^{12}	0.68	1,800
9. $NH + O = NO + H$	6.3×10^{11}	0.5	0
	5.0×10^{11}	0.5	5,000

TABLE 5.2 (Continued)

Reaction	$k_f = AT^N \exp(-E/RT)$		
	A($\frac{cm^3}{mole\ sec}$)	N	E(cal/mole)
10. $NH + O = N + OH$	3.16×10^{11}	0.5	8,000
	1.0×10^{12}	0.5	100
11. $NH + OH = N + H_2O$	5.0×10^{11}	0.5	2,000
	1.6×10^{12}	0.56	1,500
12. $N + HO_2 = NH + O_2$	$\geq 1.0 \times 10^{11}$	0	0
13. $NH + N = N_2 + H$	6.3×10^{11}	0.5	0
14. $NH + NO_2 = HNO + H$	2.0×10^{11}	0.5	5,000
15. $NH + O + M = HNO + M$	1.0×10^{16}	-0.5	0
16. $NH_2 + H = NH + H_2$	1.4×10^{11}	0.67	4,300
17. $NH_2 + O = NH + OH$	9.2×10^{11}	0.5	0
18. $NH_2 + O = HNO + H$	2.1×10^{12}	0	0
	$>5 \times 10^{12}$	0	0
19. $NH_2 + OH = NH + H_2O$	3.0×10^{10}	0.68	1,300
20. $NH_2 + NH_2 = NH + NH_3$	1.7×10^{11}	0.63	3,600
21. $NH_2 + O_2 = NH + HO_2$	1.0×10^{13}	0	50,500
22. $NH_3 + H = NH_2 + H_2$	1.9×10^{11}	0.67	3,400
23. $NH_3 + O = NH_2 + OH$	1.5×10^{12}	0	6,000
24. $NH_3 + OH = NH_2 + H_2O$	4.0×10^{10}	0.68	1,100
25. $NH_3 + O_2 = NH_2 + HO_2$	5.0×10^{11}	0.5	56,000
26. $N + NO = N_2 + O$	3.1×10^{13}	0	334
27. $N_2O + M = N_2 + O + M$	1.42×10^{14}	0	51,280
28. $N_2O + OH = N_2 + HO_2$	3.16×10^{13}	0	15,000
29. $N_2O + NO = N_2 + NO_2$	2.0×10^{14}	0	50,000
30. $NO + M = N + O + M$	1.41×10^{21}	-1.5	153,000
31. $NO + H = N + OH$	2.22×10^{14}	0	50,500
32. $NO + O = N + O_2$	1.72×10^{9}	1	38,640
33. $NO_2 + H = NO + OH$	3.16×10^{14}	0	1,500
34. $NO_2 + O = NO + O_2$	1.0×10^{13}	0	1,000
35. $NO + HO_2 = HNO + O_2$	7.2×10^{10}	0.5	10,800
36. $NO + HO_2 = NO_2 + OH$	1.0×10^{13}	0	3,000
37. $HNO + NH = NO + NH_2$	2.0×10^{11}	0.5	2,000
38. $NH_3 + NO = HNO + NH_2$	5.0×10^{14}	0	50,000
39. $NO + H + M = HNO + M$	5.37×10^{15}	0	-600
40. $HNO + O = NO_2 + H$	5.0×10^{10}	0.5	3,000
41. $NO_2 + N = N_2O + O$	5.0×10^{12}	0	0
42. $N_2O + H = NH + NO$	1.0×10^{11}	0.5	30,000
43. $N_2O + H = N_2 + OH$	7.94×10^{13}	0	15,000
44. $N_2O + O = NO + NO$	6.23×10^{13}	0	25,400
45. $N_2O + O = N_2 + O_2$	6.23×10^{13}	0	25,400
46. $N_2O + NH = HNO + N_2$	1.0×10^{11}	0.5	3,000

TABLE 5.2 (Continued)

Reaction	$k_f = AT^N \exp(-E/RT)$ A($\frac{cm^3}{mole\ sec}$)	N	E(cal/mole)
47. $HNO + H = H_2 + NO$	1.0×10^{13}	0	2,500
48. $HNO + H = NH + OH$	2.0×10^{11}	0.5	23,000
49. $HNO + O = NH + O_2$	1.0×10^{11}	0.5	7,000
50. $HNO + O = NO + OH$	5.0×10^{11}	0.5	0
51. $HNO + OH = NO + H_2O$	7.08×10^{13}	0	2,630
52. $HNO + N = NH + NO$	1.0×10^{11}	0.5	2,000
53. $HNO + N = N_2O + H$	5.0×10^{10}	0.5	3,000
54. $NH + H + M = NH_2 + M$	2.0×10^{16}	-0.5	0
55. $NH_3 + M = NH_2 + H + M$	5.75×10^{15}	0	77,000
56. $NO_2 + M = NO + O + M$	1.1×10^{16}	0	65,571
57. $HCN + OH = CN + H_2O$	2.0×10^{11}	0.6	5,000
58. $CN + H_2 = HCN + H$	6.0×10^{12}	0	5,300
59. $CN + OH = NCO + H$	5.6×10^{13}	0	0
60. $CN + O_2 = NCO + O$	3.2×10^{13}	0	1,000
61. $HCN + O = NCO + H$	5.2×10^{12}	0	8,100
62. $CN + O = CO + N$	6.3×10^{13}	0	2,400
63. $NCO + H = NH + CO$	5.0×10^{11}	0.5	6,875
	2.0×10^{13}	0	0
64. $NCO + O = NO + CO$	5.0×10^{11}	0.5	6,875
	2.0×10^{13}	0	0
65. $CN + CO_2 = NCO + CO$	3.7×10^{12}	0	0
66. $CN + OH = HCN + O$	3.16×10^{12}	0	3,000
67. $CN + HNO = HCN + NO$	4.0×10^{11}	0.5	0
68. $CN + H + M = HCN + M$	3.16×10^{16}	-0.5	0
69. $CN + NH = HCN + N$	1.0×10^{11}	0.5	2,000
70. $CN + NH_2 = HCN + NH$	5.0×10^{10}	0.7	2,000
71. $CN + NH_3 = HCN + NH_2$	7.0×10^{10}	0.7	2,000
72. $CO + OH = CO_2 + H$	1.51×10^{7}	1.3	-765
73. $CO + O_2 = CO_2 + O$	3.16×10^{12}	0	50,000
74. $CO_2 + M = CO + O + M$	1.0×10^{15}	0	100,000
75. $CO + HNO = CO_2 + NH$	1.0×10^{11}	0.5	7,000
76. $CO_2 + N = CO + NO$	2.0×10^{11}	0.5	30,000
77. $CO + NO_2 = CO_2 + NO$	2.0×10^{12}	0	30,000
78. $CO + N_2O = CO_2 + N_2$	1.0×10^{11}	0	20,000
79. $CO + HO_2 = CO_2 + OH$	1.0×10^{11}	0	10,000
80. $H_2 + OH = H_2O + H$	2.19×10^{13}	0	5,150
81. $H_2O + O = OH + OH$	6.76×10^{13}	0	18,350
82. $H_2 + O = H + OH$	1.82×10^{10}	1	8,900
83. $O_2 + H = O + OH$	2.19×10^{14}	0	16,800
84. $H + O + M = OH + M$	8.00×10^{15}	0	0
85. $O_2 + M = O + O + M$	3.55×10^{18}	-1	118,000

TABLE 5.2 (Continued)

Reaction	$k_f = AT^N \exp(-E/RT)$		
	$A(\frac{cm^3}{mole\ sec})$	N	E(cal/mole)
86. $H_2 + M = H + H + M$	2.45×10^{14}	0	96,000
87. $H_2O + M = H + OH + M$	1.29×10^{15}	0	105,000
88. $H + O_2 + M = HO_2 + M$	1.59×10^{15}	0	-1,000
89. $HO_2 + OH = H_2O + O_2$	5.0×10^{13}	0	1,000
90. $OH + O + M = HO_2 + M$	5.0×10^{16}	0	0
91. $HO_2 + O = O_2 + OH$	5.0×10^{13}	0	1,000
92. $HO_2 + H = H_2 + O_2$	2.5×10^{13}	0	700
93. $HO_2 + H = OH + OH$	2.5×10^{14}	0	900
94. $HO_2 + H = H_2O + O$	1.0×10^{13}	0	1,000

1. Fuel cleaning (physical and chemical cleaning, hydrodenitrogenation);
2. Combustion modifications (low excess air, staged combustion, flue gas recirculation, water injection, furnace reactants, optimum burner operation, modified burner, fuel additives, afterburners);
3. Gas treatment (flue gas treatment, catalytic devices);
4. Any combination of the above.

It has been demonstrated in several studies that staged combustion can yield significant reduction in fuel nitrogen oxidation to NO_x. One of the questions of fuel-rich operation is whether it may result in the emission of some bound nitrogen species such as HCN and NH_3. Sarofim *et al.*[30] have carried out equilibrium calculations for the combustion of fuels with H/C atomic ratios of 1.3 (representing a coal liquid) and 1.7 (representing shale oil), Fig. 5.3. From these calculations the temperature was determined for any given equivalence ratio at which the total fuel-bound nitrogen exceeded the NO_x emission standards. The adiabatic flame temperature as a function of equivalence ratio is also included in Fig. 5.3, from which figure the following conclusions may be drawn. –

1. The equilibrium-bound nitrogen concentrations fall below the present U.S. nitrogen oxides emission standards only when the equivalence ratio reaches a particular value for a given fuel (equivalence ratio = 1.25 for $CH_{1.7}$ and 1.4 for $CH_{1.3}$).
2. It is pointed out, also, that most bound nitrogen species concentrations that are experimentally-determined for equivalence ratio >1.2 are considerably in excess of equilibrium values. This suggests kinetic limitation of these reactions. As can be seen from Fig. 5.2, the temperatures can be raised for fuel-rich mixtures because of the increasing gap between the equilibrium temperature and the adiabatic temperature. This condition can be met in gas turbine operation where adiabatic compression produces high inlet air temperature which, in turn, can raise adiabatic flame temperatures under high-load operating conditions.

The O/C atomic ratios on the plots in Fig. 5.3 indicate the range of equivalence ratios under which sooting has been observed in premixed flames and well-stirred reactors

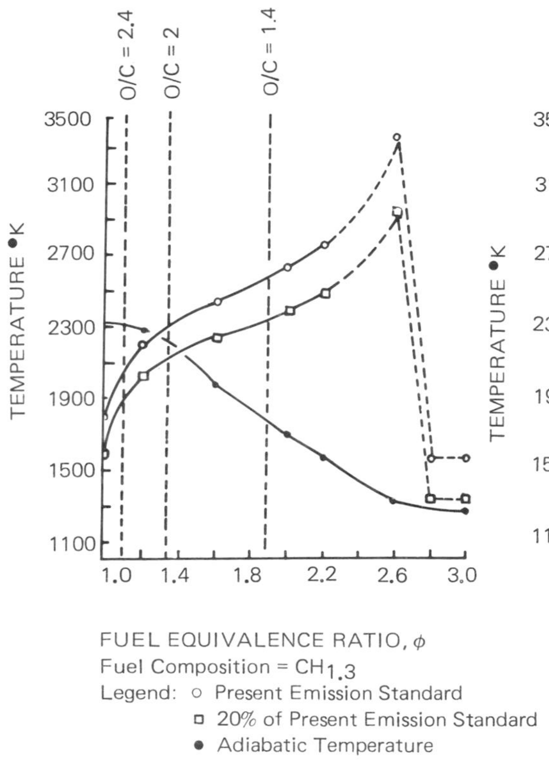

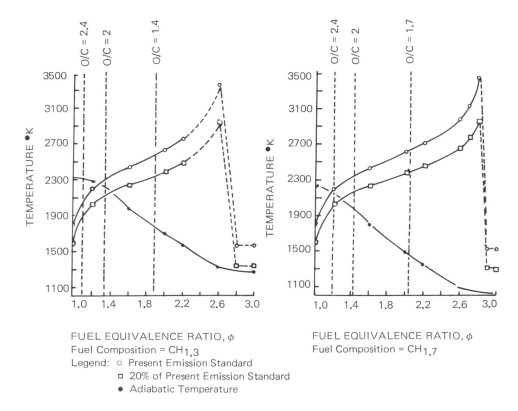

Figure 5.3 Combustor Temperature Constraints for Allowable NO_x Emissions as a Function of Fuel Equivalence Ratio (Based upon Equilibrium Composition)[30]

respectively. Thus, in practical systems, strong back-mixing in the fuel-rich zone increases the O/C ratio at which carbon is formed.

NO_x formation in the combustion of condensed phase fuels is controlled by several physical processes, including both homogeneous gas-phase reactions of the volatile pyrolysis products of the fuel, and heterogeneous gas-solid reactions of the remaining char. The fate of fuel-nitrogen in the following two heterogeneous processes is considered here: oxidation of char-bound nitrogen to form NO_x, and catalytic reduction of NO_x on the carbon surface to yield N_2.

In considering the first of these processes, we concentrate largely on the coal combustion. Of equal interest, of course, is the combustion of liquid fuels. Modeling of liquid droplet combustion, however, at least in the simpler cases of doped or distillate oils, often need not involve consideration of heterogeneous effects. Besides the known decreasing conversion of fuel-nitrogen to NO_x with increasing fuel-nitrogen or/and equivalence ratio, it is well known that changes in droplet size, fuel/air mixing (that is, flow aerodynamics) influence fuel-nitrogen conversion[31,32]. These effects are rationalized by the observation that, essentially, all of the chemistry influencing the formation of NO_x for distillate oil combustion takes place in the gas phase. Indeed, fuel-nitrogen is released as volatiles which burn essentially as a diffusion (or partially premixed) flame about the shrinking droplet (depending upon aerodynamic features). With certain kinds of fuels, increase in droplet size during pyrolysis (or combustion) has also been observed[24]. Much less, however, is known about the combustion of the residual fuel oils that contain most of the nitrogen in petroleum. These tend to form a nitrogen-containing residue during droplet combustion[33] (high asphaltine-content oils may form coked cenospheres), which may be quite similar in nature to the nitrogen-containing char formed in the coal combustion. The second of the heterogeneous processes, (that is, reduction of NO to N_2 on the carbon surface) can occur to some extent in any sooting system, irrespective of whether it is liquid or solid-fuel fired. Even greater reduction takes place with the presence of char. It is well known that the devolatilization of coal nitrogen is kinetically controlled. As such, for the temperatures and residence times encountered in practical combustors, a certain amount of nitrogen will remain in the char to undergo heterogeneous oxidation as the char burns out. It is believed that this fuel-nitrogen is converted primarily to NO according to

$$\text{char (C, N)} \xrightarrow[\text{oxidation}]{} CO + NO$$

and that, in secondary steps, the NO so formed may either participate in further gas phase reactions, be reduced to N_2 in the char (or soot, if any) or survive as NO.

Though the reduction of NO in the presence of char was known to come about in the absence of oxygen[34], it is only recently that this effect has been recognized to occur to a significant extent even in the presence of oxygen[35]. This has potential implications for reducing NO_x from hydrocarbon combustion.

The NO/carbon surface (catalyzed) reaction has been studied by numerous investigators[36-39] and the diversity of results obtained has not yet led to a clear formulation of the mechanistic details of the reaction(s) that occur, although a clear picture is gradually emerging. Most studies have been conducted at temperatures considerably below those representative of pulverized coal combustion. Nevertheless, the general consensus is that the NO/carbon reaction is first order with respect to NO concentration, produces CO, CO_2, and N_2 as products, with the CO/CO_2 ratio increasing with the temperature, suggesting a change in reaction mechanism. It is not even known with certainty, at present, what the primary reactions are of NO on the carbon surface. Most likely, they are:

$$C + 2NO \rightarrow CO_2 + N_2$$

$$C + NO \rightarrow CO + \tfrac{1}{2}N_2$$

$$CO + NO \xrightarrow[\text{(catalyze)}]{} CO_2 + \tfrac{1}{2}N_2$$

Song[40] extended the NO/char kinetic studies to combustion temperatures. In this study, char particles were allowed to react with NO in the hot zone of a heated laminar flow furnace and the conversion of NO to N_2 was monitored. The reaction was treated as first order in NO. External gas film diffusion resistance was shown to be insignificant, and the intrinsic kinetics for a reaction governed by internal pore diffusion resistance and surface reaction resistance were derived from a plug flow. The results showed that the effectiveness factor decreases with increasing temperature, indicating a transition from a regime of chemical reaction control at low temperatures to a regime of internal pore diffusion control at higher temperatures. An Arrhenius plot of the rate constant yielded an activation energy of 32.7 Kcal/mole for the temperature range 1250-1750 K. The reduction rate constant per unit BET surface area is given by

$$k = 5 \times 10^{-5} \exp\left[\frac{-32{,}700}{RT}\right] \frac{\text{moles}}{\text{sec m}^2 \text{ ppm}}$$

The char/O_2 intrinsic reaction rate constant is about two orders of magnitude faster than char/NO reaction at 1500 K[40]. The effectiveness factor for the char/NO reaction is about a factor of 20 greater than that for the char/O_2 reaction. The char/O_2 reactivity decreases with char burnout whereas the char/NO reactivity does not, implying that the char/NO reaction might compete effectively with the char/O_2 reaction. The reduction of NO_x is strongly dependent upon temperature and char availability. Reduction is shown to be quite sensitive to the nature of the catalytic (carbon) surface. Soot and carbon black can yield two orders of magnitude difference in kinetic constants.

NO_x Emission and Reduction from Practical Combustion Systems

Gupta *et al.*[41] studied the pollution emission characteristics from a tangential-axial entry type of swirl burner. Four different flames, produced by various combinations of air and fuel introduction and burner exit geometry, were studied in detail. The measurements showed that virtually complete fuel burnout and the lowest NO_x concentration are produced by axial fuel entry and a convergent/divergent exit nozzle, Fig. 5.4. The low NO_x concentrations are due to the convergent exit nozzle substantially increasing the size of the recirculation zone, recirculating colder combustion products, and thus quenching the reactions that form NO_x. Nevertheless, axial/radial fuel entry produced only slightly more NO_x. It was clearly shown that high levels of NO_x as well as H_2 and CO were produced at the exit near to the region of highest temperature. Nevertheless, as burnout proceeded downstream, the free hydrogen and carbon monoxide reduced some of the NO_x that had been formed to nitrogen, with the result that only small concentrations of NO_x (and negligible CO and H_2) resulted in the combustion products. It is evident that further reduction of NO_x may be obtained by combinations of staged combustion and increased levels of recirculation. Virtually complete burnout of the natural gas fuel occurred with axial/radial fuel entry and with axial/fuel entry and a convergent/divergent nozzle. Both axial fuel entry and tangential fuel entry with a straight exit left small but significant proportions of the fuel unburnt. Meyer and Mauss[42] showed how low levels of NO_x ($\approx$50 ppm) may be obtained by stratified burning, using a distillate liquid fuel containing only 0.01 per cent nitrogen. Fuel was injected into a primary swirling air stream, surrounded by a secondary coaxial, nonswirling, air stream. Two combustion regions were distinguishable, one in the primary swirling air stream, the other associated with the secondary air stream. The lowest levels of NO_x production ($\approx$50 ppm) were obtained with a swirl number of 0.93 in the primary air flow. It was also shown that flue gas recirculation could be used to reduce NO_x concentration by up to 40 per cent. Several workers have shown[43-46] even greater reductions of NO_x concentration and that the external flue gas recirculation principally affects the nitric oxide formed from atmospheric nitrogen. Low excess air combustion was shown to help, mainly in reducing the

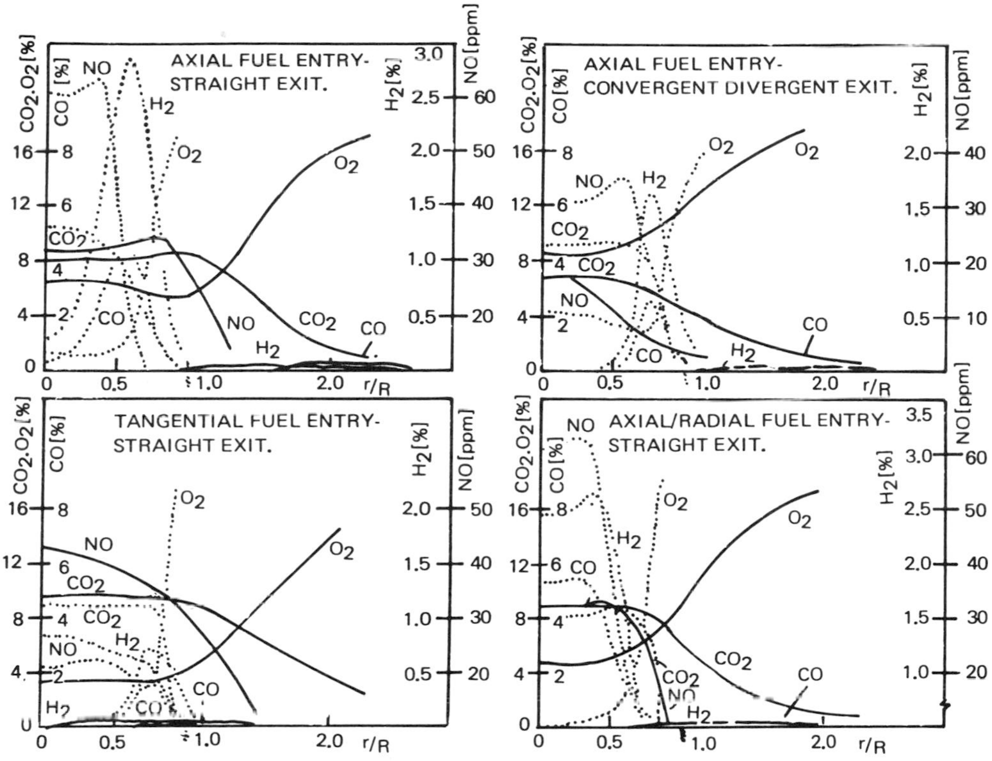

Figure 5.4 Radial distribution of gas concentrations.[41] . . . $X/D = 0$, — $X/D = 2.0$

nitric oxide formed from fuel nitrogen. It thus is most effective in controlling emissions from high nitrogen-content fuels.

Heap *et al.*[47,48] have shown that high emissions of NO_x may occur with the International Flame Research Foundation, Ijmuiden, movable block type swirl burner with pulverized coal as fuel (≈700 ppm), the emission being strongly dependent upon the available oxygen during the combustion of the volatile coal fractions. Pulverized coal was injected through a series of different injectors at the burner throat, with varying percentages of primary air. Figure 5.5(a) shows the variations of NO concentration with varying swirl numbers for different injectors and reveals the following features:

1. Sudden reduction of emission with injector A;
2. high emission from injector F (almost independent of swirl);
3. decreased and then increased emission with increasing swirl with injectors B and C;
4. low emission level with injector H, which is due to the high momentum of the fuel jet penetrating the reverse flow zone, reducing its size and thus reducing residence times.

The amount of primary air was also shown to affect the emission of NO, particularly with annular fuel injectors[48] (Fig. 5.5(b) and (c)). It is significant that the point of

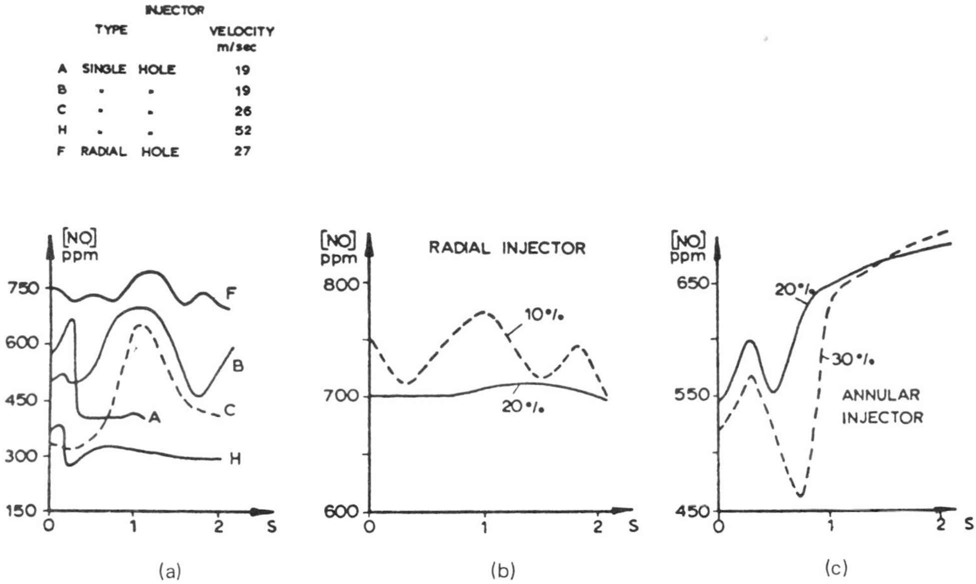

Figure 5.5 Effect of Injector Type on NO_X Emissions from an Ijmuiden Type Swirl Burner[47].

minimum NO formation is reached at a swirl number of about 0.9, similar to that reported by Meyer and Mauss[42].

Sadakata and Beér[49] have investigated local NO formation rates from experimental data obtained in a diffusion-type natural gas-fired swirl burner. A vaned-type swirler was used (vane angles 45° and 60°) and the fuel was injected axially or radially inwards from eight equally spaced holes located in the wall. Local NO formation rates in these turbulent flames were derived by solving the transport equation for a network of volume zones in the flame and using experimentally-derived data of stream function, eddy diffusivity, temperature level and NO concentration.

The stream function was calculated from results of measurements of the time mean axial velocity and of the time mean temperature. The stream function is given as

$$\psi = \int_{0}^{R} \rho \, \bar{u} \, r \, dr$$

Values of the eddy diffusivity were calculated from results of helium tracer experiments. A material balance in molar formulation was written for the helium tracer – introduced with the fuel – over a thin annulus bounded by two coaxial stream tubes in the flame. In general, designating the volume element between stream tubes ψ_o and $\psi_o + \Delta\psi$ as V_o (Fig. 5.6), the material balance for the chemical species A under steady state conditions can be given as[49]

$$\int_{V_o} r_A dv = 2\pi \int_{\psi_o}^{\psi_o+\Delta\psi} \left\{ X_A(Z_o+\Delta Z,\psi) - X_A(Z_o,\psi) \right\} d\psi$$

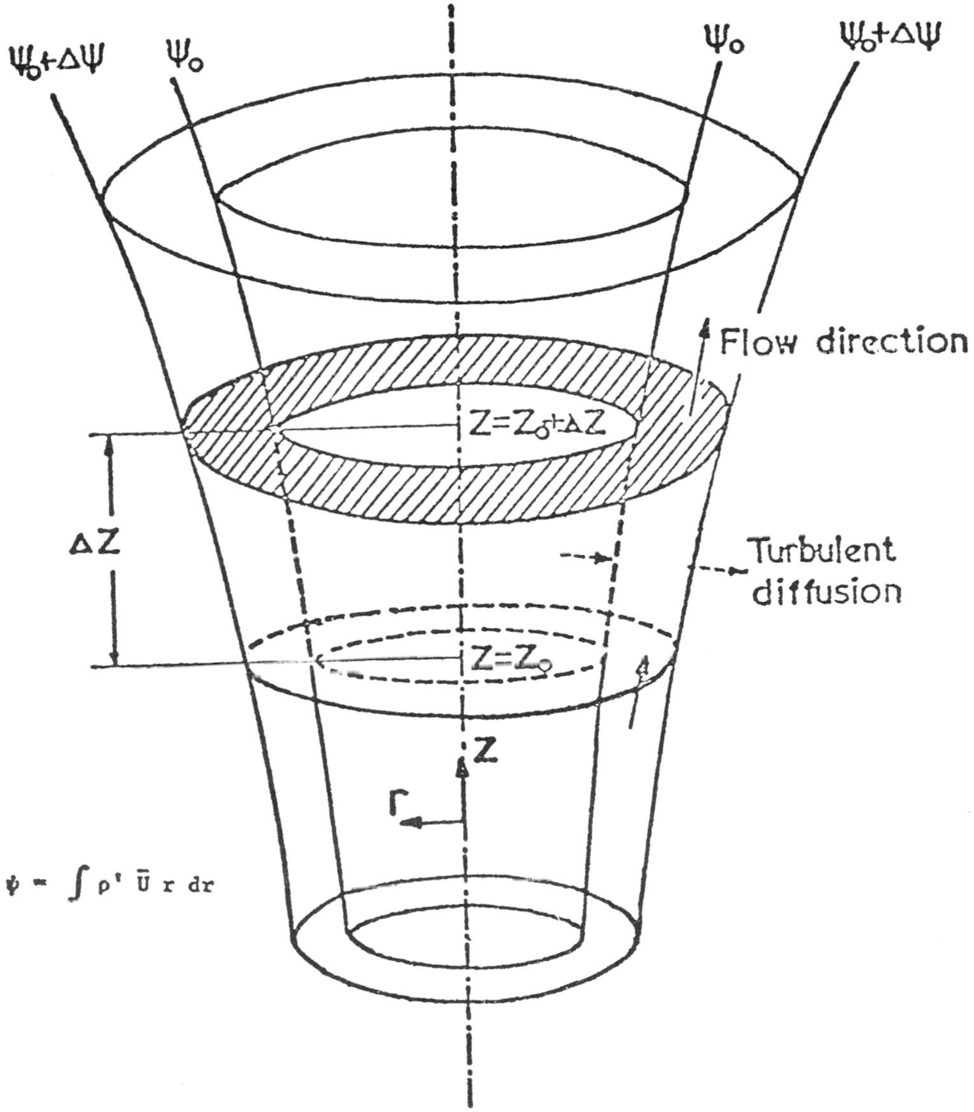

Figure 5.6 Schematic diagram of streamlines and the coordinate system: $p' = p/M$ mol/m^3; M is mixture molecular weight, kg/mol; = Σ, X, M,: X, = mole fraction of molecular species i; M, = molecular weight of molecular species i kg/mol.[49]

$$- 2\pi \int_{Z_o}^{Z_o+\Delta Z} \left[\left(\epsilon_c \, r \frac{\partial \rho \, X_A(Z,\psi)}{\partial r} \right)_{\psi=\psi_o+\Delta\psi} - \left(\epsilon_c \, r \frac{\partial \rho \, X_A(Z,\psi)}{\partial r} \right)_{\psi=\psi_o} \right] dZ$$

where r_A is the rate of formation of species A (mol/litre, s). In the above equation, terms of molecular diffusion and axial turbulent diffusion are neglected. When ΔZ, $\Delta\psi$ are small, and for the case when species A is non-reactive (such as helium) so that the reaction term $\int_V r d\nu = 0$, we can write

$$\epsilon_{c,\psi=\Delta\psi} \quad \frac{1}{\int_{Z_o}^{Z_o+Z} \left(r \frac{\partial \rho \, X_A(Z,\psi)}{\partial r} \right)_{\psi=\psi_o+\Delta\psi} dZ}$$

$$\left[\epsilon_{c,\psi_o} \int_{Z_o}^{Z_o+\Delta Z} \left(r \frac{\partial \rho \, X_A(Z,\psi)}{\partial r} \right)_{\psi=\psi_o} dZ + \int_{\psi_o}^{\psi_o+\Delta\psi} [X_A(Z_o + \Delta Z,\psi) - X_A(Z_o,\psi)] \, d\psi \right]$$

Because of symmetry, on the axis

$$\psi = 0, \partial X_A/\partial r = 0; \ \partial\rho / \partial r = 0$$

Hence

$$\int_{Z_o}^{Z_o+\Delta Z} \left(r \frac{\partial \rho X_A(Z,\psi)}{\partial r} \right)_{\psi=0} dZ = 0$$

The radial distribution of ϵ_c can be determined successively by starting from $r = 0$, $C_{He}(Z,r)$ and $\psi(Z,r)$ being given. The assumption is made that the eddy diffusivities so determined for helium will hold also for other species such as NO or CH_4 because of the nature of turbulent diffusion.

With the functions $\epsilon(Z,\psi)$, $\psi(Z,r)$ and $C_{NO}(Z,r)$ known, material balances for NO over cylindrical shell elements in the flame can be written, and the NO formation rate (r_{NO}) can be determined according to

$$r_{NO} = \frac{2\pi}{V_o} \int_{\psi}^{\psi_o+\Delta\psi} [X_{NO}(Z_o + \Delta Z,\psi) - X_{NO}(Z_o,\psi)] \, d\psi$$

$$- \frac{2\pi}{V_o} \epsilon_{\psi_o+\Delta\psi} \int_{Z_o}^{Z_o+\Delta Z} \left(r \frac{\partial \rho \, X_{NO}(Z,\psi)}{\partial r} \right)_{\psi=\psi_o+\Delta\psi} + \frac{2\pi}{V_o} \epsilon_{\psi_o} \int_{Z_o}^{Z_o+\Delta Z}$$

$$\left(r \frac{\partial \rho X_{NO}(Z,\psi)}{\partial r} \right) \int_{\psi=\psi_o} dZ$$

The whole calculation procedure is illustrated in Fig. 5.7.

The NO formation rates so determined were compared with those predicted from local gas concentrations and temperatures based on the Zeldovich kinetic model. The basic reactions considered were

$$O + N_2 \rightarrow NO + N$$

$$N + O_2 \rightarrow NO + O$$

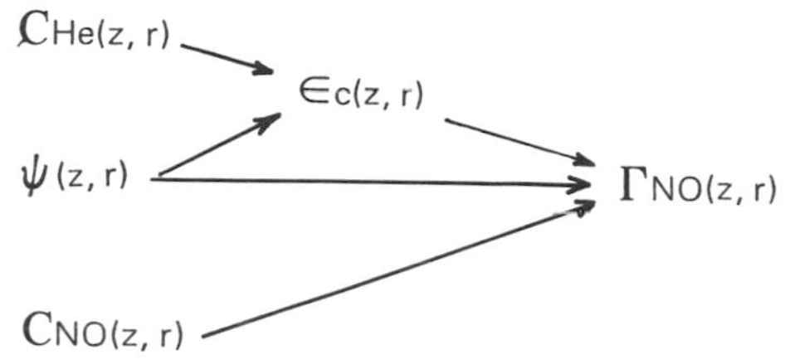

Figure 5.7 Schematic diagram of the calculation procedure: C_{He} = Helium concentration (measure); ψ = Stream function (from measurement); C_{NO} = Nitric oxide concentration (measure); r_{NO} = Rate of formation of NO (calculated).[49]

When $[NO] \ll [NO]_{equ}$, the rate of NO formation reaction can be approximately given on the basis of the steady-state approximation of N, as

$$r_{NO} = 2k_f[N_2]\,[O] \text{ mol/litre.s}$$

where k_f is the rate constant of the first reaction on the Zeldovich kinetic model and is given as

$$k_f = 13.6 \times 10^{10} \exp(-75.4 \times 10^3/RT) \text{ litre/mol.s}$$

When [O] is in equilibrium with $[O_2]^{1/2}$

$$[O] = \bar{K}[O_2]^{1/2} \text{ mol/litre}$$

Where $\bar{K} = 1.6 \times 10^2 \exp(-59.0 \times 10^3/RT)$ mol$^{1/2}$/litre$^{1/2}$

$$\text{Hence,} \quad r_{NO} = 2k_f\bar{K}[N_2]\,[O_2]^{1/2}$$

NO formation rates so calculated are given in brackets in Fig. 5.8. As can be seen from the comparison of NO formation rates determined from measurements and those predicted using the Zeldovich rate equation there is reasonable agreement throughout the flame except in the main reaction zone where the rates determined experimentally were about two orders of magnitude higher than those predicted. Evidence of NO destruction in the recirculation zone was found.

Calculations were made to take into account the effect of the fluctuating temperature upon the rate of formation of NO in the flame to see whether the rates so predicted will

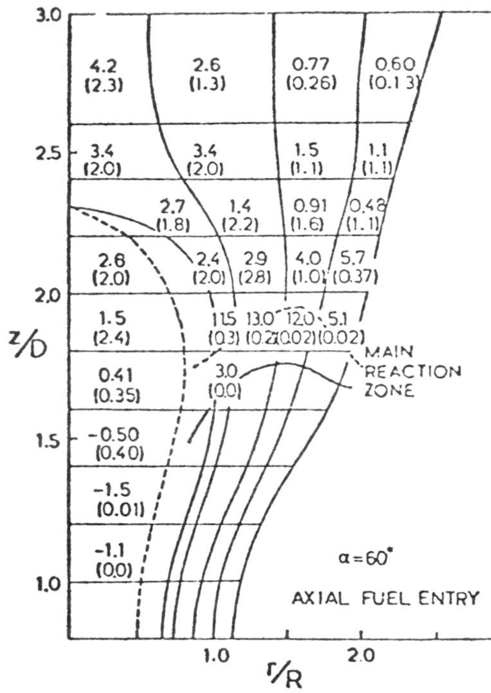

Figure 5.8 NO formation rates in the flame. Γ_{NO} averaged in each flame zone [10^{-8} mol/1 sec]; Figures in brackets are calculated values based on the Zeldovich kinetic model.[49]

be in better agreement with those calculated from experiments. As an input to these calculations, measured temperature fluctuation distributions were used, and as an approximation, sinusoidal and random temperature-time distributions were assumed.

The effect of the temperature fluctuations is – as could be expected – significant. Values of r_{NO} calculated for the region $\psi = 5\psi_o$ to $10\psi_o$ were found to be four to six times higher than those calculated for mean temperatures. Notwithstanding the important effect of the temperature fluctuations upon the rate of formation of NO this was insufficient for giving a full explanation for the large departure of the calculated rates from those determined experimentally.

With respect to the effect of the temperature fluctuations it can be argued that the measurements using electronically compensated thermocouples could follow transients only up to the frequency range of 1KHz and it is conceivable therefore that near-adiabatic temperatures that might have existed on the boundaries of fuel-rich and lean eddies could not be detected.

Gupta *et al.*[50] reported emission levels from a multi-annular swirl burner and showed that this burner has a high potential for minimizing NO_x emissions (emission levels ≈30 ppm) while operating at high temperatures (1800°C) due to the excellent control achieved over the aerodynamic flow structure and the combination of very high turbulence levels and a central recirculation zone of only moderate to small size. Thus, residence times at high temperature are minimized substantially, reducing the formation rate of Zeldovich or prompt NO_x. The multi-annular swirl burner is also attractive for its potential application as a gas-turbine combustor. In this context, the various annuli in the burner can be constructed in a telescopic arrangement (variable geometry to suit the power and altitude conditions). The problem of film cooling can be overcome by using part of the combustion air in the outermost annuli and allowing it to mix downstream with the rest of the hot combustion gases. This configuration of the burner (two-stage combustion process) has the further advantage of reducing NO_x from fuels containing high fuel-bound nitrogen.

Awerbuch[51,52] virtually eliminates NO_x formation, despite operating his swirling, pulsating combustors at high temperatures. The pulsating nature of the flow and the two-stage nature of the combustion process ensures a reducing atmosphere in the first stage of the combustor and a very rapid flame and combustion process (of period 20-50 Hz). Thus, the reactions that form NO_x are not sustained long enough to allow high production rates, and any NO_x that is formed is reduced in the fuel-rich first stage (remembering that the Zeldovich NO formation rate is relatively slow compared with combustion rates).

Substantial progress has been made in the reduction of NO_x emissions from swirl burners and boiler systems over the last few years. Some of the currently-in-use (or potential) NO_x reduction techniques are: low excess air, burner modifications for air and mixing control, staged combustion, increased burner spacing, improved windbox or plenum air distribution, flue gas recirculation, reduced air preheat, water injection, injection of ammonia.

Regardless of whether the source is atmospheric or fuel nitrogen, high NO_x is, in general, caused by high temperatures and high O_2 concentrations. These conditions are found in very localized adiabatic regions where air is present in the primary combustion zone near the burner throat. Long residence times at these conditions also increase the NO_x formation, particularly from atmospheric nitrogen. The statistical occurrence of these high NO formation pockets is minimized by local fuel richness, which must be accomplished in such a manner, that it does not cause problems of combustion safety or operation. This fuel richness control can be so localized that individual flame zones, and not necessarily the whole burner, can be made fuel rich even when immersed in high excess air.

Whole burners may be made fuel-rich through two-stage combustion, a technique that is in use in many systems. It consists of introducing some of the combustion air into the furnace through over-fire air ports (so-called NO_x ports) or through burners to which the fuel flow has been terminated, or locally eliminating adiabatic stoichiometric zones. The active burners are thus operated at fuel/air ratios well above stoichiometric. The average O_2 concentration and temperature at the burner are reduced, and so is the nitric oxide formation rate. Some of the nitrogen-bearing organic molecules are cracked to form N_2; or, if NO should form in the flame fronts, it acts as an oxidizer within the fuel-rich core. The fuel that is not completely burned at the burner face combines with the air introduced at other points in the furnace to complete the combustion. In this "second-stage" combustion, the temperatures are relatively low because the fuel and air are at this point diluted by combustion products that have lost heat through the tremendous heat absorption of the furnace water walls.

Flue gas recirculation into the combustion air provides a diluent, the heat capacity of which lowers the peak combustion temperature.

Reduced air preheat is another way of reducing peak temperature, but in this method there is no dilution. Severe penalties in fuel economy (about 2 per cent per 55°C in air temperature, or 2.5 per cent per 55°C in stack-gas temperature) are incurred if the stack-gas temperature is not lowered by some other method such as transfer of some of the heat to the boiler feedwater.

Water injection in any appreciable amount also involves large losses in boiler efficiency but is very similar to flue gas recirculation in the diluent heat capacity effect on peak combustion temperature. The method has been used on a few large boilers to extend peak load when it is limited by a specific NO_x regulation, but normally it is unacceptable because of the fuel penalty and the questionable value when considering fuel conservation, thermal pollution and net emission gain.

The temperature of the cooled product gas entrained off the firing water wall by the flame has a strong influence on NO_x emission. In one oil-fired boiler with high combustion intensity, NO_x emissions were lowered 50 per cent by cleaning deposits off the firing wall during a boiler shutdown. The NO_x gradually increased to three-quarters of its former level after six months as wall deposits again accumulated.

Injection of ammonia to reduce NO_x to N_2 was shown to be effective when the gas was injected into the combustion products at a temperature of about 960°C, the NO being reduced primarily to molecular nitrogen (N_2) and H_2O. Ammonia emissions could be minimized and maintained at less than 10 ppm if the ammonia were injected at a temperature slightly higher than the peak effectiveness temperature because the excess reducing agent is consumed by excess oxygen. Subsequent work[53] has extended this technique to a furnace and has proved its effectiveness in reducing NO emissions, optimum results being experienced when the NH_3/NO initial ratio was 2.0, giving an NO reduction ratio (Final/Initial) of 0.2. Muzio[53] concludes that the technique is more expensive than burner modifications and should be considered only when absolutely necessary to reduce NO emissions to a minimum.

Russian work on measuring NO_x from coal-fired swirl burners[54,55] is largely in agreement with that of Breen[56]. In general, NO_x levels appear to be somewhat higher than those obtained from Western systems. Recirculation of exhaust gases appears to be a very prevalent method of reducing NO_x emissions, coupled with two-stage combustion (in new burner designs) and minimization of excess air levels in existing designs.

The above comments on boilers are also generally applicable to tangential fired boilers[54,57]. In general, highest levels of NO_x formation are in the initial sections of the individual flames formed by each burner before the central vortex starts to dominate the flow structure, and thus techniques to reduce NO_x are those that apply to individual burners. Kotter *et al.*[54] showed that most of the NO_x formed in a tangentially fired boiler was due to fuel-bound nitrogen and that coarser pulverization of the fuel could lower the intensity of gasification of the fuel's nitrogen and thereby promote a reduction in NO_x emissions. NO_x concentrations in the exhaust ranged from 0.22 to 0.39 g/m^3 with exhaust gas recirculation, and 0.61 g/m^3 without any recirculation.

Coal-fired wet-bottom cyclone combustors in the West produce higher levels of NO_x than swirl burners for the following reasons[45]:

1. Combustion temperatures are high to melt the slag and ensure wet bottom operation. Thus, production of Zeldovich NO_x can be high.
2. The formation of NO_x from fuel-bound N_2 is also favored in coal-fired systems as:

(a) The coal particles are rapidly brought into contact with an O_2-rich environment due to the rapid mixing of primary and secondary air.
(b) High Nusselt and Sherwood Numbers for the particles with strong convective transport exchange.

Typical NO_x emissions from a coal-fired cyclone combustor are in the range of 1000-1200 ppm.

Russian work on cyclone combustors appear to have come to different conclusions with respect to NO_x emissions. Glebov *et al.*[46] indicate that Russian coal-fired cyclone combustors produce only about 10 per cent more NO_x than equivalent systems, using swirl burners, and that techniques such as exhaust gas recirculation, minimization of excess air and redistribution of the tangential air supplies are effective. Russian work on reducing NO_x levels has been particularly successful with oil-fired cyclone combustors[43,46,59] by utilizing the concept of two-stage combustion. This is combined with rapid quenching of the second stage of the combustion process by a heat transfer surface and low excess air operation (≈3%). NO_x levels as low as 0.15 g/m^3 can be produced (compared to emissions from an equivalent, old-fashioned, high-emission combustor of up to 1.3 g/m^3).

It is also significant to note that concentrations of SO_3 decreased from 0.0035 to 0.0015 per cent as the air level was reduced from 10 per cent to 2.5 per cent. The corresponding reduction in dew point temperature for sulphuric acid is from 150°C to 85-90°C, thus substantially reducing the danger of damage due to corrosion.

The excellent flame stabilization characteristics of cyclone combustors may be used to burn poor quality fuels efficiently at low temperatures (that is, flame front temperatures of 850°-1300°C)[60,61]. Under such conditions very low levels of NO_x emission are produced (≈10 ppm for gaseous fuels)[61]. It is necessary to ensure that solid particles remain separate and do not melt, hence operational temperatures have to be kept below 1200-1300°C, as in the case of the work of Agrest, where the resulting separated ash (fuel vegetable refuse) was sold as fertilizer because of its high potash content[62,63].

Emission of nitric oxides has usually been classified merely in terms of NO and NO_x emission. Recent work has revealed significant production of NO_2 on the boundaries of flames produced by swirl burners[64-65]. The effect seems primarily to be due to rapid quenching processes in the burner and is thought to be formed via NO oxidation by HO_2 free radicals. Fig. 5.9(a) shows the radial variation of NO_x, NO, NO_2 and per cent NO_2 at a position six diameters downstream of the combustor inlet. Both primary and secondary air supply were swirled with a similar swirl number. As can be seen, highest levels of NO are formed on the centerline (corresponding to highest temperature levels with this swirl burner configuration and downstream axial station) with a rapid radial decay of NO concentration. NO_2 is formed nearly uniformly across the central section of the burner and has a small peak at the interface between the two flows where quenching effects are maximized. Fig. 5.9(b) shows that when the direction of swirl of the primary air is reversed, practically all the NO_2 generated is NO_x for both velocity ratios shown. In this case, with the very rapid mixing of the two flows, flame quenching and dilution, very little or no NO is formed and a complex reaction between the fluid dynamics of the flow and active chemical species produces predominantly NO_2.

Although overall NO_x levels were low in this case with counter swirling primary and secondary air, low combustion efficiency resulted, indicating the reason for the low NO_x

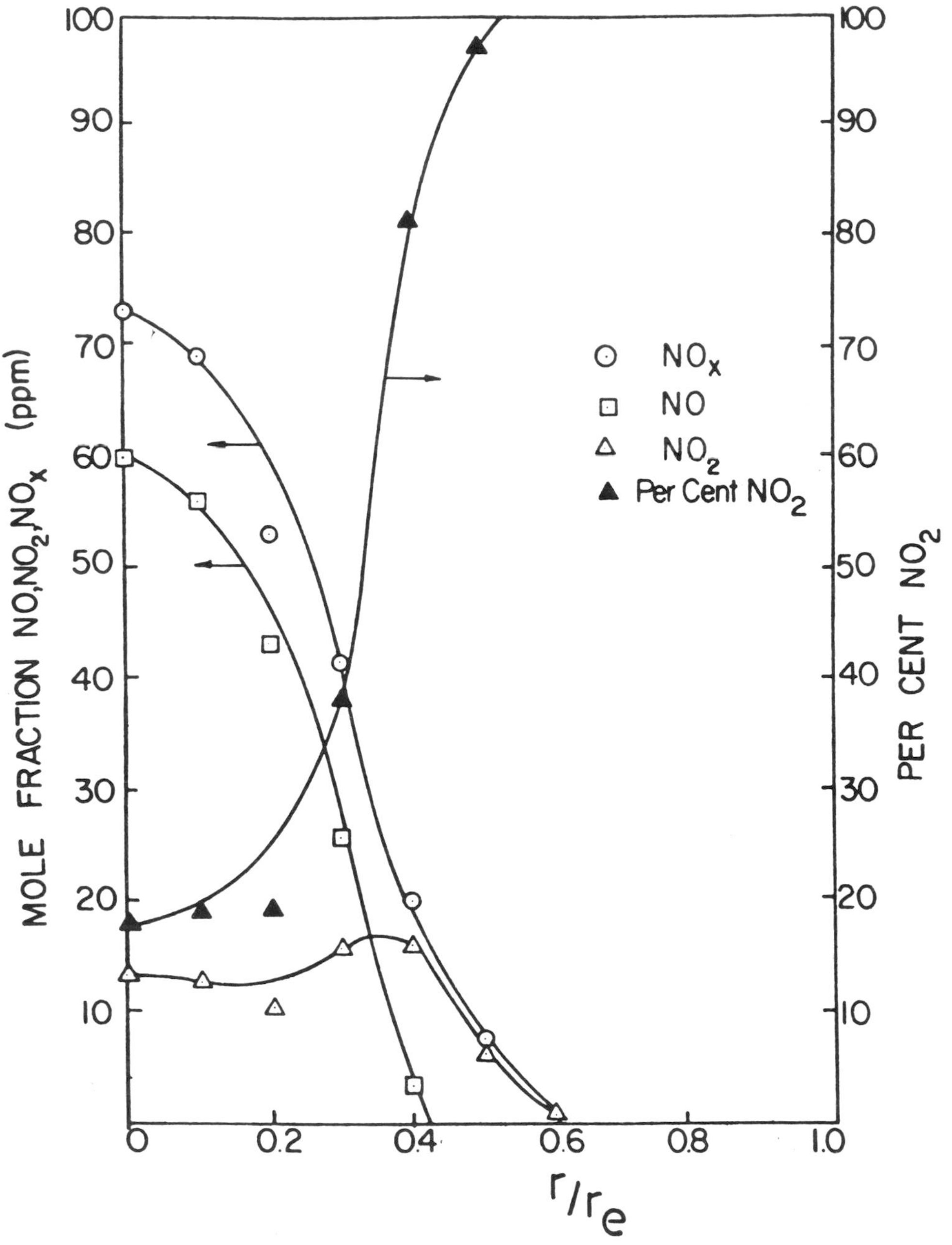

Figure 5.9 (a) Pollutant Emission Characteristics from a Co-Swirling Primary and Secondary Air Supplies (Fuel = Methane, S secondary air = 0.559, S primary air = 0.523, U primary air = 1.5 secondary air, U secondary air = 23.3 m/s)

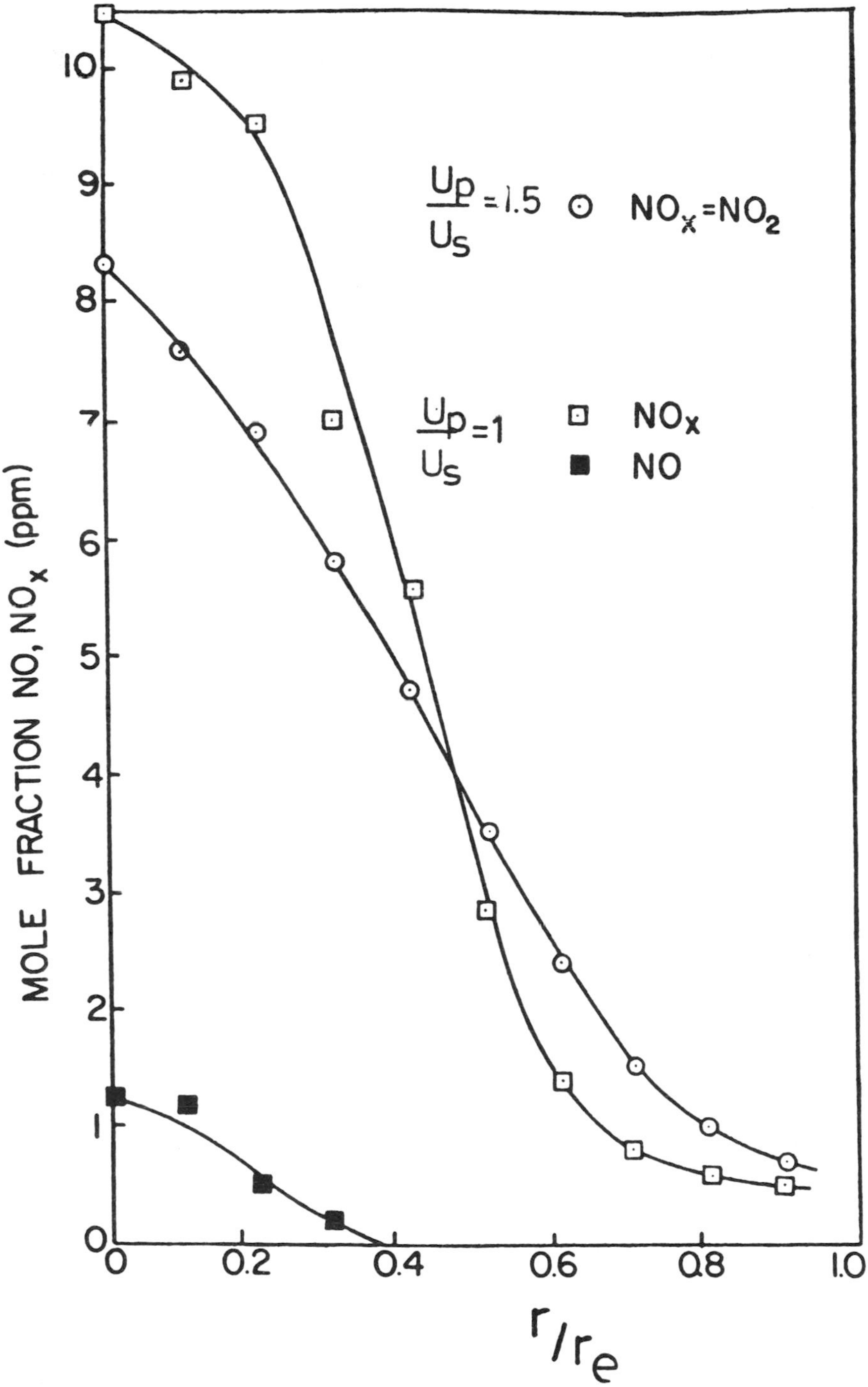

Figure 5.9 (b) Pollutant Emission Characteristics from a Counter-Swirling Primary and Secondary Air Streams (Fuel = Methane, S secondary air = –0.559, S primary air = 0.523, U secondary air = 23.3 m/s)

levels, that is, low temperature levels. Recent work by Claypole[65] has confirmed this trend by detecting high concentration levels of NO_2 near the flame envelope boundary from swirl burners with swirl numbers between 0.5 and 2.

Gas turbine combustors produce specific problems in reducing NO_x levels[8,66]. As with more conventional systems, the main factor governing NO_x formation is temperature; emission increases exponentially with flame temperature ($NO_x \propto e^{0.009T}$)[8], other parameters being important only insofar as they affect flame temperature. Thus, any attempt to reduce NO_x is inevitably tied up, again, by reduction of reaction temperature. 'Hot spots' also need to be eliminated from the reaction zone.

Reductions in both flame temperature and residence time are readily accomplished by increasing the flow of air into the primary zone, but this also produces an increase in CO and UHC. In fact, as basic feature of nearly all methods of emissions reduction is that they represent 'trade-offs' between CO and UHC, on one hand, and NO_x, on the other. This point may be illustrated by plotting CO emissions versus NO_x emissions for a typical gas turbine combustor, Fig. 5.10. This method of presenting emissions data, as advocated by Verkamp *et al.*[57], is instructive because it enables true advances in emission technology to be distinguished from mere 'emission trades.' For any given combustor the CO/NO_x emission characteristic remains sensibly constant, with the upper and lower extremities of the curve corresponding to operation at idle and full power respectively. The main advantage to the designer in most of the emission reduction techniques described below is in allowing movements along the curve over and above those dictated by changes in engine power setting. Nevertheless, real progress in emissions technology is achieved only by displacement of the CO/NO_x characteristic nearer to its origin.

The development of low NO_x combustors is proceeding along two main lines. The most direct approach is through various minor modifications to conventional designs, for example, by changes in linear geometry and airflow distribution, by the adoption of more sophisticated methods of fuel injection, and by the practical exploitation of new wall-cooling techniques that are more economical in their use of cooling air[8]. The merit of this approach is that the combustor retains its existing general size and configuration, and improvements can be made without trespassing far outside the bounds of established technology. Its main drawback is that the end product must inevitably be a compromise of some kind in regard to emissions and other aspects of combustion performance.

The other approach is essentially a rejection of the present design philosophy, which is based on heterogeneous diffusion flames and is fairly conservative in its distribution of fuel and air. Of the various advanced concepts now being actively studied, the three most promising appear to be variable geometry, staged combustion, (that is, Vorbix low pollution gas turbine combustor) and prevaporization/premix systems[8,66,67]. Extensive work has been carried out by UTRC on pollutant formation directed towards gas turbine combustor technology[68]. Concentration levels of the pollutants NO, NO_2, CO, and unburned hydrocarbons were measured at the exit of an axisymmetric combustor over a significant range of operating conditions. In addition, detailed species concentrations, temperature, and velocity maps were obtained throughout the combustor for several representative operating conditions. Gaseous fuel (natural gas, methane, or propane) issued through a central, round tube and the mixing and burning occurred with the airstream within the 1.8 m-long cylindrical combustor. Liquid propane was used as the fuel in some of the tests. Major combustor input parameters were varied over substantial ranges: over-

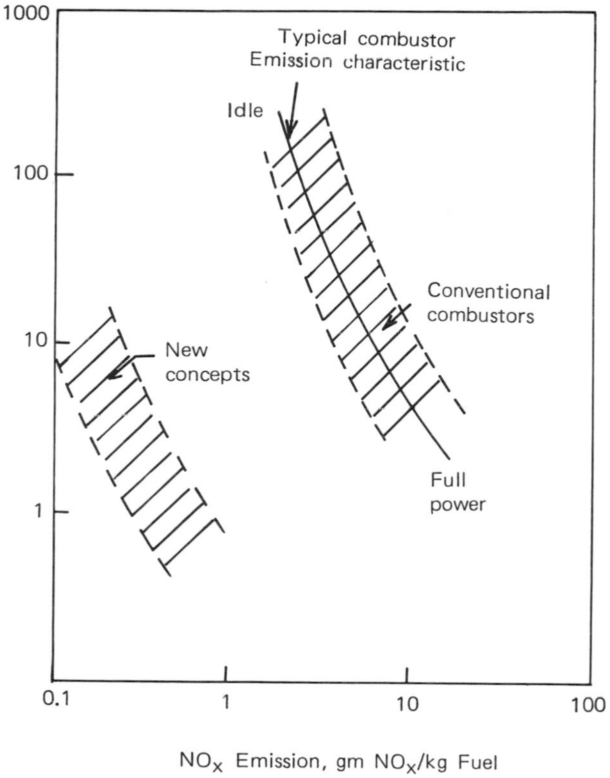

Figure 5.10 Emission Characteristics of Conventional and Advanced Combustors[12]

all fuel-air equivalence ratio, 0.5-1.3; air-fuel velocity ratio, 1.0-40.0; inlet air swirl number, 0.0-0.6; air flow rate (kg/sec) 0.09-0.14; inlet air temperature (°K), 730-860 and combustor pressure (atm), 1.0-7.0. It was found that elevated pressure and swirl result in a shift from chemistry- to mixing-limited behavior and create 'unmixedness' in the flow-field, producing high local temperatures in an annular region around the centerline, which, in turn, enhances NO formation and consumption of hydrocarbons. Aerodynamic flame stabilization, achieved without the benefit of swirl or physical flame holders in systems having large air-fuel momentum flux ratios, produces strong stirring that results in reduced temperatures, low NO formation, and hydrocarbon consumption rates.

The NASA Lewis annular or vortex combustor includes a unique concept that has demonstrated substantial potential for lower levels of NO_x emissions[66,69]. The combustor is divided into 48, 72 or 120 individual swirl-can modules arranged in two or three concentric rows, respectively; these distribute combustion uniformly across the annulus. Early designs of these modules with swirler plates did not pay much attention to fuel atomization and mixing within the individual module, all of which are now designed specifically for low oxides of nitrogen emissions. Results show that swirl-can combustors produce oxides of nitrogen levels substantially lower than conventional combustor designs. These reductions are attributed to reduced dwell-time resulting from short combustion length, and quick mixing of combustion gases with diluent air, and to uniform fuel distributions resulting from the swirl-can approach. At low power conditions, the levels of carbon monoxide and unburnt hydrocarbon emissions would normally rise to quite high values, but these can be reduced somewhat by radial staging of fuel into just one or two module rows. The evidence about the effect of swirl on pollutant formation shows that precise effects depend on the precise burner configuration being considered[1]. As far as NO_x is concerned, the effect of swirl may or may not enhance its production, depending on which of the following effects predominates. Generally, increasing the degree of swirl increases –

1. entrainment of cooled combustion products and thereby decreases thermal NO;
2. local oxygen availability, thereby increasing fuel NO and possibly also prompt NO;
3. combustion intensity and so increases thermal NO.

Prompt NO may be dealt with under the second category, where swirl increases local oxygen availability. There are two effects of this. Hydrocarbon radicals react more with oxygen rather than forming a nitrogen-containing hydrocarbon radical (essential in prompt NO mechanism), and so reduce prompt NO formation. On the other hand, any nitrogen containing free radical has more oxygen available with which to react, which leads to the greater production of prompt NO. There is little evidence as yet to decide which of these competing swirl effects predominates.

Although it is clear that hydrocarbon combustion is not completely understood, most of the trends are properly predicted. To demonstrate this, as well as the ability of the model to predict observations on actual combustors, some comparisons with data from gas-turbine type burners have been made. For this purpose, Edelman and Harsha[70] simply assumed that the primary zone is the source of NO and that the entire primary zone is a single perfectly stirred reactor.

Figure 5.11 shows comparisons of predictions with measured NO_x emissions from a variety of jet engines. The data as represented is a correlation determined by Lipfert[71]. The predictions were made assuming an equivalence ratio of unity ($\phi = 1$) and a constant residence time of about 2 ms. Lipfert showed the importance of combustor inlet temperature with his correlation, and the predictions are in complete agreement with this observation.

Water injection is regarded as one possible control measure for NO_x emissions. Edelman and Harsha[72] applied their multiphase stirred reactor model to the jet engine combustor data, and the comparison is shown in Fig. 5.12. Excellent agreement is shown for the smaller size droplets and for steam injection. The small difference between steam and the small droplet predictions is in complete agreement with the experimental observations. The predictions also show that the effectiveness of liquid water injection decreases rapidly with increasing droplet size.

5.3 OXIDES OF SULFUR EMISSION

Oxides of sulfur (SO_x) are formed in a combustion system because of the presence of sulfur in the fuel (coal or oil) and is preferentially converted to SO_2 or SO_3 in the high-temperature combustion zone. Minimization of SO_3 formation is important for alleviating combustor/furnace corrosion and sulfuric acid plumes. Most of the coal mined in the US (approximately 87 per cent) cannot meet the new source performance standard

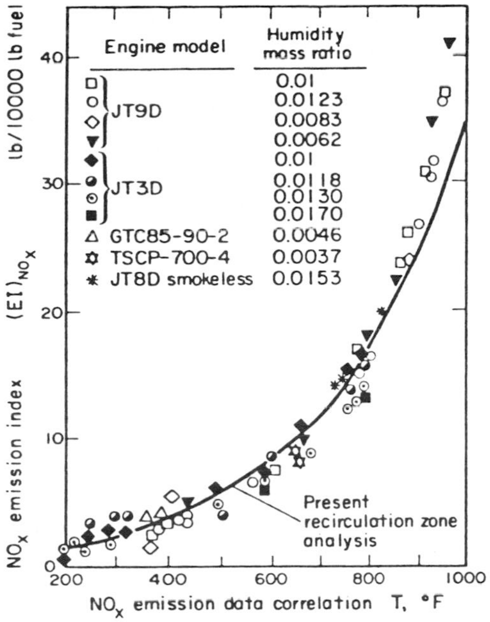

Figure 5.11 Comparison of theory with correlation for turbojet engine emissions data.[71]

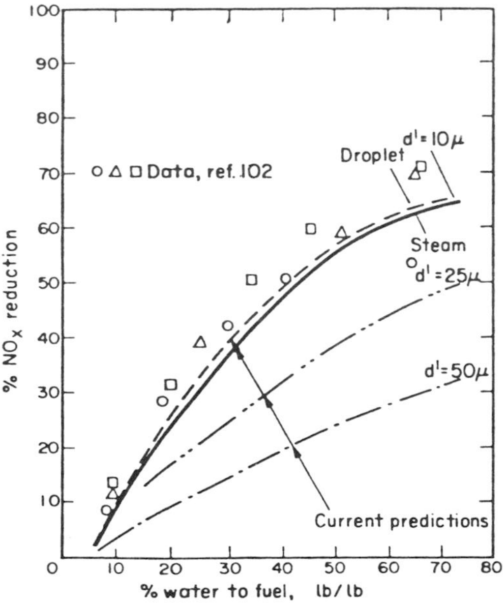

Figure 5.12 Comparison, present theory/turbine combustor data-effect of water and steam injection upon NO_x reduction[72]

mainly because of its high sulfur content. Sulfur exists in coal in three forms: sulfate, pyrite, and organic. Sulfate sulfur contents are less than 0.05 per cent by weight. Since it is water soluble, it can easily be washed out with water. Pyritic sulfur is a heavy mineral particle with a specific gravity of about 5.0. It can be separated from coal, the specific gravity of which is 1.8, by grinding to a small size and subsequent use of various techniques of specific gravity separation. Organic sulfur, tightly bound to the molecular matrix of coal, cannot be removed by mechanical means. As sulfuric acid has a low dew point, in some regulations its hydrates are considered as particulates. These hydrates may even increase plume particle agglomeration, leading to large corrosive particle 'fallout.' It is thus possible by lowering excess levels to reduce particulate emissions below legal maximum even on oil-fired units when the particulate emission is of the above-mentioned form. Excess air levels must not be reduced too far, otherwise particulates will increase again, due to incomplete combustion.

Chemical cleaning is a relatively new approach to removing sulfur from coal. In this method, the sulfur is converted into either elemental sulfur or a water-soluble compound. The elemental sulfur is removed from the coal by steam, vacuum vaporization, or solvent extraction with toluene or kerosene. The water-soluble compound, usually inorganic salt, is washed out, when an aqueous solution of the leaching reagent is separated from the coal.

Several methods of chemical beneficiation have been reported in literature. The more developed processes among them are the Battelle Process[73] and the Meyers Process[74].

The Battelle Process

The Battelle Process consists of five stages: coal preparation, hydrothermal treatment, separation, drying, and leachant regeneration. First, the raw coal is ground up (generally, 70 per cent minus 200 mesh), and goes to a slurry tank for mixing with a chemical leachant (up to 10 per cent NaOH and about 2 per cent $Ca(OH)_2$). It is then pumped into pressure vessels, where it is heated for up to 30 minutes at pressure between 350 and 2500 lbs/sq. in. and temperatures between 225° and 350°C. Here, the pyritic and organic sulfur are converted, primarily, to sodium sulfide. The treated slurry is cooled in a heat exchanger, and the desulfurized coal is separated from the spent leachant in a centrifugal filter. The desulfurized coal is then dried in a dryer, Fig. 5.13.

The spent chemical solution is sparged in a regeneration tower with carbon dioxide, converting sodium sulfide to hydrogen sulfide and sodium carbonate. The ash and fuel components are also precipitated by the carbon dioxide and filtered out. If desired, the hydrogen sulfide can be converted to elemental sulfur, for example, by the Claus Process. The sodium carbonate solution is reacted with lime to yield sodium hydroxide solution and a precipitate of calcium carbonate. The sodium hydroxide solution is concentrated by another filtration and recycled. The limestone is calcined to lime and carbon dioxide, both of which are re-used in the process.

According to Battelle, nearly all inorganic sulfur and up to 70 per cent of the organic sulfur could be removed from bituminous coals. The process also extracts environmentally hazardous metals from the coal, including beryllium, arsenic, barium, and lead. This treatment does not remove a significant amount of ash. Nevertheless, most of the remaining ash can be removed by rinsing the coal with a dilute acid. For example, coals from Ohio, Kentucky, West Virginia, and Pennsylvania contain 4.6 per cent to 13.2 per

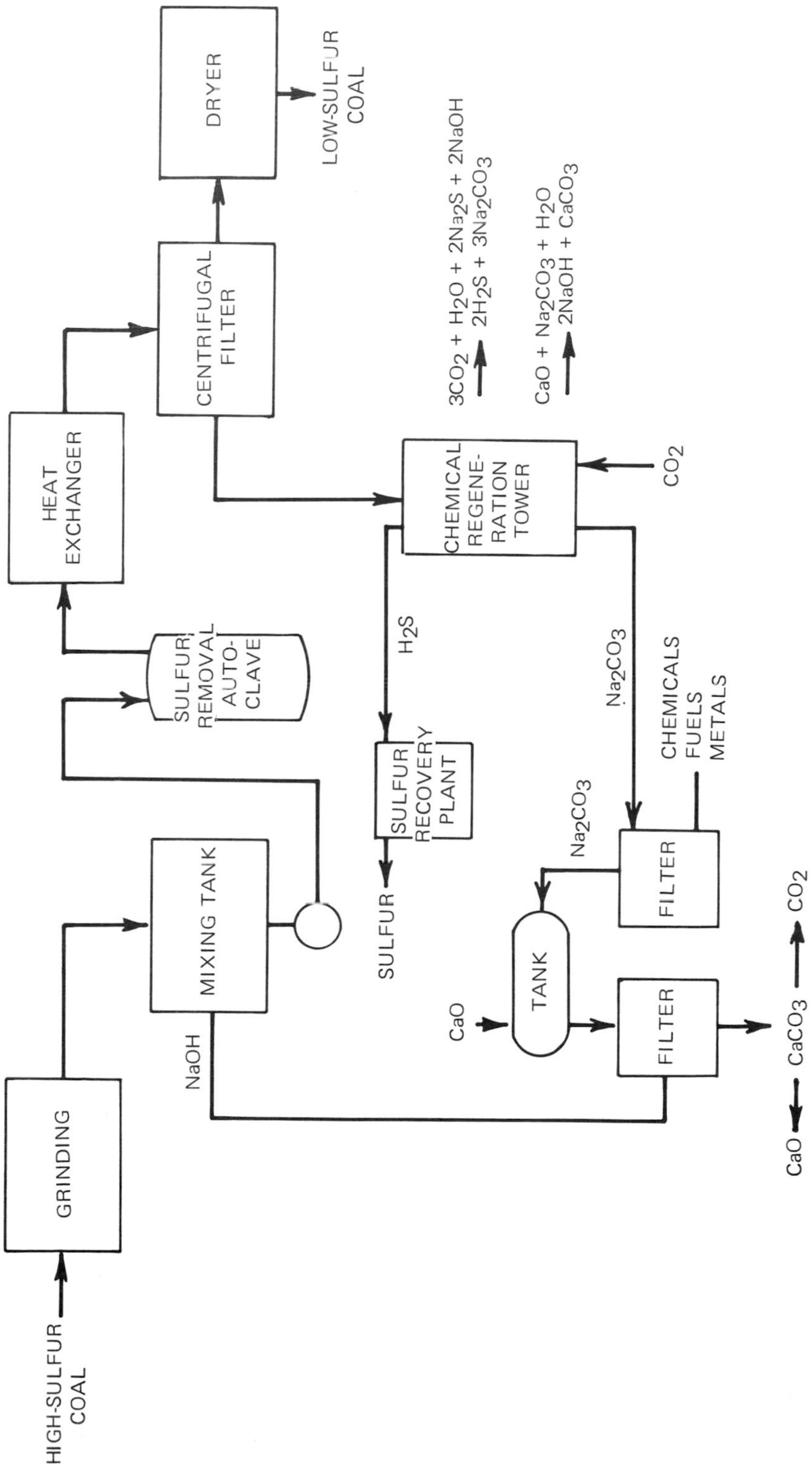

Figure 5.13 Battelle Process[73]

cent ash. After hydrothermal treatment and acid de-ashing, the ash contents of these coals were in the range between 0.7 per cent and 5.3 per cent. Stambough, the chief inventor, believes that the process is far cheaper than solvent refining and liquefaction processes, and is probably less expensive than stack gas scrubbing. He estimates the costs of the process as somewhere between \$10 and \$15 per ton of coal (about 40 to 60 cents per million Btu). Battelle also claims that the process is environmentally superior to stack gas scrubbing, in that it does not produce large volumes of waste, since the reactant chemicals are regenerated, recycled, and reused.

Battelle claims that the process produces better feedstock for combustion and coal conversion processes. The small portion of the sodium hydroxide remaining in the dried fuel after leaching reacts with part of the unextracted sulfur during combustion to produce nonvolatile compounds, further reducing sulfur dioxide emissions. Gasification and liquefaction can be performed at lower temperature and pressure with treated coal because it no longer cakes[75].

The Meyer's Process

In Meyers's Process[74], the slurry of coal in aqueous ferric sulfate solution is heated at 100°C for about 1 hour at atmospheric pressure to oxidize the pyritic sulfur to form free sulfur and sulfate.

$$FeS_2 + 4.6\ Fe_2(SO_4)_3 + 4.8\ H_2O = 10.2\ FeSO_4 + 4.8\ H_2SO_4 + .8\ S$$

The desulfurized coal is separated from the leachant solution, and washed to remove residual iron salts. The free sulfur is then removed from the coal by steam, vaccum vaporization, or solvent extraction, Fig. 5.14. The spent leachant is regenerated by oxidation with air or oxygen from ferrous ion to ferric ion.

$$2.4\ O_2 + 9.6\ FeSO_4 + 4.8\ H_2SO_4 = 4.8\ Fe_2(SO_4)_3 + 4.8\ H_2O$$

Although only pyritic sulfur is removed, the efficiency of sulfur removal is superior to the mechanical method, which is capable of removing only 70 per cent of sulfur from coal. Recently, Meyers and his colleagues at TRW performed a comparison study of Meyers's process and physical cleaning, via float-sink testing, on run-of-mine coal samples obtained from 35 US coal mines, representative of current US production. Meyers's process could remove 90-99 per cent of the pyritic sulfur from the lignites of both the Appalachian Basin and Interior Basin and 59-80 per cent of the pyritic sulfur from the western coals.

Other Processes

Many other methods of chemical beneficiation of coal can be found in the literature and patents. Most of them are still in the stage of laboratory scale investigation. A few of the more developed methods are mentioned below.

Sareen[76] (ammonia/oxygen system) and his associates of Ledgemont Laboratory, Lexington, Massachusetts, recently reported that almost all of the pyritic sulfur and up to 25 per cent of the organic sulfur were removed from Illinois #6 coals (bituminous) by oxidation of the coal sulfur at 130°C and 300 psi oxygen pressure in an ammonia-based system. Friedman[77] (oxidative desulfurization) and associates of Pittsburgh Energy

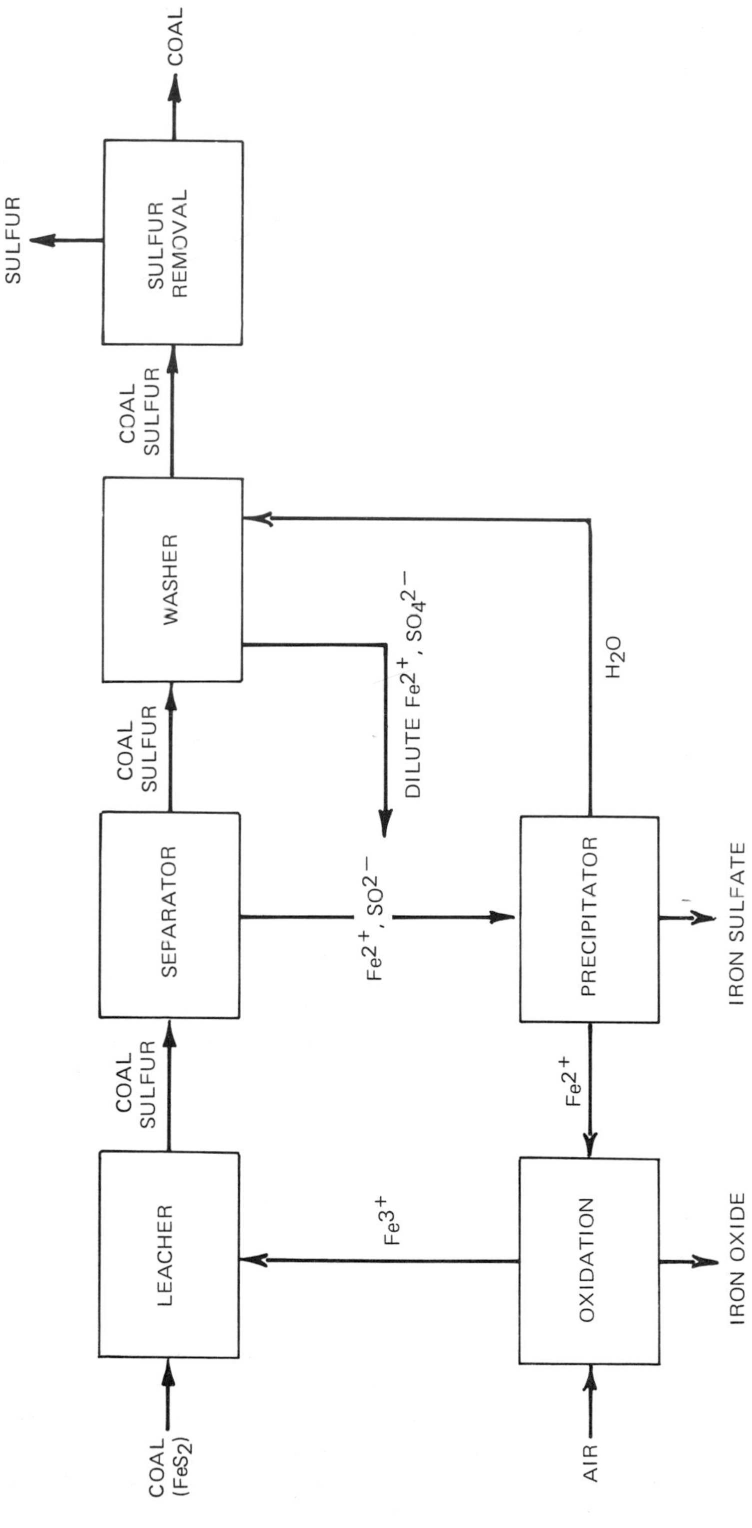

Figure 5.14 Meyer's Process[74]

Research Center reported that air oxidation of an aqueous slurry of bituminous coal at pressures up to 1,000 psi and temperatures of 140°C to 200°C could convert more than 90 per cent of pyritic sulfur and up to 40 per cent of organic sulfur into sulfuric acid, which could be separated from the desulfurized coal by filtration. Ganguli[78] (Chlorinolysis) and his colleagues at the Jet Propulsion Laboratory, California Institute of Technology, used a simple method of chlorinolysis to remove 60 per cent of organic sulfur, 90 per cent of pyritic sulfur, and 30 per cent of sulfate sulfur from high sulfur (4.77% S) bituminous coal at a moderate temperature and atmospheric pressure. Smith[79] (peroxide-acid) of Laramie Energy Research Center, Laramie, Wyoming, treated high sulfur coals at room temperature with solutions containing both hydrogen peroxide (10-17%) and sulfuric acid (0.1-0.3 normal), and reduced the sulfur content 30 per cent to 55 per cent and ash 8 per cent to 40 per cent. Organic sulfur was not significantly affected.

Potential

The claims and estimates made by the developers of chemical methods of cleaning coal seem to suggest that chemical beneficiation has definite advantages over other methods of solving sulfur emission problems.

Mechanical beneficiation is one of the most developed and cheapest methods of removing sulfur from coal. Nevertheless, only up to 70 per cent of pyritic sulfur can be removed by this method, whereas chemical beneficiation can remove practically all pyrites from coal, in most cases. The mechanical methods can suffer severe coal loss in the reject stream, whereas the rejection loss is negligible in chemical beneficiation. Lignites and sub-bituminous coals cannot be efficiently handed by a mechanical method because of their high initial moisture content, which is not a limiting factor for chemical cleaning.

Most of the chemical beneficiation methods have a significant advantage over the mechanical method in that they can remove organically bound sulfur from the coal matrix. Organic sulfur can also be removed by solvent refining, gasification, and liquefaction processes. These processes, however, are more expensive than chemical beneficiation because of the complexity of design and more severe process conditions.

Stack gas scrubbers at present in operation are notorious for their unreliability and are plagued by the need to dispose of the huge amounts of sludge they produce. The chemical method does not produce as much sludge because it is a closed-loop system in which the spent reagents are regenerated and recycled. Since chemical beneficiation attacks the emission problem at its source, namely in the coal, rather than in the flue gas produced, and also with chemical reactions that have proved to proceed quantitatively, it may prove to be more reliable.

Despite the promising claims, chemical beneficiation is still in its infancy. Many technical questions remain to be answered. Chemical reagents used must be inexpensive, highly selective to the species to be removed, water soluble before and after the reaction, and easily regenerable. The need to use for the reaction vessels material that is resistant to the chemicals is an important factor in deciding technical feasibility. The properties of the treated coal and its effect on combustion, including residual ash, or as feedstock for gasification and liquefaction processes must also be investigated.

Trindale *et al.*[80] reported an experimental study, together with an economic analysis of the process, to elucidate processing conditions of magnetic cleaning of coals by using high gradient magnetic separation techniques in coal slurries. It was shown that magnetic cleaning of coals can remove practically all the liberated pyritic sulfur and a portion of the other minerals. The experimental study confirmed the importance of the key independent variables, for example, particle size and liberation, slurry velocity, field intensity and packing characterization.

It is known that SO_3 formation can be substantially reduced by operating with low excess air rates when burning coal or oil. Problems arise with flame control and soot formation, however. Wendt *et al.*[81] have shown that SO_3 (as well as NO_x) levels can be reduced by burning the fuel with moderate excess air, sufficient to suppress soot and maintain stable flame, and to inject additional clean fuel downstream of the primary combustion zone. This principle of 'reburning' must be clearly distinguished from that of two-stage air addition which is known to be effective in the reduction of NO_x, but cannot be easily applied to 'difficult' high C/H ratio, and high nitrogen and sulfur content fuels because the primary combustion zone must then be sub-stoichiometric. Reburning allows some SO_3 and NO_x to be formed in the primary combustion zone, but destroys a large fraction of these pollutants in the secondary zone by reducing reactions involving CH_4 or CO.

Tager *et al.*[82] have shown how SO_3 emission can be substantially reduced by using a cyclone combustor (fired with high sulfur oil) in which combustion is arranged to occur in two stages, one inside the device; the other in the exhaust region. Provided rapid heat transfer (that is, to water tubes) occurs in the second stage SO_3 emission can be reduced by up to a factor of 4 when operating with excess air levels of less than 3 per cent. Awerbuch[83,84] demonstrated that SO_3 emission can also be minimized and virtually eliminated in his design of a swirling flow pulsating combustor in which a two-stage fuel-rich/fuel-weak combustion process occurs of variable frequency (20-50 Hz). High temperatures ($>1400°C$) staged combustion and a very fast combustion process (due to the pulsating nature of the flame) ensures minimum SO_3 emission.

Fuel additives such as magnesium oxide, which are used to coat boiler tubes, can reduce SO_2 to SO_3 conversion in convective heat transfer regions of the boiler by adversely affecting catalysis of the reaction by the boiler tubes.

Sulfur can be eliminated from a fuel by prior treatment, as described earlier, but the process is expensive[85]. Wet scrubbing of the exhaust gases is another possibility but typically reduces overall efficiency of a modern electricity generating station from 40 per cent to about 27 per cent when it is remembered that the cleaned exhaust gases have to be reheated to ensure efficient dispersal by the chimney or stack.

5.4 SMOKE AND PARTICULATE EMISSION AND HEAT RECOVERY

Smoke and particulate emission are conveniently grouped together here for discussion in this section. Solid particulates can range in shape from spherical if formed by condensation and then solidification to highly irregular forms. Initially, spherical particles may increase in size by coagulation and become non-spherical. The shape and especially the size distribution of particles are important parameters since the particle removal method primarily depends on the size of the particles to be removed.

In combustion systems, the emission of smoke and particulates results from the production of finely divided particles in fuel-rich regions of the flame. With oil flames and pressure jet atomizers the main soot-forming region lies inside the fuel spray in a region where local pockets of fuel and fuel vapour are enveloped in recirculating burnt products moving upstream towards the fuel spray. Especially in high temperature high intensity flames, soot may be produced in considerable quantities.

In medium to large boiler plant, levels of smoke emission have for many years been used to indicate combustion efficiency of a plant. In general, as excess air levels are reduced, a point is reached where smoke emission starts to increase dramatically due to the formation of numerous fuel-rich areas in the flame. Excess air levels in commercial boiler units can be as low as 2 per cent with "fine tuning", although many older units run with substantially higher levels. For many decades it has been axiomatic that optimum heat recovery has been obtained when at least a light haze was seen issuing from a chimney, thereby indicating low excess air levels[85,86]. Energy savings that can be achieved by increasing combustion efficiency in most commercial systems are almost negligible.

The main emphasis then, on reducing smoke emission is due to legislation on pollution in much of the Western World. With respect to swirl burners it is necessary to match the method of introduction of the fuel to the aerodynamic characteristics of the swirling flow so produced. Beér and Chigier[87] have shown that maximum fuel burnout with a liquid fuel fired swirl burner occurs when the oil-spray angle is so arranged that the liquid fuel is fired into regions of maximum shear and turbulence intensity on the boundary of the recirculation zone. Similar comments apply to pulverized coal and gaseous flames.

With pulverized coal flames a careful matching of the primary pulverized coal-carrying air stream (typically 20 per cent of the total air flow), with the rest of the swirl burner is necessary to ensure high levels of fuel burnout. Examples of this are given in Chapter 4 of Ref. 1. The coal-carrying duct also acts as a form of bluff body, especially when annular or radial fuel injectors are used, and sometimes it is found necessary to swirl the primary air supply (Fristrom and Westenberg, Chapter 4)[1].

With solid and liquid fuels maximum fuel burnout and minimum smoke emission seems to occur with Swirl numbers less than 1. Drake and Hubbard[88] showed for a liquid fuelled industrial-type swirl burner that minimum emission of smoke and unburnt solids occured when the secondary air supply (comprising >80 per cent of the total) had a fairly moderate degree of swirl ($S \cong 0.9$), the primary air flow being unswirled. Wroblewska *et al.*[89] swirled both the primary and secondary air supplies to their swirl burner using a swirl number of 0.65 for higher calorific value coals (highest momentum flux from secondary air supply) 0.45 for lower calorific value coals (equal momentum fluxes from the primary and secondary flows).

Cyclone combustors do not suffer greatly from problems of smoke emission, in particular with solid fuels, wherein the slag can be removed in the "wet" or liquid form for the following reasons:

1. Centrifugal forces tend to retain larger soot particles.
2. Long residence times in the cyclone chamber combined with high temperature levels with "wet" bottom operation ensures high fuel, and particulate burnout rates.
3. An afterburning region is formed in the exhaust region (*see* Chapter 5 Gupta, Lilley and Syred)[1], in which smoke can be burnt.

4. And discussed later, cyclone combustors can be operated with low levels of excess air (=2%).

For a boiler-fired with swirl burners; typically, combustion heat recovery is some 80-90 per cent efficient, most of the losses going up the stack both as latent and sensible heat. Flue or stack gas temperatures are generally above 120°C. Fig. 5.15 indicates losses and boiler heat recovery levels in a fossil-fueled electricity generating plant. Losses due to unburnt combustible range from 0.3 per cent with coal to 0.1 per cent with oil-fired systems[85].

In gas-turbine combustors, where swirl vanes are often used for flame stabilization purposes, in the primary zone, smoke formation is dependent on the complete combustor system, including the dilution stages and the fact that the combustor has to operate over a far wider operating range than burners in conventional boiler systems[8].

STACK HEAT LOSS, PERCENT

	TOTAL	SENSIBLE	LATENT
Gas	13	3	10
Oil	10	4	6
Coal	9	5	4

Boiler heat recovery, percent

Fuel	Coal	Oil	Gas
Excess air	25	10	8
Stack heat loss	9	10	13
combustible	0.3	0.1	0
auxiliary power	6	4	4
Net Boiler	84.5	85.7	82.8
Overall Cycle Efficiency: 38 to 42%			

Cycle improvement factors

Variable	Change	Fuel decrease, %
(Excess air	–5%	0.25
Boiler exit gas temperature	–20 to 23°C	1.0
Steam temp.	+28°C	0.7
Reheat temp.	+28°C	0.6

Figure 5.15 Losses and Boiler Heat Recovery in Fossil-Fueled Electricity Generating Plant.[85]

In the primary zones of gas turbine combustors featuring spray fuel injection, the pattern of burning is highly complex. Since soot is not an equilibrium product of combustion, its formation is influenced as much by the physical processes of atomization, evaporation and fuel/air mixing as by reaction kinetics.

During the first portion of its trajectory each individual fuel drop suffers loss by evaporation due to heat transmitted from the flame. If the liberated fuel vapour then mixes with air it will burn in the manner of a premixed flame. As drag forces gradually deplete its momentum the fuel drop eventually reaches a certain critical velocity, which depends on its size, below which it becomes completely surrounded by an attached diffusion flame[90]. This diffusion mode of combustion is often a prime cause of the high rates of soot formation and smoke that characterize spray combustion.

The proportion of fuel burned in the diffusion mode may be reduced by increasing the relative velocity between the fuel drops and the surrounding gas and by reduction in fuel drop size[90]. Nevertheless, if improved atomization is accompanied by lower spray penetration the smoke output may actually increase[91]. This is what happens with pressure atomizers and is the main reason for the high smoking tendencies of duplex and dual-orifice atomizers when operating at high pressures.

Even when the overall fuel/air ratio in the primary zone indicates sufficient oxygen for complete combustion, imperfections in mixing can give rise to local regions in which pockets of fuel vapour are enveloped in oxygen-deficient gases at high temperatures. Under these conditions increasing the flow of air into this zone is usually very beneficial. If this additional air is accomplished by an increase in liner pressure drop, the combined effects of more oxygen, lower temperature and improved mixing can drastically reduce soot formation and smoke. Unfortunately, this approach is limited, since adverse effects include those on ignition and stability as well as CO and UHC emissions at idle.

Soot-forming propensity of a liquid fuel increases with aromatic content, boiling point and carbon/hydrogen ratio. Fuel additives have been used with varying degrees of success to reduce smoke emission[8].

Particulate, or solids emission is a problem primarily associated with solid fuels, synthetic and heavy fuel oils. Two types of boiler or furnace can be considered:

1. Dry, in which the solids in the boiler are removed (periodically) as a powder or ash. Only a small proportion of the solids produced remain in the boiler.
2. Wet, in which the solids melt to form a slag, which is tapped off on a regular basis.

For (1) above, particulate emissions to atmosphere can be quite high because much of the coal ash is carried over by the exhaust gases and thus exhaust gas cleanup techniques are required, including cyclone dust separators and/or electrostatic precipitators. Combustion systems using pulverized coal and swirl burners nearly always operate in a "dry" mode. Coal-fired cyclone combustors nearly always operate in a "wet" mode and thus require high temperature levels (approx. 1600 to 1700°C) in order to keep the resulting slag mobile enough to facilitate removal. The cyclone effect, however, traps most particulate matter and ensures that stack gas particulate clean up systems need not be so extensive as with dry, swirl-burner fired boilers.

A typical modern permitted level for particulate emissions is 0.043 g/J (New York State)[85].

Particulates Removal Methods

Particulate matter may be removed from the flue gases by a number of methods, some of which are discussed below. In the natural fallout, often referred to as sedimentation, the particles "drop out" in free fall with the terminal velocity by

$$u = \frac{2(\rho_{part} - \rho_\infty) D g v}{C_D A_P R e \mu}$$

where
- μ is the viscosity of the medium
- v is the particle volume
- D the particle diameter
- A_p the particle frontal area
- Re the Reynolds number, $uD\rho_\infty/\mu$
- C_D the drag coefficient

For Stokes flow $C_D = 24/Re$, $Ap = \pi R^2$, and $v = \frac{4}{3}\pi R^3$, so that

$$u = \frac{2(\rho_{part} - \rho_\infty)(2R)4R^3 g}{(3)(24)(R^2)(\mu)}$$

$$u = \frac{2(\rho_{part} - \rho_\infty)R^2 g}{9\mu}$$

The drag coefficient is a function of the Re and is available for spherical particles in any fluids text. For Re<1 we may use C_D=24/Re, for 3<Re<400, $C_D=24/Re+4/Re^{1/3}$ and for 1,000<Re<2X10^5, C_D=0.44 and is independent of the Reynolds number. Interpolation can be used to fill in values between these expressions.

In the coagulation process, particles come into contact and coalesce or adhere. For example, simple Brownian motion (which dominates below 0.25mm at 1 atmosphere and 20°C) may bring two particles sufficiently close to coalesce. Such coagulation is referred to as thermal since the random Brownian motion may be related to the ambient temperature. We can also force coagulation by hydro-dynamic or electrical forces. Theoretical considerations indicate that the basic equation for thermal coagulation, in which it is assumed that in each collision the particles adhere, is given by

$$\frac{dn}{dt} = -kn^2$$

The form can be justified by considering that in an aerosol with n particles per cm^3 the probability of a collision between two of them is proportional to n^2. The rate of change of particle concentration is thus $-kn^2$. Solving this simple differential equation we have

$$\frac{1}{n} - \frac{1}{n_o} = kt$$

or

$$n = \frac{n_o}{1 + kn_o t}$$

where n_o is the initial particle concentration in particles/cm^3. The constant k can be found from theory but is also determined empirically for a particular distribution and type of particle.

Gravitational coagulation, important in some pollution situations, takes place when particles of unequal size, and hence speed, collide under the action of the gravitational field. This form of coagulation is a method for cleaning aerosols out of the air by use of water spray in a wet scrubber.

Besides the removal mechanism of coagulation and fallout for smaller particles, or direct sedimentation for large particles, aerosols are also removed by washout.

The choice of particulate separation from the gases depends upon various factors such as particle size and its physical and chemical properties, the concentration and volume of the particulate to be handled; the temperature and humidity of the gaseous medium and, most importantly, the collection efficiency required.

Most commonly used collectors are: gravitational settling chambers, centrifugal separators, wet scrubbers, electrostatic precipitators, and filters.

The mechanisms by which particles are collected depend upon the particle size and velocity. Gravitational settling is an obvious mechanism, as is centrifugal force which is really just enhanced gravitational settling. Inertial impact or inertial collection depends upon the particle not following a streamline as flow goes around a collection device. Other collection mechanisms include electrostatic effects as in the case of electrostatic precipitators and direct filtration if fibers are put close enough together.

Gravitational settling chambers are only used to collect large particles above approximately 50μ. Gravitational settling chambers are often used upstream of further collection devices so that larger particulate has already been eliminated before more sophisticated removal devices are used.

In the centrifugal separators (cyclones) the centrifugal action throws the heavy particles to the side of the cyclone where they can slide down into a collector. The separator operates with two vortices as shown in Fig. 5.16. The advantage of a cyclone, which is the most common dust collector used, lies in the high separation factor given as the ratio of the radial velocity in the cyclone to the Stokes velocity in a simple settling chamber. We have

$$u_s = \frac{\rho D^2 g}{18\mu}$$

and for the radial velocity

$$v = \frac{D^2 \rho w^2}{18 R \mu}$$

$$S = \frac{v}{u_s} = \frac{w^2}{Rg}$$

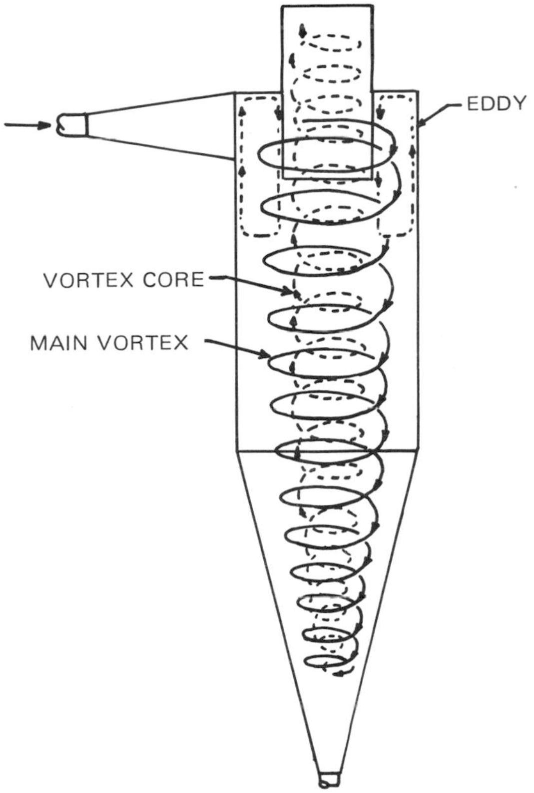

Figure 5.16 A typical cyclone for centrifugal separation of particles.

For typical parameters of R=6 inches and w=50 ft/sec we have a separation factor given by

$$S = \frac{v}{u_s} = \frac{2{,}500}{(0.5X32)} = 155$$

In practice, S ranges from 5 for large-diameter, low-resistance cyclones to 2,500 for small-diameter, high-resistance devices.

A large separation factor requires high tangential velocities and small diameters both of which result in a large pressure drop. The magnitude of our calculated separation factor indicates that cyclones will have much higher efficiencies than the settling chamber. Table 5.3 gives the efficiencies for per cent particulate collected by weight in a conventional cyclone and in a high-efficiency cyclone. The latter is one with a diameter of 9 inches or less. At peak performance a high-efficiency single cyclone would only collect particles of about 2μ diameter at efficiencies of about 50 to 60 per cent by weight.

TABLE 5.3

Efficiencies of Simple Cyclones (by weight %)

Particle size	Conventional cyclone	High efficiency cyclone
$<5\mu m$	–	50–80
$5–20\mu m$	50–80	80–95
$15–50\mu m$	80–95	95–99
$>50\mu m$	95–99	95–99

The effect of changing parameters such as body length, entry velocity, and entry shape is not readily calculated and is usually measured. The important economic parameter in a cyclone is the pressure drop, which is calculated from

$$\Delta P = \frac{KQ^2 p \rho g}{T}$$

where ΔP is in inches of water
Q is cfm of gas
p is the absolute pressure in atmospheres
ρg is the gas density in lb/ft^3
T is the temperature in K
and K is a function of cyclone diameter.

The above equation is intended to serve as a guide only for indicating the effect of variables. Data on a specific cyclone should be obtained from manufacturers' specification for accurate calculations.

Scrubbers or wet collectors come in a variety of shapes and include spray towers (without beds), cyclone, venturi and packed or floating bed scrubbers. The latter are often used in combination particulate and gaseous removal applications. The principle of the scrubber is to remove the particulate, or gas, by absorbing the material into liquid droplets directly by contact. The contact mechanism may be inertial impingement or gravitational settling. After a simple cyclone has removed the larger particles, a scrubber might be used to remove material in the size range of 0.2 to 10μ. The advantages of the scrubber system are that it can remove simultaneously particulate and gases; it has high efficiencies for small particles; and there is no particle reentrainment. Scrubbers, however, do not function well where plume rise is important since a wet plume has little buoyancy. Handling of the dirty liquid and removal of the entrained material is difficult and can cause a water pollution problem.

In the simplest form, a spray tower consists of a downward flow of water droplets sprayed into the tower and an upward flow of dirty gas. High pressure sprays produce small drops with more surface area per mass of water used and these are effective in collecting particles in the 1-$2\mu m$ range.

In the cyclone scrubber, the gas is tangentially swirled around just as in the dry cyclone. Water sprays are introduced in a variety of ways either across the cyclone from the outside wall to the centerline or down the cyclone from the top. The combined impingement and centrifugal forces clean the gas. The wet cyclone has the advantage of a higher efficiency than the dry cyclone. Nevertheless, sludge removal is more difficult than dry particulate removal.

In the venturi scrubbers the water is injected upstream of the venturi throat. The curtain of water is broken up by the gas stream into drops that collect the dirt. Inertial impact is the primary collection mechanism; consequently, the faster the gas passes through the venturi, the higher the efficiency. The disadvantage of this device is the high-pressure drop. The advantage is the high efficiency for small particles. Once again, engineering design tradeoffs are evident. Because of the high-pressure drop, power costs are high, but difficult cleaning situations may require this type of collector with its greater than 90 per cent efficiency for submicron-size aerosols.

Electrostatic precipitators are used to handle large volumes of gases from which aerosols must be removed. They have the advantage of low-pressure drop, of the order of 1 inch of water, high efficiency for small particle size, the ability to handle both gases and mists for high volume flow, and the relatively easy removal of the collected particulate. The four steps in the process are:

1. place a charge on the particle to be collected
2. migrate the particle to the collector
3. neutralize the charge at the collector
4. remove the collected particle

The electrostatic precipitator consists of a negatively-charged inner rod and a positively-charged (ground) outer cylinder. At very high voltages (25-100kV) a corona discharge occurs close to the negative electrode. The gas close to the negative electrode is thus ionized upon passing through the corona. As the negative ions and electrons migrate toward the collector electrode they, in turn, charge the passing particulate. The electric field then draws the particulate to the collector where it is deposited. The collected material is removed, usually by hitting the collector, a process called 'rapping'. If a mist is being collected, then the material runs down the collectors and is removed at the bottom.

The theoretical efficiency, that is, weight fraction collected, of an electrostatic precipitator is given approximately by the relation

$$\eta = 1 - e^{-2vL/Ru_g}$$

where u is the particulate velocity towards the electrode, typically on the order of 0.1 to 0.7 ft/sec
L is the length of collector
R is the radius of collector, if cylindrically shaped
u_g is the bulk gas velocity, 2 to 8 ft/sec

Noting that the collector area, A, is equal to $2\pi RL$ and the volumetric flow rate, Q, is given as $\pi R^2 u_g$, we can rewrite above equation as:

$$\eta = 1 - e^{-Au/Q}$$

This expression, while approximate, indicates that higher efficiencies occur for low Q, high u, and large collector area. One can obtain high efficiency, if required, by increasing the surface area. Nevertheless, in order to increase efficiency from 80 to 99 per cent one must approximately double the area; to go from 90 to 99.9 per cent requires tripling the area. An increase in flow rate reduces the efficiency and even though only a small reduction in η might occur for a slight increase in Q, this means a large increase in emissions. A precipitator dropping from 99 per cent efficiency to 97 per cent triples the emissions and it is the emissions that are the important variable. In practice, the theoretical efficiency is never attained since some reentrainment of the collector material occurs. The collectors are usually plates rather than cylinders. Plate-type collectors are used for dry particulate collection, as from power plants, while the tube type is often used for wet collection.

The electrostatic precipitator system is not without problems. Ionization of the gas occurs only in a limited temperature range so that the device can suffer a loss in efficiency if sudden changes occur in the operating conditions. Build-up of collected material can cause "spark-over" between the electrodes which, in turn, causes a high current flow and excessive power use. Build-up of material on the negative electrode can suppress the corona discharge and reduce efficiency. The resistivity of the gas-particulate combination also affects the corona and the collection efficiency. Re-entrainment of the collected material can interfere with the particle charging and result in direct release of particulate up the stack.

Filters are used in a wide variety of materials and geometries to remove particulates from gas streams; for example, bag houses consist of a large number of filter bags, arranged so that continuous removal of the collected material is possible. Since filters show an increase in pressure drop as material is deposited, some means for periodically removing the solids is required. In fact, the disadvantage of filtering is the high-pressure drop and the clogging of the filter. Advantages are high efficiency, even for very small particles, low capital costs, and ability to handle a wide range of operating conditions. The filter collection mechanisms are direct interception and inertial impact for the larger particles, and Brownian, or diffusion impact, for the smaller particulate.

A filter should be used so that it can be readily serviced and the collected particulate easily removed.

Typical collection for the various particulate removal methods discussed above is given in Table 5.4.

5.5 ALTERNATIVE FUELS

The limited reserves and inevitable depletion of oil and gas in the world forces serious consideration upon the energy consumption and to adapt radical changes in supply by increased utilization of alternative fuels – fuels manufactured from sources other than petroleum. It is expected that the limited petroleum fuels in the world would be replaced by, first, coal, shale oil, tar sands, and uranium and ultimately, by nuclear fusion and solar-based resources.

Although the increased utilization of coal is seen as the major short-term alternative, the realities of retrofit capability necessitate the use of liquid fuels for transportation and many industrial applications. The projected maximum in world oil production towards

TABLE 5.4

Collection Efficiency for Various Particulate Removal Methods

	Efficiency, %					
Collector Type	Overall	0-5	5-10	10-20	20-44	>44
Baffled settling chamber	58.6	7.5	22	43	80	90
Simple cyclone	65.3	12	33	57	82	91
Long-cone cyclone	84.2	40	79	92	95	97
Multiple cyclone – 12 in. diameter	74.2	25	54	74	95	98
Multiple cyclone – 6 in. diameter	93.8	63	95	98	99.5	100
Irrigated long-cone cyclone	91.0	63	93	96	98.5	100
Electrostatic precipitator	97.0	72	94.5	97	99.5	100
Irrigated electrostatic precipitator	99.0	97	99	99.5	100	100
Spray tower	94.5	90	96	98	100	100
Self-induced spray scrubber	93.6	85	96	98	100	100
Disintegrator scrubber	98.5	93	98	99	100	100
Venturi scrubber, 30 in. pressure drop	99.5	99	99.5	100	100	100
Wet impingement scrubber	97.9	96	98.5	99	100	100
Baghouse	99.7	99.5	100	100	100	100

the end of this century will result in a series of shifts in the use of liquid fuels, which, in turn, will result in a significant reduction in the ratio of gasoline (petrol) production to diesel, jet fuel, heating oil, and heavier industrial fuels. Refinery operations will be geared to the production of predominately light oils (for example, gasoline, jet fuel), and the industrial users (for example, combustors and furnaces) will be required to burn heavier residual fuels or coal-derived liquids of high carbon to hydrogen atomic ratio. This trend, plus the introduction of low hydrogen content liquids from coal, shale and tar sands will reduce the hydrogen content of the various distillates. The combustion of alternative fuels (synthetic fuels, synfuels) is expected to be complicated by the presence of high nitrogen content, high carbon to hydrogen atomic ratio, and high aromatic content in the fuel which results in the increased emission of NO_x, carcinogenic polycyclic aromatic hydrocarbons and soot, increased combustor linear heating, and increased ignition time[92-101].

The alternative fuels have higher aromatic and nitrogen content than today's fuels and the pollutant emission potential of alternative fuels is linked very strongly to their chemical properties. Alternative fuels emit high levels of NO_x, carcinogenic polynuclear aromatic hydrocarbons and soot, increased combustor linear heating, and increased ignition time. The effect of increasing aromatic content is to increase the formation of soot in the early stages of combustion where local fuel-rich conditions occur. The formation of soot in practical equipment is correlated better by the hydrogen content of the fuel than the analysis for total aromatics, since individual aromatics vary considerably in tendency to form soot and, also, in hydrogen content. A hydrogen content of 15 per cent corresponds to paraffinic fuels with specification jet fuel having a hydrogen content of around 14 per cent. Figure 5.17 illustrates the reasoning behind the use of per cent hydrogen rather than the aromatics content. Napthalene (6.2% H) and butyl-benzene

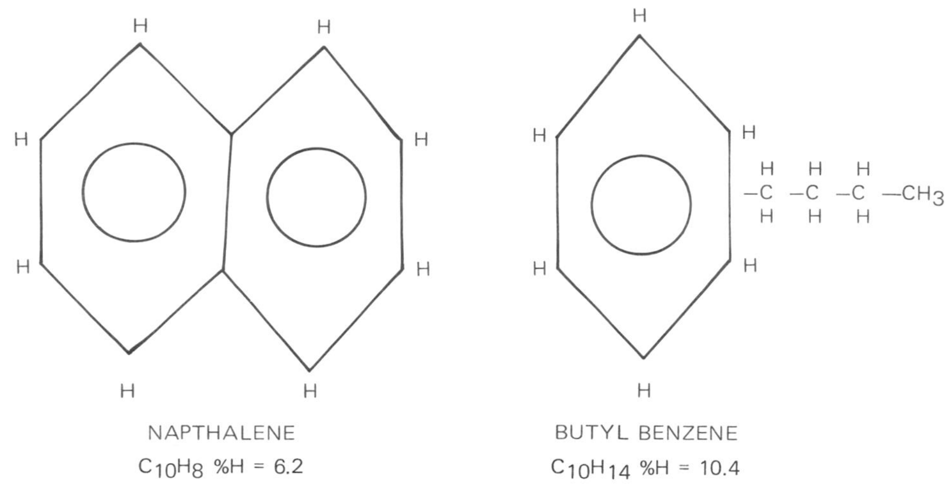

Figure 5.17 Hydrogen content of aromatics.[92]

(10.2% H), both containing 10 carbon atoms, are compared. Napthalene is well known to produce considerably more soot than butyl-benzene, so that a better correlation with per cent hydrogen can be expected. This type of correlation applies to several types of combustion systems.

Alternative Fuel Effects on Gas Turbine Combustion

The fuel characteristics most likely to affect the design of future gas turbines are fuel C/H ratio, viscosity, volatility, nitrogen content and fuel stability[92,93,97,104]. The impacts of high C/H ratio in the fuel is to increase the rates of carbon particle formation. A high C/H ratio fuel generally has increased kinematic viscosity, surface tension and specific gravity compared with Jet A fuel at room temperature. These changes in fuel properties have an adverse impact on the atomization quality of the spray when a given fuel injector is used. Increased levels of carbon particle concentrations formed in fuel-rich regions of the primary zone lead to higher linear temperatures and higher smoke emissions. Reduced volatility and increased viscosity affect droplet life-times and atomization, respectively. Volatility affects the rate of fuel vaporization in the combustor can. Since important heat release processes do not occur until gas-phase reactions take place; a reduction of volatility reduces the time available for chemical reaction within the combustion system. In the aircraft engine this can result in difficulty in ground or altitude ignition capability, reduced combustor stability, increased emissions of CO, hydrocarbons, and the associated loss in combustion efficiency. Moreover, carbon particle formation is aided by the formation and maintenance of fuel-rich pockets in the hot combustion zone. Low volatility allows rich pockets to persist because of the reduced vaporization rate. Again, increased soot can cause additional radiative loading to combustor liners.

The desired formation of a finely dispersed spray of small fuel droplets is adversely affected by viscosity. Consequently, the shortened time for gas-phase combustion reaction and the prolonging of fuel-rich pockets experienced with low volatility can also occur with increased viscosity. Ignition, stability, emissions, and smoke problems also increase for higher viscosity fuels.

Increased fuel-bound nitrogen in alternative fuels leads to increased NO_x emissions. Indications are that bound nitrogen conversion to NO_x can be minimized by early release of fuel-N in a fuel-rich combustion zone. The release of fuel-N in a high temperature combustion zone depends, in general, on the fuel type and cannot be taken from the results of equilibrium distillation. Nearly all the derived liquid fuels are believed to behave in a different manner for the release of fuel-N.

The conventional liquid fuels for transportation use an average of 1.9 for hydrogen to carbon (H/C) ratio and since combustion characteristics are a strong function of H/C ratio, it is clear from Table 5.5 that the manufacturing of synthetic fuels from coal hinges around increasing this ratio. The process used to purify and upgrade the coal-derived liquids include fractionation (distillation) and hydrotreating (hydroprocessing). Upgrading the raw coal-derived liquids by hydrotreating usually involves the addition of hydrogen in the presence of a catalyst. This process also reduces the sulfur and nitrogen content of the coal-derived fuels. In order to produce a 42 gallon barrel of refined oil from coal, approximately 384 m^3 of hydrogen is required. The hydrogen alone is estimated to cost about $25 per barrel by 1980. An additional cost element is due to the increased thermal losses relative to petroleum fuels. The thermal losses can be translated into cost.

TABLE 5.5

Hydrogen to Carbon Ratio of Some Liquid Fuels[92]

	Approximate H/C Ratio	Approximate US Remaining Resources 10^{15} BTU
Petroleum	2.0	700
Oil Shale	1.9	20,000
Tar Sands	1.75	100
Coal	0.75	90,000

In the United States, approximately 34 per cent of industrial and commercial boilers in operation are oil-fired. It is expected that coal liquids may replace a portion of the petroleum-based fuel oil-direct industrial boilers with modification in the combustion process. Only minor modifications may be required in the handling and storage of coal and liquids (H-coal or SRC-II). Utilization of Exxon Donor Solvent (EDS) liquid fuel as residual fuel will depend on the extent of hydrotreatment.

Coal liquids are fairly analogous to petroleum residual fuels. Nevertheless, analysis of these coal liquids shows that their chemical compositions and certain physical properties are sufficiently different to require possible handling and combustion modifications before use in industrial boilers[102,103]. Coal liquids are more aromatic and their C/H ratios and concentrations of heteroatoms such as nitrogen and oxygen are much higher than petroleum crudes and fuels, Tables 5.5 and 5.6. Coal liquids containing residual

TABLE 5.6

Properties of No. 2 Fuel Oil and Coal Liquids

Fuel	Typical Petroleum No. 2 Fuel Oil	Raw SRC-I Recycled Solvent*	Raw H-Coal Distillate	Raw EDS 205-425°C Distillate
Elemental Composition, wt %				
Hydrogen	12.9	7.4	9.1	10.0
Sulfur	0.093	0.37	0.10	0.3
Nitrogen	0.008	0.62	0.39	0.2
Oxygen	<0.01	3.9	1.5	1.9
Trace Contaminants, ppm wt				
Titanium	<1.0	20.0		
Sodium	0.55	0.39	0.59	
Potassium	0.37	0.19	0.08	
Calcium	0.17	0.35	0.14	
Vanadium	<0.1	0.9	0.1	
Lead	–	0.9	<1.0	
Iron	0.2	61.0	10.3	
Chloride	–	35.0		
Physical Properties				
Gravity, °API	33.6	5.3	14.7	18.0
Aromatic Carbon, %	19.0	74.0	55.0	–
Flash Point, °C	67.2	82.2	90.5	91.1
Heat of Combustion MJ/kg (BTU/lb)	45.4 (19500)	39.4 (16920)	42.1 (18080)	44.2 (19000)
KV, CS at (43.3°C)	2.61	5.79	3.0	SUS @ 37.8°C = 38
KV, CS at (98.9°C)	1.09	1.48		

*SRC-I recycled solved is considered analogous to SRC-II liquid fuel.

fractions high in asphaltenes are incompatible when blended with typical petroleum fuels. The sulfur contents of both coal liquids and petroleum residuals can vary considerably. The physical properties of coal liquids are also quite variable; they depend on the type of coal used and the liquefaction process employed. Petroleum residuals have higher concentrations of nickel and vanadium (10 to 500 ppm) than coal liquids. Nevertheless, coal-derived liquids contain more iron (approximately 10 to 60 ppm).

Various types of coal liquefaction reactors are currently available. In the coal liquefaction reactor, coal is solubilized in the solvent and is further hydrogenated by the addition and/or transfer of hydrogen to remove sulfur, nitrogen and oxygen. Liquid and gaseous products are produced by hydrocracking. The severity of the reaction is measured by the extent to which hydrocracking reactions proceed.

In the SRC-I solid system, the reaction severity is low. The hydrogenation and hydrocracking reactions result in the desired product having respective sulfur and ash contents of about 0.7 and 0.1 per cent. Nitrogen contents may be slightly increased.

In the SRC-II (liquid) system, a portion of the reactor effluent slurry is recycled back to the reactor. The mineral residue in the product slurry is believed to act as a catalyst and enhance hydrocracking reactions. More hydrogen is transferred, and the main product is a distillate fuel with sulfur and nitrogen contents of about 0.3 and 0.9 per cent, respectively. Lower sulfur and nitrogen contents in the final product signify larger amounts of hydrogen sulfide and ammonia generated in the reactor, and a reaction severity greater than in the SRC-I system.

In the H-coal reactor, hydrogenation and hydrocracking reactions are activated by the addition of a catalyst, which helps minimize hydrogen consumption. The reactions are sufficiently complete to allow production of fuel oil distillate (204^{+}°C oil) with a sulfur content of about 0.6 per cent. Operating with a higher consumption of hydrogen in the reactor, the system produces syncrude with a sulfur content of 0.2 per cent. The reaction severity is higher than in the SRC system.

In the EDS liquefaction reactor, the solubilized coal is hydrocracked to liquid products, which are separately hydrogenated in a catalytic reactor to reduce the sulfur and oxygen content. The process produces a variety of liquid products with sulfur content of less than 0.1 per cent. The reaction severity in the liquefaction reactor is quite high.

In summary, the effect of system type in producing lower sulfur and nitrogen content fuels is that higher sulfur and nitrogen removal efficiencies are obtained with higher severity of hydrogenation and hydrocracking reactions. Table 5.7 shows the variation in hydrogen consumption and sulfur content of the product with the type of liquefaction system.

In the USA, approximately 55 per cent of the petroleum consumption is used in transportation (automotive, aircraft, and others). When petroleum has become so scarce and expensive that a major fraction of liquid hydrocarbons come from coal and oil shale, it is expected that substantial reduction in power generation and industrial use will result, since direct use of coal and nuclear heat will offer attractive viable options. In commercial and home heating, use of electricity plus heat pumps and solar heating or synthetic gas offer options that should in time substantially reduce the need for liquid fuels. Petrochemical use of paraffinic hydrocarbons to produce plastics, rubber and a great variety of other products is expected to grow, relative to other uses, and will place increasing stress on the high H/C ratio components that are the starting point for the bulk of these products.

TABLE 5.7

Hydrogen Consumption and Sulfur Content of Coal Liquids in Liquefaction Systems

	SRC-I (solid)	SRC-II (liquid)	H-Coal (fuel oil)	EDS
H_2 consumption, % by wt of dry coal*	2.20	4.30	3.88	3.05
% sulfur in 205^{+}°C oil	0.70	0.30	0.58	0.10

*Coal type: Illinois No. 6, Sulfur Content 3.5%

Transportation use is the largest and is expected to continue to depend primarily on liquid fuels for the rest of this century. Here the opportunities of substitution for petroleum are limited because of the requirement for high energy density and clean combustion requirements. It can be expected that with time it will become an increasing fraction of the total, petrochemicals are also growing and demanding an increasing portion of the high quality fractions of the available liquid hydrocarbons.

Industrial use and electric power generation use of fuel oil is currently growing extremely rapidly because of the substitution of oil for gas. Eventual substitution of coal for fuel oil is expected to reduce this use before or around 1990. The heavy fuel oil used here is of higher boiling fraction range than fuels used in the transportation sector. Reduction in its use will allow its conversion to lower boiling materials falling in the transportation fuel range. A summary of these trends is as follows: (a) increased use of paraffinic hydrocarbons (diesel oil, kerosene-type jet fuel, petrochemical feed); (b) decreased demand for high boiling aromatic fuels (fuel oil); and (c) stable or somewhat decreased demand for internal combustion engine gasoline and home heating oil.

In 1974, stationary combustion sources accounted for 75 per cent of the United States' energy consumption and 65 per cent of this energy was consumed by power systems (for example, combustors, boilers). The major factors involved in the use of alternative fuels in stationary sources are: fuel preparation, combustion characteristics, and pollutant emission potential. Fuel preparation is a mechanical problem and will be specific to a particular alternative fuel. The physical properties of a fuel may be such that it must be stored and transported under certain conditions to insure its delivery at the burner in a form suitable for burning. Certain forms of solvent-refined coal are solid at low temperatures and must be heated for transportation and atomization.

Several combustion characteristics are important when considering the impact of conversion to alternative fuels. Boilers are fired by turbulent diffusion flames in which the fuel and combustion air are introduced into the combustor separately. Ignition stability is normally achieved by insuring feed back of heat to the base of the flame by the recirculation of hot combustion products and active chemical species by using swirl or a bluff-body flame stabilizer. Several options are available to improve stability should conversion introduce problems: the fuel injection system can be modified or the strength of the recirculation zone increased. Changing the properties of the fuel can affect the heat release rate and the flame emissivity, which affects the heat flux distribution to the combustor walls. If conversion introduces the use of fuels with high ash contents, then fouling could become a problem, causing a loss in efficiency. Fouling problems may be overcome to a certain extent or even alleviated by controlling the time-temperature history of the particulate to prevent the formation of adhesive particles.

5.6 THEORETICAL APPLICATIONS

Choice of Complexity

In order to complement associated experimental studies in design and development, the improvement and use of theoretical approaches are of prime concern. Mathematical models of physical processes are needed, together with computer programs for solving the appropriate level of complexity of the resulting problem simulation. The objective of Chapters 2 and 3 was to clarify the choice, extent and usefulness of computer application, and give pointers to the available techniques and methods. Current capabilities are now demonstrated, with results serving primarily to help designers in judiciously deciding where experimental emphasis should be placed in order to meet design objectives and/or in interpolating results from a limited amount of experimental data.

Because application of the general partial differential equations is complex, time-consuming and in a developmental stage, *simplified approaches* to the problem are extremely popular. The most common models include: perfectly stirred reactors PSRs, well-stirred reactors WSRs and plug flow reactors PFRs. Models differ in the way in which these are interrelated to simulate various aspects of the mixing/reaction taking place. An important problem in finite rate chemistry is choosing an appropriate level of complexity, in view of the large number of species and chemical reactions taking place. One solution to this problem is the use of the quasi-global reaction scheme whose key element is a unidirectional sub-global oxidation step. Coupled with this are a number of intermediate reversible reactions. The model affords a useful computer time-saving as compared to a full finite-rate chemical kinetics formulation. Well-known models are categorized as integral, modular or hybrid. Modular[105-108] methods give useful qualitative trend predictions and, when amalgamated with finite difference flowfield predictions via 2-D axisymmetric[109] or fully 3-D approaches[110], excellent results are available.

Most combustion systems exhibit recirculation, and full flowfield prediction requires iterative solution techniques. *Axisymmetric simulations* give rise to 2-D elliptic problems and involve 2-D storage, stream function-vorticity ψ-ω or primitive pressure-velocity p-u-v formulation, and Gauss-Seidel point-by-point iteration or line-by-line SIMPLE (semi-implicit method for pressure-linked equations) iteration procedures, the line methods involving the TDMA (tri-diagonal matrix algorithm). The essential differences between the various available computer codes include the following: the complexity of the equation set for the simulation of the physical processes, the storage requirements, the location of variables in the grid space system, the method of deriving the finite-difference equations that are incorporated, and the solution technique. In primitive pressure-velocity variable formulations a staggered grid system is normally used, as recommended by Los Alamos for its special attributes. In computational fluid dynamics the "best" representation of the convection and diffusion terms is essential to the accuracy and convergence of the iteration scheme. At high cell Reynolds numbers a certain degree of "upstream differencing" is essential, using, for example, these techniques: upwind differencing, a hybrid formulation or the Los Alamos zip, donor cell, etc. Sample recent numerical prediction studies include Pun and Spalding[111], Gosman *et al.*[112], Roberts[113], Schorr *et al.*[114], for the ψ-ω approach and [19-28] for the *p-u-v* approach. Excellent trade-off between code complexity and quality of flowfield patterns is available via the axysymmetric approach. For example, in Jones and Priddin[147], computational results show the interesting effects of several combustor design parameters, such as degree of swirl, performance of a recirculation zone amplifier ("trip"), and effect of laterally induced secondary air supply on subsequent flowfield development and combustor performance (for example, velocity, temperature, and composition distributions, the occurrence of recirculation zones, and flame size, shape, and combustion intensity).

Practical combustor designs exhibit many nonaxisymmetric features mainly because of air and fuel inlets at discrete circumferential locations. The requirement to predict a *fully 3-D* flowfield arises. Recent significant contributions to *steady* 3-D combustor flowfield prediction are available with application to the furnace and gas turbine fields. Computationally, the techniques are very similar, except that handling very high combustion intensities in the latter case causes additional problems. Implicit techniques for 3-D flows with recirculation have the advantage of efficiency and stability in their computations. Most workers use methods that are implicit in character and solve directly for pressure and velocities, a staggered mesh system is used and some degree of upstream differencing is employed for the convection terms at high cell Reynolds numbers. *Unsteady* 3-D flow occurs in gasoline and diesel engines.

The next three sub-sections discuss differences in the choice of physical problem representation [of reciprocating engines, furnaces and gas turbine combustors].

Reciprocating Engines

Computations which deal with reciprocating engines where the simulation, although time-dependent, is often simplified via axisymmetric assumptions are now discussed[133-137].

Preliminary investigations were concerned with subsets of the total problem, and included numerical solution of 2-D unsteady spray problems where penetration and vaporization into an inert gas were assumed[133].

Axisymmetric 2-D transient calculations were performed to analyze turbulent-reacting flow in a Honda CVCC divided chamber SCE, using the semi-implicit Los Alamos ALE program and a simple constant turbulent viscosity concept. Further work is reported[134] on the compression and power strokes of the cycle, including simplified NO_x kinetics calculations when methane fuel is used. Predicted total NO in ppm residing in the engine enclosure was found to peak at a factor of 4 higher than previous 1-D calculations, thus illustrating the importance of chamber geometry and nozzle configuration.

Despite the simpler geometry (axisymmetric cylinder) and neglect of combustion, all four strokes are considered for predicting the flow and temperature in piston/cylinder assemblies[135]. The two-equation k-ϵ turbulence model is used, the computational mesh expands and contracts with the motion of the piston, and an implicitly iterative finite difference solution procedure is employed. Combustion, of course, is a much-desired modeling inclusion, which is currently omitted.

A similar isothermal turbulent flow is studied by others, with and without swirl[136]

Idealized value operation is via a centrally located orifice which opens and closes suddenly at bottom dead center or as an annular orifice of varying area which simulates the value lift profile as a function of time. The results without swirl for the annular value configuration show two eddies that persist up to top dead center. The swirl calculations performed with the sudden-value configuration show similar trends for the flowfield (almost uniform radial profiles of velocity and turbulent kinetic energy in the piston-driving stroke) and solid body rotation swirl velocity profile with very steep gradient at the cylinder wall.

Only recently have fully 3-D transient IC engine calculations been performed[137], as a sequel to earlier 2-D calculations for all four strokes of an IC engine. All results are obtained by means of an explicit time-dependent finite-difference technique. The paper is divided into two parts, dealing, respectively, with combustion simply modeled as constant volume heat addition, and finite rate chemical reactions representing gasoline-air combustion. The results represent an important application of computational fluid dynamics to a problem of vital interest.

3-D Furnaces

The interest now[138-141] is on time-steady furnace flows where the axisymmetric assumptions have, until recently, been standard. Some methods are explicit in character, and require severe time-step limitations in their solution of the time-dependent equations.

Implicit methods remove the time-step limitation, and some 3-D furnace prediction studies are now described. Computations were made[138] with the SIMPLE technique for a box-shaped furnace into which gaseous fuel and air are injected through two separate but adjacent ducts, both inclined downwards. Steady laminar flow is assumed with mixing controlled diffusion flame assumptions and constant temperature walls. Further refinements to obtain information that is more useful and reliable to designers are described in Patankar and Spalding[139], which give the formulation of a computer model for full 3-D flows in furnaces.

More complete physical modeling is incorporated in recent 3-D work[140] simulating the flames of the Gaz de France furnace in Toulouse, France and the IFRF furnace in Ijmuiden, Holland. The requirement of computational economy is strongly emphasized by the method, which employs the SIMPLE method of solution with a version of the TEACH-3E code. The two-equation k-ϵ turbulence model is used, while combustion is based on a 'fast kinetics' statistical approach. A newly developed flux model is employed for the thermal radiation.

Prediction of flames 8 and 10 of the IFRF M3 trials is also discussed by others[141], who also use a fully 3-D simulation based on the SIMPLE approach, apparently borrowing a version of TRIC from Concentration, Heat and Momentum, CHAM. The experimental trials were carried out to provide data with a calorimetric hearth for testing mathematical models. A tunnel burner operating on natural gas, fires either parallel to the hearth (flame 8) or at 25° towards it (flame 10). Predictions are based on a single set of sub-models describing the turbulent exchange of momentum, mass, energy and radiation. Quite realistic predictions of flow and velocity patterns, temperature patterns and heat flux distributions are obtained.

3-D Gas Turbine Combustors

Similarly, fully 3-D gas turbine combustor flowfields may also be predicted. In Odgers[142] some applications and limitations of 0-, 1-, 2- and 3-D models are described with regard to six different design/development stages:

(i) initial sizing
(ii) initial development testing
(iii) primary zone modeling
(iv) secondary zone modeling
(v) dilution zone modeling
(vi) changes due to alteration of ambient conditions

Perhaps the following are optimal: Use an O-D model for items (i), (ii) and (vi), a 2-D axisymmetric model for items (iii) and a 3-D nonaxisymmetric model for items (iv) and (v). Some recent contributions [110, 143-149] to 3-D gas turbine combustor prediction are now discussed.

An early computation[143] with the SIMPLE program TRIC (three-dimensional recirculating flow in cartesian coordinates) concerns a diffusion flame in a section of an annular combustor, which is idealized as being a rectangular box shape. Twelve equations are solved, including those for the two-equation k-ϵ turbulence model and a six-flux radiation model. The flow is fully 3-D and exhibits a complex recirculation pattern.

Recent 3-D prediction work[145] at UTRC includes pseudo-kinetic hydrocarbon chemistry, with the k-ϵ turbulence model, droplet vaporization and burning, and radiation effects. Solution is via the Multi-dimensional implicit Nonlinear Time-dependent MINT procedure, but results so far are not very encouraging.

Garrett AiResearch appears to be one of the few gas turbine manufacturers seriously developing and applying advanced 3-D combustor analytical design procedures to the design and development of combustion systems. Application is to premix/prevaporized combustors. Salient features are described[146,149] regarding application to the design of two different advanced full-scale/reverse-flow annular systems. Predicted fuel-air ratio profiles and isothermal plots are presented, with discussion concerning proposed modifications. These and other results give useful guides to the combustion engineer, and significant reductions in development time and cost result.

Gaseous phase diffusion flames in can-type combustors may also be predicted[148]. The k-ϵ turbulence model is used and a thick flame region is simulated via a version of the TRIP code. Predicted patterns of velocities and temperature show that qualitative trends may be simulated, but accuracy of predicted pollutant emissions would be in doubt.

A 3-D two-phase mathematical model of a Lycoming combustor is amalgamated in Swithenbank *et al.*[110]: some 30 PDEs are solved at 3402 grid points covering the flow domain and about 240 minutes of ICL1906S CP time is required for each case. Results for the finite difference phase of the study with simple chemistry are used to assign plug flow and well-stirred characteristics to the flowfield. Modular calculations provide the second phase which handles realistic chemical kinetics, unmixedness and evaporation. Presently, 13 species undergoing 18 reactions model the combustion of a typical fuel like kerosene. Concentrations of minor constituents of combustion are thus predicted with a view to detailed study of pollutant-formation mechanisms. Encouraging results are portrayed for a variety of flow types.

Results cited and discussed briefly in the above three sub-sections mostly involve swirl. As these are illustrated at length in a companion volume[1] [entitled '*Swirl Flows*'], the present descriptions have been kept short so as to give only the flavor of the multitude of possible applications to practical systems. The next two sub-sections investigate chemical aspects in the choice of problem representation.

Diffusion Flames

The simplest turbulent reacting flow of engineering interest is the free diffusion flame, where a gaseous fuel jet mixes and burns with an otherwise stationary air surroundings. It has been widely studied as it serves as a useful data base with which model results may be compared. For example, the axisymmetric coflowing hydrogen-air data of Kent and Bilger[150] have been used for comparison with a variety of different turbulent reacting flow models, including an integral, one-equation turbulent kinetic energy approach, utilizing both "laminar" shifting-equilibrium chemistry (that is, based on local mean temperature and element concentrations)[151] and "turbulent" shifting-equilibrium chemistry (involving an assumed probability density function for scalar variables)[152], a finite-difference, one-equation turbulent kinetic energy approach utilizing finite-rate hydrogen-air "laminar" chemistry[153]; a finite-difference, two-equation turbulent kinetic energy model utilizing a shifting-equilibrium chemistry model and an assumed-probability density function model for the turbulence-chemistry interaction[154] and a finite-difference, two-equation turbulent kinetic energy model utilizing a partial-equilibrium finite-rate chemical kinetics model and an assumed-probability density function approach for the turbulence-chemistry interaction[155]. In the work reported by Rhodes, *et al.*[152] and Edelman and Harsha[153] the governing equations are written in conventional Reynolds-averaged form and the turbulence model is that described by Harsha[156], while for the work described by Kent and Bilger[154] and Janicka and Kollman[155], Favre- (or mass-) averaged forms of the governing equation solved and the turbulence model is based on the two-equation turbulent kinetic energy closure described by Launder, *et al.*[157]

Figures 5.18[153] and 5.19[155] show the results obtained by two different theories [respectively] in their attempt to predict the data.[150] Clearly, these are substantial differences between the two computations, overall the results do not differ as much as the very different assumptions used in the two models might imply. In particular, the temperature and species mass fraction results obtained by Edelman and Harsha appear to indicate effects that are as much caused by an overpredicted species mixing rate as by the neglect of the turbulence-chemical kinetic interaction: Because the overall mixing rate is overpredicted over much of the flow, the predicted flame is leaner, and thus at higher temperature near the axis, than the data indicate. The centerline NO concentration prediction shown in Fig. 5.18 reflects this. The early increase in NO concentration in the fuel-rich region of the jet is well represented by the calculation, but the predicted NO proceeds to peak at a level substantially greater than the experimental data indicate. Janicka and Kollman do not present axial centerline NO concentration results, but their radial profiles of NO mole fraction at $x/d = 80$ indicate almost a factor of two under-prediction of NO concentration.

Differences in the predictions just cited can be ascribed as much to the details of the turbulence modeling as they can to the presence or lack of a turbulence-kinetic interaction model. There are, of course, other significant differences; most importantly, the

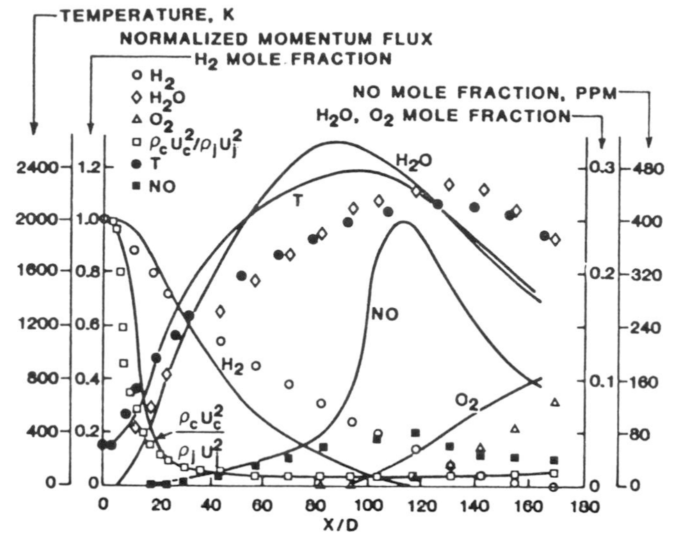

Figure 5.18 Axial profiles for reacting hydrogen/air jet, predicted with finite-rate chemistry model.[153]
[——— predictions]

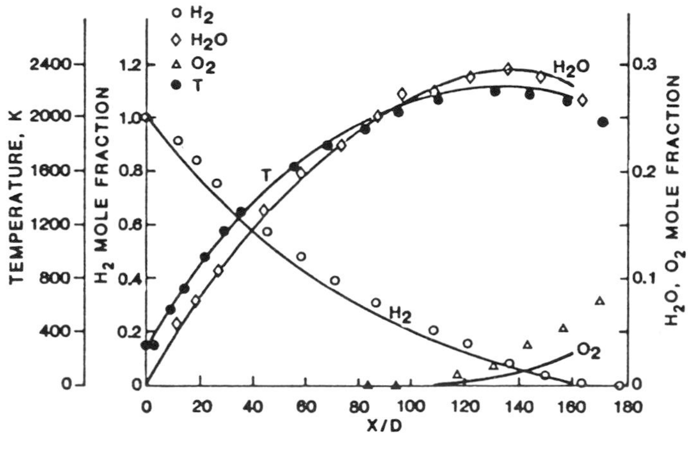

Figures 5.19 Axial profiles for reacting hydrogen/air jet, predicted with statistical combustion model.[155]
[———— predictions]

experiments show a significant overlap in H_2 and O_2 profiles which is not reproduced by computations which ignore turbulence-chemistry interactions. Nevertheless, these results highlight the observation that a major effect of the inclusion of the turbulence kinetic interaction phenomenon in a turbulent reacting flow model is to change the *shape* of the temperature and concentration distributions, rather than the *overall heat release* and *major species concentrations.* While this observation may only be true for flows which are dominated by convective transport, it is of considerable interest with regard to overall combustor performance modeling generally.

As the chemical reactivity of propane is less than that of hydrogen, more significant effects of finite-rate chemical reactions can be expected in the propane-air diffusion flame than in the hydrogen-air diffusion flame. Mao, *et al.*[158] use a flowfield and turbulence-chemistry interaction model similar to that described by Lockwood and co-workers[159,160]. The flow model employs the Reynolds-averaged conservation equations for mass, momentum, and mixture fraction; viscous dissipation, mean kinetic energy, and radiation are neglected, and the exchange coefficients for species and energy are assumed identical. Thus properties at each point in the flow are taken to correspond to the thermodynamic equilibrium state achieved when a quantity f (the mixture fraction) and (1-f) of ambient fluid, at their initial states, are adiabatically mixed at the ambient pressure of the reacting jet. Turbulent transport is modeled using the two-equation k-ϵ model as described in Chapter 2. The equilibrium assumption allows an equation of state relating local species mass fractions, temperature, and density to be constructed from adiabatic equilibrium flame computations. Average temperature, density, and species mass fraction values at each point in the flow are obtained from a single assumed-probability density function approach. Thus a probability density function is assumed for the mixture fraction, f, and the local average value of f and the variance of f are obtained through the solution of appropriate transport equations. Further ideas about the PDF approach are given in Section 2.6 of the present text.

Extremely good predictions of the details of the flame structure are then possible, as Figs. 5.20 and 21 illustrate for centerline velocity and temperature profiles. Fuel, oxygen, and nitrogen concentrations predicted for this flame are all in reasonably good agreement with the data as well. However, predictions of the product concentrations are not in as good agreement with the experimental data, as can be seen from the results shown in Fig. 5.22. It may be remarked that the errors are largest in high mixture fraction regions of the flow, where relatively arbitrary decisions concerning the degree of equilibration of the mixture have the greatest impact.

Heterogeneous Flames

Many practical flowfields inject fuel in the form of solid particles or liquid droplets, and additional problems arise resulting in combustion modeling efforts being not nearly as well-developed as those for homogeneous gas phase flames.

A number of surveys of the problems involved in modeling multiphase reacting flows have been published, of which the articles by Essenhigh[161] on solid particle combustion and Faeth[162] on droplet and spray combustion are representative examples. For droplet or particle cloud flames, a complication arises in that individual particle mechanisms have generally been investigated via single isolated droplets. In the case of spray flames the appearance of a single envelope flame surrounding the droplet cloud has been used to argue that combustion models based on single-droplet analyses are inappropriate[163]. However, the same observation can be interpreted to mean that the droplets within the cloud are evaporating and the local fuel vapor/air mixing process produces conditions conducive to combustion only in the outer region of the cloud[164].

As discussed in Chapter 2, detailed analysis of the fuel spray problem can be achieved by writing down conservation equations for the liquid phase behavior, including droplet

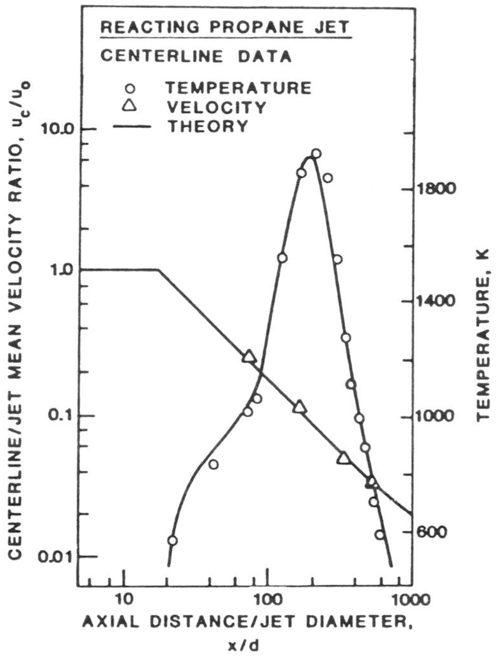

Figure 5.20 Axial variation of mean velocity and temperature for the reacting propane gas jet.[158]

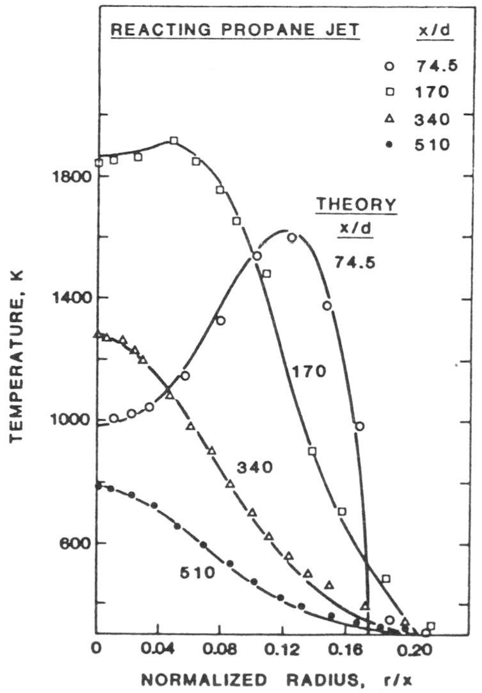

Figure 5.21. Radial variation of mean temperature for the reacting propane gas jet.[158]

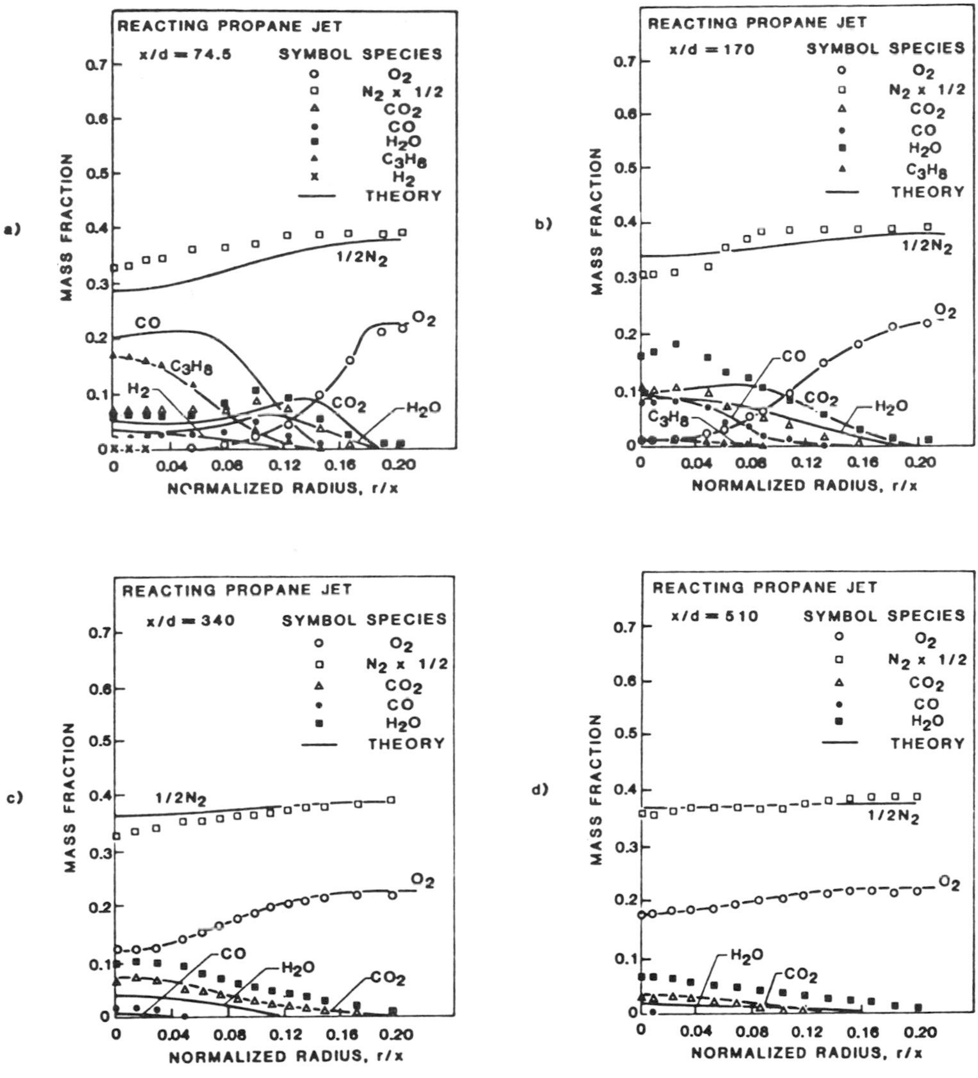

Figure 5.22 Radial variation of species concentrations for the reating propane gas jet, at four axial stations.[158]

size and number density distribution function, total mass, momentum, and energy. While in principle these equations can be solved when coupled to the appropriate gas-phase equations, the small size of the droplets produced by spray nozzles relative to typical combustor dimensions introduces a major resolution problem if the spray is to be modeled using the same technique as applied to the combustor. It is impracticable to simulate numerically the entire flowfield and still resolve the droplets to any realistic degree: A more realistic approach is one in which the characteristics of the fuel nozzle are employed to obtain the jet penetration distance and initial droplet size and number density distributions for input to a computational procedure. Given the initial droplet size and number density distribution, the problem is one of determining the rate of change of the droplet density and size distribution in the flowfield.

Turbulent drop diffusion and the effects of the presence of drops on the generation and dissipation of turbulence are ignored in most turbulent spray models. Drop life histories are calculated using transport correlations for individual drops and interactions between droplets are ignored[162]. Models of this type have been described by Crowe, *et al.*[165] and Spalding[166]. Genovese *et al.*[167] report a more general formulation in which the diffusion of the particles in a cloud relative to the gas phase can be accounted for. However, it has not been applied to the spray flame problem, so that the effects of diffusion as incorporated in this model on spray flame structure have not been determined. Clearly a current limitation on this approach is the lack of heterogeneous mixing data from which an appropriate particulate phase diffusivity can be defined.

A local homogeneous flow (LHF) model is an attractive simplification for the spray combustion process resulting from observations that the structure of a spray flame is in some respects similar to a gaseous diffusion flame. In this model, applied by Shearer *et al.*[168] to evaporating sprays and by Mao *et al.*[158] to spray combustion, the only effect of the liquid on the overall flowfield is through the equation of state on the evaluation of density at any point in the flow. The model thus implies infinitely fast interphase transport rates; the thermodynamic equilibrium assumption allows the existence of liquid at high mixture fractions of the injected fuel, but not at low mixture fractions. This spray model is embedded within the overall flowfield computational procedure.

Centerline results obtained using the LHF model for the n-pentane spray flame are shown in Fig. 5.23. Clearly the results are considerably worse than were obtained using the same model for the gaseous propane-air diffusion flame of Fig. 5.20. These results are

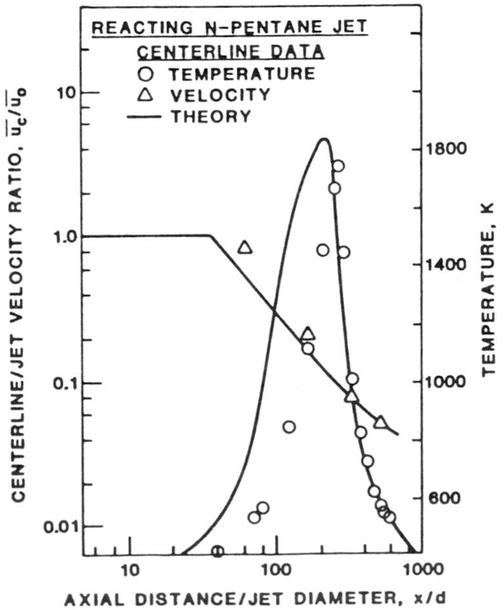

Figure 5.23. Axial variation of mean velocity and temperature for the reacting n-pentane spray flame. [158]

similar to those observed by Shearer, *et al.*[168] for the evaporating spray case. The LHF model, while providing a qualitative picture of the flowfield development, overestimates the flowfield development rate. Single-droplet calculations made using the computed LHF flowfield show that finite-rate interphase transport effects are a major cause of the discrepancy. The LHF model thus provides a lower bound on the spray combustion process, since it underpredicts the length of the spray flame by some 30 per cent and it can provide a useful first estimate, but not quantitatively correct results[158].

Clearly heterogeneous combustion is considerably less well developed than for corresponding homogeneous gas phase combustion problems. A major unknown is the effective diffusivity appropriate for particulate flowfields, while finite-rate transport and chemical-kinetic effects also play an important role.

Closure

In deciding and justifying the use of a particular procedure, one has some deliberation. One of the objectives of the present text is to clarify the choice and give appropriate advice, emphasizing computer application where appropriate. For example, at the present time the usefulness of a fully 3-D computer code *in practice* is not clear. Again, recent discussions have doubted the industrial value of this, especially when current practice and many problem areas involve use of 0-D and 1-D models, as successful application of modular and hybrid schemes reveal. 2-D and 3-D approaches do possess the possibility of being eventually capable of a higher degree of realism, but model accuracy is in doubt, time and cost requirements are large and, more specifically, many current needs do not demand them[169-171].

Model experiments designed to highlight specific sub-problems and their interactions (and *not* complex combustor flows) should receive attention for model development and validation. Areas in which further research will be most useful include: the simulation of complex chemistry, the turbulent-reaction interaction problem, the utilization of non-orthogonal and/or finite element methods of computation, and application to realistic three-dimensional problems, perhaps interfacing of a fine grid 2-D axisymmetric calculation of the primary zone and spray with a fully 3-D calculation further downstream. Computational results show some of the interesting effects of combustor design parameters on subsequent flowfield development and combustor performance. Computational experiments can be, should be and have been performed which complement test cell data describing the internal flowfield characteristics. Theoretically, it is in the area of parameter influences that computer programs show their supremacy in terms of time and cost savings as compared with experimental work. Progress will lead to more realistic and cost-effective practical combustor modeling. Continued development on the accuracy of the simulation of the physical processes involved should elevate computer modeling to an established place in practical combustor design and development programs.

5.7 EXPERIMENTAL APPLICATIONS

Flowfield Complexity

Combustion of fossil or derived fuels for the purposes of extracting energy in the form of heat is a complex process which involves strong interactions between several coupled physical, fluid mechanical and thermochemical phenomena. The combustion chambers of most furnaces and boilers must fulfill the desired requirements of fuel-air mixing, complete combustion, and cooling of the combustion products by effective heat transfer. The constraints imposed on the design are many, including those of flame stability, complete combustion at very low levels of excess air, maximum permissible refractory temperature, low levels of noise, particulates and gaseous pollutants, acceptable pressure drop. For residual fuel oils and certain coals, the minimization of deposits on, and the corrosion of, exposed metal surfaces is also required. A quantitative understanding of certain primary combustion phenomena [for example: droplet vaporization and combustion, solid particle combustion, gas phase chemical reaction kinetics, radiative heat transfer from combustion products, the mixing of reactants and combustion products, etc.] can sometimes be obtained by the design of relatively small-scale experiments which seek to isolate particular phenomena of interest. Basic combustion work of this sort has traditionally been carried out at graduate level in university or research establishments. The fundamental information obtained is of limited value if the results cannot be scaled-up with confidence for the particular application and the complex coupling between the phenomena as they exist in large-scale practical combustion systems.

In turbulent combustion processes, knowledge of the time-mean properties (for example: velocity, temperature, pressure, concentration, density) are useful but not sufficient to determine the reaction rate. The temporal characteristics of a turbulent flow are important since they govern not only the mixing process, but also the way in which the combustible mixture reacts and heat is transferred to the surroundings. They also give a great deal of insight into the pollutants emission and combustion efficiency of the system. For the modeling and prediction of the spatial distribution of reaction, it is desirable to know the turbulence properties of the fuel concentration. To date, the prediction of local changes in the distribution of reaction rates, temperatures, concentration etc. are based on empirical and/or semi-empirical relationships incorporated into the theory. In heterogeneous combustion systems, such as coal particle and liquid fuel spray flames, additional time-resolved information is required on the particle or droplet size distribution, and on the relative velocities of particles and the surrounding gas.

In order to analyze and understand combustion in stationary power plants, gas turbine engines, and internal combustion engines, the nature of turbulent flowfields must be ascertained. This is because important elements of the combustion process such as ignition, propagation and stabilization of the flame, the burn-out of the fuel and the formation of pollutants depend greatly on the transfer of heat, mass and momentum. In fact, the limiting steps in many of the combustion models developed to date is the description of the turbulent flowfield. Due to the considerable increase in the rates of transport under turbulent conditions, aerodynamic effects become more prevalent and when fuel and oxidant are not premixed prior to ignition – as in the case of the most significant industrial flame, the turbulent diffusion flame. Then flow and mixing processes determine the overall characteristics of the flame. They are indispensible also for understanding the formation and destruction of minor constituents (soot, PAH, gaseous pollutants, noise, etc.). Procedure aimed at predicting distributions of velocity, species concentration, temperature and local heat flux distribution to bonding surfaces require turbulent transport properties to be determined as a function of the local fluid state. The investigations can be experimental, semi-empirical or purely theoretical. In the theoretical approach, although the mathematical model can be used to provide the solution more cheaply and quickly as described in Chapters 2 and 3, the final results on a particular combustor geometry have to be checked and adjusted against the experimental facts. The objective of Chapter 4 was to give the choice of various methods available for determining the fundamental property and some typical results. In the present chapter some experimental applications, together with who has applied and used the methods, are being discussed. In deciding upon a particular method for a particular application, one has to decide if the method needs to be qualitative or quantitative, and intrusive or non-intrusive. The general philosophy toward measurements should be that only techniques that are sensitive to the magnitude and direction of flow and have sufficient spatial resolution should be used. No comparisons of theoretical predictions should be made with experimental data by techniques that lack these requirements for a given flow zone of interest. Flow visualization always should accompany quantitative measurements. Redundant measurements using different techniques should be made when possible. Measurements of as much flow detail as possible should be made in experiments used for developing turbulence models. Other measurements, in perhaps more practical flow conditions, should be made in enough detail to permit validation of these models. Complementary to the referencing of Chapter 4, Refs. 172-214 exemplify the possibilities for measuring many of the complex quantities in general flow systems.

Flow Visualization

For the visualization of flow, many techniques are available that have been employed in research and development. Table 5.8 shows the common methods of flow visualization and indicates which are essentially qualitative or can be used to provide quantitative data on one or more variables of the flowfield. The normal range of application for each method is also suggested.

Even though flow visualization methods date back fifty years or more, their application to combustion processes (particularly in IC and GT engines) is still a critical element in understanding how various physical and chemical processes couple with each other. Laser shadowgraphy has been used in many experiments to correlate global behavior with the detailed point measurements of the other diagnostics. In the laser shadowgraph system of Dyer *et al.*[215], a laser beam is spatially filtered, expanded, and then collimated before passing into the combustion chambers of an IC engine. A mirror bonded to the piston surface returns the incident light through a series of recollimating lenses to a translucent screen or directly on to the film plane of a camera. The resultant photographs can be highly informative in describing the qualitative features of transient complex engine processes. The placement of an acousto-optic modulator in the path of the laser beam allows the image to be created synchronously with the engine cycle in a manner analogous to a conventional strobe light[215]. Computer control of the modulator determines both the crank angle of occurrence and the duration of the laser pulse. The shadowgraph image created on the screen permits direct observation of the events occuring within the combustor in real time. The effect of variations in combustor operating parameters on the flame propagation mechanism can thus be readily determined. This provides insight that could not be gained from pressure or point measurements alone.

Holography is a recording technique which stores, on a holographic plate for later reconstruction, all of the coherent optical information that has passed through or been

TABLE 5.8

Flow Visualization Techniques

Method	Measures	Fluid and Speed
Dye or Smoke[174,185]	displacement, qualitative	low speed flows
Surface powder	displacement, qualitative	restricted to open surface liquid flow
Neutral density particles[183]	displacement, qualitative	mainly liquids
Spark discharge[183]	displacement, qualitative	restricted to low density gases
Hydrogen bubble[183]	displacement, qualitative	restricted to electrolytic fluids
Electro-chemical luminescence[183]	velocity near surfaces, qualitative	low speed special solutions
Interferometric[174,179,184,186]	density (ρ), quantitative	high or low speed gases or transparent liquids with thermal or concentration gradients
Schlieren[174,179,183,184,186]	$\frac{d\rho}{dx}$, quantitative	high or low speed gases or transparent liquids with thermal or concentration gradients
Shadowgraph[174,179,183,184,186]	$\frac{d^2\rho}{dx^2}$, quantitative	high or low speed gases or transparent liquids with thermal or concentration gradients
Direct photography[183,184,186] (imaging method)	particle size, velocity	low to moderately high speed gases or transparent liquids
Holography[174,180,183,185,186]	particle size, velocity	as that for direct photography but with relaxed depth of field limitation.

reflected from a certain volume. The key requirement for producing a hologram is that the wavefront (object wave) which emanates from the volume of interest be mixed coherently with a reproducible reference beam and recorded on a receptor (hologram). When the processed hologram is illuminated by a duplicate of the reference beam, a complete three-dimensional image of the object field is reconstructed in space in its original position relative to the hologram.

For highly luminous events typical of combustion processes, pulse laser holography yields good ambient light rejection capabilities. The ambient light plays no part in the reconstructed waveform, but does fog the hologram. The use of a cut-off filter, mechanical shutter and an intense reference beam is normally sufficient to permit the technique even in severe combustion environments where broad-band flame radiation is present.

Particle and Emulsified Fuel Combustion

Holography has been used to study the devolatilization of coal particles and explosion of emulsified water/fuel droplets[216,217]. The coal particles were simultaneously illuminated with both reflected light and transmitted light. The hologram showed the cloud surrounding the particles consists of very many small particles. The regions of devolatilization, sooting and burnout were identified[216]. Particle size information, important from the point of view of combustion efficiency and pollutant formation, can therefore be obtained by holography[216] or by laser velocimetry, which also yields information on velocity of the individual particles[172,173,176]. The data reduction associated with obtaining statistical properties of a large number of particles can be tedious in holography. It is at present the limiting factor. Some progress has been made in automated data reduction but as yet no on-line holographic particle size analyzer is available for use in flows with and without combustion. Velocity information can also be stored on a hologram by double-pulsing method.

In the explosion of emulsified fuels the idea is to fragment an originally large fuel droplet into many small droplets, thus increasing the effective evaporation rate of the fuel. The water in the emulsion superheats and homogeneously nucleates to produce a vapor-phase explosion. The flow visualization and droplet size distribution after explosion has been successfully accomplished with 2-mm diameter droplets moving at 50 to 100 m/s using a ruby laser of 15 ns pulse duration[217].

Flame Structure Visualization

The structure of turbulent flows can be obtained qualitatively with aids to direct high speed photographic visualization[183]. Other methods that have been successfully used are water model (or dye, smoke) study for flow visualization[183], interferometry[179], schlieren photography[179], shadowgraphy[215] and speckle metrology[211]. Holographic interferometry is an effective method for the visualization of coherent structures in flames. Several techniques for holographic interferometry have been defined and in each case two or more coherent waves are ultimately mixed to produce the interferogram[186]. In double exposure holographic interferometry, two exposures (one with background having no index of refraction gradients and other with the test object) are made, and upon reconstruction the two waves are mixed. In the double exposure interferogram, the instantaneous structure of the entire flame can be observed[209,216], including boundary eddies and regions of significant temperature and concentration gradients.

Velocity Measurements

In recent years major advances have evolved to allow more in-depth investigation of the fundamental physical and chemical processes occurring in combustion systems using intrusive and non-intrusive laser probes. Better understanding of these basic processes quantitatively will contribute to the design of systems that maximize both energy conversion efficiency and pollution control.

Table 5.9 gives a brief comparison of velocity measurement technique in complex flows both with and without combustion. Appropriate references are given, and the merits and limitations of each method are also discussed. Velocity measurements are essential to the understanding and optimization of the performance of combustors and individual elements of combustion and propulsion systems. Examples of such elements include combustion chambers, gas turbine combustors, internal combustion engines, turbines, compressors, and nozzles. The flows in such systems may vary from simple cold laminar flows to very complex three-dimensional recirculating turbulent flows of very hot soot-laden gases. Hot-wire anemometry, which had been standard for many years, has many inherent limitations, *see* Table which compares velocity measurement techniques.

The development in laser technologies in the last decade or so has resulted in an unprecedented growth of new diagnostic techniques complementing conventional optical methods[172-186], which could not be applied to fluid dynamics because of the inadequacy of previously available light sources. Optical methods have the best hope at present of achieving the best measurement in non-burning and combustion systems with least interference and can provide quantitative information on specific parameters of interest accurately with good time and space resolution. A summary of the laser-based techniques is given in Table 4.1, p. 185. The application of laser velocimetry to the diagnostics of propulsion systems has become quite extensive at several universities and research establishments, for example: Sandia Labs, MIT, Purdue University, G.E. (Schenectady, N.Y.) [in USA], Imperial College, UKAEA, Sheffield University [in UK], and Karlsruhe University [in Germany]. Laser Velocimetry has been developed to the stage where it can now be used as a routine practical tool and can be applied with confidence to complex flows (with or without combustion) to yield mean and fluctuating velocity, shear stresses and higher order correlations. Simultaneous measurements of instantaneous values of axial, radial and swirl velocity components can be made with a three channel laser velocimeter. The most common optical arrangement is a dual beam, real fringe, system where one beam has been frequency-shifted, for example, by a bragg cell. The frequency-shifting causes the real fringes to move through the control volume and distinguish the flow direction. A dual beam system permits a large received signal aperture, produces high signal-to-noise ratio (SNR) signals for sparse seeding, does not require critical beam alignment to obtain good signals, does not require a laser etalon as long as incident beam paths are equal, and does not require a high quality optical table[172,176]. Beams with different colors or frequency shifts can be used to measure simultaneously two or three components of velocity. LV is now practically fully developed; only minor improvements in its capability can be expected within the next few years. In industrial flames of large size, LV has been only moderately successful because of beam schlieren effects and poor SNR. Optimum signal levels are obtained with particles whose diameters are about half the fringe spacing. High SNR signals can be processed with commercially available digital

TABLE 5.9

Comparison of Velocity Measurement Techniques

Method	Comments
Pitot-static probe[177,178,187]	can be used in three-dimensional flows both with and without combustion, difficult to interpret signals in highly turbulent flows, causes flow interface, fairly inexpensive, large probe volume, problems with measurement close to solid surfaces.
Hot wire/Hot film[177]	insensitive to local flow reversal can be used in 3-D flows with proper alignment, cannot be used in high temperature conditions, signal difficult to interpret in highly turbulent flows, causes flow interference, large probe volume, problems with measurement close to solid surfaces, requires clean fluid at constant temperature for stable and long-time calibration.
Pulsed-wire anemometer	causes flow interference especially near wall, large probe volume, not very suitable in flows with high turbulence levels, moderate cost, difficult to measure near solid surfaces, requires custom design, upper limit on maximum measurable velocity, not suitable in combustion systems.
Laser Velocimeter[172,173,176,177,185]	fairly expensive, data obtained by sampling individual particles, can be used in highly turbulent flows with flow reversal, small probe volume ($\simeq$ mm^3), applicable to combustion system, non-intrusive, requires seeding of flow with particles, usually require custom design of traversing mechanism, information on particle size possible, require high power laser in combustion systems.
Photon Correlator[173,177,181]	as for laser velocimeter except that it requires no seeding to the flow, suitable for high velocity flows, requires low power laser, expensive.
Two-spot laser transit anemometer[173]	suitable for measurement near solid walls (for example, turbine blades) and high velocity flows, not suitable in highly turbulent flows with reverse flow zone, small probe volume, applicable to combustion systems, flow access through small windows compared to LV, fairly expensive.

burst counters. Photon correlation signal processing can be used with poor back-scattered signals from a lightly seeded flow and a low power laser[181]. While the photon correlation electronics is more expensive than other signal processing methods, the future of this technique is attractive.

Particle Size Measurement

Recent interests in combustion research have intensified demands for accurate and fast techniques for the measurement of particle size over a large dynamic range. But, unfortunately, there is, as yet, no single technique capable of providing size distribution information over a very large dynamic range. Each method has a certain limited range of application. A number of laser based optical techniques have been developed at various centers (for example: Imperial College, Sheffield Univ., Karlsruhe Univ., Spectron Development Labs, Stanford Univ., Univ. of Minnesota) and most of these are based on the scattering of light from particles. Optical techniques are superior because of their non-intrusive nature, and in many cases can provide data *in-situ* and on-line. See Chapter 4 for further discussion of various particle sizing methods.

Laser Probes for Combustion Chemistry

During recent years laser probes for measuring flame gas properties have advanced to the stage where they can now be utilized to determine key flow and combustion field variables. These include temperature, major constituent densities, gas velocity and correlations of these properties. A convenient overview of laser diagnostic methods is provided in Table 5.10, which groups the methods into two categories of scattering: elastic (or unshifted) and inelastic (shifted). Velocity by LV is obtained by elastic scattering which requires observation of light scattered from particles either naturally present or seeded into the flow, and upon total gas density. Space and time-resolved measurements from inelastic light scattering processes, by the type of information they yield, and their current status is given in Table 5.11.

Laser-based spectroscopic methods are assuming an ever-increasing role in combustion research due to its ability to provide *in situ*, remote, spatially and temporally resolved measurements with high sensitivity and species selectivity. The techniques appropriate to measurements of temperature and species concentration in combustion can be grouped into two categories: that is, those that are inherently spatially precise and those that are line-of-sight, but capable of spatial resolution when properly implemented. The former category includes Raman scattering, Rayleigh scattering, coherent anti-stokes Raman spectroscopy (CARS), stimulated Raman gain/loss spectroscopy and laser-excited fluorescence; the latter category includes laser absorption spectroscopy. CARS is a non-linear, light-wave mixing process capable of both high spatial and temporal resolution. In brief, two laser beams of frequencies ω_1 (pump) and ω_2 (stokes) generate an intense coherent beam at $\omega_3 = 2\,\omega_1 - \omega_2$ (antistokes or CARS) when the frequency difference $\omega_1 - \omega_2$ is tuned to a molecular vibrational resonance. The CARS signal produced is many orders of magnitude stronger than conventional Raman scattering. In CARS, fluorescent interferences are negligible since the signal for the most part is in the antistokes region. Temperature measurements are derived from the spectral distribution of the CARS radiation and concentration measurements from the signal intensity or, in certain ranges, also from spectral shapes[198,200,201]. The practical potential of CARS has been exhibited in several

TABLE 5.10

Information Obtained from Elastic and Inelastic Light Scattering

Observation	Scatterer	Scattering Process	Information	Comments
Elastic (unshifted) scattering	Particles	Tyndall (Mie)	Characterization of particle distribution	Information can be difficult to interpret for non-ideal particle systems
			Velocimetry	Particles must be small enough to follow flow fluctuations
	Gas	Rayleigh	Total density	Few particles Favorable configuration Major composition known
			Temperature	Few particles Favorable configuration Major composition known Equilibrium Difficult to instrument
Inelastic (shifted) scattering	Gas	Raman Fluorescence Nonlinear processes	Temperature and component densities	Nonequilibrium OK Wide range of signal strengths and complexities to obtain detailed data from various systems, including hostile environments

TABLE 5.11

Space and Time Resolved Measurements from Inelastic Light Scattering. All methods are suitable for nonequilibrium conditions. [RS refers to Raman scattering, CARS to coherent anti-Stokes Raman spectroscopy, and RIKES to Raman-induced Kerr effect].

Information	Environment	Method	Status	Comments
Temperature	Clean flame zones	RS	Accomplished	Do not need a priori composition Too weak for luminous systems
Major species densities	Clean flame zones	RS	Accomplished	Do not need a priori temperature for low temperatures Too weak for luminous systems
Temperature	Bright and/or particle-laden flame zones	CARS	Accomplished	Strong signal Tolerates particle loading and strong flame luminosity More difficult to instrument and interpret than RS
Major and intermediate species densities	Bright and/or particle-laden flame zones	CARS	Possible	Strong signal Tolerates particle loading More difficult to instrument and interpret than CARS for temperature
		Raman gain	Possible	Developmental alternative to CARS
Minor species densities	Bright and/or particle-laden flame zones	Fluorescence	Semi-quantitative	Strong signal
		Saturated fluorescence	Probably quantitative for some species	Reduces dependence of fluorescence on collisional quenching
		RIKES, other nonlinear processes	Possible	Developmental High experimental demands for increased quality of data

investigations and, recently, to map temperature fields in a practical combustion system (liquid-fueled combustors, a swirl burner and a JT-12 combustor can, situated in a 50 cm diameter tunnel)[201]. Tunable laser absorption spectroscopy lends itself to tomography with spatial scanning of a multiplicity of angles and can be employed for spatially-resolved field mapping.

The techniques currently being developed at a rapid pace are vibrational Raman scattering, coherent anti-Stokes Raman scattering (CARS), Rayleigh scattering, and laser fluorescence. CARS shows promise of a more sensitive method for temperature measurement in hot gases, which may be less susceptible to interference due to fluorescence and particulates. This is a currently active research field at various research establishments at, for example: Sandia Labs, United Technologies Research Center, and Office National D'Etudes Et De Recherches Aerospatiales, France. Results obtained from flames of several different sizes reveal that it is indeed a viable technique and has the potential for its application to high-intensity combustors of large size. Rotational Raman and resonant Raman are, as yet, not able to supply meaningful data in a reacting environment. Laser-induced fluorescence spectroscopy has been used and has the potential to measure several combustion intermediates, for example: Cn C_2, HCH, OH, NO, NO_2, HNO, C_2O, halogenated hydrocarbons and polycyclic aromatic hydrocarbons.

5.8 PROBLEM AREAS

Prior to discussing the state of knowledge of unsteady flows within combustion systems, it is convenient to first assess the situation regarding steady aerodynamic flows. Here all combustors must possess a swirl flame stabilizer or a bluff body for flame stabilization. The pressure energy loss is first converted to stream velocity, which decays in shear layers to turbulence. The turbulent mixing process is essential to the satisfactory operation of the stirred chemical reactor at all loadings. The rate of decay of the turbulence determines the degree of mixing in the reactor, while its location determines the size of the reactor. Knowledge of the distribution of the steady velocity throughout the combustor is thus a first step in analyzing or designing combustors. The steady flow pattern falls broadly into three classes. The first is axisymmetric flow with a toroidal vortex formed at a simple sudden expansion. Scaling laws, entrainment theory or "eddy viscosity" theories can be applied to this case in a semi-quantitative manner in cold flow, but the effects of temperature, concentration and spray evaporation are only poorly understood. The second case is confined vortex flow encountered in the various forms of cyclone or swirl combustors[1]. For cyclone combustors, Russian and German work is prominent and gives a good guide to the flow patterns to be expected. Even more ignorance prevails for the combustive flow case. The difficulty stems partly from the fact that the boundary layer repeatedly separates and interacts with the outer flow in such a manner that attempts to solve the two separately are doomed to failure. The third case is the complex three-dimensional flowfield encountered in large boilers, swirl combustors and GT and IC engines, etc. Here the problem can be described as "interacting semi-confined jets." At present there is a lack of suitable detailed measurements in practical combustion systems, which are often desired by the modelers to test and develop complex models of the phenomenon.

Laser Probes for Diagnostics

It is expected that within the coming years significant developments in laser based probes will take place for diagnosing flames and practical environments. Table 5.12 shows that the established techniques for velocity measurement allow one to determine the average

TABLE 5.12

Ordering of Predictive Needs for Combustion Modeling with Measurement Capabilities (in Increasing Level of Experimental Difficulty).

Here, Instantaneous Value X = Mean Value X + Fluctuation Value X′; LV denotes laser velocimetry; RS, Raman scattering; RayS, Rayleigh scattering; and PDF, probability density function.

Flow Field Quantities		*Measurement Techniques*
Average Momentum Flux	ρu^2	Pitot Tube
Average Velocity	u	LV, Pitot Tube
Turbulent Intensity	$\langle u'^2 \rangle$	LV
Shear Stress	$\langle u'v' \rangle$	LV
Fluctuation Mass Flux	$\langle \rho' u' \rangle$	LV + RS or RayS
Combustion Field Quantities		
Temperature T and Major Species Mass Fractions M_i	Mean and Variance of T, M_i	RS; RayS for T
	PDF for T, M_i	RS; RayS for T
		[Thermocouples (mean)]
		[Gas Sampling (mean)]
		[Absorption/Emission Spectroscopy (not 3-dimensional)]
Density	ρ	RayS; RS using ΣM_i, or T with fast chem. and ideal gas law

momentum flux, average velocity, turbulent intensities and shear stresses. In order to complete the flowfield description, temperature, major species densities and fluctuating mass flux of the flame gases are required. This is currently being investigated at various research centers and universities. Other currently-unresolved fluid dynamic problems in combustion systems are listed in Table 5.11.

In large-scale flames, optical access is a particularly difficult problem involving a full-scale dirty, vibrating, confined environment. The lack of adequate optical access is perhaps the greatest inhibiting factor at present for the acquisition of LV measurements in large flames. Even when optical windows are present there are problems with measurements very near to solid surfaces. The development of compensating optics for aberrations introduced into the light beam is well overdue. The application of fiber optics and miniaturization of optics should be encouraged. The application of fluorescent particles to study mixing, particle migration, intermittency, and other characteristics of turbulent flows appears to have considerable unresolved potential.

Furnace Flames

The flowfield in furnace flames and continuous flow combustors is very complex as a result of flow recirculation, induced by swirl or other means, which is utilized for flame stabilization. The flowfield is further complicated by the fuel spray, usually a wide-angle spray which penetrates far into the recirculation zone and with a swirl component which is independent of the primary air swirl. The turbulence level induced by these interacting flows determines the rate at which the fuel and air mix and burn and is, therefore, very important in the evaluation of combustor efficiency and pollutants emission. Scales of turbulence are defined in terms of correlations and the general description of a turbulent flowfield is given in terms of profiles of mean and RMS variations of velocity, temperature, and species concentrations. Correlations for fluctuating quantities provide shear stress for velocity components and correlations are also given between mean and fluctuating components of velocity, temperature and concentration. Until recently there was very little instrumentation available to measure fluctuating velocities. Hot-wire anemometers have been used in model cold flow combustors and their application to flow with varying density and temperature and multi-component flowfields is questionable. New ideas and developments in hot-wire anemometry should be encouraged, despite the limited potential only to simple cold flows.

The development of laser probes has now made it possible to make *in-situ* point measurements of mean and fluctuating velocity, density, temperature and concentration within a turbulent flame. Available information suggests that these fluctuating quantities can be recorded in such a form that many of the cross-correlation coefficients and other statistical quantities, that occur in the equations of turbulent combustion, can be deduced directly. A complete and comprehensive mapping of a turbulent flame (for example: mean and RMS velocity, temperature, species concentration and their correlations) has, as yet, not been accomplished. The LV is now practically fully developed and the focus now needs to be its application to hostile environments. Each application can pose unique problems, but knowledge gained in one situation can often be employed to advantage in new situations. In large industrial flames LV has been only moderately successful because of beam schlieren effects and poor signal-to-noise ratio. The developments of correlations, such as the velocity-temperature correlation ($u'T'$), using for example simultaneous LV and Raman scattering, should be encouraged. This capability needs to be developed first for benchtop measurements prior to extending to scale-model measurements. Measurements of fluctuating temperatures by frequency corrected thermocouples and optical techniques, such as two-color pyrometers and laser-schlieren interferometry, are essential to understand both combustion processes and radiative heat transfer. Due to the highly nonlinear dependence of radiation energy flow on temperature, the average temperature is almost useless in computing local radiant heat flux. Techniques for measuring the mean and fluctuating local concentration in flames of large size non-intrusively are also urgently required. A comprehensive set of such detailed measurements could allow the testing and development of mathematical models. Achievement of this goal is in sight and several investigators have demonstrated the feasibility of measuring many of the quantities and their correlations[172-218].

Fluidized Bed Combustion

During recent years, a major research effort has been exerted in the field of fluidized combustion of coal and, more recently, on the oil shale. Processes of heat and mass transfer and combustion are modeled mathematically and experiments are carried out to determine the kinetics of combustion, formation and destruction of pollutants in the bed and in the freeboard above the bed, and combustion efficiency. The freeboard reactions and sulfur retention in the freeboard are of practical significance. Information on the carry-over of particles from the fluidized bed, particle size and concentration distribution, and particle mean and temporal velocity distributions are prerequisites for further insight into the freeboard reactions. Optical methods for particle sizing and velocity measurements in fluidized bed combustors are discussed in Refs. 211-214 and are, in general, more advantageous than mechanical methods due to their high frequency response, non-intrusiveness and better accuracy. The mechanical methods have many disadvantages: the sampling process always disturbs the flowfield and, in a fluidized bed (highly turbulent system), it is particularly difficult to extract a representative sample with any degree of confidence. Also the particle agglomeration and deposition in the sampling system can alter the size distribution prior to measurement. The optical techniques discussed by Gupta[212] are: image photography, laser holography, and laser diffraction and light scattering. Each of these techniques has a certain dynamic range over which it can provide information on the size distribution.

IC and GT Engines

Detailed measurements of the turbulent flowfield are necessary for developing an understanding of the combustion process in a gas turbine (GT) engine or internal combustion (IC) engine. These processes of combustion depend very heavily on the nature of the turbulent flowfield just prior to ignition. Both the turbulent eddy size and intensity are important in determining the viability of the flame kernel and its ultimate propagation. Hot-wire anemometry has been used in IC engines with varying degrees of success. However, calibration of hot-wire anemometers is very difficult, in particular when its application is to flow with varying density and temperature, and near stagnation zones where mean velocity is low and the intensity of turbulence is very high. Besides the problem of varying density and temperature, hot-wires cannot survive at high temperatures normally encountered in combusting systems. The other apparent problem is the positioning of the wire probe under running conditions of the IC engine. Five-hole pitot probes can be used but unfortunately the probe methods have some inherent disadvantages, for example: lack of accuracy, flow disturbance by the probe, low frequency response, difficulty in positioning of the probe under engine running conditions, and hence the difficulty in the interpretation of data for mean flow and turbulence measurements. It is now possible to measure flowfield successfully with LV under actual operating conditions of an IC engine[215].

Gas turbine combustors have been almost exclusively evolved by cut-and-try methods with remarkable success. Nevertheless, to minimize pollution, heat transfer, exit temperature peaks and chamber volume, a detailed model of the system is required. The complex three-dimensional flowfield pattern is now within reasonable predictive capability. Intense efforts must be made to measure and predict the steady and fluctuating velocities, temperatures, concentrations and reaction rates for a particular combustor, with given inlet conditions and fuel spray design. Measurements are urgently needed to guide and verify the theoretical models. As compressor delivery and turbine entry temperatures rise with improving blade cooling techniques, the available combustor wall cooling air is rapidly becoming a limiting factor in engine design. Due to the adverse area/volume ratio with small gas turbines, particular attention should be paid to this problem in the development of engines of small size.

Rocket and Pulse Combustion

In the case of rocket combustion, by far the biggest problem at the present time is combustion instability. This is apparent in both space flight, in which most of the liquid-fueled engines produce vibrations, and military solid-fueled rockets, where large sums are spent overcoming the effects of combustion oscillations. In these solid propellent rockets, the part played by fluid mechanics is not fully understood. The typical sequence of interactions leading to erratic pressure peaks is as follows: a small pressure and velocity perturbation in the chamber results in an increase in burning rate having a component in phase with the pressure disturbance. An acoustic wave is initiated, which in the case of a transverse traveling mode causes an acoustic streaming motion in the opposite direction to the wave due to non-linear boundary layer effects. The acoustic pressure and acoustic erosive contributions combine to give a net gain-damping margin, and the oscillations grow to amplitudes of the order of one hundred atmospheres. Meanwhile, the acoustic streaming forms a transonic vortex within the rocket which passes out through the nozzle throat. The vortex not only causes the vehicle to roll, but also reduces the effective throat area by up to 40 per cent. The equilibrium chamber pressure depends strongly on the throat area, and up to a six-fold pressure rise has been observed. Prediction of the onset of oscillations thus demands a knowledge of the velocity-coupled acoustic erosive constant and pressure-coupled acoustic admittance. Reliable techniques to measure both these parameters are urgently required.

Pulse combustion is well-known to be a means of enhancing volumetric heat release rates and combustion efficiency. The main problem in its practical use is noise. The development of devices that can reduce noise would allow the utilization of the advantages of pulse combustion. Fluid mechanics play an important role in noise propagation and it has been demonstrated that noise from a turbulent flame can be reduced by the presence of an enclosing flame. It is well-known that oscillations are brought on by a positive feed-back mechanism, and it is fortunate that control engineers have devised several splendid methods for analyzing such systems. In particular, if the transfer functions for the various units in the feedback loop are known, then the onset of instability and the frequency of oscillation may be readily calculated from the Characteristic Equation. Thus, knowing the transfer functions for a burner and a furnace chamber permits one to predict whether the combination will be stable or unstable. There is, therefore, a need to develop methods of measuring these transfer functions.

Final Remarks

The most urgent work on the interaction between fluid dynamics and combustion is the development of real model laws. Both experimental and theoretical studies are needed. Extensive measurements should cover a wide range of dimensionless variables, and include mean and fluctuating data and correlations, so as to aid the modeler. Empirical and physical hypotheses and laws need to be further investigated, verified and refined. Computational studies should include macro- and micro-approaches, calibrate model laws and parameters with available data, and predict phenomena outside the range of previous experimental study. Here the cost effectiveness of the modeling approach reveals itself. Regarding combustion studies, after success with fluid dynamic model laws with a given fuel, extension to a wider range of fuels is required. In some cases, this may be easy [as, for example, in flows dominated by dynamics, like boundary layer combustion]. In other cases, this may be difficult [as, for example, in flows dependent on dynamic and chemical-kinetic factors, like ignition and flame stability].

Clearly, fluid dynamics plays a special role in controlling and influencing combustion processes. Most practical combustion systems have turbulent flows and are mixing controlled, and understanding of the detailed flow structure will aid the designer in modifying and controlling the combustion process. There is a justifiable need to continue establishing a sound scientific basis for fluid and particle flow characteristics in the recognition that modification and control of combustion processes can be readily achieved by modifying and controlling the flow of air and fuel through burners and the interaction between jets and recirculation flows within combustion chambers. It is convenient to cite several recent conferences and texts[219-228] which contain a wealth of information. Details about nonreacting and reacting flows are given, with both experimental and predictive evidence. New ideas about the simulation of turbulence and chemical reaction [and their interaction and pollutant formation processes] are clearly at the forefront of current research efforts with a view to their application to furnace, gas turbine and reciprocating engines flowfields. In particular, a cohesive overview of the field is provided by three recent review papers[225] on the modeling of turbulent reacting flows in practical systems from the points of view of the chemical kineticist [Westbrook and Dryer], the turbulence fluid dynamic modeler [Jones and Whitelaw], and the user [Harsha]. The last of these[226] is especially useful to persons interested in practical application of the theory to particular engineering flowfields. These conference papers, and other volumes in the Energy and Engineering Science Series elaborate further on the details given here.

References to Chapter 5

1. Gupta, A. K., Lilley, D. G., and Syred, N.: *Swirl Flows*, Abacus Press, Tunbridge Wells, England, 1984.
2. Breen, B. P., and Sotter, J. G.: *Prog. Energy Comb. Sci.*, 4, 1978, p. 201.
3. Heywood, J. B.: *Prog. Energy Comb. Sci.*, 1., 1976, p. 135.
4. Henein, N. A.: *Prog. Energy Comb. Sci.*, 1, 1976, p. 165.
5. Caretto, L. S.: *Prog. Energy Comb. Sci.*, 1, 1976, p. 47.
6. Pratt, D. T.: *Prog. Energy Comb. Sci.*, 1, 1976, p. 73.
7. Bowman, C. T.: *Prog. Energy Comb. Sci.*, 1, 1975, p. 33.
8. Lefebvre, A. H.: *15th Symp. (Intl.) on Comb.*, The Comb. Inst., 1975, p. 1169.
9. Fristrom, R. M., and Westenberg, A. A.: *Flame Structure*, McGraw Hill, New York, 1965, p. 344.
10. Kaskan, W. E.: *Comb. & Flame*, 3, 1959, p. 49.
11. Newhall, H. K.: *12th Symp. (Intl.) on Comb.*, The Comb. Inst., 1969, p. 603.
12. Verkamp, F. J., Verdouw, A. J., Tomlinson, J. G.: Impact of Emission Regulations on Future Gas Turbine Engine Combustors, *AIAA Paper No. 73-1277*, 1973.

13. Edelman, R. B., and Fortune, O.: A Quasi-Global Chemical Kinetic Model for the Finite Rate Combustion of Hydrocarbon Fuels, *AIAA Paper No. 69-86*, 1969.
14. Bowman, C. T.: *Emissions from Continuous Combustion Systems,* Plenum Press, 1972, p. 98. [Cornelius, W. and Agnew, W.G. (Eds.)]
15. Zeldovich, Y. B.: *Acta Physicochem,* USSR, **21**, 1946, p. 577.
16. Iverach, D., Basden, K. S., and Kirov, N. Y.: *14th Symp. (Intl.) on Comb.*, The Comb. Inst., 1973, p. 767.
17. Thompson, D., Brown, T. D., and Beér, J. M.: *14th Symp. (Intl.) on Comb.*, The Comb. Inst., 1973, p. 787.
18. Levy, J. M., Longwell, J. P., and Sarofim, A. F.: Conversion of Fuel-Nitrogen to Nitrogen Oxides in Fossil Fuel Combustion: Mechanistic Considerations, Report Submitted to the Energy and Environmental Research Corporation by the MIT Energy Laboratory, April, 1978.
19. Hayhurst, A. N., and McLean, H. G.: *Nature*, **251**, 1974, p. 303.
20. Fenimore, C. P.: *Comb. and Flame,* **26**, 1976, p. 249.
21. Longwell, J. P.: Plenary Lecture, *16th Symp. (Intl.) on Comb.*, The Comb. Inst., 1977.
22. Sarofim, A. F., and Bartok, W.: Methods for Control of Nitrogen Oxide Emissions from Stationery Sources, Advanced Seminar Sponsored by AIChE, New York, 1970, p. III-1.
23. Martin, G. B. and Berkan, E. E.: An Investigation of the Conversion of Various Fuel Nitrogen Compounds to NO in Oil Combustion, *70th AIChE National Meeting*, Atlantic City, New Jersey, 1971.
24. Beér, J. M., Sarofim, A. F., Timothy, L., Hanson, S., Gupta, A. K., and Levy, J. M.: *AIChE National Meeting*, Chicago, November, 1980.
25. Haynes, B. S., Iverach, D., and Kirov, N. Y.: *15th Symp. (Intl.) on Comb.*, The Comb. Inst., 1974, p. 1103.
26. Haynes, B. S.: *Combustion and Flame,* **28**, 1977, p. 113. Also see Ph.D. Thesis, University of New South Wales, Sydney, Australia, 1976.
27. Morley, C.: *Comb. and Flame,* **27**, 1976, p. 189.
28. Fenimore, C. P.: *Comb. and Flame,* **19**, 1972, p. 289.
29. Fisher, C. J.: *Comb. and Flame,* **30**, 1977, p. 143.
30. Sarofim, A. F., Pohl, J. H., and Taylor, B. R.: Strategies for Controlling Nitrogen Oxide Emissions during Combustion of Nitrogen Bearing Fuels, MIT, Department of Chemical Engineering, Internal Report, 1977.
31. Appleton, J. P., and Heywood, J. B.: *14th Symp. (Intl.) on Comb.*, The Comb. Inst., 1973, p. 777.
32. Haebig, J. E., Davis, B. E., and Dzuna, E. R.: *Env. Sci. Tech.*, **10**, 1976, p. 243.
33. Beér, J. M., and Martin, G. B.: Application of Advanced Technology for NO_x Control: Alternate Fuels and Fluidized Bed Coal Combustion, *69th AIChE Meeting*, Chicago, 1976.
34. Edwards, H. W.: *AIChE Symposium Series* No. 126, **68**, 1972, p. 91.
35. Gibbs, B. M., Pereira, F. J., and Beér, J. M.: *16th Symp. (Intl.) on Comb.*, The Comb. Inst., 1977, p. 461.
36. Shelef, M., and Otto, K.: *J. of Colloid and Interphase Science,* **31**, 1969, p. 73.
37. Bedjai, G., Orbach, H. K., and Riesenfeld, F. C.: *Ind. Eng. Chem.*, **50**, 1958, p. 1165.
38. Pereira, F. J.: Ph.D. Thesis, University of Sheffield, 1975.
39. Beér, J. M., Sarofim, A. F., Chan, L., and Sprouse, A. M.: NO Reduction by Char in Fluidized Combustion, *5th Intl. Fluidized Bed Comb. Conf.*, Washington, D.C., December, 1977.
40. Song, Y. H.: Sc. D. Thesis, MIT, 1978.
41. Gupta, A. K., Syred, N., and Beér, J.M.: *15th Symp. (Intl.) on Comb.*, The Comb. Inst., 1974, p. 1367
42. Meyer, O., Mauss, F.: *Proc. 1st European Symp. on Comb.*, Sheffield University, 1973, p. 475.
43. Tager, S. A., Talumaa, R. Yu, Kalmaru, A. M., Kazakova, N. A.: *Thermal Eng.*, **23**, 12, 1976, p. 34.
44. Brown, T. D., Mitchell, E. R., Lee, G. K.: *Proc. 1st European Symp. on Comb.*, Sheffield University, 1973, p. 487.
45. Tager, S. A., Kalmaru, A. M., Kuznetsov, N. I., Kurglov, B. I., Bulkin, Yu. P., *Thermal Eng.*, **20**, 10, 1973, p. 34.
46. Glebov, V. P., Motin, G. I., Vaknilevich, F. M., Defyunin, I. A.: *Thermal Eng.*, **22**, 3, 1975, p. 8.
47. Heap, M. P., Lowes, T. M., Walmsley, R.: *Proc. 1st European Symp. on Comb.*, Sheffield University, 1973, p. 493.
48. Heap, M. P., Lowes, T. M., Walmsley, R.: *14th Symp. (Intl.) on Comb.*, The Comb. Inst., 1973, p. 883.

49. Sadakata, M., Beér, J. M.: *16th Symp. (Intl.) on Comb.*, The Comb. Inst., 1977, p. 93.
50. Gupta, A. K., Jhawar, P., and Beér, J. M.: Combustion and Emission Characteristics of a Multi-annular Swirl Burner, *85th AIChE Meeting*, June 4-8, 1978. See also Gupta, A. K., Beér, J. M., and Swithenbank, J.: The Potential Application of a Multi-annular Swirl Burner to a Gas Turbine Combustor, paper presented at the A.R.C. Comb. Sub-Committee Meeting, *ARC 36468*, Comb. 186, December, 1975.
51. Awerbuch, N.: A propose des imeratifs d'equipmentau fuel-oil lourd des generateurs de grande puissance, La Revue Chaud-Froid-Plomberie, **329**, 1973, p. 165.
52. Awerbuch, N.: Augmentation sensible de la vitesse de combustion et intensification des es-changes thermiques par la realisation d'un regime pulsatorie controle, paper presented at the Association Technique de l'Industria due Gaz en France Congress, 1976.
53. Muzio, L. J., Arand, J. K., Teixeidra, D. P.: *16th Symp. (Intl.) on Comb.*, The Comb. Inst., 1977, p. 199.
54. Kotter, V. R., Lobov, G. V., Verzakov, V. N.: *Thermal Eng.*, **25**, 11, 1978, p. 12.
55. Babii, V. I., Verbovetskii, E. Kh. Zhukov, I. T.: *Thermal Eng.*, **24**, 3, 1977, p. 16.
56. Breen, B. P.: *16th Symp. (Intl.) on Comb.*, The Comb. Inst., 1977, p. 19.
57. Verkamp, F. J., Verdouw, A. J., Tomlinson, J. G.: Impact of Emission Regulations on Future Gas Turbine Engine Combustors, *AIAA Paper No. 73-1277*, 1973.
58. Macek, A.: *17th Symp. (Intl.) on Comb.*, The Comb. Inst., 1979, p. 65.
59. Tager, S. A., Motin, G. I., Talumaa, R. Yu., Kalmaru, A. M., Gulyaenko, A. B.: *Thermal Eng.*, 18, 4, 1971, p. 80.
60. Syred, N., Dahmen, K.: *Proc. 2nd European Symp. on Comb.*, The Comb. Inst., Orleans, France, 1975, p. 414.
61. Najim, S. A.: Ph.D. Thesis, University College, Cardiff, Wales, August, 1979.
62. Agrest, J.: *J. Inst. Fuel*, **38**, August, 1965, p. 344.
63. Schmidt, K. R.: *V.D.I. Berichte*, **146**, 1970, p. 90.
64. Oven, M. J., McLean, W. J., Gouldin, F. C.: NO-NO_2 Measurements in a Methane Fueled Swirl Stabilized Combustor, paper presented at the Central States Section Meeting of the Combustion Institute, NASA Lewis Research Center, March, 1977.
65. Claypole, T.: Ph.D. Thesis, University College, Cardiff, Wales, 1980.
66. Jones, R. E.: *Prog. Energy Comb. Sci.*, **4**, 1978, p. 78.
67. Jones, R. E.: Advanced Technology for Reducing Aircraft Engine Pollution, *ASME Paper No. 73* – WA/Aero-2 Detroit, Michigan, November 11-15, 1973.
68. Bowman, C. T. and Cohen, L. S.: Influence of Aerodynamic Phenomena on Pollutant Formation in Combustion, Vol. 1: Experimental Results, United Technologies Research Center *Report EPA-650/2-75-06/a*, East Hartford, Connecticut, July, 1975.
69. Niedzwiecki, R. W. and Jones, R. E.: *AIAA Journal*, **12**, June, 1974, p. 844.
70. Edelman, R. and Harsha, P. T.: *Prog. Energy Comb. Sci.*, **4**, 1978, p. 1.
71. Lipfert, F. W.: Correlation of Gas Turbine Emissions Data, *ASME Paper 72-GT-60*, 1972.
72. Klapatch, R. D. and Koblish, T. R.: Nitrogen Oxide Control with Water Injection in Gas Turbines, *ASME Paper 71/WA/GT9*, 1971.
73. Hammond, A. L.: *Science*, **189**, 1975. p. 128.
74. Meyers, R. A., *et al.*: *Science*, **177**, 1972, p. 1187. See also 173rd ACS Meeting, *Symp. on Fuel Chemistry*, 1977.
75. Chanhan, S. P., *et al.*: 170th ACS Meeting, *Symp. on Fuel Chemistry*, 1975.
76. Sareen, S., *et al.*: 173rd ACS Meeting, *Symp. on Fuel Chemistry*, 1977.
77. Friedman, S., *et al.*: 173rd ACS Meeting, *Symp. on Fuel Chemistry*, 1977.
78. Ganguli, P. S., *et al.*: 172nd ACS Meeting, *Symp. on Fuel Chemistry*, 1977.
79. Smith, E. B., *et al.*: 169th ACS Meeting, *Symp. on Fuel Chemistry*, 1977.
80. Trindale, S. C., Howard, J. B., Kolm, H. H., Powers, G. J., and Hottel, H. C.: *ACS Meeting*, Div. Fuel Chem., Los Angeles, California, April 1-5, 1974, p. 45, Prepr. 45, No. 2.
81. Wendt, J. O. L, Sternling, C. V., Matovich, M. A.: *14th Symp. (Intl.) on Comb.*, The Comb. Inst., 1973, p. 897.
82. Tager, S. A., Motin, G. I., Talumaa, R. Y., Kalmaru, A. M., and Gulyaenko, A. B.: *Thermal Eng.*, **18**, 4, 1971, p. 80. See also **23**, 12, 1976, p. 34.
83. Awerbuch, N.: A propose des imeratifs d'equipementan fuel-oil lourd des generateurs de grande puissance, *La Revue Chaud-Froid-Plomberie*, **329**, 1973, p. 165.
84. Awerbuch, N.: Augmentation sensible de la vitesse de combustion et intensification des es-changes thermiques par la realisation d'un regime pulsatorie controle, paper presented at the Association Technique de l'Industria due Gaz en France Congress, 1976.
85. Breen, B. P.: *16th Symp. (Intl.) on Comb.*, The Comb. Inst., 1977, p. 19.

86. Spiers, H. M.: Technical Data on Fuel, British National Committee, World Power Conference, R and R Clark Limited, Edinburgh, 1977.
87. Beér, J. M. and Chigier, N. A.: *Combustion Aerodynamics,* Applied Science, London, 1972.
88. Drake, P. F. and Hubbard, E. F.: *J. Inst. Fuel,* **39**, 1966, p. 98.
89. Wroblewska, V., Zelkowski, Jr., and Wojcicki, S.: *16th Symp. (Intl.) on Comb.,* The Comb. Inst., 1977, p. 401.
90. Sjorgen, A.: *14th Symp. (Intl.) on Comb.,* The Comb. Inst., 1973, p. 919.
91. Lefebvre, A. H.: *Cranfield International Symposium Series,* **10**, Pergamon Press, 1968, p. 21.
92. Longwell, J. P.: Plenary Lecture, *16th Symp. (Intl.) on Comb.,* The Comb. Inst., 1976.
93. Longwell, J. P.: *Prog. in Astro. and Aero.,* **62**, 1977, p. 3.
94. Heap, M. P.: *Prog. in Astro. and Aero.,* **62**, 1977, p. 116.
95. Blazowski, W. S., and Maggitti, L.: *Prog. in Astro. and Aero.,* **62**, 1977, p. 21.
96. Lefebvre, A. H., Mellor, A. M., and Peters, J. E.: *Prog. in Astro. and Aero.,* **62**, 1977, p. 137.
97. Stettler, R. J., and Hardin, M. C.: Initial Evaluation of Coal Derived Liquid Fuels in a Low Emission and Conventional Gas Turbine Combustor, General Motors Corporation Engineering Publication 6544, April, 1976.
98. Hardin, M. C.: The Combustion of Shale Derived Marine Diesel Fuel at Marine Gas Turbine Engine Conditions, Central States Section/Combustion Institute Spring Technical Meeting, Combustion of Alternate Fuels and Combustion of Coal, Battlle-Columbus Laboratories, Columbus, Ohio, April, 1976.
99. Mossier, S. A., Pierce, R. M., and Purvis, W. J.: Comparative Combustion Characteristics of Petroleum and Shale Oil Base Diesel Fuel Marine, Western States Section/Combustion Institute Spring Meeting, Salt Lake City, Utah, April, 1976.
100. Energy: *Global Prospects 1985-2000*, McGraw Hill, New York, 1977.
101. NASA Workshop on Jet Aircraft Hydrocarbon Fuels Technology, June, 1977.
102. Technology Assessment Report for Industrial Boiler Applications: Synthetic Fuels, U.S. Environmental Protection Agency Interagency Energy/Environment R&D Program *Report EPA-600/7-79-178d*, November, 1979.
103. Hittman Associates, Inc., Environmental Assessment Date Base for Coal Liquefaction Technology, Vol. I & II, Final Report. *EPA-600/7-78-184a & b, EPA Contract No. 68-02-2162,* Columbia, MD., September, 1978.
104. Sturgess, G.: Gas Turbine Combustor Design Challenges for 1980's, *AIAA/SAE/ASME 16th Joint Propulsion Conf.,* Hartford, Connecticut, Paper No. 80-1285, June 30-July 2, 1980.
105. Hammond, D. C., Jr., and Mellor, A. M.: *Comb. Sci. and Tech.,* **2**, 1970, p. 67.
106. Fletcher, R. S., and Heywood, J. B.: A Model for Nitric Oxide Emissions from Gas Turbine Engines. *AIAA Paper 71-123,* 1971.
107. Swithenbank, J., Poll, I., Vincent, M. W., and Wright, D. D.: *14th Symp. (Intl.) on Comb.,* 1973, p. 627.
108. Mosier, S. A., and Roberts, R., Low-Power Turbo-Propulsion Combustor Exhaust Emissions, III Analysis, *AFAPL-TR-73-36,* **III**, 1974. [See also **I** and **II**].
109. Harsha, P. T. and Edelman, R. B.: Application of Modular Modeling to Ramjet Performance Prediction, *AIAA Paper 78-944*, Las Vegas, Nev., July 25-27, 1978.
110. Swithenbank, J., Turan, A., and Felton, P. G.: Paper in *Gas Turbine Combustor Design Problems* (Lefebvre, A. H. ed.), Hemisphere-McGraw-Hill, New York, 1980, p. 249.
111. Pun, W. M. and Spalding, D. B.: *18th Intl. Astro. Congress,* Belgrade, Poland, 1967, Proceedings, Pergamon Press/PWN Polish Scientific Publications, 1968, p. 3.
112. Gosman, A. D., Pun, W. M., Runchal, A. K., Spalding, D. B., and Wolfshtein, M. W.: *Heat and Mass Transfer in Recirculating Flows,* Academic Press, London, 1969.
113. Roberts, L. W., Ph.D. Thesis, Imperial College, London, 1973.
114. Schorr, C. J., Worner, G. A., and Schimke, J.: *14th Symp. (Intl.) on Comb.,* 1973, p. 567.
115. El-Mahallawy, F. M., Lockwood, F. C., and Spalding, D. B.: *Comb. and Flame,* **23**, 1974, p. 283.
116. Lilley, D. G.: Swirl Flow Modeling for Combustors, *AIAA Paper 74-527*, Palo Alto, CA, June 17-19, 1974.
117. Scaccia, C., and Kennedy, L. A.: *AIAA Journal,* **12**, 9, Sep., 1974, p. 1268.
118. Anasoulis, R. F., McDonald, H., and Buggeln, R. C.: Development of a Combustor Flow Analysis, Part 1: Theoretical Studies, Tech. Report No. *AFAPL-TR-73-98*, Part'l, Air Force Aero Prop. Lab., Air Force Systems, Command, Wright-Patterson AFB, Ohio, Jan., 1974. (See also Parts 2 and 3.)
119. Kubo, I., and Gouldin, F. C.: *J. of Fluids Eng.,* Sep., 1975, p. 310.
120. Netzer, D. W.: Modeling Solid Fuel Ramjet Combustion, presented at *13th JANNAF Comb. Meeting,* Naval Postgraduate School, Monterey, CA, Sep. 13-17, 1971.

121. Schultz, R. J.: Ph.D. Thesis, Univ. of Tennessee, June, 1976.
122. Peck, R. E., and Samuelsen, G. S.: *16th Symp. (Intl.) on Comb.*, 1977, p. 1675.
123. Harlow, F. H., and Amsden, A. A.: *J. of Computational Phy.*, 8, 1971, p. 197.
124. Wieber, P. R.: Numerical Studies of Unsteady Two-Dimensional Subsonic Flows Using the ICE Method, *TM X-68288*, NASA, Aug., 1973, (N73-31240).
125. Khalil, E. E., Spalding D. B., and Whitelaw, J. H.: *Intl. J. of Heat and Mass Transfer*, 18, 1975, p. 775.
126. Lilley, D. G.: *AIAA Journal*, **14**, 6, June, 1976, p. 749.
127. Novick, A. S., Miles, G. A., and Lilley, D. G.: *J. of Energy*, 3, 2, March-April, 1979, p. 95.
128. Wuerer, J. E., and Samuelsen, G. S.: Predictive Modeling of Backmixed Combustor Flows: Mass and Momentum Transport. *AIAA Paper 79-0215*, New Orleans, La., Jan. 15-17, 1979.
129. Novick, A. S., Miles, G. A., and Lilley, D. G.: *J. of Energy*, 3, 5, Sep.-Oct., 1979, p. 257.
130. Rhode, D. L., Lilley, D. G. and McLaughlin, D. K.: *ASME Symp. on Fluid Mechanics of Comb. Systems*, Boulder, Colorado, June 22-24, 1981, p. 257.
131. Sturgess, G. J., Syed, S. A., and Sepulveda, D.: *ASME Symp. on Fluid Mechanics of Comb. Systems*, Boulder, Colorado, June 22-24, 1981, p. 241.
132. Lilley, D. G., and Rhode, D. L.: A Computer Code for Swirling Turbulent Axisymmetric Recirculating Flows in Practical Isothermal Combustor Geometries. *NASA CR-3442*, Feb. 1982.
133. Bracco, F. V., Gupta, H. C., Krishnamurthy, L., Santavicca, D. A., Steinberger, R. L., and Warshaw, V.: Two-Phase, Two-Dimensional, Unsteady Combustion in IC Engines: Preliminary Theoretical-Experimental Results, SAE Paper 76-114, Automotive Exposition, Detroit, Mich., Feb., 1976.
134. Boni, A. A., Chapman, M., Cook, J. L., and Schneyer, G. P.: *16th Symp. (Intl.) on Comb.*, The Comb. Inst., 1977, p. 1527.
135. Gosman, A. D., and Watkins, A. P.: Paper presented at *ASME/Pennsylvania State University Symp. on Turbulent Shear Flows*, University Park, Pa., April 18-30, 1977, p. 5.23.
136. Ramos, J. I., and Sirignano, W. A.: Axisymmetric Flow Model with and without Swirl in a Piston-Cylinder Arrangement with Idealized Valve Operation. *SAE Technical Paper No. 800284*, Detroit, Feb. 25-29, 1980. See also: Ramos, J. I. and Sirignano, W. A. *SAE Technical Paper No. 800286*, Detroit, Feb. 25-29, 1980.
137. Griffin, M. D., Diwaker, R., Anderson, J. D., Jr., and Jones, E.: Computational Fluid Dynamics Applied to Flows in an IC Engine, *AIAA Paper 78-57*, Huntsville, Ala., Jan. 16-18, 1978.
138. Patankar, S. V., and Spalding, D. B.: Paper in Proceedings of 4th Symp. of Flames and Industry: Predictive Methods for Industrial Flames, organized by British Flame Research Committee and Institute of Fuel, Imperial College, London, Sep. 19-20, 1972, p. 13.
139. Patankar, S. V., and Spalding, D. B.: *14th Symp. (Intl.) on Comb.*, 1973, p. 604.
140. Abou Ellail, M. M. M., Gosman, A. D., Lockwood, F. C., and Megahed, I. E. A.: *Prog. in Astro. and Aero.*, 58, AIAA, New York, 1978, p. 163. (Ed. L.A. Kennedy)
141. Pai, B. R., Michelfelder, S., and Spalding, D. B.: *Intl. J. of Heat Mass Transfer*, **21**, 1978, p. 571.
142. Odgers, J.: *AIAA Paper 77-52*, 1977.
143. Patankar, S. V., and Spalding, D. B.: Paper in *Heat Transfer in Flames* (Afgan, N. H. and Beér, J. M., eds.) Scripta Book Co. (Hemisphere-Wiley), Washington, D.C., 1974, p. 73.
144. Patankar, S. V.: Paper in *Studies in Convection* (Launder, B.E., ed.) Academic Press, London, 1975, p. 1.
145. Gibeling, H. J., McDonald, H., and Briley, W. R.: Development of a Three-Dimensional Combustor Flow Analysis, Vol. II, Theoretical Studies. United Technologies Research Center, Report *AFAPL-TR-75-59* Volume II, East Hartford, Conn., Oct., 1976.
146. Mongia, H. C., and Smith, K. F.: An Empirical/Analytical Design Methodology for Gas Turbine Combustors. *AIAA Paper 78-998*, Las Vegas, Nev., July 25-27, 1978.
147. Jones, W. P., and Priddin, C. H.: *17th Symp. (Intl.) on Comb.*, 1979, p. 399.
148. Serag-Eldin, M. A., and Spalding, D. B.: Trans. ASME, *J. of Eng. for Power*, **101**, July, 1979, p. 326.
149. Mongia, H. C., and Reynolds, R. S.: Combustor Design Criteria Validation **III** – User's Manual, *Report USARTL-TR-78-55C*, US Army Res. & Tech. Lab., Ft. Eustis, Va., Feb., 1979. [See also **I** and **II**]
150. Kent, J. H., and Bilger, R. W.: Measurements of Turbulent Jet Diffusion Flames, Technical Note F-41, Oct. 1972, Charles Kolling Research Laboratory, University of Sydney, Australia.
151. Edelman, R. B., and Fortune, O.: A Quasi-Global Chemical Kinetic Model for the Finite Rate Combustion of Hydrocarbon Fuels, *AIAA Paper 69-86*, 1969.
152. Rhodes, R. P., Harsha, P. T., and Peters, C. E.: *Acta Astro.*, **1**, April 1974, p. 443.

153. Edelman, R. B., and Harsha, P. T.: *Prog. in Astro. and Aero.*, **58**, AIAA, New York, 1978, p. 55.
154. Kent, J. H., and Bilger, R. W.: *16th Symp. (Intl.) on Comb.*, The Comb. Inst., 1977, p. 1643.
155. Janicka, J., and Kollman, W.: *17th Symp. (Intl.) on Comb.*, The Comb. Inst., 1979, p. 421.
156. Harsha, P. T.: A General Analysis of Free Turbulent Mixing, TR-73-177, Arnold Engineering Development Center, 1974.
157. Launder, B. E., Morse, A., Rodi, W., and Spalding, D. B.: Prediction of Free Shear Flows – A Comparison of the Performance of Six Turbulence Models, *Free Turbulent Shear Flows*, **I**, Conference Proceedings, NASA SP-321, 1973, p. 463.
158. Mao, C. P., Szekely, G. A. Jr., and Faeth, G. M.: *J. of Energy*, **4**, 2, March-April 1980, p. 78.
159. Lockwood, F. C., and Naguib, A. S.: *Comb. and Flame*, **24**, 1975, p. 109.
160. Gosman, A. D., Lockwood, F. C., and Syed, S. A.: *16th Symp. (Intl.) on Comb.*, The Comb. Inst., 1977, p. 1543.
161. Essenhigh, R. H.: Current Status of Fluid Mechanics in Practical Heterogeneous Combustors, Presented at the Spring Meeting, Central States Section, The Comb. Inst., NASA-Lewis Research Center, March 1977.
162. Faeth, G. M.: *Prog. in Energy and Comb. Sci.*, **3**, 1977, p. 191.
163. Chigier, N. A.: *Prog. in Energy and Comb. Sci.*, **2**, 1976, p. 97.
164. Edelman, R. B., and Harsha, P. T.: *Prog. in Energy and Comb. Sci.*, **4**, 1978, p. 1.
165. Crowe, C. T., Sharma, M. P., and Stock, D. E.: The Particle Source in Cell (PSI-Cell) Model for Gas Droplet Flows, *ASME Paper 75-WA/HT-25*, 1975.
166. Spalding, D. B.: Mathematical Models of Continuous Combustion, *Emissions From Continuous Combustion Systems*, Plenum Press, New York, 1972.
167. Genovese, J., Edelman, R. B., and Fortune, O. F.: *J. of Spacecraft and Rockets*, 8, 4, 1971, p. 352.
168. Shearer, A. J., Tamura, H., and Faeth, G. M.: *J. of Energy*, **3**, 1979, p. 271.
169. Lilley, D. G.: *AIAA Journal*, **15**, 8, Aug., 1977, p. 1063.
170. Lilley, D. G.: *J. of Energy*, **3**, July-Aug., 1979, p. 193.
171. Lilley, D. G.: *AIAA Paper No. 80-1189*, Hartford, CT, June 30-July 2, 1980. See also *AIAA Journal*, **19**, 12, Dec. 1981, p. 1562.
172. Durst, F., Melling, A., and Whitelaw, J. H.: *Principles and Practice of Laser Doppler Anemometry*, Academic Press, London, 1976.
173. The Accuracy of Flow Measurements by Laser Doppler Methods, *Proc. of the LDA-Symposium*, Copenhagen, 1975.
174. Goulard, R. (Ed.): *Combustion Measurements, Modern Techniques and Instrumentation*, A Project Squid Workshop, Academic Press, New York, 1976.
175. Lapp, M. and Penny, C. M. (Ed.): *Laser Raman Gas Diagnostics*, A Project Squid Workshop, Plenum Press, New York, 1974.
176. Thompson, H. D. and Stevenson, W. H. (Ed.): Laser Velocimetry and Particle Sizing, *Proc. 3rd Intl. Workshop on Laser Velocimetry*, Purdue University, July 11-13, 1978, Hemisphere Publishing Corp., New York, 1979.
177. Zinn, B. T. (Ed.): Experimental Diagnostics in Gas Phase Combustion Systems, *Prog. in Astro. and Aero.*, **53**, 1977.
178. Boggs, T. L. and Zinn, B. T. (Ed.): Experimental Diagnostics in Combustion of Solids, *Prog. in Astro. and Aero.*, **63**, 1978.
179. Vest, C. M.: *Holographic Interferometry*, John Wiley & Sons, New York, 1979.
180. Collier, R. J., Burckhardt, C. B., and Lin, L. H.: *Optical Holography*, Academic Press Inc., 1971.
181. Cummins, J. D. and Pike, E. R. (Ed.): *Photon Correlation Spectroscopy and Velocimetry*, NATO Advanced Study Institutes Series, Series B: Physics, Plenum Press, New York, 1977.
182. Stockham, J. D. and Fochtman, E. G. (Ed.): *Particle Size Analysis*, Ann Arbor Science Publishers Inc., 1979.
183. Merzkirch, W.: *Flow Visualization*, Academic Press Inc., New York, 1974.
184. Weinberg, F. J.: *Optics of Flames*, Butterworths, London, 1963.
185. Crossley, D. R. (Ed.): *Laser Probes for Combustion Chemistry*, ACS Symposium Series 134, American Chemical Society, Washington D.C., 1980.
186. Trolinger, J. D.: *Laser Instrumentation for Flow Field Diagnostics, AGARDograph No. 186*, 1977.
187. Günther, R.: Methods for Turbulence Measurements in Flames, *AIAA 14th Aerospace Sciences Meeting*, Paper No. 76-36, Jan., 1976.
188. Trowers, B. E. L.: Laser Beam Spread in Particle-Free Exhausts, Rocket Propulsion, Establishment, *Technical Report No. 35*, England, July 1975.

189. Kowalik, R. M., and Kruger, C. H.: Laser Fluorescence Temperature Measurements, *WSS/CI Paper No. 78-17,* 1978.
190. Setchell, R. E.: Time-Averaged Measurements in Turbulent Flames using Raman Spectroscopy, *AIAA Paper No. 76-28*, 1976.
191. Cattolica, R. J.: OH Rotational Temperature from Laser Induced Fluorescence, *WSS/CI Spring Meeting, Boulder, Colorado, Paper No. 78-18*, 1978.
192. Durst, F., and Zare, M.: Laser Doppler Measurements in Two-Phase Flows, *Report No. SFB80/TM/63*, Sonderfoschungsbereich 80, Ausbreitungs und Transportvorgänge in Stromungen, Universität Karlsruhe, July, 1975.
193. Birch, A. D., Brown, D. R., Dodson, M. G., and Thomas, J. R.: *J. Phys. D: App. Phys.*, 8, 1975, p. 127.
194. Kennedy, I. M., and Kent, J. H.: Laser Scattering Measurements in Turbulent Diffusion Flames, *AIAA 18th Aerospace Sciences Meeting, Paper No. 80-0206,* Jan., 1980.
195. Goulard, R., and Sulzmann, K. G. P.: Picosecond Techniques in Combustion Diagnostics *AIAA 18th Aerospace Sciences Meeting, Paper No. 80-0409*, Jan., 1980.
196. Ahlheim, M., and Günther, R.: Investigation of Turbulent Reaction Fields by Ionization Measurements, *AIAA 18th Aerospace Sciences Meeting, Paper No. 80-0283*, Jan., 1980.
197. Starner, S. H., and Bilger, R. W.: Measurements of Velocity and Concentration in Turbulent Diffusion Flames with Pressure Gradients, *AIAA 18th Aerospace Sciences Meeting, Paper No. 80-205*, Jan., 1980.
198. Eckbreth, A. C., Bonczyk, P. A., and Verdieck, J. F.: *App. Spectroscopy Reviews,* 13, 1, 1978, p. 15.
199. Pealat, M., and Taran, J. P.: *Optics and Laser Tech.*, Feb., 1980.
200. Setchell, R. E.: Local Turbulence Properties in Flames from Time-Averaged Raman Spectroscopy Measurements, *AIAA 17th Aerospace Sciences Meeting, Paper No. 79-0087*, Jan., 1979.
201. Eckbreth, A. C.: CARS Thermometry in Practical Combustors, *UTRC Report No. 79-82*, July, 1979. See also *Comb. and Flame*, 1980.
202. Eckbreth, A. C.: *18th Symp. (Intl.) on Comb.,* The Comb. Inst., 1981.
203. Hanson, R. K.: Combustion Gas Measurements Using Tunable Laser Absorption Spectroscopy, *AIAA 17th Aerospace Sciences Meeting*, Jan., 1979.
204. Murphree, D. L. *et al.*: *AIAA 19th Aerospace Sciences Meeting, Paper No. 81-0100,* Jan., 1981.
205. Drake, M. C. *et al.*: Probability Density Functions and Correlations of Temperature and Molecular Concentrations in Turbulent Diffusion Flames, *AIAA 19th Aerospace Sciences Meeting, Paper No. 81-0103*, Jan., 1981.
206. Stepowski, D., Puechberty, D., and Cottereau, M. J.: *Proc. 18th Symp. (Intl.) on Comb.,* The Comb. Inst., 1981.
207. Dibble, R. W., and Hollenbach, R. E.: *Proc. 18th Symp. (Intl.) on Comb.,* The Comb. Inst., 1981.
208. Gupta, A. K., Swithenbank, J., and Beér, J. M.: *J. Inst. Fuel*, Dec., 1977, p. 163.
209. Gupta, A. K., and Rossi, I.: Application of Laser Schlieren Interferometry to Burning Droplets, *AIAA 18th Aerospace Sciences Meeting, Paper No. 80-0349*, Jan., 1980.
210. Reuss, D. L.: Temperature Measurements in a Radially Symmetric Flame Using Holographic Interferometry, G.M. Research Lab. Report No. GMR-3600, F&L-720, Presented at WSS/CI Meeting, April 13-14, 1981.
211. Gupta, A. K., and Rossi, I.: *J. Inst. E.,* 1981, p. 197.
212. Gupta, A. K.: *Optical Diagnostics of Particle and Spray Size Distribution – A Review*, Dept. of Chemical Eng., MIT, Jan., 1979.
213. Walsh, P. W., Gupta, A. K., Beér, J. M., and Chiu, K. S.: Measurement of Gaseous and Solid Species Concentration in Fluidized Combustors, DOE/WVU Conference on Fluidized Bed Combustion System Design and Operation, Lakeview Inn & Country Club, Morgantown, West Virginia, Oct. 27-29, 1980.
214. Gaydon, A. G.: *The Spectroscopy of Flames,* Chapman & Hall, London, 1974.
215. Dyer, T. M., Witze, P. O., Johnson, S. C., and Smith, J. R.: Application of New Diagnostic Techniques to Combustion Studies in Engines, *AIAA 20th Aerospace Sciences Meeting*, Orlando, Florida, Jan. 11-14, 1982, Paper 82-0235. See also: Witze, P. O.: Paper at SAE Congress, Detroit, MI., Feb., 1982.
216. Wuerer, J. E., Oeding, R. G., Poon, C. C., and Hess, C. F.: The Application of Nonintrusive Optical Methods to Physical Measurements in Combustion, *AIAA 20th Aerospace Sciences Meeting*, Orlando, FL, Paper 82-0236, Jan. 11-14, 1982.
217. Sheffield, S. A., Hess, C. F., and Trolinger, J. D.: Holographic Studies of the Vapor Explosion of Vaporizing Water-in-Fuel Emulsion Droplets, 2nd Intl. Colloquium on Drops and Bubbles, Monterey, CA, Nov. 1981.

218. Powe, R. E., and Coleman, H. W.: Thermal Diagnostics for High Temperature Flows, Research Workshop held at Mississippi State University, May, 1981.
219. Dussourd, J. L., Lohmann, R. P. and Uram, E. M. (Ed.): Fluid Mechanics of Combustion (Papers presented at Conference held in Montreal, Canada, May 13-15, 1974) *ASME Book No. 100034,* 1974.
220. Fluid Mechanics of Combustion Processes, Meeting of Combustion Inst./Central States Section, March 28-30, 1977.
221. Kennedy, L. A. (Ed.): Turbulent Combustion. *Prog. in Astro. and Aero.* 58, AIAA, New York, 1978.
222. Swift, W. L., Barna, P. S. and Dalton, C. (Ed.): *Vortex Flows.* Proc. of ASME Conference, Chicago, Illinois, Nov. 16-21, 1980.
223. Combustion Modelling. *AGARD Conf. Proc. No. 275*, Feb. 1980.
224. Morel, T., Lohmann, R. P. and Rackley, J. M. (Ed.): *Fluid Mechanics of Combustion Systems*, Proc. of ASME Conference, Boulder, CO, June 22-24, 1981.
225. Morel, T. (Ed.): *Prediction of Turbulent Reacting Flows in Practical Systems,* Proc. of ASME Conference, Boulder, CO, June 22-24, 1981.
226. Harsha, P. T.: *Combustion Modeling For Practical Applications,* Ibid, 1981, p. 23.
227. Zinn, B. T. (Ed.): *Prog. in Astro. and Aero.,* 53, AIAA, New York, 1977.
228. Bowen, J. R., Manson, N., Oppenheim, A. K. and Soloukhin, R. I. (Ed.): *Prog. in Astro. and Aero.,* 76, AIAA, New York, 1981.

SUBJECT INDEX